ROUTLEDGE HANDBOOK OF SPORTS MARKETING

Sports marketing has become a cornerstone of successful sports management and business, driving growth in sports organisations and widening fan-bases. Showcasing the latest thinking and research in sports marketing from around the world, the *Routledge Handbook of Sports Marketing* goes further than any other book in exploring the full range of this exciting discipline.

Featuring contributions from world-leading scholars and practitioners from across the globe, the book examines theories, concepts, issues and best practice across six thematic parts: brands; sponsorship; ambush marketing; consumers, spectators and fans; media; and ethics and development. It examines key topics such as:

- consumer behaviour
- marketing communications
- strategic marketing
- international marketing
- experiential marketing
- and marketing and digital media

Comprehensive and authoritative, the *Routledge Handbook of Sports Marketing* is an essential reference for any student or researcher working in sports marketing, sports management, sports business, sports administration or sports development, and for all practitioners looking to develop their professional knowledge.

Simon Chadwick is 'Class of 92' Professor of Sports Enterprise in the Centre for Sports Business at Salford University, UK, and Director of Research at the Josoor Institute, part of Qatar's Supreme Committee for Delivery and Legacy, the body charged with organising the 2022 FIFA World Cup. Simon's research and teaching interests lie in the areas of sponsorship, sport marketing and commercial strategy in sport. Having previously worked at the Universities of London, where he was the founding Director of the Birkbeck Sport Business Centre, and the University of Leeds, where he was Programme Director for the MA in Advertising and Marketing, Simon is the founder and Editor of *Sport, Business and Management: An International Journal* and a former Editor of the *International Journal of Sports*

Marketing and Sponsorship. He also recently created and edits the highly regarded academic website *The Scorecard*.

Nicolas Chanavat is Senior Lecturer in Sport Marketing at the Université Paris-Saclay, France, where he has been Director of the first year of the Sport Management master's degree programme since 2010. His PhD (University Lyon I/Loughborough University) deals with multiple sponsorship effects in a mega sporting event context. Nicolas's main research interests are focused on marketing of football and mega sporting events (sponsorship and ambush marketing, branding strategies and sports organisations marketing, fan consumption). He has published several books and numerous academic articles in this field. Nicolas worked for the French soccer club, Association Sportive de Saint-Étienne (ASSE). He was also Assistant Director and Director of the volunteers programme at the FIFA France Confederation Cup in 2003 and trainer for the volunteer instructors at the 2006 Torino Winter Olympic Games. Nicolas is administrator of the French National Olympic Academy and Director of Research Grants for the French Centre for Olympic Studies. He is also marketing and strategic consultant for the museum of the Grand Stade of Olympique Lyonnais.

Michel Desbordes is a Full Professor at the Université Paris-Saclay, France, and Associate Professor at INSEEC Business School, Paris, France. He is a specialist in sports marketing with a research focus on the management of sports events, sports sponsorship and marketing applied to football. He has published 23 books (with Elsevier, UK; Editoral Piadotribo and Inde Publicationes, Spain; Economica, Les Editions d'Organisation and PUS, France) and numerous academic articles (*International Journal of Sports Marketing and Sponsorship*; *European Sport Management Quarterly*; *International Journal of Sport Management and Marketing* amongst others) in this field. Since January 2009, Professor Desbordes has been the Editor of the *International Journal of Sports Marketing and Sponsorship*.

ROUTLEDGE HANDBOOK OF SPORTS MARKETING

Edited by
Simon Chadwick, Nicolas Chanavat
and Michel Desbordes

LONDON AND NEW YORK

First published in paperback 2018

First published 2016
by Routledge
2 Park Square, Milton Park, Abingdon, Oxon OX14 4RN

and by Routledge
711 Third Avenue, New York, NY 10017

Routledge is an imprint of the Taylor & Francis Group, an informa business

British Library Cataloguing-in-Publication Data
A catalogue record for this book is available from the British Library

Library of Congress Cataloging-in-Publication Data
Routledge handbook of sports marketing / edited by Simon Chadwick,
Nicolas Chanavat and Michel Desbordes.
    pages cm
Includes bibliographical references and index.
ISBN 978-1-138-82351-8 (Hardback) — ISBN 978-1-315-74202-1 (eBook)
1. Sports—Marketing.   I. Chadwick, Simon, 1964-
GV716.R697 2016
796.0688—dc23   2015020127

ISBN: 978-1-138-82351-8 (hbk)
ISBN: 978-0-8153-9486-0 (pbk)
ISBN: 978-1-315-74202-1 (ebk)

Typeset in Bembo
by Keystroke, Neville Lodge, Tettenhall, Wolverhampton

CONTENTS

Contents

Contents

Contents

ILLUSTRATIONS

Figures

Tables

CONTRIBUTORS

Kostas Alexandris, Aristotle University of Thessaloniki, Greece

Verónica Baena, Full Professor/Chair of Marketing at Universidad Europea de Madrid, Spain

Guillaume Bodet, Université Claude Bernard Lyon-1, France

Grégory Bolle, Vice-President, Head of Strategic Planning, Maxus/GroupM (WPP), Dubai

Cheri Bradish, Ryerson University, Toronto, Canada

Christoph Breuer, Deutsche Sporthochschule Köln, Institut für Sportökonomie und Sportmanagement, Germany

Markus Breuer, Hochschule Heidelberg, Germany

André Bühler, Hochschule für Wirtschaft und Umwelt Nürtingen-Geislingen, Germany

Nicholas Burton, Brock University, Ontario, Canada

Simon Chadwick, Salford University, UK

Nicolas Chanavat, Université Paris-Saclay, France

Victor Manoel Cunha de Almeida, Instituto Coppead de Administração UFRJ, Rio de Janeiro, Brazil

Larry DeGaris, University of Indianapolis, USA

Michel Desbordes, Université Paris-Saclay, France

Geoff Dickson, Auckland University of Technology, Auckland, New Zealand

Mark Dodds, State University of New York College at Cortland, USA

Dan Funk, Temple University, Philadelphia, USA

Leah Gillooly, Alliance Manchester Business School, University of Manchester, UK

Marilyn Giroux, Concordia University, Canada

Paolo Guenzi, Department of Marketing, Università Commerciale Luigi Bocconi, Milano, Italy

Christopher Hautbois, Université Paris-Saclay, France

Sebastian Kaiser, Hochschule Heilbronn, Campus Künzelsau Reinhold-Würth-University, Germany

Nancy Lough, University of Nevada, Las Vegas, Nevada, USA

Justin Lovich, State University of New York College at Cortland, USA

Heath McDonald, Swinburne University, Melbourne, Australia

Lionel Maltese, Aix Marseille Université and Kedge Business School, France

Marc Mazodier, Hong Kong Baptist University, Hong Kong and the University of South Australia

Barbara M. B. Sá, Instituto Coppead de Administração UFRJ, Rio de Janeiro, Brazil

Ceyda Mumcu, University of New Haven, Connecticut, USA

Gerd Nufer, ESB Business School, Reutlingen University, Germany

Fabien Ohl, University of Lausanne, Switzerland

Karen Palmer, The University of Adelaide, Adelaide Business School, Adelaide, Australia

Ted B. Peetz, Belmont University, Nashville, USA

Carolin Plewa, The University of Adelaide, Adelaide Business School, Adelaide, Australia

Frank Pons, Kedge Business School and Laval University, Canada

Pascale G. Quester, The University of Adelaide, Adelaide Business School, Adelaide, Australia

Elena Radicchi, University of Florence, Italy

James T. Reese, Drexel University, Philadelphia, USA

Manfredi Ricca, Chief Strategy Officer for EMEA and LatAm at Interbrand, Italy

Christopher Rumpf, Deutsche Sporthochschule Köln, Institut für Sportökonomie und Sportmanagement, Germany

Aaron C. T. Smith, RMIT University, Melbourne, Australia

Sten Söderman, Stockholm Business School, Stockholm University, Sweden

Constantino Stavros, RMIT University, Melbourne, Australia

Gary Tribou, University of Strasbourg, France

George Vazenios, State University of New York College at Cortland, USA

Björn Walliser, University of Lorraine, France

Kate Westberg, RMIT University, Melbourne, Australia

Bradley Wilson, Facultad de Administración, Universidad de Los Andes, Bogota, Colombia; School of Media and Communication, RMIT University, Melbourne, Australia and Department of Services Management, Unversität Bayreuth, Germany

Patrizia Zagnoli, University of Florence, Italy

INTRODUCTION

Simon Chadwick, Nicolas Chanavat and Michel Desbordes

The global sports industry is now "estimated by the United Nations to account for approximately 3% of global economic activity. A recent report by PWC (2011) indicates that the sports market will be worth $145 billion by 2015, with North America accounting for 45% of global revenues, EMEA for 35%, Asia Pacific for 19% and Latin America for 5%. However, Plunkett Research (2014) believes the total size of the American sports industry is currently $485 billion. Consequently, sports are seen as big business by many people, including academic researchers. Sports continue to fulfil an important socio-cultural role across the world, providing the focus for communities, health initiatives, and so forth. There can be no doubt that sports are central to the lives and activities of innumerable people and organisations, whether they be fans in a stadium, runners taking part in a charity race, sponsors named on the side of a racing car, or local people benefitting from a sports club's community engagement programme.

As the twentieth century progressed and the North American model of sports developed (a model founded on providing good customer service linked to funding through private means, such as the sale of television and sponsorship rights), so sports marketing began to emerge as an important vehicle through which organisational goals could be simultaneously achieved. For sports such as the NBA, NFL, NHL and NASCAR, marketing developed as a basis for building a sustainable fan base, selling merchandise, securing television coverage and generating revenues. These sports set a precedent that was subsequently followed by organisations such as the International Olympic Committee, created structured marketing programmes, which in turn have been duplicated by the likes of FIFA, the PGA and the tennis Grand Slams.

As a result, the influence of and perceived necessity for sports organisations to engage in marketing has become paramount. Even in situations where there is strong state involvement in sports, the need to adopt such practices is accepted. Grassroots sports initiatives, sporting mega events and healthy lifestyle initiatives are actively marketed in order to ensure that the right people are getting the right product, delivered in the right way, in the right place and at the right time. As the importance of marketing has grown, we have seen a related growth in sports marketing research being undertaken by academic researchers and practitioners.

Academic publishing in the field of sports marketing has proliferated dramatically over the last two decades, there are now a number of established specialist journals, including *Sport*

Marketing Quarterly, the *International Journal of Sports Marketing & Sponsorship* and the *International Journal of Sport Management and Marketing*. Other journals, too, often carry sports marketing papers, such as the *European Journal of Marketing*, while there are now academic bodies that were specifically set up to further promote the discipline, America's Sport Marketing Association being one example.

It is clear, therefore, that sports marketing has an established place, not only in the sporting landscape, but also in the academic research landscape in general. Indeed, we firmly believe that sports marketing is no longer a fledgling discipline that is emerging from the generic marketing literature. Rather, it is a rapidly maturing area of research, which is rapidly developing its own unique characteristics and features. Studies now being published demonstrate that sports marketing has an identity and has developed the confidence to warrant a handbook such as this one.

As such, this *Handbook of Sports Marketing* is presented as a showcase for the latest thinking in the field, as a bold statement of confidence among the researchers working in sports marketing, and as a stimulus and motivating force for further research in the future. The *Handbook* brings together leading thinkers, researchers and writers in sports marketing, who address some of the most pressing issues in contemporary sports. Some of the issues will already be familiar to readers, some may not be, the foci of these papers are often commercial but not always so, as some papers address the socio-cultural context within which the marketing of sports is located.

Based upon the expertise of the academics who have contributed to the text, the book has been divided into six parts: brands; sponsorship; ambush marketing; customers, spectators and fans; media; marketing, ethics and development. At the beginning of each section, the reader is able to find out more about the purpose of each section and the papers appearing in it. As Editors of the *Handbook of Sports Marketing*, we believe that the contributions made to this book will enhance the current body of work in sports marketing, further adding to the growing reputation and status of the discipline. We hope readers will benefit from the range of authors and chapters that we have assembled here.

References

Plunkett Research (2014). Industry statistics sports & recreation business statistics analysis, www.plunkettresearch.com/statistics/sports-industry/ (accessed 6 May 2015).
PWC (2011). PwC outlook for the global sports market to 2015, www.pwc.com/gx/en/hospitality-leisure/changing-the-game-outlook-for-the-global-sports-market-to-2015.jhtml (accessed 6 May 2015).

1

DEFINING SPORTS MARKETING

Sebastian Kaiser and Markus Breuer

Introduction

During recent decades, sports have become an essential part of people's leisure time. Sports organizations have evolved from local institutions that were dominated by honorary employees, to professional, global players. The FIFA World Cup and the Olympic Games can be recognized as some of the most important and probably the most sought after global sports events played at a professional level. The 2010 FIFA World Cup hosted in South Africa made $2,408 million from selling TV rights and an additional $1,072 million from selling marketing rights.[1] The 2014 World Cup held in Brazil was estimated to have generated a total turnover of $4 billion for FIFA.[2] In addition to sports organizations and broadcasting stations, more and more "non-sport" corporations are becoming involved in the global sports market. According to the Qatar Foundation, one of the global players in sponsorship (for example, sponsorship of FC Barcelona), global sponsorship spending was estimated at $50 billion in 2013.[3] Producers of sports goods and sportswear, such as Nike and adidas, employ thousands of people all over the world and earn revenues of several billion dollars.

This chapter will provide an overview of sports, sports marketing and its economic background. It is structured as follows: the next two sections define the expressions *sports* and *marketing* and bring together these core ideas explaining the difference between *marketing through sports* and *marketing of sports*. The next section explains why marketing in the sports context differs from marketing for any other business segment. By virtue of the categories – suppliers, special characteristics of sports goods and special characteristics of sports demand – we will explain what makes sports marketing special. Finally, a brief outlook outlining some of the most important trends in sports marketing.

Defining sports and its meaning for sports consumers

Although the expression *sport* is widely used, it is difficult to find an appropriate definition that includes all the relevant fields of interest (from an economic perspective) and excludes all activities that should not be subject to processes like sports marketing. According to Mandelbaum (2004: 4), the expression *sport* is related to *disport*. Spectators are diverted from the burdens of normal existence. Team sports such as baseball and football offer a "particularly compelling form of drama" (Mandelbaum, 2004: 5). Similarly, Delaney and

Madigan (2009: 11) argue that the term sport has its origins rooted in the idea that it is an activity designed to divert people from the routines of everyday life. While Mandelbaum considers only the spectators (consuming professional team sports), Delaney and Madigan implicitly include athletes as well. For our purposes, it is reasonable to consider both: athletes and spectators or customers. Additional information regarding the special characteristics of sports production and consumption will be provided later.

Normally, any sports are related to some kind of effort. According to Sansone (1992: 37), sport is the ritual sacrifice of physical energy. In most cases sports include competition. Physical competition mandates that physical effort and individual skills are involved to determine a winner or loser (Delaney and Madigan, 2009: 12). However, physical energy is not a necessary part of sports in modern societies. One only needs to think of mental exercises such as chess. Even competitiveness is not essential, for example, Nordic walking shows that sports could be driven by individual ambition without being competitive. That is, instead of glory and monetary incentives, athletes are motivated by social benefits or health. In this context we define sports according to Horch (1994: 245), as an aggregate of utility creating scarce goods that are linked to sporting behavior. This definition explicitly includes passive consumption of sports, as well as individual activity culminating from competition or for individual pleasure, so long as the precondition of effort or diversion is fulfilled.

Defining marketing and sports marketing

Marketing

The expression *marketing* was already widely discussed in the United States around the turn of the twentieth century (Usui, 2008: 15). As the production capacities of companies in the business sector grew and exceeded the consumer demand, methods of how to distribute and sell goods became increasingly important. According to Ferrell and Hartline (2012: 7), marketing is many different things. Marketing can be seen as a business process like production and logistics. As a business function, the goal of marketing is the connection of organizations (producers, suppliers) and customers. It can also be seen as a process that manages the flow of products from the point of conception to the point of consumption (ibid). For simplicity reasons we will focus on the famous 4Ps of the marketing mix concept. The concept of the 4Ps dates back to the 1960s and includes the following aspects:

- Product: product variety, quality, design, features, brand name, packaging, sizes, services, warranties, returns.
- Price: list price, discounts, allowances, payment period, credit terms.
- Promotion: sales promotion, advertising, sales force, public relations, direct marketing.
- Place (distribution): channels, coverage, assortments, locations, inventory, transport (Kotler and Keller, 2012: 25).

Marketing and the marketing mix do not focus on the promotion or even on advertising, but consider the entire value chain of a company, starting with the research and development (R&D) department and the production process (product) and ending with the field of customer care (for example, returns).

Although the 4Ps model is widely taught, it suffers from a number of flaws. First, it is incomplete as many activities that are carried out by a marketer are not considered. Second, it tends to push each activity into a separate category without considering the intersections.

Third, the mutual benefit for the marketer and the consumer is neglected (Blythe, 2006: 8). Not all marketing activities are only for the benefit of the producer, some could also be providing utility to the customer. Considering these aspects, several authors built up extensions to the standard 4Ps model. Probably the best-known proposition was published by Booms and Bitner (1981), adding three more Ps (people, process, physical evidence), ending up with a 7P model. Some authors tend to distinguish different "marketing releases". In terms of "industry 4.0" and "web 2.0", they set up three stages of modern marketing activities:

- Marketing 1.0 is known to be product-centric marketing with the sole objective to sell products. The interaction between companies and consumers is limited to one-to-many transactions, indicating that it is impossible to address single consumers individually.
- Marketing 2.0 ("consumer-oriented marketing") aims at satisfying and retaining the consumers. Products and services are no longer functional but become emotional. The relationship between companies and customers is one to one, based on new technologies and decreasing costs.
- Finally, marketing 3.0 is value-driven marketing and aims at "making the world a better place". Instead of a simple interaction between company and consumer, some authors claim for a many-to-many-collaboration (Kotler, Kartajaya and Setiawan, 2010: 6).

The third stage is an inherent part of sports and its provision or consumption. For instance, when one thinks of a professional soccer game: 22 athletes and thousands in the stadium produce a unique good that is characterized by the uncertainty of outcome and is consumed by millions through TV and other media channels. However, in this case there has been no simple or direct interaction between a single company and a customer.

Sports marketing

What is sports marketing?

Sports marketing means the application of all marketing related activities, structures and thoughts to the phenomenon of sports. In this context, "sports" includes mass sports, professional (competitive) sports and sports in the media. Focusing on the supplier perspective, we can say that sports marketing is a managerial process by which the sports manager seeks to obtain what sports organizations need through creating and exchanging products and services with others (Shilbury et al., 2014: 17). To use this definition in day-to-day operations, we can put it into a sports marketing framework that outlines a step-by-step process to implement sports marketing activities. This framework includes four stages (Hoye et al., 2012: 204–205):

- Identification of sports marketing opportunities: analysis of internal and external environments, analysis of the organization, analysis of markets and consumers and consumer behavior.
- Development of a sports marketing strategy: development of a strategic sports marketing direction, development of a sports marketing strategy.
- Planning the sports marketing mix: considering price, product, promotion and place (4Ps).
- Implementation and control of the sports marketing strategy: implementation strategies, control process, sports marketing ethics.

According to Mullin (2014: 13), "sport marketing consists of all activities designed to meet the needs and wants of sport consumers[. . .]. Sport marketing has developed two major trusts:

the marketing of sport products [. . .] and the marketing of other industrial or services using partnerships and promotions with sport properties". The difference between marketing *of* sports and marketing *through* sports will be discussed in the following sections.

Marketing of sports

Marketing of sports refers to the practice of marketing as it occurs within a sports organization (Parent and Smith-Swan, 2013: 97). In this context, the term "sports organization" covers, but is not limited to: (a) sports clubs (mass sports and professional sports); (b) profit oriented sports providers; (c) media (for example, broadcasting stations, websites, etc.); and (d) production and sale of sports goods (such as clothes, rackets, etc.).

Sports club marketing implies all marketing-related activities that occur in the management of professional as well as mass sports clubs. Focusing on professional sports clubs would include:

- The entire communication towards fans and other stakeholders that act as customers. The marketer has to ensure relevant information is provided to all kinds of customers, especially fans. Due to past changes in information technology ("web 2.0"), the constant provision of information and the control of all kinds of information has become one of the crucial tasks of marketing. Moreover, marketing nowadays has to consider activities, such as customer relationship management (CRM), in its marketing strategy. CRM can be based on individualism and holistic marketing, sales and service concept based on modern IT. A good CRM policy requires a good database. This is why sports clubs compete for ingenious new ways of obtaining reliable information on their customers (Desbordes, 2012: 170).
- The selection of merchandising products and the management of the distribution channels. Licensing revenues are generated when teams grant merchandise and apparel companies the right to use their names and logos. Recently, these arrangements have been increasingly lucrative as a source of revenue for professional teams (Gladden and Sutton, 2011: 130). In addition to the direct financial effect, customers purchasing branded goods show a deep commitment to the club and the public use of merchandising products (such as jerseys) initiates a recursive process, thus increasing the brand value. The portfolio of merchandising products has to be chosen and ordered in the first step. The consequent steps include the management of inventory stocks and distribution channels.
- Negotiations with actual and potential sponsors. Sponsorship is the most important source of income for most professional sports clubs. In only a few cases, the sale of media rights outperforms the sponsorship revenue. In Europe, it is only soccer clubs that generate a major part of their revenue by selling media rights. All other clubs are constrained by their sponsorship income and a patron or investor.

All activities discussed must be executed in a mass sports club in a similar manner. However, the information management is often lot easier as the interested public is usually restricted by a city or a region. Nevertheless, demographic changes and an increase in the profit making sector make it more difficult to remain competitive.

Like any other corporation, profit-oriented sports providers, such as public baths, have to cope with the 4Ps of the marketing mix. Regarding the price, many corporations compete with non-profit service providers that might offer substitutes at lower prices, benefitting from tax exemptions or voluntary work. Therefore, any kind of promotion has to ensure that customers realize the additional value that is generated by PFOs.

The economic relationships between media (including online media) and the sports sector are long-lasting and have evolved significantly in recent years (Andreff and Bourg, 2006: 37). The media assume a hybrid role in the marketing of sports. They act as customers buying broadcasting rights from sports clubs and associations, whereas broadcasters use sports events and the coverage they receive as a marketing instrument of their own: For many years broadcasted sports events did not play an important role in the program planning, however, since global events like the Olympic Games gained importance, sports as content became more and more important. Today, broadcasting stations use sports content as a positioning tool. Revenues generated from the sale of commercials during the event might be too low to cover expenditures for the acquisition of broadcasting rights. The broadcast of sports is cross-subsidized by revenues in other fields.

In terms of the overall influence of media on sports, broadcasting stations enforced several changes in competitive sports in recent years. In order to get the media's attention, sports events had to reform forms, systems and rules of the games (for example, schedules) to meet TV requirements (Quing, 2013: 26). As a result of this influence, media is now a part of the modern magic triangle. It is formed by sports, corporations and media and describes the interdependencies between these major market players.

Sports goods producers can be regarded as suppliers for the sports industry. Although they do not underlie the restrictions for the sports organizations, they can be considered as normal for-profit corporations. The only exception is that such companies are often integrated in the entire sports value chain. When an important sports event is organized, corporations such as Nike or adidas act as sponsors and benefit from the success of athletes and teams. However, industrial enterprises can sponsor several athletes and do not suffer from individual setbacks in the same way as teams do.

Marketing through sports

Marketing through sports happens when a non-sports product is marketed through an association to sports (Smith and Stewart, 2015: 6). Sponsorship is probably the most popular example of marketing through sports. Large corporations use sports as a vehicle to promote their products and services (Shilbury et al., 2014: 16). During the 1970s, marketing through sports often served either the personal interests of the executives or as a vehicle for charitable contributions. Since the 1980s it has become a practice involving serious research, large investments, and strategic initiatives related to corporate targets (Mullin 2014: 239) and long-term oriented goals.

Because marketing through sports mainly covers sponsorship, the monetary impact strongly correlates with the sponsorship market and the possibility to reach existing as well as prospective customers. Some reasons for the sharp increase in global sponsorship expenditures include:

- More television devoted to sports programs.
- Technological developments that led to the portability of sports through cell phones, tablets, etc.
- Emergence of new sports offerings, such as mixed martial arts, or new combinations of sports and media such as e-sports.
- Globalization of sports (Mullin, 2014: 239).

The Olympic Games have been mentioned in the introduction of this chapter. The selection of the "worldwide top partners" of the IOC and the Olympic Games does not contain any sports related corporation. Current top Olympic partners are: Coca-Cola (soft drinks), Atos (IT), Dow (chemicals), GE (electronic devices), McDonald's (food), Omega (luxury watches), Panasonic (consumer electronics), P&G (personal care), Samsung (consumer electronics), and VISA (financial services). All of these sponsors share common goals that they want to achieve by their sponsorship expenditures. Sponsorship goals can be structured as follows: cognitive goals (increasing brand awareness); affective goals (support and change brand image); and behavioral goals (support and stimulate sales, increasing brand loyalty) (Lagae, 2003: 44). Depending on each individual sponsor, the importance and relevance of these goals may differ.

In addition to sponsorship engagements, several other possibilities of marketing through sports can be found in sports marketing practice. Probably the best-known is ambush marketing. An early definition can be found in Sandler and Shani (1989), saying that ambush marketing is a planned effort by an organization to identify itself indirectly with a (sports) event in order to gain at least some of the recognition that is associated with being an official sponsor. For additional information on ambush marketing, see Part III of this handbook.

Special characteristics of the sports market

Marketing of sports and marketing through sports is subject to several circumstances and recent developments that make a difference between the sports market (and its downstream markets) and other economic markets (Smith and Stewart 1999; Beech and Chadwick, 2004; Beech, Kaiser and Kaspar, 2013).

Globalization has a significant impact on the scope of sports organizations. For example, the sale of TV rights by the European major soccer leagues has become more and more important, especially for clubs that were able to build up a global brand (like Barcelona or Manchester United). From a social perspective, public requests from sports and sports organizations changed significantly during recent years. CSR and CRM became more and more important in the scene of global competition of sports organizations. Federations like FIFA are subject to discussions in the media, even legal restrictions are discussed in some countries. Individualization and sophisticated lifestyles influence the demand for sports. Former "9 to 5" jobs are increasingly replaced by lifestyles empowering workers to commit themselves beyond their working hours. Strictly-defined training hours become less important. The recent development in the media sector has changed the finance structures of competitive sports. Mass sports are still mainly financed by member contributions and donations, whereas competitive sports are mainly financed by sponsorship and the sale of media rights. As a result of the development of the new media, i.e. internet related media, clubs and federations are able to broadcast themselves by using sites such as YouTube. Today, there is no need to contract a broadcasting station to communicate with fans and spectators. Hence, increased media coverage makes sports events and tournaments more attractive for sponsors. The following section analyzes some characteristics that are special for the sports market and that should be recognized for any kind of sports marketing.

Characteristics of suppliers and the overall market structure

The main characteristic of the sports market (from the supplier's perspective) is the diversity of different sports producing organizations. Focusing on Europe, a major part of the sports facilities is provided by non-profit organizations such as clubs and associations that are subsidized by the federal state through direct payments or other advantages like tax exemptions. The goals of many sports organizations are not maximizing their profit but maximizing their success in sports events, tournaments, etc. Moreover, the sports sector is dominated by small suppliers, such as local clubs or small gyms. These market players most often face restrictions regarding their budget (for example, for promotion activities or the development of new products). Finally, smaller organizations normally show a minor degree of internal differentiation, employing only a few staff members acting as generalists.

Regarding sports as a phenomenon of competition that is determined by tournaments, league tables, etc., it is obvious that competition needs a degree of cooperation. Without any cooperation between the athletes or teams, neither sports nor sports goods (for passive sports consumption by spectators) can be provided. Additionally, in the case of professional sports production, external production factors, especially the spectator in the stadium, hall, etc., are involved in the production process. Production and consumption of sports goods are linked inseparably (Uno-Actu principle). Additionally, exogenous factors such as the weather, consumption of performance-enhancing drugs, etc., play an important role during the production process and affect the marketability of the economic result (i.e. the product). The most important result of these factors is a "systematic and structural deficit of rational behavior" (Horch, 1994; cf. Smith and Stewart 1999). The core of the product cannot be fully controlled or determined by the supplier (i.e. the athlete, team, club, gym, etc.).

Regarding the circumstances for the marketing of sports, it is impossible to promote the characteristics of the sports goods. Therefore, any promotion has to focus on the facts and circumstances of the production process itself. These facts include, but are not limited to, the objective quality of players and athletes (in comparison to other athletes based on a league table) and the importance of the contest (derby, championship, "battle for being #1").

Special characteristics of the goods produced

Regarding the special characteristics of sports goods, the predominance of services is to be mentioned first. From an economic perspective, the quality of services cannot be assessed prior to the consumption. Therefore, services can be classified as confidence goods: any consumer would need to rely on the service provider for the quality and display confidence. Otherwise, no contract will be concluded and no service will be provided. The consumer is embedded in the service provision process. As a result of the provision of services, uncertainties could occur at the level of the service provider as well as at the level of the service recipient. Special "cooperation designs" offer possibilities to reduce these uncertainties (cf. Fitzsimmons, 2011). Instruments that visualize the potential, the process and the result, and that symbolize the quality of the service, are most important in this context. Popular "signals" are, for example, certificates, photographs and other visual media providing information on the comfort of an event location, etc.

Predominant (economic) goals of sports organizations are increasing revenues and increasing numbers of members and customers. Besides these goals, sports organizations utilize promotional activities to strengthen their public recognition and the publicity of their offers. Recognition at the level of actual and prospective customers and the offer's publicity both influence the value of the sports organization's brand positively. Because the advertisement for services is more complicated compared to other goods (tangibles), it is even more important to use repeated signals describing the quality of the service. The main goal of permanent signals is to build on the organization's reputation and to be silhouetted against other competitors.

Moreover, many sports goods and services can either be described as public goods (Samuelson, 1954) or merit goods (Musgrave, 1969). Promotion of sports and promotion through sports can benefit from this aspect, provided promotion refers to sports goods' special characteristics. Because sports can create positive external effects that can be classified as public goods, sports might be subsidized. The following example might clarify this idea: Children and adolescents playing football (either in a non-profit club or in a profit oriented soccer center) train their physical fitness attributes and learn to adapt a disciplined lifestyle (development of human capital). Moreover, the game could act as an integration opportunity for children coming from low income households, immigrant families, etc. Thus, sports can play an important role in the education and building of a prosperous society. Not only the children, but the entire city or district benefit from this effect and hence, we can refer to this as a positive external effect. In many cases, the state is not able to generate these effects in a similar quality or extent with lower costs. Therefore, a public subsidy for the organized sports can be derived from the positive externalities generated by sports organizations.

Special characteristics of sports demand

The demand for sports services and goods is characterized by several special effects that influence it significantly and that should be considered in the marketing mix of sports marketing. First, active sports execution is normally performed with other individuals and as a part of some kind of social program that aims at social interaction. In nearly all cases, active sports has a social impact. Second, sports goods show a variety of exemptions from the standard demand rules. Only a few examples should be given in this context. Individual decisions suffer from bounded rationality due to the good character of some sports goods. Moreover, doing sports often can be characterized by a positive marginal utility (in contrast to the consumption of normal goods) (Heinemann, 1995). Therefore, any analysis of the demand for sports (including sports services and goods) must not rely only on the generally-accepted economic principles of consumption. These generally-accepted principles assume income changes and market prices as independent variables. However, origin and shape of preferences are neglected and the time factor is normally not considered (ibid). Finally, regarding sports and differentiating between active and passive sports consumption, individuals have to trade passive sports consumption (individuals act as consumers) against active sports exercises (individuals act as sports suppliers) in many cases.

If athletes buy sports goods (or receive sports services) they want to satisfy needs, such as health, prestige, social contacts, etc. In contrast to normal goods, the purchase of sports goods does not satisfy these needs. Furthermore, inputs like time, effort, etc., that need to be provided by the athletes are necessary for the utility. In day-to-day life the utility level that can be reached by an athlete is uncertain due to input restrictions. This leads to a reduced willingness to pay by consumers or athletes.

Regarding professional sports, the popularity of team sports and team sports events is often explained by the uncertainty of outcome hypothesis (Rottenberg, 1956). The attractiveness of a competition is influenced by the uncertainty of outcome: The more uncertain the result is, the higher is the popularity. Focusing on fans that show a deep loyalty to a club, the uncertainty of outcome hypothesis is of less importance. Group experiences (in the stadium, watching their club win or lose) become much more important for these fans, compared with neutral spectators who are only interested in the sports but not in the performance of a single team. Against this background, sports marketing faces an opportunity: If the marketer is able to strengthen the identification of the fans (consumers) with "their" team, the revenues resulting from the sale of tickets, merchandising, etc., are more and more independent from the current performance of the team. Thus, "identification with the team" is an important segmentation criterion for a target group oriented address. In this context, the new media allow adequate means to get in contact with target groups as they enable the marketer to address different groups at low costs. For the strategic planning and the identification of adequate content, it is important to identify links that allow a long-term identification with a club that is independent of the current success (independent of the current league table). According to Kaiser (2010) such links might be:

- The team's success in the past.
- The performance of individual athletes.
- Shared values (for example, a working-class background).
- A strong connection to a city or region.
- A common understanding as an underdog.

Outlook

Against the background of the past there is hardly any doubt over the ongoing professionalization of sports and its related industries. Professionalization does not focus on FPOs but will explicitly gain importance in the context of NPOs.

The technological evolution is only one additional factor influencing the marketing of sports and the marketing through sports. Marketing 3.0 was already discussed earlier; the current discussion of industry 4.0 provides an initial idea of future technologies and its impact on organizations. Any marketing in relation to sports has to consider the outstanding changes in information technology. Facebook, Google and Twitter have already changed our day-to-day life and will continue to do so. Marketing of individual athletes involves new media in order to allow a 24/7 availability of stars. Twitter posts and (user) channels on YouTube allow new possibilities in reaching millions of users and customers within seconds, irrespective of their location. In order to stay in contact with all stakeholders, sports organizations will have to consider these changes in their marketing strategy and their 4Ps. In a nutshell, sports marketing remains one of the most important tasks in relation to sports.

Notes

1 www.fifa.com/aboutfifa/finances/income.html (accessed 18 August 2015).
2 www.forbes.com/sites/mikeozanian/2014/06/05/the-billion-dollar-business-of-the-world-cup (accessed 18 August 2015).
3 www.qf.org.qa/page?a=835&lang=en-CA (accessed 18 August 2015).

References

Andreff, W. and Bourg, J.-F. (2006). Broadcasting rights and competition in European football, in Jeanrenaud, C. and Késenne, S. (eds.), *The economics of sport and the media*, Cheltenham: Edward Elgar, pp. 37–70.
Beech, J. and Chadwick, S. (2004). *The business of sport management*, London: Pearson Education.
Beech, J., Kaiser, S. and Kaspar, R. (eds) (2013). *The business of events management*, Harlow: Pearson.
Blythe, J. (2006). *Marketing*, London: SAGE Publications.
Booms, B. and Bitner, M. J. (1981). Marketing strategies and organizational structures for service firms, in J. H. Donnelly and R. W. George (eds), *Marketing of services*, Chicago: American Marketing Association, 47–51.
Delaney, T. and Madigan, T. (2009). *The sociology of sports*, Jefferson: Jefferson: McFarland & Company.
Desbordes, M. (2012). The establishment and management of sports arenas: A neo-marketing approach, in Desbordes, M. and Richelieu, A. (eds.), *Global sport marketing*, New York: Routledge, pp. 156–186.

Ferrell, O. C. and Hartline, M. (2012). *Marketing strategy*, 6th edition, Nashville: South Western Education Publishing.

Fitzsimmons, J.A. (2011). *Service management*, Boston: McGraw-Hill/Irwin.

Gladden, J. M. and Sutton, W. A. (2011). Professional sport, in Pedersen, P. M., Parks, J. P., Quarterman, J. and Thibault, L. (eds.), *Contemporary sport management*, 4th edition, Champaign: Human Kinetics, pp. 120–141.

Heinemann, K. (1995). *Einführung in die Ökonomie des Sports: Ein Handbuch*, Schorndorf: Hofmann.

Horch, H.-D. (1994). Besonderheiten einer Sport-Ökonomie, in *Freizeitpädagogik*, 16, pp. 243–257.

Hoye, R., Smith, A.C. T., Nicholson, M., Stewart, B. and Westerbeek, H. (2012). *Sport management: Principles and applications*, 3rd edition, New York: Routledge.

Kaiser, S. (2010). Kommunikationsmanagement im Sport, in Nufer, G. and Bühler, A. (eds.), *Management im Sport: Betriebswirtschaftliche Grundlagen und Anwendungen der modernen Sportökonomie*, 2nd edition, Berlin: Schmidt, pp. 437–461.

Kotler, P., Kartajaya, H. and Setiawan, I. (2010). *Marketing 3.0*, New Jersey: John Wiley and Sons.

Kotler, P. and Keller, K. (2012). *Marketing management*, 14th ed., New Jersey: Prentice Hall.

Lagae, W. (2003). *Sports sponsorship and marketing communications*, Essex: Pearson Education.

Mandelbaum, M. (2004). *The meaning of sports*, New York: Public Affairs.

Mullin, B. J. (2014). *Sport marketing*, 4th edition, Champaign: Human Kinetics.

Musgrave, R. A. (1969). *Finanztheorie*, 2nd edition, Tübingen: Mohr.

Parent, M. M. and Smith-Swan, S. (2013). *Managing major sport events: Theory and practice*, New York: Routledge.

Quing, W. (2013). Relationship between sport and media: on promoting the sound development of bilateral relations, in *2013 International Symposium: Common development of sports and modern society*, 16–18 Dec, 2013, Beijing, pp. 23–29.

Rottenberg, S. (1956). The baseball player's labor market, *Journal of Political Economy*, 64 (3), pp. 242–258.

Samuelson, P. A. (1954). The pure theory of public expenditure, *The Review of Economics and Statistics*, 36 (4), pp. 387–389.

Sandler, D.M. and Shani, D. (1989). Olympic sponsorship vs ambush marketing: Who gets the gold, *Journal of Advertising Research*, 29 (4), pp. 9–14.

Sansone, D. (1992). *Greek athletics and the genesis of sport*, Berkeley/Los Angeles: University of California Press.

Shilbury, D., Westerbeek, H., Quick, S., Funk, D. and Karg, A. (2014). *Strategic sport marketing*, 4th edition, Crows Nest: Allen & Unwin.

Smith, A. and Stewart, B. (1999). *Sports management: A guide to professional practice*. Sydney: Allen and Unwin.

Smith, A. C. T. and Stewart, B. (2015). *Introduction to sport marketing*, 2nd edition, New York: Routledge.

Usui, K. (2008). *The development of marketing management*, Hampshire/Burlington: Ashgate Publishing.

PART I

Brands

Simon Chadwick, Nicolas Chanavat and Michel Desbordes

The notion of branding in sports is one that has only recently emerged, but which has now become a focus for sports marketing practitioners and academic researchers. In some quarters, there is still a marked reluctance to conceive of teams, clubs, events and other sporting entities as brands. Critics see branding as the unnecessary commodification of sports, rendering social institutions simply as commercial properties. However, there is no doubt that many of these sporting institutions have a clear history, identity and position, which can be utilised as the basis for fan engagement, product positioning and revenue generation. As such, sports organisations have variously sought either to create clear brand identities or to release the latent equity that many of the organisations possess. Branding is thus a relatively immature activity but is nevertheless rapidly rising to prominence. This part sets out to examine some of the currently most salient issues in the field. Chapters examine how sports brands are built, how such brands can be activated in sports, and the role brands play in promoting sports properties.

2
CONGRUENCE EFFECTS IN SPORTS MARKETING
Determinants, measures, and outcomes of fit or misfit

Björn Walliser

Introduction

In sports marketing, congruence often arises as a magical concept, able to induce stronger and more positive impacts on consumer reactions than incongruent pairings. For example, an athlete endorser should have a stronger influence than an actor on the evaluation of an energy bar but not on the evaluation of a candy bar (Till and Busler, 2000). Even athletes such as Tiger Woods or Michael Phelps, who transgress social norms, might enjoy commercial success if they endorse "rebellious" products (Pokrywczynski and Brinker, 2012). Similarly, a sports team brand should anticipate greater success by leveraging its brand equity in a sports clothing line rather than a cosmetics line (Papadimitriou et al., 2004). In contrast, misfits—brands and sports entities not going well together—might damage brand equity by prompting negative reactions among consumers. It is questionable whether the sponsorship of the soccer team, Atletico Madrid, by the country of Azerbaijan is well understood by sports spectators, albeit some recent studies propose that a well-chosen misfit could benefit sponsors and sports marketing brands (for example, Trendel and Warlop, 2013).

For decades, sponsorship practitioners and scholars have suspected that congruence drives sponsorship and endorsement success. Congruence effects are arguably the most widely-used theoretical concept for explaining sponsorship effectiveness, often in interaction with other variables. Sponsorship literature thus follows research in other marketing areas, such as celebrity endorsements and brand extensions, where the role of fit had received earlier attention. Several theories provide explanations for congruence effects, though they do not all offer the same conclusions. Congruity theory (Osgood and Tannenbaum, 1955) and balance theory (Heider, 1958) both stress the importance of cognitive consistency, which motivates people to maintain uniformity in their thoughts, feelings, and behavior. According to general schema theory, information that is consistent with existing schemas tends to be better remembered and evaluated more positively (Fiske, 1982). In contrast, the encoding flexibility model (Sherman et al., 1998) posits that information consistent with prior expectations receives little attention and is poorly encoded, such that people instead turn their attention to inconsistent information that is harder to comprehend, such as incongruent pairings.

Sports sponsorship:	Shell (lubricant supplier) and the Ferrari Formula 1 team.
Sports naming rights:	Macron (sportswear manufacturer) and Bolton Wanderers F.C.
Sports (celebrity) endorsement:	Under Armour (sports apparel) and Jordan Spieth (golf).
Sports brand extension:	Liverpool F.C. and LFCTV (television channel).

Figure 2.1 Congruent pairings in key sports marketing areas

This chapter details the impact of congruence on three key areas of sports marketing: sports sponsorship, sports advertising based on endorsements, and sports brand extensions. All three areas combine two or more brands or entities in a quest for commercial success, such that congruence should be important for all of them, though the focal associations differ. For example, a sponsorship entails a match between a brand and a sports property, often an event, but sometimes a person or team (for example, Shell and the Ferrari Formula 1 team); for some, sports naming rights are also a specific form of (venue) sponsorship. When it comes to endorsements, congruence between the athlete and the brand or product is of primary concern (for example, Jordan Spieth and Under Armour sports apparel). For brand extensions, the congruence between two brands or products is most important (for example, Liverpool F.C. and LFCTV, the club's television channel).

Negotiating a sponsorship or endorser agreement demands substantial time and resources. More than one in four endorsers featured in U.S. magazine advertising represents the world of sport (Belch and Belch, 2013). If a perfect match was not necessarily required, this would alleviate much stress from sports marketing managers. If congruence had a consistent influence, it would be reassuring to take advantage of positive effects and avoid negative ones.

The following sections describe the nature, relevance, and existing measures of congruence, before documenting the outcome of congruence effects and suggesting several variables that likely mediate or moderate their impact.

Determinants of congruence in different sports marketing contexts

Many terms describe congruence, and many grounds provide theoretical bases for predicted congruence effects. That is, congruence also appears as "relevance" (Johar and Pham, 1999), "fit" (Pracejus and Olsen, 2004), "similarity" (Gwinner and Eaton, 1999), "match" (McDaniel, 1999), "compatibility" (Ruth and Simonin, 2003), and many other terms. In sports marketing, congruence refers to how well a brand goes with another entity, such as an event, athlete, or another brand.[1] Furthermore, the basic determinants of congruence—image and product features—are common across different areas of sports marketing, but its precise conceptualization differs (see Table 2.1).

As early as the 1970s, Kanungo and Pang (1973: p. 172) suggested the need for "fittingness" between a model and a product, though they did not specifically address the sports context. Misra and Beatty (1990: p. 161) led the groundwork to understanding endorsement-related fit—the so-called matchup hypothesis—by asserting: "the highly relevant characteristics of the spokesperson are consistent with the highly relevant attributes of the brand." Endorsement research (for example, Erfgen, 2011) frequently distinguishes three congruence categories: attractiveness-based (relevance of the physical attractiveness of the endorser), expertise-based (perceived expertise of the endorser for a product category, brand, or issue), and image-based (match of the endorser's image with the image of the brand). In addition, Fleck et al. (2012) observe that the perceived congruence of a (celebrity) endorser depends on the consumer's

Table 2.1 Determinants of congruence in sports marketing

Sport celebrity endorsement	Sport brand extension	Sport sponsorship
Image of the endorser (including endorser ubiquity). Expertise of the endorser. Attractiveness of the endorser. Liking of the endorser.	Image of the parent brand. Expertise of parent brand. Product category and product features (performance, team play characteristics, history, quality level, etc.).	Image of the sponsor (including sponsor sincerity and ubiquity). Product functions and benefits (product use, audience similarity, geographic origin, etc.).

attitude toward that endorser. People who like a celebrity are more likely to find them congruent, regardless of the brand being promoted.

The congruence between a parent brand and its extension has been conceptualized in various ways (for example, Apostolopoulou, 2002). Early studies (Chadwick and Clowes, 1998) define extension congruence primarily in terms of product category fit and feature similarity, that is, whether the product category of the parent brand and the extension brand are similar, and whether both brands are used in similar settings or are manufactured at the same facility. Aaker and Keller (1990) define brand extension fit as the established expertise of the parent brand in the extension's product category. Image and quality are other key dimensions of extension congruence. The team brand association scale (Ross et al., 2006) establishes several factors that might determine extension congruence in a sports context, such as the non-player personnel associated with a particular team, team performance, team history, team play characteristics, identifying marks associated with the team, organizational attributes, and even liking or disliking competitor teams. Marketing research has shown that perceived fit is mediated by the perceived credibility of the parent brand and its potential ability to launch new products (Smith and Andrews, 1995). Apostolopoulou (2002) suggests that sports fans with stronger team identification are more likely to react positively to brand extensions, regardless of perceived fit. In most cases, brand extension literature (Broniarczyk and Alba, 1994) simply defines "fit" as the extent to which consumers perceive congruence, notwithstanding the specific reasons that lead to it.

The extent to which a sponsor and sponsee are perceived as similar by sponsorship targets depends on their functionality, image, or other attributes, associations, or strategies. Fleck and Quester (2007: p. 981) tabulate definitions of congruence in sponsorship literature. For example, functional or logical fit arises from sponsor products that are used during the sponsored event. Image fit reflects a link between the image of the sponsor and the sponsee, such as Rolex supporting a prestigious golf tournament. A strategic fit might be exemplified by a beer brand sponsoring football, for the simple reason that football fans tend to consume above-average amounts of beer. A qualitative, empirical, cognitive mapping sponsorship study (Olson and Thjømøe, 2011) confirms some of these dimensions and adds new ones, identifying seven total explanations of fit: (1) using a brand's products during an event, either directly, for example, athletes' shoes, or indirectly, for example, spectators drink beer while watching a game; (2) size similarity, for example, the object and brand are both prominent or not prominent; (3) audience similarity, for example, the object's audience is also the brand's target segment; (4) geographic similarity, for example, national brand and national team; (5) attitude similarity, for example, equal liking of the brand and the object; (6) image similarity, for example, similar meaning or image of both entities; and (7) time duration of the sponsorship relation, for example, "unhealthy" beer brands still fit well with "healthy" sports, because of their longstanding sponsorship link.

Use by the participants and audience similarity turns out to be the most important predictors of fit in the context of the study done by Olson and Thjømøe (2011). Work by Woisetschläger et al. (2010) reveals that the perceived benefits of the sponsor for the sponsored entity and regional identification with the sponsor company have the strongest influence on sponsorship fit, according to fans of a soccer club. The same variables influence perceived fit in a stadium-naming context (Woisetschläger and Haselhoff, 2009). Sponsor sincerity and ubiquity contribute only modestly to perceived fit (Speed and Thompson, 2000; Woisetschläger et al., 2010).

Across various sports contexts, the different determinants of congruence appear independent. For example, if an endorser does not fit a brand in terms of image, they could still be perceived as congruent, because of their expertise or attractiveness. In the absence of a functional sponsorship fit, a sponsor and sponsee could be perceived as similar because of their image, national origin, or another dimension of fit. Therefore, brands should always be able to find some grounds on which to establish fit with a sports entity.

Measures of congruence

Congruence can be measured indirectly or directly. Indirect methods determine the overlap among associations evoked independently by each of a pair of entities. Indirect methods thus would first evaluate the associations evoked by a brand, then test the associations evoked by a celebrity or event, and finally compare the two set of associations. Direct methods instead evaluate congruence as on overall construct, using "fit" and its synonyms such as "similar," "well matched," or "congruent" as prompts. The scales in Table 2.2 reflect direct measures, which tend to be more commonly adopted by sports marketing studies.

Some direct measures are also more elaborate. Speed and Thompson (2000: p. 231) include a specific fit dimension in their five-item sponsorship scale: "The image of the event and the image of the sponsor are similar." Olson and Thjømøe (2011) propose 17 items to measure six of the seven dimensions of sponsorship fit they identified. For the "product use" dimension, they ask: "(1) How likely is it that the products from [sponsor] are used by the participants in [object]? and (2) When watching [object] on television, how likely are audience members to be using [sponsor] products?"

Table 2.2 Direct measures of overall congruence

Sponsorship literature		Endorsement literature
Simmons and Becker-Olsen (2006)	Rifon et al. (2004)	Fleck et al. (2012)
1. dissimilar ↔ similar	1. not compatible ↔ compatible	"[Brand X] and [celebrity Y] go well together."
2. inconsistent ↔ consistent	2. not a good fit ↔ good fit	"[Brand X] is well matched with [celebrity Y]."
3. atypical ↔ typical	3. not congruent ↔ congruent	
4. low fit ↔ high fit		"In my opinion, [celebrity Y] is very appropriate as a celebrity endorser for [brand X]."
5. does not make sense ↔ makes sense		

Table 2.3 Two-dimensional congruence scale (Fleck and Quester, 2007)

Expectancy	Relevancy
1. I am not surprised that this company sponsors this event.	1. That this company sponsors this event tells me something about it.
2. I would expect this company to sponsor this event.	2. With this sponsorship, I discover a new aspect of this company.
3. It was predictable that this company would sponsor this event.	

Inspired by advertising research (Heckler and Childers, 1992), Fleck and Quester (2007) validate a two-dimensional congruence scale (see Table 2.3 for the measures) based on expectancy and relevancy. Consumers clearly understand congruence more in terms of expectancy (noticing a sponsor at an event where it was expected) than relevancy (learning something about the sponsor through the event or the sport). To illustrate, Messi and Adidas would be an expected and relevant pairing, as would be Phil Mickelson and Callaway golf balls. However, KPMG would not necessarily be expected as a sponsor of golfers, but could still be considered relevant based on the strategic capacities needed by golf professionals playing a course as well as by management consultants. Expectancy explains three times more variance in the congruence construct than relevancy. An adapted version of this scale successfully measured endorsement congruence as well (Fleck et al., 2012).

Conceptual background of congruence effects

On a general level, congruence effects in sports marketing can be explained by balance theory (Heider, 1958). Consumers strive to establish harmony in their thoughts about elements they perceive as belonging together. Confronted with an entity they like, such as an athlete or sports event, together with a less-valued entity, such as a brand, consumers may form more positive attitudes toward the brand, or else a less positive attitude toward the celebrity or event. Congruity theory (Osgood and Tannenbaum, 1955) refines this approach by identifying degrees of positive and negative evaluations and anticipating that evaluations of both entities could change. Thus, consumers might form more neutral attitudes toward the liked celebrity or event and the less-liked brand.

Schema theory offers another means to explain congruence effects. Schemas are cognitive structures that represent information about objects, their attributes, and the interrelations among attributes. In a general case, information congruent with existing schemas is easier to memorize (Alba and Hasher, 1983); items consistent with existing schemas also receive affect from that schema (Fiske, 1982). In a sponsorship setting,[2] general schema theory posits that when spectators perceive that a sponsor brand fits with an existing schema (for example, a brand that fits with an event), they better remember the brand, and the affect from the event schema transfers to the brand schema (or vice versa). Predictions about schema processing outcomes are not uniform. According to one model of schema theory, expectancy-incongruent information enjoys better encoding. This "schema-pointer plus tag" model posits that incongruent information gets encoded in a specific memory location and is therefore better recognized in subsequent encounters.

The associative network (AN) approach further posits that memory consists of individual pieces of information, called nodes, that are connected. Thinking about one node (for example, event, athlete) may activate thinking about another node (for example, brand). Repeated exposures to typical sports marketing pairings strengthen the associative link of the two entities, which might also modify the evaluation of our attitude toward these objects, because attitude reflects the association between an object and its evaluation (Fazio et al., 1989). Whether expectancy-congruent information is better remembered than expectancy-incongruent information depends on the level of elaboration. In a sponsorship context, Simmons and Becker-Olsen (2006) describe interpretations of marketing stimuli as a two-stage process. First, consumers make relatively effortless inferences about sponsor stimuli on the basis of their event schemas (or inversely, make inferences about the event on the basis of their sponsor schemas), such as "This brand fits well with the event" or "Supporting this event or cause is a good thing." Second, congruent relationships do not trigger very elaborative processes, so they lead to milder, albeit positively valued thoughts. Incongruent pairings instead advance the processing to a level at which consumers assess all available inputs and potentially correct inferences they drew during the more superficial first processing stage. This more effortful processing leads to positive valuations if people can resolve the incongruity (Jagre et al., 2001). The resolution of slightly incongruent messages leads to similar (Simmons and Becker-Olsen, 2006) or possibly stronger affect; an inability to cope with strong incongruence may lead to frustration and negative thoughts (Mandler, 1982).

The encoding flexibility model (Sherman et al., 1998) confirms these processes. It posits that information consistent with prior expectations receives little attention and is not well encoded. Instead, consumers turn their attention to inconsistent information, which is harder to comprehend, such as incongruent pairings. This model also differentiates between perceptual and conceptual encoding of information. Perceptual encoding implies processing of the physical qualities of the stimulus (for example, recognizing the logo of a sports brand). Conceptual encoding relates to the attribution of meaning to a stimulus (for example, perceiving a brand as luxurious). According to the encoding flexibility model, under low elaboration, perceptual encoding is superior for incongruent information, but conceptual encoding is better for congruent information (Trendel and Warlop, 2013).

Samu et al. (1999) combine schema and AN theories to explain co-branding and advertising alliances. Whereas AN theory explains how memory of partner brands gets activated, schema theory explains the transfer of affect across activated schemas and explains how the perception of congruence changes over time.

Effects of congruence on sports marketing variables

Congruence affects sports celebrity advertising, sports brand extensions, and sports sponsorship in many ways. Table 2.4 offers an overview of studies that measure and test the influence of congruence on key marketing variables, such as memorization, attitude, and purchase intentions.

Overall effect of congruence

Sponsorship literature, that has provided the vast majority of the studies presented in Table 2.4, regularly documents positive outcomes of congruence. In most cases, congruence seems to increase rather than decrease attention to sponsors (for example, Deitz et al. 2009), sponsor memorization (for example, Rodgers, 2004), sponsor brand attitude (for example, McDaniel, 1999), purchase intentions (for example, Rodgers, 2004), and the market value of brands or companies (for example, Clark et al., 2009). Congruence benefits not only the sponsor

Table 2.4 Outcome of congruence on key marketing variables

Variable investigated	Positive effects	Negative or neutral effects
Recall/recognition.	Barros and Silvestre (2006[S]), Johar and Pham (1999[S]), Wakefield et al. (2007[S]), Cornwell et al. (2006[S]), Grohs et al. (2004[S]), Trendel and Warlop (2013[S])[3]	Trendel and Warlop (2013[S]),[4] Olson and Thjømøe (2009[S])
Image or attitude (e.g., preference, attractiveness, favorability of/for sponsor products, word-of-mouth intentions).	Simmons and Becker-Olsen (2006[S]), Speed and Thompson (2000[S]), Weeks et al. (2008[S]), McDaniel (1999[S]), Olson (2010[S]), Becker-Olsen and Hill (2006[S]), Coppetti et al. (2009[S]), Woisetschläger and Haselhoff (2009[S]), Donahay and Rosenberger III (2007[S]), Gwinner and Eaton (1999[S]), Roy and Cornwell (2003[S]), Barros and Silvestre (2006[S]), Woisetschläger et al. (2010[S]), Kim and Na (2007[E]), Papadimitriou et al. (2004[BE]), Fink et al. (2004[E]), Koernig and Boyd (2009[E])[5]	Ruth and Simonin (2003[S]), Koernig and Boyd (2009[E])
Purchase intentions.	Fink et al. (2004[E]), Koernig and Boyd (2009[E]), Papadimitriou et al. (2004[BE])	McDaniel (1999[S]), Koernig and Boyd (2009[E])[6]
Financial (stock) value of brands.	Cornwell et al. (2005[S]), Clark et al. (2009[S]), Cornwell et al. (2001[S])	

[S]Sponsorship study, [E]Endorsement study, [BE]Brand extension study

company or its shareholders but in certain conditions, it also strengthens the brand's identity, brand relationships (Becker-Olsen and Hill, 2006), and the image of sponsees (Ruth and Simonin, 2003).

There is some doubt whether the influence of fit on memorization is always positive. Some studies (Olson and Thjømøe, 2009; Trendel and Warlop, 2013) reveal that non-congruent sponsors are easier to recognize than congruent sponsors, in line with Stangor and McMillan's (1992) meta-analysis, in which recall of expectancy-incongruent information is higher overall than that for expectancy-congruent information. Some prior studies may have overestimated the positive role of congruence on memorization because they ignored spectators' tendency to infer sponsor names using congruence heuristics (Johar and Pham, 1999): if they are not sure about a sponsor of an event, spectators tend to cite brands they think would fit with the event.

A series of empirical results confirm the tenets of the match-up hypothesis for sports endorsements. Till and Busler (2000) show that respondents offer more positive evaluations of an energy bar when it is promoted by an athlete, that is, someone who should have expertise about energy products, rather than by an actor. Athlete characteristics, such as perceived attractiveness and expertise, positively influence perceived fit, which in turn influences attitudes toward the endorsed brand (Fink et al., 2004). Even unknown athletes in advertisements for sports products elicit more favorable responses, in terms of perceived expertise and purchase intent, than do non-athlete endorsers (Koernig and Boyd, 2009). But not all dimensions of fit are equally salient in all situations. The endorser characteristic most directly linked to the promoted product exerts the strongest impact. For example, the expertise of a softball player has a stronger influence on attitudes toward a softball game and ultimately intentions to buy tickets for that game than player attractiveness (Fink et al., 2004). Congruence has a positive general influence on endorsement processes, regardless of whether the endorsers are sports celebrities or unknown athletes. A single, salient (sports-related) characteristic, such as muscularity for exercise equipment, may even be enough to evoke congruence among consumers.

Congruence also is influential for the extension of existing sports brands into new product categories, though empirical evidence addressing this point is sparse. Sports managers believe fit is a key success factor for extensions (Apostolopoulou, 2002), and fans are capable of assessing the fit of extensions (Walsh et al., 2012). Sports clothing and sports camps thus produce significantly higher fit perceptions than cosmetics or banking services. Furthermore, product categories with greater fit are evaluated more positively by fans and invoke higher purchase intentions (Papadimitriou et al., 2004). Similar to endorsement and sponsorship literature, the dimensions of congruence vary by the product category of the extensions, hinting at effects of perceived typicality for sports brand extensions that are similar to those uncovered in brand extension literature in general (for example, Loken and Ward, 1990).

Mediating and moderating variables of congruence for sports marketing outcomes

The influence of congruence on memorization, brand attitudes, and other marketing outcomes is moderated and mediated by several other variables, including message elaboration, perceived brand motives, and brand prominence. It is also subject to situational traits and the personal characteristics of the consumers.

Consumers generate more thoughts if they perceive a misfit rather than fit, in a brand extension (Koernig and Boyd, 2009) or sponsorship (Becker-Olsen and Hill, 2006) context. If fit is high, perceived cognitive consistency leads to positive thoughts (Speed and Thompson, 2000). Without such cognitive consistency, consumers develop more thoughts about the misfit, including more negative thoughts toward both partners (Simmons and Becker-Olsen, 2006; Speed and Thompson, 2000; Becker-Olsen and Hill, 2006). Similarly, if an endorser does not fit, consumers have more negative, more neutral, and fewer positive ad-related thoughts than if the endorser fits with the product advertised (Koernig and Boyd, 2009). The negative thoughts due to the lack of relation in the pairing lead to feelings of frustration (D'Astous and Bitz, 1995) and negative attitudes toward both partners. Between the extremes of fit and misfit, a moderate level of fit may lead to better brand memorization and more positive attitudes than perfect fit (Jagre et al., 2001). That is, a small misfit between two entities may be beneficial, so long as it is perceived as interesting and mostly positive. For example, unexpected information leads to greater advertising message involvement and more favorable evaluations (Lee, 2000).

Increased elaboration generates thoughts not only about the misfit itself but also the context of the pairing in general (Koernig and Boyd, 2009; Simmons and Becker-Olsen, 2006). According to attribution theory, consumers try to understand why sponsors support an event or cause. Spectators who believe that sponsors have altruistic motives, perceive them as more credible and develop more positive attitudes toward them (Rifon et al. 2004; Speed and Thomson, 2000). Sponsors perceived as too aggressive or commercial instead are perceived less favorably. Colbert et al. (2005) show that congruence interacts with the type of sponsor, perceived sponsor objectives, and the type of event. For example, some large public companies in Canada do not need functional matches to be perceived favorably as sponsors, because their longstanding history of sponsorships makes them seem like "natural" sponsors to many Canadians.

Analogous to literature on "brandfests", participation in sponsorship experiences offers another way to increase congruence and brand attitudes for non-congruent sponsors (Coppetti et al., 2009; Weeks et al., 2008). Furthermore, sponsors that articulate their good intentions (Simmons and Becker-Olsen, 2006) can accommodate pairings that initially were perceived as non-congruent. Articulation and spectator experience both facilitate image transfers (Coppetti et al., 2009) and memory (Cornwell et al., 2006) for non-congruent sponsors, though not for already congruent brands. In addition to the positive main effects of congruency, activation, and altruistic articulation on brand attitudes, Weeks et al. (2008) observe a three-way interaction among these variables. For less congruent sponsorships, the positive effects of activation leverage get offset by commercially oriented articulations. For congruent sponsors using activation, perceptions of a commercial rationale do not negatively alter brand perceptions.

The more expertise a person has with a stimulus category, the more likely they are to apply schema-based processing. Experts have more compact and readily accessible schemas and use schema-inconsistent information more than novices do. In a sports context, experts are equivalent to fans; brand experience is largely influenced by brand prominence. Compared with less knowledgeable persons, event experts generate more thoughts about the event, as well as more negative thoughts about sponsor–event combinations (Roy and Cornwell, 2004). Thus, experts should be more critical of sponsor–event pairings, especially when sponsor equity is low, because experts also generate more negative thoughts for such low equity sponsors than do novices (Roy and Cornwell, 2004). Sponsors with high brand equity instead appear more congruent with the event (Roy and Cornwell, 2003) and invoke more positive brand attitudes (Rifon et al., 2004). Deitz et al. (2009) highlight how social identification with a team (i.e., fans) and need for cognition can enhance perceived fit and sponsorship responses. Identification with a team, being a fan, directly and indirectly, through perceived team–sponsor congruence, leads to more positive responses to a sponsorship.

Congruence typically appears as a static property, such that the relationship between the two entities is perceived as congruent or not. However, perceptions of congruence can change over time. Sponsors or endorsers that do not appear congruent when a deal is first announced might achieve increased matching over additional encounters. Exposure leads to habituation, if not liking, and may help people forget about mismatches. According to Dardis (2009), congruence thus mediates between exposure and brand attitude. Brand extension research also affirms that congruence is "elastic" (Dardis, 2009: p. 39), in the sense that promoting an extension is a key success factor. Consumers' perceptions of congruence thus appear to evolve over time, depending on communication efforts by the brand and learning by spectators (Cornwell et al., 2006). The Amstel Gold Race—a popular cycling event in Europe sponsored by the beer brand, Amstel—offers an extreme example. If asked explicitly, many cycling fans likely consider an alcoholic beverage and a cycling race a misfit. But over time, this longstanding sponsor has literally become part of the event (i.e., its name) and is barely perceived as a sponsor, much less an intruder or misfit. When sponsors have been with an event long enough, people tend to question the link much less.

Conclusion

Prior literature demonstrates that congruence has a positive effect on brands across three areas of sports marketing: sports sponsorship, sports celebrity endorsements, and sports brand extensions.

Considering the many determinants of congruence, brands should always be able to find some grounds on which to create fit with a sports entity. But because congruence is context-dependent, dynamic, and subjective, it remains a constant managerial challenge to determine the most convincing basis of fit. Consumers have different reasons to believe that two entities fit (or misfit), but some of these reasons are more convincing, or have better predictive power, than others.

Sports marketing managers seem to believe that congruence has a positive effect for brands with little prior exposure but a negative one for brands with a strong sponsorship presence (Henseler et al., 2007). The reality is more complicated. Evaluations of fit and positive sports marketing partnerships depend on brand-related factors, including brand prominence, brand equity, sponsorship articulation, and brand history, as well as consumer-related factors, such as brand experience, brand knowledge, and brand motive attributions.

Notes

1. This chapter does not elaborate on self-congruity or self-image congruity, which is not to be confounded with the aforementioned conceptualizations of congruence. Self-congruity refers to the match between a person's self-concept and the image of a product or service. In a sport context, self-congruity is the degree to which spectators think that an event they attend or a product they buy is congruent with their self-image (for example, Close et al., 2009).
2. Most examples in the following paragraphs refer to sponsorships, yet the conceptual framework applies equally to endorsements, brand alliances, and brand extensions.
3. Memorization measured in terms of conceptual implicit memory.
4. Memorization measured in terms of perceptual implicit memory.
5. The impact was positive when this study used an unknown athlete.
6. This study found no significant impact when a famous athlete was used.

References

Aaker, D. A. and Keller, K. L. (1990). Consumer evaluations of brand extensions, *Journal of Marketing*, 54, 27–41.

Alba, J. W. and Hasher, L. (1983). Is memory schematic? *Psychological Bulletin*, 93, 203–231.

Apostolopoulou, A. (2002). Brand extensions by U.S. professional sports teams: Motivations and keys to success, *Sport Marketing Quarterly*, 11, 205–214.

Barros, C. P. and Silvestre, A. L. (2006). An evaluation of the sponsorship of EURO 2004, *International Journal of Sports Marketing and Sponsorship*, 7(3), 192–212.

Becker-Olsen, K. L. and Hill, R. P. (2006). The impact of sponsor fit on brand equity: the case of nonprofit service providers, *Journal of Service Research*, 9(1), 73–83.

Belch, G. E. and Belch, M. A. (2013). A content analysis study of the use of celebrity endorsers in magazine advertising, *International Journal of Advertising*, 32(3), 369–389.

Broniarczyk, S. M. and Alba, J. W. (1994). The importance of the brand in brand extension, *Journal of Marketing Research*, 31(2), 214–228.

Chadwick, S. and Clowes, J. (1998). The use of extension strategies by clubs in the English Football Premier League, *Managing Leisure*, 3, 194–203.

Clark, J. M, Cornwell, T. B. and Pruitt, S. W. (2009). The impact of title event sponsorship on shareholder wealth, *Marketing Letters*, 20(2), 169–182.

Close, A. G, Krishen, A. S. and Latour, M. S. (2009). This event is me! How consumer event self-congruity leverages sponsorship, *Journal of Advertising Research*, 49(3), 271–284.

Colbert, F., D'Astous, A. and Parmentier, M.-A. (2005). Consumer perceptions of sponsorship in the arts. A Canadian perspective, *International Journal of Cultural Policy*, 11(2), 216-228.

Coppetti, C., Wentzel, D., Tomczak, T. and Henkel, S. (2009). Improving incongruent sponsorships through articulation of the sponsorship and audience participation, *Journal of Marketing Communications*, 15(1), 17–34.

Cornwell, T. B., Pruitt, S. W. and Clark, J. M. (2005). The relationship between major-league sports' official sponsorship announcements and the stock prices of sponsoring firms, *Journal of the Academy of Marketing Science*, 33(4), 401–412.

Cornwell, T. B., Pruitt, S. W. and van Ness, R. (2001). The value of winning in motorsports: Sponsorship-linked marketing, *Journal of Advertising Research*, 41(1), 17–31.

Cornwell, T. B., Humphreys, M. S., Maguire, A. M., Weeks, C. S. and Tellegen, C. L. (2006). Sponsorship-linked marketing: the role of articulation in memory, *Journal of Consumer Research*, 33(3), 312–321.

Dardis, F. E. (2009). Attenuating the negative effects of perceived incongruence of sponsorship: How message repetition can enhance evaluations of an "incongruent" sponsor, *Journal of Promotion Management*, 15(1/2), 36–56.

D'Astous, A. and Bitz, P. (1995). Consumer evaluations of sponsorship programmes, *European Journal of Marketing*, 29(12), 6–22.

Deitz, G. D., Myers, S. W. and Markley, M. (2009). A resource-matching based view of sponsorship information processing, *Journal of Current Issues and Research in Advertising*, 31(1), 75–87.

Donahay, B. and Rosenberger, P. J., III (2007). Using brand personality to measure the effectiveness of image transfer in Formula One racing, *Marketing Bulletin*, 18, 1–15.

Erfgen, C. (2011). Impact of celebrity endorsement on brand image: a communication process perspective on 30 years of empirical research, *Research Papers on Marketing and Retailing*, (40), University of Hamburg, 1–24.

Fazio, R. H., Powell, M. C. and Williams, C. J. (1989). The role of attitude accessibility in the attitude-to-behavior process, *Journal of Consumer Research*, 16(3), 280–288.

Fink, J. S., Cunningham, G. B. and Kensicki, L. J. (2004), Using athletes as endorsers to sell women's sport: attractiveness vs. expertise, *Journal of Sport Management*, 18, 350–367.

Fiske, S. T. (1982), Schema-triggered affect: Applications to social perception, in: *17th Annual Carnegie Symposium on Cognition,* eds. Margaret S. Clark and Susan T. Fiske, Hillside, NJ: Erlbaum, 55–78.

Fleck, N. and Quester, P. (2007). Birds of a feather flock together... Definition, role and measure of congruence: an application to sponsorship, *Psychology & Marketing*, 24(11), 975–1000.

Fleck, N., Korchia, M. and Le Roy, I. (2012). Celebrities in advertising: looking for congruence or likability, *Psychology & Marketing*, 29(9), 651–662.

Grohs, R., Wagner, U. and Vsetecka, S. (2004), Assessing the effectiveness of sport sponsorships: An empirical examination, *Schmalenbach Business Review*, 56(2), 119–138.

Gwinner, K. P. and Eaton, J. (1999), Building brand image through event sponsorship: the role of image transfer, *Journal of Advertising*, 28(4), 47–57.

Heckler, S. E. and Childers, T. L. (1992). The role of expectancy and relevancy in memory for verbal and visual information: What is incongruency? *Journal of Consumer Research*, 18, 475–492.

Heider, F. (1958). *The Psychology of Interpersonal Relations*, New York: Wiley.

Henseler, J., Wilson, B., Götz, O. and Hautvast, C. (2007). Investigating the moderating role of fit on sports sponsorship and brand equity, *International Journal of Sports Marketing and Sponsorship*, 8(4), 321–329.

Jagre, E., Watson, J. J. and Watson, J. G. (2001). Sponsorship and congruity theory: A theoretical framework for explaining consumer attitude and recall of event sponsorship, *Advances in Consumer Research*, 28, 439–445.

Johar, G. V. and Pham, M. T. (1999). Relatedness, prominence, and constructive sponsor identification, *Journal of Marketing Research*, 36(3), 299–312.

Kanungo, R. N. and Pang, S. (1973). Effects of human models on perceived product quality. *Journal of Applied Psychology*, 57, 172–178.

Kim, Y.-J. and Na, J.-H. (2007). Effects of celebrity athlete endorsement on attitude towards the product: the role of credibility, attractiveness and the concept of congruence, *International Journal of Sports Marketing and Sponsorship*, 8(4), 310–320.

Koernig, S. K. and Boyd, T. C. (2009). To catch a tiger or let him go: The match-up effect and athlete endorsers for sport and non-sport brands, *Sport Marketing Quarterly*, 18(1), 25–37.

Lee, Y. H. (2000). Manipulating ad message involvement through information expectancy: Effects on attitude evaluation and confidence, *Journal of Advertising*, 29(2), 29–43.

Loken, B. and Ward, J. (1990). Alternative approaches to understanding the determinants of typicality, *Journal of Consumer Research*, 17(2), 111–126.

Mandler, G. (1982). The structure of value: accounting for taste, in *Affect and Cognition: The Seventeenth Annual Carnegie Symposium on Cognition*, ed. Margaret S. Clark and Susan T. Fiske, Hillsdale, NJ: Erlbaum, 3–36.

McDaniel, S. R. (1999). An investigation of match-up effects in sport sponsorship advertising: the implication of consumer advertising schemas, *Psychology and Marketing,* 16(2), 163–184.

Misra, S. and Beatty, S. E. (1990). Celebrity spokesperson and brand congruence: An assessment of recall and affect, *Journal of Business Research*, 21, 159–173.

Olson, E.L. (2010), Does sponsorship work in the same way in different sponsorship contexts? *European Journal of Marketing*, 44 (1/2), 180–199.

Olson, E. L. and Thjømøe, H. M. (2009). Sponsorship effect metric: Assessing the financial value of sponsoring by comparisons to television advertising, *Journal of the Academy of Marketing Science*, 37(4), 504–515.

Olson, E. L. and Thjømøe, H. M. (2011). Explaining and articulating the fit construct in sponsorship, *Journal of Advertising*, 40(1), 57–70.

Osgood, C. E. and Tannenbaum, P. H. (1955). The principle of congruity in the prediction of attitude change, *Psychological Review*, 62(1), 42–55.

Papadimitriou, D., Apostolopouiou, A. and Loukas, I. (2004). The role of perceived fit in fans' evaluation of sports brand extensions, *International Journal of Sports Marketing and Sponsorship*, 6, 31–48.

Pokrywczynski, J. and Brinker, D., Jr. (2012). "Rogue" athlete endorsers: using social identity theory to assess brand fit, *Journal of Brand Strategy*, 1(3), 279–291.

Pracejus, J. W. and Olsen, G. D. (2004). The role of brand/cause fit in the effectiveness of cause-related marketing campaigns, *Journal of Business Research*, 57, 635–640.

Rifon, N. J., Choi, S. M., Trimble, C. S. and Li, H. (2004). Congruence effects in sponsorship, *Journal of Advertising*, 33(1), 29–42.

Rodgers, S. (2004). The effects of sponsor relevance on consumer reactions to internet sponsorships, *Journal of Advertising*, 32(4), 67–76.

Ross, S. D., James, J. and Vargas, P. (2006). Development of a scale to measure team brand associations in professional sport, *Journal of Sport Management*, 20, 260–279.

Roy, D. P. and Cornwell, T. B. (2003). Brand equity's influence on responses to event sponsorships, *Journal of Product and Brand Management*, 12(6), 377–393.

Roy, D. P. and Cornwell, T. B. (2004). The effects of consumer knowledge on responses to event sponsorships, *Psychology & Marketing*, 21(3), 185–207.

Ruth, J. A. and Simonin, B. L. (2003). Brought to you by Brand A and Brand B, *Journal of Advertising*, 32(3), 19–30.

Samu, S., Krishnan, S. and Smith, R. E. (1999). Using advertising alliances for new product introduction: Intercations between product complementarity and promotional strategies, *Journal of Marketing*, 63(1), 57–74.

Sherman, J. W., Lee, A. Y., Bessenoff, G. R. and Frost, L. A. (1998). Stereotype efficiency reconsidered: Encoding flexibility under cognitive load, *Journal of Personality and Social Psychology*, 75(3), 589–606.

Simmons, C. J. and Becker-Olsen, K. (2006). Achieving marketing objectives through social sponsorships, *Journal of Marketing*, 70(4), 154–169.

Smith, D. C. and Andrews, J. (1995). Rethinking the effect of perceived fit on customers' evaluations of new products, *Journal of the Academy of Marketing Science*, 23, 4–14.

Speed, R. and Thompson, P. (2000). Determinants of sports sponsorship response, *Journal of the Academy of Marketing Science*, 28(2), 226–238.

Stangor, C. and McMillan, D. (1992). Memory for expectancy-congruent and expectancy-incongruent information: A review of the social and social developmental literatures, *Psychological Bulletin*, 111(1), 42–61.

Till, B. D. and Busler, M. (2000). The match-up hypothesis: Physical attractiveness, expertise, and the role of fit on brand attitude, purchase intent, and brand beliefs, *Journal of Advertising*, 29(3), 1–14.

Trendel, O. and Warlop, L. (2013). Mémorisation des parrains: l'influence de la congruence du parrainage réexaminée à l'aide du modèle de la flexibilité de l'encodage, *Recherche et Applications en Marketing*, 28(4), 28–46.

Wakefield, K. L., Becker-Olsen, K. and Cornwell, T. B. (2007). I Spy a sponsor. The effects of sponsorship level, prominence, relatedness, and cueing on recall accuracy, *Journal of Advertising*, 36(4), 61–74.

Walsh, P., Chien, C. J. and Ross, S. D. (2012). Sport teams as brand extensions: A case of Taiwanese baseball, *Sport Marketing Quarterly*, 21, 138–146.

Weeks, C. S., Cornwell, T. B. and Drennan, J. C. (2008). Leveraging sponsorships on the internet: activation, congruence, and articulation, *Psychology & Marketing*, 25(7), 637–654.

Woisetschläger, D. M. and Haselhoff, V. J. (2009). The name remains the same for fans: Why fans oppose naming right sponsorships, *Advances in Consumer Research*, 36, 775–776.

Woisetschläger, D. M., Eiting, A., Haselhoff, V. J. and Michaelis, M. (2010). Determinants and consequences of sponsorship fit: A study of fan perceptions, *Journal of Sponsorship*, 3(2), 169–180.

3

BRAND ACTIVATION IN SPORTS ORGANIZATIONS

Frank Pons, Lionel Maltese and Marilyn Giroux

Introduction

The level of competition in the sports industry has tremendously increased in recent years and sports organizations have to fight to get a part of the sports consumer dollar. The global sports revenue should continue to grow in the coming years and generate more than $145 billion in 2015. From this, the gate revenue accounts for the largest source of income, with 32.6 percent of the total sports market. This is especially true for North America and Europe, where live events are part of the traditions. However, gate revenue has the smallest growth compared to other types of income. The second source of revenue is sponsorship with a significant 28.8 percent of the total income. Sponsorship is the most promising factor for sports organizations and teams in the coming years, with an average increase rate of 5.3 percent (PWC, 2011). However, in order to be effective, sponsorship activities need the development of differentiated and strong sports brands that can cater to potential sponsors' objectives. Therefore, being part of this extremely competitive environment, brand managers of different sports entities and organizations are focusing more on the notion of brand development, brand equity and how to better transfer more efficiently these values and equity from sports properties to sponsors. In addition, sponsorship activities are becoming more and more subtle as exposure and visibility are not sufficient objectives anymore. In this complex landscape, brand activation has become critical for sponsors to maximize their return and for properties to attract sponsors.

This chapter will first highlight the importance of brand and brand equity, then present activation strategies adapted to different sports contexts.

The importance of brand and brand equity

A brand is a name, a word, a sign, a symbol, an image, or a combination of these elements, intended to identify the products and services of a company and thereby distinguish them from those of its competitors (Kapferer, 2004; Keller, 2007). In the context of spectator sports (professional sports teams and major events), the importance of a strong brand image is even more crucial. Thus, since the mid-1990s, the brand concept has become omnipresent in the sports industry (Gladden, 2007). Increased competition from the entertainment industry has compelled sports events organizers to seek long-term sustainability through developing a more strategic approach to brands (Bauer, Sauer and Schmitt, 2005). Keller's (1993) and De Chernatony's (2001) contributions have led to the application of some elements of brand development in the area of spectator sports, modeled in three stages: identity, positioning, and strategic brand management (Couvelaere and Richelieu, 2005). Even though revenue growth may constitute the ultimate benefit to be drawn from a strong brand, Gladden (2007) posits that effective brand management yields four main benefits: regularity of revenue, the possibility of establishing a premium, greater attractiveness to sponsors, and the opportunity for brand extension.

Emphasis on brand strength has ushered in a wave of academic research and has had implications for management consisting of a push to translate brand strength into brand equity (Bodet and Chanavat, 2010; Chanavat and Bodet, 2009). In recent years, the concept of brand equity has received special attention in the marketing sector. Dubois and Jolibert (1992) attempt to grasp the concept through the following definition: "*value added through a brand name and rewarded by the market through greater profits or greater market shares*" (our translation). Clients and members of the channel might perceive this added value as a financial asset and as a set of favourable associations and behaviours. Many ratings in the financial press offer an evaluation of brand equity (Forbes and BrandZ ratings, for instance). In one of these ratings, Manchester United appears among the sports brands with the highest brand equity. Its brand equity is estimated at nearly $2.23 billion. Furthermore, 55 percent of its supporters are from Asia, where the English Premier League is the most widespread sports property. Strong brand equity becomes a factor and provides major financial leverage for the organization's strategic development (Gladden and Funk, 2002; O'Cass and Grass, 2004), allowing it to position itself in comparison to other companies with respect to media opportunities, sponsorship and brand extension.

At the academic level, numerous studies highlight the complexity of the concept of brand equity, in particular, the multidimensionality that characterizes it and the absence of consensus to date regarding its conceptualization and measurement (Schuiling, 2002). Brand equity is mainly measured through the variable "brand awareness", understood either as "brand notoriety" or as "brand image". Evaluating the impact of brand awareness on the various elements of the marketing mix can also inform as to the level of brand equity. The stronger the equity of a sports brand, the easier it is to differentiate from the branding of competitors and to become a distinct offer, even though the product does not always have concrete attributes for the consumer (Bobby, 2002; Desbordes, 2008). Strong brand equity also helps a brand transcend the sports context (event) by creating a "brand community" based on a structured set of social relations among admirers of a brand (Muniz Jr. and O'Guinn, 2001). Supporters therefore experience this connection within an event as well as outside of it (Chanavat and Bodet, 2014).

This connection may have different origins. First, self-identification may explain this connection with the sports brand and why spectators buy, consume and wear diverse products related to the team and ultimately contribute to the brand equity of the sports property. In this perspective, people identify strongly with what the team is and this association is part of their description of themselves. This is related to the cognitive processes described by Bhattacharya and Sen (2003), which stipulated that consumers compare and match different attributes (of brands) to their own characteristics like personality and traits. Fans who perceived those characteristics to be similar to them feel more proximity and connection to the team and the validation of their identity (Pritchard et al., 2010). This concept is closely related to the intensity of the identification to a team (Pritchard et al., 2010). These similarities between the fans' perceptions of the team and themselves strongly influence their identification with this specific team. People associate themselves with teams that they believe are comparable to them (actual self) or what they aspire to be (aspirational self) (Pritchard et al., 2010). Social identity is also important in understanding how strong brands can develop and favor fan engagement (Ashforth and Mael 1989). In this mindset, the consumption and affiliation with a sports brand can increase the sense of belongingness to the sport entity and other similar individuals (Kwon et al., 2002). A strong motivation for buying branded products is that fans enjoy the bonding that it creates with other supporters of the team. Supporters often feel an instant connection with the other fans of the team. Consumers think of other partisans of the team as having a lot of similarities with them, they have a lot in common, especially related interests and passion. The decision to purchase products is motivated by this factor because people want to show to others what they are, what they represent and want to be part and be a member of this special community. It seems to be a criterion for them to be included in this community of fans. Real and authentic supporters need to have products that identify themselves to the specific team. This need for affiliation is known to be an important factor and a basic need for individuals. Participants feel they share something special and common with other fans of the team. Individuals, who watch the same game or participate in the same tailgate, even if they don't know each other, view this activity as a mutual experience. People affiliate themselves easily with each other. By wearing and consuming different products, people express their love for the team and that they are part of a group of fans and once again this brand engagement and experience contribute to the reinforcement of the sports brand equity.

In an ethnographic study, Kraszewski (2008) investigated the different consumption acts of people in North Forth and their identification with the Pittsburgh Steelers, as well as the type of relationships that the franchise is able to build with fans thanks to strong team brand equity. In this city, the team's fans go to the Steelers' bar where they perform specific rituals. They asked the bar to carry Iron City beer, the only beer they would drink, as it embodies Pittsburgh's blue-collar identity. Fans also brought Steelers merchandise with them, but not only did they want typical jerseys, they only wanted products sold in Pennsylvania. Fans establish their credibility and authenticity by wearing products that are sold exclusively on the local market and enhance the brand equity locally as a complement to the more comprehensive marketing efforts of the team. In a similar fashion but with a different scope, sports organizations can rely on their brand equity and identity at a broader level. The Red Sox Nation is an excellent example of this strategy and exemplifies the role of brand equity. The expression was first used by a journalist from the Boston Globe in 1986 and showed that the Boston Red Sox were popular all over North America, not just in the Boston region. Capitalizing on their brand equity, since 2004 the franchise has offered official citizenship and access to various newsletters and exclusive merchandise items to their fans. People from all over America have joined the ranks, as well as some celebrities, including Ben Affleck, Matt Damon and Jake Gyllenhaal, who are proud to exhibit their preference for this team, thus helping to reinforce the team's brand equity and its attractiveness for potential partners.

The preceding paragraphs have focused on the importance of developing strong brand equity and show that in the particular case of sports brands, it helps them, directly or indirectly, to expand various revenue streams. For companies and communities, sports constitute an original avenue with an impressive potential for communicating through sponsoring events. Indeed, sponsorship activities are perceived as a unique marketing means that perfectly completes a marketing communication program (Roy and Cornwell, 2004; Chanavat and Desbordes, 2014).

Sponsorship can deliver increased brand recall and awareness, brand image, brand equity and purchase intentions (Chanavat and Desbordes, 2014; Barros et al., 2007; Cliffe and Motion, 2005; Cornwell, 2008; Koo et al., 2005). In addition, it can be an excellent way to differentiate the brand from other competitors (Fahy et al., 2004). Perceived as less intrusive than advertising by consumers, sponsorship is viewed as more personal and altruist and tends to become a part of people's lives (Aaker and Joachimsthaler, 2000). Sports sponsorship represents an approved tool to concretely manage its brand image, brand personality and related aspects of the brand equity. Several factors can influence the effectiveness of sponsorships. One important factor is the congruence (fit) between the sponsor and the sponsee. This congruence can be perceived in terms of sponsor product relevance or functional benefit, and also in terms of personality or image.

Sponsorship deals can represent an important part of revenues for soccer teams who benefit from their huge success and their field performance to negotiate important kit and shirt sponsorship deals. For example, Manchester United recently signed the most expensive supplier kit deal with Adidas. This agreement, which represents an impressive $100 million per year, came soon after Arsenal's $47 million per year with PUMA. In addition, teams secured multi-millions for their shirt sponsorship deal.

However, despite these successes, sponsorship is currently undergoing a significant evolution in the operational implementation and the new marketing opportunities available to sponsors. In addition, research on sports sponsorship (Chanavat and Desbordes, 2014; Cornwell and Maignan, 1998; Walliser, 2006) has often focused on operational techniques and performance from the perspective of the search for visibility and has long neglected the use and impact of public relations as well as of partner brand activation and citizen initiatives. The next section of this chapter will address these two aspects.

Activation strategies

Contrary to scientific literature where the concept of sponsorship activation is seldom studied (Weeks et al., 2008), activation has become a well-developed activity and issue. Very few researchers have attempted a clear definition, which Weeks et al. (2008) have done by trying to differentiate the concept of "leverage" from that of sponsorship activation. According to these authors, the term "leverage" is used to describe marketing-related tools, communications and any collateral activity in sponsorship investment. The term "activation" is often used with respect to situations where the public has any sort of opportunity to interact with the sponsor. In practice, www.partnershipactivation.com, conceived as a think tank, addresses activation as the answer to a key question for professionals in the field of communications and sports sponsorship: "How to connect fans to brands?"

Activation is therefore a concept deriving from sponsorship marketing, which can be defined as operational methods of sponsorship implementation in events organizing with the objective of connecting fans (or the direct audience) to sponsors' brands. The relational phenomenon of connecting consumers with a brand can be seen as "bringing a brand alive on the event ground level". From a strictly operational and pragmatic perspective, several event communication tools can be used for the purpose of stimulating the connection between the direct audience and a sponsor's brand. At first centered on brand visibility, sponsorship has gradually evolved towards a more relational axis (Ferrand et al., 2009), where the sponsored entity becomes a supporter of client-provider relations management strategies, as well as of internal human relations. The classical notion of sponsorship has thus rapidly been replaced by that of sponsorship activation (Weeks et al., 2008), where the objective of connecting club fans, events or athletes to sponsor brands has become a main priority.

Activation is integrated into programs designed by advertisers so as to develop an interaction with those who are exposed to sporting competitions. Various tools are available to advertisers for attracting and interacting with fans (BtC) or companies and institutions (BtB). The following table summarizes possible sponsorship activation tools and techniques.

This presentation of activation tools shows the range of possible event communication offers used to activate a brand and to fulfill marketing objectives. From the standpoint of the

Table 3.1 Sponsorship activation tools

Sponsors' marketing objectives	Operational activation tools	Description
Visibility	Panel advertising	Billboards around grounds, fields and courts (with increased use of LED technology), radar speed gun, clock, coolers.
	Printed material	Placards (4★3), posters, programs, flyers, internal newspapers and magazines.
	Media, multimedia	Giant screens, web portals, internal TV or radio.
	Human support and equipment	Jerseys, shorts, ball boys, umpires (line judges), managers (clothing, watches), mascots, Pom Pom Girls.
	Naming	Stadium, arena, stands, team, match, competition, special event.
	Umpiring, scoring	Umpire's chair, scoring (mobile, TV, web, giant screens).
	Branding	Flags, banners, tents, printed canvas.
Relations	Public relations	VIP and hospitality areas.
	Web marketing, Web 2.0	Banners, mailing, newsletters, news feeds, audio and video, forum, chat, blog, Facebook, Twitter, Flickr.
	Mobile marketing	WAP sites, news feeds, cards.
	Conventions, seminars	Organization of conventions or seminars, which can be internal or open to the public depending on the topic.
Participation	Activities, games	Activities and games for the public to participate in, as well as activities broadcast during game intermissions, sponsored by certain companies.
	Stands, testing facilities	Commercial stands, product and service placement, testing facilities (cars, mobiles, micro-computers).
	Supporting objects	Use of objects for communication support (for example, the PMU hand or BNP Paribas "tap tap").
Involvements	Official supplier	The partner provides know-how and expertise for the event: technologies, catering, transportation, security, environment, energy, waste management.
	Cause-related marketing, eco-citizen sponsorship	Partners, organizers and associations set up programs in defense of certain causes (humanitarian, environmental, educational, solidarity), attempting to harmonize the participating partners' expertise and expectations.
	Sponsored days	With the organizer's assent, the partner sponsors one or several theme days related to the partner's social commitments (women, children, solidarity).

offeror (event organizer), personalizing the sponsorship offer is a crucial aspect for setting up the optimal activation system corresponding to the marketing needs of the client (sponsor). In practice, sponsors often hire specialized agencies to design their activation programs. The latter can pinpoint the needs of their client, i.e. the future partner, and negotiate the desired actions with the event offeror. However, many sporting event producers have started developing this kind of expertise, like UEFA recently, and PSG. Their knowledge of the offer and their capacity to anticipate the needs of partner brands help them to personalize activations.

The question now is whether the financial and human investment in an activation program is cost-effective. Although a thriving area of academic research, measurement of the impact of sponsorship often remains, at a practical level, limited to measuring media impact and equivalent advertising. Beyond hardly quantifiable declared objectives and expected returns, the search for or preservation of competitive advantages is a core concern of partner brands. For brands such as Coca-Cola, which primarily target individuals, activation techniques aiming to maximize the interaction between the sponsor's brand and the exposed public often use media and digital tools. The objectives for services brands are different and often oriented towards perceptions of the reputation of partner companies reaching a BtB and BtC public. The choice of activation programs and their deployment integrates internal and external actions where the search for interpersonal interactions remains central. Consequently, efficiency measurements must capture relational objectives rather than simple visibility metrics.

Most of the time, event and sports marketing agencies are solicited by sponsors to design and implement activation programs. The Tour de France and its caravan are known for their activation system promoting numerous brands, which interact with the public at every stage of the competition. The copyright holder and organizer, Amaury Sport Organisation (ASO), recently established an internal activation cell designed to replace agencies. The advantage of this lies in its capacity to pinpoint the sponsor's needs and to adapt the activation system to a sporting event. UEFA, too, is increasingly developing in-house marketing actions intended for activation partners for the Champions League, Europa League and Euro of soccer. Considering the wide range of possible activation operations, personalization of offer has become a major issue. Thus we propose the following approach to formalizing a personalized activation program:

1   Analysis of the sponsor's needs either directly on the basis of a brief or by studying the group's marketing strategy.
2   Personalization of a partner's offer by mounting a specific adaptive file containing proposals corresponding to the known or anticipated objectives of the future partner.
3   Operational implementation of the activation program for the event on the ground.
4   Comprehensive evaluation of the program through the development of contextual indicators capable of objectifying expected returns.
5   Helping the program move forward in line with the evaluation results and creating a sustainable dynamic.

The specific case of eco-responsible activations

In order to stand out from the crowd and with a view to making sponsorship more socially conscious, many advertisers have moved towards a new form of responsible sponsorship and activation (Bayle et al., 2011; Babiak and Wolfe, 2006). In France, major groups historically linked to the public sector (for example, Française des Jeux, EDF, GDF Suez, Veolia, La Poste) have rapidly adopted this style of support and communication. Very few academic studies have focused on this trend, in particular with respect to the expected returns for sponsors who adopt this responsible approach to their activation activities.

In this respect, several key factors must be taken into consideration in order to build an ecosystem whose main ambition is to create an interaction between targets for exposure and the partner brand. The first stage in configuring such a marketing system consists of choosing objectives for the sponsor, on the basis of which – the second stage – appropriate activation tools for attaining these objectives are then selected. The third stage involves constructing the core of the ecosystem, namely, the creation and mobilization of a community to apply the set of activation actions capable of boosting the notoriety and promotion of the new ecosystem's brand. The next stages focus on evaluating returns of objectives (ROO) in connection with the sponsor's strategy for managing its relationship with the client. The sixth stage involves readjusting objectives ahead of the next annual cycle of implementation of the comprehensive sponsorship program.

Box 3.1   Fondation La Française des Jeux: Wear your trainers at the office! *Mets tes baskets dans l'entreprise!*

La Française de Jeux is a major European lottery operator, offering enjoyable, responsible and safe sports games and betting for the general public. In 1993, La Française des Jeux created the first Fondation d'Entreprise (Company Foundation) dedicated to sports, whose action focused on two main areas: sports and solidarity. As such, every year, the Fondation Française des Jeux supports more than 50 projects and helps more than 350 high-level athletes.

In the context of its eco-citizen activation programs, La Fondation Française des Jeux partnered with ELA, an association of parents and patients uniting their efforts in the fight against leukodystrophies. Since 1994, ELA has been organizing a "Wear your sneakers and fight disease" week in schools. La Française des Jeux subsequently involved partners from the business world in this solidarity campaign. The concept put forward by the Fondation Française des Jeux consists in inviting employees of partner companies to wear trainers to work and measure the steps they take with pedometers. For each step, the partner contributes one centime to ELA. A communication campaign bringing together all partners and sporting shows is also planned for the event.

One such day-event, which took place on May 19, 2010 in Vitrolles, Bouches du Rhône, engaged 690 partners of La Française des Jeux at three of the group's sites, for a participation rate of 62 percent. A total of 250 employees took part in the activities. At national level, 14 companies joined the system (including PPR, Puma, Boursorama, Allianz, Generali, Veolia, Mitsubishi). Some 19 million steps were measured, corresponding to a €163,000 contribution made to ELA.

The benefit of this citizen activation operation was to raise funds for an association and to raise awareness among many employees. The internal company dynamic was also impacted thanks to a friendly day of solidarity. The media coverage of this original approach earned various actors significant visibility. Finally, the positioning of La Française des Jeux was promoted to current and potential commercial targets and key influencers intrinsically suited to sports betting (adult population with sufficient purchasing power for this act of consumption).

Source: Case study carried out by *Observatoire de l'expérience de consommation dans les stades et arénas* Kedge Business School (2011)

In France, many formerly public organizations, now privatized, for example, Française des Jeux, La Poste, Veolia, EDF, SNCF, prioritize eco-citizen approaches in their choice of activation programs. Among sports sponsorship actors, La Française des Jeux and Groupe Generali are most active.

Taking into consideration the objectives of each sponsor, the activation tools of an eco-citizen sponsorship operation also include the entire range of those presented in Table 3.1 (visibility, relations, participation and involvement). The activation methods of eco-citizen sponsorship can be framed according to two positionings:

- The copyright holder establishes its eco-citizen strategy and proposes to its partners to integrate its system by activating their sponsorship mainly in the areas related to the core of their business or to their own CSR policy. In this case, activation programs are planned by the event organizer (Babiak and Wolfe, 2006), while partners validate the operational methods.
- The sponsor imposes its CRS approach in the framework of its eco-citizen activation, and the copyright holder adapts its offer so as to satisfy its client's project specifications. In this context, partners often solicit specialized agencies to design, monitor and evaluate the activation program.

BNP Paribas's "We are Tennis" *ecosystem*

In 2013, BNP Paribas celebrated its 40th year of partnership with Roland Garros. A major partner of tennis and tennis events (Davis Cup, Fed Cup, Roland Garros, ATP and WTA tours), BNP Paribas developed a new community system called "We are Tennis" three years ago. At first, it was only a live portal for information on tennis along with a blog and social media presented by journalists attending tennis events worldwide. The portal included signposting and stands featuring the colours of the brand and offering numerous activities, including the possibility of commenting live on match points or uploading videos on Internet during tournaments.

BNP Paribas had oriented its sponsorship strategy towards two objectives:

- Visibility of the brand on the court and therefore a robust search for notoriety; and
- Exploiting the opportunity that events offer to develop relationships by inviting present and prospective clients, individuals and companies (hospitality service).

The "We are Tennis" ecosystem introduced a third objective: becoming an operator by galvanizing the community of tennis fans under an umbrella brand. Besides the physical support enabling the organization of activities stands, the citizen element was recently integrated into the system through the operation "We are Tennis at Heart."

An analysis of BNP Paribas's overall system and choice of activation methods regarding each tennis event it supported shows that two classic activities are always implemented: optimization of BNP Paribas's brand visibility and public relations operations. The third objective was developed by the group three years ago with the aim of becoming a more involved participant by interacting with tennis fans on site and online. This is what is meant by creating an ecosystem in the form of an expanding community. The possibility of sharing digital and sporting and other community content online, coupled with numerous activities and games, allows for interaction with event-exposed targets and with fans of professional

Table 3.2 The "We are Tennis" ecosystem

Objectives	Choice of activations	Ecosystem creation
Visibility	Back-court tarps, printed material, media, ball boys, Hawk Eye, branding.	Communication (notoriety) regarding the "We are Tennis" ecosystem (other than back-court tarps): TV, press, branding.
Relationships	Hospitality, PR, large public stands, game-gifts (tennis balls, trophy awards).	Promotion (emulation) of the "We are Tennis" ecosystem: Stands, games, participatory sponsorship.
Reputation	Social media, blog, fan community of the "We are Tennis" brand, live and offset content, "We are Tennis at Heart" (hospitals, star program).	Creating interaction (CRM–FRM): expanding community: "We are Tennis" virtual community.

tennis players. It is important to note that this activity, which is at the core of the community ecosystem, is stimulated in two ways:

- Visibility of the brand and therefore of the "We are Tennis" ecosystem on all printed material (except panel advertising on tennis courts), as well as on media, enabling the development of its notoriety; and
- A reception area for BNP Paribas guests (stands for the general public and hospitality areas) integrating various competitive games and activities.

The "We are Tennis" ecosystem is integrated into BNP Paribas's overall sports sponsorship strategy and is thus composed of a set of activations including a central digital activation, thus establishing an interaction between tennis fans and the "We are Tennis" brand, supported by peripheral activations acting as stimulants in terms of notoriety and emulation. Finally, thanks to this system, BNP Paribas has the opportunity to integrate its sponsorship actions as an ecosystem into its customer relationship management policy with a view to creating and maintaining customer loyalty. In this regard and in the context of sporting events, the brand purveyor can plan to develop its Customer Relationship Management (CRM) strategy by incorporating a Fan Relationship Management (FRM) strategy, as such benefiting from the emotional impact induced by exposure to the event in question.

Conclusion

The purpose of this section was to present a conceptual and an operational approach to the sponsorship action and offer and its activations. In an economic system where the pursuit of competitive advantages remains a major priority for companies, the search for differentiation can be optimized through ecosystem constructs co-created by copyright holders, certain specialized agencies, and partner brands. The use of activation tools is part of a range of increasingly dominant strategy options at the managerial level, even though academic studies in this field remain relatively limited. For example, thanks to its "caravan," the Tour de France is likely considered by many product-producing businesses as a spectator sport producer that provides fertile ground for activations. The creation of new sporting avenues should increase offers and will enable partners to interact with certain targets in modern stadiums and arenas, thus generating a plethora of activation initiatives, even though it remains difficult for sponsors and copyright holders to evaluate returns on investments in an objective and comprehensive manner. The importance of building client relationships in marketing nevertheless suggests that activation holds great promise for the future.

References

Aaker, D. A. and Joachimsthaler, E. (2000). The brand relationship spectrum. *California Management Review*, 42(4), 8–23.

Ashforth, B. E. and Mael, F. (1989). Social identity theory and the organization, *Academy of Management*, 14(1), 20–39.

Babiak, K. and Wolfe, R. (2006). More than just a game? Corporate social responsibility and Super Bowl XL, *Sport Marketing Quarterly*, 15(4), 214–222.

Barros, C. P., Barros, C. D., Santos, A. and Chadwick, S. (2007). Sponsorship brand recall at the Euro 2004 soccer tournament. *Sport Marketing Quarterly*, 16(3), 161–170.

Bauer H., Sauer, N. and Schmitt, P. (2005). Customer based brand equity in the team sport industry, *European Journal of Marketing*, 39(5/6), 496–513.

Bayle E., Chappelet, J. L., François, A. and Maltese, L. (2011). *Sport & RSE: vers un management responsable*, Brussels: Editions De Boeck.

Bhattacharya, C. B. and Sen, S. (2003). Consumer–company identification: A framework for understanding consumers' relationships with companies, *Journal of Marketing*, 67(2), 76–88.

Bobby, D. (2002). Can a sports club be a brand?, *Sport Business International*, April.

Bodet, G. and Chanavat, N. (2010). Building global football brand equity: Lessons from the Chinese market, *Asia Pacific Journal of Marketing and Logistics*, 22(1), 55–66.

Chanavat, N. and Bodet, G. (2009). Sport branding strategy and internationalisation: A French perception of the "big four" brands, *Qualitative Market Research, An International Journal*, 12(4), 460–481.

Chanavat, N. and Bodet, G. (2014). Experiential marketing in sport spectatorship services: A customer perspective, *European Sport Management Quarterly*, 14(4), 323–344.

Chanavat, N. and Desbordes, M. (2014). Le parrainage sportif multiple événementiel : atouts, défis et conditions de succès, *Revue Gestion* (HEC Montréal), 38(4), 27–36.

Cliffe, S. J. and Motion, J. (2005). Building contemporary brands: A sponsorship-based strategy. *Journal of Business Research*, 58(8), 1068–1077.

Cornwell, T. B. (2008). State of the art and science in sponsorship-linked marketing. *Journal of Advertising*, 37(3), 41–55.

Cornwell T. B. and Maignan, I. (1998). An international review of sponsorship research, *Journal of Advertising*, 27(1), 1–21.

Couvelaere, V. and Richelieu, A. (2005). Brand strategy in professional sports: The case of French soccer teams. *European Sport Management Quarterly* 5(1): 23–46.

De Chernatony, L. (2001). A model for strategically building brands. *Brand Management*, 9(1), 32–44.

Desbordes, M. (2008). Le marketing du sport en question, *Revue Française de Marketing*, 4–5(219), 5–9.

Fahy, J., Farrelly, F. and Quester, P. (2004). Competitive advantage through sponsorship: A conceptual model and research propositions. *European Journal of Marketing*, 38(8), 1013–1030.

Ferrand A., McCarthy, S., and Zintz, T. (2009) *Marketing des organisations sportives. Construire les réseaux et les relations*, Brussels: Editions De Boeck.

Gladden, J. (2007). Managing sport brands, in Mullin, B. J., Hardy, S. H., and Sutton, W. A. (eds), *Sport Marketing*, Champaign, IL: Human Kinetics, p. 539.

Gladden, J. M. and Funk, D. C. (2002). Developing an understanding of brand associations in team sport: empirical evidence from consumers of professional sport, *Journal of Sport Management*, 16(1), 54–81.

Kapferer, J. N. (2004). *The new strategic brand management: Creating a sustaining brand equity long term*, Paris: Editions d'Organisations.

Keller, K. L. (1993). Conceptualizing, measuring, and managing brand equity, *Journal of Marketing*, 57(1), 1–22.

Keller, K. L. (2007). Advertising and brand equity, in Tellis, G. J., Ambler, T. (eds), *Handbook of Advertising*, Thousand Oaks: Sage Publications, p. 54–70.

Koo, G., Quarterman, J. and Flynn, L. (2006). Effect of perceived sport event and sponsor image fit on consumers' cognition, affect, and behavioral intentions. *Sport Marketing Quarterly*, 15(2), 80–90.

Kraszewski, J. (2008). Fandom, and the management of home Pittsburgh in Fort Worth: Football bars, sports television, sports, *Journal of Sport and Social Issues*, 32(2), 139–157.

Kwon, H. H. and Armstrong, K. L. (2002). Factors influencing impulse buying of sport team licensed merchandise, *Sports Marketing Quarterly*, 11(3), 151–163.

Muniz, A. M. and O'Guinn, T. C. (2003). Brand community. *Journal of Consumer Research*, 27(4), 412–432.

O'Cass, A. and Grass, D. (2004). Service brands and communication effects. *Journal of Marketing Communication*, 10 (December), 15–35.

PricewaterhouseCoopers (2011). Outlook for the global sports market to 2015, A report from PricewaterhouseCoopers International Limited.

Pritchard, M. P., Stinson, J. and Patton, E. (2010). Affinity and affiliation: The dual-carriage way to team identification, *Sport Marketing Quarterly*, 19(2), 67–77.

Roy, D. P. and Cornwell, T. B. (2004). The effects of consumer knowledge on responses to event sponsorships. *Psychology and Marketing*, 21(3), 185–207.

Schuiling, I. (2002). La force des marques locales et ses determinants spécifiques par rapport aux marques internationales: Applications dans le marché alimentaire. Thèse de doctorat, Presses de l'université Catholique Louvain.

Walliser, B. (2006). Recherche en parrainage. Quelle évolution et quels résultats?, *Revue Française de Gestion*, 163, 45–58.

Weeks, C. S., Cornwell, T. B., Drennan, J. C. (2008). Leveraging sponsorships on the internet: Activation, congruence, and articulation, *Psychology and Marketing*, 25(7), 637–654.

4

THE STRATEGIC BRANDING OF A FOOTBALL CLUB

The case of Interbrand and Shakhtar Donetsk

Paolo Guenzi and Manfredi Ricca

Branding and the world of sports

There are four key aspects to consider when evaluating a product's brand equity (Aaker, 1991):

1   Perceived quality.
2   Brand loyalty.
3   Brand awareness.
4   Brand associations.

Just as for any organization, each of these aspects is essential for sports clubs as well, in order to create advantageous relationships with fans and with other key stakeholders, particularly current and potential sponsors. When a team has strong brand equity, its offering is perceived as high quality, its fans are unconditionally loyal, its brand name is widely recognized and its brand enjoys a positive image. All these factors can generate broader media coverage, lucrative merchandising activity, higher ticket sales with more season passes, and a more upbeat atmosphere during sporting events, making it easier to find sponsors.

The importance of branding in sports, especially for sports teams, is illustrated by the high number of academic publications on topics such as brand equity (for example, Ross, 2006; Gladden and Milne, 1999; Bauer, Sauer and Schmitt, 2005; Richelieu and Pons, 2006), brand associations (for example, Ross, James and Vargas, 2006), brand personality (for example, Braunstein and Ross, 2010), brand extension (for example, Apostolopoulou, 2002; Walsh and Lee, 2012), brand dilution (Walsh and Ross, 2010), brand architecture in professional sports leagues and teams (Kunkel, Funk and Hill, 2013), human brands in sports (Carlson and Donavan, 2013), the impact of sponsorship on a club's brand equity (Henseler, Wilson and Westberg, 2011), the impact of logos on brand personality in sports (Watkin and Gonzenbach, 2013), brand alliances (Yupin, Mengze and Goldfarb, 2009), brand recall and recognition for sports organizations (Walsh, Kim and Ross, 2008), and sports brand positioning (Ferreira, Hall and Bennett, 2008).

According to Gladden, Irwin and Sutton (2001); the variables that impact brand equity can be grouped into three macro-categories:

1   The characteristics of the product offered by the sports organization (with a club, for instance, the players and the coach, which equate to success on the field and quality of play).
2   The specific traits of the sports organization (its history and tradition).
3   The characteristics of the geographic and competitive context of the sports organization, as well as its ability to impact the market (for example, through local media coverage).

Worth noting is that in this model, for a professional sports club a winning record is only one of the determinants of brand equity, and not necessarily even the most important one. Other significant variables include the number and quality of potential target customers, the intensity of competition in the club's home territory, the team's history and traditions, the decisions concerning club management from a technical or sports standpoint. Beyond these considerations, marketing activities also serve to increase the club's brand equity, in particular, by growing brand awareness and creating and managing the brand image with respect to the final customers (fans and spectators), the media, and business partners.

It has been suggested that spectator-based brand equity in sports is ultimately comprised of brand awareness and brand associations (Ross, 2006), and these brand components have the potential for significant impact on the sports organization's revenue streams, such as ticket and licensed merchandise sales. Gladden and Funk (2002) investigated brand associations in the specific field of sports and developed the Team Association Model (TAM): starting from the three categories proposed by Keller (1993), i.e. attributes, benefits and attitudes, sixteen dimensions were identified as potential constructs believed to underlie brand associations in sports. Later, Ross, James, and Vargas (2006) developed the Team Brand Association Scale (TBAS), which identifies eleven types of brand associations held by consumers in the professional sports setting. These associations are: (1) the non-player personnel associated with a particular sports team (Non-player Personnel); (2) the quality, performance, or success of a team (Team Success); (3) the history of a particular sports team (Team History); (4) the stadium and community in which the team calls "home" (Stadium Community); (5) specific characteristics that a team displays on the field of play (Team-play Characteristics); (6) the identifying marks associated with a specific sports team (Brand Mark); (7) the sports organization's dedication to fans of the team (Organizational Attributes); (8) eating and consuming beverages at the stadium (Concessions); (9) associating with others such as friends and other fans of team (Social Interaction); (10) the competition among teams that are known to be historically significant competitors (Rivalry); and (11) an individual's enduring affiliation to a particular sports team (Commitment).

When a team enjoys strong brand equity, this sets a virtuous circle in motion as outlined below:

1   Marketing processes that aim to enhance the team's brand equity (for example, by attracting the attention of the general public, the media, and sponsors; beyond having a winning track record) make a major contribution to improving customer equity as well.
2   Customer equity, which the club generates by attracting new fans, leads to a broader customer base on one hand, and more intense involvement and loyalty of long-time fans on the other. This gives a sizable boost to the number of season-ticket holders and spectators at live matches and through different media. Beyond this, fans are also more likely to buy club merchandise, which prompts the organization to pursue brand extension strategies. All this paves the way to acquiring media equity.

3   Media equity refers to the attention and interest that various media dedicate to an organization. When a sports organization has a dedicated, loyal, highly-involved fan base, the media can count on a broad, stable audience. For the club, this translates into more media coverage, which equates to greater brand exposure, continually reinforcing brand awareness and resulting in higher-value contracts with these media for broadcasting rights for team matches.

4   Media equity, in turn, means increasing possible touchpoints with potential customers (who are often fans of other clubs when matches are broadcast on television). In this way, the club grows the target market for its offering.

5   So customer equity and media equity mutually reinforce one another, and this process is closely linked to the team's ability to attract and connect with other companies (through sponsorships and various other kinds of partnerships), establishing and building lucrative relationships with them. There are certain key factors that would attract a company looking to tap into the communicative and promotional potential of associating its brand with a sports club: a team with a broad, active customer base on one hand (from fans to occasional television viewers), and on the other, a platform provided by media coverage of the team and team activities.

6   A team's brand equity also translates into its ability to attract all-star athletes and the most qualified human resources for club management. The image of a winning club – more importantly one with a promising future – represents powerful forces of attraction for top-tier players and coaches (Gilson, 2000). After all, these are the people with the power to build up the team's brand equity, because world-class athletes and coaches help the club draw the attention of the general public, media and sponsors.

According to Richelieu et al. (2008), the process of managing brand equity for a sports organization such as a football club should start with a precise definition of the identity of that organization. This identity should then serve as a guideline for developing a consistent marketing positioning strategy, which lays the foundation for coordinated marketing initiatives. Taken together these initiatives should convey to the market a certain perception of brand equity, a perception based on tangibles and intangibles. The first include the logo, the mascot, and the stadium; the second refer to a sense of belonging and community among the club's fans.

The process of building brand equity is shaped in part by internal factors that the sports organization can control (for example, merchandising, websites and web channels, organizing tournaments and recruiting top-level athletes and coaches, and so forth). Other factors are external, such as rivalries with other teams, the image of the home city or region, as so on.

This overview of the literature on branding in sports highlights the lack of empirical investigations on the processes of strategic development of a new brand and strategic re-branding of an existing brand (Milligan, 2009). Furthermore, the extant literature is largely based on empirical analyses run in the United States. Therefore, here we focus on the case of the strategic re-branding of an existing club in Ukraine.

Shaktar Donetsk: history of the club

Football Club Shakhtar Donetsk was formed in May 1936 and was initially named Stakhanovets, from Aleksei Stakhanov, a coal-miner in the Donbass region and propaganda celebrity in 1935. The team changed its name in July 1946 to Shakhtyor, the Russian word for "miner". In the 1960s, the club reached the finals of the USSR Cup three times, winning it twice in 1961 and

1962. In 1980 and 1983, Shakhtar brought home the crystal USSR Cup to Donetsk and in 1983, it won the USSR Super Cup. In the newly independent Ukraine, Shakhtar and Dynamo Kyiv became perennial first place competitors. The team won the Ukrainian Cup three times in 1995, 1997 and 2001. The club won their first Ukrainian Premier League title in the 2001–02 season. They were also victorious in the 2001–02 Ukrainian Cup. In 2004, coach Mircea Lucescu won the 2003–04 Ukrainian Cup, and after three months, for the first time in club history the club made it to the UEFA Champions League group stage. They won their second Premier League title in the 2004–05 season and retained the Premier League crown in the 2005–06 season, when they managed to win their first Super Cup title. Shakhtar regained the title in the 2007–08 season, when they were also victorious in the Ukrainian Cup. Shakhtar's attendance levels at league matches have continually risen over the years to a point where they averaged 36,983 spectators over the 2011–12 Premier League season. In 2009, they became the second Ukrainian team to win a European competition (and the first since independence), and the first to win the UEFA Cup. Shakhtar won the Premier League title in the 2009–10 season. The 2010–11 season was also very successful for Shakhtar: they reached the quarter-final stage of the Champions League, they won the Premier League, Ukrainian Cup, and the Super Cup. In 2011, the IFFHS gave Shakhtar a special award for making the biggest progress of the decade among football clubs. They then went on to win the Premier League and Ukrainian Cup in the 2011–12 season. In the 2012–13 season Shakhtar won the Premier League, Cup and Super Cup. Shakhtar won the 2014 United Supercup, a tournament between the top-two placed clubs of Ukraine and of Russia, which strengthened Shakhtar's status as the strongest club in Eastern Europe. At the end of the 2013–14 season, Shakhtar won the Ukraine Premier League and the Ukrainian Super Cup.

Rebranding Shakhtar: formulating a new strategy

In the mid-2000s, the new management team set out two *strategic objectives* for the five years to follow:

1　Augment the weight of the team on the international scene, ensuring that Shakhtar would become a regular player in European competitions, aiming to bring home the top European trophies.
2　Consolidate the role of the club at a local level, establishing Shakhtar as major promoter of the culture of football in the Ukraine.

The club's management was convinced that to reach these objectives, the image of Shakhtar had to evolve from a post-Soviet era football team to the pride of all of Eastern Europe. The management team realized that what was lacking was a deep understanding of the team's values among the Ukrainian football fans. This knowledge would provide the foundations for designing a strategy that would make the team's objectives attainable. What followed was the club's decision to invest in market research to fill this knowledge gap.

The findings were encouraging. Shakhtar enjoyed a positive image among its own fans and football fans in general. The team was recognized as having ambition, technical quality, a desire to grow, willingness to invest and a forward-looking attitude: all associations that the new strategic plan could leverage. At the same time, though, the perception emerged that many of these positive factors had not yet translated into success at an athletic or managerial level. Case in point, opinion on the most recent team logo (see Figure 4.2 later) wasn't particularly positive.

The management team realized that the lack of a clear brand identity was the main reason the team didn't have a distinctive positioning among football fans. Specifically, preserving the existing, unclear identity would work against communicating change. This prompted the club to turn to a consulting company specialized in branding, Interbrand, which would develop a branding strategy to establish a new brand identity, complete with a new set of brand elements and an appropriate brand architecture.

Interbrand

Interbrand, a division of Omnicom Group (NYSE: OMC), is a global branding consultancy company founded in London in 1974. The company's focus is the creation and management of brand value, a notion it developed in the 1980s using its breakthrough Brand Valuation methodology, allowing to identify a brand's financial worth. Interbrand combines diverse left- and right-brain branding disciplines to assist companies with market intelligence, strategic advice, experience creation, and activation. Today, Interbrand is the largest company of its kind in the world, with more than 30 offices around the world. Interbrand defines a brand as:

> A living business asset, brought to life across all touchpoints, which, if properly managed, creates identification, differentiation and value. Value from a consumer perspective is the promise and delivery of an experience; from a business perspective it is the security of future earnings.

There are different ways of looking at brand equity. However, the notion of brands as powerful business assets implies the ultimate measure of success should be sustainable economic value, and this should apply to a sports brand, too. There are two ways in which a brand builds value: by generating higher expected earnings by making a promise, and by mitigating their risk by delivering upon that promise. In the case of a football club, there are several interconnections that link the brand to the business value. To give one example, a stronger brand is more attractive to football talent, creating a higher likelihood of sports success and, therefore, the opportunity for higher revenues through rights, attendance and merchandising.

Beyond that, brands are crucial to football clubs for two reasons. First, they are key to preference and loyalty. Whilst in other categories the brand plays a role alongside other factors such as product performance, in football the role of brand is dominant, and outbalances the actual performance (sports results). Second, brands in football solve the often critical tension between business and passion. They bridge the two hemispheres by being an asset and a symbol; brands ensure that passion is converted into business sustainability. Conversely, brands are the insurance policy against business choices, which compromise on the ethos and the values of the club. These were the deepest principles with which the Shakhtar brand development process was approached.

The new Shakhtar brand

To cast the new brand in the same mold that shaped the values and ambitions of the club, the management turned to Interbrand, tasking the company with developing a brand identity to reflect the excellence that the club was striving to achieve, to set up a clear and sharp brand positioning, and to create an updated, representative visual identity. This is how Manfredi Ricca, Managing Director of Interbrand's Italian office, and leader of the project, explains how these objectives were achieved:

Even before we started, the Club had always shown a strong sensitivity toward the brand, managing it carefully and consistently. So as we began working with the club's management we realized we were partnering with an uncommon organization, unified by a common sense of purpose, a high level of professionalism, and a genuine ambition. The Club was extremely disciplined in managing the brand's touchpoints (communication, website, merchandising, and so on). However, what was missing was a shared, sharp definition of what the brand should stand for, and compelling design codes that could do justice to the club's status and vision. I believe that our most important contribution was to use the brand to make the business and sports strategy visible and understandable internally and externally. In other words, we changed the conversation from "logo" to "brand"; a shift that came natural to a club that, not by chance, hired a brand consultancy rather than the typical design or ad agency, however competent. Brands are powerful catalysts for change, and the Shakhtar story is a compelling example of that.

The rigorous process that Interbrand crafted for the Shakhtar brand's development can be summed up as depicted in Figure 4.1.

We kicked off the project by carrying out an in-depth analysis, including reviewing all existing research material as well as holding dozens of hours of interviews with the management, the technical staff and even the players. This enabled us to immerse ourselves into the Club's vision, both in terms of sport and business, and to identify the role that the brand should play. We soon realized that the brand wasn't expressing the platform of excellence that the club had begun to build, from the world-class management team to the magnificent sports center, from the medical center to the new stadium (then under construction), which would be the first in Eastern Europe to earn a five-star UEFA rating. All this laid the foundations for the Brand Definition – a concise but compelling summary of Shakhtar's philosophy, bringing together Vision, Mission, Values and Personality. The Brand Definition represents the brand's DNA, and guides everything that the brand has to be, say, and do. We defined Shakhtar's Mission as being the ambassador of Ukrainian football in the world, and of international football in the Ukraine. A critical role, which in a way sees the Club as the celebration of a city and a region.

This foundation was designed to inspire the entire experience created by the brand – ideally from the team's playing style to the communication and all that's in between, including the brand architecture, i.e. the portfolio of brands associated to the Shakhtar brand (among which the Donbass Arena brand). The new Shakhtar brand was launched in December 2007, a tough time for the club from a sports perspective. It served as a kind of reboot in many ways.

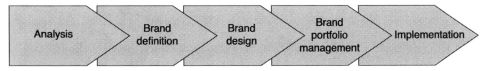

Figure 4.1 Interbrand's model for the development of the Shakhtar Donetsk brand

Source: Picture courtesy of Interbrand

Developing a branding strategy is a process that begins by clearly determining what the brand is meant to represent, which positioning it will have within the relevant context and how it can serve the business objectives. The brand identity emerging from Interbrand's work with the club's management consisted of the following elements:

Vision. To be the ambassador of Ukrainian football in the world and of international football in Ukraine, promoting the culture of the sports in the country.

Mission. To be the team that redefines the boundaries and the standards of excellence in football in Ukraine.

The next step was to identify the values underpinning this identity, values that would serve to more clearly delineate brand positioning.

Youth

Loyalty

Determination

Knowledge

Interbrand developed a concise Brand Proposition that captures the brand's overall ethos: "Beyond boundaries".

New brand elements: the logo

Between 1936 and 2007 the team logo changed several times: a blue hexagon with a red "C" in the centre and a jack hammer on top (1936); a black and white symbol with the club's name (1946); two crossed hammers inside a circle with the name "Shakytyor Donetsk" (1965); and the previous logo (Figure 4.2), which didn't get favorable reviews from the sample of fans interviewed for the study. In fact, it was seen as quite traditional, predictable (with its round shape, a football in the centre, and a green pitch), and muddled (using three languages: Ukrainian, Russian, and English).

The centrepiece of the new visual identity is the new logo developed by Interbrand (see Figure 4.3) that encapsulates a variety of meanings. It capitalizes on the origin of the club as the coalminers' team through the traditional orange and black colours, expressing the contrast

Figure 4.2 The team logo: 2006

Source: Picture courtesy of Interbrand

Figure 4.3 The new logo

Source: Picture courtesy of Interbrand

between the darkness of mines and brightness of the sun. The lower black part of the logo focuses on the club's origins by reintroducing the year of foundation and the symbol of miners' labour: the crossed hammers. Both were disappointingly absent in the preceding logo. This not only communicates the club's heritage, but also reflects President Rinat Akhmetov's desire: "I am proud of having been born and brought up in Donetsk. Donetsk is the capital of Donbass, a symbol of hard labour. I want the world to know about this region."[1]

A flame burns in the centre of the upper part of the logo, symbolizing the natural energy entrapped in the earth of the coalmining region of Donbass, and the "flame of passion" driving the Club's supporters, players, officials. The flame is surrounded by a black shape, evoking the mine galleries and the fact that energy is trapped within every chunk of coal. The strongly distinctive pointed shape of the logo reflects the value of determination, providing a strong sense of direction. The sharpness of its design evokes the renowned "fighter character" of the team. The shape is a courageous break from the standard shapes of the football industry.

The strategic meaning and implications of the development and launch of the new logo should not be underestimated and are clearly pointed out in the words used by the club's top managers during the official presentation of the new logo:

> Our previous crest was not revealing our ambitions. If we conducted an opinion poll to find out what people were thinking about a football club that have such a crest, you would hear them saying: this is a team from the middle of the league table and all they can do is winning the third place in the domestic championship. These are not our ambitions. We decided after a thorough consideration, to change the crest that would tell three main things about our team: where we come from, who we are and where are we heading to. We were born in an industrial region. Our fans are strong courageous and hard-working people. Who we are – we are the club that live up to European standards. And, finally, where we are heading to – our plan is to win European trophies. We shall become one of Europe's strongest clubs. We shall be representing the entire nation on the European football stage.
>
> *Rinat Leonidovich Akhmetov, President*[2]

> For our Club this is a very serious, significant event. This is not only the change of an emblem. This is the idea of the philosophy of our club, which consists of our brand's mission, values, essence, and finally our purposes. This is not simply about fancy pictures. This is the expression of our past, present and future. Our symbol expresses the aggressiveness of our plans, which compel us to establish standards in football. And in this we see the basic mission of our club.
>
> *Sergey Palkin, CEO*[3]

New brand elements: the name

One of the complexities in rebranding the club lay in the local cultural sensitivity, something that gains a tragic status at the time of this writing, when Donetsk is one of the epicentres of unrest and violence in the context of Ukraine's unstable political situation. The club already had a name: shakhtar means miner in Ukrainian. This name has always been a point of pride for the club, underscoring its origins as the miners' football representative. In keeping with the research findings, the first objective of the project was to sort out the confusion surrounding the languages and lettering used in the logo: Russian, the commonly spoken language in the

Donbass region, or Ukrainian, the official language? With the local Cyrillic, or the more internationally widespread Latin script? Ultimately the decision was based upon the agreed mission as the "ambassador of Ukrainian football", which directed the decision towards the use of the Ukrainian–Cyrillic combination.

The new brand architecture

The next step was to align the club's entire product and communication strategy with the new brand strategy. To do so, Interbrand developed a brand architecture with the goal of defining exactly where and how to use the Shakhtar brand without diluting it. The brand architecture was built on three hierarchical levels, with the purpose of achieving effectiveness and efficiency in communication. First, the Shakhtar masterbrand represents the vertex of the portfolio. Using a masterbrand-driven approach enables each component of the portfolio to leverage the equity of the Shakhtar brand in a broader context. The second level consists of sub-brands, which identify specific activities that the club manages either directly or by partnering with other organizations. Sub-brands are used, for example, for specific communication activities. The club owns an official website (around 14.7 million hits during the 2011–12 season), a club newspaper (150,000 copies sold during the same season), an in-house newsletter, pre-match distribution programmes (letters and flyers), an online television channel (FCSD.tv), all marked with the corporate logo. Figures 4.4 and 4.5 show some examples.

The third and final level is made up of endorsed brands, i.e. brands with their own unique images but which tap into the positive associations of the master brand. An example is the Donbass Arena, which has its own logo, inspired by the club's identity (Figure 4.6). A close, but separate, design personality achieves precisely this goal, communicating the relationship between the club and the stadium. The logo is widely used in the stadium to characterize restaurants, membership clubs, etc. (see Figures 4.7, 4.8 and 4.9).

The new logo has also supported a strong increase in revenue-generating activities (see Figure 4.10). For example, merchandising sales grew by 30% for the 2008–09 season compared to the previous year, as a result of providing a contemporary, distinctive identity and leveraging an excellent distribution chain. This consists of seven official Shakhtar Donetsk stores, including the impressive 390-square-metre Fan Shop in the Donbass Arena.

 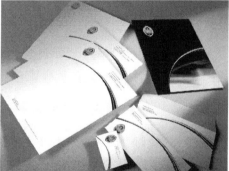

Figures 4.4 and 4.5 Examples of using the Shakhtar logo in the club's communication activities

Source: Pictures courtesy of Interbrand

Figure 4.6 The Donbass Arena logo

Source: Picture courtesy of Interbrand

Figures 4.7, 4.8 and 4.9 Examples of using the Donbass Arena logo in the stadium

Source: Pictures courtesy of Interbrand

Figure 4.10 A preliminary study for Shakhtar's merchandising, displaying the logo's power

Source: Picture courtesy of Interbrand

Shakhtar Donetsk today

The club's victories and its positive commercial results are the result of a long-term project developed by Ukrainian magnate, Rinat Akhmetov, who took over as club president on 11 October 1996. Akhmetov had the ambition to see his club compete on the same level as the great European clubs, not only in the quality of play, but the managerial approach as well. The first investments were concentrated on raising the bar on technical skills: Akhmetov hired coaches and players with international stature, and also opened a football school and the Kirsha training centre, one of the most innovative sports facilities in Europe. The centrepiece of all this is the Donbass Arena, the first UEFA five-star stadium in Eastern Europe. The 50,000-seat venue offers high entertainment value thanks to four mascots, music and mega-screens inside the arena that are used not only to display information, but also simply for audience enjoyment (for example, the "kiss cam"). There are also 500 monitors that show press conferences and similar events in addition to advertising. Often, the stadium hosts other activities as well, such as concerts by Ukrainian celebrities, cheerleading shows, and personalized initiatives such as small opera performances for the "Diamond Club" (the most prestigious members), or children's entertainment for the "Family Club".

The club's communication has also been ramped up considerably. The official website, http://shakhtar.com, is in Ukrainian but is also translated into Russian, Portuguese and English; foreign fans can even download it in pdf format on their cell phones. The club also has a magazine that is distributed throughout the television station that broadcasts programs dedicated exclusively to Shakhtar. The club also has its own YouTube channel.

The successful growth of Shakhtar is witnessed by many performance indicators:[4] the average attendance at the stadium grew from 27,300 spectators in the 2009–10 season, to 37,050 in the 2011–12 season, which is largely above the average attendance of the major European championship. In the same time period, season ticket holders grew from 17,500 to 23,200 and visitors of the club's website grew from 9.5 million to 14.7 million people. The club's Facebook fans in the 2011–12 football year exceeded 59,000, which was four times more than in the previous season. Income from commercial activities grew by 20% in the same period, and average spending for merchandising grew by 7%. More than 23,500 team scarves and 3,500 team t-shirts were sold. In the 2011–12 season, revenues from commercial activities accounted for 49% of total revenues, higher than all of the top 20 European clubs with the exception of a couple of German teams (Deloitte, 2013).

Shakhtar's success can be attributed to a combination of factors. Beyond an impressive improvement in the team's athletic performance, the quality of management throughout the organization is noteworthy, and the creation of a brand with an identity and a positioning that stand out in the world of football at a national and international level. A fundamental aspect in achieving the club's ambitious goals has been working on the club's brand equity.

Shakhtar Donetsk has become one of the best-managed football brands in Europe, has diversified revenue sources, has an excellent reputation for first-rate management and a variety of assets: one such asset is its brand. From the post-Soviet club it once was, Shakhtar is now recognized as one of the rising stars on the European football scene. In 2014, Shakhtar's team and management relocated to Western Ukraine as a consequence of the tragic events in the Donbass Region, following political unrest and the ensuing annexation of Crimea by the Russian Federation. Despite the upheaval, Shakhtar finished second place in the 2014–15 Ukrainian Premier league.

Notes

1. Shakhtar Donetsk 2009 Calendar.
2. http://shakhtar.com/en/news/5756
3. Press conference December 6th, 2007, Donetsk. Partly recorded on www.ukrrudprom.com/digest/dfghgfg061207.html
4. Shakhtar Donetsk Annual Report 2011–2012.

References

Aaker, D. (1991). *Managing brand equity.* New York: Free Press.

Apostolopoulou, A. (2002). Brand extensions by U.S. professional sport teams: Motivations and keys to success. *Sport Marketing Quarterly,* 11(1), 205–214.

Bauer, H. H., Sauer, N. E. and Schmitt, P. (2005). Customer-based brand equity in the team sport industry: Operationalization and impact on the economic success of sport teams, *European Journal of Marketing,* 39(5/6), 496–513.

Braunstein, J. and Ross, S. (2010). Brand personality in sport: Dimension analysis and general scale development. *Sport Marketing Quarterly,* 19(1), 8–16.

Carlson, B. D. and Donavan, D. T. (2013). Human brands in sport: Athlete brand personality and identification, *Journal of Sport Management,* 27(3), 193–206.

Deloitte (2013). Football Money League Report.

Ferreira, M., Hall, T. K. and Bennett, G. (2008). Exploring brand positioning in a sponsorship context: A correspondence analysis of the Dew Action Sports Tour, *Journal of Sport Management,* 22, 734–761.

Gilson, C. (2000). *Peak performance: business lessons from the world's top sports organizations,* Harper Collins.

Gladden, J. M. and Funk, D. C. (2002). Developing an understanding of brand associations in team sport: Empirical evidence from consumers of professional sport. *Journal of Sport Management,* 16(1), 54–81.

Gladden, J. and Milne, G. (1999). Examining the importance of brand equity in professional sports. *Sport Marketing Quarterly,* 8(1), 21–29.

Gladden, J., Irwin, R. and Sutton, W. (2001). Managing North American professional sport teams in the new millennium: A focus on building brand equity. *Journal of Sport Management,* 15, 297–317.

Henseler, J., Wilson, B. and Westberg, K. (2011). Managers' perceptions of the impact of sport sponsorship on brand equity: Which aspects of the sponsorship matter most? *Sport Marketing Quarterly,* 20(1), 7–21.

Keller, K. (1993). Conceptualizing, measuring, and managing customer based brand equity, *Journal of Marketing,* 57(1), 1–22.

Kunkel, T., Funk, D. C. and Hill, B. (2013). Brand architecture, drivers of consumer involvement, and brand loyalty with professional sport leagues and teams, *Journal of Sport Management*, 27(3), 177–192.

Milligan, A. (2009). Building a sports brand, *Journal of Sponsorship*, 2(3), 231–240.

Richelieu, A. and Pons, F. (2006). Toronto Maple Leafs vs Football Club Barcelona: How legendary sports teams built their brand equity. *International Journal of Sports Marketing and Sponsorship*, 7(1), 231–250.

Richelieu, A., Lopez, S. and Desbordes, M. (2008). The internationalisation of a sports team brand: The case of European soccer teams. *International Journal of Sports Marketing & Sponsorship*, 10(1), 29–44.

Ross, S. D. (2006). A conceptual framework for understanding spectator-based brand equity. *Journal of Sport Management,* 20, 22–38.

Ross, S. D., James, J. and Vargas, P. (2006). Development of a scale to measure team brand associations in professional sport. *Journal of Sport Management,* 20, 260–279.

Shaktar Donetsk (2012). Annual Report, 2011–2012.

Walsh, P. and Lee, S. (2012). Development of a brand extension decision-making model for professional sport teams. *Sport Marketing Quarterly*, 21(4), 232–242.

Walsh, P. and Ross, S. (2010). Examining brand extensions and their potential to dilute team brand associations. *Sport Marketing Quarterly*, 19(4), 196–206.

Walsh, P., Kim, Y. and Ross, S. D. (2008). Brand recall and recognition: A comparison of television and sport video games as presentation modes. *Sport Marketing Quarterly*, 17(4), 201–208.

Watkins, B. A. and Gonzenbach, W. J. (2013) Assessing university brand personality through logos: An analysis of the use of academics and athletics in university branding. *Journal of Marketing for Higher Education*, 23(1), 15–33.

Yupin Y., Mengze, S. and Goldfarb, A. (2009) Estimating the value of brand alliances in professional team sports, *Marketing Science* 28(6), 1095–1111.

5

SPORTS AND CITY BRANDING

How useful are professional football clubs for branding Europe's cities?

Christopher Hautbois

Introduction

Over the past 15 years, cities all over the world have become involved in international competitions; their common goal is to attract visitors, residents and businesses. In general, one can argue that a place with a positive reputation is more able to gain attention, resources, people, jobs and money. Consequently, place reputation has become a key element in cities' global strategies. Managers of urban development are now having to generate a virtuous circle. They need to consider a holistic approach that includes "hard" factors, such as tourism, economic development, the social organization of the city, infrastructure, people, local policies, tax regime and accessibility. Nevertheless, according to several branding specialists, it is becoming more and more difficult for mega-cities to differentiate themselves using only these "hard" factors. Designing and promoting "soft" factors, such as friendly local people, entertainment and leisure services, and art heritage and traditions, are now assumed to have a greater importance. These elements appear to be crucial for cities seeking to become creative destinations. According to Morgan, Pritchard and Pride (2011), cities that want to improve their place reputation by becoming creative destinations need to engage in a virtuous circle that encapsulates six interconnected elements: (1) tone (ambience, attitudes of its people, heritage, narratives); (2) tradition (culture, history, authenticity[1]); (3) tolerance (welcome people, regardless of race, religion, ethnic background or sexual persuasion); (4) talent (host incoming talented human capital to enhance local economy and tourism competitiveness, promote new ideas or lifestyles); (5) transformability (able to embrace new technologies but also to think differently, because in difficult times there may be a tendency to retreat into safe thinking and knowledge markets); (6) testimonies (stories told by tourists, students, residents and business people of a destination can add or subtract to the real equity of a place's reputation).

In every case, place or destination[2] brands have to manage complex relationships between brand, image, reputation and identity (Morgan et al., 2011). Thus, place reputation can be a point of interest for city governments in charge of local development and for academics. There is a need for cities to better understand the way in which they can differentiate themselves from direct competitors and enhance their branding skills in terms of their strengths. Over the past ten years, place and destination branding have become a major field of research. During the 2000s, several publications (including Anholt, 2005; 2006a; 2006b;

51

2008; Dinnie, 2008; Fan, 2005; Florian, 2002; Kavaratzis, 2004; Lucarelli and Berg, 2011; Papadopoulos, 2004 and Van Ham, 2008) suggested the fundaments of this fairly new theoretical field. In addition, since 2004, one particular journal, *Place Branding and Public Diplomacy*, has addressed the lack of information and knowledge of this field.

To date, the literature about place branding has aimed to look at the best way to build good place reputation. Several options have been studied, including: culture,[3] festival,[4] fashion,[5] folklore dancing,[6] food and beverage[7] and hallmarks events.[8] However, one of the main ways that a place can build a positive reputation is through sports. Sports can be particularly useful, because they are a worldwide phenomenon that matches the international ambition of many cities. For this reason, since the beginning of the 2000s, many cities and countries have based their urban development plans on sports. Consequently, an increasing number of journal papers have been published on this topic in major international reviews.

This chapter aims to provide both theoretical and managerial perspectives about place branding through sports. More precisely, it stresses the branding relationships between professional football clubs in Europe and their host cities. The key research questions of this chapter are: How useful are professional football clubs in a city branding strategy? How damaging is it for place branding if a professional football club becomes too famous or is made into a worldwide brand (i.e. the club brand becomes a competitor of the city brand)? Can a good place reputation be useful for football club branding strategy? How do the different local stakeholders manage the relationships between places and football clubs and any co-branding strategies?

Place branding: sports as a relevant tool

Places and destination branding: a (not so) particular form of branding

Is place a common product? Can a city be seen as a regular product? Are common branding concepts helpful when branding a city? Following Keller's (1993) definition of a brand,[9] one can postulate that destination can be assimilated into a brand. Indeed, "Most researchers in this area seem to be willing to accept definitions of city branding that are analogous to product branding whilst acknowledging the special nature of a city as an entity" (Anttiroiko, 2014). Thinking of towns as brands, Kapferer (2008) suggested that

> [A] town . . . is first and foremost a human, local and immovable reality (that is not to say it is unchangeable), anchored in history, culture and its ecosystem. [. . .] The brand cannot be built without it. It must be reckoned with. The construction of the brand should first of all involve a consensus among the town's key actors.

Cai (2002) considered that a destination image brand can be defined as "perceptions about the place as reflected by the associations held in tourist memory". Thus, a consensus does exist to say that a destination or a place can be considered as a regular brand or product. However, there are some specificities that make place branding different from other types of branding.

The first places to develop branding strategies were cities involved in the tourism business, where the local turnover was directly correlated to tourist flow. Today, branding strategies extend more widely, affecting most medium-size and large cities. The latter compete in terms of attracting visitors, tourists, residents and businesses. From a broad perspective, brand city managers have to focus on attributes, visual associations, overall reputation and identity. This poses a major challenge because if a tourist, potential resident or business person already has a prejudice against a city, positive facts and aspects about the place do not necessarily gain the attention they deserve. Conversely, a well-perceived city may have many factual disadvantages, even though it is seen favorably at the time of decision-making. Thus, it has become more and more important to pay attention to place image and reputation. This is significant because, according to Morgan et al. (2011), "it's incredibly difficult to persuade people to change their minds about places and their notions of whether somewhere is an attractive place to live, work, study, holiday or even travel". Using Simon Anholt's Nation Brands Index, the authors identified that since 2005, the date of the Index's launch, only two cities of the 3,400 taken into consideration (distributed throughout the world) saw their international image change significantly. Furthermore, Herstein and Jaffe (2008) suggested that there are ways for a city to transit from a negative to a positive image. Baker (2012) made a similar point, stating that "when a city has a negative image that has evolved over decades, it's very difficult, if not impossible, to change it in a short term". Prebensen (2007) claimed that a destination's image can be influenced by three sources of information: organic image (for example, what we learn about a destination at school, in books, or hear about on the news and through word of mouth), induced image (the result of promotional material and destination marketing efforts) and modified-induced image (the result of personal experience of the destination). These different elements challenge the city governments in two main ways. First, local managers who are in charge of branding the destination can influence only one (induced image) of the three sources of information that impact on image. Second, it can take a long time to change a destination's image or reputation. This poses a problem, in that mayors, councillors and elected urban developers do not know how long they will maintain their authority over their city. As a result, a city branding strategy does not intrinsically fit well with the time restrictions imposed on city governments.

The concept of city brand can be defined as "the unique, multi-dimensional blend of elements that provide the city with locally grounded differentiation and relevance for all its target audiences" (Anttiroiko, 2014). Earlier, Baker (2012) provided the following definition: "a place brand is the totality of thoughts, feelings and expectations that people hold about a location. It's the reputation and the enduring essence of the place and represents its distinctive promise of value, providing it with a competitive edge." With regard to the concept of city branding, we should also recognize that several other analogous terms exist in the literature, including: place branding, location branding, destination branding, city marketing, place marketing, place promotion, place production, place shaping and place making. Whilst these terms vary in their meaning to some degree (see Anttiroiko, 2014), they all refer in some way to local development. Whatever the term used and the case studied, two main phases can be identified: brand audit and brand development. In 2006, Prophet, a consulting company, gave more details about the city branding process and suggested eight different steps.[10] This process is clearly defined and city governments have to brand their city according to the strengths and opportunities provided within its boundaries. However, whilst the eighth step requires us to measure the efficiency of the process, we still have little evidence of how cities have branded successfully (Parkerson and Saunders, 2005). What we observe is that the best examples of city branding are those that are best known, in other words, cities that are at the top of the global urban hierarchy (for example, Amsterdam, Barcelona, Hong Kong, New York, Seoul, Singapore and Toronto). Confirmation of the importance of large cities in the branding process can be found in the 2013 GfK's City Brands Index of brand and asset strengths in major worldwide cities. Paris emerged as the number one city brand, followed by Sydney and London (see Table 5.1).

Table 5.1 Global top 10 city brands

Top 10 city brands
1 Paris
2 Sydney
3 London
4 Rome
5 New York
6 Barcelona
7 San Francisco
8 Los Angeles
9 Vienna
10 Madrid

Based on the following six categories: presence, place, prerequisites, people, pulse, potential

Source: GfK's City Brands Index

Two comments can be made about Table 5.1. First, this list of branded mega-cities does not reflect the realities of most cities around the world. For example, "For many of them, the mission is rather to increase the awareness of the target audience that the city exists" (Anttiroiko, 2014). However, the globalization and internationalization of business and tourism appear as new and big challenges for most of the cities, regardless of their size.[11] This process pushes cities to state their branding process (i.e. definition of objectives and SWOT, segmenting and positioning) and to subdivide it into successive logical steps. Second, it is necessary to further explore the values associated with a brand. Such an investigation was carried out by Westerbeek and Linley (2012). The figure they provided (Figure 5.1) shows the possible associations between city brands and brand identity or values.

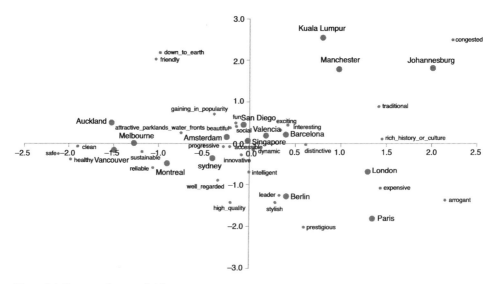

Figure 5.1 Perceptual map of cities

Source: Westerbeek and Linley 2012

Sport-based branding strategies

Westerbeek, Turner and Ingerson (2002) assumed that "increasingly, cities are basing their city marketing efforts around hallmark events in order to maximize the benefits to be achieved from event-driven tourism, sponsorship and media exposure". This sporting event-based option, which allows cities to be (re)branded, has also been supported by Rein and Shields (2007), Heslop, Nadeau and O'Reilly (2013) and Herstein and Berger (2013b). The sporting events that gain most attention are the Summer and Winter Olympic Games and the FIFA World Cup. Others, for example, Commonwealth Games, motorsport Grand Prix,[12] Rugby World Cup[13] and Super Bowl,[14] have been studied to a lesser degree. Whatever the kind of sporting event, it seems that the entertainment industry, of which sports events are a vital part, is particularly influential with regard to creating, facilitating, strengthening and changing people's perceptions about places (Kotler and Gertner, 2002). Referring to the brand personality concept, and to the existing literature on sponsorship, Westerbeek and Linley (2012) considered that this concept also applies to place and country marketing. According to them, "it could even be argued that cities that attract events in order to (re)position their image and build their brand can be likened to corporate sponsors who, for similar reasons, decide to sponsor individuals, organizations or events". As a result, the fit between a destination brand and one or more major sporting event brands is of particular interest.

As previously mentioned, the Olympic Games are seen as the most powerful platform for rebranding a city. They are reputed to have two kinds of impact: on image and on local economy (including the labor market[15]). These two impacts refer to the common objectives of city planners. During the bidding process, the latter usually claim that hosting this event will leverage the image of their city. Consequently, several surveys have been conducted to measure the impact of such events. With regard to image impact, one should consider the case of Seoul. This city's branding strategy was designed in parallel with the city's involvement in international bids and the hosting of sporting events. The process started with the hosting of the 2002 FIFA World Cup in Korea and Japan. The 2008 Olympic Games in Beijing have also been studied several times, in order to identify their impact on China's image. First, in an *ex-ante* perspective, Berkowitz et al. (2007) analyzed the opportunity to use the 2008 Olympics as a marketing tool to maximize the global equity of the China brand. Preuss and Alfs (2011) and Chung and Woo (2011) went on to address the effects on China's country image of hosting the 2008 Olympic Games, as an international marketing strategy. A second-level objective was to study the way the changed image of the country contributed to changing its product image. They found a significant difference in the overall image of China two months after the Olympics, compared with the overall image of the country two months before. However, no significant change in China's product image has been found. Gibson et al. (2008) and Chen and Funk (2010) studied the relationship between destination image, travel intentions and tourist characteristics. The respondents perceived China and the Beijing

---

"Melbourne has been named winner of the 2014 SportsBusiness Ultimate Sports City [. . .] for the second time and also recognized as the world leader in Sports Venues and in Event Strategy, at an Awards announcement at the SportAccord Convention in Turkey. [. . .] Others cities short listed were Berlin, Cape Town, Singapore and Sydney"

Figure 5.2 Melbourne, the world's ultimate sports city

Source: Victorian Major Events Company, Media release, 14 April 2014

Olympic Games positively and destination image was significantly predictive of the intention to travel to China and the Olympic Games. Finally, Zeng et al. (2011) focused on the impact of the 2008 Beijing Olympic Games on China's image in the international TV media (nine countries). Chalip, Green and Hill (2003), Avraham (2004) and Hede (2005) also used a media approach in their respective researches. The latter analyzed the efficacy of the Australian telecast of the 2004 Athens Summer Olympic Games in developing positive perceptions and attitudes of Greece as a tourist destination. With regard to the impact on the host country's image, Armenakyan et al. (2012) carried out a cross-national, longitudinal study of Canadian and US respondents in order to examine the (positive) impact of the 2010 Vancouver Olympic Games on the images of the host country, Canada, and the Olympic Games itself.[16] However, according to Herstein and Berger (2013a), hosting a mega-sporting event is not enough to rebrand a city or leverage its image. Indeed, over the last 30 years, many millions of dollars have been spent with little success in leveraging the image of host cities. Two cities were studied by the authors. The Barcelona model shows how a city can leverage its image, using the Olympic Games to become more familiar to millions of potential tourists. The London model shows how an entire country can also profit from the fact that its capital is hosting the Olympic Games.

With regard to the impact of image, hosting[17] hallmark events is a good way to attract tourists. According to Westerbeek et al. (2002), people are often drawn to destinations because of the hallmark (sporting) events staged there, rather than the region itself. In 2001, the 11th report of the Tourism Forecasting Council stated that 1.7 million tourist visits were estimated in Sydney between 1997 and 2004 as a direct response to the Olympic Games. During 2000, however, visits for the period were estimated to be 20 percent of this total.

In terms of strategy design, Herstein and Berger (2013b) considered that city planners can use four re-branding strategies related to sporting events: mega events, international events, medium events and minor events. The first two event types can be useful to local businesses if decision makers ensure that people all over the world see their city as a leisure, tourism and consumption center and not just as a sports arena. The last two event types are helpful in fostering residents' civic pride (Maennig and Porsche, 1999). Another area of interest is to look at the use of single-purpose events to build a city brand versus the use of a genuine long-term, multi-event portfolio. Chalip and Costa (2005), Ziakas and Costa (2011) and Westerbeek and Linley (2012) all supported the option of a multi-event portfolio and the idea of founding a city branding strategy on hosting recurrent events.

As previously established, mega sporting events (especially the Olympic Games) are often taken into consideration by city governments, who aim to (re)brand their city and to position it in a worldwide competition. They are also considered by academics, who see the Olympic Games as an interesting case to study. Such interest can be explained by the fact that when a city government bids for a sporting event, there is a real strategy and ambition to host this event, on a certain date and with a return of investment that has been well analyzed and targeted. In such a strategy, a voluntary choice has been made by the community. Alternatively, a city can (re)brand itself through its professional sports clubs. Few studies of this strategy exist in the literature, which is surprising, bearing in mind that many cities in the world have become well known because of the professional sports clubs that they host. Thus, it is of interest to study the role of professional sports clubs, particularly football clubs, in branding European cities. This chapter seeks to address this lack of research in co-branding strategies between professional football clubs and their host cities.

Method

The key research questions of this chapter are: How useful are football professional clubs in city branding strategies? How are city governments able to use the powerful brand of local football clubs in order to enhance their city brand? Is it damaging for place branding if football professional clubs become too famous or become a worldwide brand, limiting the city brand development? In order to answer these questions, two complementary surveys have been designed. This double approach allowed the crossing of data and provided an overview of the strategic relationships between the football club brand and the city brand. This method also offered an opportunity to gather general data about several football clubs in Europe. From this general data, special and interesting cases could be further explored. For both approaches, data was collected between December 2014 and March 2015.

Qualitative approach: a study of three well-known professional clubs in football history

For our research, several football clubs were deemed suitable for our analysis. Three main criteria were then taken into consideration: nationality of the club (with the goal to diversify as much as possible); the importance of the club in football history (the fact that each club could be perceived as a legendary club on a European or national scale); the trophies and titles of the club (in terms of national and European championships won or the domination of the club in the short- or medium-term period). Using these three criteria, the clubs of FC Barcelona, Manchester United and AS Saint-Etienne were selected. An interview was carried out with one or more experts in each club in order to analyze the relationship between the professional football club and the city from a branding perspective. The table below provides additional information about these three clubs and the interviews carried out.

Quantitative approach: a study of the four most major football championships in Europe

The second approach we used was based on a questionnaire sent to all clubs in the Premier League championship (n=20), Bundesliga championship (n=18), Calcio championship (n=20) and Liga championship (n=20). In addition, another questionnaire was sent to the host cities of football clubs that belong to the Premier League championship (n=13[18]), Bundesliga championship (n=17), Calcio championship (n=15) and Liga championship (n=16). As a result, a questionnaire was sent to a theoretical sample of 139 respondents. However, we faced problems in delivering this questionnaire, because of an incorrect email address in 29 cases. In addition, 16 respondents answered that they were not the right person to complete the questionnaire and were not able to forward it to the relevant person. Thus, our final sample was 96 respondents. At the time of writing this chapter, 18 correctly completed questionnaires (10 clubs and 8 cities) were received and analyzed (a response rate of 0.19). The questionnaire asked the respondents to rate the extent to which they agreed or disagreed with different statements on a 7-point Likert scale. The first part of the questionnaire asked the respondents about the existence of a branding strategy for the football club and the city. The second part was about the influence of the city on the club's ability to meet certain key goals, but also about the influence of the club on the city's ability to meet certain key goals. Finally, the question enquired as to the nature of the perceived relationships between the football clubs and cities from a branding perspective.

Table 5.2 Information about the three cases studied

Club	FC Barcelona	Manchester United	AS Saint-Etienne
Nationality	Spanish	British	French
Date of creation	1899	1878	1919
Number of national titles (cups and championships)	61	35	17
Number of European titles (cups and championships)	12	6	0 (1 final)
Expert interviewed	Antonio Davila	Claude Boli	(1) Lionel Boucherp (2) Stéphane Devrieux
Function	Professor at the IESE Business School	Historian, specialist on Manchester United	(1) Councillor in charge of sporting events (2) Local tourism manager
Date and duration of the interview	9 March (35 minutes)	11 February (60 minutes)	(1) 9 February (65 minutes) (2) 19 February (55 minutes)
City	Barcelona	Manchester	Saint-Etienne
Population	1,600,000	512,000	172,000
Number of professional football clubs	2	2	1
Tourists	13,200,000 overseas tourists per annum	988,000 overseas tourists per annum (second in the UK after London)	43,000

Results and discussion

Three different contexts for three different city branding strategies

The results presented below are based on the interviews of experts shown in Table 5.2.

The football clubs as a symbol of rebirth

In order to study city branding, it is important to look at the background of the cities and to better understand where they have come from. This section aims to provide some detail of the local background of all three cities studied. Furthermore, it explores how local football clubs came into being after economic troubles faced by the cities.

> In my opinion, there are three things about Manchester that have to be put into their historical context. First of all, we need to remember that Manchester was the birthplace of the industrial revolution. Manchester's ability to respond to situations comes from that history. It's often thought that the suburbs, places where people can live and work, had their origins in Manchester. Finally, this city has been known since the 1980s as a place of deindustrialization, which has damaged Manchester's image as a symbol of Victorian England. In the 1980s, music, particularly pop and New Wave, became one of Manchester's trademarks. [...] From the 1990s, the international success of Manchester United, has brought new life to this city through its

industrial heritage [a sort of renewal]. So, whether we're in England or elsewhere, when people speak about Manchester they inevitably mean Manchester United.

Claude Boli (Manchester)

Saint-Etienne has a strong heritage, a strong industrial past, a past that is linked with the mail-order business Manufrance, which was set up here. It's all part of our history, but this history is still being written today, only in a different way. Our ambition is to change the city's image. That's why we have an ongoing campaign called "Do you know how Saint-Etienne will change the world?" It highlights design-based activities, such as the International Design Biennale. There's also the modern art museum that houses the second most important collection after the Pompidou Centre in Paris.

Lionel Boucher (Saint-Etienne)

A football club with a strong identity suitable for urban development

The three football clubs studied have a very strong brand, internationally for Manchester United and FC Barcelona and nationally for AS Saint-Etienne. In all three cases, the existence of these clubs has a strong and positive influence on local development, place reputation and business.

If the club does well, businessmen here can sell their products abroad. Some companies have even decided to mark their products with the "made in Manchester" logo. It's become a mark of quality. The attraction of football has led to some companies setting themselves up in Manchester so as to benefit from the city's "aura". Thanks to all this, Manchester is seen less as a Northern town where it rains all the time.

Claude Boli (Manchester)

As I said, today Manchester United is seen as the city's international showcase. Nonetheless, Manchester's past, its industrial heritage, the music scene that still carries on, is being reinvented. This is especially obvious with the transformation of former industrial buildings into modern loft apartments, which now form a part of the city's identity. Football has contributed to Manchester's renaissance. And it's not just Manchester United; from 2000 on, Manchester City has also contributed to the renewal of a city that now has two leading clubs, with two different, but complementary, histories. Thanks to them, the city is seen differently by those who live here. That said, the Manchester brand has historically been based more on Man United than on Man City. The success of the Manchester brand was based on the sporting success of Man United. Everyone knows that City is a foreign force. It's not English. Even though United belongs to the Glaser family, it's not the same thing. Really, there's no rivalry between the Manchester brand and the United brand.

Claude Boli (Manchester)

The club continues to generate enthusiasm with our associates in the rest of France. Very often, we're chosen to host exhibitions or events because they're fans of ASSE and they want their event to take place in the city. Admittedly, ASSE is a club that has a large fan base all over France, including in towns where there are big football clubs, like Toulouse.

Stéphane Devrieux (Saint-Etienne)

Saint-Etienne is a football town. Even if we try to develop other areas of the town, we'll still have to invest in football, because it's the number one subject when we're talking about our town, it's our main sound box.

Lionel Boucher (Saint-Etienne)

I really think that the FC Barcelona is one of the attributes of the Barcelona city brand. The FC Barcelona is sometimes known as the club of the Catalonia. But for branding, I think that the club is more internationally known as the club of Barcelona. People don't know what Catalonia is but they know what Barcelona is and what this city refers to in terms attributes.

Antonio Davila (Barcelona)

The influence of a football club on city branding: maintaining a tricky balance between the advantages and disadvantages

Each of these three football clubs has a strong brand and has a positive influence on city reputation. However, it's the business of the city planners to limit the negative influence that these brands could have if they became too strong, dominating other assets in the city.

Sport helps us to sell land, that's certainly true. [. . .] Firstly, ASSE allows us, as much on a national as a local level, to capitalise on our positive image, to our benefit. Equally, though, we want to make sure that it doesn't overshadow everything else. The town of Saint-Etienne isn't just about its football club, as prestigious as it is, it's also important in terms of its local history and the history of sport in the country. We want to show off everything that we have to offer. In my opinion, what we have is a win–win partnership between the town and the club.

Stéphane Devrieux (Saint-Etienne)

It's clear that you can't just focus on the results of one club. By their very nature, these results are random. They don't come out as you'd like. . . So, you could say that the club is very important and of great interest to the town in terms of pride, the activities that take place here, a sense of community, of living here together. [Despite this], Saint-Etienne cannot yet see itself as being a brand. Until now, this hasn't been a priority. We're not in the position of Lyon or Amsterdam, which has "Iamsterdam' as its brand, but this can change.

Lionel Boucher (Saint-Etienne)

Today, the town's tourist offering rests on three pillars. First, business tourism, with its conferences and seminars, where we try to welcome more and more people to Saint-Etienne. Then, there's urban tourism, which builds on our cultural offering. [. . .] Urban tourism is based on offering short breaks. One of the main ways we've carried out this second strategy is through the Design Biennial, which we organised in 2006. This event has been a big help to us, especially when in 2010 Saint-Etienne became the first UNESCO City of Design in France. The final point is concerned with the development of our natural heritage. Close to Saint-Etienne, accessible only five minutes from the town, is the regional park of Pilat.

Stéphane Devrieux (Saint-Etienne)

The Barcelona city has two Professional football clubs. I do not think that this is a problem to brand the city. I consider that this gives you two opportunities to make people come to the city. Of course, the FC Barcelona has the same name as the city which is very helpful and this is much famous team than Espanyol. Beside, the city of Barcelona is famous for these professional clubs but to me this counts only for 10 percent of the awareness of the city. This city is also known for architecture, quality of life, entrepreneurship. . .

Antonio Davila (Barcelona)

European football clubs: are they globally helpful for city branding strategies?

As mentioned in the methods section, both a qualitative study and a quantitative survey were carried out. Data about the city government's perception, of the influence of the local football club on place reputation is now given.

According to the city governments, the three most important effects of a professional football club on city branding were found to be civic pride (6.5), tourism activity (5.7) and incoming residents (5). Moreover, respondents considered that on a 7-point Likert scale (1=negative; 7=positive), the global average influence of a professional club on place reputation was highly positive (6.3). In addition, the perceived influence of football clubs on place reputation was not correlated with the number of seasons in the first division ($r=0.086$), the number of national titles ($r=-0.061$), or the number of international titles ($r=-0.034$). Rather, this positive influence was correlated more with the size of the local population ($r=0.5$).

Another lesson from our quantitative analysis is that we also need to consider the influence of the place reputation on the football club branding and business. Data about the perception of this influence by the respondents[19] is now given.

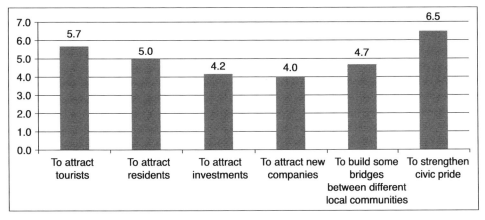

Figure 5.3 Effects of a professional football club on city development

Note: rating on a 7-point Likert scale (1=disagree; 7=agree) to the question: "Do you consider that the local professional football club, in terms of its image, awareness, and values is helpful for the city to . . .?"

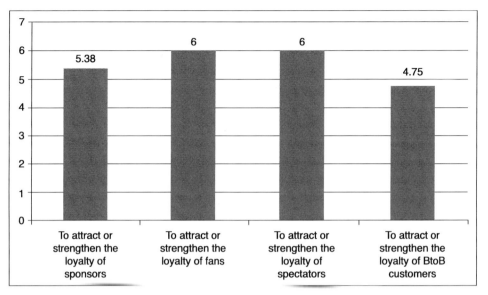

Figure 5.4 Effects of place reputation on football club development

Note: rating on a 7-point Likert scale (1=disagree; 7=agree) to the question: "Do you consider that the image, the awareness, the value of the host territory or city are helpful for your club to . . .?"

The influence of place reputation was generally perceived as being positive for the football clubs, especially in terms of fans' and spectators' loyalty (6.0), but also because of sponsors' loyalty (5.38) and BtoB customers' loyalty (4.75). The overall perception of the influence of the city brand on the football club brand was positive (5.12).

The quantitative approach concluded that the relationship between the football clubs and their host cities is based on a positive co-branding. Even if this effect was perceived as being more positive for the city (6.3) than for the football club (5.1), from a marketing perspective, one brand does seem to help the other. Thus, one can conclude that there the city brand and the football club brand do not compete; rather, they form part of a positive co-branding strategy.

Discussion

According to the data collected, it seems that the existence of a professional football club can be used by city planners to engage in a virtuous circle, as described by Morgan et al. (2011). The quantitative data gathered, and both the Saint-Etienne and the Manchester cases, highlight the fact that the existence of a local football club had a positive impact on place reputation, as well as on tourists' intention to visit, on companies' intention to invest locally and on local companies, who mentioned on their products or in their communication plans that their headquarters are based in these towns. These observations can form the fundaments of this virtuous circle.

In comparing the data collected on football clubs and from publications on city branding through sporting events, it is necessary to mention that, in both cases, media exposure appeared decisive to branding the city. In order for a football club to have a positive influence on a city brand, the city needs to be associated with the football club and this association has to be exposed by the media. This is a key element because, without media exposure, the potential of using the football club to brand the city will not be reached. One of the advantages provided by a professional football club is to bring media to the city.

In addition to this media exposure, the association between a club and a city brand needs to be strengthened over the long term. As emphasized by Morgan et al. (2011), "it's incredibly difficult to persuade people to change their minds about places". Even if quantitative data shows that there is no correlation between the number of seasons that the football club has played in the first division, interviews have confirmed that, in order to use the club brand to brand the city, the club has to be part of the local and city history. The history of the club, its status as a legend, its long-term association with the city, the existence of several generations of local fans who've attended matches in the stadium, are an efficient way for city planners to take advantage of the club to enhance the city brand. From this perspective, our case studies of football clubs have produced findings that are in line with existing literature on hosting sporting events. Both the football club and the city need a long time period to positively influence a place reputation.

According to quantitative data collected, however, there is no correlation between the number of titles and the perceived effect of the football club on city brand. The interviews also confirmed that long-term positive results give a city government more opportunities to brand the city and to improve place reputation. In others words, the existence of the club is maybe not enough on its own. By taking these results into consideration, it may be possible to optimize the city brand strategy. They may appear less important if the football club's brand is strong and has worldwide appeal. Even if a club is no longer competitive, it can nevertheless be used in a city brand strategy if it is a legendary club. "Legend" or "history" are two good concepts to use when engaging in a communication plan.

In each of our three cases, the city government needed to be involved in a city brand strategy based on the local football club. As previously mentioned, Prebensen (2007) claimed that a destination's image can be influenced by three sources of information (organic image, induced image and modified-induced image). As a result, city planners must be active, especially in terms of induced image, when it is necessary to integrate the opportunity provided by the club in the global city brand strategy and any plans to make the city more attractive. For example, Manchester placed a giant Manchester United poster at Manchester Airport so that people who arrive in the city can see it, along with the implied message "you are arriving at the city of Manchester United". This strategy forms part of the Marketing Manchester Agency's plans, which seek to

> develop the Manchester brand and to focus on the contemporary and traditional strengths of the city-region's culture, create world-class events programme, [. . .] position Manchester as a vibrant international destination, ensure that Manchester is further established as one of the Europe's leading business destinations and support the enhancement of the tourism product in Great Manchester.
>
> *www.marketingmanchester.com*

Following this example, and looking at the data collected from our sample, one can conclude that there is no competition between football club and city branding. This point was one of the research questions of this chapter. Both qualitative and quantitative data confirm that there is no negative influence of the football club on the city brand. Rather, it seems very likely that a positive circle can be created that benefits both structures. Managers who were asked to complete the questionnaires insisted on the positive co-branding that exists between the club and the city.

Two final comments can be made. First, the interviews confirmed that it is important to correctly position the football club within the city branding strategy. The city planners control neither the existence of the club (the city government is not the owner of the club and is not able to decide if the club can keep on playing in the first division), nor its results, thus, using the club in a branding strategy adds a degree of uncertainty. If the club produced poor results over the medium and long term, or if it was relegated to division 2, then the city's branding plans would have to completely change. On this point, the use of a football club to brand the city is not widely covered in the existing literature, which has largely dealt with branding from the perspective of hosting sporting events. Of course, hosting a mega sporting event can also bring uncertainty, because before hosting can take place, cities have to engage in a bidding process (Ingerson and Westerbeek, 2000). Once the bid has been won, however, the opportunity for the city to design a branding strategy is fixed; it does not depend on the results. That is why a mega sporting event is a relevant vehicle for branding a city. Second, the experts interviewed suggested that a local football club should not be used the sole vehicle in city branding. The club should be a part of a portfolio of opportunities used by the city government, taking into consideration the timing, the current objective and the agenda. This result is in line with previous recommendations on sporting events put forward by Chalip and Costa (2005), Ziakas and Costa (2011) and Westerbeek and Linley (2012), who supported the option of a multi-event portfolio and the idea of founding a city branding strategy on hosting recurrent events. In this portfolio, city planners should also ensure that the football club does not overtake other opportunities in the city's branding strategy. The data collected confirms that mayors, councilors and city governments wanted their city to be known only through its football club.

Conclusion

As mentioned in the introduction and the section on theoretical background, little is known about the usefulness of a professional football club to city branding. This is quite surprising because many cities throughout the world, especially those in Europe, are known through their local professional club. Most existing publications about the role of sports in the enhancement of place reputation have dealt with sporting events hosted by cities. This assessment can be explained in two ways. First, hallmark sporting events, such as the Olympic Games and the FIFA World Cup, are powerful events that can brand cities. Thus, it is logical that many publications have dealt with them. Second, whilst city governments can drive an offensive campaign when bidding to host sporting events, they have no influence on the existence or performance of a local football club, an organization that is distinct from the city government. As a result, whilst city governments can plan to brand their city by hosting a sporting event, they cannot do the same by "creating" a football club. They can only take advantage of a club that already exists. The fact that the city governments are powerless to "create" a professional football club may account for why the existing literature has, until now, focused more on major sporting events.

This chapter can be seen as a first step; one that serves as a call to others to explore further. However, it does draw the conclusion that a professional football club can be a support for a city brand strategy, because of the knowledge we already have about the use of hallmark sporting events. During our survey, the chief revenue and marketing officer of Valencia FC claimed that "the club was the best ambassador of the city". Nevertheless, this work is still a work in progress. More data needs to be collected if we are to refine the current results and explore other hypotheses. What is the precise impact of a club's performance and the number of seasons in the first division on the city brand, on tourism activity and on local business? Is the size of a city important in terms of enhancing the city brand? Do we observe the same effects on city brands for all European championships?

Notes

1. According to Gilmore (2002), a destination's brand message should be "an amplification of what is already there and not a fabrication".
2. This can be defined as places that have tourism-oriented business. A survey conducted for the World Tourism Organization in 2009 stated that 60% of brands are focused only on tourism.
3. Anttiroiko (2014) shed light on Seoul's case, which in the 2000s used the cultural sector and a slogan ("Seoul, the soul of Asia") to enhance its competitiveness in tourism. Baker (2012) focused on how the movie *Australia* helped to brand and market a location to make it attractive to tourists.
4. Cannes' case (France).
5. Milan's case (Italy).
6. Rio de Janeiro's case (Brazil).
7. Munich's case (Germany).
8. De Carlo (2011) discussed Milan's case; the city hosted Expo 2015.
9. "A brand can be defined as a name, term, sign, symbol or design or combination of them which is intended to identify the goods and services of one seller or group of sellers and to differentiate them from those of competitors" (Keller, 1993).
10. Step 1: Define clear objectives. Step 2: understand the target audience. Step 3: identify current brand image. Step 4: set the aspirational brand identity. Step 5: develop the positioning. Step 6: create value propositions. Step 7: execute the brand strategy. Step 8: measure access.
11. A similar comment can be made for nations. Most countries have a destination brand: "100 Percent Pure New Zealand", "South Africa it's possible", "YourSingapore", "Incredible India". Even Afghanistan positions itself as the "Last unconquered mountains of the world".
12. See, for example, McCartney (2005).
13. See, for example, Jones (2001).
14. See, for example, Kim and Walker (2012).
15. See, for example, Hagn and Maennig (2007) for data about the labour market effects of the 2006 FIFA World Cup.
16. Using a co-branding framework, authors also go further in demonstrating that the "2008 Beijing Olympics were not successful in reputation and image enhancement of either the Olympics brand or of China. However, the Canadian mega-events outcomes were positive for both partners": country and OG.
17. Or bidding. Cornelissen (2004) tested the impact on African countries' image of bids for sporting events they were involved in.
18. One city hosts several football clubs.
19. Most of the time, respondents were commercial directors, brands or sales managers, and marketing officers of football clubs.

References

Anholt, S. (2005). Some important distinctions in place branding. *Place Branding and Public Diplomacy*, 1(2), 116–121.
Anholt, S. (2006a). Is place branding a capitalist tool? *Place Branding and Public Diplomacy*, 2(1), 1–4.
Anholt, S. (2006b). Public diplomacy and the place branding: where's the link? *Place Branding and Public Diplomacy*, 2(1), 271–275.
Anholt, S. (2008). Place branding: is it marketing or isn't it? *Place Branding and Public Diplomacy*, 4, 1–6.
Anttiroiko, A.-V. (2014). *The political economy of city branding*, Abingdon: Routledge.
Armenakyan, A., Heslop, L. A., Nadeau, J., O'Reilly, N. and Lu, I. R. R. (2012). Does hosting the Olympic Games matter? Canada and Olympic Games images before and after the 2010 Olympic Games. *International Journal of Sport Management and Marketing*, 12(1/2), 111–140.
Avraham, E. (2004). Media strategies for improving an unfavorable city image. *Cities*, 21(6), 471–479.

Baker, B. (2012). *Destination branding for small cities: the essentials for successful place*, Portland: Creative Leap Books.

Berkowitz, P., Gjermano, G., Gomez, L. and Schafer, G. (2007). Brand China: Using the 2008 Olympic Games to enhance China's image. *Place Branding and Public Diplomacy*, 3, 164–178.

Cai, A. (2002). Cooperative branding for rural destinations. *Annals of Tourism Research*, 29, 720–742.

Chalip, L. and Costa, C. A. (2005). Sport event tourism and the destination brand: towards a general theory. *Sport in Society*, 8(2), 218–237.

Chalip, L., Green, B. C. and Hill, B. (2003). Effects of sport event media on destination image and intention to visit. *Journal of Sport Management*, 17(3), 214–234.

Chen, N. and Funk, D. (2010). Exploring destination image, experience and revisit intention: a comparison of sport and non-sport tourist perceptions. *Journal of Sport Tourism*, 15(3), 239–259.

Chung, W. and Woo, C. W. (2011). The effects of hosting an international event on country image: the 2008 Summer Olympics case, *International Journal of Sports Marketing & Sponsorship*, 12(4), 281–300.

Cornelissen, S. (2004). Sport mega-events in Africa: processes, impacts and prospects. *Tourism and Hospitality Planning & Development*, 1(1), 39–55.

De Carlo, M. and Lei, C. (2011). Repositioning city brands and events: Milan, in N. Morgan, A. Pritchard, R. Pride (Eds) *Destination brands. Managing place reputation*, London: Elsevier.

Dinnie, K. (2008). *Nation branding: concepts, issues, practice*, Oxford: Butterworth-Heinemann.

Fan, Y. (2005). Branding the nation: What is being branded? *Journal of Vacation Marketing*, 12(1), 5–14.

Florian, B. (2002). The city as a brand, in V. Patteeuw, *City branding: image building & building images*, Rotterdam: Nai Publishers.

Gibson, H., Xueqing, C. Q. and Zhang, J. J. (2008). Destination image and intent to visit China and the 2008 Beijing Olympic Games. *Journal of Sport Management*, 22, 427–450.

Gilmore, F. (2002). A country: Can it be repositioned? Spain: The success story of country branding. *Brand Management*, 9, 281–293.

Hagn, F. and Maennig, W. (2007). Labour market effects of the 2006 Soccer World Cup in Germany. *Working Paper*, 08/2007.

Hede, A. (2005). Sports-events, tourism and destination marketing strategies: an Australian case study on Athens 2004 and its media telecast. *Journal of Sport Tourism*, 10(3), 187–200.

Herstein, R. and Berger, R. (2013a). Hosting the Olympics: A city's make-or-break impression, *Journal of Business Strategy*, 34(5), 54–59.

Herstein, R. and Berger, R. (2013b). Much more than sports: Sports events as stimuli for city re-branding, *Journal of Business Strategy*, 34(2), 38–44.

Herstein, R. and Jaffe, D. E. (2008). The children's city: The transition from a negative to a positive city image, *Place Branding and Public Diplomacy*, 4, 76–84.

Heslop, L. A., Nadeau, J. and O'Reilly, R. (2013). Mega-event and country co-branding: image shifts, transfers and reputational impacts, *Corporate Reputation Review*, 16, 7–33.

Ingerson, L. and Westerbeek, H. (2000). Determining key success criteria for attracting hallmark sporting events. *Pacific Tourism Review*, 3(4), 239–253.

Jones, C. (2001). Mega-events and host-region: Determining the true worth of the 1999 Rugby World Cup. *International Journal of Tourism Research*, 3, 241–251.

Kapferer, J.-N. (2008). *The new strategic management*, London: Kogan Page.

Kavaratzis, M. (2004). From city marketing to city branding: towards a theoretical framework for developing city brands. *Place Branding and Public Diplomacy*, 1(1), 58–73.

Keller, K. L. (1993). Conceptualizing, measuring and managing customer-based brand equity. *Journal of Vacation Marketing*, 18, 147–155.

Kim, W. and Walker, M. (2012). Measuring the social impacts associated with Super Bowl XLIII: Preliminary development of a psychic income scale. *Sport Management Review*, 15, 91–108.

Kotler, P. and Gertner, D. (2002). Country as brand, product and beyond: a place marketing and brand management perspective. *Brand Management*, 9(4/5), 249–261.

Lucarelli, A. and Berg, P.O. (2011). City branding: A state of the art review of the research domain, *Journal of Place Management and Development*, 4(1), 9–27.

Maennig, W. and Porsche, M. (1999). The feel-good effect of a mega sports events. Recommandations for public and private administration informed by the experience of the FIFA World Cup 2006, *IASE/NAASE Working Paper Series*, 08–17.

McCartney, G. (2005). The impact of the 50th Macao Grand Prix on Macao's destination image. *International Journal of Event Management Research*, 1(1), 46–65.

Morgan, N., Pritchard, A. and Pride, R. (2011). *Destination brands. Managing place reputation*. 3rd edition, London: Elsevier.

Papadopoulos, N. (2004). Place branding: evolution, meaning and implications. *Place Branding*, 1(1), 36–49.

Parkerson, B. and Saunders, J. (2005). City branding. Can goods and services branding models be used to brand cities, *Place Branding and Public Diplomacy*, 1(3), 242–264.

Prebensen, N. K. (2007). Investing in an event: The case of a sledge dog race in Norway "The Finnmarkslopet". *Event Management*, 11(3), 99–108.

Preuss, H. and Alfs, C. (2011). Signaling through the 2008 Beijing Olympics, using mega sport events to change the perception and image of the host. *European Sport Management Quarterly*, 11(1), 55–71.

Rein, I. and Shields, B. (2007). Place branding sports: strategies for differentiating emerging, transitional, negatively viewed and newly industrialised nations. *Place Branding and Public Diplomacy*, 3(1), 73–85.

Tourism Forecasting Council (2001). The 11th report of the tourism forecasting council, *Tourism Forecasting Council*, February.

Van Ham, P. (2008). Place branding: the state of art. *The Annals of the American Academy of Political and Social Science*, 616(1), 126–149.

Westerbeek, H. M., Turner, P. and Ingerson, L. (2002). Key success factors in bidding for hallmark sporting events, *International Marketing Review*, 19(2/3), 303–322.

Westerbeek, H. M. and Linley, M. (2012) Building city brands through sport events: theoretical and empirical perspectives. *Journal of Brand Strategy*, 1(2), 193–205.

Zeng, G., Go, F. and Kolmer, C. (2011). The impact of international TV media coverage of the Beijing Olympics 2008 on China's media image formation: a media content analysis perspective. *International Journal of Sports Marketing and Sponsorship*, 12(4), 319–337.

Ziakas, V. and Costa, C. A. (2011). Event portfolio and multi-purpose development: establishing the conceptual grounds. *Sport Management Review*, 14(4), 409–423.

PART II

Sponsorship

Nicolas Chanavat, Simon Chadwick and Michel Desbordes

Although sponsorship is not an exclusively sporting phenomenon, over the last four decades sponsorship has become synonymous with sports. Indeed, in many markets across the world, sports account for the significant majority of all spending by sponsors. Sponsors view sports as one way of reaching target audiences and getting people to notice them. Sports are also a route through which a corporation can build its image. There are B2B benefits too: sponsorship is often the focus for corporate hospitality and networking, and for the joint development of new products and technologies. For sports, at one level sponsorship is a source of revenue; at another, it can form the basis for a collaborative relationship with a sponsor and a way to engage fans and customers. For the fans, sponsorship can be contentious (some see it as the over-commercialisation of sports) but also hugely beneficial, for instance, in the way sponsorship programmes create an experience around sports properties they are linked to. In this context, chapters presented in this part address a range of issues pertinent to sport in the twenty-first century, notably, the role of data in sponsorship, how sponsorship decisions are made, the link between objectives and evaluation in sponsorship, what the impacts of sponsorship can be (especially in a global context), and the link between sponsors and athlete endorsers.

6

COMPUTING THE IMPACT OF SPONSOR SIGNAGE EXPOSURE WITHIN SPORTS BROADCASTS

Christopher Rumpf and Christoph Breuer

Introduction

Despite the continuous growth of sponsorship as a branding tool, the evaluation of sponsorship performance is still at a limited stage. The most frequently used evaluation technique is based on a media analytical approach known as exposure analysis. Exposure analysis accounts for seconds of sponsor–brand visibility, and thus, gives an indication of the opportunities to be seen (Cornwell, 2008). However, most sponsors seek to achieve economic or psychological objectives with their sponsorship instead of merely being visible. Therefore, a main criticism of exposure analysis relates to the fact that it does not account for the impact of sponsorship (Shilbury et al., 2009). It is also noteworthy that exposure analysis only allows for ex-post evaluation: that is, *after* a sports event took place. However, for decision makers it would be even more important to have a reliable estimate of sponsorship performance before investing a share of the marketing budget.

This chapter is dedicated to the measurement and evaluation of sponsorship performance. First, we will critically discuss current approaches of sponsorship evaluation before the concept of attention is introduced. We will explain how eye-tracking can be used to assess visual attention to sponsor signage. Then, we will discuss findings from a lab study on the impact of exposure. The models derived from the study serve as the basis of an innovative evaluation system. Finally, we will conclude by explaining the system's application in sports business.

Evaluation approaches in sponsorship research

A widely-used approach for the evaluation of sponsorship is called exposure analysis and reveals the seconds of visibility for any sponsor signage in the media, particularly on TV. Exposure analysis helps to answer the question of how long a sponsor signage was visible within a certain sports telecast and consequently, how many opportunities to be seen were derived. At the same time, the audience reach dedicated to the sports telecast is assessed. The amount of exposure is then put in relation to the audience ratings on a program-by-program basis and accumulated over a certain time span (for example, a season). Based on such index values (so-called sponsoring contacts) sponsorships can be benchmarked against each other (Felten, 2007).

Despite its simplicity and transparency, exposure analysis is criticized by leading thinkers in research and industry (Meenaghan and O'Sullivan, 2013). "Sponsoring contacts" reveal the extent to which a brand was presented on television, however, it remains unclear whether sports viewers have perceived the sponsorship message. Thus, exposure analysis provides data on the inputs, but no insight into whether or not the sponsorship generates any outputs for the brand. Thus, sponsorship managers base their decisions on the probability of having contacted the sports viewer, whereas no conclusions can be drawn on the impact of their activity (Tripodi et al., 2003).

Current research shows that the impact of sponsor signage exposure depends on the position of the sponsor signage at the venue (for example, Breuer and Rumpf, 2012; Olson and Thjømøe, 2009). Sponsorship platforms offer a wide variety of signage positions, for example, apparel, interview backdrops or perimeter boards. To date, the influence of the sponsor signage position is not considered by the media analytical approach of sponsorship evaluation.

Furthermore, the size of signage exposure and the surrounding clutter is neglected, even though we know from vision science that small stimuli in an overloaded environment are less likely to be perceived compared to large and exclusively presented stimuli (for example, Palmer, 2002). As "sponsoring contacts" do not consider the position, size and clutter of exposure, all sponsor signage appearances have the same weight on the index value. For example, large and exclusive logo exposure on a player's jersey is accounted for in the same way as very small signage on a brand-overloaded interview backdrop. Based on this reasoning, exposure analysis offers a very limited basis for managers' decision making. It can provide general guidance towards the maximization of brand visibility, but it is useless when it comes to the analysis of sponsorship outcome. However, the outcome for the brand should be regarded as the key success criterion for sponsorship activities.

Cornwell, Weeks and Roy (2005) classify sponsorship outcomes as cognitive, affective and behavioral. Cognitive outcomes typically focus on the target group's awareness of the sponsor–sponsee relationship and image transfer, whereas affective outcomes mean brand liking and preference. Behavioral outcomes reflect whether or not there is a change in the target groups purchase behavior due to sponsorship.

To assess sponsorship outcomes, market research carries out phone interviews and on-site or online surveys to collect data on the consumers' response. In most cases, the same questions are asked before and after the event to calculate the deviation between pre- and post-event results that indicate the impact of sponsorship (Crompton, 2004; Gwinner, Larson and Swanson, 2009).

Even though the survey-based approach provides the sponsorship manager with some comprehensive figures, the method is faced with serious problems. First, experimental studies show that cognitive outcomes are biased in favor of prominent brands. Given all other variables being equal, well-known brands are more likely to be recalled than non-prominent competitors. This phenomenon is due to the fact that consumers not only retrieve sponsor-event-associations from memory, but also use constructive processes such as heuristics to identify sponsors. To put it in other words, consumers tend to believe that big brands are more capable of sponsoring sports properties than small brands (Pham and Johar, 2001).

Affective outcomes, such as brand liking and preference, are biased towards the mood of consumers (Hoyer and MacInnis, 2010). Therefore, consumers are more likely to make positive sponsor–brand evaluations in a state of euphoria (for example, after a successful match), whereas the same brand might be evaluated less favorably after an unexpected defeat of the favored team. This situational bias means a serious constraint to the validity of affective outcome measures. Moreover, the measurement of behavioral outcomes is highly problematic because most companies use a number of marketing activities (for example, advertising), which makes it difficult to isolate the impact of a sponsorship activity on purchase behavior (Tripodi et al., 2003).

Attention as an intermediary measure

We suggest a new approach for the evaluation of sponsorship performance based on the "economics of attention" (Simon, 1971). This framework builds on the scarcity of attention deriving from the ratio between visible information and the receiver's cognitive capacity to process such visible information. In most situations the amount of cognitive capacity is insufficient to process all visible information in our environment. Consequently, a mechanism called "attention" selects the most salient and relevant information to be processed on higher cognitive levels, whereas the other information remains unconsidered (Davenport and Beck, 2001).

Sports viewers are usually exposed to more visual information than they can process at one point in time. Therefore, the human information processing system filters out most information to protect against information overload (Jacoby, 1984).

Only when the viewer's attention is devoted to sponsorship signage can the information be processed by the sports viewer. Thus, we argue that attention can only be captured by visible sponsorship signage and sponsor–brand awareness requires attention. According to these propositions, attention means an intermediary construct between sponsor signage visibility and the sports viewers' awareness of the sponsor–sponsee relationship. Figure 6.1 illustrates that the amount of information decreases from the visibility level to the attention level, and from the attention level to the awareness level.

To understand how sports viewers select sponsorship signage to be processed, it is useful to introduce the two-component framework of attention (Itti and Koch, 2000; Treisman and Gelade, 1980). The first component, saliency-based attention, can be described as an automatic mechanism that drives the viewer to select stimuli based on the perceptual saliency of visual features (Pieters and Wedel, 2004). Whereas saliency-based attention works very quickly and almost without cognitive control, the second component, top-down attention, is slower and responsible for conscious experiences (Treisman and Gelade, 1980). That is, in the case of top-down attention, the viewer has deliberate control over the allocation of their cognitive capacity.

When sports-interested people watch sports, top-down attention is most likely to be devoted to the game or race action in order to follow the sports competition (for example,

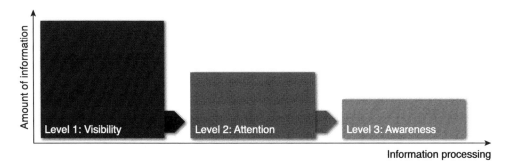

Figure 6.1 Brand-related information processing

progress of the race, ball movement, scoring). However, we argue that sponsorship signage captures the viewer's saliency-based attention through automatically activated processes. In the context of sports events, simple brand logos or names are exposed to the sports viewer, who is usually experienced in processing "advertising fragments" without top-down attention (Pham and Vanhuele, 1997). Therefore, we can build on the general assumption that sponsorship signage, to a large extent, is processed automatically by saliency-based attention.

Inspired by the neural architecture of the human visual system and building on feature integration theory (Treisman and Gelade, 1980), the model of saliency-based visual attention (Itti and Koch, 2000) suggests that objects in the visual field are not processed equally. Only those objects the viewer perceives as visually salient draw the viewer's automatic attention, whereas other objects require the viewer's voluntary effort (i.e., top-down attention) in order to be processed (Itti and Koch, 2000). Thus, sponsorship signage must win the competition for saliency or receive the viewer's top-down attention, which is rather unlikely in an attracting sports environment. In the model of saliency-based visual attention, saliency is derived from the visual properties of color, intensity and orientation, which are "extracted" from the visual scene. Each visual property becomes analyzed in terms of its features, for example, color is broken down into red, green, blue, etc. Based on the network of visual features, a so-called "saliency map" is created in which one object captures the visual attention in a winner-takes-all manner (Itti and Koch, 2000).

Measurement of attention

Given that gaze direction is highly correlated with attention (Henderson and Hollingworth, 1999), eye-tracking methodology has been used in several studies to measure the participants' attention to sponsorship signage (for example, Breuer and Rumpf, 2012; d'Ydewalle and Tasmin, 1993; Le Roy and Vivier, 2008). Compared to alternative measures of attention, namely, memory measures that are dependent on top-down attention, eye-tracking is also capable of detecting preconscious allocation of attention. As we argue that attention for sponsorship signage is mainly captured through a saliency-based process, memory measures must be regarded as an insufficient indicator of attention (Rosbergen, Pieters and Wedel, 1997).

The fundamental principle of eye-tracking is to measure the direction of the gaze by recording the position of the pupils with high frequency as horizontal and vertical coordinate values. As the focus of the gaze can change not only through the movement of the eyeballs, but also through head movements, modern systems measure the pupil position and the position of a reflection point on the cornea of the eye (Duchowski, 2007). On the basis of the relationship between the position of the pupils and the position of the corneal reflection on the eye, the eye tracking system can calculate the direction of the gaze independently of head movement. For this purpose, infrared light is beamed from a fixed lighting source onto the test person's face, while a special infrared camera records the reflected light.

On the recorded video image, the eye tracking system can identify the test person's pupils as dark circles because the beamed light is absorbed by the pupils. The cornea reflects the infrared light very strongly, which is why the corneal reflection appears as a bright point on the video image and is identified by the system (Holmqvist et al., 2011).

Even though eye-tracking allows for a precise measurement of gaze direction, it does not, per se, reveal whether the sports viewer's gaze is oriented to sponsor signage. Therefore, so-called areas of interest (AOI) are marked within the sports broadcast. Due to the short length of fixation (100–400 milliseconds), this marking should be done frame-by-frame. The manual work process can be supported by the automatic algorithms of modern computer software. Given a complete marking of AOIs, it is possible to automatically evaluate how long and frequently a sports viewer's gaze enters into a certain AOI in order to draw conclusions about the attention for sponsor signage.

Empirical findings on the impact of exposure

To analyze the impact of sponsor signage visibility on the viewers' attention and awareness, lab studies provide a good surrounding as several potential biases can be controlled. In a recent study, four sports (football, handball, biathlon, Formula 1) were tested by using a mix of research techniques (exposure analysis, eye-tracking, questioning). By doing so, the visibility of sponsor signage (exposure time, on-screen size, on-screen clutter), visual attention (glance duration) to sponsor signage, and brand awareness (spontaneous sponsor recall) were assessed. Brand-related (brand familiarity, prior purchase behavior) and individual variables (sports involvement) were measured by a questionnaire.

Based on the derived multi-level data, regression models for each type of sports were estimated, explaining the degree of visual attention to sponsor signage. The exposure variables (signage position, on-screen time, on-screen size, and on-screen clutter) were entered as predictors, whereas the degree of personal involvement served as control variable. The likelihood of brand awareness was estimated by logistic regression. The model of sponsor–brand awareness reflects the predictors glance duration, prior brand familiarity and prior purchase behavior. Interestingly, we found an S-shaped relationship between glance duration and sponsor–brand recall. Hence, the viewer's awareness is highly increased on a low attentional level, then the effect "flattens out" and finally grows again on a high attentional level.

Furthermore, the statistical models reveal that the choice of signage positions has a significant impact on capturing viewer attention, independent of their exposure time. In particular, sponsor signage located on the athletes' apparel (or at least close to sports action), provides a greater chance of attracting viewer attention than sponsor signage in the periphery. In an effort to maximize the efficiency of sponsorship communication, decision makers should therefore choose signage positions at the venue that generate the best ratio between exposure time and attention.

The exposure–attention ratio of particular signage positions (for example, interview backdrop) can vary between venues or due to different camera placements. An interview backdrop, for example, can either hold a single sponsor message, or it can be visually overloaded by more than twenty smaller logos. The efficiency of sponsorship communication highly depends on the size and exclusiveness of sponsor signage exposure.

The study reveals that increasing the size of the sponsor signage helps significantly to draw attention to the sponsor. Thus, decision makers are advised to select positions that allow for large signage presentations. Additionally, the exclusiveness of signage exposure is relevant for capturing visual attention. On-screen clutter will significantly reduce the attention of sports viewers. Therefore, sponsorship managers should consider sponsorship information overload as a threat to their communication objectives. For example, a jersey holding more than five sponsor logos should be avoided, because the impact of exposure on visual attention will be marginal.

Application in sports business

Based on the data derived from the lab study, multivariate regression models were estimated. The model equations were connected to build a computer-based system for the evaluation

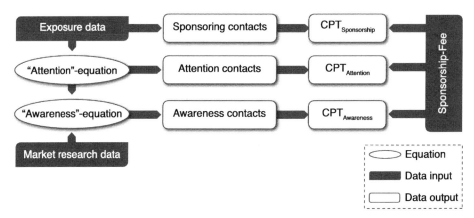

Figure 6.2 Modeling process

of sponsorship performance. Figure 6.2 illustrates the structure of the evaluation system. Starting with the "attention"-equation, exposure data (i.e., signage position, exposure time, size, clutter) is used to calculate the number of "attention contacts" for each sports program in which the specific sponsor signage appeared. "Attention contacts" reflect the number of sports viewers who have devoted their visual attention to certain sponsor signage. The number of "attention contacts" is then entered into the "awareness"-equation calculating the number of "awareness contacts" by also considering market research data (i.e., brand familiarity, prior brand use). "Awareness contacts" denominates sports viewers who have become aware of a certain sponsor–sponsee relationship.

To also reveal the efficiency of a sponsorship investment, the costs per thousand (CPT) are calculated by the evaluation system. For this purpose, the sponsorship fee needs to be taken into account. The CPT is calculated on three levels: "$CPT_{Sponsorship}$" indicates the conventional price value based on the amount of visibility, whereas "$CPT_{Attention}$" and "$CPT_{Awareness}$" indicate the sponsorship's impact on attention and awareness, respectively.

The application of the evaluation system provides decision makers with solid indicators of sponsorship effectiveness (gained attention and awareness) and sponsorship efficiency (costs per gained attention and awareness). The evaluation system is highly compatible with current methods of media and market research in sports business as it makes use of secondary data (exposure data and market research data). It can be applied in three essential phases of sponsorship management: the negotiation phase (i.e., sponsorship manager compares various sponsorship proposals), the implementation phase (i.e., sponsorship manager makes use of communication rights) and the adjustment phase (i.e. sponsorship manager adapts the sponsorship communication strategy).

During the negotiation phase, the sponsorship manager is faced with the problem of selecting the most efficient sponsorship activity from a number of options. After pre-selecting those options that match best with the brand's target group, the sponsorship with the greatest amount of attention at the lowest costs needs to be identified. Although the sponsorship fee is given by the right holder, the attention for sponsor signage is hard to predict based on conventional methods. By using exposure data from the prior season or event, the evaluation system carries out ex-ante evaluations of certain scenarios. The option that offers the best ratio between predicted attention contacts and costs is to be selected.

In the implementation phase, most sponsors rely on performance indicators from media analysis such as seconds of visibility or "sponsoring contacts", although exposure data cannot reflect sponsorship effectiveness. The evaluation system overcomes this shortcoming by calculating the "attention contacts" and the "awareness contacts". The use of the latter two indicators is recommended because they reveal the actual impact of signage exposure on the viewer's visual and cognitive processing.

In the adjustment phase, the sponsorship manager needs to assess the extent to which changes in certain communication conditions will affect sponsorship effectiveness. Most rights holders frequently adjust their marketing concept by changing, for example, the size of their sponsor pool or modifying the communication tools at the venue. Thus, sponsors raise the question of whether the planned adjustments lead to a change in the value of their sponsorship. In order to support the manager's decision making, the evaluation system is capable of running various simulations of sponsorship performance in terms of attention and awareness. Thus, the manager can find out whether a certain adjustment is worth the additional costs.

Even though the evaluation system provides several merits compared to conventional sponsorship evaluation, it is not free from limitations. The predictions by the evaluation system are based on experimental data patterns and therefore it builds on the (unproved) assumption that the identified relationships are also valid in the real world. The artificial character of a lab situation might lead to the criticism that the viewer's behavior in a natural environment may deviate from the behavior in the lab.

Evaluation of a football sponsorship

The practical relevance of the evaluation system was tested with regards to several high-tier and low-tier sponsorships in football, handball, biathlon and Formula 1. To run the system, sponsors provided exposure data and market research data for at least one season. In the remainder of this chapter, the case of a football sponsorship is presented to illustrate the applicability of the evaluation system.

The predicted output for the football sponsorship is displayed on the visibility, attention and awareness level in Table 6.1. "Sponsoring contacts" on the visibility level indicate the amount of possibilities of having contacted a viewer. "$CPT_{Sponsorship}$" reflects the costs per 1,000 "sponsoring contacts". Although "sponsoring contacts" simply consider visibility, "attention contacts" reveal how far specific sponsor signage captured the sports viewers' attention. That is, only sports viewers who put their gaze on the signage are accounted. In this context, "$CPT_{Attention}$" reflects the costs per 1,000 contacts weighted by the attentional impact of sponsor signage exposure. Moreover, the evaluation system outputs the number of viewers who became aware of the sponsorship, so called "awareness contacts". Thus, the "$CPT_{Awareness}$" reflects the costs per 1,000 contacts weighted by the exposure's impact on awareness. In terms of "awareness contacts", the status of a brand within the target group is also considered: that is, prior brand familiarity and prior brand use.

On average, the football sponsorship reached 1,757 million "sponsoring contacts" per season. Given that the sponsorship fee was four million euros per season, the average "$CPT_{Sponsorship}$" amounts to €2.36. If we compare the four seasons on the visibility level, the results imply that the highest return on investment was achieved in the 2008/2009 season because the most "sponsoring contacts" were reached (2,023 million) and the lowest price for 1,000 "sponsorship contacts" was paid ($CPT_{Sponsorship}$=€1.98). The results on the visibility level are equal to the values derived from the conventional exposure-based approach discussed earlier.

Table 6.1 Model output

Season	Sponsorship Fee	Visibility		Attention		Awareness	
		Sponsoring contacts (in millions)	$CPT_{Sponsorship}$	Attention contacts (in millions)	$CPT_{Attention}$	Awareness contacts (in millions)	$CPT_{Awareness}$
2007/2008	4 000 000 €	1 812,00	2,21 €	47,28	2,75 €	18,00	2,12 €
2008/2009	4 000 000 €	2 022,75	1,98 €	58,09	2,24 €	17,99	2,12 €
2009/2010	4 000 000 €	1 264,60	3,16 €	45,65	2,85 €	14,54	2,62 €
2010/2011	4 000 000 €	1 928,15	2,07 €	74,05	1,75 €	22,79	1,67 €
Average	4 000 000 €	1 756,87	2,36 €	56,27	2,40 €	18,33	2,13 €

The mathematical equations take corrective influence on the attention and awareness level. It shows that the application of the evaluation system leads to different implications. Thus, the most efficient season in terms of sponsorship impact occurred in 2010/2011, when a maximum of "attention contacts" (74.05 million) and "awareness contacts" (22.79 million) was reached. This leads to the lowest costs for the sponsor in terms of attention ($CPT_{Attention}$=€1.75) and awareness ($CPT_{Awareness}$=€1.67). The sponsor found an efficient way to communicate its sponsorship to the TV audience. Based on these results, it is advisable to continue the sponsorship and to keep the adjustments with regards to signage positioning.

Conclusion

The optimal selection of sponsor signage positons, the optimizations of exposure size, and the reduction of visual clutter can be regarded as significant drivers of sponsorship impact. In this chapter we proposed a new evaluation system that takes these drivers of success into account by predicting the sports viewer's attention and awareness rather than sponsor signage visibility.

The evaluation system enables decision makers to use sports sponsorship more efficiently. The most important advantage of the evaluation system relates to the fact that managers receive information regarding a sponsorship's impact rather than a sponsorship's visibility. Hence, it offers the opportunity to link the marketing managers' decision making a lot closer to the overall marketing objectives (for example, brand awareness). Furthermore, through ex-ante scenarios the manager receives relevant information prior to making an investment.

In summary, we recommend that viewer attention and awareness should be regarded as critical indicators of sponsorship performance. As the attention capacity of sports viewers is not unlimited, it represents a chronically scarce resource from the sponsor's perspective. In this context, we suggest that maximizing the degree of viewer attention, instead of maximizing viewer exposure, should be regarded as the main challenge for sponsorship management.

References

Breuer, C. and Rumpf, C. (2012). The viewer's reception and processing of sponsorship information in sport telecasts. *Journal of Sport Management*, 26, 521–531.

Cornwell, T. B. (2008). State of the art and science in sponsorship-linked marketing. *The Journal of Advertising*, 37, 41–55.

Cornwell, T. B., Weeks, C. S. and Roy, D. P. (2005). Sponsorship-linked marketing: Opening the black box. *The Journal of Advertising*, 34, 21–42.

Crompton, J. L. (2004). Conceptualization and alternate operationalization of the measurement of sponsorship effectiveness in sport. *Leisure Studies*, 23, 267–281.

Davenport, T. H. and Beck, J. C. (2001). *Attention economy: Understanding the new currency of business.* Boston: Harvard Business School Press.

Duchowski, A. (2007). *Eye tracking methodology: theory and practice* (2nd edn.). London: Springer.

d'Ydewalle, G. and Tasmin, F. (1993). On the visual processing and memory of incidental information: Advertising panels in soccer games. In D. Brogan, A. Gale and K. Carr (Eds.), *Visual Search 2* (pp. 401–408). Bristol, PA: Taylor & Francis.

Felten, J.-B. (2007). Defining industry standards for sponsorship performance: A German perspective. *Journal of Sponsorship*, 1, 62–67.

Gwinner, K. P., Larson, B. V. and Swanson, S. R. (2009). Image transfer in corporate event sponsorship: Assessing the impact of team identification and event-sponsor-fit. *International Journal of Management and Marketing Research*, 2, 1–15.

Henderson, J. M. and Hollingworth, A. (1999). High-level scene perception. *Annual Review of Psychology*, 50(1), 243–271.

Holmqvist, K., Nyström, M., Andersson, R., Dewhurst, R., Jarodzka, H. and van de Weijer, J. (2011). *Eye tracking: A comprehensive guide to methods and measures.* Oxford: Oxford University Press.

Hoyer, W. D. and MacInnis, D. J. (2010). *Consumer behavior* (5th edn.). Mason: South-Western Cengage Learning.

Itti, L. and Koch, C. (2000). A saliency-based search mechanism for overt and covert shifts of visual attention. *Vision Research*, 40, 1489–1506.

Jacoby, J. (1984). Perspectives on information overload. *Journal of Consumer Research*, 10, 432–435.

Le Roy, I. and Vivier, J. (2008). Game, Set, Match! Brand eye tracking on TV sport programmes. In ESOMAR (Ed.), *World Multi Media Measurement 2008* (pp. 1–10). Amsterdam: Esomar.

Meenaghan, T. and O'Sullivan, P. (2013). Metrics in sponsorship research: Is credibility an issue? *Psychology & Marketing*, 30, 408–416.

Olson, E. L. and Thjømøe, H. M. (2009). Sponsorship effect metric: assessing the financial value of sponsoring by comparisons to television advertising. *Journal of the Academy Marketing Science*, 37, 504–515.

Palmer, S. E. (2002). *Vision science: Photons to phenomenology* (3rd edn.). Cambridge: MIT Press.

Pham, M. T. and Johar, G. V. (2001). Market prominence biases in sponsor identification: Processes and consequentiality. *Psychology & Marketing*, 18, 123–143.

Pham, M. T. and Vanhuele, M. (1997). Analyzing the memory impact of advertising fragments. *Marketing Letters*, 8, 407–417.

Pieters, R. and Wedel, M. (2004). Attention capture and transfer in advertising: Brand, pictorial, and text-size effects. *Journal of Marketing*, 68, 36–50.

Rosbergen, E., Pieters, R. and Wedel, M. (1997). Visual attention to advertising: A segment-level analysis. *The Journal of Consumer Research*, 24, 305–314.

Shilbury, D., Westerbeek, H., Quick, S. and Funk, D. (2009). *Strategic sport marketing* (3rd edn.). Sydney: Allen & Unwin.

Simon, H. A. (1971). Designing organizations for an information-rich world. In M. Greenberger (Ed.), *Computers, communications, and the public interest* (pp. 37–72). Baltimore: Johns Hopkins Press.

Treisman, A. M. and Gelade, G. (1980). A feature-integration theory of attention. *Cognitive Psychology*, 12, 97–136.

Tripodi, J. A., Hirons, M., Bednall, D. and Sutherland, M. (2003). Cognitive evaluation: Prompts used to measure sponsorship awareness. *International Journal of Market Research*, 45, 435–455.

7

A DATA-DRIVEN APPROACH TO SPONSORSHIP PLANNING

Multiple sponsorship selection

Larry DeGaris, Mark Dodds and James T. Reese

Introduction

Sponsorship is "an investment, in cash or in kind, with an activity, in return for access to the exploitable commercial potential associated with that activity" (Meenaghan, 1991). In other words, a sponsor pays money to a property for the ability to communicate to the fans attracted to that property. It is important that the sponsor chooses the best property in order to achieve its objectives. In order to make that choice, a sponsor must evaluate potential properties. The continued increases in sponsorship rights fees means there is a lot on the line financially when choosing sponsorship properties.

Prior to choosing a property, a sponsor should create a policy to identify goals and objectives attainable with a sponsorship. This policy can be effective to choose the optimal proposal (Meenaghan, 1991). A sponsor should identify clear goals for the sponsorship, such as reaching a defined target audience (either demographic or geographic), generating incremental sales, attracting media attention, increasing brand awareness, or enhancing brand image (Liu, Srivastava and Woo, 1998; Meenaghan, 1991).

Sponsors often seek properties that "fit" their brands. Traditionally, "fit" is the perception of the congruence between the sponsor and the property (Speed and Thompson, 2000). It is usually either functional or image related (Otker and Hayes, 1987). The sponsor then needs to define what congruence means to them. Some may look at personality fit, similar image and values, even corporate mission statements (Cunningham, Cornell and Coote, 2009; Dees, Bennett and Ferreira, 2010; Simmons and Becker-Olsen, 2006). Sponsorship managers may look at a narrow audience such as a female head of household with children as a demographic fit (Mayo and Bishop, 2010).

Despite the importance of sponsorship selection, very little research has been done in the area. What little research exists suggests that sponsors would benefit from a more rigorous, systematic approach to sponsorship selection. For example, gender has been found to influence the sponsorship selection decision process. Johnston's research indicates that female managers adhere to a firm's sponsorship criteria more closely than male managers (Johnston, 2010). This insight suggests that no matter what criteria is utilized, a male manager may choose a property based on something other than empirical data support, such as previous experience, a "gut feeling", or a personal affinity for the property. It is important to choose the right property because a poor selection will not create the desired impact and would be a waste of valuable funds and other resources (Day, 2010).

Sponsors often point to measurement as being one of sponsorship's biggest challenges. Most often, however, measurement is viewed in the context of evaluation: what sponsors are getting for their sponsorships. Given the high stakes and potentially corrupting influences in the sponsorship planning process, data and measurement can play a vital role in planning as well. For sponsorship properties, the use of data and measurement can help support their sponsorship sales efforts. For sponsors, data and measurement can help to justify programs in addition to empirically-supported sponsorship strategies (DeGaris, 2008b).

Despite the fact that most sponsors hold multiple sponsorships, often within the same sports, most published sponsorship research focuses only on single sponsorships (Chanavat, Martinent and Ferrand, 2009). Even after deciding to enter a particular sport, sponsors must choose among sponsorship levels and properties, such as leagues, teams, and individuals. Moreover, the few research studies that examine multiple sponsorship contexts look at the aggregate effects and do not measure the relative contributions of different sponsorship relationships.

To date, there is very little empirical support to guide sponsors' decisions in selecting from among an array of choices. The small body of research about sponsorship selection indicates that sponsors rely heavily on very basic measures. Based on a survey of industry executives, Pearsall (2009) noted that sponsors are most likely to look at demographics, attendance, and fan passion in making a decision about sponsorships. According to the survey, 46% of sponsors consider "psychographics" when planning a sponsorship.

It is also important to consider sponsorship activation plans while considering which properties to sponsor. As Cornwell (2008) notes, there is an urgent need for more research in marketing activities-linked sponsorships, or sponsorship leveraging. As Simmons and Becker-Olson (2006) found, when a property does not "fit" a sponsor, the sponsor can take steps to make it fit through advertising, public relations, promotions, or other sponsorship-linked marketing communications. Along these lines, Reisman and Eccleston (2013) argue that "receptivity" to sponsorship is a more important criterion for sponsorship selection than fan passion. Based on the results of a national survey of 2,750 U.S. adults, they identified segments of sports fans who report varying degrees of receptivity to sponsors' efforts. That is, even if a sponsorship property fits a sponsor's demographics and brand image, and has passionate fans, the sponsorship must be actionable (i.e., "activation-able").

Therefore, the purpose of this chapter is to draw on examples from baseball in the U.S. to provide a framework for a data-driven approach to selecting sponsorship properties. Building on existing frameworks for sponsorship selection, the approach includes demographics, attitudes, and leveraging opportunities. Although baseball has a modest profile outside the United States, the multi-level structure (for example, elite professional, lower-level professional, amateur, and grassroots) presents sponsorship options that are common to most sports. In sponsoring soccer in Europe, for example, sponsors must choose among leagues by country (La Liga, Serie A, etc.), within countries (Premier League, Championship, etc.), teams within each league, individual players, and events (FIFA World Cup, Champions League, Europa, FA Cup, etc.). Therefore, the current study examines the three dominant baseball organizations in the United States (Major League Baseball, Minor League Baseball and Little League Baseball) and their role in a sponsorship-linked integrated marketing communications strategy.

Integrated marketing communications

Integrated marketing communications (IMC) is a strategic marketing approach that coordinates all marketing communication tactics, including sales promotions and sponsorships (Ciletti, 2011). IMC allows marketing communication to build relationships with consumers by creating a consistent message across the all message platforms. All marketing communications need to convey a single message to the customer to break through clutter and eliminate brand confusion. Sponsorship represents a platform upon which sponsors can integrate marketing communications – advertising, PR, sales promotions, etc. – not another promotional tool.

Sales promotions

Sales promotions are short-term incentives designed to stimulate product sales. Sales promotion tactics may include coupons, sweepstakes and contests, premium giveaways, athlete or coach autograph signings, bundling or price reductions for purchasing multiple products, and loyalty cards. Many of these sales promotions may be implemented through technology using social media platforms. Sales promotions often interrelate with other aspects of the marketing mix including advertising, personal selling and public relations (Cormier, 2011).

Sponsorships are a great tool to leverage existing sales promotions (DeGaris, West and Dodds, 2009). Research confirms that sales promotion participation is strongly linked to fan avidity, and fans participate in promotions because they are fun and have sports ties, which results in driving sales through the sport-linked sales promotion.

Sponsorship as a catalyst

Sponsorships can drive direct and indirect sales. Some packages include on-site sales, pouring rights and merchandise opportunities that companies use to offset the cost of the sponsorship. Although practitioners often find difficulty with isolating the impact a sponsorship has on sales given the influence of advertising, sales promotions and other marketing mix elements, DeGaris and West (2013) found an increase in soft drink consumption depending on effective sponsorship activation tactics. Therefore, a sponsorship should be integrated with other marketing communication tools strategically in order to be most effective.

Baseball organization background

Major League Baseball (MLB)

Professional baseball has existed within the United States since the mid-1800s (Eagleman, 2011). In 1903, two major leagues, the National League (NL) and the American League (AL), containing eight teams each, combined to hold a post-season championship series, now referred to as the World Series (Eagleman, 2011). Today, there are 30 teams in MLB; both the NL and AL have 15 teams each (Team-by-team information, 2015). MLB franchises are dispersed throughout North America ("Goodbye", 2011).

The franchises are located within the largest metropolitan areas within North America ("Baseball markets", 2015). In fact, the largest markets within the United States and Canada without an MLB team are Montreal, Quebec (3,426,350); Portland, Oregon (2,265,223); Vancouver, British Columbia (1,986,965); and Sacramento, California (1,796,857).

Cost to attend

The sports publication, *Team Marketing Report*, publishes an annual fan cost index for MLB that ranks the average ticket prices for all 30 major league clubs. The Fan Cost Index comprises the prices of four adult average-price tickets, two small draft beers, four small soft drinks, four regular-size hot dogs, parking for one car, two game programs and two least expensive, adult-size adjustable caps. On average, it costs a family of four $210.46 to attend an MLB game. Despite the cost, MLB reported a total attendance of more than 70 million during 2014 (MLB Press Release, 2014).

Minor League Baseball (MiLB)

Minor League Baseball is a hierarchy of professional baseball leagues one level below Major League Baseball. Many Minor League teams are official affiliates of Major Leagues teams used for the development of players. Minor League Baseball, founded in 1868 and headquartered in St. Petersburg, Florida, consists of 160 teams in 43 states across the United States. Additional leagues and teams also exist in South America. The duration of the season is typically 70 games per team from April to early September (Minor League Baseball, 2013).

Cost to attend

Team Marketing Report also publishes the average ticket prices and a fan cost index for Minor League Baseball. As there are so many minor league teams across the United States (approximately 160), the report summarizes ticket prices based on the level of play (for example, AAA, AA, A, Rookie League, etc.). The Fan Cost Index for MiLB is a little different from MLB as the report looks at tickets for adults and children. The average cost to attend an MiLB game ranges from $56.37 in the Rookie league to $70.03 at the highest level (Triple-A), substantially lower than that for MLB.

Little League Baseball (LLB)

As early as the 1880s, a variety of baseball leagues were operated in the state of New York for pre-teen children. Due to a variety of circumstances, such as a lack of funding and an inadequate number of volunteers, the leagues were unable to flourish (Little League Baseball, 2014). In 1925, the American Legion, which still exists today, was formed for boys aged 15–19 ("History of American Legion baseball", 2015). However, a void still remained for younger boys who wanted to play organized baseball.

In 1938, Carl Stotz came up with the idea of starting a youth baseball league for his nephews and the local boys in Williamsport, Pennsylvania. His vision was to provide a "wholesome program of baseball for the boys of Williamsport, as a way to teach them the ideals of sportsmanship, fair play and teamwork" (Little League Baseball, 2014: p. 8). Stotz named the new organization Little League and the first game was played on June 6, 1939 (Little League Baseball, 2014). Little League baseball was born.

A Board of Directors guides each individual league, usually consisting of between five and twenty-five adult volunteers from the community. There are now more than 6,500 Little League programs in nearly 90 countries around the world ("Structure", 2015). A group of 10–20 leagues in a specific area makes up a Little League district and reports to the respective district office. Groups of districts are classified into one of five national regions in the United

States and report to regional directors. Regional offices are located in Warner Robbins, Georgia; San Bernardino, California; Indianapolis, Indiana; Bristol, Connecticut; and Waco, Texas. There are also four offices that serve the Little League international regions. They are located in Puerto Rico, Canada, Hong Kong, and Poland. All regional offices report to the International Headquarters located in South Williamsport, Pennsylvania (Little League Baseball, 2014).

Media

On August 26, 2013, Little League Baseball announced an 8-year contract extension to 2022 for multi-platform (television and digital) broadcast rights with ESPN worth $76 million (Brigandi, 2013). This is more than double the previous deal of $30.1 million, which ran from 2007 to the end of the 2014 season. Either ESPN or its broadcast partner ABC has televised every Little League World Series final since 1963 (Cook, 2013).

Cost to attend

Since its formation in 1939, there has never been a cost to attend a Little League World Series event at the international headquarters in South Williamsport, PA ("World Series," 2015). Most of the attendance is composed of family members of the players and would be very small. However, the 2014 Little League World Series drew an average of 12,895 fans to the 32-game tournament with two games exceeding 30,000 (Beauge, 2014). There is no Fan Cost Index for Little League Baseball. However, prices are affordable at Little League games and families can get the types of food and beverages, but less alcohol, that you would expect to find at any baseball game. According to Wood (2015), you can find traditional menu items such as hotdogs, hamburgers, chicken fingers, pulled pork sandwiches, roast beef sandwiches, corn on the cob, cotton candy, funnel cakes and Cracker Jacks. Traditional soft drinks, water, Gatorade, lemonade, and fruit smoothies are also available.

This study examines demographics, attitudes, and activation propensity among the three major baseball properties in the United States. Then the results are compared for similarities and differences in order to answer the study's research question: How can sponsors select sponsorship properties to best meet their objectives?

Methodology

Data for this study was drawn from a larger industry study that analyzed baseball sponsorships, including Major League Baseball, Minor League Baseball, and Little League Baseball (DeGaris, 2008a). Data was collected from a telephone survey of 1,000 baseball fans (defined as at least a "6", where 1 means "not interested at all" and 10 means "extremely interested", on at least one form of baseball: the sport of baseball in general; Major League Baseball; Minor League Baseball; Little League Baseball).

Demographic information

Demographic profiles of sports audiences help to guide sponsors in establishing a baseline fit for their sponsorships. Sponsors seeking younger consumers would seek sponsorship properties that can provide access to their marketing targets. Like most sports audiences, the respondents in the study were predominantly male (57.8% to 42.2%), older, affluent, and educated (see Table 7.1).

Table 7.1 Survey demographics

Male	57.8%
Female	42.2%
Average age: male	46.6
Average age: female	47.2
Average household income: male	$62,540
Average household income: female	$56,322
College graduate/Some college: male	57.6%
College graduate/Some college: female	60.0%

Fan avidity information

Fan avidity measures are important because sponsors attempt to leverage the passion fans have for the sports they love into marketing outcomes. In general, the more passionate the fan, the more successful the sponsorship. It is interesting to note consistent fan avidity levels between "Baseball in general" and "Major League Baseball", suggesting that respondents may equate fan avidity in baseball to mean fan avidity in MLB only. It is also noteworthy that MiLB score tends to be lower than LLB, despite the higher level of play. In addition to past experiences in playing youth baseball, involvement with LLB may extend to being a parent of a player or a volunteer with the local organization.

Although baseball fans are more likely to be male, both genders are baseball fans at mostly similar levels, but differ slightly with respect to specific baseball properties (see Table 7.3). Both men and women are fans of MLB at similar levels (8.4/8.2) and MiLB (4.9/4.9), however, men are less interested in LLB than women (4.9/5.6), suggesting a segment of passionate "Little League Moms". The relative lack of baseball sponsorships targeting female fans might be a result of confusing a higher percentage of men being fans with men being bigger fans. Results of this study indicate that is simply not the case. To the contrary, female baseball fans represent a largely untapped opportunity for sponsors. Moreover, this dynamic is likely to extend to other sports because of the prevalence of male sports fans comprising larger numbers within respective fan bases.

Although baseball tends to attract an older audience in general, younger fans are as passionate about the sports as older fans, supporting the axiom that "fans are fans"; they might be greater or fewer in number but fans share the passion for the sports. Major League Baseball attracts a consistent level of interest across all age categories with the mean ranging from 8.2 to 8.4 (see Table 7.4).

However, in LLB, the 35–44 age group shows highest interest level overall (5.7). This may be explained by interest in this type of baseball being driven by a personal connection. If a child is participating in baseball (typically parented by the 35–44 category) then interest in

Table 7.2 How interested are you in the sport of baseball (1=not at all interested; 10=Extremely interested)

	Baseball in general	Major League Baseball	Minor League Baseball	Little League Baseball
Mean	8.3	8.3	4.9	5.2

Table 7.3 How interested are you in the sport of baseball, by gender (1=not at all interested; 10=Extremely interested)

	Major League Baseball		Minor League Baseball		Little League Baseball	
	Male	Female	Male	Female	Male	Female
Mean	8.4	8.2	4.9	4.9	4.9	5.6

Table 7.4 Major League Baseball: fan avidity based on age (1=not at all interested; 10=Extremely interested)

	18–34	35–44	45–54	55+
Mean	8.2	8.4	8.3	8.4

Table 7.5 Little League Baseball: fan avidity based on age (1=not at all interested; 10=Extremely interested)

	18–34	35–44	45–54	55+
Mean	5.5	5.7	5.3	4.6

LLB rises. The data indicates lower interest in 45–54 and 55+ when those children grow out of LLB (see Table 7.5).

Although baseball fans report similar levels of interest, the points of attachment differ. Almost two-thirds (64.1%) of fans in the study say they are biggest fans of their favorite team, much higher than the sport of baseball in general (30.4%) or their favorite players (5.5%). This potentially has huge implications for sponsorship selection because sponsors must choose among league, team, and player relationships. Given the strong following for "baseball in general", sponsors looking to identify with the broader sports and not just the local team must decide which assets collectively define the sports, and for whom.

Sponsors are interested in live event attendance as opportunities to reach fans directly, providing opportunities for experiential marketing and product sampling, for example. This is a major strength of baseball as a potential sponsorship property. Attendance comparisons of the three properties reveal numerous insights into the leagues. It is important to note that although this study measured the number of games attended, the total number of possible games is different per league. The MLB season has 162 regular season games, the MiLB season may contain 70 games and the LLB season may have 10–20 games per season.

When comparing the high interest level associated with MLB and the corresponding frequency of games attended, an explanation may be that the fan avidity for MLB is media driven. Because 28.8% of the respondents attend one or two games, this suggests a high media impact for the fan to choose which particular game to attend. This data also suggests the choice of game may be dependent on the promotion offered at that game.

Minor League Baseball has the lowest number of games attended. This may be attributed to the smaller markets and lower stadium capacities of the MiLB teams. Almost two-thirds of

Table 7.6 The number of games attended (frequency)

	Major league baseball	Minor league baseball	Little league baseball
None	44.8	65.5	55.8
1–2	28.8	22.9	10.7
3–5	15.2	7.1	8.2
6+	11.1	4.4	25.4

Table 7.7 Fans' media behavior

How often do you…? (Daily)	
Watch baseball news on television, such as Sportscenter or your local news	58.5%
Follow baseball in the newspaper	43.8%
Watch baseball games on television	31.0%
Watch baseball news, such as Baseball Tonight or This Week in Baseball	24.8%
Visit Internet sports sites for baseball news, such as ESPN.com or Foxsports.com	24.3%
Visit Internet sports sites such as MLB.com	15.0%
Follow baseball in magazines	3.9%

the fans in the study surveyed did not attend a MiLB game. Conversely, Little League Baseball has the highest percentage of frequent attendees ("six or more" games attended) among all the properties tested. For sponsors, LLB's opportunity to reach fans directly through more frequent attendance is mitigated by the challenge of implementing promotional programs at the grassroots level.

Although live attendance is a strength for MLB because of the number of games and sizes of the venues, mediated audiences can deliver substantial value to sponsors on their own and as part of a larger integrated sponsorship that includes experiential marketing elements. Fans in the study actively consume baseball related media, with more than half (58.5%) following baseball daily on television news (see Table 7.7). Sponsors should look to fans' media behavior to identify a potential fit with their current marketing programs and goals. Nearly two-thirds of fans in the study say their favorite team is outside their local area, with only 30.5% saying their favorite team is in their hometown. Although fans' emotional attachments are local in that they focus on teams, the teams are likely to be more broadly geographically distributed, placing a greater emphasis on media behavior, especially digital assets and national television.

Fan attitudes toward corporate sponsorship

Generally, baseball fans like corporate sponsorship. More than 43% of baseball fans like sponsorship in baseball as opposed to 24% who dislike corporate sponsorship. This difference is important to a marketer because attitudes toward sponsorship in general can affect attitudes toward a specific sponsorship. In addition, more than 58% of all baseball fans think corporate sponsorship is very or extremely important to the sport, with another 30% believing it's somewhat important. Comparatively, however, these numbers are low.

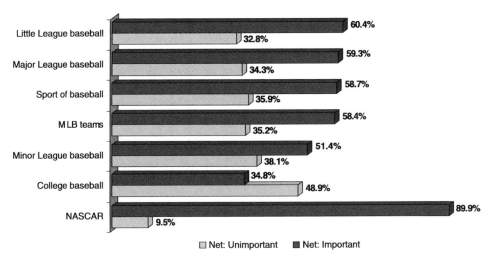

Figure 7.1 The importance of sponsors

Source: SRS NASCAR Sponsorship Study (2006)

A similar study of NASCAR fans (SRS NASCAR Sponsorship Study, 2006) yielded much higher sponsorship favorability, with 80% of NASCAR fans saying they "like" corporate sponsorship in NASCAR.

Based on the results of the survey, we see a high importance of corporate sponsors for LLB, though still well below NASCAR levels (see Figure 7.1). This may be explained by the business model of the Little League organizations, with LLB being a blend of sports and cause-related marketing. Little League Baseball and each individual, local group is a non-profit organization that provides recreation for young boys and girls. The fans, many of whom are the parents of the players, understand the direct impact of the sponsorship revenue for the organization. This revenue is used for field renovation, improving facilities, purchasing safety equipment. In fact, much of the sponsorship sales activity is conducted by the parents themselves.

Sponsorship leveraging

Despite the weak favorability, there is evidence that baseball sponsorship drives incremental sales, with 33.8% of baseball fans saying they support sponsorships through purchasing sponsor products. In contrast to the weak favorability toward sponsors, and fortunately for sponsors, baseball fans are broadly receptive to sponsors' leveraging efforts.

Nearly a third (28.9%) of fans in the study say they have participated in a baseball sponsor's consumer sales promotion (i.e., contest or sweepstake, premium, loyalty program) during the past 12 months. Participation in baseball sponsors' promotions increases with fan usage or avidity. More than a third (37.3%) of "super fans" (the top quartile as measured by media behavior) participated in a contest or sweepstake, 14.5% received a premium item, and 5.9% participated in a loyalty or rewards program. Sponsors' baseball tie-ins seem to trigger interest and participation among the sport's most avid fans.

Further, there is evidence to suggest that the participation is incremental and attributable to sponsors' links to baseball. Nearly a third (31.5%) of fans who participated in a sponsor's promotion in the past 12 months say that they do not like to participate in promotions, suggesting that the baseball tie-in motivates incremental participation among fans who are not predisposed to participate.

In addition to promotional participation at the ballpark, there is evidence to suggest that baseball sponsorships can drive traffic at retail. Baseball fans make a concerted effort to seek out sponsor's products. More than 17% of baseball fans specifically search for baseball sponsor products at retail. When combined with the data indicating baseball fans purchase baseball sponsors' products, it can be concluded that sales promotions, including point-of-purchase displays, couponing, etc., is important to create sponsorship awareness.

Conclusions and recommendations

Sponsorship can be an effective investment to build brands and drive incremental sales. However, the investment needs to be planned effectively and strategically, especially in light of increasing sponsorship rights fees. Sponsorship needs to be selected with the overall marketing communications program in mind. Tactical decisions should be data-driven and there must be an overall "fit" between the property, the brand, and the marketing communications plan. Because there are three distinct baseball organizations with different benefits, a manager needs to analyze the marketing objectives, decide what promotional tactics can best achieve the brand's marketing goals, then choose the sponsorship property to deliver the message.

MLB teams are the major point of attachment for fans. Because the individual teams are in the largest markets within the United States, a sponsor may choose to sponsor an individual team to focus on a particular market. The individual team would create more interest in a promotional tactic specifically tied to the home team. However, this strategy misses out on the large number of fans who live outside the home market. Digital properties and targeted advertising might mitigate the loss, but it might make sense for some sponsors to seek a national platform, especially if they do not wish to run the risk of alienating fans of opposing teams.

MLB league sponsorships provide a platform that may be executed with a national campaign. MLB receives national media exposure through game broadcasts on many channels, game highlights on national and local television stations, game recaps in newspaper and magazines and has a significant presence on social media sites such as MLB.com. MLB is supported by both genders and fan avidity is consistent through the age demographics.

Although MiLB may be seen as a national organization, it is a strongly local sponsorship property lacking the fan passion in other baseball properties. A national campaign would be difficult due to the limited national media associated with minor league baseball. However, MiLB is a family friendly, low-cost entertainment option with extensive on-site promotional options.

LLB combines elements of traditional commercial sponsorships with a pure, grassroots marketing opportunity. The LLB World Series is a property that offers national (and international) media exposure. However, the individual leagues are community-based where a small market may have numerous little leagues within its boundaries. The media is very limited. Aside from the LLB World Series, there is no national media coverage. Typically, there is very little broadcast media even from local media. Small, local newspapers and websites run by the league itself, tends to be the only media associated with the leagues. Local sponsors can promote their brands with naming rights at the field or of the individual teams. Activation has to be on-site. However, the high frequency attendance suggests a successful promotion may extend over multiple visits. For instance, a local restaurant may offer a new coupon every week to stimulate several visits as opposed to one coupon with a long expiration date. LLB sponsorships are very successful for brands geared toward children or "little league moms" aged 35–44.

Although favorability toward baseball sponsors is tepid compared to the highly sponsor-loyal NASCAR fans, baseball fans represent a fertile market for promotional efforts. High levels of receptivity to and participation in sponsors' promotions, combined with high levels of live attendance, present baseball as a strong opportunity for sponsors' experiential marketing and consumer promotions. For sponsors with a strong emphasis on these marketing programs, baseball sponsorships might be a good fit even if demographics and attitudes match poorly.

Finally, sponsorships should be considered part of a portfolio, which together lead to achieving sponsorship goals. A brand may choose to incorporate a national campaign then support it with individual team sponsorship. In this case, the national campaign would increase brand awareness and the individual team sponsorship would generate a favorable attitude toward the brand. For example, Bank of America identified itself as the "Official Bank of Baseball", a trademarked designation of their own making. In order to support their status, Bank of America signed national sponsorship agreements with Major League Baseball, Little League Baseball and Softball, Minor League Baseball, and the National Baseball Hall of Fame ("Bank of America", 2007).

As this chapter shows, there are many differences among the three dominant baseball organizations within the United States. In order to maximize success, a potential marketer must match its goals and tactics with the baseball property that best achieves those objectives. Each property reaches its target audience differently, which allows a sponsor to activate its brand to meet its marketing objectives.

References

Bank of America loads the bases for baseball fans by launching first full season of MLB Extra Bases Credit Card Program (2007). http://newsroom.bankofamerica.com/press-release/consumer-banking/bank-america-loads-bases-baseball-fans-launching-first-full-season-ml (accessed 18 April 2015).

Baseball markets by Al Streit. (2015). Baseball Almanac. Retrieved from www.baseball-almanac.com/articles/baseball_markets.shtml

Beauge, J. (2014). Little League attendance up over 2013, but not a record, www.pennlive.com/little-league-world-series/2014/08/little_league_world_series_att.html (accessed 5 September 2014).

Brigandi, B. (2013, August 27). Little League, ESPN reach 8-year, $76 million deal, http://sungazette.com/page/content.detail/id/596257/Little-League--ESPN-reach-8-year--76-million-deal.html?nav=5011

Chanavat, N., Martinent, G., and Ferrand, A. (2009). Sponsor and sponsees interactions: Effects on consumers' perceptions of brand image, brand attachment, and purchasing intention. *Journal of Sport Management*, 23, 644–670.

Ciletti, D. (2011). Integrated Marketing Communication, In Swayne, L. and Dodds, M. *Encyclopedia of Sports Management and Marketing*, Vol. 2 (pp. 686–689). Thousand Oaks: Sage Publications, Inc.

Cook, B. (2013, August 26). Little League, reflecting youth sports TV demand, doubles its money from ESPN. Forbes, www.forbes.com/sites/bobcook/2013/08/26/little-league-reflecting-youth-sports-tv-demand-doubles-its-money-from-espn/

Cormier, J. A. (2011). Sales Promotions, In Swayne, L. and Dodds, M. *Encyclopedia of Sports Management and Marketing*, Vol. 3 (pp. 1319–1323). Thousand Oaks: Sage Publications, Inc.

Cornwell, T. B. (2008). State of the art and science in sponsorship-linked marketing. *Journal of Advertising* 37(3), 41–55.

Cunningham, S., Cornell, T. B. and Coote, L. (2009). Expressing identity and shaping image: The relationship between corporate mission and corporate sponsorship. *Journal of Sport Management*, 23, 65–86.

Day, H. (2010). Editorial: Choosing well, making an impact and then moving on. *Journal of Sponsorship*, 4(1), 4.

Dees, W., Bennett, G. and Ferreira, M. (2010). Personality fit in NASCAR: An evaluation of driver-sponsor congruence and its impact on sponsorship effectiveness outcomes, *Sport Marketing Quarterly*, 19, 25–35.

DeGaris, L. (2008a). *2007 Baseball Sponsorship Study*, Colorado Springs: Sponsorship Research & Strategy.

DeGaris, L. (2008b). Sport marketing consulting strategies and tactics: Bridging the academy and the practice. *Choregia: Sport Management International Journal*, 4(2), 11–20.

DeGaris, L. and West, C. (2013). The effects of sponsorship activation on the sales of a major soft drink brand. *Journal of Brand Strategy*, 1(4), 403–412.

DeGaris, L., West, C. and Dodds, M. (2009). Leveraging and activating NASCAR sponsorships with NASCAR-linked sales promotions. *Journal of Sponsorship*, 3(1), 88–97.

Eagleman, A. (2011). Major League Baseball, In Swayne, L. and Dodds, M. *Encyclopedia of Sports Management and Marketing*, Vol. 2 (pp. 797–801). Thousand Oaks: Sage Publications, Inc.

Goodbye NL Central, hello AL West. (2011, November 17). http://buthomps87.wordpress.com/2011/11/17/goodbye-nl-central-hello-al-west/

History of American Legion baseball. (2015). The American Legion. Retrieved from www.legion.org/baseball/history

Johnston, M. (2010). Illuminating the dark corners of sponsorship decision making. *Journal of Sponsorship*. 3(4), 365–378.

Little League Baseball (2014). LLBWS Media Guide. Retrieved from www.littleleague.org/media.htm

Liu, J., Srivastava, A. and Woo, H.-S. (1998). Transference of skills between sports and business. *Journal of European Industrial Training*, 22(3), 106.

Mayo, D. and Bishop, T. (2010). Fixed rights to activation ratios can harm sponsorship ROI. *Journal of Sponsorship*, 4(1), 12.

Meenaghan, T. (1991). The role of sponsorship in the marketing communication mix. *International Journal of Advertising*, 10, 36.

Minor League Baseball (2013). Amusement Media, Inc. Retrieved from www.amusement-media.com/Amusement-Media/minorleaguebaseball.html

MLB Press Release (2014). MLB records seventh best attendance total ever in 2014, http://m.mlb.com/news/article/96990912/mlb-records-seventh-best-attendance-total-ever-in-2014

Otker, T. and Hayes, P. (1987). Judging the efficiency of sponsorship: Experience from the 1986 Soccer World Cup, *European Research*, 15, 3–8.

Pearsall, J. (2009). Sponsorship performance: What is the role of sponsorship metrics in proactively managing the sponsor–property relationship? *Journal of Sponsorship*, 9(2), 115–122.

Reisman, M. and Eccleston, J. (2013). Decoding the modern sports fan. *Journal of Brand Strategy*, 2(2), 189–206.

Simmons, C. J. and Becker-Olsen, K. L. (2006). Achieving marketing objectives through social sponsorships. *Journal of Marketing*, 70(4), 154–169.

Speed, R. and Thompson, P. (2000). Determinants of sport sponsorship response. *Journal of the Academy of Marketing Science*, 28(2), 226–238.

SRS NASCAR Sponsorship Study (2006). Colorado Springs: Colorado.

Structure of Little League baseball and softball. (2015). Little League. Retrieved from www.littleleague.org/learn/about/structure.htm

Team-by-team information. (2015). Major League Baseball. Retrieved from http://mlb.mlb.com/team/index.jsp

Wood, J. (2015). Summer forever, www.stadiumjourney.com/stadiums/howard-j.-lamade-stadium-s959/

World Series general info. (2015). Little League, www.littleleague.org/media/llbbwsgeneralinfo.htm

8

SPORTS SPONSORSHIP DECISION MODEL

A conceptual model proposition

Barbara M. B. Sá and Victor Manoel Cunha de Almeida

Introduction

Professional sports have gained recognition in the corporate environment as an extremely lucrative market that attracts investments and provides countless opportunities for enterprise (Shannon, 1999). By the end of 2014, it was estimated that the global sports market will have grossed more than $140 billion (PwC, 2011). Most sponsorship investment has been directed towards sports, which already accounts for 70% of this type of investment in the USA (International Events Group, 2014). It is estimated that the 2014 FIFA World Cup earned $1.4 billion from sponsorship deals, with more than 20 global enterprises choosing to link their brands to the most important football (soccer) event in the world (Valim, 2014).

As with the Rio 2007 Pan American Games, many companies were attracted by opportunities to associate their brands with sports in Brazil (Ramiro, 2007). According to Rosa (2009), it is expected that the 2014 FIFA World Cup and the 2016 Olympic Games in Rio will lead to a 40–50% increase in investments in marketing in Brazil and the country should obtain more than $800 million exclusively from sponsorship deals of these events.

There are many options for companies that wish to develop ties with sports through sponsorship, but executives should think strategically to evaluate the opportunities and select those that have the greatest potential to help them achieve their desired goals (Farrely, Quester and Greyser, 2005). However, the lack of knowledge regarding the best way of investing in sports marketing often leads companies to begin a process marked by frustrated attempts or unexpected successes in the development of their sponsorship strategies (Davies and Tsiantas, 2008).

The literature abounds with studies that separately analyse the different elements of a sports sponsorship decision-making process: the strategic decision to invest in sports (Fullerton and Merz, 2008; Mason, 2005; Papadimitriou, Apostolopoulou and Dounis, 2008); the objectives of sports sponsorship (Cornwell and Maignan, 1998); different types of sports sponsorship activation (Fullerton and Merz, 2008; Miloch and Lambrecht, 2006); measuring the results of this type investment (Davies and Tsiantas, 2008; Lagae, 2005); and evaluation models to select sponsorship opportunity (Copeland, Frisby and McCarville, 1996;

McCook, Turco and Riley, 1997). When it comes to the creation of a portfolio of sponsorships, it is suggested that managers should also take into consideration the interactive system that is built by the multiple properties (Chanavat, Martinent and Ferrand, 2010), because the fit of sponsored properties helps create a brand showing consistency and clarity (Chien, Cornwell and Pappu, 2011).

Some of the authors mentioned highlight gaps in this field of research and suggest that new studies should be developed in order to: (a) increase knowledge of the process involved in acquiring this type of investment (Arthur, Scott and Woods, 1997); (b) investigate the dynamics of the sponsorship process (Copeland, Frisby and McCarville, 1996); (c) lead advances in the understanding of sponsorship processes (Meenaghan, 2001); (d) enable comparisons to be made between sponsorship practices and effects (Walliser, 2003); and (e) verify the effectiveness of alternative strategies to leverage or activate sponsorship (Speed and Thompson, 2008).

Although many studies have been developed in recent years, none of them analyse these issues in the integrated fashion that would make it possible to establish a clear connection between motivation, selection, activation and measurement of the results of sports sponsorship. This chapter intends to contribute to the expansion of knowledge in the sports sponsorship by investigating the phenomenon from the sponsors' perspective. The aim is to understand the decision-making process by gaining a greater understanding of a company's motivations for making the investment, identifying how opportunities are selected, how activation actions are planned and executed and how sports sponsorship results are measured.

Theoretical references

Sports sponsorship consists of a set of activities linked to a communication process that uses the marketing of sports and the lifestyle associated with it to transmit messages to a specific target audience (Mullin, Hardy and Sutton, 2004). It constitutes an association with sports established as an alliance that provides strategic partners with opportunities to add actions to the marketing mix and thus get better marketing activity results (Morgan and Summers, 2005).

Objectives of sports sponsorship

It is essential that companies clearly define what they aim to achieve with sponsorship in order to obtain the best return (Lee and Ross, 2012). In a typical sports sponsorship partnership, the sponsor provides resources in the form of funds, products or services in exchange for an association with an element that is external to the company and which offers promotional opportunities to enhance the value of its brand from the customers' perspective (O'Reilly and Madill, 2007; Pichot, Tribou and O'Reilly, 2008).

Attempting to achieve a broad understanding of what companies expect from sports sponsorship, this study classifies the objectives identified in the literature into six groups: (1) corporate objectives, such as return on investment (Koo, Quarterman and Flynn, 2006), conquering markets (Davies and Tsiantas, 2008), developing new business (Irwin and Asimakopoulos, 1992), increasing sales and undertaking competitive actions (Cornwell, Pruitt and Clark, 2005; Davies and Tsiantas, 2008); (2) brand objectives, such as improving corporate brand image (Irwin and Asimakopoulos, 1992), company or brand awareness and product or brand positioning (Cornwell, Pruitt and Clark, 2005; Davies and Tsiantas, 2008); (3) product objectives, such as product development, testing and launch (Barrand, 2005; Davies and

Tsiantas, 2008; Rines, 2000); (4) audience objectives, such as consumer perception towards the brand (Cornwell, Pruitt and Clark, 2005), customer satisfaction and loyalty, and recognition of the company as a sponsor (Davies and Tsiantas, 2008; Gwinner and Swanson, 2003); (5) relationship objectives, such as involvement with the community (Meenaghan, 1983), hospitality or development of a closer ties with employees (Cornwell, Pruitt and Clark, 2005; Davies and Tsiantas, 2008), and also media exposure or reaching opinion formers (Copeland, Frisby and McCarville, 1996); and (6) executives' personal objectives (Meenaghan, 1983).

Sponsorship selection: sports modality, type of sponsorship and sports property

Sponsors have become more selective in their choice of sports sponsorship, not only due to the increase in the amount invested in sports in recent years, but also to the number of proposals that appear on a daily basis (Lardinoit and Derbaix, 2001; Walliser, 2003). Establishing realistic objectives and choosing activities carefully can enable the company to maximise the results of a sponsorship (Davies and Tsiantas, 2008). The choice of sports sponsorship should be based on a rational decision using selected criteria (Meenaghan, 1983) and set out in a detailed plan included in the marketing communication, encompassing the selection of the type of sponsorship, the execution of the action, its integration with marketing communication and the measurement of the effects of sponsorship communication (Lagae, 2005).

The similarities between each sponsorship in a portfolio affect brand meaning and clarity (Chien, Cornwell and Pappu, 2011) and the existent interaction between sponsors and sponsored properties can influence brands' cognitive and affective dimensions (Chanavat, Martinent and Ferrand, 2009). Also, a sponsor–sponsee partnership that seems incongruent might not have a positive influence on a customer's behavioural and emotional responses to the brand (Nickell, Cornwell and Johnston, 2011). Companies should take into account the characteristics of the sports modality before taking the decision to sponsor (Lagae, 2005). This is the best way of identifying whether there is a fit between the sport's potential reach and the company's area of interest, and whether the audience that follows the sports intersect the company's target audience. Each sports modality affects consumers' emotions in different ways (Wann et al., 2008) and affects evaluations regarding the sponsoring company's endorsement of its products (Martin, 1996). Sponsors should select the opportunities that will better represent the image their companies desire to have (Ensor, 1987).

Another factor companies should consider is the type of sports sponsorship in which they wish to invest. Eight types of sports sponsorship were identified in the studies investigated: (1) sponsorship of sports teams; (2) individual sponsorship and endorsement of sports celebrities; (3) sponsorship of sports organizations or entities; (4) sponsorship of sports events; (5) sponsorship of sports facilities; (6) sponsorship of sports transmissions; (7) sponsorship of technologies; and (8) licensing (Fullerton and Merz, 2008; Lagae, 2005; Rines, 2000). Although there are many options for investment in sports, it is not always easy to make a choice and it is necessary to assess the opportunities and risks associated with each alternative to be certain that the company's objectives will be achieved (Rines, 2000). Selection should be made carefully, as a sponsee's image can be transferred to the sponsor (Cornwell and Maignan, 1998); also, multiple sponsorship interactions have the power to affect the brand image (Chanavat, Martinent and Ferrand, 2010). Knowing that each type of sponsorship requires a different investment, companies should question whether it is better to bet on a single type of sports sponsorship or on a combination of actions (Lardinoit and Derbaix, 2001).

Selecting the sports property is an important task when a company chooses sports sponsorship as a way of achieving internal or external marketing objectives (Pichot, Tribou and O'Reilly, 2008). Sports property is the term used to describe organizations, events or athletes sponsored by companies as part of their marketing strategies (Farrelly, Quester and Greyser, 2005: p. 341). Sports can provide various properties, such as teams, competitions, individuals, events or static advertising. It is precisely through a sports property that sports sponsorship occurs (Rines, 2000). A sports property can also be a major event, celebrity, entity, a developing athlete or even an event that is still unknown (Amis, Pant and Slack, 1997).

As sponsors wish to create involvement with an appropriate sports property (Madrigal, 2000), the professionals involved in selection should observe whether there is a clear fit between the company's image and marketing strategy, and the characteristics of the property being sponsored (Ensor, 1987). Various authors highlight the need for strategic decisions in the selection of the best property in order to achieve the company's aims (Farrelly, Quester and Greyser, 2005; Meenaghan, 1998). To better select a sports property, all available options should be carefully considered before taking a decision so that the choice contributes to ensuring that the company is able to achieve the objectives proposed with the sports sponsorship action, and consequently, that investments in sports are not seen as being costly and yielding disappointing returns (Papadimitriou, Apostolopoulou and Dounis, 2008).

Activation of sports sponsorship

Activation is defined as a set of strategic initiatives adopted by companies to position themselves in sports marketing (Fullerton and Merz, 2008). The term is also used to describe the activity developed through actions that exploit the property's potential to achieve specific marketing objectives. Activation contributes to the formation of a link between sponsor, sponsee, customer and sales (Rines, 2000).

The growing number of sponsors and the demand for companies' more effective financial controls has forced companies to imagine more creative and innovative solutions for the activation of their sports sponsorships (Miloch and Lambrecht, 2006). An activation strategy requires communication that clearly publicizes the association between sponsor, sponsee and a specific audience (Westerbeek and Smith, 2002).

Activation is able to influence a brand's recognition and recall rates as well as increase an event's level of familiarity. The recognition of sponsoring companies that activate their sports sponsorships can be as much as twice as those that do not (Miloch and Lambrecht, 2006). The disciplines typically used for activation of sports sponsorship are: the brand, promotions, hospitality, merchandising, relationship marketing and advertising (Rines, 2000), development of B2B strategies, internal communication, internet agreements and greater public relations efforts (Miloch and Lambrecht, 2006).

Measurement of sports sponsorship

Walliser (2003) explains that the evaluation of the results of investments in different types of sports sponsorship has constituted an important issue for marketing professionals who, due to the increasing cost of sports sponsorships, have been questioning the effectiveness of their actions (Lardinoit and Derbaix, 2001).

The measurement of sponsorship is a complex activity (Lagae, 2005) and is usually performed using models and scales developed for other forms of advertising. From the consumers' perspective, this assessment is normally performed in terms of the levels of recognition achieved, attitudes created or altered, brand recall, whether it is instantaneous or not, and level of press coverage (Bennett, 1999). Some measures used by companies to assess the impacts of sports sponsorship on consumers are: public awareness; change of attitude in relation to the brand's image, undertaken comparatively before and after the execution of the action; measures of affinity, evaluated in market research; and evaluation of the impact on sales, purchase intention and loyalty (Meenaghan, 2005). Despite academic efforts to develop more precise evaluation measures, the tests of association and recognition that have been proposed are merely superficial measures of the impacts of sponsorship that do not contribute to a better understanding of the ways consumers involve themselves in sports (Meenaghan, 2001).

Conceptual model

The Sports Sponsorship Decision Model (SSDM) proposed in this study (see Figure 8.1) was developed using the theoretical references to serve as the conceptual framework for the analysis. According to the SSDM, a company interested in investing in sports sponsorship should establish clear objectives that serve as a basis for the sponsorship selection decision, which can begin with the choice of (1) sports modalities or (2) types of sponsorship aligned with established objectives. The company should consider the opportunities and restrictions that occur when trying to match (3) sports modalities and types of sponsorship, given that not all sports modalities provide opportunities for all types of sponsorship and vice versa. Once the sports modalities and types of sponsorship have been defined, the company should select sports properties, the concrete locus of the sports sponsorship action. Once again, the nature of the sports property (4) should be aligned with the company's objectives. The company should also consider the restrictions between (5) sports properties and sports modalities and between (6) types of sponsorship and sports properties. The company should then decide on sponsorship activation actions to fully exploit the sports property's potential. These actions should be aligned with the opportunities and restrictions that result (4') from the nature of the sports property, (5') the sports modality and (6') the type of sponsorship.

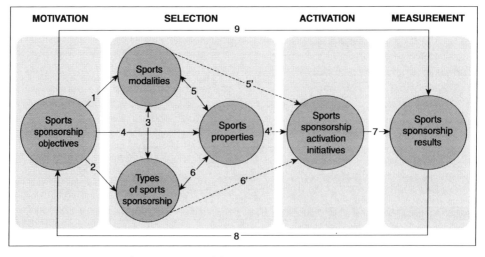

Figure 8.1 Sports Sponsorship Decision Model (SSDM)

The next step is to decide on the indicators that will be used to measure the results of the sponsorship, considering (7) the results expected from sponsorship activation actions and (8) the objectives initially defined. Finally, the company should use the results as a tool to refine (9) the objectives to be achieved through sports sponsorship.

Methodology

This chapter aims to contribute to the expansion of knowledge in the sports marketing area, more specifically regarding the theme of sports sponsorship, by investigating the phenomenon from the sponsors' perspective. The main objective is to understand the sports sponsorship decision-making process by analysing companies' motivations for making these investments, identifying how opportunities are selected, how activation actions are planned and executed and how the results of sports sponsorship are measured.

We decided to use the case analysis method to conduct the investigation. "Case study" can be defined as a description of a managerial situation (Bonoma, 1985) usually conducted when the researcher intends to obtain a better understanding of a given theme (Eisenhardt, 1989) typically by deeply analysing a restricted number of situations (Campomar, 1991) in the real context where they happen (Yin, 2001: p. 19). To achieve the aim of this research, the following four research questions were proposed:

1 What motives lead companies to become involved with sports and what objectives do they expect to achieve by investing in sports sponsorship?
2 How do companies select sports sponsorship opportunities and what criteria do they use to choose those they wish to become involved in?
3 How does the activation of sports sponsorship occur?
4 What are the indicators used by companies to measure the results of sports sponsorship?

Due to the nature of these questions, we conducted an exploratory study and developed it in two stages. During the first one, in-depth interviews were performed with eight sports sponsorship specialists, professionals who had worked in sports agencies as mediators of the relationship between sponsors and sponsees. The aim of these interviews was to acquire deeper knowledge of the phenomenon investigated as well as verify the adequateness of the semi-structured interview guide for the subsequent interviews with sponsors in order to perform an external triangulation of the information collected from the informants. In addition, complementary information regarding each sponsoring company was researched in secondary sources, reinforcing the validity of the study through external triangulation (Bonoma, 1985).

After the first round of investigation, we conducted another set of in-depth interviews with six executives in charge of the sports sponsorship areas from their companies. These executives represent a total of four companies selected for the purpose of this study, based on the criteria that, together, they embrace most types of sponsorships identified in literature. Petrobras is one of the biggest oil companies in the world and has been investing in sports since the 1980s. It has sponsorship agreements encompassing different sports, events, and entities, among others. Ipiranga is also an oil company that invests in athletes, teams, and events, mostly in race sports. Unimed-Rio is a medical insurance enterprise that chooses to sponsor athletes from different disciplines and supported one of the most well-known soccer teams in the country for 15 years. Finally, Olympikus – a big Brazilian sporting goods company – has licensing agreements, and was also the technological supplier of sports equipment to athletes, teams and sports organizations.

The analysis was performed using the critical realism approach. This approach holds that the existence of reality depends on our perception of what is real and that the analysis of this reality is only possible by understanding the cause and effect relations that exist in what is observed. By using this approach, researchers are able to reinforce the degree of analytical generalization of their findings and the ability to replicate them (Welch et al., 2011).

In order to apply the proposed method, first, a case-by-case analysis was performed to identify patterns. Second, the cases were compared to search for similarities and divergences in each of the categories of analysis: (a) objectives of sports sponsorship; (b) selection of sports sponsorship; (c) activation of sports sponsorship; (d) measurement of the results of sports sponsorship.

Discussion of results

What motives lead companies to become involved with sports and what objectives do they expect to achieve by investing in sports sponsorship?

The analysis of the four cases investigated suggests that companies that sponsor sports do so for different reasons: corporate or business, brand, product and relationship objectives, or to take advantage of tax breaks and even for personal reasons and also to link the company to a property with a high level of visibility, credit and success. The interviewees highlighted increased sales and brand visibility as important objectives for sponsors, as had been mentioned by previous researchers (Cornwell, Pruitt and Clark, 2005; Davies and Tsiantas, 2008). Their main aim is to conquer space in Brazil's most significant media groups, especially on television. The interviewed executives believe that sports sponsorship creates closer ties between the brand and customers by enabling corporate hospitality (CH) opportunities to interact with strategic customers as well as providing sales opportunities in stands set up at sports events or even in the points of sale, which can be used to undertake actions that communicate the company's involvement with sports, thus attracting more customers.

Other objectives observed were the expansion of existing business, as observed by Davies and Tsiantas (2008) and the development of new business (Irwin and Asimakopoulos, 1992). Companies attribute part of their success in closing deals with investors and in their strategies to conquer new markets to sports sponsorship. Objectives linked to the personal interests of executives as highlighted by Meenaghan (1983) as well as relationship actions with different interest groups also appeared in the interviews.

A particular characteristic of the Brazilian market also emerged from the interviews. Since the promulgation of the Federal Sport Incentive Act in the year 2000, Brazilian companies can use 1% of taxes owed to sponsor projects approved by the Ministry of Sport. Tax breaks have encouraged the development of sports sponsorship actions but the companies investigated in the study were still organizing themselves to use these benefits in their relations with sports while awaiting the outcome of ongoing adaptations to the law. Table 8.1 summarizes the study's main findings and relates them to the objectives identified in the literature.

How do companies select sports sponsorship opportunities and what criteria do they use to choose those they wish to become involved with?

Some of the companies investigated have a specific area responsible for sports matters. These sectors manage the strategies, execution and measurement of the results of sports sponsorships undertaken. In various cases investigated these sectors with decision-making powers are

Table 8.1 Sports sponsorship objectives

Categories of Analysis	Olympikus	Unimed-Rio	Petrobras	Ipiranga
Corporate: increase sales, increase ROI and conquer new markets.	Increase sales. Guarantee the company's ROI. Consolidate the company's position in Latin America.	Increase sales of health plans.	Increase sales incentivized by promotions linked to sports. Consolidate the company's position in Latin America.	Draw more consumers to the stations to consume Ipiranga's products and services.
Brand: improve brand knowledge, awareness and image, change the public's perception of the company and its products.	Increase brand knowledge and awareness with more visibility and exposure. Position itself and be recognized as a brand of quality products and Brazilian sports brand. Endorse the quality of products winning consumers' trust and improving the brand's image.	Increase knowledge and awareness of the brand in the domestic and Brazilian market. Reinforce the positioning of health and wellbeing through association with sports.	Increase brand knowledge and awareness in new markets. Position itself as a brand with high-performance and technological products and a Brazilian company that invests in the development of Brazilian sports. Endorse the quality of products winning consumers' trust and improving the brand's image. Publicize investments in renewable energy.	Increase visibility of the brand, gaining more knowledge. Position itself as a brand with high-performance and technological products and reinforce the message of "In love with cars like all Brazilians". Endorse the quality of products winning consumers' trust and improving the brand's image.
Product	Develop products with sponsees.	Not observed.	Develop, test and improve products jointly with sponsees.	Develop, test and improve products jointly with sponsees.
Relationship with strategic customers, opinion formers, the community and collaborators.	Not observed.	Develop a relationship with strategic customers in CH and with collaborators with the presence of the athletes in the company.	Develop a relationship with strategic customers in CH. Develop close ties with opinion formers and in surfing events.	Develop a relationship with strategic customers in CH. Facilitate the integration of new retailers by maintaining the sponsorship that was formerly Texaco's.
Personal	Not observed.	Not observed.	Not observed.	Some retailers may have personal reasons for sponsorship.

composed of one person or a small group of people. Companies' sports sponsorship strategies also vary from case to case. Most companies plan their actions, whether they involve initiating a new relation or renewing an existing contract, around one year in advance. In most cases it is the individual or entity seeking sponsorship that approaches the companies to request a sponsorship, as observed in previous studies (Lardinoit and Derbaix, 2001; Walliser, 2003), but the opposite can also occur when companies see an opportunity to link their brand to a sports property.

The study revealed that only Petrobras employs specific software to support managers in the sports sponsorship decision-making process. The other companies were unaware of the existence of any kind of software that could help them take decisions related to sports sponsorship. In the cases investigated, no signs were found of an ideal set of evaluation criteria for the selection of sports sponsorship. Each company examines its necessities and translates these interests into factors that could help them determine whether or not to select a sports sponsorship opportunity, in line with the idea of evaluating benefits and risks of establishing the partnership (Rines, 2000). The following criteria emerged from the interviews: visibility, budget availability, congruence between the sports property and the sponsor's brand; attributes of the sports property and those desired by the brand; the audience interested in the property and the sponsor's target audience. In addition, companies also observed the potential of the properties evaluated to: increase sales, have an impact on the relevant target audience, develop a relationship with different audiences, exploit sports sponsorship with the company's internal audience, generate spontaneous media, generate a return on investment, and activate sports sponsorship. Sponsorship coverage and alignment with company strategy complement the selection criteria observed.

As regards sports modalities, the specialists said in their interviews that this was the first decision to be taken in the selection of sports sponsorship. The investigation of the cases also showed that various companies consider that the sports modality is an important criterion although they also chose according to types of sports sponsorship or specific sports properties. Companies seek sports modalities that are capable of contributing to achieve planned strategic marketing objectives (Ensor, 1987; Pichot, Tribou and O'Reilly, 2008), or possess attributes close to those desired for the sponsor's brand, following the idea of a need for congruency in the sponsor–sponsee relationship (Nickell, Cornwell and Johnston, 2011). Properties that have an interested audience and show characteristics that are congruent with the brand of the sponsoring company are also attractive. This can be observed in the cases of Petrobras and Ipiranga, that maintain links with motor racing, or Olympikus and its sponsorship of Olympic sports and football. These three companies have products that can be related to the sports sponsored, perhaps suggesting that the reason for prioritising involvement in a specific modality depends on the existence of products or services related to it.

In most of the cases observed, sports sponsorships are not chosen essentially according to the type of sponsorship. This may give the impression that this is a secondary decision but there have been cases in which the choice of type of sponsorship was the most important. The types of sports sponsorship seem to be more important as a selection criterion when they represent some kind of risk. Some companies that allege not having a preference for any particular type of sponsorship declare that they do not establish ties with athletes or are very cautious about sponsoring teams. In the case of athletes, bad behaviour inside or outside sports can end up being linked to the sponsor's brand. Image transfer from the sponsored property to the sponsor had been mentioned by other studies as a result of sponsorship (Cornwell and Maignan, 1998) but the negative impact of these relationships was what emerged. Poor performance can also lower the expected return on an investment in sponsorship, given that its natural consequence is less space in the media. As regards teams, companies' main concern is the question of rivalry, especially between football teams, where the passion of one group of supporters' can mean the aversion of the other group.

Sports sponsorship can also involve exploiting an opportunity in the form of a sports property. Olympikus revealed that it became interested in the Brazilian Olympic swimming champion Cesar Cielo when he reached the top of the ranking. Another example of this type of opportunism can be seen in major sports events as they represent a unique chance for companies that wish to establish strong ties with sports like Petrobras, the main sponsor of the 2007 Pan American Games. For some companies, the sports property is what really matters in sports sponsorship. After all, a link to a sports property constitutes the very nature of sponsorship. Table 8.2 summarizes the main points highlighted in the interviews, showing that the selection criteria identified in this study correspond to those identified in the literature.

How does the activation of sports sponsorship occur?

Activation can occur through advertising, the use of electronic media, corporate hospitality actions, promotional actions and using properties for actions inside the company. These kinds of strategies had already been identified by Rines (2000) and Miloch and Lambrecht (2006). In the cases investigated, when companies use advertising to activate their sponsorships they create campaigns that highlight their support for sports as well as transmitting the desired messages. Companies can also activate sponsorships using electronic media. Specific websites to talk about the sponsorships, websites for the properties, online games and profiles in social media are examples of the forms of activation through the internet most widely used by the companies investigated. Corporate hospitality, which is already recognised as an important marketing tool by companies (Cornwell, Pruitt and Clark, 2005; Davies and Tsiantas, 2008), constitutes another form of activation. It improves sponsoring companies' networking capabilities, promotes greater product exposure and enables companies to develop engagement programs for employees. For these employees, motivational speeches are also an important form of activation. Table 8.3 presents a summary of the main activation actions identified in the study.

What are the indicators used by companies to measure the results of sports sponsorship?

The companies investigated evaluate their sponsorship investments by employing the same models typically used to assess other communication actions, as had already been identified by Lagae (2005). Traditional forms of advertising evaluation are commonly used in the cases investigated, as Bennett (1999) highlighted. The assessment is usually based on reports that present information on the visibility of sponsoring brands and sports events related to the property sponsored. Regarding the sponsor's visibility, reports typically address brand exposure in terms of frequency and length (inches) of citations and reviews on press media, as well as broadcast media (minutes). The data obtained is compared with what would be paid for traditional media. In addition, information can be gathered on the sports events, such as the attendance of each event and its corresponding media coverage. Interviews also revealed the use of indicators that come from market studies such as the "Top of Mind" research – a study promoted by media vehicles that indicates the most remembered companies according to specific criteria – to evaluate the effects of sports sponsorship on the perception of sponsoring companies' brands.

Table 8.2 Sports sponsorship selection

Categories of Analysis	Olympikus	Unimed-Rio	Petrobras	Ipiranga
Strategy	Greater involvement with sports from the mid-1990s. Investments planned nearly one year in advance.	Greater involvement with sports observed in 1998 with the beginning of a partnership with Fluminense FC.	Great involvement only with motor racing until the 1990s, after which it invests in other modalities. Interest in using the Federal Sports Incentive Act. Decisions planned nearly a year in advance and others even earlier.	Resumes sponsorship of tarmac motor racing in 2009. Interest in using the Federal Sports Incentive Act. Planning together with other communication areas nearly a year in advance.
Decision	Specific department responsible for sports-related decisions. Receives around 10 proposals per day, but is also pro-active in searching for interesting properties.	Specific department responsible for sports-related decisions. Did not specify exactly how many proposals it receives but evaluates all individually.	Single department responsible for sports-related decisions. Was not able to specify the exact number and only evaluates proposals that fulfil the directives' pre-requisites.	Sports-related decisions taken by the same area that deals with institutional communication. Receives around 80 sports sponsorship projects for evaluation every year.
Tools	Not observed.	Not observed.	Uses its proprietary evaluation tool called MetriCom.	Uses a spreadsheet containing the most important evaluation criteria.
Criteria	Visibility, congruence with what the brand produces, value, impact and sales increase potential. Short and long-term complementary sponsorships.	Seek properties with attributes desired for the brand. Verifies visibility, estimated audience, activation potential ability to generate returns, budget, internal exploitation potential. One-off and long-term sponsorships that complement Unimed do Brasil initiatives. Close and partnership-based relations with sponsees.	Activation potential, degree of adherence with communication policy, cost, coverage, relationship potential, estimated audience, spontaneous media potential. Fulfil directives of each sponsorship program and observe criteria stipulated by government bodies. One-off projects such as the 2007 Pan American Games and renewable ones (rally and others). Exclusive sponsorships and sponsorship deals with preference for long-term partnerships.	In motor racing, alignment with brand strategy, broad coverage, nationwide visibility. In other sports, it is sufficient to have good brand visibility and exposure. One-off and renewable sponsorships (aiming at visibility and exposure).

Modality/ Type/ Property	Popular modalities (soccer and volleyball), sports entity (Brazilian Olympic Committee) and specific properties (sponsorship deal with broadcaster Rede Globo in the 2010 FIFA World Cup).	Involvement with distinct sports, preferentially with athletes. In the case of football the company sponsors teams and participates on a one-off basis in facilities and events. Does not sponsor risky or combat sports.	Involvement with different modalities. Selection according to the coverage of a type of partnership. Does not sponsor individual athletes.	Concentration on off-road and tarmac racing. Investment in events, teams, drivers and transmissions. One-off involvement with other modalities.
Risks	Behaviour of individual athletes requires very careful selection.	Exercises caution with certain modalities due to attributes it does not wish to associate with the brand.	Rivalry between teams, limited duration partnerships with drivers.	Risks associated with regionalized actions that can create discomfort with retailers and the general population.

Table 8.3 Sports sponsorship activation

Categories of Analysis	Olympikus	Unimed-Rio	Petrobras	Ipiranga
Advertising	Use of the image of the sponsored property in company communication. Creation of teams that use the brand name in competitions.	Creation of teams that use the brand name in competitions.	Use of the image of the sponsored property in company communication. Creation of proprietary teams and events, acquisition of naming rights.	Use of the image of the sponsored property in company communication. Creation of teams with the company name.
Use of electronic media	Presence in only a few social media networks, but an intense one. Creation of a tool for socialization between ordinary sports practitioners. Use of the corporate website to communicate and activate sports sponsorship with spaces for interactivity between fans and athletes. Creation of online games.	Incipient use of social media. Communication of sports sponsorship on the corporate website.	Present in all main social media networks with constant updating of information. Development of websites to communicate sponsorships. Development of online games and authorization to use the brand in electronic games.	Present in only a few social media networks, sparse use and rare information. Development of websites to communicate sponsorships.
Corporate hospitality	Not observed.	Use of CH for relationship actions with strategic customers, stakeholders and the internal audience.	Use of CH for relationship actions with strategic customers and negotiation of new deals.	Use of CH for relationship actions with internal audience and customers and negotiating of new deals.
Promotional actions	Distribution of promotional material.	Distribution of promotional material.	Distribution of promotional material and promotional actions with customers in the points of sales and through the internet.	Distribution of promotional material and promotional actions with customers in the points of sales and creation of a sales stand at the event location.
Use of properties for actions in the company	Not observed.	Participation of sponsored athletes in motivational speeches for the internal audience.	Not observed.	Participation of racing drivers in the company's social actions.

Another way of evaluating the impact of sponsorship on companies' brands is to verify whether there was public recognition of the initiatives undertaken, which had also been identified in previous researches (Davies and Tsiantas, 2008; Gwinner and Swanson, 2003). The results of activation actions are also evaluated by observing the interactions that occur inside a hospitality centre, which contribute, for example, to the closing of deals and an increase in product sales. Another kind of evaluation is to observe the evolution in the quality of products used by the sponsored athlete or team. This was seen in the case of motor racing, with Ipiranga and Petrobras improving their products, and also Olympikus, which even developed specific products jointly with its sponsees. The study, however, found no evidence of models that can measure precisely how much of this improvement is due exclusively to sports sponsorship, corroborating the lack of measurement tools for evaluating sponsorship deals identified in the literature (Speed and Thompson, 2008; Walliser, 2003). Table 8.4 summarizes the main findings on this topic.

Contributions to academic research and managerial practice

The main contribution of this study lies in the proposal – based on the theoretical references and empirical validation using case studies – of the Sports Sponsorship Decision Model (SSDM), a model that articulates the main decisions that companies wishing to sponsor sports may have to face. It constitutes the first academic attempt to model the sports sponsorship decision-making process considering motivation; selection of modalities; types and sports properties; activation; and measurement of results; identifying how these elements interrelate to foster results aligned with company strategies. The SSDM model suggests that sports sponsorship strategies should consider these four blocks of elements so that the process is undertaken in an integrated fashion, ensuring that stage execution is aligned with planning and consistent with company objectives.

This investigation also provided empirical evidence to support previous findings of the sports sponsorship literature. It revealed that the companies investigated see this type of investment as an opportunity to enhance the value of their brands with their target audiences (O'Reilly and Madill, 2007; Pichot, Tribou and O'Reilly, 2008) and have different objectives when they involve themselves with sports through a sports sponsorship agreement. In the cases investigated, the study identified corporate, brand, product, relationship and personal objectives that had already been identified in the literature by other authors such as, for example, Meenaghan (1983), Kuzma, Shanklin and McCally Jr. (1993), Gwinner (1997) or Cornwell and Maignan (1998). It is necessary to establish clear objectives to be achieved with the actions independently of a company's motive for choosing to invest in sports sponsorships. Whenever possible, companies should seek congruence between the property sponsored and their business, as mentioned also in other investigated studies (Chien, Cornwell and Pappu, 2011). It should be highlighted that companies that have a clear vision of the objectives they expect to achieve through sports sponsorship seem to find it easier to select the opportunities that contribute to furthering their interests and reject those that do not fit.

We also verified that no pattern can be found in the choice of sports sponsorship actions by the companies investigated. They have been learning from their mistakes in order to improve their opportunity selection process, corroborating the literature's findings that the evolution of sponsorship skills depends on companies' ability to learn from their successes and failures (Kuzma, Shanklin and McCally Jr., 1993). It was also observed that although the companies investigated showed some level of activation of their sponsorships, especially through the successful development of portals, games and social media profiles, the results of

Table 8.4 Sports sponsorship results

Categories of Analysis	Olympikus	Unimed-Rio	Petrobras	Ipiranga
Visibility	Visibility reports with media impact developed by specialized firms and by entities and those seeking sponsorship.	Visibility reports with media impact developed in the media prepared by specialized firms and by entities and those seeking sponsorship.	Visibility reports with impact developed in the media prepared by specialized firms and by entities and those seeking sponsorship.	Visibility reports with media impact and frequency prepared by specialized firms.
Brand	Research to evaluate brand recognition and remembrance or recall.	Recognition and recall evaluated in Top of Mind research.	Qualtative research prepared jointly with other company communication areas.	Annual research to evaluate the company's positioning, recall, perception mobilization and change in the public's consumption habits.
Activations	Not observed.	Surveys of the company's target audience regarding receptivity of its actions.	Research developed by the company to evaluate results.	Not observed.
Sales	Reports of sales of CR Flamengo shirts, for example.	Unable to establish a direct relation with investments in sports sponsorship.	Closing of deals.	Increasing sales during promotion periods.
Products	Development and testing of products jointly with athletes.	Not observed.	Technical gains achieved with tests performed with teams.	Not observed.
Tools	Not observed.	Not observed.	Use of MetriCom, a proprietary project evaluation tool	Not observed.

this study indicate that there are still many opportunities for the development of activation actions. This study's findings also suggest that initiatives that provide consumers with interaction opportunities can lead them to forge closer ties with companies. Given that sports is a theme that provokes interest and emotion, this relation can become even more intense.

This chapter did not identify any satisfactory model to evaluate the results of sports sponsorship. The empirical evidence corroborates the literature's findings, which show that as the methods currently used are based on models developed to measure the results of advertising (Lee, Sandler and Shani, 1997), they are inefficient (Bennett, 1999) to evaluate a complex tool like sports. However, it should be emphasised that despite all the difficulties, some activations performed by the companies investigated in this study make it possible to evaluate the direct effects of sports sponsorship. This may suggest that establishing assessment parameters for concrete activation actions would allow a more direct and less abstract measurement. However, this is a theme that needs to be explored more fully. The gap regarding forms of measurement remains to be filled and opens up a vast field of investigation into methods, models and variables that facilitate the evaluation of investment results.

References

Amis, J., Pant, N. and Slack, T. (1997). Achieving a sustainable competitive advantage: a resource-based view of sport sponsorship. *Journal of Sport Management,* 11(1), 80–96.

Arthur, D., Scott, D. and Woods, T. (1997). A conceptual model of the corporate decision making process of sport sponsorship acquisition. *Journal of Sport Management,* 11(3), 223–233.

Barrand, D. (15 Jun 2005). Licensing: why brands are banking on sports. *Promotions & Incentives,* 13–14.

Bennett, R. (1999). Sport sponsorship, spectator recall and false consensus. *European Journal of Marketing,* 3(3/4), 291–313.

Bonoma, T. V. (May 1985). Case research in marketing: opportunities, problems, and a process. *Journal of Marketing Research,* 22(2), 199–208.

Campomar, M. C. (Jul/Sep 1991). Do uso do "estudo de caso" em pesquisas para dissertações e teses em administração. *Revista da Administração,* 26, 95–97.

Chanavat, N., Martinent, G. and Ferrand, A. (2009). Sponsor and sponsees interactions: effects on consumers' perceptions of brand image, brand attachment and purchase intention. *Journal of Sport Management,* 23, 644–670.

Chanavat, N., Martinent, G. and Ferrand, A. (February 2010). Brand images causal relationships in a multiple sport event sponsorship context: developing brand value through association with sponsees. *European Sport Management Quarterly,* 10, 49–74.

Chien, P., Cornwell, T. and Pappu, R. (2011). Sponsorship portfolio as a brand-image creation strategy. *Journal of Business Research,* 64, 142–149.

Copeland, R., Frisby, W. and McCarville, R. (1996). Understanding the sport sponsorship process from a corporate perspective. *Journal of Sport Management,* 10(1), 32–48.

Cornwell, T. B. and Maignan, I. (1998). An international review of sponsorship research. *Journal of Advertising,* 27(1), 1–21.

Cornwell, T. B., Pruitt, S. W. and Clark, J. M. (2005). The relationship between major league sports' official sponsorship announcements and the stock prices of sponsoring firms. *Journal of Academy of Marketing Science,* 33(4), 401–412.

Davies, F. and Tsiantas, G. (2008). Selection of leveraging strategies by national Olympic sponsors: a proposed model. *International Journal of Sports Marketing & Sponsorship,* 9(4), 271–289.

Eisenhardt, K. M. (October 1989). Building theories from case study research. *The Academy of Management Review,* 14(4), 532–550.

Ensor, R. J. (Sep 1987). The corporate view of sports sponsorship. *Athletic Business,* 11(9), 40–43.

Farrelly, F., Quester, P. and Greyser, S. A. (Sep 2005). Defending the co-branding benefits of sponsorship B2B partnerships: The case of ambush marketing. *Journal of Advertising Research,* 45(3), 339–348.

Fullerton, S. and Merz, R. (2008). The four domains of sports marketing: a conceptual framework. *Sport Marketing Quarterly,* 17(2), 90–108.

Gwinner, K. and Swanson, S. R. (2003). A model of fan identification: antecedents and sponsorship outcomes. *Journal of Services Marketing,* 17(3), 275–294.

International Events Group. (9 January 2014). *IEG,* disponível em IEG: www.sponsorship.com/About-IEG/Press-Room/Sponsorship-Spending-Growth-Expected-to-Slow-As-Ma.aspx (accessed 29 May 2014).

Irwin, R. L. and Asimakopoulos, M. K. (1992). An approach to the evaluation and selection of sport sponsorship proposals. *Sport Marketing Quarterly,* 1(2), 43–51.

Koo, G., Quarterman, J. and Flynn, L. (2006). Effect of perceived sport event and sponsor image fit on consumers' cognition, affect and behavioral intentions. *Sport Marketing Quarterly,* 15(2), 80–90.

Kuzma, J. R., Shanklin, W. L. and McCally Jr., J. F. (1993). Number one principle for sporting events seeking corporate sponsors: meet benefactor's objectives. *Sport Marketing Quarterly,* 2(3), 27–32.

Lagae, W. (2005). *Sport Sponsorship and Marketing Communications: an European Perspective.* Harlow: Prentice Hall.

Lardinoit, T. and Derbaix, C. (2001). Sponsorship and recall of sponsors. *Psychology & Marketing,* 12(2), 167–190.

Lee, M., Sandler, D. M. and Shani, D. (1997). Attitudinal constructs towards sponsorship: scale development using three global sporting events. *International Marketing Review,* 14(3), 150–169.

Lee, S. and Ross, S. D. (2012). Sport sponsorship decision making in a global market: an approach of Analytic Hierarchy Process (AHP). *Sport, Business and Management,* 2(2), 156–167.

Madrigal, R. (2000). The influence of social alliances with sports team on intentions to purchase corporate sponsors' products. *Journal of Advertising,* 29(4), 13–24.

Martin, J. H. (1996). Is the athlete's sport important when picking an athlete to endorse a nonsport product? *Journal of Consumer Marketing,* 13(6), 28–43.

Mason, K. (2005). How corporate sport sponsorship impacts consumer behavior. *The Journal of American Academy of Business,* 7(1), 32–35.

McCook, K., Turco, D. and Riley, R. (1997). A look at the corporate sponsorship decision-making process. *Cyber-Journal of Sport Marketing,* 1(2).

Meenaghan, J. A. (1983). Commercial Sponsorship. *European Journal of Marketing,* 17(7), 5–69.

Meenaghan, T. (1998). Current developments & future directions in sponsorship. *International Journal of Advertising,* 17(1), 3–28.

Meenaghan, T. (Feb 2001). Understanding sponsorship effects. *Psychology & Marketing,* 18(2), 95–122.

Meenaghan, T. (2005). Evaluating sponsorship effects. In J. Amis and T. B. Cornwell (eds), *Global Sport Sponsorship,* pp. 243–264. Oxford: Berg.

Miloch, K. S. and Lambrecht, K. W. (2006). Consumer awareness of sponsorship at grassroots sport events. *Sport Marketing Quarterly,* 15(3), 147–154.

Morgan, M. J. and Summers, J. (2005). *Sports Marketing.* Southbank: Thomson.

Mullin, B. J., Hardy, S. and Sutton, W. A. (2004). *Marketing Esportivo* (2a ed.). (C. A. Soares, Trad.) Porto Alegre: Artmed/Bookman.

Nickell, D., Cornwell, B. and Johnston, W. (2011). Sponsorship-linked marketing: A set of research propositions. *Journal of Business & Industrial Marketing,* 26(8), 577–589.

O'Reilly, N. J. and Madill, J. J. (2007). Evaluating social marketing elements in sponsorship. *Social Marketing Quarterly,* 13(4), 1–25.

Papadimitriou, D., Apostolopoulou, A. and Dounis, T. (2008). Event sponsorship as a value creating strategy for brands. *Journal of Product & Brand Management,* 17(4), 212–222.

Pichot, L., Tribou, G. and O'Reilly, N. (2008). Sport sponsorship, internal communications, and human resource management: an exploratory assessment of potential future research. *International Journal of Sport Communication,* 1(4), 413–423.

PwC. (1 December 2011). *Changing the game: Outlook for the global sports market to 2015,* disponível em PwC: www.pwc.com/sportsoutlook (accessed 14 June 2014).

Ramiro, D. (25 April 2007). O Pan como vitrine. *Istoé Dinheiro.*

Rines, S. (2000). *Driving business through sport: An analysis of Europe's sport sponsorship industry, business opportunities and best practices* (1st ed.). International Marketing Reports Ltd.

Rosa, B. (17 October 2009). Salto Olímpico na Publicidade. *O Globo, Caderno de Economia,* p. 17.

Shannon, J. R. (1999). Sport marketing: an examination of academic marketing publication. *Journal of Services Marketing,* 13(6), 517–534.

Speed, R. and Thompson, P. (2008). Determinants of sport sponsorship response. *Journal of Academy of Marketing Science,* 28(2), 226–238.

Valim, C. (23 May 2014). *A Guerra das marcas na Copa*, disponível em Istoé Dinheiro: www.istoedinheiro. com.br/noticias/negocios/20140523/guerra-das-marcas-copa/157381.shtml (accessed 14 June 2014).

Walliser, B. (2003). An international review of sponsorship research: extension and update. *International Journal of Advertising,* 22(1), 5–40.

Wann, D. L., Grieve, F. G., Zapalac, R. K. and Pease, D. G. (2008). Motivational profiles of sport fans of different sports. *Sport Marketing Quarterly,* 17(1), 6–19.

Welch, C., Piekkari, R., Plakoyiannaki, E. and Paavilainen-Mäntymäki, E. (2011). Theorising from case studies: Towards a pluralist future for international business research. *Journal of International Business Studies* (42), 740–762.

Westerbeek, H. and Smith, A. (2002). Location dependency and sport sponsors: A factor analytic study. *Sport Marketing Quarterly,* 11(3), 140–150.

Yin, R. K. (2001). *Estudo de Casos: Planejamento e Métodos* (2a ed.). Bookman: Porto Alegre.

9

EFFECTS OF MULTIPLE SPONSORSHIP ACTIVITIES

Propositions and framework

Nicolas Chanavat, Michel Desbordes and Geoff Dickson

Introduction

Sponsorship activities, including ambush marketing, rarely occur in isolation from other sponsorship activities. A large portion of research takes the view that sponsorship is dyadic, failing to recognize that other organizations or brands have a sponsorship relationship with the sponsee (Cornwell, 2008). In other words, studies that investigate dyadic sponsorship (or ambush marketing) relationships do not reflect the real world. An analysis of multiple sponsorship will reflect real-world complexity. Therefore, "sponsorship shall be considered as a network of players rather than a link between a sponsor and a sponsee" (Walliser, 2006: 31). Multiple sponsorship occurs when two or more organizations are associated, either directly or indirectly, with the one sponsorship property (for example, event, organization, individual, facility). The indirect dimension also includes the ambush marketing activities that are present in so many high profile sporting events. A review of the literature reveals that nothing has been done to simultaneously examine the interaction effects between these sponsorship stakeholders.

Some scholars recognize the plural nature of sponsorship (Chien, Cornwell and Pappu, 2011; 2012; Groza, Cobbs and Schaefers, 2012). Groza et al. (2012) analyzed the effects that sponsors have on the sponsored enterprise. However, previous studies have not investigated the interaction between the cognitive, affective and conative reactions of the consumer across multiple sponsorship stakeholders. This is despite the interaction between the different sponsorship having consequences for the relevant brands.

Recent conceptual frameworks are trying to better comprehend the way sponsorship works without considering multiple sponsorship. For instance, Kim, Stout and Cheong's (2012) framework of how sponsorship affects the image of the sponsor was developed from an information-processing perspective. Depending on the consumer's processing capabilities, sponsorship information is processed either holistically or analytically. Each mode is theorized to play an important role in impacting several components of the sponsor's image. Despite its singular, rather than plural focus, the interactions identified by Kim et al. are useful when endeavoring to study the impact of sponsorship. The proposed conceptual model seeks to extend this research by considering multiple sponsorship. The model is pioneering but grounded in previous sponsorship research, and offers scholarly and practitioner utility.

Given this context, this research proposes an innovative framework for sponsorship relationships. The goal is a conceptual model which simultaneously takes into account the interaction effects between organizations that are associated, either directly or indirectly, with the one sponsorship property, and the relationships between brand image, brand attachment and purchase intention. The model explains how sponsorship stakeholders can affect the other brand image of other stakeholders.

Brand image "refers to the set of associations linked to the brand that consumers hold in memory" (Keller, 1993: 2). This definition of brand image is used in this research to measure consumers' brand cognition. Attachment represents "the degree of linkage perceived by an individual between him/herself and a particular object" (Schultz, Kleine and Kernan, 1989: 360). Spears and Singh (2004) define purchase intention as "an individual's conscious plan to make an effort to purchase a brand" (p. 56). Attachment and purchase intention represent consumers' affective and conative reactions respectively.

In this perspective, an overview of the research on multiple sponsorship activities is presented. The authors also propose a theoretical framework that takes into account realities in the field. Simultaneously, future research propositions are suggested.

Overview

Research considering the plural nature of sponsorship

There is a discrepancy between academic research and the realities of sponsorship. Most academic research on sponsorship focuses on the relationship between a sponsee and only one sponsor. This is despite sponsorship memorization and recognition research demonstrating that sponsees have multiple sponsors (Nanopoulos, 2008). In effect, the majority of sponsorship studies are investigating an "individual", "single" or "exclusive" sponsorship. Only a few studies – Ruth and Simonin (2003; 2006), Carrillat, Lafferty and Harris (2005), Chien, Cornwell and Stokes (2005) and Chanavat, Martinent and Ferrand (2009) – explicitly investigate "multiple sponsorship".

Ruth and Simonin (2003) were the first to investigate the simultaneous involvement of multiple sponsors with a single sponsee. More specifically, they investigated the impact of these sponsors on consumer attitudes towards the sponsee. The results suggest that attitudes towards the co-sponsors (i.e. Coca-Cola and an unspecified co-sponsor) are positively linked to attitudes towards the sponsee. Consequently, the results show that stigmatized sponsors (for example, alcohol or tobacco brand) will influence consumer attitudes towards the event. Furthermore, the results of this research highlight interactions between the stigmatized sponsors, the nationality and the perceived sponsor-event fit. This research reveals that the assessment of co-sponsors may be improved in a context of multiple sponsorship. Brands can benefit from the direct positive effects of the event and indirect effects of other co-sponsors that are held in high regard by consumers.

Carrillat et al. (2005) investigated the influence of single and multiple sponsorship on consumer attitudes and purchase intentions. They examined two co-sponsors (FedEx and Alltel) in the context of the 2004 Olympic Games in Athens. The results reveal that the effect of sponsorship on the attitude and intention to purchase of the consumer is stronger towards a less familiar brand whatever the situation studied (single sponsorship or multiple sponsorship). In other words, the existence of co-sponsors does not modify the influence of sponsorship on the attitude towards a little-known sponsor. If the presence of several partners seems to lessen the process of transfer from the sponsee to the one of the sponsors, this study suggested that an attitude transfer, coming from other co-sponsors, offsets this process. Consequently, in comparison to a single sponsorship, the impact of the sponsorship on the affective (attitude) and conative (intention to purchase) dimensions does not seem to be attenuated within multiple sponsorship. The results of this study could not validate Gwinner's hypothesis (1997) that a high number of sponsors associated with the same event may curb the transfer of image process of that event towards involved sponsor brands.

Furthermore, Chien et al. (2005) propose a theoretical framework to explain image transfer within sponsorship portfolio. This model, adapted from works by Gwinner (1997) and McCracken (1989) comprises three phases: construction of the event's image, exposure to the multiple sponsorship situations, and development of brand image through the event. In contrast to previous brand-image research, this study suggested that interaction between two sponsors of the same event impacts sponsee–sponsor evaluations. The authors postulate that the congruence between partners impacts the interaction effect. Because images of the events may become closely linked to the brand, it is important to take multiple sponsors into account. In this perspective, the effects of incompatible partnerships must be considered so that the desired image is not tarnished.

Ruth and Simonin (2006) recognized that most events are sponsored by more than one company. Using a fictional event, they examined whether co-sponsors dilute the effects of the sponsorship. Using an exclusive approach, Ruth and Simonin first demonstrated that a stigmatized sponsor would negatively influence consumer attitudes towards the event. However, as the number of co-sponsors increased, the negative attitudes towards the event were attenuated. This is despite evidence that an additional sponsor would normally increase negative attitudes towards the event.

In the context of sponsorship portfolios, Groza et al (2012) investigated the effect of sponsor–sponsee congruence on the sponsee's brand equity. The results of the first study reveal that sponsor–sponsee incongruence is most problematic for sponsees with incongruent title sponsors. The second study shows that increasing the number of congruent sponsors could reduce the impact for the sponsee of title-sponsor incongruence.

Multiple sponsorship is a real-world practice

The lack of academic interest in multiple sponsorship strongly contrasts with the reality of sponsorship practices (Ruth and Simonin, 2006). Although some studies utilize the plural nature of sponsorship operations, they do not comprehend all the implications. In a nutshell, consumer reactions to multiple sponsorship have rarely been measured (Chien et al., 2011; 2012; Groza et al., 2012; Ruth and Simonin, 2006). We are confident that, "the association of several sponsors on the same shirt (five to six sometimes) may blur the perception of each" (Tribou and Augé, 2009: 113). Therefore, it is necessary to understand the relationships between and among sponsors and their sponsees. Despite its importance, attitude does not enable us to understand all the reactions generated by the sponsorship.

Another reality of sponsorship is ambush marketing (Meenaghan, 1994). There is growing understanding of the potential associations between sponsored entities and ambushers (Mazodier, Quester and Chandon, 2011; Scassa, 2011). Consequently, any model that seeks to improve our understanding of real-world sponsorship, must consider ambush marketing alongside the official sponsorship. This is certainly the case for multiple sponsorship.

We suggest the analysis of the potential effects caused by multiple sponsorship with regard to the consumer. Cognitive, affective and conative reactions of the individual towards co-sponsee entities, sponsors and ambushers within the framework of a given sporting event should be examined.

Theoretical framework and propositions

Towards an innovative theoretical and conceptual framework

Bacharach (1989: 496) stressed, "a theory is a statement of relations among concepts within a set of boundary assumptions and constraints. It is no more than a linguistic device used to organize a complex empirical world". Some research has attempted to theorize the effects of sponsorship on consumer behaviour. Nevertheless, previous studies on sponsorship highlight the complexity and the difficulty of explaining how it works. Cornwell, Weeks and Roy (2005) are concerned that many studies on sponsorship offer no theoretical explanations. In this perspective, Walliser (2003: 88) argues that there is no dominant theory among the many theoretical explanations of sponsorship. He contends, "Several theoretical frameworks would probably need to be mobilized and adapted to specific situations in order to explain the effects of sponsorship" (p. 88).

This section develops a theoretical and conceptual framework that explains consumer reactions to multiple sponsorship. The aim is to highlight the relevance of a theoretical approach and to formalize research propositions. The relations in this model are developed in purposeful sequence. The propositions are shown in Figure 9.1. A theoretical foundation will be provided for each series of propositions. The entire theoretical framework is presented in Table 9.1.

Propositions: multiple sponsorship and cognitive reactions

Sutton and Staw (1995) argue that a prediction without logic should not be considered a theory. In this section, we consider the effectiveness of multiple sponsorship on the cognitive reactions of consumers (P1a, P1b, P1c, P1d). It is anticipated that these reactions lead to significant links between the cognitive components of involved brands.

Activation and spreading theory

Our theoretical approach to cognitive components is based on cognitive psychology and more particularly, memory models and associative networks. Rooted in the theory of spreading activation, memory models under the form of networks (Anderson, 1983; Collins and Loftus, 1975; Wyer and Strull, 1989) provide explanations of how multiple sponsorship works. Multiple sponsorship requires people to create or reinforce the associations linked to the brand image of involved entities. Since the 1980s, mainstream marketing research has investigated brand associations and brand image (Aaker, 1991; Keller, 1993). With a strong brand, organizations can more easily create a positive image (Keller, 2003). Sports organizations can leverage their brands (Desbordes and Richelieu, 2012; Chanavat and Bodet, 2009; Richelieu and Pons, 2009). In this context, the majority of previous sponsorship research examines the cognitive response of consumers (for example, Chanavat et al., 2009; Groza et al., 2012; Gwinner and Eaton, 1999; Lee and Cho, 2009; Speed and Thompson, 2000). Considered collectively, the results suggest an image transfer occurs between the sponsor and the sponsee.

Brand image, according to Keller (1993), is based on the theory of long-term semantic networks and the principle of information. Memory is characterized as a network with nodes and links. Information is stored in a node. Nodes are linked to other nodes by links of varying strength. In this way, a brand is a node to which other nodes are linked, nodes that are the associations to the brand. This network of nodes and links represents the knowledge of the brand by consumers. Thus, when a node is stimulated, activation spreads through the whole network related to the brand. Other nodes can be activated. For a node to be activated, it is necessary that the level of activation reach a specific threshold. With multiple sponsorship, the individual is exposed to the official sponsors, the sponsee and any ambush sponsors. The nodes and links related to all these entities may consequently be activated simultaneously.

Learning "means adding new nodes, new links and/or reinforcing existing links" (Grunert, 1996: 91). Thus, an individual, exposed simultaneously to multiple brands through multiple sponsorship, will activate nodes and create links between these as well as the connected associations. In this way, the principle of spreading activation may explain how brand images are created or reinforced by multiple sponsorship.

Theories of transfer and endorsement: the double transfer phenomenon

The transfer theory is capable of incorporating cognitive (meaning) and affective (feeling) reactions.[1] This theory is based on the endorsement theory of McCracken (1989). The multiple sponsorship concept incorporates sponsors, their sponsees and ambushing organizations. Each involved brand, laden with meaning and affect, is likely to interact with others. Consequently, these theories may contribute to potential links between the components of, on one hand, image, and on the other hand, affect, of multiple sponsorship entities. If transfer theory is key to the understanding how single sponsorship works, then it will likely have some explanatory value for multiple-sponsorship interactions. Propositions P1a, P1b and P1d are relevant to this theoretical framework.

Sponsorship can enhance the image of the sponsor's brand. This is a consequence of an image transfer from the sponsee towards the sponsor (Gwinner and Eaton, 1999). Ganassali (2009: 3) notes that consumers will subconsciously transfer,

> the perceived features of the sponsee (person, event, activity, etc.) onto the sponsor. The transfer would take place in that way than in the other because sponsees generally involve consumers deeply and their perceptions are more rooted and less mobile than those they have about brands and companies.

Nevertheless, little research has looked into the cognitive impact of the sponsor onto the sponsee. This study assumes this process occurs in a situation of multiple sponsorship. This proposition is reinforced by the results from Ruth and Simonin (2003, 2006). These authors suggest that co-sponsors may impact the cognitive perception of the sponsee. The research on the effectiveness of multiple sponsorship did not take the plurality of co-sponsored entities into account. The small volume of research conducted focused on the study of several sponsors within the framework of an event (Carrillat et al., 2005). Multiple sponsorship may create relations between the cognitive dimensions of the sponsee and that of the sponsor. The direction of the transfer (sponsee => sponsor; sponsor => sponsee) thus represents an important issue.

For example, our model would allow us to measure the most effective partnerships to reinforce the perceived image of Nike by a New York Jets fan. What image components of the entities sponsored by Nike are transferred or impact the brand image of the kit supplier?

Is it the image of their quarterback Michael Vick? Is it more generally the values connected to the New York Jets franchise? Is it the brand image of the NFL?

Consequently, the first proposition (P1a) deals with the interactions between the cognitive dimensions of the co-sponsored entities and those of the sponsor.

P1a: Multiple sponsorship creates relations between the cognitive dimensions of the sponsee and that of the sponsor.

In this perspective, this study supposes that in a situation of multiple sponsorship, the attitude towards a given sponsor has a positive influence on the attitudes towards other co-sponsors. Furthermore, to our knowledge, the literature on brand management and marketing in professional sports has not considered the potential links perceived by the consumer between various sports entities whatever their nature. Yet *branding* is the most important asset for a professional sports organization (Bauer et al., 2005). The brand power of a professional sports organization often determines team identification and purchase behaviours (Richelieu and Pons, 2006). In addition, an organization brand equity can generate income despite poor on-field success (Gladden and Milne, 1999). Any sports-brand owner should develop its brand equity through a marketing approach (Ferrand and Torrigiani, 2005). In sports, the objective of brand equity is to establish a strong link between the consumer and the club (Suckow, 2009). In this context our model allows us to measure the interactions of perceived images by an MLS fan towards the New York Red Bulls, the Red Bull Arena and Thierry Henry (a New York Red Bulls player). Given these elements, and independent of the possible links between co-sponsored entities and sponsors, this study thus proposes:

P1b: Multiple sponsorship creates interrelations between the cognitive dimensions of the co-sponsored entities.

Beyond the sponsor-interactions, the issue of knowing if multiple sponsorship generates interactions between the image components of a same brand is raised. Thus, the cognitive components relating to the image of Thierry Henry would be measured (for example, "All-time best scorer of the French soccer team", "best Arsenal FC player", "New York Red Bull star", "World and European champion", "cheat", "arrogant") with regard to MLS fans. Our model would enable us to measure the cognitive components of the image of the brands studied. Therefore, the propositions P1c asserts that multiple sponsorship creates relations between the cognitive dimensions of brands.

P1c: Multiple sponsorship creates interrelations through causality links between the image components of a brand.

Given the abundance of brands associated with a property, we propose that interactions are generated between an ambush sponsor and the sponsee. For instance, the applications of our model would allow us to simultaneously evaluate the McDonalds–IOC–USOC sponsorship in the context of the Subway–Michael Phelps sponsorship. Therefore, we propose the following:

P1d: Multiple sponsorship creates interactions between the cognitive dimensions of the co-sponsored entities and those of the ambusher.

Propositions: multiple sponsorship and affective reactions

The second series of propositions are concerned with the impact of multiple sponsorship on the affective reactions of consumers (P2a, P2b and P2c). Here it is considered that multiple sponsorship will create significant links between the affective dimensions of the relevant brands.

In this context, we rely on the transfer theory and the principle of affective conditioning. There is evidence of an affect transfer between sponsee and sponsor (Cornwell et al., 2005). Some works examined specifically the affective dimension and also demonstrated sponsee–sponsor interactions (for example, Hansen, Halling and Christensen, 2006). These dyadic interactions underpin multiple sponsorship as each affect-laden entity may interact with others. For example, Tissot is the official watch and timekeeper of NASCAR. Danica Patrick, a NASCAR driver, is also a brand ambassador for Tissot. The proposed model can determine the partnerships that have the greatest impact on the affect developed by a NASCAR fan towards Tissot. Is it the partnership developed with the Sprint Cup Series or the partnership established with Danica Patrick? Thus, a new proposition is offered, relating to the impact of multiple sponsorship on the affective components of the brands involved.

P2a: Multiple sponsorship creates interactions between the affective dimensions of the co-sponsored entities and that of the sponsor.

To our knowledge, the research on multiple sponsorship has not considered the multiplicity of co-sponsored entities. Furthermore, the literature on brand management and marketing in professional sports shows that the attachment towards an athlete may influence the affect towards the club they belong to. For example, Chanavat and Bodet (2009) demonstrated that some French fans supported Chelsea (an English Football Club) because Didier Drogba (a player with French heritage) played for them.

Our model permits the simultaneous measurement and analysis of affective links perceived by a fan towards the NBA, the Los Angeles Lakers and Kobe Bryant (Lakers player). Is the affect developed towards the franchise stronger? Is this affect influenced by the affect developed towards the player? That multiple sponsorship creates links between the affective dimensions of the co-sponsored entities is the focus of the next proposition:

P2b: Multiple sponsorship creates interrelations between the affective dimensions of the co-sponsored entities.

Ambush marketing (Meenaghan, 1994; 1998) is common in commercial sports (Desbordes and Richelieu, 2012). Chanavat and Desbordes (2014) show that ambushers could be very imaginative at the expense of official sponsors and that social networks can be powerful publicity channels. Ambush marketing takes many distinctive forms depending on the strategy and the ingenuity of the ambusher (Séguin and Ellis, 2012). Overall, ambush marketing has a triple-objective: (1) divert attention from the official sponsor towards the ambusher; (2) constrain the official sponsor's operations; (3) modify the reaction of sports spectator audiences to the benefit of the ambusher (Chanavat, Desbordes and Ferrand, 2013). As mentioned previously, recent research identifies potential associations between sponsees and ambushers (Mazodier, et al., 2011; Scassa, 2011). Considering the potential effects of ambush marketing on the fan's reactions will reflect real-world situations. Consequently, we suggest the analysis of the potential effects caused by multiple sponsorship with regard to the consumer. To date, sponsorship research has not considered the potential impact of an ambusher on multiple co-sponsors of a sporting property. Thus, one can rightfully wonder what roles are played by Adidas sponsees in the development of the Nike affect towards a Chicago Bulls and Derrick Rose fan? Therefore, we offer a new proposition (P2c) regarding the multiple sponsorship and the affective dimensions of co-sponsored entities and those of the ambusher.

P2c: Multiple sponsorship creates interrelations between the affective dimensions of the co-sponsored entities and that of the ambusher.

Propositions: Multiple sponsorship and cognitive, affective and conative reactions

Cognitive reactions are things that a consumer *knows*, or things that they *think*. Sponsorship researchers have examined cognitive reactions that were based on brand-related (i.e. brand equity, brand image or brand association) interactions between sponsor and sponsee. Chanavat et al. (2009) stress that few researchers have studied sponsor–sponsee or ambusher–sponsee fit and that scholars failed to clearly examine the relations between brands in this context. The affective refers to things that a consumer feels and the things that are valued. Affective outcomes of sponsorship activities, such as attitude, liking, preference, psychological attachment or favourable thoughts, have been examined in sponsorship literature. The conative aspect of the mind is the least well understood, but may be the most important. Conation refers to those things you will *actually do* when striving. Only a few researchers have investigated conative reactions of fans to sponsorship.

We propose significant links between the cognitive, affective and conative reactions of the consumer towards co-sponsored entities and a brand within the framework of a multiple sponsorship operation. P3a, P3b and P3c represent the third series of propositions.

In the context of advertising effectiveness, Beerli and Santana (1999) argue that it is necessary to consider the cognitive, affective and conative dimensions. Though not identical, sponsorship is similar to advertising (Meenaghan, 1991). These behavioural reactions allow the effects of sponsorship on an individual to be measured. Sponsorship must have some sort of mental impact before influencing the behaviour of an individual (Poon and Prendergast, 2006).

Advertising persuasion theory: hierarchy of effects model

These propositions are based on the cognitive models of persuasion and information processing, and the hierarchy of effects model (Lavidge and Steiner, 1961). Grouped in pairs, the six advanced steps correspond to the three main dimensions of advertising communication: cognitive dimension (fame and knowledge of the product), affective dimension (assessment, preference and development of an attitude towards the product) and conative dimension (conviction or purchase intent and product purchase). Poon and Prendergast (2006) utilized the hierarchy of effects model to assess sponsorship effectiveness. Pyun and James (2011) suggest that sports are an advertising platform capable of fostering positive attitudes towards advertising. The model proposed by the authors involves antecedents (beliefs), a consequence (attitude towards the advertisement), and attitude regarding sports as a moderator of the association between beliefs about, and attitude towards, advertising through sports.

Little academic research offers a combined analysis of the relations between the cognitive, affective and conative components of sponsorship effects. The known interactions between sponsor and sponsee in a single sponsorship situation (for example, Koo, Quarterman and Flynn, 2006; Madrigal, 2000, 2001), provide a sensible foundation for multiple sponsorship. This knowledge offers an explanation of the potential interdependency between the cognitive, affective and conative dimensions of the individual towards brands within multiple sponsorship (P3a, P3b and P3c). Despite the dearth of research, this study suggests interactions between co-sponsored entities, sponsors and ambushers. Support for our view is provided by Carrillat et al. (2005), who highlight the affective and conative relations between a property and several co-sponsors. Bridgestone is a partner of the Bridgestone Arena, the venue used by NHLs Nashville Predators. In this situation of multiple sponsorship, how does a consumer determine their affect towards Bridgestone? Can the affective reaction of the consumer impact purchase intentions? The idea that multiple sponsorship activates cognitive, affective and conative reactions in the consumer towards the sponsor reflects the cognitive => affective => conative sequence within the hierarchy of effects model.

P3a: Multiple sponsorship activates the cognitive, affective and conative perceptions in this sequence: cognitive => affective => conative.

The specificity of multiple sponsorship leads us to take the multiplicity of involved entities in an operation of multiple sponsorship into account. Adidas was simultaneously a partner of the Fédération Internationale de Football Association (FIFA), the Argentine Football Association, and Lionel Messi within the context of the 2014 FIFA World Cup. Our model incorporates the contribution of these three sponsorships towards the intention to purchase Adidas products. To what extent does each partnership with the federation influence the image of Adidas? What partnership influences the affect developed towards the kit supplier? Does the partnership with the player dominate? Could it be considered sufficient? Given this, we formulate the proposition that multiple sponsorship activates cognitive and affective perceptions towards the sponsee and the affective and conative perceptions towards the sponsor according to the hierarchy of effects model (Lavidge and Steiner, 1961).

P3b: Multiple sponsorship activates the cognitive and affective perceptions of the sponsee and the affective and conative perceptions of the sponsor according to the sequence: cognitive => affective => conative.

Ambush marketing is likely to impact the effectiveness of sponsorship. Nike is simultaneously a partner of Cristiano Ronaldo and the Portuguese Football Federation, which participated in the Adidas-sponsored 2014 FIFA World Cup. In this context, our model would allow us to determine whether a Portuguese consumer is more or less likely to purchase Nike or Adidas products at the end of the event. Furthermore, does the fan's image of the Portuguese team dominate and does it determine their affect towards Nike? Does the consumer's affective reaction favour purchase intent towards Nike?

Consequently, we assert that multiple sponsorship activates the cognitive and affective perceptions of the sponsee and the affective and conative perceptions of the sponsor according to the hierarchy of effects model (Lavidge and Steiner, 1961).

P3c: Multiple sponsorship activates the cognitive and affective perceptions of the sponsee and the affective and conative perceptions of the ambusher in this sequence: cognitive => affective => conative.

Multiple sponsorship: a conceptual model

The ten propositions can be presented in a conceptual model (see Figure 9.1). Different entities were chosen to illustrate the model: sporting event (sponsee 1), sports team (sponsee 2), sponsor and ambusher.

Three psychological constructs have been chosen in the conceptual model of this study (cognitive => brand image; affective => brand attachment; conative => purchase intention). It should be noted that, overall, several other marketing constructs can be integrated in the model (for example, attitude towards the team, brand familiarity, fan loyalty, brand love or team identification). For example, fan loyalty is the strength of the relationship between a sports consumer's attitude and repeat patronage (Bee and Kahle, 2006). In all instances, to simplify the comprehension of the multiple sponsorship model, only three constructs have been chosen for our research.

Table 9.1 aims to summarize and clarify the presentation of the theoretical frameworks of the research proposals.

Managerial implications

Our model encourages the consideration of the plural nature of sponsorship. The model provides a more authentic real-world understanding of multiple sponsorship and its impact on consumer perceptions and behaviours.

This model demands a reconsideration of how sponsorship effectiveness is measured in operations. There are implications for many sponsorship stakeholders: sponsors, ambusher, clubs, federations, athletes, rights holders, marketing agencies. The model can foresee strategic management and strategic marketing implications. For example, sports organizations with a strong brand image can leverage their relationship with existing sponsors to extract greater value from new sponsor. The benefit for the new sponsor is that they derive value, not just from their relationship with the sponsee, but also from the other sponsors.

Table 9.1 Recap of the theories relating to the research perspectives

Models / Theories	Relevance in the framework of research perspectives	Reactions of the relevant consumer	Relevant propositions
Theories in advertising persuasion. Hierarchy of effects model by Lavidge and Steiner (1961).	Allows observation of the effects related to multiple sponsorship activities on the consumer's reactions.	Cognitive, affective and conative.	P3a, P3b and P3c
Activation and spreading theory.	Contributes to explaining the reinforcement or creation of the brand image of entities involved in a situation of multiple sponsorship.	Cognitive.	P1a, P1b, P1c and P1d
Transfer and endorsement theories.	Contributes to explaining the links between brand components and the affective dimensions of involved entities in a situation of multiple sponsorship.	Cognitive and affective.	P1a, P1b, P1d, P2a, P2b and P2c

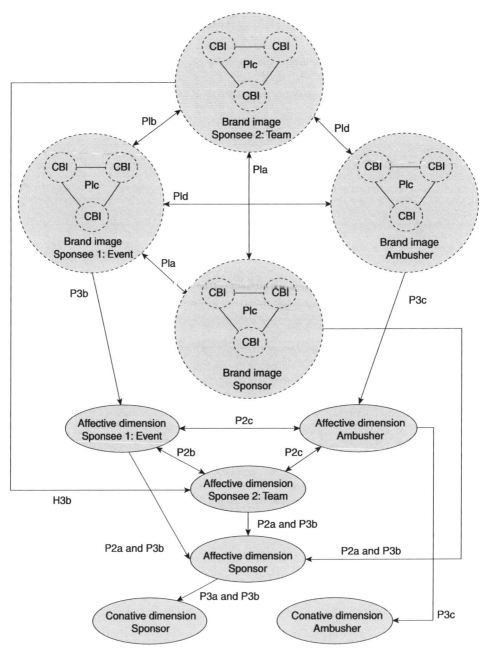

Figure 9.1 A conceptual model of multiple sponsorship

Note: The acronym "CBI" means "component of brand image". Please note that in order to facilitate the reading of this model, the direct links between all the components of brand image studied do not appear. Theoretically, multiple relations are possible. In addition, two components of brand image can represent all cognitive dimensions associated with each brand studied.

Furthermore, this new type of analysis may favour the measurement and comparison of potential effects between sponsors and ambushers. In the case of companies, it would be a tool that would contribute to the measurement of the performance of their sponsorship policies and to the protection of their rights against ambushers. For the sake of performance, genuine reflection on the choice of sports entities to sponsor is necessary. Rights sellers would need to propose a "sports entities package" and a measurement protocol that would determine the effectiveness of multiple sponsorship activities. Furthermore, a development (negative or positive) of the perceived affect by consumers towards the sponsored entity might, for instance, be integrated into the sponsorship contract.

Limitations, perspectives and conclusion

This conceptual model is grounded in a real-world phenomenon: a sponsorship does not exist in isolation, sponsorship co-exists with other sponsorships. Almost all sponsees are simultaneously associated with multiple brands. An organization will almost certainly have sponsorship with several properties. All of these occur in the context of ambush marketing. It is not possible to understand sponsorship effectiveness without recognizing the multiplicity of sponsorship contracts and the myriad of brands associated with a sporting event. Sponsorship is a complex phenomenon with numerous interactions. Our model highlights the cognitive paradigm and the importance of the mental processes underpinning consumer's behaviour. This work provides a foundation for better understanding of sponsorship effects.

Two main limits to this work can be highlighted. First, if the proposed model integrates numerous constructions, others could have been included. Second, the model is deductive and was not tested empirically. The proposed model requires structural equation modelling to simultaneously test the potential relations. Bacharach (1989: 508) emphasized,

> Although path and structural equation (for example, LISREL) models provide a systematic format for expressing the assumed relationships among variables and estimating the strength of these relationships, the actual ordering of the variables and the nature of their relationship (for example, causal, simultaneous) can only take place on the assumptive level.

So whilst useful, SEM will not illuminate the entire story.

In any case, our understanding of dyadic sponsor–sponsee relationships is well-developed. Multiple sponsorship provides an opportunity for understanding sponsorship that is otherwise unattainable. We expect this innovative model to create a better understanding of multiple sponsorship and be used as a work basis for new research. Beyond the theoretical developments, entities involved in sponsorship activities will appreciate this work and the perspectives it brings to their practice.

Note

1. The measure of affective reactions affect the second and third series of propositions. Nevertheless, in order to facilitate the understanding of the reader, it was necessary to present the double transfer phenomenon from the beginning of this chapter.

References

Aaker, D. A. (1991). *Managing brand equity: Capitalizing on the value of a brand name*, New York: The Free Press.

Anderson, J. R. (1983) *The architecture of cognition*, Cambridge: Harvard Press.

Bacharach, S. B. (1989). Organizational theories: Some criteria for evaluation, *The Academy of Management Review*, 14(4), pp. 496–515.

Bauer, H. H., Sauer, N. E. and Schmitt, P. (2005). Customer-based brand equity in the team sport industry, *European Journal of Marketing*, 39(5/6), pp. 496–513.

Bee, C. C. and Kahle, L. R. (2006). Relationship marketing in sports: A functional approach. *Sport Marketing Quarterly*, 15, pp. 102–110.

Beerli, A. and Santana, M. D. J. (1999). Design and validation of an instrument for measuring advertising effectiveness in the printed media, *Journal of Current Issues and Research in Advertising*, 21(2), pp. 11–30.

Carrillat, F. A., Lafferty, B. A. and Harris, E. G. (2005). Investigating sponsorship effectiveness: Do less familiar brands have an advantage over more familiar brands in single and multiple sponsorship arrangements, *Brand Management*, 13(1), pp. 50–64.

Chanavat, N. and Bodet, G. (2009). Sport branding strategy and internationalization: A French perception of the "Big Four" brands, *Qualitative Market Research: An International Journal*, 12(4), pp. 460–481.

Chanavat, N. and Desbordes, M. (2014). Towards the regulation and restriction of ambush marketing? The case of the first truly social and digital mega sport event: Olympic Games London 2012, *International Journal of Sport Marketing and Sponsorship*, 15(3), pp. 79–88.

Chanavat, N., Desbordes, M. and Ferrand, A. (2013). Faut-il avoir peur de l'ambush marketing? *Jurisport*, 128, pp. 41–45.

Chanavat, N., Martinent, G. and Ferrand, A. (2009). Sponsor and sponsee interactions: Effects on consumers' perceptions of brand image, brand attachment and purchasing intention, *Journal of Sport Management*, 23(5), pp. 644–670.

Chien, P. M., Cornwell, T. B. and Pappu, R. (2011). Sponsorship portfolio as brand image creation strategy, *Journal of Business Research*, 64, pp. 142–149.

Chien, P. M., Cornwell, T. B. and Pappu, R. (2012). Rejoinder to commentary on Chien, Cornwell, and Pappu (2010): Advancing research on sponsorship portfolio effects, *Journal of Business Research*, 65(1), pp. 117–121.

Chien, P. M., Cornwell, T. B. and Stokes, R. (2005). A theoretical framework for analysis of image transfer in multiple sponsorships, *Proceedings of the 2005 ANZMAC Conference*, Broadening the Boundaries, The University of Western Australia, Perth, Western Australia.

Collins, A. M. and Loftus E. F. (1975). A spreading activation theory of semantic processing, *Psychological Review*, 82(6), pp. 407–428.

Cornwell, T. B. (2008). State of the art and science in sponsorship: Linked marketing, *Journal of Advertising*, 37(3), pp. 41–55.

Cornwell, T. B., Weeks C. S. and Roy, D. P. (2005). Sponsorship-linked marketing: opening the black box, *Journal of Advertising*, 34(2), pp. 21–42.

Desbordes, M. and Richelieu, A. (2012). *Global sport marketing*, Abingdon: Routledge.

Ferrand, A. and Torrigiani, L. (2005). *Marketing of Olympic sport organisations*, Champaign: Human Kinetics.

Ganassali, S. (2009). L'analyse des dimensions affective et symbolique du transfert d'image en parrainage: Louis Vuitton et la Coupe de l'America, Actes du 25ᵉ Congrès International de l'AFM, Association Française de Marketing, London.

Gladden, J. M. and Milne, G. R. (1999). Examining the importance of brand equity in professional sport, *Sport Marketing Quarterly*, 8(1), pp. 21–29.

Groza, M., Cobbs, J. and Schaefers, T. (2012). Managing a sponsored brand: The importance of sponsorship portfolio congruence, *International Journal of Advertising*, 31(1), pp. 63–84.

Grunert, K. G. (1996). Automatic and strategic processes in advertising effects, *Journal of Marketing*, 60, October, 88–101.

Gwinner, K. P. (1997). A model of image creation and image transfer in event sponsorship. *International Marketing Review*, 14(1), pp. 145–158.

Gwinner, K. P. and Eaton, J. (1999). Building brand image through event sponsorship: the role of image transfer, *Journal of Advertising*, 28(4), pp. 47–57.

Hansen, F., Halling, J. and Christensen, L. B. (2006). Choosing among alternative parties to be sponsored for supporting brand strategies, based upon emotional responses, *Journal of Consumer Behaviour*, 5(6), pp. 504–517.

Keller, K. L. (1993). Conceptualizing, measuring, and managing customer-based brand equity, *Journal of Marketing,* 57, pp. 1–22.

Keller, K. L. (2003). Brand synthesis: The multidimensionality of brand knowledge. *Journal of Consumer Research*, 29(4), 595–600.

Kim, K. Stout, P. A. and Cheong, Y. (2012). The image management function of sponsorship: A general theoretical framework, *International Journal of Advertising*, 31(1), pp. 85–111.

Koo, G. Y., Quarterman, J. and Flynn, L. (2006). Effect of perceived sport event and sponsor image fit on consumers' cognition, affect, and behavioral intentions, *Sport Marketing Quarterly*, 15, pp. 80–90.

Lavidge, R. J. and Steiner G. A. (1961). A model for predictive measurements of advertising effectiveness, *Journal of Marketing*, 25(6), pp. 59–62.

Lee, H.-S. and Cho, C.-H. (2009). The matching effect of brand and sporting event personality: Sponsorship implications, *Journal of Sport Management*, 23, pp. 41–64.

Madrigal, R. (2000). The influence of social alliances with sports teams on intentions to purchase corporate sponsors' products, *Journal of Advertising,* 29, pp. 13–24.

Madrigal, R. (2001). Social identity effects in a belief-attitude-intentions hierarchy: Implications for corporate sponsorship, *Psychology and Marketing,* 18, pp. 145–165.

Mazodier, M., Quester, P. and Chandon, J.-L. (2011). Unmasking the ambushers: Conceptual framework and empirical evidence, *European Journal of Marketing*, 46(1/2), pp. 192–214.

McCracken, G. (1989). Who is the celebrity endorser? Cultural foundations of the endorsement process, *Journal of Consumer Research,* 16(3), pp. 310–321.

Meenaghan, T. (1991). The role of sponsorship in the marketing communications mix, *International Journal of Advertising*, 10, pp. 35–48.

Meenaghan, T. (1994). Point of view: Ambush marketing: immoral or imaginative practice? *Journal of Advertising Research*, 34(5), pp. 77–88.

Meenaghan, T. (1998). Ambush marketing: Corporate strategy and consumers' reactions. *Psychology and Marketing*, 15(4), 305–322.

Nanopoulos, P. (2008) Le co-parrainage: définition et hypothèses de recherche. Actes des 3èmes Journées Internationales sur la Communication Marketing Hors Media, Nancy, France, 27–28 mars 2008, http://etudiant.icn-groupe.fr/com/recherche/colloque/ Nanopoulos.pdf (accessed 1 May 2015).

Pyun, D. Y. and James, J. D. (2011). Attitude toward advertising through sport: A theoretical framework. *Sport Management Review*, 14, pp. 33–41.

Poon, D. T. Y. and Prendergast, G. (2006). A new framework for evaluating sponsorship opportunities, *International Journal of Advertising,* 25(4), pp. 471–488.

Richelieu, A. and Pons, F. (2006). Toronto Maple Leafs vs Football Club Barcelona: How two legendary sport teams built their brand equity, *International Journal of Sports Marketing & Sponsorship,* May, pp. 231–250.

Richelieu, A. and Pons, F. (2009). If brand equity matters, where is the brand strategy? A look at the National Hockey League (NHL), *International Journal of Sports Marketing and Management*, 5(1), pp. 34–45.

Ruth, J. A. and Simonin, B. L. (2003). Brought to you by brand A and brand B, *Journal of Advertising*, 32(3), pp. 19–30.

Ruth, J. A. and Simonin, B. L. (2006). The power of numbers: Investigating the impact of event roster size in consumer response to sponsorship, *Journal of Advertising,* 35(4), pp. 7–20.

Scassa, T. (2011). Ambush Marketing and the right of association: Clamping down on references to that big event with all the athletes in a couple of years, *Journal of Sport Management*, 25(4), pp. 354–370.

Schultz, S. E., Kleine, R. E. and Kernan, J. B. (1989). These are a few of my favorite things: Toward an explication of attachment as a consumer behavior construct. *Advances in Consumer Research. Association for Consumer Research (U.S.)*, 16, pp. 359–366.

Séguin, B. and Ellis, D. (2012). Ambush marketing. In Robinson, L., Chelladurai, P., Bodet, G. and Downward, P. (Eds), *Handbook of Sport Management*, Abingdon: Routledge.

Spears, N. and Singh, S. N. (2004). Measuring attitude toward the brand and purchase intentions, *Journal of Current Issues and Research Advertising*, 26, pp. 53–66.

Speed, R. and Thompson, P. (2000). Determinants of sports sponsorship response, *Journal of the Academy of Marketing Science*, 28(2), pp. 227–238.

Suckow, C. (2009). Literature review on brand equity in professional team sport: a German perspective on ice hockey, *International Journal of Sport Management and Marketing*, 5(1/2), pp. 211–225.

Sutton, R. I. and Staw, B. M. (1995) What theory is not, *Administrative Science Quarterly*, 40(3), pp. 371–384.

Tribou, G. and Augé, B. (2009) *Management du sport: Marketing et gestion des clubs sportifs* (3ème édition), Paris: Dunod.

Walliser, B. (2003) An international review of sponsorship research: Extension and update, *International Journal of Advertising*, 22(1), pp. 5–40.

Walliser, B. (2006) *Le parrainage : Sponsoring et Mécénat*, Paris: Dunod.

Wyer, R. S. and Strull, T. K. (1989) Person memory and judgment, *Psychological Review*, 96(1), pp. 58–83.

10

CELEBRITY ATHLETE ENDORSERS

A critical review

Ted B. Peetz and Nancy Lough

Part 1

Arnold Palmer is regarded as one of the greatest golfers of all-time. His significance to the game of golf is unquestioned, however, it can be argued his biggest impact occurred off the course. Although endorsements have been a marketing strategy used for centuries, Palmer helped to usher in a new era of the celebrity athlete endorser. His ascent to stardom in the 1950s aligned with the beginning of sport's television age. Palmer's ability, style and good looks made him the perfect spokesman for companies seeking to benefit from his popularity. The strategy he utilized to parlay his athletic accomplishments with advertising success has become the template for today's celebrity athlete endorser. McCracken (1989) defined a celebrity endorser as "an individual who enjoys public recognition and who uses this recognition on behalf of a consumer good by appearing with it in an advertisement" (p. 30). Companies have utilized celebrity athletes like Arnold Palmer because it is believed that they can attract and hold consumers' attention (Charbonneau and Garland, 2005), enhance believability of the advertisements (Kamins et al., 1989), differentiate product images (Friedman and Friedman, 1979) and increase brand loyalty (Bush, Martin and Bush, 2004). An example of a company who blatantly acknowledges the impact a celebrity athlete endorser like Arnold Palmer can have on their brand, is Ketel One Vodka who ran an advertisement stating: "Dear Ketel One Drinker, We know you're not influenced by what other people drink, however, we thought you might like to know Arnold Palmer drinks Ketel One".

Endorsements and sponsorships can appear synonymous at first glance. Endorsements have been labeled as "personality sponsorships" and sports marketers have agreed that endorsements fall within the sponsorship category. Both concepts approach their marketing outcomes in slightly different ways. A sponsorship is usually considered as a broader marketing tactic, which seeks to gain exposure through the commercial potential of a specific event or property. Sponsors typically pursue similar outcomes in using this approach as they would when implementing a celebrity athlete endorsement, such as supporting overall organizational objectives, marketing goals and promotional strategies. A sponsorship allows the sponsor the opportunity to capitalize on the number of spectators of a particular event and to associate themselves with the positive brand attributes the event or property holds. An endorser's effectiveness, on the other hand, comes from their ability to reach target markets in a more direct manner. The culturally relevant images, symbols and values celebrity athletes embody help to extend and strengthen the connection with consumers that many sponsorship attempts cannot accomplish. The increased use of new technologies for delivering marketing messages has also increased ways to utilize celebrity athlete endorsers and make more enduring connections with consumers. Social media, for example, can give the appearance of a more authentic testimony. Support and promotion from celebrity athletes' personal Twitter accounts has become so muddled it can obscure the lines between a paid endorsement and a friendly recommendation. The Advertising Standards Authority (UK) and the Federal Trade Commission (USA) have been investigating this new trend in endorsements and outline that the hashtag #ad should follow any endorsement claim made on a personal Twitter account (Varney, 2013). The fact that a hashtag needs to be applied to a celebrity athlete's paid marketing messages to distinguish it from social media chatter is testament to the power an endorsement by a celebrity athlete can provide a product or service.

The potential reach of sponsorships through associations with events and companies is impressive and "personality sponsorships" often help to solidify this connection with consumers. As Advertising Age (2001) explained, "Other creative tactics and techniques change with the fashion of the day but the testimonial is such a workhorse selling tool that it never goes out of style" (p. 10). Endorsements traditionally have featured consumers due to their similarity to target audiences (Ohanian, 1990). Also known as typical person testimonials, these persuasive messages involve a person unfamiliar to the audience who endorses a product in an advertisement. Research suggests that using a "typical person" acts as a minor cue to influence the persuasiveness of an advertising message (Petty, Cacioppo and Schumann, 1983). In contrast to the average consumer testimonial, the use of a celebrity acts as a more direct cue relating to a number of factors such as trustworthiness or expertise. For example, when athletes are used to promote a sports product they use in competition, consumers are likely to acknowledge that they have expert knowledge of the product based on their experiences. McCracken (1989) noted that a testimonial can be implemented using four endorsement styles. The most straightforward of these styles is the explicit mode and features the endorser declaring, "I endorse this product". The implicit mode is when an endorser states "I use this product", while the imperative mode has the endorser explain, "You should use this product". The final endorsement style is the co-present mode where a celebrity only appears with the product. The co-present mode is often a favorite method of using celebrity athlete endorsers because it allows a sponsor to benefit from the meanings associated with the athlete and allows the consumer to align those meanings with their self-images. Effective pairings are often due to an easy to understand connection between endorser and product where the meanings associated with the endorser are easily conveyed and valued.

Investing in endorsements

Companies with confidence that celebrity athlete endorsers are an effective way to reach their target audiences are willing to pay large sums to connect with high-profile star athletes. The amount of money spent on athlete endorsers is truly staggering. Even though Arnold Palmer retired from golf years ago, he continues to make large sums of money through endorsement deals. According to *Forbes* magazine, Palmer made $1.8 million during his professional golf career, yet he earned an estimated $40 million off the course in 2013 alone (Badenhausen, 2014a). The Top 10 highest paid currently active celebrity athlete endorsers earned more than $350 million in endorsement royalties in 2013 (Badenhausen, 2014b). These impressive numbers are a far cry from the $75 reportedly paid in 1905 to Honus

Wagner to endorse Louisville Slugger Baseball Bats (Mullin, Hardy and Sutton, 2014). A select number of today's athletes enjoy significant leverage in their endorsement contracts, adding testimony to the value companies place on these figures to promote their products. Although paying an athlete to endorse a brand is still common, other forms of compensation have been devised to entice athletes to hawk their products. For example, basketball player, Kevin Durant, re-signed with athletic apparel provider, Nike, for an estimated $265 million over ten years, but that number is flexible and could reach $300 million with royalties he receives from shoe sales (Rovell and Stein, 2014). Another basketball star, Lebron James profited an estimated $30 million from the stock options he earned by endorsing the headphone company Beats by Dre when the company was purchased by Apple (Smith, 2014). Company expenses often reflect the significance they place on using a celebrity athlete endorser in their marketing messages. Nike, for instance, typically spends about 10% of its revenues on "demand creation", which is a term they use to describe the advertising expenses and costs associated with endorsement deals (Stock, 2014).

When an athlete attains celebrity status the result can be a high level of importance with consumers that companies hope to capitalize on. Although the cost of using this marketing strategy has risen exponentially over the years the goals of using celebrity athletes have remained the same: grab the consumer's attention, create positive associations with the product or service, and positively impact revenue. A recent study has validated the use of celebrity athlete endorsers by showing a firm's decision to use this strategy has a positive pay-off on product sales in an absolute sense and relative to the firm's competitors. Elberse and Verleun's (2012) research showed that signing a high-profile athlete to endorse a brand "on average generates a 4% increase in sales, which corresponds with around $10 million in

Figure 10.1 Early example of a co-present mode endorsement

additional sales annually and nearly a .25% increase in stock returns" (p. 163). Marketing literature has supported that a well-executed endorsement deal with a successful athlete can substantially impact how a company is perceived as well as their bottom line.

Risks associated with celebrity athlete endorsers

The benefits of using a celebrity athlete endorser are well documented, however, a number of risks exist when using this marketing tactic. No matter how perfect a crafted image may be, there is always the possibility of a negative event, association or comment greatly affecting the way the athlete and their endorsement are perceived. Some studies have shown that unflattering conduct by an endorser can cause consumers to hold lower opinions of the athlete and that those opinions will become associated with the products they endorse. What makes this connection even more significant is that consumers typically pay more attention to negative information than to positive publicity linked to the endorser.

Scandals involving infidelity, substance abuse, violence, and other detrimental activities have caused marketers to evaluate the risk–reward ratio associated with this strategy. National Football League Hall of Famer, O.J. Simpson, is a cautionary tale of a once bankable athlete whose persona instantly changed from American sports hero to accused double murderer. The fear some companies have in using celebrity athlete endorsers is understandable given the seemingly constant reports of athletes being involved with undesirable events. One strategy used to combat the negative publicity associated with embarrassing or upsetting behavior is using deceased celebrities or animated characters who still offer a wealth of symbolism and meaning to a company, yet pose no threat of doing something that could tarnish a brand's image. Another common strategy for companies is to purchase insurance policies to lessen the harmful effects of a damaging incident.

The substantial amount of money an athlete can make by lending their endorsement to a brand has caused many celebrities to tie their image to multiple products. Consumers are skeptical of celebrities who are paid to deliver support for a brand or product. This skepticism is heightened when a celebrity athlete endorses more than one product. Overexposure as an endorser can weaken the distinctiveness, likability and credibility of an athlete and can adversely affect the brands they endorse.

It is not uncommon for athletes to suffer injuries that can greatly impact their exposure and performance. Olympian Liu Xiang became a national hero and cultural icon after winning China's first gold medal in men's track and field in 2004, however, his effectiveness as an endorser was limited due to untimely injuries during the 2008 and 2012 Olympics. If companies are using athletes to promote distinct brand attributes to separate them from the competition, having an athlete who is frequently injured or unreliable does not send a strong message.

There is a large range of negative events that can impact the relationship between endorser, brand and consumer. Whether it is an insensitive comment made over social media or breaking the law, no company using this strategy is immune to the negative actions of endorsers. Athletic apparel manufacturer, Nike, has experienced the impact of being associated with controversy surrounding some of their athletes. During one week in September 2014, Nike had to cancel endorsement deals with three of their athletes: sprinter Oscar Pistorius (culpable homicide), and National Football League running backs Ray Rice (domestic violence) and Adrian Peterson (child abuse). A few marketers may push the mantra, "any publicity is good publicity", however, many would warn about placing short-term economic gains before intangible impacts and sustaining a strong brand image. Although the risks of using celebrity athletes as endorsers are ever present, their popularity has continued to remain near the forefront of advertising campaigns.

Companies have embraced using athletes as endorsers because few professions are as highly revered as professional athletics. The cultural shift from being an athlete to being a celebrity athlete has caused many companies to utilize these figures in endorsements of a wide-range of products. The perceived benefits of this marketing strategy have led to endorsements now being one of the most popular forms of retail advertising. Researchers have studied this phenomenon to gain a better understanding of what makes an effective endorser. Brooks and Harris (1998) noted,

> the common fault with all these efforts is that athlete endorsement is often discussed without any apparent theoretical understanding of the phenomenon. The papers frequently fall victim to a significant element of hype and contain little, if any, critical analysis of what the endorsement process is all about (p. 35).

A major issue with the analysis of this subject is that there is no agreement as to the dimensions or factors that make-up endorser effectiveness. Although the number and types of factors associated with this construct are still debated, a number of models have been developed that have allowed further analysis and clarification of endorser effectiveness. It should be noted that analyzing endorser effectiveness is a difficult task and the factors associated with endorser effectiveness are often not viewed the same way by all consumers. The following section will outline the development of the most commonly used models and critically examine how they have shaped our understanding of celebrity endorser effectiveness.

Part 2

Source models

In an exploratory study of this topic, Roy (2006) stated, "A review of literature suggests that there are four basic models that deal with the issue of celebrity endorsements" (p. 140). Those four models include the source credibility model (Hovland, Janis and Kelley, 1953; Hovland and Weiss, 1951; McGuire, 1968) the source attractiveness model (McGuire, 1985), the match-up hypothesis (Mowen, Brown and Schulman, 1979), and the transfer of meaning process (McCracken, 1989). Each of these models offers a framework to examine the effectiveness of celebrity athlete endorsers. The models are also highly applicable to sports due to a celebrity athlete's ability to impact consumer attitudes. A number of factors related to endorsers have been tested to gauge their impact on the advertising message. As the study of this concept has gained more attention, these models have provided the theoretical basis for the selection of factors included in examinations. By no means do these models encapsulate all the factors and situations that can arise in a consumer's evaluation of an endorser's marketing communication, but they provide a better understanding of how this phenomenon has been analyzed over the past 60 years.

Source credibility model

The source credibility model (Hovland et al., 1953) is recognized as being the first widely accepted model to identify the factors impacting the effectiveness of an endorser. Source credibility has been defined as "the believability of the endorser, spokesperson or individual in an advertisement" (Clow et al., 2011 p. 25). The model has its origins in social research and asserts that a credible source will elicit positive responses from its intended audience. The model contends that expertise and trustworthiness are the most vital factors associated with endorser credibility. These two factors have become commonplace in endorser research due to their presumed impact on consumer behavior. Establishing credibility of a source is a critical element in gaining acceptance from the message recipient. If a consumer finds an endorser credible, "they may forgo the effortful task of scrutinizing the message and, instead, unthinkingly accept the conclusion as valid" (Priester and Petty, 2003 p. 409).

Research has shown that a consumer's favorable assessment of a source's expertise will positively influence their effectiveness (Ohanian, 1990). Expertise refers to "the knowledge, experience or skills possessed by the endorser" (Erdogan, 1999 p. 298). The status of celebrity athlete endorsers in society allows them to provide expert opinions on a number of products, but especially on products they use during competition. For example, few would argue the expertise of Olympic gold medal sprinter, Usain Bolt, when it comes to his knowledge and experience with running shoes. Messages coming from an expert endorser are accepted with greater agreement than the same message from a non-expert. The expertise factor is often highlighted in advertisements of new products or products that require more than a surface level understanding because believability of the message is increased when a celebrity holds an expert position in the mind of consumers (Kamins et al., 1989). Similar to the other factor within the model, trustworthiness, the *perception* of expertise among the target audience is ultimately what determines the effectiveness of this factor (Hovland et. al., 1953; Ohanian, 1991). These connections also help to create positive word of mouth associations. It is not surprising that this factor has been linked with the intention to purchase products (Ohanian, 1991). Therefore, a company utilizing this marketing strategy would be wise to establish endorser expertise in their promotions.

The other factor included in the source credibility model is trustworthiness. When discussing endorsements it is intuitive that trustworthiness would be a factor that is included. Ohanian (1990) explained, "the trust paradigm in communication is the listener's degree of confidence in, and the level of acceptance of, the speaker and message" (p. 41). If an endorser is viewed as being untrustworthy, it may not matter what product or brand attributes they are describing because consumers will not have confidence in the message. Trustworthiness is a powerful factor in marketing messages and the perceived trustworthiness of the source has been shown to create a greater attitude change than perceived expertise. American professional cyclist, Lance Armstrong, is an example of an endorser who greatly changed the level of trust he had obtained with the public when he admitted to taking performance enhancing drugs during his career. His confession created a mass withdrawal from sponsors who wanted to distance themselves from the tarnished athlete. In addition, a group of consumers sued Armstrong for false advertising for his endorsements of FRS energy products that he claimed were his "secret weapon" (Schrotenboer, 2014). Although Armstrong successfully defended the lawsuit, legal action is definitely a strong statement as to the public's perception of the disgraced cyclist. According to research, consumers who distrust an athlete like Armstrong would be more likely to critically examine advertising messages that came from him, while an athlete with a perceived high level of trustworthiness would be less likely to have their marketing communications scrutinized.

In Ohanian's (1990) seminal work on celebrity endorsers, she included attractiveness in the source credibility model as a factor influencing the persuasiveness of an endorser's marketing communication. The inclusion of this factor was based on theoretical and empirical observations. You only need to turn on the television or browse through a magazine to

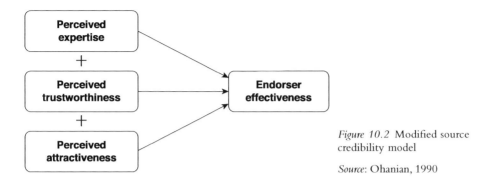

Figure 10.2 Modified source credibility model

Source: Ohanian, 1990

understand the importance marketers place on the physical attractiveness of an endorser. Attractive endorsers consistently receive higher evaluations of likability compared to spokespersons who are unattractive (Ohanian, 1990). When basing marketing decisions on the attractiveness of an endorser, advertisers hope to gain from the dual effects of physical traits and an athlete's celebrity status. Aligned with the source credibility model, researchers have found that celebrity athlete endorsers who were viewed as an expert were also viewed as being significantly more attractive and liked than someone who was viewed as a non-expert (Buhr, Simpson and Pryor, 1987). One celebrity athlete endorser who garners significant attention due to his attractiveness is footballer, David Beckham. His skillfulness on the pitch has often been overshadowed by his good looks. As Cashmore and Parker (2003) stated, there is more than one David Beckham, he is a fashion icon, sports star and trend setter. Beckham's magnetism has allowed him to continue to grow his brand, attaching himself to products ranging from air travel to chocolate, even though his playing days are over.

It is important to note that the physical appearance of an endorser is not the only way a consumer evaluates attractiveness. Like all factors associated with the source models, attractiveness has been operationalized in many ways. For example, images of a strong, powerful female athlete can be a source of inspiration and empowerment for women. The exposure can also aid in helping build the attractiveness of a sports league. When the Women's National Basketball Association (WNBA) was first established, one of its star players, Lisa Leslie, helped to create positive associations with the league through many traits that fans found attractive. Although she had physical beauty she also had power, she was the first women to dunk in a professional game, and had a fun personality. Val Ackerman, former President of the WNBA, noted, "It's vital to us to have our star players part of popular culture, part of television shows, and to be seen as not just part of the sports landscape but part of the cultural landscape" (Mullin, 2003, para. 12). Lisa Leslie was able to convey the image and message the WNBA wanted to send to the public. The associations people connected with Lisa Leslie made her a sought-after endorser by a long list of companies. Her perceived attractiveness, trustworthiness and expertise provides supporting evidence of why the source credibility model is still widely accepted, even 60 years after it was first conceived.

Source attractiveness model

It took more than 30 years before another endorsement model was introduced that received a similar level of acceptance in the evaluation of endorser effectiveness as the source credibility model. The source attractiveness model came as a result of a number of attempts to further analyze endorser communication and both models have become an essential part of our understanding of the endorsement process (McCracken, 1989). As Brooks and Harris (1998) noted, "both the source attractiveness and source credibility models have been validated to some degree in the literature, and each provides an intuitively appealing reason why an athlete should be an effective endorser" (p. 41). This particular model identifies familiarity, similarity and likeability as dimensions of attractiveness. The concept of attractiveness is more than physical appearance. Attractiveness as it applies to this model can be someone's affinity for an endorser's personality, intellectual skills, lifestyle or other appealing traits (Erdogan, 1999). Most people would naturally conclude that if an endorser is viewed as likeable, familiar and similar to the intended audience, the greater the likelihood their message would be accepted.

Familiarity is described as "the knowledge of a source through exposure" (Erdogan, 1999, p. 299). With the increase of media outlets, especially those devoted to sports coverage, athletes have garnered more exposure than ever before. Athletes who attain this level of familiarity with the general public are often viewed as stars. It seems reasonable that a company who is utilizing the endorsement strategy would want someone who is recognizable with the target market. A celebrity athlete endorser who is familiar to an audience is said to be have the ability to break through the media clutter and hold viewers' attention. Athletes have benefited greatly from the exposure they receive in the media. For example, the continued growth in women's sports has strengthened the reach for female athletes due to the increased coverage they receive in the media. Research has shown that females prefer to purchase sporting goods endorsed by their favorite female athletes and are supportive of female sports (Bush et al., 2004). A tennis superstar like Serena Williams, for instance, should be able to elicit greater attention and consumer action when endorsing a product compared to an unfamiliar source promoting the same item. As long as sports remain a popular viewing option, the familiarity of athletes should make them appealing to companies looking to use a spokesperson to sell their products.

The factors included in the source attractiveness and source credibility models are not independent of each other. An example of this includes whether or not a person views an endorser as being similar. Similarity is defined as the perceived resemblance a respondent feels exists between themselves and the source (Erdogan, 1999). Researchers have theorized that people trust individuals who are similar to them. Patzer (1985) posed the "likes attract" hypothesis, which stated that consumers respond positively to endorsers who are similar. Interestingly, the author suggested using above-average-looking endorsers because people usually inflate their own attractiveness. Cialdini (2007) expanded on the idea by explaining this notion holds true if the similarity includes areas such as opinions, personality traits or lifestyle. Burgoon (1976) noted "if similarity breeds attraction, and if both influence credibility, people should prefer as the ideal source someone similar to themselves" (p. 201). The traits associated with the concept of similarity can also be explained as either in-group or out-group characteristics. Brewer (1979) explained that the in-group members tend to hold other in-group members in higher regard compared to out-group members. Sports fandom offers plenty of opportunities for social interaction and comparison between fan bases. This interaction allows people to navigate through in-groups and out-groups. If a celebrity endorser is someone who is viewed as part of the in-group of the targeted audience, the source attractiveness model asserts that it will be more effective than using someone who is viewed as an out group member.

Likeability is the last factor included in the source attractiveness model and is a construct that can include physical and behavioral characteristics (McCracken, 1989). This factor falls within the concept of endorser attractiveness, which is a basic component of source

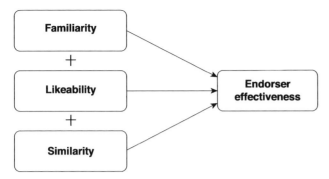

Figure 10.3 Source attractiveness model

Source: McGuire, 1985

effectiveness (McGuire, 1968). Likeability can be influenced by the number of products a celebrity athlete endorses. A study by Tripp, Jenson and Carlson (1994) found that as the number of products a celebrity endorsed grew, their credibility and likability dropped. However, if a celebrity is viewed as an expert in a product category they are more liked. Reinhard and Messner (2009) conducted a study that found the greater the consumer's cognitive motivation to process a persuasive message, the less important were peripheral cues such as an endorser's likability. However, the tendency to consider endorser likability as a factor in evaluating the persuasiveness of a message increased when the consumer's cognitive motivation was low. This finding suggests that likability can be an effective aspect of a product's advertising, especially if the product being endorsed requires little thought during the buying process. For example, the cereal brand, Wheaties, first started using athletes on their product packaging in the 1950s but they were very particular with who graced the box. It was important to the Wheaties brand that the athlete was viewed as exceptionally likeable to the point of being a role model. Two-time gold medalist vaulting legend, Bob Richards, was the brand's first spokesman ("The Box", 2014). He was strong, likeable, and an advocate for physical fitness. His likeability allowed for the message to persuade with ease: Wheaties is the "Breakfast of Champions".

Limitations with the source models

A plethora of studies have been designed and conducted over the last 60 years, which analyzed factors deemed relevant in the effectiveness of celebrity athlete endorsers. Although the source credibility and source attractiveness models have provided some clarification and theoretical structure to the discussion, there continues to be a lack of consistency as to the number and types of factors influencing source effectiveness (Ohanian, 1990). McCracken (1989) noted that these models do not capture all aspects concerning the endorsement process. The author goes on to state that the models fail to explain endorsement's most fundamental features. Plenty of companies have encountered situations where endorsers have not had the effect on consumers they had intended. Although the source models may help to address how an athlete is viewed, they fail to examine why they are viewed that way. "For the model's purposes, as long as the credibility and attractiveness conditions are satisfied, *any* celebrity should serve as a persuasive source for *any* advertising message" (McCracken, 1989, p. 311). The source models therefore have a singular focus on the endorser without addressing the product being endorsed. Another criticism of the source models is that they only make claims regarding an endorser's credibility and attractiveness without addressing their role as a message medium. The source models may explain that one athlete is perhaps more likable or attractive than another athlete but they fail to address how they "differ from a symbolic or communications point of view" (McCracken, 1989, p. 312). Ultimately, critiques of the source models admit that certain characteristics of a source are important, but how those factors affect the meaning associated with the product is vital in understanding the effectiveness of an endorser.

Match-up hypothesis

The match-up hypothesis (Mowen et al., 1979) is a concept that was created to further examine the effectiveness of an endorser and one of the first attempts to take into account the significance of the product in the endorsement process. The match-up hypothesis explores the appropriateness of fit between the endorser, the target market and the product. One criticism of the match-up hypothesis is that there are no established rules to assess whether or not a good fit exists between a product or brand and endorser. Even though the understanding of what creates "fit" is still vague, a number of studies have been conducted that have explored the concept though traditional endorser effectiveness factors.

Several studies have focused on a match or fit between a celebrity endorser and products centered on physical attractiveness. The "match" in these studies showed that messages for beauty products promoted by celebrities who were physically attractive were most effective. Expertise is also a factor that can be enhanced based on congruence between endorser and product. Celebrity athletes are often viewed as having expertise when it comes to products that involve high social and psychological risk (Friedman and Friedman, 1979). Celebrity athletes are often used in advertisements for automobiles, for instance, because of the high social risk involved when someone is perceived to be driving a beat-up or non-stylish car. Because their images can depend on aligning themselves with products that support their personas, a consumer may feel more confident selecting a product that is closely connected with a celebrity athlete.

The strength of congruence between an endorser and a product or brand can be based on the perceived similarity of the two. A study analyzing athletes who endorsed energy bars found athletes were better able to increase brand attributes than actors (Till and Busler, 2000). In this example, it is logical that athletes would have better product fit with energy bars than actors. In some instances the strength of a celebrity's image can overpower the product they are endorsing. This phenomenon is known as the "vampire effect" and often occurs when the consumer believes there is a poor fit between the endorser and product. An infamous example of the "vampire effect" was the use of American football player, Joe Namath, in an advertisement for Hanes Beautymist Pantyhose. Although the advertisement received a lot of attention for the unexpected use of a male endorser, Joe Namath's celebrity status overpowered the message ultimately causing the product to be an afterthought. A strong fit between product and endorser also influences the believability of the endorsement. When the endorser–product match-up is not strong it will likely give the appearance that the endorser is only participating for financial gain and not because of their belief in the product.

The positive or negative perceptions consumers have about an endorsement come from the meaning they attribute to the celebrity athlete. In some cases "match-ups" between product and endorser can alter how both are perceived. This phenomenon is especially visible with female celebrity athlete endorsers who can be viewed as "sell outs" if they try to capitalize on their fame and good looks by endorsing products in an overly sexualized manner. Racecar driver Danica Patrick has been frequently criticized for showcasing her looks to promote products rather than relying on her talent as a driver. Within the marketing culture, the "sex sells" strategy is often believed to be the most effective way to use females in endorsements, even when this idea has been shown to be counterproductive. Highlighting attractiveness of an athlete for a beauty product is logical and appropriate, however, simply employing the "sex sells" strategy does little if the goal is to align your product with other traits like performance or reliability. Tennis star Maria Sharapova is an example of a female athlete who has been able to balance the line of looks and credibility. Harvard Business School professor, Anita Elberse, explained that Sharapova is a perfect match for the Canon PowerShot digital camera because, "she possesses a number of qualities that fit with the brand being powerful but with precision, and having a sense of style" (Gilbert, 2007). The message to take from the match-up hypothesis is that celebrity athlete endorsers have powerful meanings associated with them, and often, so do the products they endorse; it is critical to the success of an endorsement that the fit between the two is harmonious.

The transfer of meaning process

The transfer of meaning process (McCracken, 1989) explores the meaning a person associates with an endorser and how their interpretation affects the persuasiveness of the advertising message. In this process a consumer often has aspirational motives and will symbolically identify with a particular sports star by purchasing products endorsed by the athlete. The transfer of meaning occurs when the meaning connected to a celebrity athlete endorser becomes associated with the product they endorse. If successful, the meaning is transferred to the consumer when they purchase the product. Peetz, Parks and Spencer (2004) explained, "the effectiveness of athletes' endorsements of sports products (or products in general) depend upon successful transfer of meaning from the athlete to the product and, ultimately the consumer" (p. 142). For example, an athlete like basketball legend, Michael Jordan, is someone who is associated with powerful meanings, those meanings could include traits such as cool, confident and athletic. According to the transfer of meaning process, a product that he endorsers, like an athletic shoe, will take on the meaning of being cool, confident and athletic. If the process is successful, the consumer will adopt the meanings associated with the product and apply it to their own self-image.

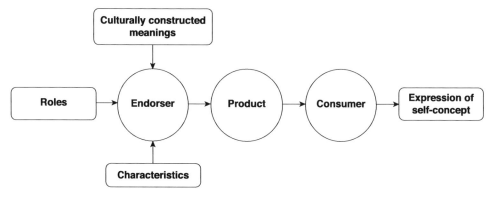

Figure 10.4 Transfer of meaning process

Source: McCracken, 1989

The transfer of meaning process is specifically applicable to celebrity athlete endorsers because of the powerful meanings they often project. Advertising is a tool used to communicate culturally constructed meanings and due to the many dimensions associated with endorser effectiveness, celebrity athlete endorsers can often "deliver meanings of extra subtlety, depth and power" (McCracken, 1989, p. 315). If relevant, meanings are not projected to a consumer then the result will most likely be an unresponsive consumer. When someone purchases an endorsed product it does not always mean the process has been completed. In order to complete the transfer of meaning process, a consumer must claim the meaning associated with the product and endorser. Levy (1959) argued that people claim meanings and behave in a particular way to stay consistent with their sense of self. It is suggested that advertisers research the meanings and symbolism associated with endorsers to determine whether they are desirable for the brand or product because these meanings are a significant part of what an endorser brings to the endorsement process (McCracken, 1989).

Part 3

Sports endorsement research

Investigations into endorser effectiveness place emphasis on any type of celebrity that receives public recognition (McCracken, 1989). Athletes are naturally included in this research because of their popularity and exposure within society. The models and conceptual frameworks presented in this chapter provide a strong understanding of the endorsement process and factors deemed critical to the success of an endorser. However, as noted previously, the endorsement effectiveness is a multifaceted construct and the models currently associated with endorsements do not provide a complete understanding of this phenomenon. Due to their strong presence in marketing strategy, sports scholars have expanded on traditional endorser research to specifically examine the celebrity athlete endorser.

A more recent investigation into celebrity athlete endorser effectiveness was the creation of a scale to examine the factors most critical to the success of an athlete endorser. Grounded in the theoretical framework of the two previously mentioned source models the study aimed to create a valid and reliable measuring tool to assess celebrity athlete endorser effectiveness. A wide-ranging assortment of factors impacting this construct have been examined, however, an instrument containing all six attributes (expertise, trustworthiness, attractiveness, likability, familiarity and similarity) included in the source credibility and source attractiveness models had not been analyzed (Peetz, 2012). The researcher felt that examining all six of the factors included in the two most widely recognized source models was necessary to gain a more complete understanding of celebrity athlete endorser effectiveness.

Peetz (2012) examined the perceptions of a college student population on advertisements utilizing celebrity athletes. College students are an attractive demographic to sports marketers because of their high levels of interest in sports celebrities (Stotlar, Veltri and Viswanathan, 1998). The initial phase of the study included asking a convenience sample of fifty students ($n=50$) to list as many athletes as they could remember in three minutes. The two celebrities, one male and one female, with the most mentions were used in the final instrument. The two athletes who garnered the most responses were basketball player, Kobe Bryant, and tennis player, Serena Williams. Next, those athletes were positioned in mock advertisements for a cellular phone and a survey was sent out electronically to a college student population. The participants ($n=813$) viewed the advertisement then answered six questions pertaining to each of the six factors included in the source credibility and source attractiveness models for a questionnaire that included 36 items.

Once the surveys had been administered, data analysis was conducted to discover the nature of the factors influencing responses to the hypothetical advertisements. From the factor analysis calculated, an interesting result became evident: both celebrity athletes had factor solutions that included the same set of factors. Ultimately, the finalized questionnaire included four questions pertaining to attractiveness from the source credibility model and four questions for the factor familiarity from the source attractiveness model. A new factor was also uncovered that the author labeled as compatibility, which included a combination of one question concerning expertise (source credibility) and two questions on the factor similarity (source attractiveness). In this study, compatibility is defined as "the strength in relationship between the consumer and the celebrity athlete endorser" (Peetz, 2012 p. 81). As a result of this study, a simplified scale encompassing a mixture of factors from the two most widely used endorsement scales was created. What is more intriguing is the newly created compatibility dimension, which may become viewed as a vital factor in how celebrity athlete endorsers are perceived.

The compatibility factor appears to incorporate not only factors from the source modeled but also elements of the other two widely used endorsement models. Although interpretation of the findings within the newly developed scale were not completed considering the match-up hypothesis or the transfer of meaning process, it does offer a compelling argument for future research on this concept. New examinations into celebrity athlete endorser effectiveness might want to place greater emphasis on the idea of the "relationship strength" a consumer feels toward an endorser and the product. If applied to the match-up hypothesis, compatibility would theoretically increase if the product and endorser had a strong fit. In addition, within the transfer of meaning process a compatible endorser would likely generate stronger and more powerful meanings for the consumer. This study is just one example of how our understanding of endorser effectiveness has continued to evolve. With a phenomenon as multifaceted as the celebrity athlete endorser, it will likely remain a topic that receives considerable attention from academics and sports marketers.

Table 10.1 Brief evolution of research examining celebrity endorsers

Author(s)	Concept	Significance
Mowen, Brown & Schulman (1979)	Match up Hypothesis	One of the first endorser frameworks to consider the product as well as the endorser.
McGuire (1985)	Source Attractiveness Model	Used a person's evaluation of similarity, familiarity and likability to determine endorser effectiveness.
McCracken (1989)	Transfer of Meaning Process	Examined the meaning people attach to celebrity endorser.
Ohanian (1990)	Source Credibility Model	Modified previous endorser credibility research and determined trustworthiness, expertise and attractiveness as significant factors.
Peetz (2012)	Endorser Effectiveness Scale	Factor analysis that examined all factors within the source attractiveness and credibility models resulting in the creation of an new factor, compatibility.

Conclusion

Sponsorships have long been used in sports marketing as a viable strategy for building associations between brands and consumers. Sports marketers have agreed that "personality sponsorships" more commonly referred to as endorsements fall within the sponsorship category. Endorsements of celebrity athletes are believed to solidify the connection with consumers, and are valued by companies for their reach capacity. The culturally relevant images, symbols and values celebrity athletes embody work to extend and strengthen the connection with consumers, which is something sponsorships rarely accomplish. When an athlete attains a certain level of celebrity status, they often garner a high level of importance among consumers, which is precisely what companies hope to capitalize on.

The three primary goals sought when using celebrity athletes have remained consistent: (1) grab the consumer's attention, (2) create positive associations with the product or service, and (3) positively impact revenue. So despite the high cost, the use of this marketing strategy has risen exponentially over the years. Risks are inherent in all marketing strategies, and endorsements are no exception. Injuries, insensitive comments on social media, or behavior problems often compromise the athlete-brand association and diminish the value, because no matter how perfect a crafted image may be there is always the possibility of a positive association turning negative. Even overexposure as an endorser can become a risk, because it weakens the distinctiveness, likability and credibility of an athlete and can thereby adversely affect the brands they endorse.

To counter perceptions of risk and establish credibility for this key sports marketing strategy, four models have been utilized to evaluate the effectiveness of celebrity athlete endorsements. The source credibility model (Hovland et al., 1953; Hovland and Weiss, 1951; McGuire, 1968) the source attractiveness model (McGuire, 1985), the match-up hypothesis (Mowen et al., 1979), and the transfer of meaning process (McCracken, 1989) have all been used extensively in scholarly work. Most often, research on celebrity athlete endorsers has examined the characteristics of the source (athlete) that affect the effectiveness of the message. Peetz (2012) evaluated the six factors from the two source models, including expertise, trustworthiness, attractiveness, familiarity, likability and similarity. In his work, the new factor of compatibility emerged, along with support for familiarity and attractiveness factors. The effectiveness of athlete endorsers can be an elusive concept as consumer characteristics influence perceptions and can vary widely. Considering the gender of the target market and the endorser is one strategy too often overlooked, despite findings showing a match will "improve endorser credibility through greater trustworthiness" (Boyd and Shank, 2012, p. 338). Clearly, the use of celebrity athletes as endorsers will continue long into the future. With the considerable investment in endorsements increasing each year, those using this core marketing strategy could benefit from a deeper understanding of how to best match their products and brand image with endorsers to maximize the appeal among their target markets.

References

Advertising Age (2001). FTC Target, *Advertising Age*, 72 (December 17), 10.

Badenhausen, K. (2014a, February 27). Highest paid retired athletes. www.forbes.com/sites/kurtbadenhausen/2014/02/27/the-highest-paid-retired-athletes/ (accessed 18 August 2015).

Badenhausen, K. (2014b, June 11). Floyd Mayweather heads list 2014 list of the world's highest paid athletes. www.forbes.com/sites/kurtbadenhausen/2014/06/11/floyd-mayweather-heads-2014-list-of-the-worlds-highest-paid-athletes/ (accessed 18 August 2015).

Boyd, T. C. and Shank, M. D. (2004). Athletes as product endorsers: The effect of gender and product relatedness. *Sport Marketing Quarterly*, 13(2), 82–93.

Brewer, M. B. (1979). In-group bias in the minimal intergroup situation: A cognitive-motivational analysis. *Psychological Bulletin*, 86, 307–324.

Brooks, C. M. and Harris, K. (1998). Celebrity athlete endorsement: An overview of the key theoretical issues. *Sport Marketing Quarterly*, 7(2), 34–44.

Buhr, T., Simpson, T. and Pryor, B. (1987). Celebrity endorsers' expertise and perceptions of attractiveness, likability and familiarity. *Psychological Reports*, 60, 1307–1309.

Burgoon, J. K. (1976). The ideal source: a reexamination of source credibility measurement. *Central States Speech Journal*, 27, 200–206.

Bush, A. J., Martin, C. A. and Bush, V. D. (2004, March). Sports celebrity influence on the behavioral intentions of generation Y. *Journal of Advertising Research*, 108–118.

Cashmore, E. and Parker, A. (2003). One David Beckham? Celebrity, masculinity, and the soccerati. *Sociology of Sport Journal*, 20(3), 214–231.

Charbonneau, J. and Garland, R. (2005). Talent, looks or brains? New Zealand advertising practitioners' views on celebrity and athlete endorsers. *Marketing Bulletin, 16*, 1–10.

Cialdini, R. B. (2007). *Influence: The psychology of persuasion*. New York: Harper Collins.

Clow, K. E., James, K. E., Sisk, S. E. and Cole, H. S. (2011). Source credibility, visual strategy and the model in print advertisements. *Journal of Marketing Development and Competitiveness*, 5(3), 24–31.

Elberse, A. and Verleun, J. (2012). The economic value of celebrity endorsements. *Journal of Advertising Research*, 52(2), 149–165.

Erdogan, B. Z. (1999). Celebrity endorsement: a literature review. *Journal of Marketing Management*, 15(3), 291–314.

Friedman, H. H. and Friedman, L. (1979). Endorser effectiveness by product type. *Journal of Advertising Research*, 19(5), 63–71.

Gilbert, S. J. (2007, October 29). Marketing Maria: Managing the athlete endorsement. http://hbswk.hbs.edu/item/5607.html (accessed 18 August 2015).

Hovland, C. I. and Weiss, W. (1951). The influence of source credibility on communication effectiveness. *Public Opinion Quarterly*, 15, 635–650.

Hovland, C. I., Janis, I. K. and Kelley, H. H. (1953). *Communication and persuasion*. New Haven: Yale University.

Kamins, M. A., Brand, M. J., Hoeke, S. A. and Moe, J. C. (1989). Two-sided versus one-sided celebrity endorsements: The impact on advertising effectiveness and credibility. *Journal of Advertising*, 18(2), 4–10.

Levy, S. J. (1959). Symbols for sale. *Harvard Business Review*, 37(4), 117–124.

McCracken, G. (1989). Who is the celebrity endorser? Cultural foundations of the endorsement process. *Journal of Consumer Research*, 16, 310–321.

McGuire, W. J. (1968). The nature of attitudes and attitude change, In Lindzey, G. and Aronson, E. (Eds), *Handbook of Social Psychology* (2nd ed.). Reading, MA: Addison-Wesley, 136–314.

McGuire, W. J. (1985). Attitudes and attitude change, In Lindzey, G. and Aronson, E. (Eds), *Handbook of Social Psychology*, New York: Random House, 233–346.

Mowen, J. C., Brown, S. W. and Schulman, M. (1979). Theoretical and empirical extensions of endorser effectiveness. In N. Beckwith et al. (Eds.), *Marketing educators conference proceedings*. Chicago: American Marketing Association, 258–263.

Mullin, L. (2003, January 6). Leslie nabs new endorsements. www.sportsbusinessdaily.com/Journal/Issues/2003/01/20030106/This-Weeks-Issue/Leslie-Nabs-New-Endorsements.aspx?hl=Kraft%20Foods%20Inc&sc=0 (accessed 18 August 2015).

Mullin, B., Hardy, S. and Sutton, W. (2014). *Sport Marketing* (4th ed.). Champaign: Human Kinetics.

Ohanian, R. (1990). Construction and validation of a scale to measure celebrity endorsers' perceived expertise, trustworthiness, and attractiveness. *Journal of Advertising*, 19(3), 39–52.

Ohanian, R. (1991). The impact of celebrity spokespersons' perceived image on consumers' intention to purchase. *Journal of Advertising Research,* 46–54.

Patzer, G. L. (1985). *The physical attractiveness phenomenon*. New York: Plenum Press.

Peetz, T. B. (2012). Celebrity athlete endorser effectiveness: Construction and validation of a scale (Doctoral dissertation). http://digitalscholarship.unlv.edu/thesesdissertations/1609 (accessed 18 August 2015).

Peetz, T. B., Parks, J. B. and Spencer, N. (2004). Sport heroes as sport product endorsers: The role of gender in the transfer of meaning process for selected undergraduate students. *Sport Marketing Quarterly*, 13, 141–150.

Petty, R. E., Cacioppo, J. T. and Schumann, D. (1983). Central and peripheral routes to advertising effectiveness: The moderating role of involvement. *Journal of Consumer Research*, 30, 135–146.

Priester, J. R. and Petty, R. E. (2003). The influence of spokesperson trustworthiness on message elaboration, attitude strength, and advertising effectiveness, *Journal of Consumer Psychology*, 13(4), 408–421.

Reinhard, M. A. and Messner, M. (2009). The effects of source likeability and the need for cognition on advertising effectiveness under explicit persuasion. *Journal of Consumer Behavior*, 8, 179–191.

Rovell, D. and Stein, M. (2014, August 31). Nike keeps Durant with megadeal. Retrieved from: http://espn.go.com/nba/story/_/id/11443079/kevin-durant-oklahoma-city-thunder-stays-nike-shoe-company-matches-armour-offer (accessed 18 August 2015).

Roy, S. (2006). An exploratory study in celebrity endorsements. *Journal of Creative Communications*, 1(2), 139–153.

Schrotenboer, B. (2014, February 26). Lance Armstrong wins endorsement lawsuit. Retrieved from: www.usatoday.com/story/sports/cycling/2014/02/26/lance-armstrong-frs-false-advertising-ruling/5840623/ (accessed 18 August 2015).

Smith, D. (2014. June 12). LeBron James' big payday from the Apple-beats deal could help his team land another NBA star. www.businessinsider.com/lebron-james-nets-30-million-from-apple-beats-deal-2014-6 (accessed 18 August 2015).

Stock, K. (March 20, 2014). Is Nike Spending Too Much on Superstars? Bloomberg Businessweek. www.businessweek.com/articles/2014-03-20/is-nike-spending-too-much-on-superstars (accessed 18 August 2015).

Stotlar, D. K., Veltri, F. R. and Viswanathan, R. (1998). Recognition of athlete endorsed sports products. *Sport Marketing Quarterly*, 7(1), 48–56.

The Box (2014). September 25, 2014: www.wheaties.com/feature/the-wheaties-story/ (accessed 18 August 2015).

Till, B. D. and Busler, M. (2000). The match-up hypothesis: Physical attractiveness, expertise and the role of fit on brand attitude, purchase intent and brand beliefs. *Journal of Advertising,* 29(3), 1–13.

Tripp, C., Jenson, T. D. and Carlson, L. (1994). The effects of multiple product endorsements by celebrities on consumers' attitudes and intentions. *Journal of Consumer Research*, 20, 535–547.

Varney, C. (2013, October 9). Celebrity twitter ads: Regulations, allegations, and selling out. [Blog post] www.brandwatch.com/2013/10/celebrity-twitter-endorsements-regulations-allegations-and-selling-out/ (accessed 18 August 2015).

11

A SPORTING (MIS)MATCH?

Assessing the objectives pursued and evaluation measures employed by sports sponsors

Leah Gillooly

Introduction

Despite difficult economic conditions, expenditure on sponsorship as a communications vehicle continues to grow as the scope of sponsorship activities expands to include ever more properties and associations. IEG reported global sponsorship expenditure of $43.5 billion in 2008 (Sponsormap, 2009a), growing to $55.3 billion in 2014 (IEG, 2015). Therefore, sponsorship remains an ever expanding area of interest both academically and to practitioners seeking return on their marketing investments. The nature of sponsorship objectives has been the subject of considerable interest, with an array of notable surveys on the most commonly pursued objectives across a range of countries (Abratt and Grobler, 1989), sectors (Armstrong, 1988) and vehicles (e.g. sports, arts, charitable causes) (Witcher et al., 1991). More recently, authors have turned their attention to not only assessing but also categorising sponsorship objectives (Nufer and Bühler, 2010; Hartland, Skinner and Griffiths, 2005). As sponsorship has matured as a communications vehicle, so there is evidence of an increasing sophistication in the objectives pursued by sponsors, with a notable shift from tactical to strategic and from short-term transactional to long-term relationship-building goals (Farrelly, Quester and Burton, 2006).

While the objectives set by sponsors continue to evolve, the other side of the coin concerns the measurement of sponsorship outcomes and whether such measures are evolving concurrently. The issue of sponsorship evaluation has been referred to as the greatest challenge facing sponsors and as an area of weakness within the sponsorship domain (Copeland, Frisby and McCarville, 1996). Sponsorship objectives and the evaluation of sponsorship are therefore intricately linked (Tripodi, 2001) and the growing requirements to evidence return on investment (RoI) of marketing activities will only heighten the need to evaluate performance against stated objectives. This chapter presents the results of a mixed methods investigation, first exploring the objectives pursued by sports sponsors through a content analysis of global sponsorship announcements and second, through a series of semi-structured interviews with Sponsorship Managers, examining the objectives being pursued and evaluation measures employed by a range of brands involved in sponsorship of major sporting properties in the United Kingdom. Therefore, conclusions can be drawn concerning the current 'state of play' as regards the nature of sponsorship objectives and the match, or mismatch, between objectives pursued and evaluation measures of sports sponsorship. As such, this chapter updates our understanding of the current activities of sponsors in terms of objectives and evaluation, building on previous studies and identifying shifts in the orientation of sponsorship as a communications tool.

Literature review

Sponsorship objectives

Sponsorship can offer brands the opportunity to achieve multiple objectives (Ukman, 2004), and the nature of the objectives pursued is likely to vary considerably between sponsored properties, product categories and levels (e.g. community versus elite). With a growing focus on RoI, it is unsurprising that objectives directly impacting on bottom line sales/market share are becoming increasingly common (Apostolopoulou and Papadimitriou, 2004). However, market research carried out by Sponsorium indicates that sponsors are starting to pay more attention to CSR-related elements of sponsorship deals (McCullagh, 2009), with Plewa and Quester (2011) arguing that this may be a particularly relevant objective for local/regional sponsorships.

Despite a surge in interest in sponsorship and CSR, arguably the most frequently cited sponsorship objective is building brand awareness (Zinger and O'Reilly, 2010; Cornwell, Roy and Steinard, 2001). Most recently, IEG's survey of sponsorship decision-makers found awareness benefits to be the most important (Performance Research, 2014). Often vying with awareness for the top ranking in surveys of sponsorship objectives is corporate or brand image enhancement. In line with the theoretical framework of Keller (1993), Yang, Sparks and Li (2008) found evidence of sponsors in China pursuing what they termed brand equity objectives of awareness and image, while Roy and Cornwell (1999) found corporate/brand image enhancement to be the most common objective among both product and service firms.

In line with the pursuit of image benefits, sponsorship can be used to reach defined target markets based not only on demographic profiles but also on shared values (Barrand, 2006). As such, sponsorship may be used to achieve objectives relating to brand positioning (Hartland et al., 2005), or repositioning. Depending on the nature of the sponsor's products/services, sponsorship can also provide a perfect environment for brands to showcase their products (Howard and Crompton, 2004) being used in the sporting arena. However, awareness, image-benefits and targeting specific markets/clients can all be thought of as intermediate to the ultimate goals of building sales and brand loyalty.

Several studies indicate sales as the most important objective pursued by US sponsors (Lough, Irwin and Short, 2000; Lough and Irwin, 2001). Such a view is supported by the IEG survey, in which sales/trial/brand usage was considered highly important by 47 per cent of respondents (Performance Research, 2014). The sponsorship of sports by alcoholic and soft drinks brands is often associated with a focus on sales, for example through on-site product sampling (Nufer and Bühler, 2010) or obtaining pouring rights at a sporting venue. In an interesting comparison between sponsorship in general and sponsorship of women's sports, Lough and Irwin (2001) found that image benefits were considered most important for sponsors of women's sports, while overall (when including (the much larger number of) male sports), sales objectives were ranked as most important. The authors conclude that the female sports sponsorship market is less developed than that of male sports and suggest that as sponsorship matures, there is a shift from image-based to sales-based objectives.

There is also growing evidence of a further shift in sponsorship objectives, in line with changing marketing orientations from a transactional to a relational paradigm (Grönroos, 1994), where brands are seeking to develop long-term, mutually beneficial relationships with customers. A strength of sponsorship is its ability to allow brands to develop an attachment with target audiences (Ferreira, Hall and Bennett, 2008) by associating themselves with emotional brands such as sports teams (McManus, 2002). The importance of relationship building was borne out by Farrelly et al. (2006), who identified, through interviews with sponsors, a move away from the pursuit of awareness and image benefits to a focus on developing connections with consumers. Fostering customer relationships through sponsorship may ultimately lead to increased brand loyalty (Henseler, Wilson and Westberg, 2011). In a 2002 study of sponsorship managers by IEG, the number one objective of sponsors was building brand loyalty (Levin, Beasley and Gamble, 2004), while increasing brand loyalty was considered an important objective by 63 per cent of sponsorship decision-makers in the 2014 IEG survey (Performance Research, 2014).

Along with the shift in general sponsorship orientation, it is also likely that the nature of objectives pursued by sponsors will evolve over the lifetime of their sponsorship deals. Verity (2002) proposes a hierarchy of sponsorship effects, starting with building awareness, leading to positive, top-of-mind image associations, brand preference and ultimately to brand purchase and loyalty. This was evidenced by Cliffe and Motion's (2005) case study of Vodafone New Zealand, which initially used sponsorship to build brand awareness in a new market, before moving to more sophisticated objectives of communicating brand values through sponsorship experiences and developing emotional connections with the target market. Therefore, sponsorship is firmly positioned, both theoretically and empirically as a communications tool through which brands can develop a sustainable competitive advantage (Amis, Pant and Slack, 1997).

The vast spectrum of opportunities with a range of sports properties also makes sponsorship an appropriate medium for pursuing objectives relating to stakeholders other than the end consumer, with staff recruitment (Ukman, 2004) and employee relations (Apostolopoulou and Papadimitriou, 2004) goals increasingly being pursued by sponsors. Equally, sponsorship is frequently undertaken to enhance trade relations (Lough and Irwin, 2001) and for influencing wider stakeholders including governments and investors (Collett, 2011). From the above discussion, it is clear to see that sponsorship is capable of achieving a multitude of objectives, cementing its position as a valuable tool in the armoury of brands. However, the multi-faceted nature of sponsorship also presents a challenge to those trying to develop measures of sponsorship effectiveness (Houlder, 2008).

Sponsorship evaluation

With ever growing sponsorship expenditures, evaluation of sponsorship effectiveness is becoming crucial, with fewer sponsors in IEG's 2014 study reporting a zero spend on sponsorship measurement than in previous iterations of the survey (Performance Research, 2014). However, there are still considerable gaps in our understanding relating to the measurements of sponsorship effectiveness (Cliffe and Motion, 2005; Ashill, Davies and Joe, 2001) and in tight economic times, corporations may begin to question the use of sponsorship faced with a lack of empirical evidence of its RoI (Becker-Olsen and Hill, 2006).

While advertising and other promotional media have long-established methods and traditions of evaluation, sponsorship has somewhat lagged behind, with Smolianov and Aiyeku (2009) reporting that according to S:COMM Research in 2003, 70 per cent of traditional media campaigns were measured, compared with only 28 per cent of sponsorship campaigns. However, perhaps in light of the growing importance of demonstrating RoI, the 2014 IEG survey reports that 51 per cent of sponsors spend up to 1 per cent of rights fees and 27 per cent spend 1 to 5 per cent of rights fees on evaluation (Performance Research, 2014).

From the above figures, there is a generally encouraging trend towards greater use of sponsorship measurement. Nonetheless, measuring sponsorship effectiveness is still widely viewed as a problem faced by sponsors (Hartland et al., 2005) and in a study of Norway-based sponsors, Thjømøe, Olson and Brønn (2002) found a general lack of use of appropriate sponsorship evaluation tools/techniques, with a lack of effective means to measure results being a commonly cited reason for brands not using sponsorship. Similarly, a 2007 European Sponsorship Association survey revealed that only 11 per cent of sponsors felt their organisations measured sponsorship's RoI effectively, with 58 per cent believing their organisations to be ineffective at measuring RoI (Houlder, 2008). Despite the recognition of the importance of sponsorship evaluation, the question remains, therefore, as to the nature and usefulness of the evaluation measures employed.

Sponsorships which use regular, objective feedback and measurement tend to yield the greatest benefits (Zinger and O'Reilly, 2010) and there are numerous proprietary sponsorship evaluation tools available, for example Sponsormap's (2009b) Sponsorship Performance Matrix, while many consultancies offer sponsorship evaluation, often based on media coverage metrics. However, the use of media equivalencies is widely criticised for inflating the value of sponsorship by directly comparing the impact, for example, of a sustained 60-second advert, with 60 seconds of exposure to sponsorship signage during a sporting fixture (Parker, 1991) and for lacking relevance to brands with already high brand recall (Crompton, 2004). Equally, measuring sponsorship effectiveness based on media equivalency assumes that exposure will lead to changes in consumer perceptions about a sponsoring brand (Quester and Farrelly, 1998).

Many academic studies have also examined the impact of sponsorship using measures of sponsorship and brand recall and recognition (Lardinoit and Derbaix, 2001; Johar and Pham, 1999). As with all measures of business performance, the sponsorship evaluation measures should be tied closely to stated objectives (Arthur et al., 1998). However, the use of recall and recognition measures, perhaps because they are easy to employ and interpret (Howard and Crompton, 2004), has not been limited to those pursuing awareness-related objectives (Herrmann, Walliser and Kacha, 2011). With the growing importance of objectives other than awareness, the use of such measures is questionable (Herrmann et al., 2011) as they do not capture how consumers are engaging with sponsorships (Meenaghan, 2001). Equally, while sponsorship recall and recognition measures can facilitate comparisons between sponsors of an event, it is likely more meaningful for brands to compare their performance against competitors, rather than against other sponsors in different product categories (Herrmann et al., 2011). Therefore, there is an apparent mismatch between objectives considered to be important and the measures employed in practice (Smolianov and Aiyeku, 2009).

While awareness measures have predominated, in line with the importance of image as a sponsorship objective, many studies have also explored the effectiveness of sponsorship at building corporate (Pope, Voges and Brown, 2009; Stipp, 1998) and brand image (Nufer and Bühler, 2010; Chanavat, Martinent and Ferrand, 2009), using dimensions including attitude towards the brand (Lardinoit and Quester, 2001), sympathy towards the brand (Nufer and Bühler, 2010) and brand personality (Carrillat, Harris and Lafferty, 2010). However, a considerable problem is that many sponsorship objectives within the 'image' domain remain vague (Fenton, 2005), thus rendering the development of appropriate measures problematic.

Moving beyond the popular areas of awareness and image, studies measuring sponsorship effectiveness become scarcer. However, a few studies have explored sponsorship effectiveness on a more behavioural level, including examining the impact on purchase intention (Ko et al., 2008) and brand loyalty (Sirgy et al., 2008; Levin et al., 2004). More broadly, Speed and Thompson (2000) developed a sponsorship evaluation scale, which assessed sponsorship response in line with the hierarchy of effects concept, measuring impact on interest in the brand, favourability towards the brand and willingness to use the sponsoring brand. Equally, in one of few such studies, Jensen and Hsu (2011) assessed sponsorship effectiveness by measuring the impact of sponsorship investment on overall business performance (measured by financial indicators such as total revenue and earnings per share). However, while representing a bottom line measure of sponsorship effectiveness, this approach perhaps lacks direct relation to the range of sponsorship objectives pursued. Lund (2006), in response to the range of objectives (not only marketing) pursued through sponsorship, suggests the Intellectual Capital Framework as a tool for evaluating sponsorship, although again its usefulness will be determined by the specific objectives pursued by individual sponsors.

From the above discussion of literature, we can see that there is a dual thrust acting upon the sponsorship environment: first, a marked shift in the nature of objectives being pursued by sponsors and, second, a growing need to evaluate RoI in sponsorship. However, perhaps the greatest challenge facing those trying to measure sponsorship effectiveness (in all of its guises) is the problem of isolating the impact of sponsorship from the effects of other marketing communications (Nufer and Bühler, 2010; Zinger and O'Reilly, 2010). Thus, the complexity of the sponsorship objectives being pursued perhaps makes developing one single sponsorship evaluation methodology unrealistic (Houlder, 2008). Nonetheless, this should not deter sponsors from evaluating their sponsorships and the challenge remains to develop creative ways of assessing effectiveness against objectives.

The following section will outline the methodology employed in this study, before moving on to discuss the results obtained and draw conclusions relating to the objectives pursued through, and evaluation of the effectiveness of, contemporary sports sponsorship.

Methodology

In line with the exploratory nature of the research in mapping the objectives pursued and evaluation methods employed by sports sponsors, this study adopts a mixed methodology, incorporating a content analysis of press statements relating to sponsorship announcements and a series of semi-structured interviews with Sponsorship Managers (or equivalent) in a range of large, UK-based organisations.

In order to facilitate the quantitative analysis of objectives being pursued by sports sponsors, an online search was made for press reports relating to sponsorship announcements from the top 30 monthly worldwide sponsorship deals from October 2008 to October 2011, as published in *SportBusiness International* magazine. The criterion for inclusion of the final sample was that a publically available press report must contain a quote from a representative of the sponsoring organisation, which made reference to the objectives to be pursued through the sponsorship deal. Consequently, of the 1,020 sponsorship deals within the sample period, data on objectives was available for 713 sponsorship deals. The reported objectives, along with the sport, sponsor product/service category and type of sponsorship was recorded and analysed using SPSS. Tables 11.1, 11.2 and 11.3 below provide a summary of the sports, sponsorship types and sponsor product/service categories of the final sample. In order to analyse the data, sponsorship objectives

Table 11.1 Sports sponsored

	Frequency	Valid percent
Football	225	31.6
Olympic	69	9.7
Golf	36	5.0
Tennis	31	4.3
Venue	43	6.0
Sailing	19	2.7
Motor Sport	71	10.0
US Team Sports (inc. College Sport)	86	12.1
Rugby (League & Union)	33	4.6
Other	100	14.0
Total	713	100.0

Table 11.2 Sponsorship type

	Frequency	Valid percent
Team	278	39.0
Event	259	36.3
Organisation	101	14.2
Personality	33	4.6
Venue	42	5.9
Total	713	100.0

Table 11.3 Sponsor product/service category

	Frequency	Valid percent
Financial services	110	15.4
Sports clothing, equipment & organisations	85	11.9
IT & telecommunications	74	10.4
Alcoholic drinks	37	5.2
Soft drinks	21	2.9
Travel, tourism & entertainment	65	9.1
Cars/automotive	72	10.1
Gambling & lottery	22	3.1
Energy/power/gas/electricity	23	3.2
Oil/petrol	26	3.6
Other	178	25.0
Total	713	100.0

were cross-tabulated with sponsor product/service category and sponsorship type, using chi-squared analysis, to examine if there were any significant differences between the objectives pursued by different sponsors relating to these categories.

Evidently, the use of press statements means that the analysis is relying on self-reported objectives which the sponsors were willing to articulate in the public domain. As such, and acting as a limitation of this study, it is possible that some element of 'window-dressing' or masking of true commercial objectives could have taken place in order to protect commercially sensitive information and present both sponsor and sponsored property in the best light. Consequently, this limitation should be borne in mind when interpreting the findings of the content analysis. In order to compensate for the limitation of using statements made in the public domain, the press statement analysis was complemented by conducting interviews with Sponsorship Managers.

Semi-structured telephone interviews were carried out with nine managers with sponsorship responsibilities in a range of large, UK-based corporations. Respondents were purposely sampled to reflect the organisation's sponsorship activity, with the final sample determined by willingness to take part in the study. The sponsoring firms represent a broad range of product and service industries, with both a B2B and B2C focus, including financial services, telecommunications, travel and professional services. All of the brands in the study were involved in sponsoring elite-level sport, including events, sports teams and individual athletes, with a well-known national or international profile. The quotes presented below are selected for their ability to illuminate the discussion and are not attributed to a particular sponsor in order to protect the identities of the brands involved. Anonymity was granted to all participants as a condition of taking part in the research.

Interviews lasted between 25 and 45 minutes and covered a range of sponsorship-related topics, including those concerned with objectives and evaluation measures reported in this chapter. With sponsors operating across different product and service industries, a semi-structured interview format was adopted in order to capture the sponsorship objectives in the words of the sponsorship practitioners themselves. Questions and outline topics for discussion were sent to respondents prior to the interviews to allow them to reflect on the sponsorship objectives and evaluation procedures of the organisation and gather any relevant information to prepare for the interview. This prior consideration can result in respondents giving more guarded responses than if questions are asked spontaneously, which could pose a limitation, particularly in light of the interviews attempting to compensate for the use of public statements in the quantitative phase of the study. However, several respondents requested a copy of the questions, thus this was seen as necessary to elicit cooperation in the research. A copy of the interview questions used is included below in the Appendix. All interviews were recorded and transcribed verbatim. Transcripts were then subjected to thematic analysis using NVivo.

Results

Sponsorship objectives

As can be seen in Table 11.4, by far the most commonly cited objective in the press statements related to image (39 per cent), largely couched in terms of positive image transfer, with a further 2 per cent referring specifically to brand positioning. Notably, within the interviews with Sponsorship Managers, less mention was made of the pursuit of image-related objectives than in the press statements. Nonetheless, in certain contexts, reference was made to borrowing the image associations of 'success', 'credibility' and 'being seen as [the] Olympic firm', while others referred to using sponsorship to reinforce a brand's 'leadership positioning'. However, these are very general attributes and lack specific detail. While some managers referred to

Table 11.4 Cited objectives from press statement content analysis

	Frequency	Valid percent
Image	277	38.8
Targeting market segments	125	17.5
Brand awareness	113	15.8
Showcasing products/brand	101	14.2
Customer engagement	28	3.9
Image (positioning)	13	1.8
Corporate social responsibility	12	1.7
Community relations	11	1.5
Sales	11	1.5
Product development	8	1.1
Relationship development	8	1.1
Brand development	4	.6
Profit	1	.1
Promotional leverage	1	.1
Total	713	100.0

using sponsorship for 'enhancing stature', or developing 'trust', these notions were predominantly expressed in discussions of why sponsorship was undertaken, rather than when discussing specific objectives.

The distinction between objectives and motivations for undertaking sponsorship may account for the prevalence of image-related mentions in the press statement analysis, with sponsors actually articulating why they undertook sponsorship rather than what they hope to get out of it. As such, perhaps here we see a mismatch between motivations and objectives, with brands being influenced by image congruence and image benefits when selecting sponsorships but having end goals related to aspects other than image. Therefore, while brand image may be seen as a stepping stone to higher order brand objectives such as loyalty or purchase intention, one can question whether appropriate sponsorship decisions are being taken as any sponsorship should be undertaken based on its ability to achieve its objectives.

Image was followed by targeting market segments (18 per cent) and brand awareness (16 per cent) within the most mentioned objectives. However, the pursuit of 'brand awareness' was more prevalent in the interviews, across a range of sponsor product/service categories, with one example of sponsorship being used to build awareness for a new brand. With the growing maturity of the sponsorship market, many sponsors have long-term associations with sport; therefore, in line with the contention of Lough and Irwin (2001), and supported by interview findings, there may be an evolution of objectives, with sponsorship initially being used to build awareness, before moving on to higher order elements of brand building as the sponsoring brands grow and mature.

Within the overall results from the press statements, some significant differences in objectives did occur across different sponsor product/service categories and different types of sponsorship (e.g. event, team, venue, individual). As shown below in Table 11.5, using chi-square analysis, a significant difference was found between the objectives pursued by sponsors from different product/service categories ($\chi^2=224.639(60)$, p < 0.000). A notable difference was found in terms of the pursuit of awareness objectives, which was cited by 30 per cent of

Table 11.5 Sponsor product/service category: objective cross-tabulation

Industry			Objective							Total
			Brand awareness	Image & positioning	Targeting market segments	Showcasing products/brand	Customer engagement & relationship development	CSR & community relations	Other	
Industry	Financial Services	Count	33	31	26	0	11	9	0	110
		% within product category	30.0%	28.2%	23.6%	.0%	10.0%	8.2%	.0%	100.0%
	Sports clothing, equipment & organisations	Count	4	53	8	11	1	1	7	85
		% within product category	4.7%	62.4%	9.4%	12.9%	1.2%	1.2%	8.2%	100.0%
	IT & telecommunications	Count	9	22	5	26	10	2	0	74
		% within product category	12.2%	29.7%	6.8%	35.1%	13.5%	2.7%	.0%	100.0%
	Alcoholic drinks	Count	2	15	15	1	2	0	2	37
		% within product category	5.4%	40.5%	40.5%	2.7%	5.4%	.0%	5.4%	100.0%
	Soft drinks	Count	4	7	6	1	1	1	1	21
		% within product category	19.0%	33.3%	28.6%	4.8%	4.8%	4.8%	4.8%	100.0%
	Travel, tourism & entertainment	Count	8	25	20	6	2	4	0	65
		% within product category	12.3%	38.5%	30.8%	9.2%	3.1%	6.2%	.0%	100.0%
	Cars/automotive	Count	17	29	16	7	2	0	1	72
		% within product category	23.6%	40.3%	22.2%	9.7%	2.8%	.0%	1.4%	100.0%
	Gambling & lottery	Count	5	11	3	1	2	0	0	22
		% within product category	22.7%	50.0%	13.6%	4.5%	9.1%	.0%	.0%	100.0%

(continued)

Table 11.5 (continued)

		Objective							Total
		Brand awareness	Image & positioning	Targeting market segments	Showcasing products/ brand	Customer engagement & relationship development	CSR & community relations	Other	
Energy/power/gas/ electricity	Count	7	5	2	5	1	2	1	23
	% within product category	30.4%	21.7%	8.7%	21.7%	4.3%	8.7%	4.3%	100.0%
Oil/petrol	Count	2	12	2	3	1	1	5	26
	% within product category	7.7%	46.2%	7.7%	11.5%	3.8%	3.8%	19.2%	100.0%
Other	Count	22	80	22	40	3	3	8	178
	% within product category	12.4%	44.9%	12.4%	22.5%	1.7%	1.7%	4.5%	100.0%
Total	Count	113	290	125	101	36	23	25	713
	% within product category	15.8%	40.7%	17.5%	14.2%	5.0%	3.2%	3.5%	100.0%

financial services brands, 24 per cent of automotive and 23 per cent of gambling brands, compared with only 16 per cent overall. Brands in these sectors face stiff competition and as such it is crucial to gain high levels of brand awareness in order to get into consumers' consideration sets for purchase. This can be contrasted with sports clothing/equipment, only 5 per cent of which cited awareness as an objective. While this is also a competitive industry, purchase, particularly of sports clothing, also involves a hedonic motivation and as such, image was an objective for 62 per cent of brands in this category (compared to 41 per cent overall). Equally, the pursuit of image-related objectives is also significantly more important for sponsors which perhaps lack inherently attractive characteristics, such as transport brands, of which 69 per cent cited image objectives. In this case, sponsorship may be used by brands to differentiate themselves from their competitors, by borrowing the intangible image associations from sponsored properties.

Supporting the data from the quantitative analysis, interviewees reported using sponsorship to 'engage with our target audience'. In particular, the interviews suggest that sponsorship, through its ability to reach a diverse range of consumers in an environment where they are comfortable, is being used to reach 'new audiences that perhaps wouldn't normally consider [the brand]'. However, the focus of sponsorship is not only on acquiring new customers, as one sponsor reports using it to 'drive very strong affinity with customers, both existing and new ... and thereby reduce churn and drive acquisition'. Here, then, we see sponsorship moving from targeting market segments to encompassing a notion of 'driv[ing] brand loyalty' in terms of developing an affinity with consumers.

Interestingly, from the press statements, showcasing products/brands was cited as an objective by 14 per cent of sponsors, which can likely be explained by the timing of the analysis, which covered the time when many sponsorship deals were signed for the London 2012 Olympic Games, the 2010 FIFA World Cup and the EURO 2012 Football Championships. In line with this, a significant difference ($\chi^2 = 94.685(24)$, $p < 0.000$) was found between objectives pursued using different types of sponsorship (team, venue, event, personality), as shown in Table 11.6 below. Showcasing products was found to be an objective of 22 per cent of event sponsors, compared with 14 per cent overall, as sports events provide high-profile, challenging environments, in which (particularly B2B) brands can demonstrate their capacity to deliver for the best clients in the most demanding of circumstances. The power of sports events to allow sponsoring brands to demonstrate their products/services is captured by one Sponsorship Manager, who talks of how event sponsorship is used as a 'showcase for the firm in terms of a super-credential of the work we can do'.

Contrasted with the use of events for sponsors showcasing products/services, the press statement analysis revealed a greater tendency to use venue sponsorship for awareness-related objectives (25 per cent, compared with 16 per cent overall). Such a finding is logical, with venue sponsorship often entailing naming rights, which confer significant media coverage and visibility to brands. Equally, venue sponsorship was used more for achieving community relations/CSR objectives (14 per cent), compared with sports sponsorship overall (3 per cent). Such sponsorship, by contributing to funding the construction of new stadia, can help sponsors be seen as giving something back to the local community.

Unlike the evidence from the literature, there appears little evidence of a shift towards the pursuit of more relational objectives from the press statement analysis, with only 4 per cent of sponsors citing customer engagement as an objective and 1 per cent citing relationship development. However, the interviews did reveal a trend, particularly among B2B brands, of the use of sponsorship for pursuing objectives relating to relationship development, with one interviewee reporting 'using it to develop existing relationships and to help facilitate new

Table 11.6 Sponsorship type: objective cross-tabulation

			Objective							Total
			Brand awareness	Image & positioning	Targeting market segments	Showcasing products/brand	Customer engagement & relationship development	CSR & community relations	Other	
Sponsorship Type	Team	Count	44	132	38	26	18	6	14	278
		% within Sponsorship Type	15.8%	47.5%	13.7%	9.4%	6.5%	2.2%	5.0%	100.0%
	Event	Count	43	89	46	58	11	5	7	259
		% within Sponsorship Type	16.6%	34.4%	17.8%	22.4%	4.2%	1.9%	2.7%	100.0%
	Organisation	Count	9	37	31	11	5	6	2	101
		% within Sponsorship Type	8.9%	36.6%	30.7%	10.9%	5.0%	5.9%	2.0%	100.0%
	Personality	Count	5	25	2	0	0	0	1	33
		% within Sponsorship Type	15.2%	75.8%	6.1%	.0%	.0%	.0%	3.0%	100.0%
	Venue	Count	12	7	8	6	2	6	1	42
		% within Sponsorship Type	28.6%	16.7%	19.0%	14.3%	4.8%	14.3%	2.4%	100.0%
Total		Count	113	290	125	101	36	23	25	713
		% within Sponsorship Type	15.8%	40.7%	17.5%	14.2%	5.0%	3.2%	3.5%	100.0%

relationships'. Interestingly, the use of sponsorship to pursue relationship development objectives is not limited to consumers, with one interviewee reporting the use of sponsorship to 'develop relationships with our major retail and trade customer base'. As such, the relationship development potential of sponsorship remains significant and while the number of sponsors citing such goals in the press statements is small, the evidence from the interviews suggests that relational objectives are becoming increasingly relevant for sponsors in both B2B and B2C markets.

While the above suggests the use of sponsorship to pursue brand objectives of image, awareness and loyalty, in the words of one Sponsorship Manager, while brands are interested in 'tapping into the hearts and minds of the fans . . . we're certainly doing it for more direct commercial gain'. Such a view is echoed by several Sponsorship Managers, with statements of: 'ultimately we want to sell [products]' and 'first and foremost, [it is] to drive revenue'. Thus, the pursuit of the other objectives is, in many cases, a stepping stone towards the ultimate objective of sales and/or revenue. While sales is only infrequently mentioned in academic studies of sponsorship objectives, this may be more associated with the difficulty of ascribing sales to sponsorship, rather than its lack of importance among practitioners. Although the press statements talked largely in terms of image-benefits, the Sponsorship Managers, in the interviews, are positioning sponsorship firmly as a tool for driving sales and revenue. As such, there is a clear shift in emphasis, perhaps driven by the drive to demonstrate sponsorship's RoI. Equally, it may be that in public statements, sponsors are less likely to talk of overt commercial objectives, perhaps conscious that there remains some resistance to what is perceived as excessive commercialisation of sport.

Despite the focus of some sponsors on sales, one interview respondent was more cautious on the link between sponsorship and sales, suggesting that sponsorship is used to drive 'brand preference', rather than being an overt sales tool. In the words of the Sponsorship Manager: 'the idea is that when people have a need [for the product] that they will then consider you because they already have a connection with the brand'. Therefore, consistent with previous research and ongoing academic debate (Chanavat et al., 2009; Hoek et al., 1997), the findings from this study find opinions divided on the ability of sponsorship to impact sales.

Moving away from a consumer focus, CSR/community relations was mentioned as an objective by one Sponsorship Manager, in this case, using sponsorship to 'invest in our local community' by sponsoring a team based in the town where the brand is headquartered. As such, this objective seems to still be relevant in some cases, but often on a local, rather than national or global, scale. Finally, within the interviewee sample, objectives in relation to recruitment and employee relations were also mentioned, with sponsorship acting as a way for brands to 'engage and motivate our employees'. This is of particular note in the context of event sponsorship, which can, in the words of one Sponsorship Manager, be used as a point of differentiation when trying to attract employees: '[we] use [the sponsored event] to help us differentiate our recruitment brand . . . we're the only firm that can offer the opportunity to work on [the sponsored event], so for us it's a big differentiating factor'. Thus, from the point of view of setting objectives, sponsorship can be utilised as a source of differentiation not only among consumers but also among (potential) employees.

The above discussion has highlighted the diverse range of objectives currently being pursued by sports sponsors. Therefore, and in the words of one Sponsorship Manager, 'especially in the current climate where you're very accountable for how you're spending your marketing dollar, [and] everyone's checking return on investment', the discussion will now proceed to explore the findings from the interviews in relation to current sponsorship evaluation measures and the (mis)match between these and objectives pursued.

Sponsorship evaluation

Unsurprisingly, in the current environment, many interviewees discussed the importance of undertaking evaluation of their sports sponsorships, with one Sponsorship Manager asserting that evaluation is 'an essential part of the sponsorship in order to ascertain its effectiveness'. However, several admit that evaluation remains neglected to some extent, with one Manager admitting: 'if I was honest, we don't do enough evaluation', going on to say that 'I'd love to do more but it's often a product of time and budget'. However, in some cases, evaluating sponsorship outcomes is not considered a priority when allocating time and resources, with one Sponsorship Manager explaining that the brand made 'a strategic decision that we wouldn't spend our time trying to measure to the nth degree', instead saying that 'we'd rather spend our time making things happen and activating and leveraging the sponsorship'. Given the sophistication of the sponsorship in question, this may initially seem at odds with the overall strategy, however the claim made here is likely to have more to do with the nature of the objectives of the brand, relating to showcasing expertise and using sponsorship to build new client relationships in a B2B context (which are easier to track more informally than for B2C brands due to the lower volume of client relationships), than a lack of concern for whether sponsorship is delivering results. The brand in question does assess whether the sponsorship contributed to them winning a particular contract, but this is done in a very general sense.

Among those Sponsorship Managers who reported measuring sponsorship effectiveness, one reported using intermediate measures such as 'how many people clicked on the ads [and] whether they entered the ticket competitions'. These measures assess consumer engagement with sponsorship activations, yet they provide no indication of whether consumers go on to have further interactions with the brand. Similarly, several Sponsorship Managers reported using 'tracking studies', measuring 'awareness and what people's perception of the brand is' as a result of the sponsorship. In some cases, this tracking takes the form of 'qualitative research at events' assessing metrics such as 'awareness and affinity and what they thought of the event and would that … increase their preference towards [the brand].' In the case of one particular sponsor, the stated objectives related to engendering loyalty among existing customers and driving new customer acquisition, with the evaluation consisting of, in the words of the Sponsorship Manager, tracking 'spontaneous brand awareness, which is a key metric that directly correlates with brand consideration and brand purchase'. While such claims have some academic support (Hoyer and Brown, 1990), tellingly the interviewee goes on to suggest that evaluation is: 'more about spontaneous brand awareness [because] it's very hard to determine how many of those [sport] fans have ended up staying with [the brand] or how many of them have been converted from another brand'.

Therefore, while there is some evidence that by measuring spontaneous brand awareness, they are tapping into a driver of brand consideration and purchase, the reality may be more that they are measuring what is easily measurable, rather than directly measuring against stated objectives. As with all of the interviews, these quotes are specific to individual brands and therefore no claim is made as to their generalisability to other sponsoring brands. However, it is telling that such practices exist and it is therefore not unreasonable to assume that many brands may be measuring awareness-related aspects of their sponsorship, which might correlate with sales- or loyalty-related objectives, because measuring the direct sales or loyalty effects is too complex. In fact, several sponsors reported the difficulty of measuring against their actual objectives, with one Sponsorship Manager saying that while they track sales around the times and locations of sponsored events and measure sales in markets where sponsorship activation has taken place, the actual increase in sales attributable to sponsorship is 'almost impossible to measure'. This is equally the case with objectives concerned with relationship development, with one Sponsorship Manager explaining that 'what's harder [than using media values] is tracking the investment that you make in hospitality with key business partners'. Thus, it is unsurprising that brands resort to measuring awareness, which is an easy metric to assess, regardless of the objective.

From the above discussion, it appears that the overall pattern is that tracking awareness and consumer opinions still predominates with, to a lesser degree, some attempt to measure sales. Thus, there is a mismatch to some extent, between objectives and evaluation measures employed. While many sponsors are aware of the importance of measuring the return on their sponsorship, the diverse nature of the objectives pursued makes this measurement difficult. Therefore, the development of more comprehensive, varied sponsorship evaluation tools is imperative and presents a challenge to both academics and practitioners.

Conclusion

From the analysis of the press statements and interview data it appears that awareness, once the most commonly pursued objective by sponsors, is becoming of lesser importance. While awareness objectives remain important for certain sponsors, the interview findings suggest that this is often an early sponsorship objective and over time sponsors' objectives evolve towards targeting market segments, relationship development, brand loyalty and sales. Image-related objectives were most often cited in the press statements, yet received little attention from interviewees. It is suggested that in press statements brands talk more of reasons why they engage in sponsorship, rather than what they specifically want to get out of the sponsorship relationship. This reluctance to discuss business objectives in the press statements may also be a means of tempering the commercial focus in the face of resistance against the commercialisation of sport. The use of event sponsorship by both B2B and B2C sponsors to showcase products/services/expertise is particularly prevalent as the scale and range of sporting events increase. Thus we see a shift in sponsorship away from mere exposure goals to the provision of goods and services as a means of demonstrating the sponsoring brands' capabilities on the biggest worldwide stages.

Within the interviews, a range of objectives concerned with relationship development and brand loyalty were identified, but, in the current climate, an overriding theme was that ultimately sponsorship was about driving sales and revenue, with the other objectives acting as a conduit towards this. Moving on to the evaluation of sponsorship, many interviewees identified this as an area of real importance but also of weakness, claiming that the ultimate goals of sales are difficult to assess. Therefore, use is still made of awareness and brand opinion measures, which may correlate with sales, as a means of evaluating the return on sponsorship. We can see that the objectives being pursued by sponsors have evolved significantly to involve a focus not only on consumers but also on employees and other stakeholders. However, sponsorship evaluation techniques have not evolved concurrently, and in the face of growing scrutiny and the need to demonstrate discernible RoI, sponsorship risks losing its appeal, not because it does not work, but because sponsors do not know how to effectively demonstrate how it delivers bottom-line value. As such, sponsorship evaluation still remains a challenge; one which is becoming increasingly complex as objectives evolve, but also one which is becoming increasingly important to ensure the continued growth and success of sponsorship as a viable tool for achieving business objectives.

References

Abratt, R. and Grobler, P. S. (1989) The evaluation of sports sponsorships. *International Journal of Advertising*, 8 (4), 351–362.

Amis, J., Pant, N. and Slack, T. (1997) Achieving a sustainable competitive advantage: a resource-based view of sport sponsorship. *Journal of Sport Management*, 11 (1), 80–96.

Apostolopoulou, A. and Papadimitriou, D. (2004) "Welcome home": motivations and objectives of the 2004 Grand National Olympic sponsors. *Sports Marketing Quarterly*, 13 (4), 180–192.

Armstrong, C. (1988) Sports sponsorship: a case-study approach to measuring its effectiveness. *European Research*, 16 (2), 97–103.

Arthur, D., Scott, D., Woods, T. and Booker, R. (1998) Sport sponsorship should . . . a process model for the effective implementation and management of sport sponsorship programmes. *Sport Marketing Quarterly*, 7 (4), 49–60.

Ashill, N. J., Davies, J. and Joe, A. (2001) Consumer attitudes towards sponsorship: A study of a national sports event in New Zealand. *International Journal of Sports Marketing & Sponsorship*, 2 (4), 291–313.

Barrand, D. (2006) Developing and delivering. *SportBusiness International*, June, 34–34.

Becker-Olsen, K. L. and Hill, R. P. (2006) The impact of sponsor fit on brand equity: the case of nonprofit service providers. *Journal of Service Research*, 9 (1), 73–83.

Carrillat, F. A., Harris, E. G. and Lafferty, B. A. (2010) Fortuitous brand image transfer: investigating the side effect of concurrent sponsorships. *Journal of Advertising*, 39 (2), 109–123.

Chanavat, N., Martinent, G. and Ferrand, A. (2009) Sponsor and sponsees interactions: effects on consumers' perceptions of brand image, brand attachment, and purchasing intention. *Journal of Sport Management*, 23 (5), 644–670.

Cliffe, S. J. and Motion, B. (2005) Building contemporary brands: A sponsorship-based strategy. *Journal of Business Research*, 58 (8), 1068–1077.

Collett, P. (2011) *Sponsorship – past its 'sell by' date?* Available at: http://blogs.cisco.com/truthmarketing/sponsorship-%E2%80%93-past-its-%E2%80%98sell-by%E2%80%99-date/ (accessed 24 October 2011).

Copeland, R., Frisby, W. and McCarville, R. (1996) Understanding the sport sponsorship process from a corporate perspective. *Journal of Sport Management*, 10 (1), 32–48.

Cornwell, T. B., Roy, D. P. and Steinard, E. A. (2001) Exploring managers' perceptions of the impact of sponsorship on brand equity. *Journal of Advertising*, 30 (2), 41–51.

Crompton, J. L. (2004) Conceptualization and alternate operationalizations of the measurement of sponsorship effectiveness in sport. *Leisure Studies*, 23 (3), 267–281.

Farrelly, F., Quester, P. and Burton, R. (2006) Changes in sponsorship value: competencies and capabilities of successful sponsorship relationships. *Industrial Marketing Management*, 35 (8), 1016–1026.

Fenton, W. (2005) Sports sponsorship in first place. *Brand Strategy*, 191 (April), 37–39.

Ferreira, M., Hall, T. K. and Bennett, G. (2008) Exploring brand positioning in a sponsorship context: a correspondence analysis of the Dew Action Sports Tour. *Journal of Sport Management*, 22 (6), 734–761.

Grönroos, C. (1994) Quo vadis, marketing? toward a relationship marketing paradigm. *Journal of Marketing Management*, 10 (5), 347–360.

Hartland, T., Skinner, H. and Griffiths, A. (2005) Tries and conversions: are sports sponsors pursuing the right objectives? *International Journal of Sports Marketing & Sponsorship*, 6 (3), 164–173.

Henseler, J., Wilson, B. and Westberg, K. (2011) Managers' perceptions of the impact of sport sponsorship on brand equity: Which aspects of the sponsorship matter most? *Sport Marketing Quarterly*, 20 (1), 7–21.

Herrmann, J-L., Walliser, B. and Kacha, M. (2011) Consumer consideration of sponsor brands they do not remember. *International Journal of Advertising*, 30 (2), 259–281.

Hoek, J., Gendall, P., Jeffcoat, M. and Orsman, D. (1997) Sponsorship and advertising: a comparison of their effects. *Journal of Marketing Communications*, 3 (1), 21–32.

Houlder, F. (2008) The importance of sponsorship measurement, in B. Speight (ed) *The future of sports marketing* (2nd edition), London, Sport Business Group, 71–84.

Howard, D. R. and Crompton, J. L. (2004) *Financing sport* (2nd edition), Morgantown, WV, Fitness Information Technology Inc.

Hoyer, W. D. and Brown, S. P. (1990) Effects of brand awareness on choice for a common, repeat-purchase product. *Journal of Consumer Research*, 17 (2), 141–148.

IEG. (2015). New year to be one of growth and challenges for sponsorship industry. Available at: http://www.sponsorship.com/iegsr/2015/01/06/New-Year-To-Be-One-Of-Growth-And-Challenges-for-Sp.aspx (accessed 8 March 2015).

Jensen, J. A. and Hsu, A. (2011) Does sponsorship pay off? An examination of the relationship between investment in sponsorship and business performance. *International Journal of Sports Marketing & Sponsorship,* 12 (4), 352–364.

Johar, G. V. and Pham, M. T. (1999) Relatedness, prominence, and constructive sponsor identification. *Journal of Marketing Research,* 36 (3), 299–312.

Keller, K. L. (1993) Conceptualizing, measuring, and managing customer-based brand equity. *Journal of Marketing,* 57 (1), 1–22.

Ko, Y. J., Kim, K., Claussen, C. L. and Kim, T.H. (2008) The effects of sport involvement, sponsor awareness and corporate image on intention to purchase sponsors' products. *International Journal of Sports Marketing & Sponsorship,* 9 (2), 79–94.

Lardinoit, T. and Derbaix, C. (2001) Sponsorship and recall of sponsors. *Psychology & Marketing,* 18 (2), 167–190.

Lardinoit, T. and Quester, P. G. (2001) Attitudinal effects of combined sponsorship and sponsor's prominence on basketball in Europe. *Journal of Advertising Research,* 41 (1), 48–58.

Levin, A. M., Beasley, F. and Gamble, T. (2004) Brand loyalty of NASCAR fans towards sponsors: The impact of fan identification. *International Journal of Sports Marketing & Sponsorship,* 6 (1), 11–21.

Lough, N. L. and Irwin, R. L. (2001) A comparative analysis of sponsorship objectives for US women's sport and traditional sport sponsorship. *Sport Marketing Quarterly,* 10 (4), 202–211.

Lough, N. L., Irwin, R. L. and Short, G. (2000) Corporate sponsorship motives among North American companies: A contemporary analysis. *International Journal of Sport Management,* 1 (4), 283–295.

Lund, R. (2006) Assessing sponsorship through the intellectual capital framework. *The Marketing Management Journal,* 16 (1), 181–187.

McCullagh, K. (2009) Sponsors placing heavier focus on CSR. Available at: http://www.sportbusiness.com/news/168988/sponsors-placing-heavier-focus-csr (accessed 13 March 2012).

McManus, P. (2002) Clubs play the community card. *Sports Marketing* (January), 8–9.

Meenaghan, T. (2001) Understanding sponsorship effects. *Psychology & Marketing,* 18 (2), 95–122.

Nufer, G. and Bühler, A. (2010) How effective is the sponsorship of global sports events? A comparison of the FIFA World Cups in 2006 and 1998. *International Journal of Sports Marketing & Sponsorship,* 11 (4), 303–319.

Parker, K. (1991) Sponsorship: The research contribution. *European Journal of Marketing,* 25 (11), 22–30.

Performance Research (2014). *2014 Performance Research/IEG sponsorship decision-makers survey.* Available at: http://www.performanceresearch.com/sponsor-survey-2014.htm (accessed 12 May 2014).

Plewa, C. and Quester, P.G. (2011) Sponsorship and CSR: is there a link? A conceptual framework. *International Journal of Sports Marketing & Sponsorship,* 12 (4), 301–317.

Pope, N. K., Voges, K. E. and Brown, M. (2009) Winning ways: immediate and long-term effects of sponsorship on perceptions of brand quality and corporate image. *Journal of Advertising,* 38 (2), 5–20.

Quester, P. and Farrelly, F. (1998) Brand association and memory decay effects of sponsorship: The case of the Australian Formula One Grand Prix. *Journal of Product & Brand Management,* 7 (6), 539–556.

Roy, D. P. and Cornwell, T. B. (1999) Managers' use of sponsorship in building brands: service and product firms contrasted. *International Journal of Sports Marketing & Sponsorship,* 1(4), 345–360.

Sirgy, M. J., Lee, D-L., Johar, J. S. and Tidwell, J. (2008) Effect of self-congruity with sponsorship on brand loyalty. *Journal of Business Research,* 61 (10), 1091–1097.

Smolianov, P. and Aiyeku, J. F. (2009) Corporate marketing objectives and evaluation measures for integrated television advertising and sports event sponsorships. *Journal of Promotion Management,* 15 (1/2), 74–89.

Speed, R. and Thompson, P. (2000) Determinants of sports sponsorship response. *Journal of the Academy of Marketing Science,* 28 (2), 226–238.

Sponsormap (2009a) Global sponsorship spend remains positive for 2009. Available at: http://www.sponsormap.com/global-sponsorship-spend-remains-positive-for-2009/ (accessed 13 March 2012).

Sponsormap (2009b) Evaluating sponsorship performance – some recent findings from SponsorMap. Available at: http://www.sponsormap.com/sponsorship-performance/ (accessed 13 March 2012).

Stipp, H. (1998) The impact of Olympic sponsorship on corporate image. *International Journal of Advertising,* 17 (1), 75–87.

Thjømøe, H. M., Olson, E. L. and Brønn, P. S. (2002) Decision-making processes surrounding sponsorship activities. *Journal of Advertising Research,* 42 (6), 6–15.

Tripodi, J. A. (2001) Sponsorship – a confirmed weapon in the promotional armoury. *International Journal of Sports Marketing & Sponsorship,* 3 (1), 95–116.

Ukman, L. (2004). *IEG's guide to sponsorship.* Chicago, IEG.

Verity, J. (2002) Maximising the marketing potential of sponsorship for global brands. *European Business Journal,* 14 (4), 161–173.

Witcher, B., Craigen, J. G., Culligan, D. and Harvey, A. (1991) The links between objectives and function in organizational sponsorship. *International Journal of Advertising,* 10 (2), 13–33.

Yang, X. S., Sparks, R. and Li, M. (2008) Sports sponsorship as a strategic investment in China: perceived risks and benefits by corporate sponsors prior to the Beijing 2008 Olympics. *International Journal of Sports Marketing & Sponsorship,* 10 (1), 63–78.

Zinger, J. T. and O'Reilly, N. J. (2010) An examination of sports sponsorship from a small business perspective. *International Journal of Sports Marketing & Sponsorship,* 11 (4), 283–301.

Appendix 1 – Pre-circulated Interview Questions

1 What sponsorships are [brand] currently involved in? (select the most high profile/ appropriate for further probing)
2 Why have you chosen to use sponsorship over other communications vehicles?
3 How long has the current sponsorship deal been going?
4 How long is the deal in total?
5 Why did you select this particular sponsorship?
6 What choice criteria were used in selecting this sponsorship?
7 Who is the primary target market you are trying to reach through this sponsorship?
8 What are your objectives for the sponsorship of [property]?
   a) (if image-related: What images did you want to be transferred? What images are being transferred? How do you know this?)
9 When were the sponsorship objectives set?
10 Are you achieving your stated objectives?
11 How often are the objectives reviewed/re-evaluated?
12 Who is responsible for setting the sponsorship objectives?
13 What benefits does [brand] get from this sponsorship?
14 What benefits are offered to your consumers through your partnership with [property]?
15 What support activities do you use to exploit/communicate your sponsorship?
16 How closely do you cooperate with the rights holder, e.g. joint promotions, meetings, updates, evaluation?
17 What role does sponsorship play in the wider communications/branding strategy of [brand]?
18 How do you evaluate the success of your sponsorships?
19 What measures do you use to measure sponsorship effectiveness?
20 Who is responsible for sponsorship evaluation (brand, rights holder, agency)?
21 What support, if any, do you get from [property] in terms of evaluation?
22 Do you see sponsorship as playing a long-term role in the communications/brand strategy of [brand]?

PART III

Ambush marketing

Nicolas Chanavat, Simon Chadwick and Michel Desbordes

As sports sponsorship has evolved as a phenomenon, so, too, have challenges and threats to it. One of these in particular has emerged as a significant issue for sponsors and the properties with which they are associated. Ambushing is now over thirty years old, but rather than showing any sign of abating, appears to be proliferating in number and gaining in creativity and innovation. Ambushing can distract, confuse or undermine official sponsorships, and may also be viewed as being immoral or illegal. Such is the threat posed by it that major sports properties, such as the Olympic Games, oblige host nations to pass legislation aimed at protecting official sponsors. There are other approaches to protecting against ambushers; sponsors and event owners seem keen to strongly engage fans to mitigate the effects of ambushing. Conversely, ambushers appear to see creativity, innovation and sometimes aggression, as the route to diminishing official sponsorships. As these contests play out across the sporting world, fans and customers seem either unaware of or indifferent to ambushing and ambushers. However, this remains something of a moot point requiring further attention. Chapters in this part consider prevailing issues pertaining to ambushing, specifically, what ambushing is, what its effects are and the ways it might be regulated and controlled.

12

A THEORETICAL AND EMPIRICAL OVERVIEW OF AMBUSH MARKETING IN SPORTS

Gerd Nufer and André Bühler

Introduction

For many companies, it is major international sporting events (in particular the Football World Cup or the Olympic Games) that constitute the ideal platform for the integration of their target group-specific marketing communication into an attractive sports environment. Sports event organizers sell exclusive marketing rights for their events to official sponsors, who, in return, acquire exclusive options to utilize the event for their own advertising purposes. Ambush marketing is the method used by companies that do not hold marketing rights to an event, but still use their marketing activities in diverse ways to establish a connection to it. There is still widespread debate and confusion about the topic. Ambush marketing is often defined in different ways, by different people, according to their position as either supporters or opponents of the practice.

The principles of ambush marketing

The philosophy of ambush marketing consists of achieving conventional marketing objectives with unconventional methods. The general intention is that a relatively small investment generates the greatest possible impact. The phenomenon of ambush marketing is not new, but in recent years it has become significantly more professional. The growing aggressiveness in communications and sponsorship markets has resulted in the fact that ambush marketing can be observed worldwide and continues to grow.

Definition of ambush marketing

Ambush marketing was first mentioned by Bayless (1988: 1) as "a popular tactic . . . to take advantage of . . . an event". This simple, unambiguous definition describes the false association by a company not sponsoring an event, with a view to deriving similar benefits as the official sponsors. Another early definition of ambush marketing originates from Meenaghan (1994: 79). He describes ambush marketing as "the practice whereby another company, often a competitor, intrudes upon public attention surrounding the event, thereby deflecting attention toward themselves and away from the sponsor". More than a decade later, Farrelly, Quester and Greyser (2005: 341) define ambush marketing as "a quasi-parasitic appropriation of the brand value of an event by competitors who time a purposeful use of the sports theme during and around the event they seek to ambush". A very recent definition originates from Chadwick and Burton (2011: 714):

> Ambush marketing is a form of associative marketing which is designed by an organization to capitalize on the awareness, attention, goodwill, and other benefits, generated by having an association with an event or property, without the organization having an official or direct connection to that event or property.

In summary, ambushers want to promote and sell products through an association with the (sports) event in the same manner as official sponsors that have paid to do so.

In popular sources, ambush marketing is frequently used synonymously with terms such as "coattail marketing", "parasitic marketing" and "free-rider marketing". Official sponsors define these ambushes on high-priced advertising rights as "theft" and emphasize the illegal aspects of ambush marketing (Payne, 1998; Townley, Harrington and Couchman, 1998). However, there are also proponents, who see ambush marketing as a legitimate power that facilitates more efficiency in the sponsorship market. "All this talk about unethical ambushing is . . . intellectual rubbish and postured by people who are sloppy marketers" (Welsh, 2002: w.p.).

This shows that there is still disagreement about the definition of ambush marketing. Because of the widespread character of ambush marketing, for the following analysis a comprehensive definition will be applied. Ambush marketing is the practice by companies of using their own marketing, particularly marketing communications activities, to give an impression of an association with the event to the event audience, although the companies in question have no legal or only underprivileged or non-exclusive marketing rights for this event sponsored by third parties. Thus, ambushers want to promote and sell products through an association with the event as official sponsors are allowed to do.

Objectives of ambush marketing

The idea of ambush marketing is to capitalize on the success of sports sponsorship without taking on the intrinsic obligations of an official sponsor. The objectives of ambush marketers are therefore largely identical to those of the sponsors, but are to be attained with reduced financial expenditure (Burton and Chadwick, 2009; Pechtl, 2007). The objectives of ambush marketing can be deduced from the objectives of sponsorship. Their primary function is the achievement of communicative (psychological) aims (see Figure 12.1).

Ultimately, the exploitation of the marketing potential of a sports event implies the targeting of economic objectives such as sales, revenue, market share and profit. This is to be understood as directly related to the range of event-related products and services (Pechtl, 2007).

The pre-economic (psychological) objectives are situated primarily in the area of communication impact. Like sponsors, ambushers target psychological objectives such as attention to their own advertising, the increase of their awareness levels as well as a sense of being up to date. They aspire to achieve image enhancements through their (supposed) sponsorship (goodwill), as well as an image transfer from positive attributes of the sport event to the image of the product or the company. In addition to these goals, ambush activities also feature explicit competition-oriented objectives. The intent is to diminish the

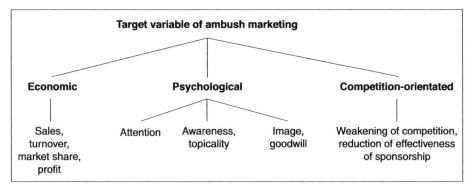

Figure 12.1 Objectives of ambush marketing

Source: Nufer, 2013: 34

communication–political effectiveness of the sponsorship, thereby weakening the competition (for example, by obviating the exclusivity of the sponsorship, the reduction of the share of voice of the sponsors or obstructing the sponsors' advertising) (Nufer, 2013).

Structuring the manifestations of ambush marketing

A novel approach to structuring the various manifestations of ambush marketing is presented in this section, classified into different categories, case groups and cases (Nufer, 2013).

Differentiating the fundamental categories of ambush marketing

In the first step, three basic categories of ambush marketing are differentiated. To begin with, it can be differentiated between direct ("blatant") and indirect ("subtle") ambush marketing. It is characteristic of direct ambush marketing for actions to target the marketing rights of the event organizer or the event sponsors without deviation. Indirect ambush marketers, on the other hand, use the sports event as the motive for their own marketing activities, which is why indirect ambush marketing is prevalent primarily in the area of communications. In literature, this fundamental differentiation has been established (Du Toit, 2006; Wittneben and Soldner, 2006; Pechtl, 2007). The aforementioned dichotomy is complemented by a third category that can best be designated as dominant destructive-aggressive ambush marketing: The essential objective of actions in this category is to diminish the effectiveness of official sponsorships with predatory methods. The obstruction of sponsors' measures is an attack on a direct competitor of the ambusher, in effect, weakening the competition (McKelvey and Grady, 2008; Nufer, 2010).

Differentiating ambush marketing case groups per category

In a second step, these three categories are further broken down into case groups, in which similar cases are grouped together. Within the scope of direct (blatant) ambush marketing, direct ambushing approaches that are motivated primarily by product policy and predominantly pursue (mainly short term) economic objectives are distinct from direct ambushing activities, whose motivation and implementation are focused primarily in the realm of communications policy and which therefore prioritize (mainly medium term) psychological objectives. Within the scope of the first case group, event-associated products are created and marketed in an unauthorized manner. The second case group involves communicative pretense to a sponsorship that, in reality, does not exist (Du Toit, 2006; Nufer and Bühler, 2013b).

Initially, indirect (subtle) ambush marketing is subdivided into ambush marketing by intrusion and ambush marketing by association. Whereas under ambush marketing by intrusion, all ambush activities that can be characterized as "capitalising on the opportunity" are subsumed within the scope of a sports event, ambush marketing by association can be further differentiated: "Agenda setting" encompasses all ambush marketing measures that can be subsumed under "positioning by topicality" and focus on the event as a communications platform (Pechtl, 2007). "Fun ambushing" (Nufer, 2005) and "philanthropic ambushing" (Nufer and Geiger, 2011) constitute two special cases of ambush marketing by association. The category "dominant destructive-aggressive ambush marketing" is not differentiated into any distinguishable case groups.

Typology of the manifestations of ambush marketing

In the third step, a total of 21 cases of ambush marketing subsumed in the individual categories and case groups are distinguished from one another. Figure 12.2 summarizes the observations with regard to structuring the manifestations of ambush marketing.

Most of these 21 cases of ambush marketing have a focus on marketing communications. In these descriptions, the examples shown have made it obvious that a clear cut differentiation is not always possible, but that overlaps do occur. What this means is that some ambush activities have multiple characters and could (or even should) be ascribed to two (or possibly more) parallel cases. Neither does the systematisation claim to be complete. Based on the highly innovative content of ambush marketing, with its constantly new creative activities, this is rather a snapshot of the current situation. The applied structure is therefore not rigid, but flexible and open, in order to allow for new cases to be subsequently included and integrated.

Examples of eye-catching cases of ambush marketing

This section presents and analyses two particularly striking examples of ambushing activities that were observed in the context of the 2006 and 2010 Football World Cups (Nufer, 2010; 2013).

Before and during the 2006 World Cup in Germany, Bavaria, a beer brand owned by the Dutch Heineken group, distributed about 250,000 samples of imitation lederhosen in orange, the Dutch national colour, bearing the advertising imprint "Bavaria" (see Figure 12.3).

The intention was to have the Dutch fans wear these lederhosen during their World Cup stay in what was supposedly the "lederhosen country" of Germany and especially to display these prominently during their stadium attendances. This strategy was initially successful, as thousands of Dutch fans showed up wearing them at the Netherlands vs. Ivory Coast group stage game in Stuttgart, consciously or subconsciously acting as disseminators transporting unauthorised advertising into the stadiums. In order to protect the official sponsors, a rapid decision by the organisers was called for. FIFA invoked Rule 10 of the ticket terms and conditions, which stated: "advertising, commercial, political or religious articles of all types, including banners, symbols and flyers . . . are inadmissible and . . . may not be brought into the stadium if the organisation committee has grounds to assume that these will be displayed in the stadium." The FIFA Rights Protection Team saw to it that all unauthorised Bavaria

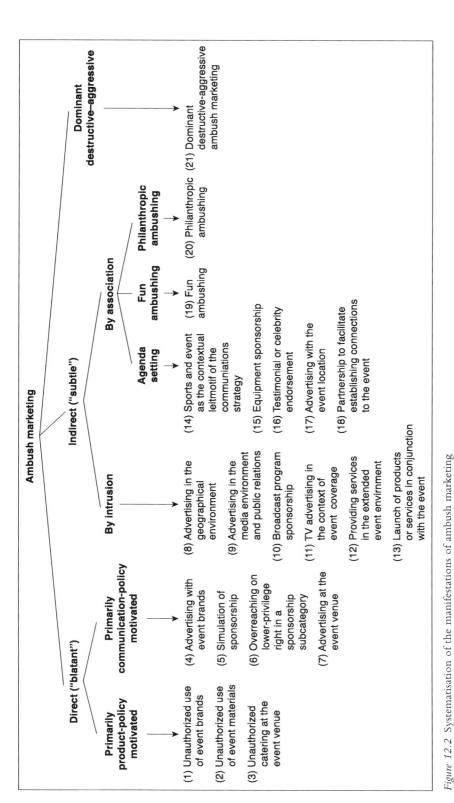

Figure 12.2 Systematisation of the manifestations of ambush marketing

Source: Nufer, 2013: 58

Figure 12.3 Ambush marketing case, "Bavaria", 2006

Source: Nufer, 2013: 44

advertising items remained outside the stadium gates, more than 1,000 Dutch fans had to remove their lederhosen otherwise FIFA would have barred them from entering the stadium. Although ultimately a repelled ambush attempt, the operation produced a tremendous amount of attention for Bavaria. The fact that more than 1,000 fans followed a World Cup game in the stadium in their underpants was picked up with great interest by the media.

During the 2010 World Cup in South Africa, Bavaria also relied on ambush marketing and again attained a high level of media attention, this time with the so-called "beer babes". The spectators at the Netherlands vs Denmark preliminary round game in Johannesburg included 36 young women, who showed up in the orange-coloured mini-dresses of the brewery. This time the Bavaria brand name was only evident on a small label on the seam (see Figure 12.4).

Once again, FIFA was rigorous in dealing with this action, removing the women from the stadium and even briefly had their alleged ringleaders arrested. Then the situation exploded. The World Football Association filed a suit in court against the planned promotion. The Dutch embassy assured the women of legal support. While Bavaria's advertising intent in 2006 with the clearly visible logo on the lederhosen was obvious, the brewery's calculation in 2006 was infinitely more subtle. On site, in front of and in the stadium, the action was initially not recognised as ambush marketing. Thus, the "beer babes" were easily able to make their way into the stadium. Who pays attention to a few orange-clad girls (with a barely visible Bavaria logo) in a stadium, when thousands of orange-clad Dutch fans are already there? It was only with the intervention of FIFA that the ambush marketing activity was exposed as such and became public knowledge. Only this way did an initially harmless incident, in terms of advertising effectiveness, make it into the media reports and achieve such an immense PR impact, which is precisely what Bavaria wanted to achieve.

The Bavaria lederhosen from 2006 are at first advertising with the event location, also a kind of fun ambushing (both indirect ambush marketing by association). The activity grew

Figure 12.4 Ambush marketing case, "Bavaria", 2010

Source: Nufer, 2013: 44

at the World Cup venue Stuttgart to advertising in the geographical environment (indirect ambush marketing by intrusion). It would have culminated to advertising at the event venue (direct, primarily communications-policy motivated ambush marketing) if the RRP team hadn't intervened at the last minute.

The Bavaria beer babes from 2010 are definitely a more subtle form of ambush marketing. Without the intervention of FIFA, this ambush marketing activity would never have appeared in the media (reference in the media environment and public relations), and would never have become public knowledge (news in the context of the event coverage). This is cool, calculated ambush marketing straight from the drawing board. Based on their ambushing experience from the 2006 World Cup, this case is an example for an innovative and well-planned form of indirect ambush marketing by intrusion.

Empirical study on ambush marketing

The following analyses are based on a comprehensive primary statistical data collection that was conducted in the frame of a particular event: at the time of the 2006 FIFA football World Cup in Germany. As part of this survey, 2,109 people were interviewed before, during and after the World Cup (Nufer, 2010). The results of this study may help to better understand the effectiveness of ambush marketing and to evaluate forthcoming ambush marketing activities.

Research design

For the selection of the sampling units, a process of simple random sampling was used and was based on additional standards in order to guarantee the comparability of the individual subsets and survey waves. Three standard attributes were defined for the empirical survey: age, sex and education of the interviewees. Adolescents in Germany constitute the specific survey target group. Previous empirical surveys have shown that younger groups are particularly receptive to sports advertising, achieving above average results primarily with high school and college students (von der Lippe and Kladroba, 2002). This study concentrates on teenagers aged 13–18 years and includes equal numbers of boys and girls. Care was taken to include students of all three major school types in Germany: "Hauptschule" (secondary modern school), "Realschule" (middle school), "Gymnasium" (grammar school). What was called for was an identity for the subsets and interview waves in terms of the parameters of these demographic characteristics in order to obtain largely structurally identical groups, thereby enabling a meaningful comparison of effects to be conducted.

The empirical data collection was performed in three independent waves. The reference measurement took place in March and April, i.e. 2–3 months prior to the start of the World Cup. The comparison measurement during the World Cup was performed in the third week of the tournament, at the exact point in time when the group stage had been completed and thereby 48 of the total of 64 games had been played. The follow-up survey was performed in September and October, i.e. the same interval after (2–3 months) as the first survey was prior to the World Cup. In order to obtain independent subsets for the statistical data analysis, stringent care was taken to interview each participant only once, as the first round of questions regarding recollection of sponsoring activities sensitizes their attention with the result that a follow-up interview with the same person can no longer be considered independent (Opfer, 1997; Stenger, 1986).

Perception of brands and companies in the context of sports

Brand perception is the basic prerequisite for the success of communications activities. The following analyses concerning perception of World Cup sponsors and ambushers are based on the data collected in the second survey wave. Only those who indicated that they are watching or watched the World Cup are included.

Unaided recall

Unaided recall is measured in terms of perceived official World Cup sponsors. Consequently, only naming the 15 official main and the six German sponsors is correct. These 21 brands and companies were displayed on stadium billboards and therefore visible to television viewers.

Table 12.1 depicts the top 50 responses with reference to unaided recall, i.e. all companies and brands that were named by at least five test respondents in the study conducted during the World Cup. The brands are ranked according to the frequency with which they were named during the World Cup (figures highlighted in bold print) and, for purposes of comparison, the frequency with which they were named in the post-World Cup survey are indicated alongside. In addition, the change from the during and after comparison has been calculated and the difference regarding World Cup sponsors assessed for its significance (Mann-Whitney U tests for two independent samples with non-metric variables; Bühl 2006). Official World Cup sponsors continue to be highlighted in dark or pale grey, while all other companies listed have been named erroneously.

Table 12.1 Results of unaided recall

Rank	Brand	During		After		Change	Significance	
		Absolute	*Relative*	*Absolute*	*Relative*			
1	McDonald's	381	**59.5 %**	268	46.1 %	−13.4 %	0.000	↓★★★
2	adidas	332	**51.9 %**	257	44.2 %	−7.7 %	0.008	↓★★
3	Coca-Cola	298	**46.6 %**	208	35.8 %	−10.8 %	0.000	↓★★★
4	Telekom	184	**28.8 %**	149	25.6 %	−3.2 %	0.224	
5	Nike	129	**20.2 %**	101	17.4 %	−2.8 %		
6	Nutella	120	**18.8 %**	148	25.5 %	+6.7 %		
7	Puma	114	**17.8 %**	84	14.5 %	−3.3 %		
8	Hyundai	108	**16.9 %**	33	5.7 %	−11.2 %	0.000	↓★★★
9	OBI	91	**14.2 %**	86	14.8 %	+0.6 %	0.773	
10	MasterCard	87	**13.6 %**	40	6.9 %	−6.7 %	0.000	↓★★★
11	Yahoo	68	**10.6 %**	31	5.3 %	−5.3 %	0.001	↓★★★
12	Vodafone	60	**9.4 %**	54	9.3 %	−0.1 %		
13	Bitburger	57	**8.9 %**	33	5.7 %	−3.2 %		
14	Philips	40	**6.3 %**	3	0.5 %	−5.8 %	0.000	↓★★★
	Toshiba	40	**6.3 %**	4	0.7 %	−5.6 %	0.000	↓★★★
16	Media-Markt	35	**5.5 %**	25	4.3 %	−1.2 %		
17	Postbank	34	**5.3 %**	23	4.0 %	−1.3 %	0.263	
18	Gillette	24	**3.8 %**	9	1.5 %	−2.3 %	0.018	↓★
19	Emirates	20	**3.1 %**	2	0.3 %	−2.8 %	0.000	↓★★★
20	Continental	19	**3.0 %**	16	2.8 %	−0.2 %	0.822	
	Reebok	19	**3.0 %**	10	1.7 %	−1.3 %		
22	O₂	18	**2.8 %**	3	0.5 %	−2.3 %		
23	Fujifilm	17	**2.7 %**	11	1.9 %	−0.8 %	0.374	
	Burger King	17	**2.7 %**	13	2.2 %	−0.5 %		
	Google	17	**2.7 %**	10	1.7 %	−1.0 %		
26	EnBW	16	**2.5 %**	8	1.4 %	−1.1 %	0.158	
	Pepsi	16	**2.5 %**	17	2.9 %	+0.4 %		
28	Budweiser	14	**2.2 %**	2	0.3 %	−1.9 %	0.005	★★
	Canon	14	**2.2 %**					

(Continued)

Table 12.1 (Continued)

Rank	Brand	During		After		Change	Significance
		Absolute	Relative	Absolute	Relative		
30	Allianz	13	**2.0 %**	13	2.2 %	+0.2 %	
	Mercedes	13	**2.0 %**	13	2.2 %	+0.2 %	
	Xbox	13	**2.0 %**				
33	Avaya	12	**1.9 %**	6	1.0 %	-0.9 %	0.223
	Premiere	12	**1.9 %**	6	1.0 %	-0.9 %	
35	Sony	11	**1.7 %**	16	2.8 %	+1.1 %	
	Warsteiner	11	**1.7 %**	10	1.7 %	0.0 %	
37	Deutsche Bahn	10	**1.6 %**	14	2.4 %	+0.8 %	0.287
	Siemens	10	**1.6 %**	7	1.2 %	-0.4 %	
	Snickers	10	**1.6 %**	12	2.1 %	+0.5 %	
40	Deichmann	9	**1.4 %**				
41	Kreissparkasse	8	**1.3 %**	8	1.4 %	+0.1 %	
42	Oddset	7	**1.1 %**	0	0.0 %	-1.1 %	0.012 ★
	Bwin	7	**1.1 %**	30	5.2 %	+4.1 %	
	Erima	7	**1.1 %**				
	Krombacher	7	**1.1 %**	7	1.2 %	+0.1 %	
46	Yellow Strom	6	**0.9 %**				
47	Hamburg-Mannheimer	5	**0.8 %**	2	0.3 %	-0.5 %	0.313
	Axe	5	**0.8 %**	3	0.5 %	-0.3 %	
	Intersport	5	**0.8 %**	4	0.7 %	-0.1 %	
	Samsung	5	**0.8 %**	4	0.7 %	-0.1 %	

★   p <= 0,05 significant
★★   p <= 0,01 very significant
★★★   p <= 0,001 highly significant

The results for the unaided recall survey conducted during the World Cup vary considerably for the 21 World Cup sponsors:

- The top three brands (McDonald's, adidas and Coca-Cola), which were mentioned by about half of the interviewees, can be particularly pleased with their results.
- Among the main sponsors, the lowest rates in the adolescent target group were scored by Fujifilm, Budweiser and Avaya, with less than 3%.
- The average unaided recall value of the 21 World Cup sponsors is 13.4% (main sponsors: 17.1%; German sponsors: 4.2%).
- As far as the unaided recall values are concerned, it appears that the non-sponsors Nike, Nutella and Puma easily join the ranks of the official sponsors and achieve individual values of up to 20%. Vodafone, Bitburger and Media-Markt are also erroneously named more frequently than many actual World Cup sponsors.

If one compares the unaided recall values attained by the World Cup sponsors during the World Cup, with their scores three months after the end of tournament, the following is striking:

- In most cases a significant decline in unaided recall is apparent in the during and after comparison for the World Cup. Only the main sponsors, Deutsche Telekom, Continental, Fujifilm, Avaya, and the German sponsors, OBI, Postbank, the energy group EnBW, the rail operator Deutsche Bahn and the insurance company Hamburg-Mannheimer tend to maintain their summer levels.
- On average, the recall capacity for World Cup sponsors falls by 3.8% (main sponsors: -5.2%, German sponsors: -0.4%).

The companies named erroneously can be explained as follows:

- Nike and Puma were, and still are, active as sports equipment providers for numerous teams. Therefore, although they were not represented on stadium billboards, they did have a strong presence on the playing field (for example, players' shirts and shoes).
- As the program sponsor, Bitburger presented all public service television broadcasts on the ARD and ZDF channels. The Bitburger commercials were aired immediately prior to kick-off, in the halftime break and following the final whistle of all game broadcasts on German television.
- Nutella has been running advertising with German national players for an extended period of time, including the time frame of the survey. Vodafone has been operating as the sponsor of European Champions League football for years. In its 2006 marketing communications, Media-Markt focused on the theme "We will be world champions". It becomes clear that these brands and companies are very closely linked with the themes of football and the World Cup, which evidently led to confusion among the respondents.
- Other companies are erroneously named when the respondents recall the sponsor's sector but not the specific name and then err when they provide a response. The fact that Nike, Puma, Reebok, Vodafone, O_2, Bitburger, Burger King, Google and Pepsi were named can be explained in this manner.
- Mercedes-Benz is occasionally named erroneously, since the automobile company has been active as the sponsor of the German national team for many years.

Approximately one third of all responses are erroneous. Furthermore, it is astonishing that of the 640 respondents who indicated that they were following games during the World Cup, 95 openly admitted they were unable to recall any brands. Another 22 did not respond to this question, which leads us to the conclusion that they too were unable to recall any brands. A total of 18.3% of people interviewed during the World Cup appear not to have been affected in any way by sports-related advertising.

Aided recall

In the context of this analysis, the participants were given a list of 16 selected brands to check off. Of the official sponsors, those companies it could be assumed that the young consumers would know and use were specifically chosen. Among these were five main sponsors: Coca-Cola, McDonald's, Yahoo, Deutsche Telekom and adidas as well as OBI, a German sponsor for the 2006 World Cup. The other ten brands that were presented were non-sponsors and direct industry competitors of the World Cup sponsors, either ambush marketers (Nike, Puma, Nutella, Vodafone, Media-Markt and Burger King) or simply dummies placed as a distraction (Google, Pepsi, Reebok and Snickers).

Table 12.2 Results of aided recall

Rank	Brand	During	After	Significance	
1	adidas	**81.3 %**	76.6 %	0.046	
2	McDonald's	**79.2 %**	77.5 %	0.454	
3	Coca-Cola	**78.0 %**	77.5 %	0.829	
4	Telekom	**56.4 %**	53.0 %	0.234	
5	Nutella	**49.5 %**	64.4 %	0.000	↑★★★
6	Nike	**41.4 %**	42.2 %	0.787	
7	Puma	**40.3 %**	38.0 %	0.416	
8	Vodafone	**30.9 %**	35.3 %	0.107	
9	OBI	**29.2 %**	24.6 %	0.070	
10	Media-Markt	**23.6 %**	21.3 %	0.347	
11	Yahoo	**20.8 %**	14.3 %	0.003	↓★★
12	Google	**11.9 %**	13.4 %	0.415	
13	Pepsi	**10.2 %**	8.6 %	0.354	
14	Burger King	**9.8 %**	9.6 %	0.904	
15	Reebok	**8.4 %**	11.2 %	0.106	
16	Snickers	**4.4 %**	5.7 %	0.296	

In Table 12.2 these brands are arranged in a ranking based on their aided recall values during the World Cup (official main sponsors are again highlighted in dark grey, while German sponsors are highlighted in pale grey). The differences in the during and after comparison were tested for their significance (Mann–Whitney U tests for two independent samples with non-metric variables).

The main results are:

- The first four places are occupied by four main sponsors. The German sponsor OBI is mid-table. Yahoo is the sole main sponsor to attain a very low rank.
- With an average recall of 57.5%, the selected World Cup sponsors achieve good results (by way of comparison, the average value is 23.0% for non-sponsors).
- All five of the main sponsors included (adidas, Coca-Cola, McDonald's, Deutsche Telekom and Yahoo) are more or less able to distinguish themselves from their non-sponsor industry competitors Nike, Puma, Pepsi, Burger King, Vodafone and Google, by a significant margin.
- Additional interesting aspects are revealed by a comparison of aided recall measured during the World Cup with that compiled several months after: the results are largely identical. In 14 of 16 cases there is no significant difference in the during and after comparison. Of the World Cup sponsors considered, only Yahoo had to deal with a very significant reduction of its score. On the other hand, the non-sponsor, Nutella, managed a real feat: even after the World Cup, the brand was able to very significantly increase its already excellent score.

Analysis of the reasons for confusing ambushers with official sports sponsors

In the following, the focus is on the data collected during the World Cup and circumscribed in terms of the filter variable "followed the World Cup". The analyses below are based on the study of whether and, if so, to what extent, the interviewees were able to differentiate World Cup sponsors from ambushers and dummies among the great variety of brands and companies included on the list presented to determine aided recall.

Determination of confusion

In order to do this, the number of World Cup sponsors correctly identified by each interviewee is initially added up. An individual quotient of correctly identified World Cup sponsors in proportion to the number of all official World Cup sponsors contained in the question regarding aided recall may be calculated from this (in this case, six). This sponsor quotient features a range of values from 0 (worst possible result: none of the six sponsors are identified) to 1 (best possible result: all of the sponsors are identified).

$$\text{Sponsor quotient} = \frac{\sum \text{World Cup sponsors identified}}{\sum \text{World Cup sponsors queried}}$$

Similarly, a calculation is made for each interviewee as to how many non-sponsors they erroneously considered to be World Cup sponsors. Based on this, a second quotient is generated that relates this value to the total number of ambushers and dummies (in this case, a total of ten) appearing on the list. The non-sponsor quotient also features a range of values from 0 to 1, whereby in this case, 0 is the best possible result (the interviewee did not confuse any of the ten non-sponsors with a World Cup sponsor) and 1 is designated as the worst possible result (the interviewee incorrectly declared all non-sponsors as official sponsors).

$$\text{Non-sponsor quotient} = \frac{\sum \text{Non-sponsor incorrectly declared as World Cup sponsors}}{\sum \text{Ambushers and Dummies queried}}$$

Subsequently, an individual confusion coefficient is calculated for each interviewee. Here, the difference between the sponsor quotient and the non-sponsor quotient is determined. The result of this subtraction formula, as per its definition, fluctuates within a value area of –1 to +1. The value –1 designates the worst case scenario, i.e. the test person did not recognize a single World Cup sponsor but mistook all the ambushers and dummies for the official sponsors. The value +1, on the other hand, can be interpreted as the best case scenario, i.e. all sponsors listed were correctly recognized and all non-sponsors also identified as such. The confusion coefficient thus indicates the extent to which each individual interviewee allowed themselves to be misled by ambush marketing or dummies.

$$\text{Confusion coefficient} = \text{sponsor quotient} - \text{non-sponsor quotient}$$

With regard to the evaluations below, the interviewees are grouped in different confusion clusters depending on their individual confusion coefficients, in terms of the value area (see Table 12.3).

It becomes apparent that in the context of the present empirical study that only clusters 1 and 3 occur, thus a mistaken identification in the sense of very severe confusion has not been determined for a single interviewee. The majority of the interviewees are to be assigned to cluster 2.

The purpose of the following observations is to ascertain what factors led to the confusion of the World Cup viewers and are therefore substantially responsible for non-sponsors being mistaken for official World Cup supporters. Answering this question allows us to extrapolate

Table 12.3 Characterization of the confusion clusters

Confusion cluster	Specificity of the confusion coefficient	Share of the sample	Characterization
1	<0.5 to 1	28.3 %	Slightly confused
2	<0 to 0.5	57.2 %	Confused
3	<-0.5 to 0	14.5 %	Severely confused
4	-1 to -0.5	0 %	Very severely confused

what influences on the interviewees promote the effectiveness of ambush marketing and thereby possibly compromise the effectiveness of the World Cup sponsors' activities.

Bivariate analyses

An analysis was conducted of the influence of a total of 21 recorded variables on the extent of the interviewees' confusion, evaluated in terms of their affiliation to various confusion clusters. In Table 12.4 the results of all bivariate analyses that were conducted regarding the state of confusion or mix-up are aggregated in one overview. The smaller the p-value,

Table 12.4 Results of the bivariate tests regarding ambush marketing

Influencing factors	Variables	Correlation to confusion	
		Significance	Interpretation
Individual attributes	Age	0.006★	Correlation exists, but no clear trend
	Sex	0.017★	Confusion among girls more prevalent than among boys
	Education	0.000★★★	The lower the level of education, the more frequent the confusion
Sports type-specific involvement	Interest in football	0.003★★	The greater the interest in football, the rarer the confusion
	Play football	0.011★	Correlation exists, but no clear trend
	Interest in World Cup	0.114	No correlation
	Number of World Cup games watched	0.020★	The more games watched live on television, the less confusion occurs
Product or company-specific involvement	Use Coca-Cola	0.466	Overwhelmingly no correlation
	Use McDonald's	0.408	
	Use Yahoo	0.469	
	Use Deutsche Telekom	0.060	
	Use adidas	0.150	
	Use OBI	0.004★★	

Influencing factors	Variables	Correlation to confusion	
		Significance	Interpretation
Sports advertising-specific involvement	Attitude to sports advertising	0.716	No correlation
	Intention to purchase based on sports advertising	0.041★	Correlation exists, but no clear trend
Event knowledge	Knowledge of event	0.000★★★	The greater the knowledge of the event, the rarer the confusion
Sponsorship knowledge	Knowledge of sponsorship rights	0.000★★★	The greater the knowledge of sponsorship rights, the rarer the confusion
Attitude towards sponsorship and ambush marketing	I don't care if a company that uses the 2006 World Cup in its advertising is an official sponsor or not.	0.458	No correlation
	Only companies that support the World Cup financially as official sponsors should be allowed to advertise using the World Cup	0.028★	The greater the approval, the rarer the confusion
	Companies who are not World Cup sponsors should not use their advertising to create the impression that they are somehow involved with the World Cup	0.487	No correlation
	If a company is not a World Cup sponsor but uses its advertising to pretend that it is, I think that it's smart and savvy	0.212	No correlation

the stronger the influence of the individual factor, which is indicated by the number asterisks. In addition, the direction of the effect of significant influences is verbally interpreted.

However, the explanation for the confusion of World Cup sponsors with ambush marketers or dummies cannot be merely monocausal. The fact is that the confusion is influenced by a variety of determinants in parallel or their interdependencies. Further, multivariate analyses have to answer questions such as: "What are the differences between slightly confused, confused and severely confused consumers?" "Which variable-characteristics are essentially relevant for affiliation to the three diverse confusion clusters?"

Limitations of the study

To date there have been very few empirical analyses as to the effects of ambush marketing, in business administration and sports economics. In the context of the comprehensive study that has been conducted, of which only selected results have been presented here, an effort has been made to close that gap. However, the results of this study cannot be generalized for a variety of reasons:

- The object of the research was a specific sponsorship event, namely, the 2006 FIFA Football World Cup.
- In the context of the present study, only psychological target variables were measured.
- The analysis focused exclusively on the target group adolescents aged 13–18.
- The study focused primarily on the official main sponsors and selected ambushers. It is not really surprising that the brands that were able to achieve the best effectiveness ratings were often those with which the adolescents are most likely to have contact.
- Adolescents in Germany were interviewed for this study. One can assume the fact that the 2006 World Cup was held in Germany did have some impact on the results of the study (the interviewees' high degree of interest in an event held in their own country, strong accompanying media coverage).

Conclusion and outlook

The main results of the empirical impact evaluation may be summarized as follows. Ambush marketing helps non-sponsors to achieve comparable or even greater impact than the official event sponsors. Ambushing campaigns above all compromise the effectiveness of sponsorship, as official sponsors are forced to share the attention of the target group with additional advertisers as freeriders using the theme of the event for their own benefit.

Ambush marketing remains controversial and will continue to be the subject of contentious discussions. From the perspective of the event organizers and sports sponsors it represents an understandable threat, while from the perspective of the ambushers it offers the opportunity to reach the target audience in an attractive environment and at affordable cost. However, ambush marketing may by no means be relegated to the status of a "dirty word" of sports marketing on the basis of its controversial nature. Instead, ambush marketing should be classified as a competitive tool in conjunction with a sporting event. The fact that ambush marketing is often a "race between the hare and the tortoise", in which the organizers take on the role of the hare should therefore be viewed as a sign of functioning competition in which all the participating players deploy their specific "weapons": official sponsorship against creativity (Pechtl, 2007; Nufer, 2013).

The concept of ambush marketing has a negative connotation and at first glance inevitably produces a negative estimation of this phenomenon. One could extrapolate that there are ambushing forms that are not objectionable, neither in legal-statutory nor ethical and moral terms.

The overall conflict potential that ambush marketing generates may be summarized as follows. The interests of the organizers in monopolising the marketing rights for a sports event exist in a relationship of legal tension with the advertising freedom of companies who seek to use the event for advertising even without making a sponsor's contribution. Therefore, a closer contemplation of ambush marketing must always differentiate. A limited extent of event protection would be a proper and appropriate solution. Ultimately, this involves a political value judgment as to what is to be considered the higher ranking interest (Wittneben and Soldner, 2006). It is important to determine an adequate median so that the financing of sports mega events is secured, and at the same time, fairer competition among advertiser companies is enabled, as per the saying "if you don't stand out from the pack, you're out" (Schulte, 2007: 138).

This chapter structured the phenomenon of ambush marketing. It contained empirical research results concerning the effects of ambush marketing in sports. For a detailed analysis of legal and ethical aspects of ambush marketing see, for example, Hartland and Williams-Burnett,

2012; Ellis, Scassa and Séguin, 2011; Heermann, 2011; Grady, McKelvey and Bernthal, 2010; McKelvey and Grady, 2008; Noth, 2007.

References

Bayless, A. (1988). Ambush Marketing is becoming a popular event at Olympic games. *Wall Street Journal*, 8 February, 1.

Bühl, A. (2006). *SPSS 14. Einführung in die moderne Datenanalyse.* 10th ed. München: Pearson.

Bühler, A. and Nufer, G. (Eds). (2014). *International sports marketing: Principles and perspectives.* Berlin: Erich Schmidt Verlag.

Burton, N. and Chadwick, S. (2009). Ambush marketing in sport: An analysis of sponsorship protection means and counter-ambush measures. *Journal of Sponsorship* 2(4): 303–315.

Chadwick, S. and Beech, J. (Eds). (2006). *The marketing of sport.* Harlow: Prentice Hall.

Chadwick, S. and Burton, N. (2011). The evolving sophistication of ambush marketing: A typology of strategies. *Thunderbird International Business Review* 53(6): 709–719.

Crow, D. and Hoek, J. (2003). Ambush marketing: A critical review and some practical advice. *Marketing Bulletin* 14(1): 1–14.

Du Toit, M. (2006). Ambush marketing. www.bowman.co.za/LawArticles/Law-Article.asp?id= 1079997814 (accessed 1 March 2010).

Ellis, D., Gauthier, M. E. and Séguin, B. (2011). Ambush marketing, the Olympic and Paralympic Marks Act and Canadian national sports organisation: Awareness, perceptions and impacts. *Journal of Sponsorship* 4(2): 253–271.

Ellis, D., Scassa, T. and Séguin, B. (2011). Framing ambush marketing as a legal issue: An Olympic perspective. *Sport Management Review* 14(3): 297–308.

Eschenbach, F. (2011). *Erfolgsfaktoren des Ambush-Marketing. Eine theoretische und empirische Analyse am Beispiel der Fußball-Europameisterschaft 2008.* Wiesbaden: Gabler.

Farrelly, F., Quester, P. and Greyser, S. A. (2005). Defending the co-branding benefits of sponsorship B2B partnerships: The case of ambush marketing. *Journal of Advertising Research* 45(3): 339–348.

Grady, J., McKelvey, S. and Bernthal, M. (2010). From Beijing 2008 to London 2012: Examining event-specific Olympic legislation vis-à-vis the rights and interests of stakeholders. *Journal of Sponsorship* 3(2): 144–156.

Hartland, T. and Williams-Burnett, N. (2012). Protecting the Olympic brand: Winners and losers. *Journal of Strategic Marketing* 20(1): 69–82.

Heermann, P. W. (2011). *Ambush Marketing bei Sportveranstaltungen.* Stuttgart: Boorberg.

Hoek, J. and Gendall, P. (2002). Ambush marketing: More than just a commercial irritant? *Entertainment Law* 1(2): 72–91.

Johnson, P. (2008). *Ambush marketing: A practical guide to protecting the brand of a sporting event.* London: Sweet & Maxwell.

Levinson, J. C. (2007). *Guerilla marketing: Easy and inexpensive strategies for making big profits from your small business.* 4th ed. Boston: Houghton Mifflin.

Lyberger, M. R. and McCarthy, L. (2001). An assessment of consumer knowledge of, interest in, and perceptions of ambush marketing strategies. *Sport Marketing Quarterly* 10(2): 130–137.

McDaniel, S. R. and Kinney, L. (1996). Ambush marketing revisited: An experimental study of perceived sponsorship effects on brand awareness, attitude toward the brand and purchase intention. *Journal of Promotion Management* 3(1/2): 141–167.

McDaniel, S. R. and Kinney, L. (1998). The implications of recency and gender effects in consumer response to ambush marketing. *Psychology & Marketing* 15(4): 385–403.

McDonald, J. and Davidson, J. (2002). Avoiding surprise results at the Olympic Games. *Managing Intellectual Property* 115: 22–27.

Macintosh, E., Nadeau, J., Seguin, B., O'Reilly, N., Bradish, C. L. and Legg, D. (2012). The role of mega-sports event interest in sponsorship and ambush marketing attitudes. *Sport Marketing Quarterly* 21(1): 43–52.

McKelvey, S. and Grady, J. (2008). Sponsorship program protection strategies for special sport events: Are event organizers outmaneuvering ambush marketers? *Journal of Sport Management* 22(5): 550–586.

Meenaghan, T. (1994). Point of view: Ambush marketing: Immoral or imaginative practice? *Journal of Advertising Research* 34(9/10): 77–88.

Meenaghan, T. (1996). Ambush marketing: A threat to corporate sponsorship? *Sloan Management Review* 38(1): 103–113.

Meenaghan, T. (1998). Ambush marketing: Corporate strategy and consumer reaction. *Psychology & Marketing* 15(4): 305–322.

Noth, M. (2007). *Trittbrettfahren durch Werbung bei Sportveranstaltungen: Rechtliche Beurteilung von Ambush Marketing und ähnlichen Werbeformen*. Bern: Stämpfli.

Nufer, G. (2005). Ambush Marketing: Angriff aus dem Hinterhalt oder eine Alternative zum Sportsponsoring? In Horch, H.-D., Hovemann, G., Kaiser, S. and Viebahn, K. (Eds). *Perspektiven des Sportmarketing. Besonderheiten, Herausforderungen, Tendenzen*. Köln: Deutsche Sporthochschule, 209–227.

Nufer, G. (2010). *Ambush Marketing im Sport: Grundlagen – Strategien – Wirkungen*. Berlin: Erich Schmidt Verlag.

Nufer, G. (2013). *Ambush marketing in sports: Theory and practice*. London and New York: Routledge.

Nufer, G. and Bühler, A. (Eds). (2012). *Management im Sport: Betriebswirtschaftliche Grundlagen und Anwendungen der modernen Sportökonomie*. 3rd ed. Berlin: Erich Schmidt Verlag.

Nufer, G. and Bühler, A. (Eds). (2013a). *Marketing im Sport: Grundlagen und Trends des modernen Sportmarketing*. 3rd ed. Berlin: Erich Schmidt Verlag.

Nufer, G. and Bühler, A. (Eds). (2013b). *Ambush Marketing im Sport*. In Nufer, G. and Bühler, A. (Eds). *Marketing im Sport. Grundlagen und Trends des modernen Sportmarketing*. 3rd ed. Berlin: Erich Schmidt Verlag, 445–474.

Nufer, G. and Geiger, C. (2011). Ambush Marketing im Sport: Systematisierung und Implikationen für Ambusher. *Sciamus – Sport und Management* 2(2): 1–18.

O'Reilly, N., Lyberger, M., McCarthy, L., Séguin, B. and Nadeau, J. (2008). Mega-special-event promotions and intent-to-purchase: A longitudinal analysis of the Super Bowl. *Journal of Sport Management* 22(4): 392–409.

O'Sullivan, P. and Murphy, P. (1998). Ambush marketing: The ethical issues. *Psychology & Marketing* 15(4): 349–366.

Opfer, G. (1997). Monitoring und Day-after-Recall im Sportsponsoring: Methodische Anforderungen an Werbewirkungs-Messungen. Hamburg.

Payne, M. (1998). Ambush marketing: The undeserved advantage. *Psychology & Marketing* 15(4): 323–331.

Payne, M. (2003). Ambush marketing, www.guerilla-marketing-portal.de/doks/pdf/ppp_ambush-marketing-2003.pdf (accessed 2 August 2006).

Pechtl, H. (2007). Trittbrettfahren bei Sportevents: das Ambush-Marketing. Wirtschaftswissenschaftliches Diskussionspapier Nr. 1/2007, Rechts- und Staatswissenschaftliche Fakultät, Universität Greifswald.

Pitt, L., Parent, M., Berthon, P. and Steyn, P. G. (2010). Event sponsorship and ambush marketing: Lessons from the Beijing Olympics. *Business Horizons* 53(3): 281–290.

Preuß, H., Gemeinder, K. and Séguin, B. (2008). Ambush marketing in China: Counterbalancing Olympic sponsorship efforts. *Asian Business & Management* 7(2): 243–263.

Sachse, M. (2010). Negative Kommunikationseffekte von Sponsoring und Ambush Marketing bei Sportgroßveranstaltungen. Wiesbaden: Gabler.

Sandler, D. M. and Shani, D. (1989). Olympic sponsorship vs. 'ambush' marketing: Who gets the gold? *Journal of Advertising Research* 29(4): 9–15.

Sandler, D. M. and Shani, D. (1993). Sponsorship and the Olympic Games: The consumer perspective. *Sport Marketing Quarterly* 2(3): 38–43.

Schulte, T. (2007). *Guerilla Marketing für Unternehmertypen*. 3rd ed. Sternenfels: Verlag Wissenschaft & Praxis.

Séguin, B. and O'Reilly, N. J. (2008). The Olympic brand, ambush marketing and clutter. *International Journal of Sport Management and Marketing* 4(1): 62–84.

Shani, D. and Sandler, D. M. (1998). Ambush marketing: Is confusion to blame for the flickering of the flame? *Psychology & Marketing* 15(4): 367–383.

Shilbury, D., Quick, S. and Westerbeek, H. (2009). *Strategic sport marketing*. 3rd ed. Crows Nest: Allen & Unwin.

Skildum-Reid, K. (2007). *The ambush marketing toolkit*. Sydney: McGraw-Hill.

Stenger, H. (1986). *Stichproben*. Heidelberg: Physica.

Townley, S., Harrington, D. and Couchman, N. (1998). The legal and practical prevention of ambush marketing in sports. *Psychology & Marketing* 15(4): 333–348.

Von der Lippe, P. and Kladroba, A. (2002). Repräsentativität von Stichproben. *Marketing ZFP* 24(2): 139–145.

Welsh, J. (2002). Ambush marketing: What it is and what it isn't, www.poolonline.com/archive/issue19/iss19fea5.html (accessed 17 August 2004).

Wittneben, M. and Soldner, A. (2006). Der Schutz von Veranstaltern und Sponsoren vor Ambush-Marketing bei Sportgroßveranstaltungen. *Wettbewerb in Recht und Praxis* 21(10): 1175–1185.

Zanger, C. and Drengner, J. (2005). *Eventreport 2004: Die Wirkungen von Ambush Marketing bei sportlichen Großevents.* Chemnitz: Technische Universität.

13

AMBUSH MARKETING IN SPORTS

Simon Chadwick, Nicholas Burton and Cheri Bradish

Introduction

On 16 June 2006, the Netherlands and the Côte d'Ivoire met in a group stage match at the 2006 FIFA World Cup in Stuttgart, Germany; a game remarkable more for the action on the terraces and outside the ground than for the play on the pitch. As part of a marketing campaign centered on the World Cup and Dutch football supporters, Netherlands-based brewery Bavaria staged a promotional giveaway offering fans orange, Bavaria-branded "leeuwenhose", or "lion pants", in special cases of beer throughout Holland. The campaign proved a great success, as thousands of Dutch supporters descended on Germany for the World Cup clad in Bavaria-lettered lederhosen, setting the stage for one of the most audacious event-related guerrilla marketing campaigns in European sports history. Stadium officials and FIFA's brand police met leeuwenhose-adorned supporters outside the stadium, requiring fans to remove the offending merchandise or be refused admission in an effort to protect official sponsors, Budweiser, from unwanted competition. FIFA's reaction garnered international media coverage, applauding Bavaria's ingenuity and condemning FIFA's draconian response. More importantly, Bavaria's efforts to "ambush" the tournament – to associate or align with the event without an official marketing partnership with FIFA – ignited a new era in sponsorship protection and public awareness of ambush marketing and brand management in sports, and introduced ambush marketing to the world as a key player in sports marketing.

Ambush marketing: in the beginning . . .

The history and development of ambush marketing is presented here, contextualizing the emergence and evolution of ambush strategies from the 1984 Los Angeles Summer Olympic Games to the present day.

First emergent in 1984 as a result of changes implemented by the 1982 FIFA World Cup and the 1984 Los Angeles Summer Olympic sponsorship programmes, ambush marketing is defined as *the marketing communications activities of a brand seeking to capitalize on the attention, awareness, fan equity, and goodwill generated by having an association with an event or property, beyond the official or authorized rights of association delivered by that event or property.* As a result of growing uncertainty regarding the financial security and viability of sporting events in the 1970s and early 1980s, FIFA and the International Olympic Committee (IOC) implemented major structural reforms to their sponsorship programmes, incorporating rights bundling (the combining of assets and rights owned by the events into comprehensive, inclusive sponsorship packages) and category exclusivity (securing one sponsor from each major product category) into their sponsorship programmes. These changes served to limit the number of "official" sponsors of their events, and to increase the value of those sponsorships, revolutionizing the sale and distribution of sports sponsorship assets, and encouraging a progressive growth in the marketing value of sports events and properties.

The reforms enacted by Ueberroth and the Los Angeles organizing committee made the 1984 Olympic Games the most successful in Olympic history to that point and inspired changes throughout the sports sponsorship industry. The IOC created The Olympic Partner (TOP) sponsorship platform, combining category exclusivity, rights bundling, and a multi-tiered sponsorship framework, in order to further grow sponsorship revenues and build upon the success of the Los Angeles Games. These structural changes ushered in a period of progressive growth in sponsorship expenditure and subsequent managerial and strategic sophistication. Whereas in 1984 the global sponsorship industry was estimated to be worth $2 billion (Meenaghan, 1991), the International Events Group valued the global sponsorship market for 2014 to be approximately $55.3 billion (International Events Group, 2014), a growth of $30.9 million since 2002 alone (International Events Group, 2006). Within this international sponsorship market, Europe and European sports account for a significant share of spending; in 2013, the European Sponsorship Association estimated the industry's value to have exceeded €26 billion, a growth of more than 15% over the preceding four years (European Sponsorship Association, 2014). Although estimates vary, sports account for approximately 50–75% of all sponsorship investment worldwide, with particular emphasis on major international properties, such as the IOC Summer and Winter Olympics, the FIFA World Cup, and the UEFA European Championships (Mintel, 2006).

Despite these advances, the sponsorship reforms to come from the 1984 Olympic Games equally inspired the advent of ambush marketing. Prior to 1984, any company willing to pay for the rights to associate with the Olympic Games or FIFA World Cup had the opportunity to do so for a nominal fee. The increased competition for sponsorship rights, and the increased expenditure necessary for official partners to secure an association, ultimately forced market rivals who previously held simultaneous official partnerships with the Olympics into direct competition for corporate sponsorship rights. The new framework thus encouraged non-sponsor brands to identify alternative means of affiliating with the event, and gave rise to ambush marketing as competitive marketing practice for brands left out of the sponsorship families of major events.

The earliest examples of ambushing – such as Kodak's sponsorship of the United States Track and Field team for the 1984 Los Angeles Games – represented overt and direct attempts to weaken or undermine the official sponsorship partnerships of direct market rivals, in this instance official sponsors and industry competitors Fuji. Such early examples of ambush marketing capitalized on marketing opportunities and activities today viewed as wholly legitimate and acceptable: individual team, nation, or federation sponsorship, broadcast partnerships, and the exploitation of outdoor advertising media at and near event facilities, with the express intent of competing directly with a market rival for consumer awareness. This predominantly competitive, sabotage-based form of ambushing which emerged inspired its nomenclature, and ultimately guided the initial discussions – professional and theoretical – of ambush marketing's place and purpose in sports marketing.

This competitive, rivalry-based ambush marketing defined the formative stages of ambush marketing as a form of marketing communications, as major international brands vied for place and presence around the Olympics in the late-1980s and early 1990s. This era of ambushing inspired famous campaigns such as the American Express ambush of Visa around the 1992 Albertville Winter Olympic Games, 1992 Barcelona Summer Olympic Games, and 1994 Lillehammer Winter Olympic Games, proudly proclaiming that fans "don't need a visa" to travel to the host countries of each Games. This direct, explicit approach to ambush marketing continued until the 1996 Atlanta Summer Olympic Games, where brands outside of the IOC family began to realize and exploit the multitude of marketing options available to non-sponsors, and ambushing as a commercial and not-competitive activity was fully embraced. The Atlanta Games became a marketing phenomenon with brands, such as Nike, Puma, Converse, Pepsi, and hundreds more, activating around the event, signalling ambush marketing's true emergence as an event marketing alternative.

The Atlanta Olympic Games saw ambushing brands launch international marketing campaigns focused on the Games, construct elaborate off-site marketing and hospitality centres for visitors to the Games, and activated throughout the Games using major events, athletes, and themes surrounding the Games as a means of attaching their brands to the event. Sportswear manufacturer, Puma, for example, incurred heavy fines from the IOC and marketing regulatory bodies for outfitting British sprinter, Linford Christie, with Puma-logo styled contact lenses for a press conference ahead of the 100m men's sprint final. Competitors, Nike, also mounted an elaborate ambush of the Games, designing gold, highly visible spikes for gold medallist Michael Johnson, the face of the American Olympic team. The ambush marketing attempts that emerged in Atlanta evidenced a creativity and bravery on the part of the ambushers previously unseen in other events. Specifically targeted campaigns against official sponsors, such as American Express's ambush attempts in Barcelona and Lillehammer, were replaced by highly associative, suggestive, and subversive marketing efforts, using the colours, symbology, themes, and key players of the event to craft more innovative ambush campaigns. This move inspired continued developments in ambush tactics through the 1996 UEFA European Championships and 1998 FIFA World Cup, as ambush marketing grew in scope and scale.

Despite this pronounced shift in the mid-1990s, the perception of ambushing as an aggressive, attack-minded form of marketing communications has dominated academic and professional discourse around ambushing and sponsorship. Ambush marketing has historically been portrayed as a tactical, parasitic activity aimed at devaluing the official sponsorship of a market rival or intentionally confusing consumers as to the identity of an official sponsor. This rights-holder espoused view of ambushing has undermined a progressive evolution in ambush marketing media and strategy, influenced by the success of ambushers at the 1996 Atlanta Olympics and the interventionist activities implemented by commercial rights holders and official sponsors to limit and prohibit ambush marketers.

Interventionism in sports sponsorship

Beginning in 1992 with the Barcelona Summer Olympic Games, as the concerns of IOC and their sponsors with regard to ambush marketing grew, sponsorship programmes at the highest levels of sports have undergone a marked transformation in adopting a more stringent, regulated framework for the protection of sponsorship rights and relationships. The prominence and availability of ambushing opportunities around events witnessed necessitated a reaction from major rights holders and event organizers designed to better protect their corporate partners and condemn the activities of non-sponsoring brands.

The response elicited proved the catalyst for the development of counter-ambush marketing activities, broadly categorized into two major forms: proactive, marketing-oriented counter-ambush strategies, which place greater responsibility on sponsors to leverage and better communicate their relationship with a property in an effort to limit potential ambush opportunities, and minimize the detrimental effects of ambush marketing efforts; and the employment of reactive, rights holder-based interventionist tactics, such as the enforcement of legal protection by rights holders, and the utilization of increasingly rigid intellectual property rights infrastructures and legislations available, in an effort to prohibit the illegal association of non-sponsoring brands with an event or property. The result of these initiatives has been widely felt throughout European and international sports sponsorship: as sponsorship agreements and programmes have become more strictly protected and enforced, the management of corporate partnerships as dyadic and synergistic relationships has grown. However, the interventionist activities and policies put in place have equally encouraged a rise in the creativity and innovation of ambush marketers, and has forced non-sponsoring brands to identify new, unique, and increasingly clever and subversive opportunities by which to leverage against the commercial appeal of major events.

The earliest forms of counter-ambush activities relied upon predominantly reactive, ex post facto defence tactics employed by event staff and major federations. Chief amongst these reactive interventionist measures was the development of "name and shame" public relations activities, intended to capitalize on the unethical and immoral perception of ambushing perpetuated by commercial rights holders and to drive public opposition to ambush marketers. Press conferences, such as Reebok's response to Nike's activities around the 1996 Atlanta Summer Olympics, appealed to consumers' sense of justice and fair play in marketing in the hopes of courting public support and turn opinions against Nike. As part of a wide-reaching ambush campaign, Nike erected a temporary store on the limits of the Olympic village, and partnered with Sports Illustrated on a special insert triumphing Nike-endorsed athletes and US-sports federations; official United States Olympic Committee sponsors Reebok responded by condemning Nike's efforts, stating: "Shame on them. They're undercutting people and companies and products and services that will go to make the ultimate success of their own athletes" (Myerson, 1996).

Such appeals, on ethical grounds, ultimately proved ineffective as ambush marketers received additional coverage and attention and public opinion offered little remedy for the implicated sponsors. Ambushers felt little deterrence from such public condemnation, and instead grew more bold and confident in staging ambush campaigns, inviting the added media coverage naming and shaming afforded them.

Simultaneously, a growing push towards contractual and legal regulation for sponsorship agreements emerged, affording sponsors greater protection against explicit intellectual property rights infringements and reinforcing the terminology and responsibilities of both sponsor and sponsee. The legal protection against ambush marketing has guided much of the subsequent sponsorship enforcement initiatives implement. However, the success of legal manoeuvres in preventing ambush marketing has been marginal: major sporting events, such as the Olympics or FIFA World Cup, report hundreds of ambush marketing incidents every year, but the majority of those investigated are small-scale or local businesses using protected phrases or imagery in promotions. In such instances, cease and desist letters, or court-ordered injunctions, offer immediate relief and protection against illegal ambush campaigns from smaller enterprises unwilling or unable to challenge court injunctions or risk facing legal action. However, cease and desist letters have provided little protection against larger, more creative or surreptitious efforts, which are careful not to infringe upon the intellectual property rights of organizers and rights holders. As such, the legal precedence for ambushing is largely undeveloped.

Further complicating the legal defense, past court findings have typically favoured ambush marketers in cases not involving direct infringements of intellectual property rights. Cases of alleged ambush marketing have proven difficult to assert, as most ambushing efforts fall outside the law, and manifest instead as competitive marketing practices wholly within the legal rights of the ambushing brand. Typically, ambushers have taken great care and precision to avoid potentially illegal campaigns, abstaining from the use of protected marks, symbols, and words, or making direct reference to the event targeted. As such, the legal precedent set by cases such as the National Hockey League vs. Pepsi-Cola Canada (1990), and the New Zealand Rugby Football Union (NZRFU) vs. Canterbury International Ltd. (2001), have favoured the ambush marketer, further complicating the legal protection against ambush marketing sought by sponsors and rights holders. Nevertheless, the enforcement of intellectual property rights remains a fundamental component of sponsorship protection and ambush prevention for most major events and properties. This reliance on legal protection ultimately inspired the development of event-specific ambush marketing legislation for the largest governing bodies and rights holders, such as the IOC.

The use of specific trademark and intellectual property rights legislation as a means of deterring and prosecuting ambush marketers began with the Australian government's adoption of the Sydney 2000 Games (Indicia and Images) Protection Act in 1996 as protection for the 2000 Summer Olympic Games. By the late-1980s, Australia had already enacted legislation protecting Olympic symbols and marks, as have many other participating and host countries in the years since. However, organizers for the Sydney Olympics sought new means of protecting the 2000 Olympics following the pronounced commercialization and rampant ambush marketing experienced during the 1996 Atlanta Games, and implemented bespoke ambush marketing legislation designed to govern Olympic sponsorship rights and advertising during the Games as a means of limiting potential ambush opportunities. Such legislation now exists in all Olympic host countries around the globe, including Greece, Italy, Russia, and the United Kingdom.

This event-specific ambush marketing legislation has granted major event hosts such as the International Olympic Committee enhanced intellectual property rights protection above and beyond the standard allowances for copyright and trademark protection, including protection in some countries extending to imagery and terminology deemed too similar to protected marks. The legislation employed further grants rights holders immediate injunctive relief against alleged infringements and ambush marketers, as well as increased financial and legal penalties and remedies for organisations and individuals found in violation of the legislative protection. Given the short time-frames during which most sporting events take place, and the often quick, creative campaigns released by ambush marketers, such measures provide potentially invaluable protection for sponsorship programmes.

Proactive sponsorship relations

Unfortunately for events and properties, ambush marketing's evolution and rise in prominence has seen its growth continue despite the enactment and enforcement of such legislations. The legislative efforts of the International Olympic Committee and other major events' rights holders have shown initiative in preventing possible ambush marketing campaigns and have secured enhanced rights protection for corporate partners, important elements of contemporary sponsorship protection. However, the creativity and innovation of ambushers shown in circumventing the legal frameworks in place, and in identifying new opportunities unguarded against by rights holders, has defined ambush marketing in recent years, and merely reinforced the difficulty faced by rights holders and host governments in preventing ambush marketing's proliferation.

Arguably more effective have been advancements in the management of sponsorship relations by rights holders and sponsors witnessed over time, developments that have redefined the roles and responsibilities of both parties and encouraged greater collaboration in maximizing the value and visibility of official sponsorship agreements. Sponsors and rights holders have increasingly embraced a more comprehensive, positive approach to the activation of sponsorship, adopting multi-tiered, extensive marketing campaigns in order to prevent would-be ambushers, and increase sponsorship effectiveness.

Amongst those strategies adopted in refining sponsorship strategy, perhaps none have been more important than the cooperation between organizers and broadcasters in distributing broadcast advertising and the more effective activation of a sponsor's association. Rights holders have taken a more proactive involvement, endeavouring to block-out possible ambush opportunities, and limit the immediate threat faced by corporate partners. To this effect, sponsorship contracts have grown in sophistication, more clearly establishing the rights and responsibilities of sponsor and sponsee, and ensuring that properties and events play a more active role in the promotion and activation of sponsors' associations and marketing communications activities.

Furthermore, following the increasingly opportunistic, adventurous ambush marketing campaigns emergent around the 1996 Atlanta Summer Olympic Games and 1998 FIFA World Cup, the International Olympic Committee and UEFA both initiated new protocols on the sale of broadcast advertising rights during their events, restricting immediate access to broadcast audiences for potential ambushers. Organizers of major events have equally taken greater control of the use and distribution of tickets, in an effort to deter their use in ambush promotions, and implemented extensive on-site policing and regulation of brand visibility and marketing. Such measures have become instrumental in ensuring "clean" venues for official partners and in keeping ambush marketers away from event sites, whilst alleviating much of the marketing clutter around major events caused by competing marketing communications and non-sponsor messaging.

Integral to this push for clean venues has been the establishment of protected marketing exclusion zones around event stadia and host sites. In 2000, UEFA and marketing partners, International Sports and Leisure (ISL), implemented restricted-access marketing zones around host stadia and event locales for the European Championships in Belgium and the Netherlands. Outdoor marketing media around and near the host football grounds – to a radius of 3km – was secured by UEFA and ISL, to be used by official sponsors or kept clean for the duration of the tournament, thus ensuring that ambush marketers were kept away from all advertising opportunities in the immediate vicinity of the matches.

Such efforts have grown in time – the 2008 Beijing Summer Olympic Games featured a protected marketing radius of 30km – yet merely reinforced the ingenuity of ambushers. In order to capitalize on China's first Olympic Games in 2008, Pepsi launched an extensive marketing campaign featuring Chinese basketball star, Yao Ming, throughout Shanghai, avoiding the restricted marketing space in Beijing whilst establishing a presence around the Games in one of China's biggest cities. Similarly, at the 2008 ATP/WTA French Open at Roland Garros, sportswear brand K–Swiss ambushed the event by staging a guerilla promotion on the limits of the tournament's protected property, placed a car being crushed by a metre-diameter purple tennis ball on a main access route in plain view of pedestrian and public transit access to the stadium. Comparable efforts have become commonplace around major golf events, along train lines, and in airports as a means of giving ambush marketers access to fans and consumers en route to events, rather than within the grounds or in the arena, areas more heavily policed and protected.

This push towards more marketing-based, proactive sponsorship protection has been an important development in sponsorship relations. Whereas the predominantly reactive, rights protection initiatives employed have largely proven ineffective in preventing or limiting ambush opportunities – and encouraged a more intelligent, creative, surreptitious approach on the part of ambushers – the move towards a more positive ambush prevention approach has limited non-sponsor communications immediately competing with sponsors, and has served to reinforce and promote sponsorship relations around major events. Nonetheless, the inherent impact of those rights protection and interventionist activities employed by right holders has been a pronounced evolution in the strategy and media employed by ambush marketers, and a proliferation in ambush strategies and media. Marketers have increasingly uncovered new and innovative ways of circumventing the rights protection and counter-ambush marketing programmes in place around major events, expanding their marketing activities beyond exclusion zones, adopting more associative, suggestive imagery and terminology, and capitalizing on the ever-growing number of opportunities available to leveraged against the value of sports. Ambushing has thus emerged as an alternative to official event sponsorship, providing non-sponsors a means to capitalize on the consumer, spectator, and media interest surrounding major sporting events, outside of the parameters and capital costs of official sponsorship.

The many sides of ambush marketing: contemporary and future challenges

The impact of ambushing's proliferation, and the interventionist frameworks enacted and employed by commercial rights holders is next discussed, with particular emphasis on European events and examples including the 2006 FIFA World Cup, the 2008 UEFA European Championships, and the 2014 Sochi Winter Olympic Games.

Whilst the discussion of ambush marketing's evolution, and the progressive adaptation of interventionist measures employed by commercial rights holders and official sponsors, has inherently driven the study of ambush marketing and consideration of its merits and place in sports marketing, the view of ambushing as something in need of preventing or protecting against is ultimately one of many perspectives in need of acknowledging. Historically, much of the theoretical and professional literature has been influenced and guided by the pejorative, parasitic definitions of ambush marketing prescribed by major rights holders. Multiple stakeholders' perspectives offer relevant views in the discussion and debate surrounding ambush marketing, including those of sponsors, consumers, and ambush marketers themselves.

Ambushing to ambushers

From the point of view of alleged ambush marketers, the legitimacy and strategy of ambush marketing is clear. Major sporting events offer a consumer outreach and visibility across target markets unlike any other medium. As such, sports and event marketing represent fundamental components of many brands' marketing communications portfolios, leveraging the cognitive, affective, and emotive connections made by consumers with sports. Whilst rights holders like the IOC and FIFA have bemoaned ambushing as an unethical, parasitic practice, the expectation that major international brands and marketers should abstain from competitive marketing practices merely out of a sense of fair play is unrealistic. It could be argued that for major international corporations to ignore mega-sporting events and not seek to use sports as a vehicle for marketing would be an abdication of duty and irresponsible from a commercial perspective. For brands unable to secure official event or property partnerships, or for whom such an approach may not reflect the brand's image or reputation, ambush marketing – when used in conjunction and with respect to the legal and legislative frameworks in place – represents a legitimate and viable alternative to official sponsorship.

Myriad strategies and marketing activities are available to brands wishing to pursue an unofficial relationship with a property through ambush marketing; creative campaigns utilizing suggestive or clever imagery, symbology, terminology, music, colours, themes, or characters may allow non-sponsors a means of circumventing the legal and legislative frameworks protecting sponsorship, whilst simultaneously aligning their brand with the intended country or event or team in the minds of consumers. In 2006, for example, German airline Lufthansa ambushed the FIFA World Cup by painting the nose cones of their fleet of aircraft with black and white footballs. Such a simple act fell foul of no regulations or laws protecting FIFA's sponsors, but served as an intelligent reminder of Germany's national airline's presence and created a subtle link between the brand and the World Cup that summer. Likewise, the 2008 UEFA European Championships saw Puma ambush rivals and official sponsors Adidas through the creation of an interactive campaign allowing fans to set their mobile's ringtone as their country's trademark song or chant, and have it played automatically each time the country scored. More recently, many companies – including clothes retailer, American Apparel – ambushed the 2014 Sochi Winter Olympic Games, by developing promotional campaigns focused on gay and lesbian rights, a response to the debate surrounding human rights and civil liberties in Russia prior to the Games.

Ambushing brands have equally been successful in leveraging existing associations with member teams, countries, or participating athletes, or in activating marketing campaigns before, during, and after an event. Such strategies maximize exposure and consumer awareness of the ambush attempt, and ensure an authority and legitimacy in the ambusher's actions. Major international brands, such as Pepsi and Nike, have long exploited such legal and authentic practices and leveraged endorsement agreements with athletes and celebrities in line with major events as a means of capitalizing on the opportunity such events present. Nike's "Courage" campaign in the summer of 2008, for instance, made no reference – overt or implied – to the Beijing Olympic Games, yet featured a variety of Nike-endorsed athletes competing in Olympic and non-Olympic sports. The creative campaign was released and run in time for the Beijing Games as a way to connect the company with the Summer Olympics, and further build upon Nike's immense marketing reach.

More recently, the proliferation of marketing media and advertizing opportunities around mega-sporting events – particularly with the advent and growth of social and digital media – has afforded ambushing brands a creative and innovative means of activating in real-time and capitalize on current affairs and major incidents at events, and establish a relevance and presence in the minds of fans unlike ever before. Brands like Specsavers, Kit-Kat, and Oreo have cleverly used social media platforms, such as Twitter and Facebook, to release digital advertisements playing on major events and incidents in games across sports, such as the disallowed England goal scored against Germany at the 2010 FIFA World Cup, and the power outage experienced during the 2013 NFL Super Bowl. Such campaigns evidenced an immediacy and relevance available to ambush marketers in securing an association with the games, unavailable to official sponsors requiring authorization from rights holders for any activation around their sponsorships, and demonstrate a creativity and ingenuity on the part of the ambushing brands.

In employing such creative, associative strategies to ambush events, the majority of contemporary ambush marketing cases represent strategic, intelligently-crafted marketing campaigns, and not the parasitic or aggressive, competitive marketing attacks aimed at industry rivals, which inspired ambushing's name. In light of this direction, and the legitimate approach embraced by ambushers, the term "ambush" marketing merits reconsideration. Although ambush marketing is an accepted and established term within professional and academic circles, the emphasis on the ethical and moral implications of ambushing is outdated and misrepresentative of current affairs. Terms such as pseudo-sponsorship, or parallel-event marketing perhaps better describe the activities and intents of major event ambushers in the twenty-first century, a trend worth greater consideration.

Commercial rights holders

Unfortunately, despite the advances made in ambush strategy and creativity, much of the dialogue surrounding ambush marketing continues to come from major rights holders such as the IOC, UEFA, and FIFA, who continue to propagate the pejorative view which originated in the 1980s. The reasons behind this perspective are clear: in providing brands with an alternative to official sponsorship, and potentially cluttering the event marketing environment with competing marketing communications, ambush marketing potentially devalues sponsorship for rights holders and sponsors alike. If the effectiveness of a sponsor's activation is negatively impacted by an ambush marketer's campaign, or if consumers are confused as to the identity of the true sponsor, the value of that partnership to the sponsor could be questioned. Moreover, if brands who would be bidding against market rivals to officially sponsor an event – and thereby raising sponsorship values – remove themselves from the auction process in favour of ambushing the event, the revenues generated by sponsorship programmes could be impacted.

Ambush marketing, therefore, represents an important concern for commercial rights holders to manage, and a potential threat to the long-term financial security of sports. The revenues contributed by sponsors to event hosts and governing bodies account for 30–50% of all turnover for major commercial rights holders, and are thus a sizable contributor to sport's viability and continued success. Thankfully, to date, no evidence of such detrimental effects have been seen in sponsorship: partnership agreements have continued to grow in value and scale over the course of ambush marketing's development, and no major partners have withdrawn from a sponsorship agreement in order to assume a role as an ambush marketer. Nevertheless, the potential threat to sport's bottom-line, and to the long-term value and future of sponsorship, guarantees that the illegitimate, parasitic view of ambushing maintained by commercial rights holders will continue to define ambushing and dictate the interventionist measures employed at all major sporting events.

The sponsors' view

Interestingly, despite the inherently threatened, pejorative view of ambush marketing held by rights holders, the impact of ambushing on sponsors has inspired a different view amongst major event partners. Whilst those early examples of ambushing presented sponsors with direct competition and saw rival companies overtly and explicitly attack their partnerships, over time greater distance has been established between sponsors and the significant majority of ambush marketers. Contemporary practices represent at worst competitive advertising and marketing between rivals, and pose little more than a minor inconvenience for those sponsors maximizing the value and potential of their official associations. For sponsors, ambush marketing is no longer an attack on their brand or partnership, instead a source of competition for consumer attention, awareness, and market share; a competition that has ultimately forced sponsors to improve their sponsorship agreements and activations. With the advances made in sponsorship protection and relations, the competition created by ambush marketing has led to a rise in sophistication and strategy on the part of sponsors, and advances in sponsorship theory and practice.

Imperative to this development has been the acknowledgement that sponsors and ambush marketers inherently have different aims and objectives at the core of their marketing activities. Whereas ambush marketers seek to leverage marketing the value of sports in order to gain attention and awareness, to reaffirm an unconventional or cavalier brand image, or to reinforce their presence and place in sports, sponsors at the highest levels have the option to look beyond simple market share or consumer recognition and build their activations around larger, more focused, and more far-reaching objectives. The authority and opportunity provided by official sponsorship agreements afford brands a multitude of available commercial and corporate objectives to fulfil, from business to business relationship-building, to corporate social responsibility activation, to brand image development, above and beyond the seemingly minor threat posed by ambush marketing.

Sponsorship has thus undergone a similar and simultaneous transformation to ambush marketing, growing in ambition, scope, and strategy. The advances made at the highest levels of sports sponsorship have influenced sports marketing relations and programmes throughout sports, and encouraged an increasingly relational approach to rights holders' sponsorship portfolios. The rights protection policies implemented by rights holders, and interventionist frameworks now commonplace for major events, have further reinforced the sophistication and professionalism of sponsorship practices, and required greater management and accountability on the part of major event sponsors. The resultant advances have helped redefine sponsorship as an integral form of marketing communications, and have facilitated an exponential rise in sponsorship value for rights holders and sponsors.

The consumer perspective

Ultimately, the success and impact of sponsorship and ambush marketing is reliant on the perspectives and behaviours of consumers, the deciding vote in the debate over ambush marketing's place in sports marketing. Rights holders have consistently sought to influence public opinion and encouraged the view of ambush marketers as unethical as a means of protecting their corporate partners, however, evidence of any negative perceptions on the part of consumers is scarce. Little evidence exists to suggest that consumers share that view: studies conducted around the 1996 Atlanta Olympic Games, 1998 FIFA World Cup, and 2000 UEFA European Championships evidenced a pronounced apathy on the part of fans and consumers. The assumption made by the likes of the IOC that consumers should be concerned about ambush marketing relied heavily on the belief that fans understood and valued Olympic sponsorship and sponsorship regulations. Instead, however, consumers' views spoke to a wide-ranging confusion and disinterest in the division between "official" and "unofficial" sponsors of major events, with little consideration for the ethics of ambush marketing activities. Such a view highlights the need for greater collaboration and communication on the part of sponsors and sponsees in establishing the role and importance of sponsorship for sport's financial viability, and continued progression towards more synergistic sponsorship programmes.

The ethical discussion regarding ambush marketing has most recently shifted focus onto commercial rights holders, and the draconian, overly-restrictive interventionist activities implemented to prevent ambush marketing. Increasingly, as event-specific legislations have grown in purview and the protections afforded to events like the Olympics have expanded, public pressure and questions over the need for and reach of such measures have arisen. The legal and legislative measures enacted to protect against ambushers have raised concerns over civil liberties infringements and anti-competitive practices, raising doubts over the ethical practices of rights protection activities and moving the debate regarding ambush marketing's moral and ethical basis away from ambushers and onto commercial rights holders. The overzealous and draconian efforts taken by some organizers and host governments have overshadowed the legal discussion of ambushing in recent years. Restrictions imposed on spectators entering venues in South Africa at the 2003 Cricket World Cup, for example, banning school children from entering the premises carrying canned beverages or wearing branded t-shirts, and legal action threatening local restaurants for perceived ambush marketing efforts in Canada in preparation for the 2010 Winter Olympics, have brought negative attention onto the measures in place to protect sponsors to a broader audience, and highlighted the rigor with which such means are enforced.

This was perhaps no more apparent than at the 2012 UEFA European Championships in Poland and Ukraine, where UEFA came in for heavy criticism following its response to an ambush marketing stunt involving Danish striker, Nicklas Bendtner. After scoring against Portugal in the tournament's group stage, Bendtner lowered his shorts to reveal branded, green under-shorts bearing the name of Irish bookmakers, Paddy Power. Bendtner was fined €100,000 for his actions, despite pleading his ignorance of the competition's regulations prohibiting player involvement in on-field ambush marketing campaigns. The severity of Bendtner's fine stood in stark contrast to UEFA's response to racial abuse and fan misconduct at the event, which earned the Spanish and Russian football federations penalties of €20,000 and €30,0000, respectively. The Croatian federation, too, faced sanctions for racist behaviour amongst its support, being fined €80,000 for its second offense. The sizable difference in fines between Bendtner's ambush and serious human- and civil-rights offenses drew criticism from fans, the media, and footballs alike, all of whom questioned the priorities of UEFA and other commercial rights holders where sponsorship protection is deemed more important than ensuring fair and equitable treatment for supporters and athletes at the event.

Similarly, the 2010 FIFA World Cup in South Africa and 2012 Summer Olympic Games in London sparked controversy in their local communities over the legislation enacted to protect sponsorship. Both host countries implemented stringent intellectual property rights protection that heavily restricted any marketing opportunities for local businesses around the events, regardless of their intent or possible impact on sponsors. South African businesses and citizens questioned the value of hosting major events like the World Cup if their own local economy is unable to benefit from or exploit the properties in any way. Likewise, aggressive brand protection activities in London threatened heavy fines and possible legal action for offending or infringing businesses across the city, igniting debate over the monopolistic power granted to the Olympics and their marketing partners in host countries.

The ethical concerns regarding ambush marketing have shifted from the place and propriety of ambush marketers onto the need for severity of rights protection measures, telling in the pervasive view of ambush marketing amongst consumers. As ambush marketing has embraced a more associative, opportunistic approach, the moral questions surrounding its legitimacy and intent have faded. The concern today is how best to protect and promote sponsors, whilst acknowledging and respecting consumers', supporters', and local businesses' civil and commercial rights, a not insignificant development in ambush marketing's constantly growing history.

Case: ambush marketing and the 2012 London Summer Olympic Games

This chapter now presents the case of the 2012 London Summer Olympic Games, providing a brief examination of the effects and impact of ambush marketing on sponsorship delivery for the Games, and the subsequent influence the 2012 London Games have had on ambush marketing theory and practice.

London and the British Olympic Association were awarded the right to host the 2012 Summer Olympic Games on 6 July 2005, a watershed moment for British sports and potentially for European sports marketing. Upon its announcement, the 2012 London Summer Games would represent a return to Europe for the world's largest multi-sports event, and London's first opportunity to host the world's best athletes since 1948. Perhaps most significantly, however, the 6 July decision ushered in a new era in British sponsorship and sports marketing regulation, a move whose impact would be felt across Europe.

Following the success of the Sydney 2000 Games (Indicia and Images) Protection Act in protecting Olympic sponsors in Australia, the International Olympic Committee's bid process for potential host cities requires candidate cities to ensure the provision of specific legislative protection for Olympic-owned intellectual property during the planning, preparation, and staging of the Games, and bespoke governmental protection enacted in order to safeguard Olympic sponsors and eliminate possible ambush marketing opportunities. Within the guarantees provided by the British Olympic Association and the London Olympic Games bid committee were assurances of enhanced and revised intellectual property rights for the Olympic marks, and the creation of a "Brand Protection Task Force" to control outdoor media. Moreover, the promises made by the United Kingdom and the Department for Culture, Media and Sport included a promise to secure 99% of all outdoor advertising media controlled by the British Airports Authority, with contingencies included to acquire the remaining 1% upon the completion or termination of existing long-term contracts.

These interventionist rights protection initiatives guaranteed by the London Olympic Games bid committee represented the preliminary framework for the 2012 Olympic Games' counter-ambush activities, and inherently reflected the state of ambush marketing and nature of ambush activities popular at the time of London's bid preparation.

The resultant legislation designed to govern the 2012 Olympic Games – the "London Olympic Games and Paralympic Games Act 2006" – was enacted a year after the announcement of London's successful bid. This act, designed to monitor and aid in the organization of the upcoming Games, featured five major sections, of which only one dealt with the commercial aspects of the Olympics, specifically, the advertising and marketing surrounding the Games, meant to protect against ambush marketing. The legislation set out guidelines and contingencies for advertising and trading standards before, during, and after the Games, as well as amendments to the existing "Olympic Symbols etc. (Protection) Act 1995" already in place to control Olympic intellectual property.

Amongst the clauses included, specific mention was given to additional protection granted for Olympic marks and intellectual property, requiring monitoring and reporting provisions for alleged infringements, revised terminology in defining those marks granted special protection, and extended coverage for any infringements deemed similar to already protected marks. Additional measures were put in place to address previously known ambush marketing strategies, such as proximity advertising, ticket giveaways, illegal merchandising, and increased penalties for offending individuals and enterprises were further incorporated.

Unfortunately, the measures implemented in Britain's event-specific legislation and rights protection guidelines highlighted two of the key dangers faced by commercial rights holders and sponsors in developing sponsorship protection strategies. First, the stipulations and contingencies included sought primarily to prevent and protect against those forms of ambush marketing seen previously at other Olympic Games and major international events, such as the use of outdoor advertising space at airports, and public transit hubs around the city. However, as evidenced throughout ambush marketing's existence, ambushers have proven adept and agile in adjusting to such regulations, and have consistently circumvented the restrictions in place and identified new, creative, and opportunistic marketing alternatives. Second, the strict brand protection activities and "ambush marketing police" teams charged with monitoring and reporting potential offences around the city contravened public opinion on ambushing and sponsorship protection, and served to further alienate supporters and businesses from the Games, a potentially costly mistake on the part of LOCOG's sponsorship protection team.

The resultant Games, and marketing environment around the event, may prove to be a major watershed moment in European sports marketing. Ambush marketers, such as Paddy Power, Nike, Beats by Dre, Puma, Mizuno, and countless others, succeeded in marketing around the London Olympics and generating considerable buzz for their efforts, despite the interventionist measures in place. Nike, for example, designed an elaborate international creative campaign titled "Find Your Greatness", making heavy use of the place-name London around the world in their marketing before, during, and following the Games. More directly, Beats by Dre earned tremendous visibility in-competition by outfitting athletes in headphones to wear during warm-ups and in pre-race routines.

The success enjoyed by ambushers in associating with the London Games reaffirmed for organizers and rights holders the challenge they face and inherent need, which exists for sponsors and rights holders to embrace a more proactive, forward-thinking approach to rights protection. Perhaps most importantly, though, the public and media discourse around the London Games and ambush marketing surrounded the draconian measures in place, and the overly enthusiastic brand police charged with monitoring alleged infringements of the Olympic legislation. Public interest stories such as that of the British Sugarcraft Guild, a bakery who were prohibited from icing cakes with "London 2012" to celebrate their annual baking competition, sparked controversy and firmly cast the spotlight on Olympic sponsors and marketers. Similar stories emerged across London as the "brand police" charged with protecting the event's intellectual property rights proved overzealous, and alienating local business and citizens as a result.

The lasting impact of these failures – and of the wealth of marketing controversies and shortcomings seen at the 2014 Sochi Winter Olympic Games – were evident in late 2014 as the International Olympic Committee accepted and approved two important sponsorship-related reforms within their 20+20 Recommendations for 2020, changes that will see the IOC and local organizing committees take a more synergistic, proactive stance on Olympic sponsorships relations. The recommendations approved look to encourage greater engagement between international sponsors and national-level organizing committees as a means of strengthening sponsorship programmes and policies in the host countries. Furthermore, the plans in place will seek to incorporate TOP Olympic sponsors in community, cultural, and socially-responsible initiatives, as a means of reinforcing the value and role Olympic sponsors play in the delivery and success of international sports.

These recommendations, whilst not specifically targeting ambush marketing, evidence a move on the part of the IOC and their sponsors towards a more proactive approach to sponsorship and sponsor-relations. The ultimate success of these recommendations remains to be seen, however, in the wake of the London Olympics, and the continued success of ambush marketers operating around major sporting events around Europe and throughout the world, it is clear that a change in sponsorship is needed, and a new approach to rights protection and ambush protection is required.

Conclusion

The emergence and proliferation of ambush marketing is an important consideration within sports business and marketing. The implications of ambush marketing for stakeholders across the sports and events marketing industry are wide-reaching, from commercial rights holders, to event host cities and countries, to official sponsors, to participating athletes, teams, and federations, to fans and supporters in-stadium and at home. The challenges and opportunities presented by ambush marketing for sports marketing and management practitioners, and scholars, are thus manifest.

To date, the emphasis in ambush marketing theory and practice has been on the prevention of and protection against potential ambush attempts, and has seen a growing interventionism in the rights management protocols of major events. Event-specific legislation, enhanced contractual protection for sponsors, and heavily-restrictive event regulations for athletes and spectators have all become commonplace for events such as the Olympic Games, the FIFA World Cup, and the UEFA European Championships, and continue to filter through the sports-events landscape. However, these increasingly stringent measures implemented by event owners have merely encouraged ambush marketers to identify and exploit more creative, innovative, and intelligent marketing opportunities in order to leverage against the rising commercial value of major events. This evolution has seen ambush marketing move away from the more aggressive, direct, attack-minded campaigns of ambushing's early history, towards a decidedly more strategic, opportunistic marketing alternative for brands operating in and around sports.

As such, it is incumbent upon event owners and official sponsors to better understand the challenges presented by ambush marketing for sponsorship relations and returns, and to identify more effective, efficient, and responsible means of protecting their investments and partnerships. Sponsors and rights holders have progressively moved towards a more collaborative, cooperative approach to sponsorship agreements, and have embraced a more proactive stance on sponsorship activation and rights protection, designing synergistic partnerships in an effort to better leverage sponsorship associations and establish greater ownership of the event marketing landscape. Such measures could be influential in the future of ambush marketing and sponsorship management.

Where ambush marketing – and event sponsorship management and relations – go from here, remains to be seen. Recent developments have seen ambushers circumvent ambush marketing legislation and event marketing regulations through digital and social media, the use of key event themes and social issues, and cavalier in-stadium guerrilla efforts. Regardless of their intent, or the media they employ, ambush marketing today is defined by the ability of marketers to remain one step ahead of commercial rights management initiatives and the laws governing event marketing; the challenge for sponsors and rights holder is therefore set.

Recommended reading

Ambush marketing as an area of academic study is a relatively young and developing field of research. Sandler and Shani (1989) and Meenaghan (1994; 2001) offer an important foundation for ambush marketing theory, and examine the early nature, objectives, and possible implications of ambushing for sponsors, commercial rights holders, and consumers. These early studies established a number of key directions in ambush marketing studies, including the ethical and moral debate over ambush marketing's place in sports marketing, the legality of ambush marketing campaigns, and the effects of ambush marketing attempts on sponsorship-linked marketing recall and recognition amongst consumers.

Subsequent studies by Crompton (2004), McKelvey and Grady (2008), and Séguin and O'Reilly (2008), have furthered the study of ambushing and its relationship with sponsorship management and explored the variety and validity of myriad counter-ambush marketing practices and protocols, and offer invaluable insight into the challenges faced by commercial rights holders in protecting their corporate partners and their investments. Finally, and most recently, research by Chadwick and Burton (2011), Scassa (2011) and Humphreys et al. (2010) have extended the study of ambush marketing into new areas, and have explored the management and marketing strategy underlying ambush attempts, the power dynamics at play within – and legitimacy of – event-specific government legislation protecting Olympic marks, and the psychological and cognitive effects of ambush marketing on information processing. These studies, and more, provide a valuable multi-disciplinary look into the effects and implications of ambush marketing, and represent a worthy foundation for continued study.

References

Chadwick, S. & Burton, N. (2011). The evolving sophistication of ambush marketing: a typology of strategies. *Thunderbird International Business Review*, 53(6), 709-719.

Crompton, J.L. (2004). Sponsorship ambushing in sport. *Managing Leisure*, 9(1), 1-12.

European Sponsorship Association (2014). ESA sponsorship fact sheet 2014. London: ESA.

Humphreys, M.S., Cornwell, T.B, McAlister, A.R., Kelly, S.J., Quinn, E.A. & Murray, K.L. (2010). Sponsorship, ambushing and counter-strategy: effects upon memory for sponsor and event. *Journal of Experimental Psychology*, 16(1), 96-108.

International Events Group (2006). IEG Sponsorship Report. Chicago: IEG.

International Events Group. (2014). IEG Sponsorship Report. Chicago: IEG.

McKelvey, S. & Grady, J. (2008). Sponsorship program protection strategies for special sport events: are event organizers outmanoeuvring ambush marketers? *Journal of Sport Management*, 22(5), 550-586.

Meenaghan, T. (1991). Sponsorship – legitimising the medium. *European Journal of Marketing*, 25(11), 5–10.

Meenaghan, T. (1994). Point of view: Ambush marketing: immoral or imaginative practice? *Journal of Advertising Research*, 34(5), 77-88.

Meenaghan, T. (2001). Understanding sponsorship effects. *Psychology & Marketing,* 18(2), 95–122.

Mintel (2006). Sport marketing and sponsorship UK 2006. London: Mintel International Group Ltd.

Myerson, A. R. (1996). Olympic sponsors battling to defend turf. *The New York Times.* www.nytimes.com/1996/05/31/business/the-media-business-advertising-olympic-sponsors-battling-to-defend-turf.html?src=pm (accessed 14 August 2008).

Sandler, D.M. & Shani, D. (1989). Olympic sponsorship vs. "ambush" marketing: who gets the gold? *Journal of Advertising Research*, 29(4), 9-14.

Scassa, T. (2011). Ambush marketing and the right of association: clamping down on references to that big event with all the athletes in a couple of years. *Journal of Sport Management*, 25(4), 354-370.

Séguin, B. & O'Reilly, N. (2008). The Olympic brand, ambush marketing and clutter. *International Journal of Sports Marketing & Sponsorship*, 4(1/2), 62–84.

14

TOWARDS THE REGULATION AND RESTRICTION OF AMBUSH MARKETING?

The case of the first truly social and digital Olympic Games: London 2012

Nicolas Chanavat and Michel Desbordes[1]

Introduction

The increase of the cost of entry for sponsors seems to have favored an implicit association with an event, considering the myriad of professional sports entities involved (athletes, teams, players, coaches, referees, etc.). In light of this, the IOC (International Olympic Committee) requires that candidate host countries for the organization of the Olympic Games adopt specific regulations in order to protect the Olympic symbols.

There was no specific law dealing with ambush marketing during the London 2012 Olympic Games. The Olympic brand is only protected by one international agreement, the Nairobi Treaty on the Protection of the Olympic Symbol (Nairobi Treaty, September 26th 1981, WIPO). However, three laws may apply. First, the Olympic Symbol etc. (Protection) Act 1995 aims to prevent unauthorized commercial association with the Olympic trademark. Second, the London Olympic Games and Paralympic Games Act 2006, complementary to the 1995 law, aims to reinforce the protection of intellectual property rights in relation to the event and in particular to implement legal sanctions. Finally, the London Olympic Games and Paralympic Games (Advertising and Trading) (England) Regulations 2011 ensure control over a number of advertising activities, providing the London police with the power to act against unauthorized advertising.

Despite reinforcement of the legislation, the London Olympics, which constituted the first truly digital games, highlighted a widespread growth of the practice where brands showed a lot of imagination at the expense of official sponsors.

In line with the implementing decree of "Rule 40" of the Olympic Charter, it was prohibited for athletes to be seen in advertising between July 18th and August 15th 2012 for brands that were not an official sponsor of the London Olympic Games. However, photos of Michael Phelps associated with the Louis Vuitton brand were revealed on the internet before the authorized date. Paddy Power, a British online betting operator, chose to sponsor a small event in a tiny French village in Burgundy called London and publicize it, in an attempt to be seen as an official sponsor. Along similar lines, Jamaican sprinter, Yohan Blake, took the risk of being disqualified by wearing a Richard Mille watch during the 100 meters final. Moreover, Beats by Dre headphones were handed out to athletes to wear on Olympic sites although Panasonic was the official sponsor. Another example occurring at the 2012 Olympic Games is the American athlete, Nick Symmonds, who deployed a creative strategy to create a buzz by lining up for the 800 meters with a bandage on his shoulder concealing a temporary tattoo of a brand, Hanson Dodge Creative. Finally, Nike launched an advertising campaign called "Find Your Greatness", featuring athletes residing in London.

Even if the Olympic charter foresaw any sanctions, neither athletes nor businesses seem inclined to miss out on such an opportunity to promote their brands. If the ambush technique has been known for many years, the transformation of its practice across social networks seems to be opening up a new and fertile field of action, whether academic or professional. Therefore it appears essential for legal experts to work on new, more effective protection measures as the illegal character of ambush marketing seems very uncertain at this time. In all events it needs to be taken quite seriously by decision makers like IOC and sponsors. They must find ways to protect official partners specifically from social ambush.

Background

The Olympic Games have become the largest sports-related property in the world since 1984 (Séguin and O'Reilly, 2005). The eleven main partners of the IOC generated €730 million in revenue between 2010 and 2012, which represents almost half of the revenue of the international organization. In return, sponsors own the right to associate themselves (under certain conditions) to the Olympic Games and Olympic brands. The value of these marketing rights and the efficiency of their operations are nevertheless attenuated when unauthorized entities use Olympic brands and symbols. Therefore, sponsors must face the creativity of the messages of pseudo-sponsors that are favored by social networks.

Clearly, the development of social networks since the Beijing 2008 Olympic Games has reinforced the battle between official sponsors, ambushers or entities trying to associate themselves with the event without paying for the rights to do so. During the Beijing Games there were, for instance, fewer than 1 million Twitter users; today there are more than 500 million accounts, at least 140 million of which are considered active.

On Saturday, August 4th 2012, Michael Phelps won his eighteenth gold medal during his last Olympic race. The American swimmer became the athlete to win the most medals in the history of the Olympics, ahead of Larissa Latynina (eighteen medals) with the 22 medals he won in 2004, 2008 and 2012. Photographers from all over the world captured the moment and instantly broadcasted the images around the globe. This was a fabulous publicity opportunity for the Swiss watch brand Omega, which was contractually associated with the Olympics and the athlete.

On Monday, August 13th 2012, people discovered the first pictures of Michael Phelps associated with the luxury brand Louis Vuitton. It was then discussed as to whether the champion should be stripped of his London medals. In fact, the IOC reproached him for publishing these pictures two days before the legal date. According to the implementing decree of "Rule 40" of the Olympic Charter, athletes were not supposed to be seen in advertising between July 18th and August 15th 2012 for a brand other than those sponsoring the London Olympics. The media coverage of these pictures, which was largely relayed by the international press and social networks, is likely to provoke confusion or a wrongful attribution and understanding in the mind of consumers.

These facts emphasize an old issue: that of the regulation and restriction of ambush marketing operations. Evidently the pseudo-sponsorship phenomenon has rapidly developed over the last twenty years, especially due to its efficiency during large-scale sports events such as the Olympic Games.

Objective

Considering the creativity of pseudo-sponsors, we can rightfully wonder how sponsors and organizers owning rights have learned how to fight against ambush marketing operations. What regulation enables them to deal with ambush practices? How effective are such legal provisions? To what extent are social networks involved in ambush marketing operations? What were the implications for those taking part in the latest Olympic Games? The multiplication of ambush marketing practices gives rise to several questions.

This chapter deals with the regulation and restriction of ambush marketing in this context through the case of the first truly social and digital London 2012 Olympic Games. It has three main objectives. First, to highlight and analyze the legal tools that help reinforce the protection of the Olympic brand and therefore the rights of its sponsors. Second, to investigate several ambush marketing cases that arose during the 2012 Games and underline a widespread growth of the practice, insofar as brands proved imaginative at the expense of official sponsors. Finally, it aims to discuss the consequences of the development of the phenomenon which proved social networks were effective publicity channels.

Implementation

The ambush marketing concept

Historically, the word "ambush marketing" (or pseudo-sponsorship) was outlined from the perspective of the sports property (McKelvey, Sandler and Snyder, 2012). Meenaghan (1994: p. 79) defines ambush marketing as: "the practice whereby another company, often a competitor, intrudes upon public attention surrounding the event, thereby deflecting attention toward themselves and away from the sponsor." Ambush marketing operations may be divided into several categories according to the nature of the practices and their extent. These operations generally have a triple-objective: (1) divert the attention away from the event towards the pseudo-sponsor; (2) attenuate the effectiveness of the official sponsor's operations; (3) modify the reaction of sports spectator audiences to the benefit of the ambusher (Chanavat, Desbordes and Ferrand, 2013).

It is commonly considered that the phenomenon appeared at the Montreal Olympic Games in 1976 (Ferrand, Chappelet and Séguin, 2012). Within the framework of its marketing strategy for the 1984 Olympic Games in Los Angeles, Kodak sponsored the broadcasting of the Games on ABC in particular, as well as the official movie of the American athletics team. The intention for Kodak was to attenuate, in a well-thought-out and planned manner, the effects of the sponsorship won by Fuji, the official partner of the event. Contrary to common belief, ambush marketing is therefore not a recent phenomenon. During the 1988 Seoul Olympic Games, each sponsor had at least one competitor that used an ambush marketing strategy. British athlete, Linford Christie, wore contact lenses showing the colors of his equipment manufacturer Puma during a press conference at the 1996 Atlanta Olympic Games. However, at the time, Reebok owned the commercial rights to the event.

In any event, the pseudo-sponsorship phenomenon has developed rapidly over the last twenty years, especially because of its effectiveness. Furthermore, as the cost of entry for sponsors increases, it appears easier to be implicitly associated with an event considering the multitude of professional sports entities involved (athletes, teams, players, coaches, referees, etc.). Furthermore, the proven effectiveness of pseudo-sponsors has led us ponder to what extent sponsors and property owning organizers have learned how to fight against ambush marketing operations.

New practices

In order to deal with the increase of pseudo-sponsorship operations, sponsors and property-owning entities have multiplied initiatives. Now they: (1) put pressure on organizers so that they protect the event; (2) have associated ground sponsorship and broadcasting sponsorship; (3) anticipate the promotional efforts of competitors; (4) must exploit secured sponsorship rights; (5) may systematically sue in case of acknowledged infringement. However, this debate is not closed, especially regarding the multiplication of sponsorship contracts.

Ambush marketing strategies are very common since football players play in teams that have collective contracts with manufacturers, while the players also have individual contracts for their boots with manufacturers who are often a competitor. The message is scrambled (Desbordes and Richelieu, 2012). One instance of this is the former Paris Saint-Germain player, David Beckham, who wore the swoosh brand on his shirt because Nike was the official manufacturer of the team, even though he is linked to adidas through an individual contract.

Before UEFA Euro 2012, Nike was sanctioned by the advertising regulatory authority after tweets from English player, Wayne Rooney, mentioning the Nike #Makeitcount campaign. The tweets proved to be hidden advertising referring to the British team and the Euro 2012 soccer tournament, the official sponsor of which was adidas.

The issue for rights owners is to fight ambush marketing, since pseudo-sponsors benefit from the perceived value of an event by reaping its benefits without being contractually tied to it. However, overreaction often means increased coverage. Using this approach, ambush marketing operations are increasingly visible on interactive media such as YouTube, Twitter and Facebook. In this perspective, social media constitutes a difficult area in order to control the dissemination of information. Clearly, this context is favorable for the action of ambush marketing called social ambush.

Towards a reinforcement of ownership and the Olympic brand

Two main threats for the Olympic property can be highlighted: the violation of the Olympic brand and ambush marketing activities. In this rather favorable context for parasitic marketing, the IOC wished to reinforce protection for the rights of its partners. For instance, the committee initiated an extensive international awareness and caution campaign against ambush marketing to the benefit of its commercial partners and the Olympic movement. The LOCOG (London Organizing Committee of the Olympic and Paralympic Games) was the most restrictive OCOG (Organizing Committee of the Olympic Games) in history as it attempted to thwart ambush marketing. The commercialization of the Olympic Games falls under the exclusive authority of the IOC and the LOCOG. Without their prior authorization it is prohibited to mention the Olympic Games in the use of logos, appellations or other methods when advertising products and services.

The Olympic brand is only protected by one international agreement, the Nairobi Treaty on the Protection of the Olympic Symbol (Nairobi Treaty, September 26th 1981, WIPO); there was no specific law dealing with ambush marketing during the London 2012 Olympics, however, three laws may apply.

First, the Olympic Symbol etc. (Protection) Act 1995 aims to prevent unauthorized commercial association with the Olympic trademark. The purpose of this law is to prohibit the use of terms and logos associated with the Olympic Games, such as the Olympic motto, "Citius, Altius, Fortius", or simply the use of the terms "Olympic(s)", "Olympiad(s)" or "Olympian" or of any similar term (for example, Olympix), without prior authorization.

Second, the London Olympic Games and Paralympic Games Act 2006, complementary to the 1995 law, aims to reinforce the protection of intellectual property rights in relation to the event and in particular to implement legal sanctions. This law specifically forbids verbal and nonverbal representation that may lead people to imagine an association with the London Olympic Games. It offers an open list of language elements suggesting any form of association with the Games, such as "Games", "2012", "Medals" or "London", as such terms belong to the Olympic property. Expressions such as "Come to London in 2012" and "Watch the Games here this summer" are also affected by this law. This regulation was considered draconian by the advertising industry (Blackshaw, 2009).

Finally, the London Olympic Games and Paralympic Games (Advertising and Trading) (England) Regulations 2011 ensure control over a number of advertising activities. This set of rules provides the London authorities with the power to act against unauthorized advertising.

Consequently, the IOC requires that candidate host states for the organization of the Games pass specific laws. Within this framework, host countries have enacted specific legislation to protect the Olympic symbols and to fight ambush marketing since the 2000 Sydney Olympic Games.

The Olympic Charter and the development of social and digital ambush marketing

As with a lot of global sporting events, sponsorship is big business and the Olympics is the premium event in terms of attracting sponsorship and ambush marketing. In all events there are neither specific legal tools nor international agreements that prohibit ambush marketing and protect official sponsorships. However, some provisions from the Olympic Charter work around these actions.

According to the "Rule 40" implementing decree of the Olympic Charter (2011: p. 77):

> Except as permitted by the IOC Executive Board, no competitor, coach, trainer or official who participates in the Olympic Games may allow his person, name, picture or sports performances to be used for advertising purposes during the Olympic Games.

According to the IOC, "during" means nine days before the official opening ceremony and up to three days after the closing ceremony. By agreeing to participate in the 2012 London Olympic Games under these conditions, each participant accepts this rule. If the participant, their federation or sponsors do not abide by the conditions of participation, the participant is liable to sanctions. In other words, during the 2012 London Olympic Games, participants and other authorized individuals were not authorized to promote a brand in a forum article, a tweet or on any social network. In line with "Rule 40" therefore, Michael Phelps could have been sanctioned. Pictures of the swimmer were indeed associated with the Louis Vuitton brand and appeared on the internet.

LOCOG has even approached Twitter, who has agreed to prevent brands from exploiting the social media for Olympic ambush marketing attempts. This will likely mean non-sponsors will not be allowed to buy promoted tweets against hashtags such as #London2012. Furthermore, LOCOG has dealt with Foursquare to prohibit ambushers from making check-ins around the locations of the Olympics.

Evidently it seems that new technologies have a greater impact on the perception of sports events by consumers. Social media has modified the way business is done. People spend so much time on Facebook, Twitter and other social media platforms. Indeed, the use of social networks proved to be very intense during the London Games: 100,000 pictures on Instagram (over 650,000 related to the Games), 116 million posts on Facebook, 12 million additional fans of athletes' Facebook pages, 150 million tweets, 393 Weibo posts. This phenomenon has consequences on sponsorship and ambush marketing operations. Hence, the London Olympics represents an extraordinary opportunity to create long-term customer loyalty, locally and universally. In this context, the 2012 London Olympic Games symbolizes the first truly social and digital games that seemed to favor ambush marketing.

The first truly social and digital games are the talk of the town in term of ambush marketing

The IOC wishes to protect the rights of its partners by implementing suitable provisions and measures. The idea of safeguarding the values of Olympic partners is the basis of Olympic marketing (Séguin and O'Reilly, 2008). However, if the IOC did its best to reinforce regulation in order to avoid non-partner brands reaping any benefit from the 2012 London Games, the staging of these Games seems to have demonstrated that social networks can be effective advertising channels. They serve to develop the economic and marketing power of athletes and play a role in the development of sports brands. The 2012 London Games showed that this practice is tending to become widespread. During these Games, ambush marketing cases were numerous and brands proved to be very imaginative in this field, at the expense of official sponsors.

Beyond the previously mentioned Phelps–Louis Vuitton case, other instances of ambush marketing situations were listed within the framework of 2012 London Olympic Games. Here are six other cases.[2]

Paddy Power, a British online betting operator, chose to sponsor a small event in France, in a small village in Burgundy called London, in order to appear on British London billboards as an official sponsor. Paddy Power actually sponsored an event called egg-and-spoon race, consisting of carrying an egg on a spoon placed between the runner's teeth. It was possible to read the following slogan, "Official sponsor of the largest athletics event in London this year! There you go, we said it", on the streets of London during the Games. This "subtle" use of the name of the village of London in France served to create a buzz and confusion in the mind of spectators in London, UK.

Jamaican sprinter, Yohan Blake, took the risk of being disqualified by wearing a Tourbillon luxury watch during the 100 meters final. The very flashy, ergonomic and reliable watch with a brand new structure was tailor-made by Richard Mille. The young athlete, who was designated as ambassador of the Swiss watchmaker for 2013 should have worn an Omega timepiece as Omega was the official sponsor of the Games. The fact that he wore this half-a-million-dollar watch caused a sensation, especially on social networks and served to increase the popularity of the ambusher brand. The disqualification of the athlete and a hefty fine was discussed after he wore this accessory during the race and on the podium. It should be noted that his teammate, Usain Bolt, left his King Power Hublot watch in the changing room.

Beats by Dre headphones were handed out to athletes to wear on Olympic sites although Panasonic was the official sponsor. Ambassadors were numerous, and among them the "Baltimore bullet", Michael Phelps. The brand sent headphones to the different delegations and especially swimmers who appeared in the Olympic village with the headphones, a situation which ensured such a sensation that the Sol Republic brand also offered headphones to swimmers. Both brands then went on handing out headphones to other athletes in warm up stadiums and in cycling velodromes. These operations seem to have ensured a more significant jump in sales for Beats by Dre than for the official sponsor Panasonic.

The American athlete, Nick Symmonds, also learnt how to benefit from the Olympic Games. It all started with an auction placed on eBay by the athlete at the beginning of 2012 and won by Hanson Dodge Creative for $11,100. This amount allowed the agency to have its logo and Twitter account inked on the athlete's shoulder to create a buzz on the internet. This buzz was increased by the propagation of videos over social networks. According to IOC regulations, Symmonds was not authorized to compete with the temporary tattoo visible on his shoulder during the Games. However, the mere fact that he lined up in the 800m with a bandage on his shoulder was an original strategy that increased attention. He later revealed the reason for this bandage on his twitter account, disclosing the brand, Hanson Dodge Creative.

Nike had been running "Find Your Greatness", a publicity campaign centered on athletic greatness, in towns called London around the world, rather than just in London, UK. Nike's videos were broadcast more than the "Take the stage" videos by official sponsor, adidas, and they allude to the Olympic Games but do not name them. The buzz-stealing approach is similar to Nike's "Write the Future" campaign during the 2010 FIFA World Cup in which it also surpassed adidas' official sponsorship. Londoners of South Africa, Jamaica, Nigeria, the United States and other countries are showcased in a one-minute television commercial, as well as a series of sports-specific shorter films, to demonstrate that even if you play far away from the dazzle of the Olympics, your greatness is no less important. The campaign is stimulated with a global Twitter-promoted hashtag, #findgreatness, designed to ignite conversation about how athletes find their own greatness everywhere.

The Tetley Tea brand launched a light-hearted social media marketing campaign on Twitter to capitalize on the Olympic fever sweeping the UK. The Tata-owned brand rolled out operations, supporting Team GB, from its "Tetley Tea Folk" Twitter account. Posts turned actual Olympic events into tea and cake-themed competitions, such as the Ar-cherry event, which saw Victoria Sponge pitted against Bakewell Tart, and Jam-nastics, which saw Chocolate Fudge Cake come first ahead of Scone and Battenburg. Tetley was driving brand engagement by getting fans to choose nominees for the events before voting on the winners. The High-tea jump actually witnessed Carrot, Lemon Drizzle, Chocolate Fudge and Victoria Sponge compete for the gold medal. Other events included Ju-dough and Tea-kwon-do, again, cake-based popularity contests designed to increase engagement. Further Olympic-based operations had the brand send a consignment of Tetley tea to British swimmer Jo Jackson, who thanked the company on Twitter. The Tetley Tea Folk, which formed the basis of the Olympic social media operations, were reintroduced by the brand after a ten-year absence, however, they featured less prominently in advertising operations as the brand launched a new approach, introducing the "Make Time. Make Tetley" strapline.

Conclusion

Sponsorship of major sporting events constitutes large business. Sandler and Shani (1989) were among the first to investigate ambush marketing, which they suggested occurred when a non-sponsor of an event attempted to pretend to be an official sponsor. Ambush marketing represents a very good opportunity for advertisers who are not the official sponsors of the event, while ambush marketing becomes a source of frustration for the brands that have given the sponsorship fees. Notwithstanding that it is an issue of critical relevance, there are few researchers or authors presently conducting in-depth research on ambush marketing as it relates to Olympic marketing (IOC, 2011).

It should be noted that no OCOG had ever imposed such restrictions in order to prevent pseudo-sponsorship operations. Nevertheless, even if the Olympic charter foresees sanctions, notably, neither athletes nor businesses seem inclined to miss out on such an opportunity to promote their brands. Therefore, this analysis of the London Games is in line with the conclusions of O'Sullivan and Murphy (1998: p. 339) who underlined that "Legal issues clearly arise, but the body of case law is as yet slight." McKelvey and Grady (2008) noted that it is unrealistic and naïve to consider that assurances or "guarantees" in the contracts between event organizers and host countries or cities can provide a "silver bullet" against the legal marketing operations of non-sponsors.

Through this research we wish to highlight that a multiplication of the legal measures developed in order to face ambush marketing operations during the 2012 Olympic Games was not sufficient. According to Sandler and Shani (1998: p. 375) "ambush marketing can be effective only if a significant number of consumers do not possess sufficient knowledge about the rights of official sponsors." With the increase of smartphone or tablet ownership, the 2012 London Olympic Games was presented as the "first social Olympic Games" or "sociolympics". With Olympic viewers becoming more social, it is no surprise that sponsorship and ambush marketing campaigns started to incorporate social media engagement components. If the ambush has been known for many years, the transformation of its practice across social networks seems to be opening a new and fertile field of action, whether academic or professional.

Therefore, we could wonder whether the multiplication of ambush marketing operations might indeed persuade brands to avoid associating themselves with the Olympic Games on a long-term contractual basis. Without their support, is the IOC not in danger of reconsidering its economic model and jeopardizing the viability of the Games? Moreover, what is the future for legitimate IOC official sponsors in the digital marketplace? It appears that the money spent on sponsorship arrangements has increased in parallel to the rise in ambush marketing campaigns in the traditional and in the online and social media space. The 2012 London Olympic Games provides an interesting insight into future practice, protections and issues related to addressing ambush marketing in virtual space. The online space brings with it a supplemented level of complication and risk to sponsorship opportunities.

Organizations should seek legal advice and think carefully about any campaigns if they plan to associate their products or services with the Olympics and major sporting events, particularly if a competitor is an official sponsor. Rights owners should also seek advice and consider a strategy to moderate the risk of rights being reduced as a result of ambush by digital marketing. In all events, as the decision-maker, the IOC must find ways to protect official sponsors from social ambush. Indeed, the IOC and sponsors should improve social media monitoring and provide athletes with better training on how to use social platforms during the Olympics in order to protect the rights of sponsors. For instance, the Olympic organizers could have a social media "command center": a rather grand description of a dedicated team of workers who use software to monitor social media and network on a bank of screens. Olympic organizers and sponsor brands could also be organized to reply to worrying tweets or blogs quickly. Further training for athletes on how to use Twitter responsibly during the Olympics may also reduce sponsorship annoyances. Each day of the London Olympics reportedly saw more tweets posted than during the whole of the Beijing Games. This represents a sign of how quickly and considerably the digital landscape has improved over the years. This should also be a warning to organizers such as the IOC, FIFA (Fédération Internationale de Football Association) or UEFA (Union of European Football Associations). For example, the organizing committee for the 2016 Rio Olympic Games, as well as brands planning to sponsor the 2016 Games, need to keep apace of emerging social and digital platforms and how they change the dynamic of its sponsorship deals. Moreover, it appears essential for legal experts to work on new, more effective protective measures as the illegal nature of ambush marketing seems very uncertain at this date. We can rightfully consider that pseudo-sponsorship operations cause harm to the development of the Olympic movement itself.

Notes

1. Both authors want to thank the *International Journal of Sports Marketing and Sponsorship* where the original version of this chapter was published in April 2014. See www.imrpublications.com/journal-landing.aspx?volno=15&no=3
2. Other pseudo-sponsors took advantage of the 2012 London Olympic Games without being contractually tied to the event: Red Bull, Virgin Media, Puma, Mizuno and Specsavers are some examples that are not specifically dealt with in this paper.

References

Blackshaw, I. (2009). Protecting major sporting events with particular reference to the 2012 Olympic Games, *Entertainment and Sports Law Journal*, January.

Chanavat, N., Desbordes, M. and Ferrand, A. (2013). Faut-il avoir peur de l'ambush marketing? *Jurisport*, 128, 41–45.

Desbordes, M. and Richelieu, A. (2012). *Global sport marketing*, Abingdon: Routledge.

Ferrand, A., Chappelet, J-L. and Séguin, B. (2012). *Olympic marketing*, Abingdon: Routledge.

IOC (2011). Olympic movement marketing history, Olympic Studies Centre.

London Olympic Games and Paralympic Games Act 2006 (2006). Implementation decree, www.legislation.gov.uk/ukpga/2006/12/contents (accessed 18 August 2015).

London Olympic Games and Paralympic Games (Advertising and Trading) (England) Regulations 2011 (2011). Implementation decree, www.legislation.gov.uk/ukdsi/2011/9780111515969 (accessed 18 August 2015).

McKelvey, S. and Grady, J. (2008). www.humankinetics.com/acucustom/sitename/dam/067/225_mckelvey_sponsorship_pr1.pdf (accessed 18 August 2015).

McKelvey, S., Sandler, D. and Snyder, K. (2012). Sport participant attitudes toward ambush marketing: An exploratory study of ING New York City marathon runners, *Sport Marketing Quarterly*, 21, 7–18.

Meenaghan, T. (1994). Ambush marketing: Immoral or imaginative practice, *Journal of Advertising Research*, 34, 77–88.

Olympic Charter (2011). Implementing decree of Rules 7 to 14, art. 1.3, www.olympic.org/Documents/Olympic%20Charter/Charter_fr_2010.pdf (accessed 18 August 2015).

Olympic Symbol etc. (Protection) Act 1995 (1995). Implementation decree, www.legislation.gov.uk/ukpga/1995/32/contents (accessed 18 August 2015).

O'Sullivan, P. and Murphy, P. (1998). Ambush marketing: The ethical issues. *Psychology & Marketing*, 15(4), 349–366.

Sandler, D. M. and Shani, D. (1989). Olympic sponsorship versus ambush marketing: Who gets the gold?, *Journal of Advertising Research*, 29(4), 9–14.

Séguin, B. and O'Reilly, N. (2008). The Olympic brand, ambush marketing and clutter. *International Journal of Sports Marketing and Sponsorship*, 4(1), 62–84.

PART IV

Customers, spectators and fans

Nicolas Chanavat, Simon Chadwick and Michel Desbordes

In an age of global media, commercial partners and celebrity athletes, fans still remain at the heart of sports: they support teams, become members of clubs, attend events and buy sponsors products. Fans are co-producers of the sports product and a source of revenue; they generate atmosphere and are often deeply engaged with sports properties. As a result, fans are taken seriously by practitioners seeking to ensure they remain committed to their club or event, and by academic researchers who have remained keen to understand the nature of fans and their fandom. The chapters in this part embrace a number of interesting and perpetually important issues. Getting fans and keeping them is a major issue for many sports marketers, which requires a deep understanding of what motivates fans and how they engage with sports properties. Chapters address these issues and examine the ways fans differ from and are similar to one another. Once engaged with a property, knowing how fans consume sports is paramount, especially as many fans who, for example, attend a sporting event, will expect an experience and contribute to delivering it. Further chapters consider issues pertaining to behaviour and experience.

15

RELATIONSHIP MARKETING IN SPORTS

Building and establishing longstanding relations in the business of sports

André Bühler and Gerd Nufer

Introduction

As long as there have been professional sports, there have been deep relationships on different levels. For example, sponsorship (or patronage as it was called in the early days) was mostly based on personal relations between the local benefactors and their favourite sports club. Regarding media, clubs always maintained special relationships with selected journalists. The bond between fans and their clubs was always a close and mutually beneficial one. All these relationships existed from the start of the sports business. Therefore, relationship marketing is nothing new in the context of sports. Many sporting organisations always knew to value a deep and good relationship with their stakeholders and practised relationship marketing without being aware of it. Successful sports managers, however, take the old wisdom and turn it into a modern relationship marketing approach by structuring the various relationships in order to make them more effective and profitable for the own sporting organisation and the various stakeholders. This has been well illustrated in a study conducted by Bühler (2006) who carried out qualitative interviews with representatives of English Premier League and German Bundesliga clubs. The results of his study acted as an inspiration for further publications (for example, Bühler and Nufer, 2010; 2013) as well as an inspiration for writing this chapter, which illustrates the many facets of relationship marketing and the possibilities it offers in the context of the sports business.

The principles of relationship marketing

Two decades ago, Buttle (1996: p. 1) came to the following conclusion when talking about the evolution of marketing:

> Marketing is no longer simply about developing, selling, and delivering products. It is progressively more concerned with the development and maintenance of mutually satisfying long-term relationships.

Indeed, managing relationships with customers and other interest groups has become the core of marketing. In the age of globalisation, competition is increasing. With product and service quality becoming a common standard in many industries and no longer being a major source of competitive advantage, organisations are especially adopting a Customer Relationship Marketing (CRM) approach as a means of differentiating themselves. CRM is a strategic orientation assuming that the customer prefers to have an ongoing relationship with one organisation rather than with changing organisations. Based on this assumption and because it is less expensive to retain satisfied customers than to attract new ones, marketers focus on building and keeping groups of profitable, loyal customers by moving them into long-term, mutually beneficial relationships (Sandhusen, 2008; Bruhn, 2013).

Development of relationship marketing

Berry (1995: p. 236) concluded that relationship marketing "is an 'old new' idea but with a new focus". The concept of relationship marketing can be traced back to as early as the Middle Ages, when merchants were already aware of how important it was to maintain a relationship with the customer. One only has to think of the ancient Middle Eastern proverb: "As a merchant you'd better have a friend in every town" (Grönroos, 1994: p. 347). However, with the beginning of the industrialisation and its resulting mass production, as well as constant growth of business organisations, the level of personal contact between buyer and seller has considerably decreased and the customer was often turned from a relationship partner into a market share statistic (Harwood, Garry and Broderick, 2008).

Academic and practitioner interest in relationship marketing took off to the extent that many marketers viewed it as the new key marketing issue. Indeed, many marketing experts propose that there has been a "paradigm shift" away from the traditional transaction marketing approach towards a more relationship-oriented one during the last few years (Sandhusen, 2008; Bruhn, 2013). Transaction marketing considers the satisfying of customer needs as an exchange of goods and services for money. With its short-term goal of making the sale through single transactions and minimal communication or interaction, it contrasts sharply with the relational-based approach. Relationship marketing puts major emphasis on close, personal and long-term provider–customer relations as well as on high interactions, and focuses on the maintenance of existing customers rather than on the acquisition of new ones (Nufer, 2006; Bruhn, 2013). Depending on the products sold and customers served, both relationship and transactional marketing can coexist in a company's strategic marketing plan. Conditions under which transactional marketing is most likely to apply include generic commodities or low-value consumer products and services, as there are usually no or low costs associated with switching suppliers, so customers have little interest in building a particular relationship with the provider but prefer transactions. Relationship marketing is most appropriate in competitive, saturated markets with few key providers or suppliers, where switching costs are high and when there is a consumer's ongoing need and desire for a certain product or service (Sandhusen, 2008; Harwood et al., 2008). Table 14.1 provides an overview of the main differences between relationship marketing and transactional marketing.

An initial starting point for relationship marketing was the notion that in order to retain customers in the long term, marketing exchanges need to be seen not just as transactions between the seller and the buyer, but as a set of activities in which relationships are developing. Another factor influencing the development of relationship marketing was the maturing of service marketing in the service industry: The dimensions of customer care and quality arose and overlapped with the traditional marketing philosophy. Advances in the information and

Table 15.1 Main differences between relationship marketing and transactional marketing

Criterion	Relationship marketing	Transactional marketing
Primary object	Relationship	Single transaction
General approach	Interaction-related	Action-related
Perspective	Evolutionary-dynamic	Static
Basic orientation	Implementation-oriented	Decision-oriented
Long-term vs. short-term	Generally takes a long-term perspective	Generally takes a short-term perspective
Fundamental strategy	Maintenance of existing customers	Acquisition of new customers
Focus in decision process	All phases focus on post-sales decisions and action	Pre-sales activities
Intensity of contact	High	Low
Degree of mutual dependence	Generally high	Generally low
Measurement of customer satisfaction	Managing customer base (direct approach)	Monitoring market share (indirect approach)
Dominant quality dimension	Quality of interaction	Quality of output
Production of quality	The concern of all	Primary concern of production
Role of internal marketing	Substantial strategic importance	No or limited importance
Importance of employees for business success	High	Low
Production focus	Mass customisation	Mass production

Source: Henning-Thurau and Hansen (2000: 5); Bruhn (2009: 15); Bühler and Nufer (2013: 357)

communication technology further facilitated the effectiveness of relationship marketing (Nufer, 2006; Bruhn 2013). Therefore, the relationship marketing orientation is bringing together service, quality and marketing philosophies.

Definition of relationship marketing

Relationship marketing has arisen from a number of academic disciplines, such as economics, psychology and sociology. The term "relationship marketing" has been used since the early 1990s, but there is still no consensus about an agreed definition of relationship marketing. Even the meaning of the two-letter acronym "RM" is contested: some understand it as relationship marketing, others use the acronym for relationship management. There have also been several substitute terms for relationship marketing, "loyalty marketing", "personalised marketing", "database marketing", "interactive marketing", all looking at the same – relationship marketing – from more or less different points of view (Buttle, 1996). However, one of the most comprehensive definitions comes from Bruhn (2013: p. 12):

> Relationship marketing includes all measures of the analysis, planning, implementation and controlling in order to serve the company regarding the initiation, stabilisation, intensification and recovery as well as the termination of business relations concerning the stakeholders, especially the customers.

In addition to customers, the main stakeholders of a company are suppliers, intermediaries and competitors, according to Meffert, Burmann and Kirchgeorg (2012).

Importance of relationship marketing

With the increasing duration of relationships with customers, and thus customer loyalty, the profitability of a consumer as part of the business's general profit increases. At the beginning of a relationship investments have to be made (acquisition costs). However, due to the newly-won consumer's demand for the company's products and services, a basic profit is assumed to be made shortly afterwards. If the company manages to establish a long-term relationship with the consumer, and if the customer is loyal to the company, a further increase in profit can be expected due to a more efficient saturation of customer–related turnover and revenue potentials (profits from cross selling). The basis for this assumption is that growing trust in the company will lead to an increase in the customer's purchase frequency and intensity. Moreover, a long-term customer relationship leads to better knowledge of consumers, as well as better-informed consumers, which in turn leads to decreased operational costs for each consumer over time. Another important effect resulting from consumer relationships are reference effects provided by satisfied customers through positive word-of-mouth communication. Non-consumers usually rate the opinion or judgement of other customers above the communication messages of companies. Consequently, for a company, satisfied long-term customers are the best advertisers and a great potential of free advertisement. A further effect of relationship marketing implementations is seen in the possibility of charging increased prices. Within long-term relationships, customers begin to appreciate the value of the product or service at such a rate that the price elasticity of demand increases (Friedrichs, 2005; Diller, 2000; Morgan, Crutchfield and Lacey, 2000; Meffert and Bruhn, 2013; Bruhn, 2013).

Instruments of relationship marketing

In order to establish a long-term relationship with customers, companies can select from a wide range of various relationship marketing instruments. The most important instruments will be introduced in the following (Bühler and Nufer, 2010; 2013).

Customer magazines are an effective tool for companies to inform their customers on a regular basis and therefore remind the customers of the company. The electronic version of customer magazines are newsletters distributed by email. They are less expensive than printed magazines, however, they are not quite effective in view of the numerous spam emails customers receive each day. A very effective instrument are bonus programmes in combination with loyalty cards (for example, frequent flyer programmes with airlines or cashback programmes at supermarkets). Customer events, such as open days where customers are allowed to cast a glance behind the scenes of a company, are another relationship marketing instrument because the experience provided might strengthen the bond between customer and company. Even more effective are exclusive customer events, where access to the event is limited. Many radio programmes provide such events, for example, private concerts of famous musicians for a limited number of people. Because tickets are not on sale, people have to listen to the radio programme the whole day in order to gain the opportunity to win them. Such exclusive events provide a once in a lifetime experience and lead to a stronger bond between the customers and the company. Another relationship marketing instrument is the joint product development, where customers are invited to take part in the product development of companies. For example, Vitamin Water (an affiliated brand of the

Coca-Cola Company) asked their Facebook fans to create a new flavour. Ten thousand customers took part in that project, discussing various tastes, sending in suggestions regarding the labelling and voting for the actual product. Vitamin Water then produced the new flavour and offered it under the name "connect", with the slogan "made by fans, for fans on Facebook". The whole project was a huge success and helped to establish a stronger relationship between the customers and the brand (Bühler and Nufer, 2013). An effective complaints management is another important relationship marketing instrument. Many companies view complaining customers as a nuisance. However, customers taking the trouble to complain should be viewed as a very good source of information in order to improve the company and its products. Therefore, companies should take complaints seriously by installing a systematic complaint management, which forwards the respective complaint to the right department and always keeps the complaining customers informed. Consequently, complaining customers feel themselves esteemed and that might lead to a positive relationship between the company and the customers (Stauss and Seidel, 2014).

Relationship marketing in sports

In recent years, relationship marketing has become a key topic in the sports sector. However, while the concept of managing relationships with customers is well established in the sporting goods industry, sporting organisations have just started to adopt the concept of relationship marketing. The fact that many sporting organisations are nowadays acting like commercial enterprises has strongly influenced the adoption of relationship marketing, above all on the professional level. Bühler and Nufer (2010: p. 25) proposed the following definition of relationship marketing in sports:

> Relationship Marketing in sports refers to the establishment and maintenance of positive, enduring and mutual beneficial relations between professional sporting organisations and their stakeholders.

Professional sporting organisations are thereby defined as "clubs, associations or teams that are involved in spectator sports on a professional level" (Bühler and Nufer, 2010: p. 51). The following section describes the stakeholders of a professional sporting organisation in further detail.

Professional sporting organisations and their main stakeholders

Some decades ago, many sports clubs and associations operated on a non-professional level with voluntary staff. In the early days, gate receipts were the only source of income. Nowadays, sporting organisations can be compared with medium-sized companies in terms of annual turnover and number of employees (Bühler and Nufer, 2014). Gate receipts are only one of many revenue sources of professional sporting organisations, and one that has become less important in comparison to the other revenue streams. The biggest share of sports entities' annual turnover today comes from television income and sponsorship revenues. Merchandising and other commercial revenues (for example, hospitality and licensing) is another important source of income, at least at the top level. Further money might come from shareholders or external investors. This is well illustrated in the case of some English and French football clubs who were taken over by foreign businessmen. Another revenue stream could be the fees paid by the members of the sports organisation. Clubs such as FC Barcelona or FC Bayern Munich

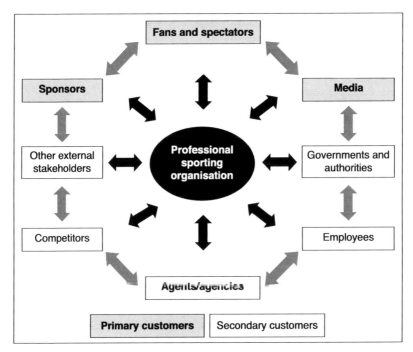

Figure 15.1 Primary and secondary customers of professional sporting organisations

Source: Bühler and Nufer (2013: 364)

have more than one hundred thousand members. In addition, some associations such as the German Football Association (DFB) count more members (6.85 million in 2014) than the national political parties. The money generated from the membership fees might therefore amount to a significant income stream for some sports entities.

However, not all sports entities are the same; one should not make any generalisations. Professional sporting organisations differ not only in the sport involved but also in their size and importance. English football clubs are bigger and attract more people than a Swedish handball team, for example. However, it is also true that the basics are nearly the same for each sporting organisation. They have to deal with the unique characteristics of the business and the sport product as well as with the various market players. Therefore, it is just fair to conclude that all professional sports entities have the same type of stakeholders. Figure 14.1 provides a general overview of the various stakeholders of a professional sporting organisation.

A customer is defined as someone who purchases a product or a service. According to this simple definition, three groups of primary customers can be identified: fans, sponsors and the media. All three groups pay the sporting organisation in order to get something in return. Fans purchase tickets, sponsors buy communication rights and television channels pay a lot of money for the broadcasting rights. The other stakeholders usually do not pay the sporting organisations. Employees and suppliers, for example, even get paid. However, from a modern marketing point of view, companies have to treat their stakeholders like customers in order to engage in a positive relationship, which benefits both parties. Therefore, it is proposed to view all internal and external stakeholders as secondary customers of professional sporting organisations.

The stakeholders mentioned in Figure 15.1 are described as follows:

- Fans and spectators: The whole business of sports is based on people who are prepared to pay money for the various sports products. Fans, supporters and spectators are the main customers of professional sporting organisations and their relationship can be described as a customer-supplier relationship.
- Sponsors: In the early days, local businessmen supported their favourite sports club for reasons of patronage. Over the years, patronage became commercial sponsorship with companies realising that sports is a perfect communication tool. Nowadays, professional sports would not be possible without revenues generated from sponsorship. However, not only have the sponsorship fees increased in the last years, but also the number of sponsors of each and every sports entity. Clubs have multiple sponsors nowadays and therefore they have to deal with various relationships. The relationship between professional sporting organisations can be described as a business-to-business relationship in view of the fact that both sponsor and sponsee are enterprises.
- The media: The business-to-business relationship between professional sporting organisations and the media is a two-way process because both need each other and both benefit from each other. Television channels, newspapers, radio stations, websites, publishers and all other types of media need content for their customers. Sports delivers not only games or competitions but also good stories. Sports entities, on the other hand, need publicity in order to develop their brand and make them more known. The relationship between sporting organisations and the media is an interesting one because there are a number of factors, which can benefit as well as damage the relationship as described later.
- Competitors: Professional sporting organisations have a number of competitors. First, there are the direct national competitors (clubs of the same national leagues) and direct international competitors (clubs competing in the same international competition). Then there are competitors of different national and international leagues within the same sport (for example, clubs in lower leagues or other international competitions). Here, sporting organisations not only compete on the field but also off the field for sponsorship revenues, players and fans. Then there are competitors of different sports (for example, cricket is competing with rugby for attention and the customers' money). Last, but not least, sporting organisations compete with the entertainment industry (cinemas, theatres, television) as a whole. Here, the sports entity competes for people's time and money. For example, a customer might have the option to spend the evening watching a movie in the local cinema or attending a game of the local football club. However, competitors don't necessarily have to compete with each other, but could also seek collaboration. After all, the relationship between sporting organisations and their various competitors can be seen as a very special business-to-business relationship.
- Agents/agencies: Some agencies have specialised in selling marketing rights on behalf of the respective sports entity. For example, Sportfive (a division of the French media group Lagardère) markets individual rights for the Pan American Games, the Men's Handball Champions League, the Argentine Rugby Union, the World Rally Championship, the Rugby Six Nations Tournament, the Swedish ice hockey league and many more. Sportfive therefore engages in many relationships with various sporting organisations. In order to make the relationship with agencies a successful one, sporting organisations have to apply relationship marketing techniques in this context as well.
- Employees: As described earlier, many sporting organisations can be viewed as medium-sized companies in terms of people working for the company full time. In this respect,

human resource management (HRM) becomes more and more important. Furthermore, sporting organisations are increasingly looking for high-potentials on a top management level. In order to attract and subsequently keep professionals, sports entities have to seek a positive relationship with their employees.

- Governments and authorities: Governments and authorities have an interest in professional sports in view of the fact that major sport events (such as the Football World Cup or the Olympic Games) not only put the respective country or city in the global limelight, but also attract millions of tourists to visit the country or city. In addition, sports entities are huge taxpayers and employers. However, sporting organisations have to collaborate with national and local authorities (such as the police) in order to secure their home games. Furthermore, professional sporting organisations benefit from governments as well in view of the fact that public money has been spent tremendously in order to subsidise the building or modernisation of sport venues. It is essential for sporting organisations to establish and maintain a good relationship with the government and authorities.

- Other external stakeholders: Professional sporting organisations have a number of other external stakeholders, for example, investors and shareholders. Some sport clubs (especially in British football) have gone public in order to attract more money. In the early days, the main shareholders of football clubs were fans who wished to call at least a small part of their favourite club their own. However, as soon as commercialisation of sports began, professional investors realised that shares of sport clubs can be a profitable investment. Professional sporting organisations, which are listed on the stock exchange, have to establish and maintain a positive relationship with their shareholders for the sake of their company. Furthermore, a sporting organisation is involved in many relationships with various suppliers, such as companies supplying copy paper for the back office or a service provider taking care of the sports club's IT system. A positive relationship approach is needed in view of the fact that a long and healthy relationship between buyer and supplier benefits both. Besides suppliers and sponsors, sporting organisations maintain various relationships with other business associates, for example, companies with which the sporting organisation collaborates on a non-sponsorship level such as producers of merchandising. Furthermore, retailers selling and distributing the sports entities' merchandising is another example of a business associate. Finally, the hometown or the local community can be another important external stakeholder of a professional sport club. A lot of those are non-for-profit organisations (for example, the local retirement home), which collaborate with the local sporting organisation. This relationship is determined more by social issues than by commercial ones, though.

The relationship between professional sporting organisations and their primary customers – fans, spectators, sponsors and the media – will be explained in detail in the following sections.

The relationship between professional sporting organisations and their fans

Fans and spectators are often described as "the lifeblood" of the sports business. Without fans there would be no live audience in the stadia, no recipients for the media, no target group for sponsors and therefore no income for professional sporting organisations. Hence, fans and spectators are not only a primary customer group for sports entities, but also their most important one. Consequently, sporting organisations must try to establish a healthy and long-term relationship with their fans.

The association between professional sporting organisations and their fans can be described as a two-way relationship. Fans need their clubs as an integral part of their lives and sports entities need their fans in order to survive, in financial terms and as an organisation. It is difficult to characterise the relationship between sporting organisations and their fans in view of the different levels of emotional attachment. Sometimes the relationship is one of love and hate. Fans love their team when it gets promoted and they hate it if relegated. Sport stars and teams can be heroes one day and losers the next. In sports, there is often only black or white because not all supporters have the intellectual ability (or the emotional distance) to differentiate. Therefore, the relationship quality between sporting organisations and their fans often depends on the performance on the pitch. If a team is doing well, the relationship is likely to be a good one. If the team is doing not so well, the relationship is likely to suffer. There are various examples (especially in Italian and German football) where fans were abusing and attacking players of their team because of poor performance on the pitch. Nearly every sports club has some troublemakers in their fan base. Sporting organisations are well-advised not to ignore these troublemakers, but to address them appropriately. However, it has to be noted that the majority of sports fans seek a positive relationship with their favourite club.

Although most sports fans are very committed to their favourite team, more and more sports entities find it difficult to establish a good and longstanding relationship with their supporters, let alone attract new ones. Good relationships don't come for free, they normally require a lot of work and investment. The process towards healthy and valuable relationships is not an easy one, especially not for sporting organisations with few resources, but there really is no alternative in today's business of sports. The process itself consists of many steps and involves various important tasks. Sporting organisations need to know who their customers are, where they can find them and how they can address them. Consumer research is therefore an inevitable prerequisite for relationship marketing. Once the relevant data has been obtained, sports entities are able to define their target groups and build relevant customer groups. Based on segmentation sporting organisations are able to design special offers to each group and offer extraordinary services to their fans. Another important step in the process of establishing longstanding relationships with supporters is to involve them by the use of different relationship marketing instruments. The aim is, of course, to satisfy the needs of the fans. However, there will always be some unsatisfied customers complaining. It is important to take these complaints seriously and to offer a satisfying complaint management system. The last step of the implementation process of a systematic relationship management programme is the evaluation and controlling of each element.

An emerging problem for sports entities is the heterogeneity of their fan base. In the early days, the vast majority of sports supporters were men, aged between 18 and 50. Nowadays, an increasing number of women support sports clubs and more and more families can be seen in sports venues attending live matches. Furthermore, sports spectators differ not only in terms of gender and age, but also in terms of income, social class and appearance. People in business suits watch the game as well as people in replica shirts on the standing terraces. People supporting a club inside and outside the stadium are a mix of different needs and intentions. The heterogeneity of their supporter base makes it so difficult for professional sporting organisations to fulfil the various needs of their fans. Since it is almost impossible to cater for every supporter's individual characteristics, professional sporting organisations are well-advised to group fans to segments by variables they have in common. These common characteristics allow developing a specific relationship marketing approach for all fans in this segment. Overall, fan segmentation is the basis for fan orientation and relationship marketing aiming at fans. Based on the fan segments, the sports entity is able to develop specific marketing strategies for each fan segment. In addition, the communication strategy can be adapted according to the characteristics of each segment. The basic rule in general marketing – one that applies to relationship marketing in sports as well – is to focus on a limited number of important variables. Possible variables that could be used for segmentation are geographic, demographic, psychographic, and behavioural variables (Bühler and Nufer, 2013).

The secret of relationship marketing is not only to serve the different segments, but also design special offers in order to fascinate the customers and give them a reason to stay with the company. A very important aspect in this context is the consumption behaviour of fans. Supporters often express their emotional attachment to their favourite sports club by catching special offers. Some sporting organisations soon realised that they can sell fans nearly everything and that fan loyalty can be a cash cow for sports entities. However, there is a fine line between doing good and exploiting fans. Sporting organisations should always remember to treat their fans fairly and not as captive consumers who don't have a choice. Fans are quite loyal to their sports club but that loyalty isn't blind (Bühler, 2006).

Very effective tools to establish healthy and long-term relationships with fans are interactive features (for example, a discussion forum on the club's website where fans can engage in a constructive dialogue with the club), member clubs and kids clubs, fan loyalty programmes and a systematic complaint management system (Bühler and Nufer, 2010, 2013).

The relationship between professional sporting organisations and their sponsors

Professional sporting organisations have multiple sponsors nowadays. Thus, sports entities have to deal with different types of sponsors and therefore with different types of relationships. For example, the relationship with the main sponsor can be more intense than with a lower sponsor. Nevertheless, sports entities have to manage the relationships with all of their sponsors properly.

In order to manage the relationship between sports entities and sponsors properly, it is very important to understand the relational aspects of sports sponsorship. However, sports sponsorship has been seen by the sponsorship literature for many years as a pure transaction based on a contractual agreement. The transactional view of sponsorship reflects reality to some extent in view of the fact that some sports sponsorships agreements are mainly transactional in nature. For example, there are definitely some sponsors looking for short-term sponsorships rather than long-term agreements, because they have short-term objectives in mind. Some sponsors also tend to be opportunistic in their behaviour by assessing the relative costs relating to the respective sponsorship deal. The same is true for sponsees. Some sports properties need short-term money and therefore look for the best deal in financial terms on a short-term basis. Support for this view comes from a study undertaken by Chadwick and Thwaites (2005), who note that many sponsorship deals in professional English football are short-term orientated. They also point out that many sponsors and sponsees move on to other sponsorship partners once the contractual obligations have been fulfilled. This leads to the conclusion that many sponsorship deals are little more than contractual obligations between sponsees and sponsors who have convergent objectives or interests at a particular point in time. In other words, sponsees and sponsors might try to exploit each other's attractiveness for a short period of time (so-called "one season stands") and therefore reduce the relationship to a purely opportunistic one.

However, reducing sponsorship to a simple transaction may be somewhat limited as to do so ignores the consideration that sponsors and sponsees may commit other resources than money and communication rights to the sponsorship deal. For example, they invest their time, their people, and their know-how in order to make the sponsorship work. Chadwick and Thwaites (2005: p. 337) advise sponsors and sponsees not to view "sponsorship as an exclusively short-term transaction" in view of the fact that "greater long-term benefits may be attainable from a closer, more strategic, network related association". Support for this view comes from Cheng and Stotlar (1999: p. 1), who suggest that it is important to "reconsider sport sponsorship as a durable partnership". They even compare sponsorship with marriages and conclude that "both require long-term commitments to assist each other in reaching mutual fulfilment". Therefore, sports sponsorships should also be viewed as a business-to-business relationship between professional sporting organisations and their sponsors.

Identifying the factors for successful relationships in sports sponsorship is a first step into the right direction. Based on some fundamental studies regarding the relational aspects of sports sponsorship (for example, Chadwick, 2004; Farrelly and Quester, 2005; Bühler, 2006; Bühler, Heffernan and Hewson, 2007) five main factors, which seem to be essential factors for successful relationships in the context of sports sponsorship, can be identified:

- Trust is an essential variable in the relationship between sports entities and sponsors. In order to build up trust, professional sporting organisations have to make sure that they deal fairly and openly with their sponsors. This implies that sports entities should not make any promises they cannot possibly keep, as breaking promises reduces the confidence the sponsor has in the sponsorship partner. Open dealings also imply the courage to communicate unpleasant truths such as problems or conflicts. The same applies for the sponsoring company as well.

- Mutual understanding of each other's objectives is another crucial factor regarding successful sports sponsorships. Professional sporting organisations have to make sure that they understand the objectives and the needs of their sponsorship partner. Only then can sports entities help their sponsor to reach the partner's objectives. Sponsors, on the other hand, have to understand the requirements of the sports club (primarily the financial needs, but also the focus on sporting performance) and the pressure sporting organisations face in view of the public and media interest.

- Sports entities should see their sponsors as long-term partners rather than as companies spending money for a few seasons. Sponsorship partners who look for long-term success would be well-advised to build up a relationship with each other and to take the concept of relationship quality into consideration when doing so. The segmentation into "transactional-orientated" and "relational-orientated" sponsors might help professional sporting organisations in their decision whether to establish a long-term partnership based on the evaluation of their sponsor's relationship orientation. Nowadays, more and more companies seek long-term alliances with their sponsorship property. However, every sponsorship agreement ends sometimes for various reasons (for example, because the sponsorship partners have achieved their objectives or found better partners to do so). In this respect, it is very important to "split up" in a professional and fair manner.

- Successful sports sponsorships are also based on effective communication between sponsor and sponsee. Communication can take many forms. Some sponsorship partners keep in touch on a regular basis by phone, email or face-to-face meetings. In this respect, it is important that sporting organisations make sure that they provide important information about themselves and recent developments. Some professional sporting organisations have established a regular newsletter for their sponsors, including articles about past events, birthdays of key decision makers or an outlook to future happenings. Other sports entities provide information exclusively for sponsors. For example, the main sponsors of the German Bundesliga club Hertha BSC Berlin receive information regarding new players or other important issues before the information is made public. Therefore, sponsors gain the perception of having an exclusive information advantage. Communication between sports entities can take part on an individual basis or in a group setting where several sponsors are invited to spend an evening together in order to talk about various issues related to the sponsorship and other subjects.

• Cooperation is another important issue when it comes to successful sports sponsorships. Involvement in each other's marketing and planning efforts is one form of cooperation and makes sense in view of the fact that it helps to achieve both partners' sponsorship objectives. Sponsors have more marketing skills than sporting organisations and could therefore support the sports entities in marketing issues, whereas professional sporting organisations could provide sponsors with sports-related know-how in order to improve their communication with sports fans.

The relationship between professional sporting organisations and the media

Sports is an important driver for the media. However, the media is equally important for professional sporting organisations for various reasons. First, revenues generated from the sales of broadcasting rights are an essential income stream for sports entities. Second, the media can help to boost the image of a sports club or association. Third, the media can be an effective political tool for sporting organisations when it comes to influencing the public opinion and political decision makers.

The relationship between professional sporting organisations and the media can be best described with the image of Siamese twins: both need each other to survive. In view of this interdependency, both parties are well-advised to seek a positive relationship.

Cooperation between sporting organisations and the media takes place on a personal level involving close contacts and even amicable relations between representatives of sports entities and the media. In general, the media is represented by journalists, commentators, editors, chief editors and the owners of media companies. People representing the sporting organisation can be the owners or the presidents of the sports entity, members of the management, coaches, players and employees responsible for media relations. The most obvious relationship exists between journalists and the official spokespersons of a sports entity. Many sporting organisations have established their own press or communication departments with an official press spokesperson at the top of it. The communication managers within the sports entities' press departments write and release press handouts, organise press conferences and coordinate interview requests. They also check and evaluate the coverage and try to sort out problems that arise. Most communication managers and press spokespersons know the local editors well and have established a personal relationship, characterised by a sense of mutual understanding. Communication often takes place on an informal level. Should problems occur they can be solved easily with a phone call or a brief face-to-face meeting. One of the most important issues in these relationships is trust. Journalists have to trust that the sports entities' press spokespersons will provide them with correct information and deal with them fairly and openly, whereas communication managers of clubs and associations have to trust that editors will not misuse the given information. Another relationship exists between journalists and the top management of sporting organisations. Presidents, managing directors or commercial managers of sports clubs often maintain longstanding relationships with (chief) editors of the local media or even the owners of media companies. Here again, the relationship is supposed to be mutually beneficial in view of the fact that both parties exchange information and news. Journalists might find it easier to get an interview with clubs' representatives than those who do not engage in positive relationships. However, members of a sporting organisation's top management might prevent the publication of a problematic story because of a longstanding relationship with the chief editor of a newspaper. On a sporting level a number of relationships exist. Coaches and managers, for example, often maintain friendly contact with journalists. Therefore, those journalists might receive exclusive information in return for less critical coverage. However, sport is a fast moving business and coaches are hired and fired often, which makes it difficult for media representatives to establish trusty relationships. That is also true for relationships between journalists and players. Some journalists try to establish amicable relations with players in order to get exclusive information. In turn, players might make use of such a relationship when it comes to contract or transfer negotiations. A positive article in the newspaper can boost the image and the personal market value of the respective player. These relationships – especially those that take place on a personal level – might benefit both sides but could also lead to potential conflict of interests. Objectivity and trustworthiness is a key issue in journalism and must always be guaranteed. On the other hand, sports entities and their representatives should be professional enough to maintain a certain balance in dealing with the media.

Besides the more personal level, cooperation between sporting organisations and the media can take place on an organisational level. More and more sports entities are seeking for specific media partnerships. This special form of collaboration is a combination of media cooperation and sponsorship. Often, local and regional companies act as "the official media partner" of a certain sports club. The ultimate form of media partnerships is the acquisition of sporting clubs by media companies. In the late 1990s, Rupert Murdoch, the famous global media tycoon, and his media network (including News Corporation, Fox Entertainment, BSkyB) bought considerable shares of major sports entities as the following examples show. In 1998, Fox Entertainment purchased the Los Angeles Dodgers (baseball) for $311 million, and gained a foothold in the US–American sports franchise market with a 40 per cent interest in the New York Rangers (ice hockey) and the New York Knicks (basketball). In 1999, BSkyB tried to buy Manchester United for £623 million but the bid was eventually blocked by the Mergers and Monopolies Commission. Instead, BSkyB gained part-ownership in the English football clubs Chelsea FC, Leeds United, Manchester City, Manchester United and Sunderland FC, with a 9.9 per cent stake in each club, which was the maximum percentage allowed for ownership in multiple clubs in the UK at the time (Andrews, 2003). Acquisitions like these are a clear commercial investment and involve some logic: media companies owning sports entities (partly or entirely) can influence the clubs' media strategy and – most of all – have a say when it comes to broadcasting negotiations. Furthermore, having a sporting organisation in the portfolio is a prestigious thing for media companies. However, collaboration on this level should be viewed critically. The relationship between a sports entity and a media corporation is unlikely to be a healthy one if the media company cares more about its short-term profits than about the long-term future of the respective sports club or organisation.

In order to establish and maintain a good relationship with the media, many options are available for sporting organisations. The working conditions for the media (including journalists, editors, commentators, camera operators and technicians) have to be of good quality. The flow of information is an essential factor in this context. Most sports entities distribute press releases on a daily basis. The bigger sports clubs hold press conferences featuring managers, selected players or officials nearly every day, the smaller clubs provide such an opportunity before and after each game, at least. In this respect, a growing number of sports entities provide a special service for smaller papers or stations enabling them to follow the press conference through livestream on the internet and thereby having the option to ask questions online. Furthermore, press spokespersons and communication managers of sporting organisations chat with the media on the phone every day in order to provide information and answer questions. In addition, more and more sports entities provide an own password-protected media section on their website where registered journalists can log in and download information and pictures. A very important point in terms of information flow is the availability of players for individual interviews. Some players are more in demand than others and therefore star players cannot meet every request. The press departments of sports clubs have the difficult task of balancing the number of interviews without disappointing the media. They must also make sure that their players deal with the media professionally. After all, dealing with the media is part of the players' job and some clubs even provide journalists with the players' mobile numbers. With regard to players' access, it is important that clubs establish and communicate a strict policy. The preparation for a game should not be disturbed and the private life of players should not be covered without prior authorisation. In order to establish and maintain positive relationships with the media, many sporting organisations invite media representatives on special occasions. For example, some clubs invite close journalists to attend their summer or winter training camps at the clubs' expense. Some other sports entities invite editors to social events such as gala dinners or charity balls hosted by the respective sporting organisation.

Another opportunity to strengthen the bond between the sporting organisation and the media are away games in international cup competitions. For example, some football clubs invite the local media to travel with them to UEFA Champions League games taking place in major European cities where the media then stays in the same hotel as the team and takes part in the post-match gala. Although such events are a good opportunity to maintain good relationships, they can also damage relations with the media when journalists perceive such invitations as some kind of bribe. In this respect, sporting organisations should be sensible and always emphasise that they do not expect a service in return or a favour. Another less expensive relationship marketing tool is the establishment of a database including personal and professional data of each journalist, editor, commentator or other media representative the sporting organisation is dealing with. A birthday card, seasonal greetings, or birthday presents for the kids are small assiduities that contribute to a positive relationship. Often, it is not the present itself but the fact that the sporting organisation remembered and cared about the individual media representative.

Conclusion

Relationship marketing in sports is not only a very interesting topic but also an evolving area. Professional sporting organisations need to keep up-to-date with the development in order to be able to successfully adapt general relationship marketing trends to their specific context and needs. The successful management of relationships as well as the useful application of relationship marketing techniques will contribute to the overall success of any sporting organisation. In contrast, sports properties that neglect the importance of healthy relationships or are not able to implement a systematic relationship management programme will find it more difficult to stay competitive in the business of sports.

References

Andrews, D. (2003). Sport and the transnationalizing media corporation. *The Journal of Media Economics*, 16(4): 235–251.

Berry, L. (1995). Relationship marketing of services: Growing interest, emerging perspectives. *Journal of the Academy of Marketing Science* 23(4): 236–245.

Bruhn, M. (2009). *Relationship Marketing: Das Management von Kundenbeziehungen*. 2nd ed. München: Vahlen.

Bruhn, M. (2013). *Relationship Marketing: Das Management von Kundenbeziehungen*. 3rd ed. München: Vahlen.

Bühler, A. (2006). Professional football sponsorship in the English Premier League and the German Bundesliga. Berlin: Dissertation.de

Bühler, A. and Nufer, G. (2010). *Relationship marketing in sports*. Oxford: Routledge.

Bühler, A. and Nufer, G. (2013). Relationship Marketing im Sport. In Nufer, G. and Bühler, A. (Eds) *Marketing im Sport. Grundlagen und Trends des modernen Sportmarketing*. 3rd ed. Berlin: Erich Schmidt Verlag, 353–382.

Bühler, A. and Nufer, G. (Eds) (2014). *International sports marketing: Principles and perspectives*. Berlin: Erich Schmidt Verlag.

Bühler, A., Heffernan, T. and Hewson, P. (2007). The soccer club–sponsor relationship: Identifying the critical variables for success. *International Journal of Sports Marketing & Sponsorship* 8(4): 291–309.

Buttle, F. (1996). Relationship marketing, In Buttle, F. (Ed) *Relationship marketing. Theory & Practice*, London: Paul Chapman Publishing, 1–16.

Chadwick, S. (2004). Determinants of commitment in the professional football club/shirt sponsorship dyad, unpublished thesis, University of Leeds.

Chadwick, S. and Thwaites, D. (2005). Managing sport sponsorship programmes: Lessons from a critical assessment of English soccer. *Journal of Advertising Research*, 45(3): 328–338.

Cheng, P. S. T. and Stotlar, D. K. (1999). Successful sponsorship: A marriage between sport and corporations for the next millennium. *The Cyber-Journal of Sport Marketing*, 3(3): 1–9.

Diller, H. (2000). Customer loyalty: Fata morgana or realistic goal? Managing relationships with customers. In Hennig-Thurau, T. and Hansen, U. (Eds) *Relationship marketing: Gaining competitive advantage through customer satisfaction and customer retention*, Berlin: Springer, 29–48.

Farrrelly, F. and Quester, P. (2005). Examining important relationship constructs of the focal sponsorship exchange. *Industrial Marketing Management*, 34(3): 211–219.

Friedrichs, S. (2005). Nachhaltigkeit als Impulsgeber für ein Relationship Marketing. *Forschungsbeiträge zum Strategischen Management*, Bremen: Universität Bremen.

Grönroos, C. (1994). Quo vadis, marketing? Towards a relationship marketing paradigm. *Journal of Marketing Management* 10(5): 347–360.

Harwood, T., Garry, T. and Broderick, A. (2008). *Relationship marketing: Perspectives, dimensions and contexts*. London: McGraw Hill.

Hennig-Thurau, T. and Hansen, U. (2000). Relationship marketing: Some reflections on the state-of-the-art of the relational concept. In Hennig-Thurau, T. and Hansen, U. (Eds) *Relationship marketing: Gaining competitive advantage through customer satisfaction and customer retention*. Berlin: Springer, 3–27.

Nufer, G. (2006). Event-Marketing und Kundenbindung – Fallstudie Adidas. In Rennhak, C. (Ed) *Herausforderung Kundenbindung*, Wiesbaden: DUV, 221–247.

Nufer, G. and Bühler, A. (Eds) (2013). *Marketing im Sport: Grundlagen und Trends des modernen Sportmarketing*. 3rd ed. Berlin: Erich Schmidt Verlag.

Meffert, H. and Bruhn, M. (2013). *Dienstleistungsmarketing: Grundlagen – Konzepte – Methoden*. 7th ed. Wiesbaden: Gabler.

Meffert, H., Burmann, C. and Kirchgeorg, M. (2012). *Marketing. Grundlagen marktorientierter Unternehmensführung. Konzepte, Instrumente, Praxisbeispiele*. 11th ed. Wiesbaden: Gabler.

Morgan, R., Crutchfield, T. and Lacey, R. (2000). Patronage and loyalty strategies: Understanding the behavioural and attitudinal outcomes of customer retention programs. In Hennig-Thurau, T. and Hansen, U. (Eds) *Relationship marketing: Gaining competitive advantage through customer satisfaction and customer retention*. Berlin: Springer, 71–87.

Sandhusen, R. (2008). *Marketing*. 4th ed. New York: Barron's.

Stauss, B. and Seidel, W. (2014). *Beschwerdemanagement. Unzufriedene kunden als profitable zielgruppe*. 5th ed. München: Carl Hanser Verlag.

16

EXPERIENTIAL MARKETING AND SPORTING EVENTS

Guillaume Bodet

Introduction

When linking experiential marketing with sporting events, the first possible images that come to mind would be those of the Super Bowl, which has become a world-famous sporting contest as well as a great entertaining spectacle (Apostolopoulou et al., 2006), similar to those of the National Basketball Association's all-star or special games, or major sporting events' opening and closing ceremonies, such as the Olympic Games and some games of the Stade Français Rugby club for the European context (Bodet, 2009). These games and events are perceived as exceptional and extraordinary because of their attendance and audience, their uniqueness and the types of experiences they produce for spectators and fans. Moreover, there is almost no doubt that these experiences are planned and engineered by sports managers and result from a deliberate particular marketing strategy. It would obviously be too simplistic to say that the marketing managers are solely responsible for these experiences because it would underestimate the co-creative role of other spectators, and teams and athletes (Woratschek et al., 2014), but it is undeniable that marketing managers do have a significant role in the success of these sporting events, which can be considered as company-driven experiences according to the classification of Carù and Cova (2007). Although it is easy to identify the extremes of a spectrum, and these extraordinary experiences can be put at one extreme end of this spectrum, it is more difficult to locate other types of sports spectatorship experiences along this spectrum and particularly define what should go at the other end of it. Consequently, stating that these events and the experiences produced result from an experiential marketing strategy is not enough because it does not allow for making a distinction between what should be considered as a conspicuous experiential marketing strategy and what simply results from a "normal" and traditional marketing strategy. This is the purpose of the first section of this chapter. We will propose a definition that is based on the notions of extraordinary and ordinary experiences on one hand and enriched services on the other hand. This definition, which is not perfect because the line between ordinary and extraordinary experiences is certainly individual, subjective and contextual, allows considering the variety of sports spectators' experiences and their consequences in terms of consumer behaviour that can be positive and negative. These two aspects will respectively be discussed in the second and third sections of the chapter.

Experiential marketing and production of experiences

In order to fully understand the meaning of experiential marketing in the context of sporting events, it is crucial to understand in which circumstances the concept emerged and which marketing practices it was associated with. The first turning point in the advent of experiential marketing as an innovative and legitimate marketing approach was probably the publication of the seminal article by Holbrook and Hirschman (1982). In this article, the authors emphasised that it was reductionist to consider consumption as an activity fulfilling only or mainly instrumental benefits, relying upon products and services' objective features and characteristics. Thus, they called for an experiential view of consumption that enlarged the traditional information processing perspective by considering that fantasies, feelings and fun as consumption is "a primarily subjective state of consciousness with a variety of symbolic meanings, hedonic responses, and esthetic criteria" (Holbrook and Hirschman, 1982: p. 132). The immediate consequence of this approach is that marketers should not only focus on the rational and utilitarian components of products and services but should also appreciate their experiential aspects. This view was later promoted by various academics and practitioners, among whom Pine and Gilmore (1999) and Schmitt (1999a, 1999b) had possibly the largest echo. For them, traditional marketing, which saw consumers as rational decision-makers focusing on features and benefits, had to be replaced by experiential marketing, which saw consumers as rational and emotional, looking for holistic experiences and an identity project. Schmitt (1999a) proposed a framework to achieve this transition. However, despite a growing interest in experiential marketing, Tynan and McKechnie (2009) noticed that practitioners tended to exaggerate the positive impacts of experiential marketing, sometimes sold as a miraculous solution by consultants, and that their claims often lacked scientific evidence and reliability. From an academic point of view, the use of various terms, such as experiential marketing, production of experiences and experience marketing, consumer experience and consumption experience, has contributed to theoretical confusions. Although the experiential dimension discussed by Holbrook and Hirschman (1982) appears relevant and legitimate, particularly when focusing on what these authors called conventional goods and services, it does not apply in the same way to all products and services. From the beginning, Holbrook and Hirschman (1982) analysed that even if all products conveyed a symbolic dimension, certain products such as entertainment, the arts and leisure activities, to which we could naturally add sports, were richer in terms of symbols. The analysis could be extended to other aspects previously mentioned: fantasies, feelings and fun. In the same vein, Filser (2002) theorised a continuum of experience production identifying products with a strong functional but a weak experiential component and products with a strong experiential but a weak functional component, where sports spectacle could be situated. In this case, we can wonder what experiential marketing would mean for sports spectacles, which already have a strong experience component: if sports spectacles are mainly made of experiences, what is the difference between traditional and experiential marketing? The definition of Carù and Cova (2006) is helpful to answer this question, as for these authors, experiential marketing goes beyond the simple production of experiences and aims to provide an additional category of offers that complete the main product, and which can be originally with low or high experiential contents, to produce extraordinary, highly emotional and memorable experiences. As discussed by Carù and Cova (2007: p. 10), "an experience becomes extraordinary thanks to increasingly spectacular and surprising decors and due to the ever greater scope of the extravagances and simulations in which the consumer will be immersed".

Consistent with this definition, the innovative marketing strategy implemented by the Stade Français Paris Rugby club, analysed by Bodet (2009), can be considered as an experiential marketing strategy. Since 2005, this professional rugby club attracted massive crowds of spectators (i.e. more than 70,000) a few times a year in the Stade de France, a stadium with a capacity of slightly more than 80,000, although the club struggled to sell out its regular home ground of nearly 11,000 capacity the rest of the year (Bodet, 2009). The main strategy relied upon the addition of numerous and sometimes extravagant entertainment and shows before, at half time and after the game. These shows could be made of car parades, mini concerts, wrestling, cancan dancers, stunts, acrobatics, and fireworks to provide extraordinary experiences to the spectators. Although some of them could appear flashy, tacky and not related to rugby they could certainly be seen as providing memorable and most of the times positive emotions and experiences. In the same vein, Apostolopoulou et al. (2006) analysed the importance of Super Bowl entertainment, which can be equivalent to an experiential marketing strategy, and which comprised several elements: pre-game show, the commercials, coin toss with celebrity presence, celebrity singing the national anthem, teams entering the field, the competitiveness of the game, halftime entertainment, MVP award presentation and post-game show. Although these elements are considered enriching for the spectators' experiences and provided extraordinary experiences, it is important to note that what constitutes an ordinary experience will strongly vary between sports, levels, leagues, competitions, countries and cultural contexts. Apostolopoulou et al. (2006: p. 224) stated:

> In today's sporting world, music, mascots, cheerleaders, dance teams, and special theme nights are part of the regular game entertainment repertoire of most professional (Major and minor) and collegiate sporting events.

But if this applies to the sporting North American context, it certainly cannot be extended to all professional sports contexts around the world. Consequently, what is considered as a normal or ordinary experience in one context cannot be considered the same in another context. Ordinary experiences in a specific context will sometimes be considered as extraordinary somewhere else. The context-specific dimension of experiences was notably discussed by Richins (1997). For this reason, Lai and Bodet (2012) and Lai (2014) focused on the distinction between ordinary and extraordinary experiences in Taiwanese professional baseball games. From a qualitative study based on focus groups with fans and spectators, they identified various factors that could make games become extraordinary. Additional events, shows and entertainment organised around the games (before, at half time and after) were considered as extraordinary, which corresponds to the definition of experiential marketing used in this chapter. In terms of occasional and regular activities, cheering bands, songs for players, birthday celebrations for fans before the games, record celebrations, theme days, family days, mascots and cheer squads, opening pitch with a special guest, and fireworks can be cited (Lai, 2014). However, the fans interviewed also indicated that some sporting elements could create an extraordinary experience. It could be the case if one player achieved a particular record or if the game noticeably influenced the overall table ranking position. Regarding this later result, it is important to highlight the particular context of professional baseball in Taiwan where the league is only composed of four teams so the ranking positions do not change very often. This result demonstrates the influence of sporting and cultural contexts on the perceptions of what is considered normal and expected and what is unexpected. It is also useful to observe the non-controllability dimension of certain factors, indicating that managers are not solely responsible for the production of extraordinary experiences. This result is in line with the conceptualisation of Verhoef et al. (2009) applied to retailing environments. These authors stated (p. 32):

> Experience is created not only by those elements which the retailer can control (e.g. service interface, retail atmosphere, assortment; price), but also by elements that are outside of the retailer's control (influence of others, purpose of shopping).

The day of the game was also identified by Lai and Bodet (2012) as a factor influencing the ordinary aspect of the games because weekend games were perceived as providing more extraordinary experiences. This result can be explained by the fact that more additional activities and shows are organised during weekend games. In this particular case, the day of the game can be considered as an indirect indicator of the managerial activation of an experiential marketing strategy. The stadium dimension was also mentioned by the respondents and, beyond teams' managerial activation, some stadiums seem to be more suitable than others for providing extraordinary experiences. This result is supported by the fact that professional baseball teams in Taiwan use various stadiums for their home games and that differences in perceptions are found despite almost similar marketing actions within each stadium. The team factor was also identified as two teams were perceived as mainly providing ordinary experiences in comparison with the two other teams (Lai and Bodet, 2012). After having defined what experiential marketing means in the context of sporting events, and having identified factors and variables influencing the ordinary and extraordinary aspects of spectators' experiences, the following section will focus on the types of experiences spectators live and the way they can be segmented based on the experiences they seek, to determine whether or not an experiential marketing strategy would be suitable.

Consumer experiences in sporting events

If experiential marketing is considered as the creation and provision of extraordinary experiences through enriched products and services, it becomes necessary to define a sports spectacle's ordinary experience from a subjective consumer point of view and from a more objective service offer analysis to fully appreciate the value of additional offers. Before discussing several theoretical frameworks aimed at increasing and sometimes modelling our understanding of sports spectators' experiences, it is necessary to posit that experiences are extremely subjective and consequently diverse, intimate and individualised. However, such uniqueness does not preclude researchers and analysts from identifying similar experiential patterns and managerial levers to create categories. They can appear simplistic – erasing the complexity and richness of experiences – but they are still useful to apprehend and make sense of phenomena. In this vein, based on in-depth observations and analyses of baseball games, Holt (1995) identified four metaphors of consumption that could be generalised to most sporting events' spectators. First, consuming as experience refers to sports spectators' subjective and emotional reactions to the spectacle and directly refers to the experiential, hedonic and aesthetic view theorised by Holbrook and Hirschman (1982) previously discussed. This experience of the sports spectacle relies upon accounting activities to make sense of the baseball world and object. They also rely upon spectators making evaluations (for example, the diving leap of a fielder, velocity of a pitch in the baseball case) and appreciations (for example, feelings of excitement and awe, joy and relief, anger and disappointment) of the game and various events. Second, consuming as integration refers to the way sports spectators acquire and manipulate objects to construct their identity and self-concept. Holt (1995) noted that this activity becomes difficult with mass-produced consumption objects that can apply in a certain way to sporting events. Integration relies upon assimilating practices, which in the context of the study, require "developing the requisite baseball world knowledge and the specialised tastes that flow from this knowledge" (p. 7), such as knowing where the best seats are, for instance. Integration also relies upon producing, which refers to spectators' actions to assert and show their belonging and involvement in the sports spectacle (for example, addressing and talking to the players) and personalising where sports spectators try to establish an individualized link with the sports event or the related sports world, often through personalised dressing, signs, and comments (Holt, 1995). Third, consuming as classification refers to the way sports spectators classify themselves in reference to relevant others through interpersonal actions. When classification is done though objects, similarities can be found with integration. However, the way sports spectators interact with the objects is as important, if not more, as the objects themselves. Holt (1995) used the examples of derogatory chanting, revering a former player, staying until the end of the game or avoiding participating in the Mexican wave. Fourth, consuming as play refers to the way consumers use the sports spectacle to commune and socialize with other spectators they know or not. Based on Holt's (1995) work, Bourgeon and Bouchet (2001) developed a framework considering that certain consumption patterns and values could be combined to create four main sports spectator profiles; Bouchet et al. (2011) later developed an instrument to operationalise them.

These profiles are considered to be contextual as individuals may seek different experiences depending on the type of sporting events, their scale, the teams and athletes involved in the competition, the importance of the sporting outcome or the type of people spectators consume with. The first profile refers to sports spectators mainly seeking an aesthetic experience associated with the beauty of the contest and the display, the high level of skills demonstrated by the athletes. They are sometimes considered connoisseurs, experts who appreciate physical, technical or tactical aspects, which are not perceived or appreciated in the same way by non-experts. They are also more sensitive to the values of the sports, the implicit rules of the sports and sportsmanship behaviours. These spectators are named aesthetes. The second profile gathers supporters, characterises spectators who mainly search for a performance, a victory, a positive outcome for the team or athlete they support. They tend to be active and vocal and firmly believe they have a significant role in the performance of the team or athlete they support. The third profile named interactive refers to sports spectators who mainly search for highly emotional and shared experiences. They are as sensitive to the things happening on the sporting field as those happening around it (for example, pre-game and half-time entertainment) and in the stands. The fourth profile is the opportunistic profile. Although Holbrook and Hirschman (1982) noted the prominence of the experiential dimension in the entertainment industry, Bourgeon and Bouchet (2001) restored the significance of the utilitarian and instrumental component in sports spectacles. For these opportunist spectators, who rarely represent a majority, sporting events represent ways to achieve non-experiential objectives and provide utilities such as an improved personal image, political and business benefits. Bourgeon and Bouchet (2001) and Bouchet et al. (2011) underlined the simulation dimension of these spectators who often try to appear like other profiles to maximize the benefits they could get; politicians trying to appear like supporters or aesthetes are often observable. Bourgeon and Bouchet (2001) also identified theoretical relationships between these profiles, highlighting the fact that depending on the type of experiences lived and engineered, certain profiles will be more visible and it is probably not possible to satisfy all of these profiles with the same experiences. For instance, aesthetes look for aesthetic and beautiful displays although supporters mainly look for performance and efficiency. Consequently, a "beautiful defeat" would not satisfy supporters whereas an "ugly victory" would not content aesthetes. Based on spectators' values associated with the sports spectacle and searched experiences, Bourgeon and Bouchet (2001) established that the aesthete profile was in contradiction with the supporter profile, and that the opportunist profile was in contradiction with the interactive profile. They also considered that the opportunist and supporter profiles had a complementary relationship such as the aesthete and interactive profiles (see Bouchet et al., 2011 for details of these relationships). Despite the relevance of these relationships from a theoretical point of view, they may not be so clear-cut and some subtle combinations may appear (Chanavat and Bodet, 2014), even if no significant correlations between the profiles have been found so far (Bodet et al., 2010; Bouchet et al., 2011).

Regarding experiential marketing, which was previously defined as the provision of additional and new service components to create unique, intense, and memorable experiences, it seems that the main targeted profile is the interactive profile. This is one of the conclusions of Bodet (2009) who analysed the experiential marketing strategy implemented by the Stade Français Paris Rugby club. According to Bodet, professional sports clubs traditionally target spectators with a supporter profile by focusing on enhancing sporting performances with the best players or athletes. However, with experiential marketing, professional clubs like the Stade Français Paris Rugby target interactive spectators who want to be first of all emotionally stimulated, share, enjoy and participate (Bodet, 2009). Spectators with an opportunist profile also seem targeted and particularly trendy or famous ones because they can help increase the awareness of the sporting event and the club brand while also producing positive associations, which could enhance the club brand image (Bodet, 2009). In a qualitative analysis of spectators' experiences of Stade Français' games using an experiential marketing strategy, Chanavat and Bodet (2014) found that all profiles could be observed. Unsurprisingly, many of the spectators these authors interviewed presented an interactive profile considering the intensity and extraordinary aspects of the emotions produced. The interaction dimensions discussed by Holt (1995), socialising and communing, were also highly discussed. It seems that this type of experience is hardly consumed alone and that the social environment appears critical even if it is not the same each time, as some spectators alternate between family, friends and work colleagues (Chanavat and Bodet, 2014). Contrary to what Bourgeon and Bouchet (2001) defined theoretically, the interactive profile does not necessarily appear in opposition with the opportunist profile. Many interactive spectators seemed to present opportunistic features because many of them benefited from very low prices, free tickets and invitations to these games (Chanavat and Bodet, 2014). This contradicts the theory because spectators with an interactive profile would be expected to be willing to pay premium price to live extraordinary experiences. Spectators with an aesthete profile were also observed and some of them seemed to present a similar opportunistic pattern regarding the price of the tickets. In this particular sporting context, it could be explained by the fact that, for various reasons, these games did not systematically involve the best teams and players and then possibly not the best quality. From a marketing perspective, it would make sense to accentuate the marketing efforts to attract spectators to the games, which are not the most appealing, from a sporting point of view. For the same purpose, these games did not seem to be the most appealing for spectators with a supporter profile even if they did not appear to be a deterrent (Chanavat and Bodet, 2014). Another aspect that could negatively influence the presence of die-hard fans and supporters is the nature of the ambiance being possibly too jolly and flimsy and which does not correspond to the type of atmosphere and behaviour they expect. For them, performance and the outcome of the games are the most important and everything should be oriented towards these aspects, whereas the experiential aspects divert spectators from them. For them, having too many spectators not displaying a supporter profile, could be another case of co-destruction of value by spectators (Stieler et al., 2014). Although some supporters have a negative opinion of these enriched experiences, this does not seem to hinder them to come in this particular context. This aspect will be further discussed in the following section, dealing with the consequences of experiential marketing strategies in sporting events. It is important to note that not all spectators look for the same types of experiences and that experiential marketing, which aims to provide a certain type of them, will not fit with all spectator profiles in the same way and that this conclusion should be kept in managers' minds when deciding whether or not they should implement such strategy. Particularly, it seems that the balance of spectators' profiles appears key to maximise the co-creation of value for most spectators.

The consequences of experiential marketing in sporting events

From its origin, experiential marketing has been seen by academics and practitioners as a great managerial lever to produce various positive outcomes, such as to create brand advocacy, loyalty and word-of-mouth (Smilansky, 2009), and sometimes sold as a miraculous solution for all marketing problems, despite a lack of conceptual foundations (Tynan and McKechnie, 2009; Verhoef et al., 2009).

From anecdotal evidence and sometimes attendance and broadcasting figures, it seems that experiential marketing tends to attract more spectators, which is the case in the Super Bowl and the Stade Français' games organised at the Stade de France, as discussed in the previous sections, or "The Big Game", which is an annual rugby union game hosted by the Harlequins F.C. during the Christmas period at Twickenham Stadium. However, beyond these short-term quantitative impacts, very few empirical studies have focused on the long-term impact of the experiential marketing strategy implementation or from a more subjective point of view. Kao et al. (2007) attempted to investigate the influence of basketball games' experiential elements in Taiwan on spectators' satisfaction, repurchase and recommendation intentions, but nothing is said about the nature of the experiences created (ordinary or extraordinary), and therefore, the eventual implementation of a marketing strategy. After having contextually defined ordinary and extraordinary experiences in Taiwanese professional baseball, Lai (2014) tried to measure the impact of extraordinary experiences, and thus experiential marketing, on the relationships between consumer-perceived levels of experience, perceived service quality, satisfaction and loyalty, and found significant differences between the models. Among these differences, the influence of the perceived level of experience on consumer loyalty increased within the context of extraordinary experiences although the role of satisfaction on consumer loyalty decreased and the role of service quality increased. Consequently, it seems that in this context, extraordinary experiences more directly impact consumer loyalty and reduce the role of satisfaction on loyalty, indicating a less rational and cognitive process of evaluation from spectators (Lai, 2014). Surprisingly, extraordinary experiences increased the role of service quality on satisfaction, which could mean that service quality is valorised by extraordinary experiences although unnoticed with ordinary experiences in the context of Taiwanese professional baseball games. In this case, we could think that the activities set and the experiences created potentially increase the perceived quality of the decor, design and staging facet (Carù and Cova, 2007); the two others being the consumer's active participation and the story narrative and intrigues created. However, due to the research design of the study, no conclusion can be drawn in a long-term perspective.

Using a different approach, focusing on the subjective opinions of spectators about extraordinary experiences produced at Stade Français' rugby games, Chanavat and Bodet (2014) tried to link experiential marketing and perceived-brand equity (Aaker, 1991). Their findings tend to support the idea that experiential marketing increases brand awareness levels as it attracted to the brand and to the games people who were not familiar with it, and also raised their interest. Nevertheless, experiential marketing did not seem to be the only managerial lever improving the notoriety of the brand as many respondents also recognised the importance of promotional activities (Chanavat and Bodet, 2014). Brand image also seemed strongly influenced as many new associations characterised the brand. Most of them could be perceived as positive (for example, fun, entertainment, unique, innovative), whereas some of them could be seen at least as neutral and sometimes negative, with terms such as "arrogant", "controversial" and "boastful".

In reference to the spectator profiles discussed in the previous section, it appears that most positive associations came from spectators presenting interactive and opportunist profiles, whereas the more neutral and negative terms mainly came from spectators with aesthete and supporter profiles (Chanavat and Bodet, 2014). Not all supporters and aesthetes had a negative view of the experiential marketing strategy and if they did not show any particular interest in these enriched experiences, several of them recognised the positive impact it had on non-supporters and casual fans, attracting more people to the game and increasing the size of the rugby community as a whole. However, for few of them, these shows and experiences did not correspond to what was seen as "traditional" and "authentic" and did not match rugby values (Chanavat and Bodet, 2014). Similarities can be drawn between these comments and some results of Chanavat and Bodet (2014) and Giulianotti (2005) regarding fans' views on the commodification of sports. In this particular sporting context, experiential marketing could be seen as a Disneyisation (Bryman, 1999) of sporting events, or even a McDisneyisation (Ritzer and Liska, 1997), if these extraordinary experiences become globally standardised, reproduced and consequently, predictable. This can certainly create resistances and oppositions, and in turn diminish loyalty, among certain segments of the most traditional and identified spectators and fans, as Carù and Cova (2007: p. 11) observed:

> [F]or many consumers, an experience is more than the simple acceptance of a prepackaged offer revolving around a theme that has been chosen by the firm (thematization of the experience) – some of it must also be left unorganized so that it can become appropriable.

In a word, consumers want to co-create and be active in the creation of their own experiences and do not want to design and actively produce them, according to their own expectations and searched experiences.

Based upon an analysis of ESPN and its consumers, Holt (2004) warned brand managers not to focus too much on consumers he called *feeders* and who present many similarities with spectators with an opportunistic and interactive profile; the ones who are either targeted or the most receptive to experiential marketing strategies. Holt (2004) defined these feeders as "promiscuous fans who jump on the bandwagon of any winning team, accomplished athlete, or celebrated contest" (p. 147), as spectators who do not follow a team or an athlete but follow trends and "find little intrinsic pleasure in spectating" (p. 148). According to him, they have little attachment to the brand and are not as committed as the brand followers: die-hard fans in the context of sporting events. This analysis seems to be supported by the fact that Chanavat and Bodet (2014) did not find any noticeable positive impact by experiential marketing on brand loyalty. Following Holt's (2004) view, sporting event brands should be careful in implementing experiential marketing strategies if they mainly attract opportunist and interactive spectators (i.e. feeders) and could possibly act as a deterrent in the long term for aesthete and supporters (i.e. followers).

Conclusion

The first objective of this chapter was to define what experiential marketing is in the context of sporting events as it did not originally come from the field. Based on a literature review, experiential marketing was defined as the provision of additional offers and activities to create extraordinary, surprising and memorable experiences. Several examples were analysed before discussing the nature and the types of sporting events' experiences spectators like and seek. It was concluded that experiential marketing in sporting events was mainly used to target or was more suitable for spectators presenting an interactive or an opportunist profile. Experiential marketing appears to be a great managerial lever to attract these types of spectators to the games, increase brand awareness and create positive brand associations and perceived quality. Nevertheless, no empirical evidence suggests that it has a noticeable positive influence on brand loyalty. However, some results tend to indicate that sporting events' managers should not consider experiential marketing as a solely positive tool, and should be particularly cautious regarding its possible impact on traditional and committed fans with supporter or aesthete profiles. Considering the lack of empirical evidence regarding the consequences and effects of experiential marketing, it seems hazardous to consider experiential marketing as a marketing management solution, which fits all consumer segments and achieves all objectives. Similarly to all marketing approaches, it will work better when combined with an in-depth strategic analysis, which takes into consideration the characteristics of the sports organisation and its sociocultural context.

References

Aaker, D. A. (1991). *Managing brand equity*. New York: The Free Press.

Apostolopoulou, A., Clark, J. and Gladden, J. M. (2006). From H-Town to Mo-Town: The importance of Super Bowl entertainment. *Sport Marketing Quarterly* 15, 223–231.

Bodet, G. (2009). "Give me a stadium and I will fill it". An analysis of the marketing management strategy of Stade Français Paris rugby club. *International Journal of Sports Marketing and Sponsorship* April, 252–262.

Bodet, G., Bernache-Assollant, I. and Bouchet, P. (2010). Segmenting NBA's Chinese viewers based on their searched experiences. Presented at the 18th Congress of the European Association for Sport Management, Bridging Sport Management Across Europe, Prague.

Bouchet, P., Bodet, G., Bernache-Assollant, I. and Kada, F. (2011). Segmenting sport spectators: Construction and preliminary validation of the Sporting Event Experience Search (SEES) scale. *Sport Management Review* 14, 42–53.

Bourgeon, D. and Bouchet, P. (2001). La recherche d'expériences dans la consommation du spectacle sportif. *Revue Européenne de Management du Sport* 6, 1–47.

Bryman, A. (1999). The Disneyisation of society. *Sociological Review* 47, 25–47.

Carù, A. and Cova, B. (2007). *Consuming experience*. Abingdon: Routledge.

Carù, A. and Cova, B. (2006). Expériences de consommations et marketing expérientiel. *Revue Française de Gestion* 162, 100–113.

Chanavat, N. and Bodet, G. (2014). Experiential marketing in sport spectatorship services: a customer perspective. *European Sport Management Quarterly* 14, 323–344.

Filser, M. (2002). Le marketing de la production d'expériences: statut théorique et implications managériales. *Décisions Marketing* 28, 13–22.

Giulianotti, R. (2005). Sport spectators and the social consequences of commodification: Critical perspectives from Scottish football. *Journal of Sport and Social Issues* 29, 386–410.

Holbrook, M. and Hirschman, E. (1982). The experiential aspects of consumption: Consumer fantasy, feelings and fun. *Journal of Consumer Research* 9, 132–140.

Holt, D. B. (1995). How consumers consume: A typology of consumption practices. *Journal of Consumer Research* 22, 1–16.

Holt, D. B. (2004). *How brands become icons. The principles of cultural branding.* Boston: Harvard Business School Press.

Kao, Y. F., Huang, L. S. and Yang, M. H. (2007). Effects of experiential elements on experiential satisfaction and loyalty intentions: a case study of the super basketball league in Taiwan. *International Journal of Revenue Management* 1, 79–96.

Lai, C. H. (2014). *An evaluation of the influence of experiential marketing on spectators' behaviour in the Taiwanese professional baseball league.* Loughborough: Loughborough University.

Lai, C. H. and Bodet, G. (2012). Exploring the notions of spectators' ordinary and extraordinary experiences in Taiwanese professional baseball games. Presented at the 2012 Global Sport Management Conference, New Taipei City, Taiwan.

Pine, B. J. and Gilmore, J. (1999). *The experience economy: work is theatre and every business a stage.* Harvard: HBS Press.

Richins, M. L. (1997). Measuring emotions in the consumption experience. *Journal of Consumer Research* 24, 127–146.

Ritzer, G. and Liska, A. (1997). "McDisneyization" and "Post-tourism": complementary perspectives on contemporary tourism, in *Touring cultures: Transformations of travel and theory*, Rojek, C., Urry, J. (eds.), 96–109, London: Routledge.

Schmitt, B. H. (1999a). *Experiential marketing: How to get customers to SENSE, FEEL, THINK, ACT and RELATE to your company and brands.* New York: The Free Press.

Schmitt, B. H. (1999b). Experiential marketing. *Journal of Marketing Management* 15, 53–67.

Smilansky, S. (2009). *Experiential marketing: A practical guide to interactive brand experiences.* London: Kogan Page.

Stieler, M., Weismann, F. and Germelmann, C. C. (2014). Co-destruction of value by spectators: the case of silence protests. *European Sport Management Quarterly* 14, 72–86.

Tynan, C. and McKechnie, S. (2009). Experience marketing: A review and reassessment. *Journal of Marketing Management* 25, 501–517.

Verhoef, P. C., Lemon, K. N., Parasuraman, A., Roggeveen, A., Tsiros, M. and Schlesinger, L. A. (2009). Customer experience creation: Determinants, dynamics and management strategies. *Journal of Retailing* 85, 31–41.

Woratschek, H., Horbel, C. and Popp, B. (2014). Value co-creation in sport management. *European Sport Management Quarterly* 14, 1–5.

17

MANAGING SEASON TICKET HOLDERS

Heath McDonald

Introduction

Of all the stakeholders professional sports teams must satisfy, it is sports fans that are arguably the most important. The value of fans stems from the wide range of direct connections or associations they form with teams, which include social, emotional and financial exchanges. All teams need fans as a basic requirement for survival, but an active and engaged fan-base provides direct revenue through ticket sales and merchandise purchase and indirect benefits such as increasing broadcast rights values. Fans also create a range of media and sponsorship opportunities for sporting organizations to leverage, through their numbers and loyalty to the team.

Fans of a team can include those who "silently" support the team without attending games, those who choose to attend individual home games on a casual basis, and those who acquire team memberships or season tickets that offer a service commonly inclusive of home match attendance and other various benefits. Season ticket holders (SIH hereafter) can be viewed as the first among equals, as their repeat patronage and higher commitment makes them, in many ways, the most desirable of all customers.

Customer management is always a complex blend of understanding what a customer requires and delivering it profitably, in the right way at the right time. STH management is even more complex, particularly in a sports context. STH management is complicated, as season-ticket products constitute a *subscription* market, where purchase decisions are made infrequently (typically annually) and evaluations are usually a result of a combination of experiences over time. Customer behaviour in subscription market situations is also very different from in repertoire or casual ticket buying markets. Added to the complexity of subscription markets is the fact that most STH are drawn from the ranks of the most passionate sports fans. Their passion can make them demanding customers, requiring personalized attention that is difficult to deliver en masse.

STH make a significant financial and emotional commitment to sports teams and require careful management in return to ensure their satisfaction and continued patronage. This chapter examines the particular requirements of STH, from understanding how to attract and retain STH through to what managers can do to ensure their satisfaction.

Season ticket markets and how they are different

The offering of a team season ticket package or a membership is a common practice for sports teams worldwide, as well as various other arts and leisure organizations (for example, theatre companies, art galleries, gyms). Variations abound, and it is no longer the case that a season ticket constitutes a pass for multiple game entry. Many organizations have moved from using the term "season ticket", to other expressions such as "member" or "patron" to reflect the changing nature of the product. For sports market leaders with capacity attendance, non-ticketed memberships are now the norm and often the major product sold.

What all season ticket products have in common is that they are annually or seasonally purchased and are usually specific to a particular team, although stadium memberships exist (for example, MCC at Lords). Such products are classified as belonging to "subscription markets" with phone services, insurance, banking and utilities (see Sharp, Wright and Goodhardt, 2002, for a full discussion). In most markets, consumers purchase regularly and do so from a repertoire of competing brands to fulfil their category requirements. The key differences between subscription markets and the more commonly seen repertoire markets are that: (a) subscription products are bought infrequently, often annually; (b) consumers have much smaller repertoires in subscription markets and are often solely loyal to one provider; and (c) they often involve being formally contracted to one specific provider for the period of purchase, for example, annual mobile phone contracts.

As a consequence, subscription market behaviour differs from repertoire market behaviour on two key metrics: brands tend to satisfy a much higher percentage of consumers' category needs; and a higher number of solely loyal customers for each brand are evident. In many markets, the positive relationship between consumer satisfaction and repeat purchase has been over-stated. There is ample evidence of satisfied customers churning in typical consumer markets (Oliver, 1999). Usually, consumer churn is unintentional, as their regular brand is either physically (for example, not stocked nearby) or mentally (for example, forgotten) unavailable to them.

A sports season ticket is likely to be different, however. Sports fans rarely switch their attitudinal loyalty, thus, their main form of protest against an unsatisfactory experience is to lessen their degree of consumption. Typically, this manifests as a shift from season tickets to casual ticket purchases, or from live attendance to television viewing. Whereas in many markets a proportion of churn occurs because consumers forget which product they bought last time or their product is unavailable (out-of-stock or not stocked in that store), the high involvement of sports fans means they rarely forget about their team and will not readily substitute one team for another. The main reasons for churn among habitual sports fans are likely to be due to dissatisfaction or an inability to get to games (for example, having a newborn or moving away from the stadium). Providing a satisfying season ticket product may be more directly related to renewal (repurchase), and the management of satisfaction is potentially more important to sports teams than to most other markets.

In addition, the sports product is inherently unpredictable because its outcome relies on competitive sporting endeavour. The unpredictable nature of sporting contests has been shown to be an important motivator of consumption (Kerstetter and Kovich, 1997). Such unpredictability makes it very difficult to provide accurate or concrete information about the content or quality of sports services in advance, which increases the level of uncertainty for consumers. Participating in a marathon or watching a football match cannot be guaranteed to satisfy or meet expectations, making them high in what Zeithaml (1981) called "experience qualities".

For these reasons, sports STH can be expected to evaluate these products differently from most other consumer products, meaning that simple adaptation of typical satisfaction and service quality measures may not be appropriate here. Despite (or perhaps because of) these complexities, consumers often become most heavily involved with these products. Fisher and Wakefield's (1998) examination of sports fans typifies the paradoxical behaviour that can occur in relation to these products. They found evidence of poorly-performing teams experiencing increased support and loyalty among their fans. This phenomenon may be explained by the notion that many of these products are hedonic (pleasurable) in nature.

Traditional Customer Relationship Management (CRM) theory suggests that careful management and monitoring of customer expectations, followed by service quality standards that consistently meet those needs, are the keys to long-term success (Grönroos, 1990). Alternative views suggest that attitudes more often form in line with behaviour, such that people feel positively about brands they use and decisions they make, provided they meet their needs (Sharp, 2010). Regardless of whether attitudes form before or after behaviour, it is clear that positive attitudes correlate with repurchase, thus, managing the attitudes is important.

STH acquisition

One of the key challenges for a sports team is how to grow its connection with its existing fan-base, and encourage the transition from a supporter to a paid-up STH. This requires a shift in the relationship status, away from casual "transactional" exchanges to a "relational" connection and interactions that are based on co-operation and shared values.

A STH is a supporter who has taken the next step in terms of their personal connection and involvement with a team, but not all fans will. With the added benefit that ticket scarcity provides in driving season ticket purchases, it is clear that a large supporter base is a requirement of a large STH base. Not all teams are equal, however, in terms of how well they make this conversion and setting a STH target continues to be a point of contention for many.

Why fans choose to follow a team

Before we can consider growing a fan-base, it is important to understand what motivates people to begin supporting a particular team. There are a number of reasons people are attracted to supporting a particular sports team in the first place. These include:

1   *Past success*: There is no doubt that on-field success is a powerful customer acquisition tool. Madrigal (1995) used the term "basking in reflected glory" (BIRGing) to capture how success draws fans to a team. BIRGing, or bandwagon jumping, occurs because people like to be associated with success and the benefits it brings. However, there are also more tangible reasons why on-field success matters. Successful teams gain more exposure by playing more games (if there are playoffs or access to other tournaments, for example, the UEFA Cup), or playing in prominent games (such as championship deciders or finals). Successful teams in the previous season are also more likely to be scheduled into prime time slots in the following year. This greater exposure brings more sponsors, who in turn raise the profile of the brand through associating with it in sponsorship "activations".

2   *Family and friends*: Sports are, for most people, a conduit to connect with other people. The so-called tribal nature of sports fandom is nothing more than people gathering around a brand to form a community. For some people, the sporting experience is

primarily about spending time with the people they attend with, and very little about the teams playing or the outcome of the match. Children, strongly influenced by family, will often follow teams in order to be part of the "tribe".

3   *Player affinity*: A charismatic player can lead fans to become interested in that sport, usually by crossing over from sports to other aspects of popular culture (for example, rapping, dating a celebrity), or fans follow athletes from one team to another (see Figure 16.1). A gifted athlete will attract their own following as they embody the things that often attract people to sports: excellence, aesthetic beauty, courage. The notion of seeing "the best player of all time" can cause a huge upswell in support. In addition, you have players who evoke other factors listed here, that drive interest in new teams as they move, such as players from someone's home town or college alma mater.

4   *Geographic location*: Regional pride is often embodied in a sporting team. Supporting a team because it represents a region that someone identifies strongly with is commonplace in world sports. In the US, allegiances to college teams are often stronger and more lasting than to professional teams. The rationale being that college often is the most enjoyable time of people's lives and professional teams often relocate within the US. More recently, allegiances to certain conferences, or competitions has been found, with supporters identifying strongly with leagues based in certain regions or countries out of regional pride.

5   *Marketing aspects*: As much as hardcore sports fans might find this objectionable, many fans choose a team based on highly subjective measures such as colours, team songs, logos or mascots. This may be a logical response to having to choose a team through social pressure (for example, to be involved in work discussion on sports) and lacking other grounds, such as those listed, to guide the decision.

Why fans become STH

Being a casual attendee has its advantages over being a STH, including greater flexibility and low risk due to limited sunk costs. Why is it, then, that some supporters take their involvement with the team to the next level and become active and "paid-up" STH? The top eight reasons identified by McDonald and Stavros (2007) (with the percentage of customers citing each reason as being the primary motivation for purchase) were:

1   To financially support the team (33.1%).
2   To feel more involved with or part of the team (19.8%).
3   To gain discounted entry (i.e. save money) (15.6%).
4   To gain a reserved seat (easier access) (10.3%).
5   As a social outing (7.8%).

Figure 17.1 Example of a tweet deriding "new" fans

6   Friends or family STH wanted me to go to the games (6.0%).
7   Membership was given to me as a gift (2.4%).
8   Other (5.1%).

This list of reasons for joining is a mix of tangible and intangible motivations. They suggest that STH are highly involved consumers whose consumption is as much about self-expression and a reflection of core values as it is about entertainment or cost savings. Keep in mind that they are fans first, and so the reasons for being a fan still impact their decisions to become STH. For these fans, purchasing a season ticket is the best way for them to express their connection with the team, to revel in team success and to mix with like-minded others.

McDonald and Stavros's (2007) study identified that the motivations for joining as an STH typically follows one of two patterns, depending on whether the team has capacity issues or not. Where a team has capacity issues, there is a strong motivation for STH to join for access purposes, particularly to have a regular reserved seat. Where sell-outs are not common, this is less of a motivation, and the primary motivation is often to financially support the team. In both cases, however, feeling involved with the team is a strong motivation for joining.

STH of teams that underperformed financially the previous year tend to join as STH to support the team financially, which unfortunately does not provide long-term benefits to a team. There are two main reasons for this: if the financial problems are resolved then the original reason for joining the team disappears, but if the financial problems are not resolved in a timely fashion, the original motivational driver may be deemed a lost cause. Although it is recommended that teams note and publicly acknowledge the funds raised by STH (whether it be through memberships or extra contributions), they should avoid using a call for financial support as a marketing strategy to attract new STH. Instead, the emphasis should be on benefits the team can consistently provide: access to stadiums, improved information and a heightened feeling of fan involvement.

Member satisfaction and retention

Although acquisition is a critical and important part of STH management, marketing activities must be designed to balance acquisition with the retention of existing STH. There has been debate around where organizations should put the bulk of their efforts, but the simple facts are that acquisition is necessary for growth and replacement of unavoidable churn, and retention is often easier and lower cost. Customer retention relies on satisfying customers and maintaining high brand awareness. Satisfied customers also spread word-of-mouth, which can be a useful aid for the acquisition of new customers. Customer satisfaction is therefore critical to the success of any business and in particular in membership-based organizations that rely on maintaining enduring and interactive relationships with their customers.

Managing satisfaction levels takes a unique twist in a sports context where we know that even unhappy members are unlikely to switch their support to another team. To demonstrate their lack of satisfaction, sports team members are much more likely decrease their level of consumption and revert to being casual supporters. In addition, where many services can be difficult to assess, sports have at heart a contest, and performance in that contest is often clearly signalled to all through the scoreboard.

While we know that the STH experience with their team is complex and multidimensional, at a basic level their satisfaction (or lack of) can be expressed as the difference between their expectations of the season ticket experience and their perception of the actual experience.

So which components of the season ticket package or experience are most important in determining the overall level of satisfaction? What impact does this have on strategy and how do teams perform overall?

What matters to members?

A study of nearly 8,000 STH identified seven core drivers of member satisfaction with professional sports teams (McDonald, Karg and Vocino, 2013). Each of those broad drivers was defined by a series of specific management or team actions. Table 17.1 provides an overview.

Table 17.1 Satisfaction drivers for season ticket products

Driver	Items
Membership arrangements	Convenience of entering the ground.
	Member access to finals tickets.
	Savings on game entry fees.
	Quality of the season reserved seats.
	Speed at which membership packages were sent.
Personal involvement	Opportunities to mix with players.
	Efforts to make members feel part of the team.
	Opportunity for members to mix with other members.
	Team values the importance of its membership base.
	Members' contributions are recognized.
Home ground	As a place to watch football.
	Feeling of a "home" ground.
	Standard of facilities at the ground.
	Ease of getting to the ground.
	"Family-friendly" ground.
Service to members	Helpfulness of team staff.
	Number and range of functions.
	Quality of the events or functions.
	Value of functions.
	Staff enquiry handling.
Marketing communications	Clarity of the membership brochure.
	Content of the official team website.
	Content of the electronic newsletter, email and SMS updates.
	Efforts to keep members informed about admin decisions.
	Information provided on membership issues.
	Social media and networking.
On-field performance	Number of games won.
	Position on the ladder.
	Effort put in by players.
	Standard of the play.
Team administration	Administration of the team.
	Functioning of the team board.
	Financial position of the team.
	Promotion of the team in general.

The relevant importance of each satisfaction driver

Over the last 10 years, the satisfaction of season ticket holders has been measured using a survey tool based on the drivers shown in Table 16.1. This survey tool has been used across sports including Rugby Union, Rugby League, Cricket, Australian Football, Netball and Soccer. The results are remarkably consistent in that the drivers always account for around 70–80% of STH satisfaction. The other 20–30% of satisfaction can be attributed to random or unique events, too difficult to capture across a wide range of customers.

That said, the relative importance, and the contribution of each driver to overall satisfaction, can vary between teams and sports based on factors related to the composition of the STH base and the team's circumstances. In particular, we know that the importance of each satisfaction driver may vary with the number of years someone has been an STH and the number of games attended in a given season. For example, depending on how many games they attend, newer members may focus on tangible aspects such as membership arrangements or service to members, while more established members are more likely to focus on personal involvement and club administration. Teams that have had long losing streaks may find that on-field performance becomes an increasingly important issue, and teams that share a home ground with other sporting teams or have an ageing stadium may find that the home ground facilities are more important.

Summarizing more than 150 of these studies on various teams and sporting codes, the typical contribution of each driver to the overall satisfaction score is shown in Figure 17.2.

Influencing and benchmarking sports STH satisfaction

A common question asked by managers is: "what is a good score on satisfaction ratings?" The eternal problem with customer satisfaction measurement is that, over time, customers quickly become used to innovations (for example, digital communications) and their expectations of the service provider increase. It is here that some benchmarking is required. Table 17.2 below captures the historical minimum, average and maximum scores against each satisfaction driver as measured in one professional league's STH surveys from 2004 until 2014.

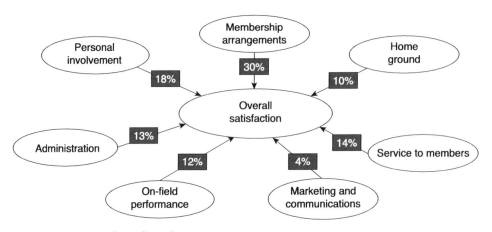

Figure 17.2 Drivers of overall satisfaction

Table 17.2 Satisfaction scores from one league: 2004–2014 (n=122 surveys)

	Minimum	*Average*	*Maximum*
Membership arrangements	6.72	7.66	8.73
Service to members	6.33	7.73	8.90
Marketing and communications	6.53	7.82	9.11
On-field performance	0.90	6.07	9.92
Personal involvement	2.59	6.72	9.43
Administration	2.60	7.08	9.21
Home ground	5.06	7.67	9.62
Satisfaction	5.44	7.38	9.20
Expectations (met or exceeded)	3.97	6.33	8.40
Renewal probability	6.38	8.93	9.76

Note: All scores are on a 0–10 scale, where 0=highly dissatisfied and 10=highly satisfied, except "expectations" where 0=well below, 5=as expected, 10=well above.

Increasing performance on individual drivers

From a management perspective, it is encouraging and empowering to note that out of the seven key drivers of STH satisfaction, all but one (on-field performance) are directly influenced by the team's commercial managers. Each of the key drivers is now discussed in more depth, with examples of activities that have influenced STH attitudes towards each component.

Membership arrangements

The umbrella term of membership arrangements captures the core tangible product offering of the team to its STH. It is not surprising that it is consistently the most important measure in terms of overall member satisfaction.

As noted earlier, the importance placed on the most tangible aspect of a team membership as defined here is relatively high for all STH, but declines with the length of membership and the number of games attended. As members' personal links with the team develop and deepen, the less likely they are to evaluate their membership experience predominantly through a cost–benefit value analysis. This has important implications for encouraging member retention and managing churn, more on that in the relevant sections that follow.

Speed of membership and ticket delivery is consistently the most important satisfaction element, yet at times still poorly executed by teams. Improving this activity should be relatively easy to execute from an internal process perspective and is highly likely to have an impact on the overall satisfaction rating. The growing trend towards outsourcing the fulfilment component of STH must be balanced with potential risks of not having control over the delivery. The key to successful fulfilment is not so much the actual time between order taking and fulfilment of that order, but the way in which customer expectations are set and met. For example, if orders taken by a certain date are promised to be fulfilled prior to Christmas, meeting that deadline is likely to satisfy the customer, regardless of the interval. Failure to do this is likely to cause significant issues for the customer (uncertainty of whether order has been lost, inability to provide promised Christmas gifts), and will result in significant dissatisfaction.

Personal involvement

In stark contrast to the highly tangible satisfaction factor previously described, personal involvement is probably the most intangible of the seven key satisfaction drivers. Despite the fact that it is a feeling more than a tangible benefit, and therefore hard to judge, STH typically consider personal involvement to be critical to their overall satisfaction.

Each of the individual dimensions that feed into personal involvement are in direct control of a team but, largely due to their intangible nature, it is often difficult to get the exact mix right. A process of trial and error is therefore largely inevitable. The contribution that personal involvement factors make to the overall importance can be expected to increase with the length of membership. As members become more familiar with the team, their loyalty and personal connection is likely to grow and they are more likely to shift from focusing as much on the tangible aspect of the membership product to assessing how well they are made to feel a part of the team.

Establishing, maintaining and developing the feelings of personal connection and involvement is also an important factor in managing member churn and renewal, particularly with new members who are most at risk. The particular dimensions of personal involvement can be leveraged to create additional membership products designed for members who are unlikely or unable to attend many games, that is membership options that offer a highly involved experience that satisfies irrespective of on-field performance and a member's ability to get to games.

Despite its importance, the overall performance rating (see Table 17.2) for personal involvement is relatively low, with only on-field performance scoring lower for most teams. To improve this, teams are encouraged to make planned, strategic efforts to increase attachment and activate greater personal involvement. Examples include loyalty schemes that reward STH based on length of membership, recognition of fans at games (especially having players thank fans) and personalized communications. Perhaps the most effective way to build personal involvement, however, is to ensure the organization is genuinely STH-centric, considering STH in all decisions and ensuring they are well informed and recognized.

Home ground

The home ground driver captures tangible and intangible dimensions of a member's experience with their home stadium. The measures used here are a simplified version of what Wakefield, Blodgett and Sloan (1996) called the "Sportscape". For teams having particular issues with low crowd attendance and satisfaction with the stadium experience, it may be useful to return to the deeper Sportscape measures to gain a fuller assessment of the fan experience at games. However, it is important to note that not all aspects of the home ground are within the control of the team. Particularly in cases where venues or stadiums are shared, there may be limits on the degree to which an individual team is able to customize the facilities to suit their STHs. The spectator experience is increasingly influenced by technology, as sports teams attempt to combat the convenience and enhanced viewing experience available at home through broadcast. Given the difficulties often faced getting to a stadium (for example, traffic, entry queues) and the impact of factors such as the weather, watching sporting events at home has become increasingly attractive due to improvements in broadcast technologies (for example, high definition, better camera angles and information) and the quality of in-home equipment (for example, large screen television, surround sound).

Teams must continue to improve the in-stadium experience if they are to compete effectively with broadcast sports. Importantly, there are some aspects of the in-stadium experience that are difficult to replicate elsewhere, notably the feeling of being part of a broader community and having a direct influence over the outcome through fan behaviour (for example, cheering, intimidating opposition players). These aspects must be enhanced and complemented by efforts to reduce barriers to attendance. Paramount here are feelings of fan safety (for example, a family-friendly environment) and ease of entry and exit. A sensory approach can be taken to managing the stadium experience, whereby all five senses are evoked to provide a feeling of "home" in the stadium (see Lee et al., 2012). Critical among the senses is touch: the stadium must be comfortable and comforting in the way it makes fans feel safe and welcome. With stadium redevelopments regularly exceeding $1 billion, there has been much attention paid to the functional aspects of the stadium environment: seating, entry points, catering and technology. However, the other senses all play a role in building a feeling of home ground.

The Seattle Sounders are a professional team playing in the American Major League Soccer (MLS) league, and have been particularly successful in encouraging attendance and a feeling of home ground in a shared stadium. Particular initiatives include a fan "march to the match", organized chants and "fight songs", a marching band, special entrances for STHs, entertainment around the ground and honour boards for STH photographs.

Service to members

Service to members broadly refers to the level of customer focus that is displayed by a team and its staff, and the opportunities given to STH to interact with each other and the team. Harking back to the SERVQUAL work of Parasuraman, Berry and Zeithaml (1991), the key aspects of customer service are reliability, responsiveness, building trust and displaying empathy. STH are characterized by a high degree of involvement with the team, and therefore could be expected to be more demanding of team service staff.

One issue notable in sports organizations is the high use of volunteer labour, and the prevalence of employees who are passionate about the organization. Many people dream of working for their favourite sports team. This has its benefits, but can be counter-productive in a service role. Highly passionate workers may lack the empathy for those fans not as engaged. They may be critical of customers who require high service levels, for example expecting "real fans" not to complain about the team. Training staff to be responsive and empathetic is therefore highly important in this context.

Another difficult aspect to manage is the interaction between STHs and between STH and the team. Simple benefits, such as allowing STH to attend functions and hear from players and coaches, become difficult as STH numbers increase. Some functions, such as family days, can be run in a manner that makes them scalable to large crowds. Others must be limited for them to be effective, but this provides an opportunity to restrict these benefits to high-tier membership products or to reward STH loyalty. Managing interactions between fans must also be done sensitively. Although it is important to build a sense of community among fans, it is again worth noting that hardcore fans are often disparaging towards new and less engaged fans. Online chat rooms, for example, can be very intimidating places for non-experts, with abuse common for "newbies". Multiple communications might need to be established to cater for the range of STH experiences sought.

Marketing and communications

The marketing and communications satisfaction component refers broadly to the key communication channels and touch points that a team has established with its membership base. As such, it includes traditional forms of communication, such as mailouts and magazines, and also emerging forms, such as social media and web content. Regardless of execution, the purpose is to keep STH informed and connected to the team.

Communication is a key tool to establishing and maintaining a sense of personal involvement among members, and as such, it is surprising that it does not rate higher in terms of its overall contribution to the satisfaction score. In terms of opportunities for improvement, qualitative discussions with STH highlight that:

- Members are critical of communications that are overly corporate and contain information that is otherwise available to the general public, or at times even out-of-date.
- They seek a behind-the-scenes perspective into team life and events or a more passionate "one-eyed" voice from the team.
- The responsibility for effective and targeted communications lies beyond that of just the marketing department. Senior management and the board also have a role to play.
- Teams should take into consideration the different needs and drivers of unique member segments and customize their communications where possible and practical.

Across the team satisfaction studies conducted, it is noteworthy that marketing and communications is often the least important driver of satisfaction (contributing only 4% in our aggregate model). Discussions with STH show the reason being that they are satisfied with the communications they receive (expectations are consistently met, lowering the importance of the element), but also that the communications they receive from the club are often "bland" or "generic", such that they are not distinguishable from media reports or other sources of information. Teams are often very conservative in their communications, and are restrained by league rules and codes of conduct, but fans expect the team to reflect their passion. For example, if the refereeing was poor, fans would like the team to speak about it in the same passionate and biased tones they do.

On-field performance

On-field performance is unique in that it is the only one of the key satisfaction drivers that is largely outside the short-term control of the team management. In a sporting context, the on-field success of a team is seen as central to the experience of being a fan and so it may be surprising to learn that winning or losing does not have a strong direct influence on the overall satisfaction score. This is because it is possible to provide a satisfying membership experience, even when the on-field results are poor. This is done through ensuring the other aspects of the membership experience are done well, and providing a buffer against the fluctuations on-field. On-field performance tends to aid STH acquisition, but does not impact greatly on STH retention. This is because most long-term STH accept that the results on-field are part of the theatre of sports, and the team is so important to their identity that even repeated failure on field does not damage their desire to stay connected to the team.

Although the direct effect is weak, there is evidence of a "halo effect" around winning and losing. More specifically, the indirect impact of winning and losing is usually stronger for satisfaction drivers such as personal involvement or team administration, and to a lesser extent on elements such as home ground and membership arrangements. The administration are held responsible for poor performance, and people feel less involved and connected to losing teams. The halo effect, overall, is not large though. Teams need to be careful to manage STH expectations of on-field performance.

Administration

Team administration might seem a strange inclusion to a scale purporting to measure the STH experience. STH can, and frequently do, judge the management and administrators of their team, and it impacts on their overall satisfaction with the season ticket product. Many season ticket products include the ability to vote for board members in general elections, something which makes STH feel part of the organization even if they seldom exercise this right.

Academic research and qualitative discussions indicate that:

- STH have a strong opinion about the performance of a board, even if they are uncertain about its exact role and responsibilities (compared with that of team management, for example). There have been examples of dissatisfied sporting team members seeing team boards overturned.
- Boards have been shown to have a strong impact on promoting a feeling of personal inclusion and therefore have a direct impact on the personal involvement element of member satisfaction.
- Boards need to be mindful of governing in an inclusive manner and taking the time and effort to explain decisions and make themselves accountable and open to scrutiny.

STH analysis of administration performance is often based on limited information, usually gleaned from annual reports or media reports. Teams can be proactive in managing perceptions of the administration in their communications efforts.

Member renewal and churn

With membership non-renewal rates often in excess of 20%, it is interesting to note that despite their high level of involvement and loyalty, members of professional sports teams churn at rates similar to customers of organizations in traditionally more volatile industries such as insurance, mobile telecommunications and supermarket retail. We know that members very rarely, if ever, switch teams, so why are the membership non-renewal rates so high? Which members are most at risk and, most importantly, what, if anything can be done about it?

Member non-renewal rates

Churn rates vary significantly from industry to industry, and a there is a wide range of official churn figures across different sports leagues internationally. At face value, churn rates among the major US leagues (the NFL, NBA, and MLB) and the English Premier League hover around an enviable 10% per annum. It is important to note that very often these averages are kept artificially low by a handful of particularly popular teams that experience almost no churn at all. The Green Bay Packers have churn reported to be under 0.05%, and consequently, a famously long waiting list with more than 100,000 on it and a waiting time now close to 1,000 seasons. Some of the other lower profile teams in these leagues experience much higher churn rates. For example, the Jacksonville Jaguars (NFL) reduced their churn rate from 32% in 2006 to a still high 26% in 2007. It is therefore very difficult to talk about a natural rate of churn among STH of professional sports teams, but comparison with other subscription markets (for example, insurance, fitness clubs, utilities) suggests that annual churn exceeding 10% is worrying.

Why members leave

Although understanding customer loyalty and purchase behaviour is core to any business, this can be particularly challenging for membership based organizations. This is often due to the annual nature of most renewals, the limited two-way dialogue between members and the organization and the broad range of reasons (tangible and intangible) that members have for joining in the first place.

Research in a broad industry context tells us that the highest proportion of churn occurs among the most recently acquired customers. We also know that while customer satisfaction is an important factor in managing churn, it alone is not a reliable predictor of non-renewal, with many satisfied customers also churning (see McDonald, Karg and Leckie 2014 for a predictive model of STH churn).

So do sports team members differ in their behaviour? Although there are some unique characteristics, in many ways the behaviour is similar to other service and membership based organizations.

Industry specific research tells us that the majority of members who don't renew do so as they are not able to attend as many games as they would like and not necessarily because they are unhappy. A 2007 study of more than 1,000 lapsed members across five large sporting teams identified that over 70% of those who did not renew their membership, did so primarily due to their inability to get to games following a change in their work or family structure.

The self-reported reasons for non-renewal were as follows. Lifestyle related reasons are in italics.

- *I can't get to the games this year due to other commitments (33.1%).*
- *Changes in family structure made it hard to get to games (30.4%).*
- Membership was not good value (14.3%).
- *Friends or family members I used to attend with no longer go to games (7%).*
- I prefer to watch football or rugby on TV (6.7%).
- I didn't think the team would win many games in the following year (6.2%).
- I'm no longer interested enough in football/rugby (2.2%).

Although member satisfaction, on its own, is not a key predictor of membership renewal, it continues to have an influence on member actions more broadly and cannot be ignored. The previously named study found a positive relationship between member satisfaction and lapsed members' intention to rejoin. In addition, a subsequent 2010 study of more than 4,500 members (McDonald, 2010), confirmed that while some non-renewers leave when satisfied overall, the total average satisfaction ratings of renewing members is higher than of those who did not renew their memberships.

The length of the member–team relationship (years of membership) also has a strong impact on the likelihood of membership renewal. Converting a fan to a member is a major achievement but it is only a part of the story, with in excess of 33% of first year members leaving at the end of their first year of membership (see Figure 17.3). First year members cannot be considered to be fully engrained in the lifestyle of a club member. They are new to the membership experience and are yet to develop links of mutual trust and commitment. The 2010 study found that new members remain "at risk" until year 4 of membership, upon which time churn likelihood stabilizes.

It is also interesting to note that excess demand (i.e., waiting list for memberships where season tickets are limited) does not reduce churn. That is, despite the waiting list, it is the

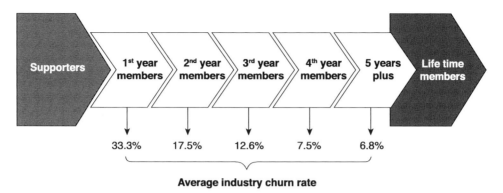

Figure 17.3 Churn rate by years of membership

newer members who form the bulk of those not renewing, and the overall churn rates for teams with limited capacity are similar to those with "unlimited" memberships on offer.

Predicting churn

Extensive experience at team level provides a degree of intuition as to the most at risk groups in terms of membership non-renewal. However, identifying and segmenting these members in order to develop targeted prevention efforts is often a challenge. Recent studies have attempted to predict churn with some success. McDonald, Karg and Leckie (2014) tracked more than 10,500 STH from five professional sports teams across two years. At the end of the first year, they developed a model to predict which STH would churn, then tracked renewal over the following season.

The churn prediction model incorporated measures of four key areas: satisfaction, probability of renewal (self-declared), games attended, and years of membership. The probability of renewal measure was the Juster scale: a 0–10 scale where 0 is labelled "a 1% chance" and 10 is "a 99% chance". Each other scale point rises from a 10% chance (1) to a 90% chance (9) in 10% increments. The Juster scale is intuitive, and has been found to be a more accurate measure than purchase likelihood measures that ask how likely someone is to do something. The Juster scale alone was found to be a good estimator of overall churn, and a reasonable predictor of churn at the individual level. That is, it tended to over-predict churn. When combined with how long they had been STH and the ticket utilization, the model could classify 81% of STH correctly as churners or stayers. This finding suggests two important things. First, STH are good at predicting their own behaviour, they know when they are likely to churn. That means staying in touch with STH is important. It also shows that although STH attach emotionally to the team, if they don't get into the habit of using the ticket over time (at least three to four years), then they will churn.

Actions to consider

The fact that up to 70% of churn is due to lifestyle changes, and therefore classified as involuntary churn outside the direct control of a team, can appear discouraging from a management perspective. The obvious answer for teams may be to actively drive additional attendance and encourage and reward renewals through various campaigns. Yet these efforts often have mixed results. Why? Because new and low attending (and therefore most at risk) members evaluate their experience and the membership product in a fundamentally different way to more established members. More specifically:

- Established members feel much more personally involved with the team and place a higher importance on this feeling, and other intangible aspects, than new members. Their attitudinal and behavioural loyalty develops over time.
- New members are much more likely to place emphasis on the tangible, easy to assess aspects of their membership such as ticketing and facilities. They have only made one purchasing decision, are new to the membership experience and are yet to develop the deeper connections of more established members.
- As members become more ingrained with the team, their loyalty grows and they shift from focusing on the tangible service delivery in a pure cost–benefit value analysis, and are more likely to renew.

The results suggest that actively establishing and promoting the intangible aspects of a team is vital in the first four years of membership and may be the key to managing churn among low attending members. If teams are able to build a strong sense of community among their newest members, and reinforce the value of those memberships to the team's success, then they may be able to shift the focus of those who are unable to get to many games.

Three broad streams of action are outlined as follows:

1 New and at risk members: focus on the intangible.
   Consider establishing new members as a unique segment in the customer relationship strategy and developing a new member management program. This program should outline the team's strategy for welcoming new members, ensuring that they know that a membership is the best way to become more involved with the team and establishing the feelings of involvement. Specific actions may include:
   - Welcome events aimed at introducing new members to various aspects of the team including key personnel.
   - Ensuring reserved ticket holders are introduced to those around them.
   - Personalized and targeted communications designed to bring a new member up-to-date on the latest team developments, events as well as news from behind the scenes.
2 Lapsed members: maintain dialogue and promote the membership community.
   Maintaining feelings of connection is also important in managing lapsed members and in any targeted "win-back" campaigns. Most lapsed members indicate that they have an intention to re-join at a later point in time, particularly over a five-year period. It is therefore important that teams maintain regular dialogue with this group and formulate a win-back strategy. Actions may include:
   - A regular and targeted communication plan developed especially for lapsed members, designed to keep them informed of the latest developments while promoting the value of the membership community and the additional insights gained only as a member.
   - Special offers and campaigns encouraging renewal, particularly by recognizing past membership.
3 Increase the barriers to exit.
   It is clear that a membership package needs to effectively balance the tangible (for example, facilities, guaranteed or discounted entry) and intangible aspects (for example,

closeness with the team, inside information). The intangible components need to be valuable enough to make memberships worthwhile even if game attendance is unlikely. The more a member feels like an integral part of the team, the less they examine the tangible aspects of product in a pure cost–benefit value analysis, and the more they focus on and value their unique experience. Teams therefore need to ensure that the membership experience is differentiated or special enough to make casual supporter status difficult to even consider. This may include:

- Sharing valuable and very clearly "member only" insight into team life on a regular basis. This may include direct communications from the coach or key players, candid reports and photographs from player events, personal insights and opinions from key staff.
- Encourage and facilitate the establishment of strong member communities. This may be through events, special forums or organized transport to and from games. In doing so teams should consider the individual needs of specific groups, for example, senior members or single females who may be overwhelmed by and therefore avoid large member functions.
- Signing STH to "auto-renewal" mechanisms (for example, automatic credit card debiting) wherever possible. The increase in renewal rates makes it worthwhile offering some discounts for those on auto-renewal.

Conclusion

The management of STH is complicated by the subscription nature of the product and the passion of the customers. With purchases only occurring annually in most cases, the opportunities for acquisition are limited. With highly involved customers, the demands placed on service staff and the product can be high. Fortunately, the research shows that if the season ticket product is well-designed to include a mix of tangible and intangible benefits, STH can be satisfied and will renew even during sustained periods of poor on-field performances from the team. Acquisition must remain a focus, even for teams with long STH wait lists, but an STH cannot be considered "rusted on" until at least three seasons of consecutive purchases. Retention efforts therefore need to be front-loaded towards these initial years, assisting the STH to connect with the team and other STH.

References

Fisher, R. and Wakefield, K. (1998). Factors leading to group identification: A field study of winners and losers. *Psychology & Marketing*, 15(1), 23–40.

Grönroos, C. (1990). *Service management and marketing: managing the moments of truth in service competition.* San Francisco: Jossey-Bass.

Kerstetter, D. L. and Kovich, G. M. (1997). An involvement profile of Division 1 women's basketball spectators. *Journal of Sport Management*, 11(3), 234–249.

Lee, S., Lee, H. J., Seo, W. J. and Green, C. (2012). A new approach to stadium experience: The dynamics of the sensoryscape, social interaction, and sense of home. *Journal of Sport Management*, 26(6), 490–505.

Madrigal, R. (1995). Cognitive and affective determinants of fan satisfaction with sporting event attendance. *Journal of Leisure Research*, 27(3), 205.

McDonald, H. (2010). The factors influencing churn rates among season ticket holders: An empirical analysis. *Journal of Sport Management*, 24, 676–701.

McDonald, H. and Stavros, C. (2007). A defection analysis of lapsed season ticket holders: A consumer and organizational study. *Sport Marketing Quarterly*, 16, 218–229.

McDonald, H., Karg, A. J. and Leckie, C. (2014). Predicting which season ticket holders will renew and which will not. *European Sport Management Quarterly*, 14(5), 503–520.

McDonald, H., Karg, A. and Vocino, A. (2013). Measuring season ticket holder satisfaction: Rational, scale development and longitudinal validation. *Sport Management Review*, 16(1), 41–53.

Oliver, R. L. (1999). Whence consumer loyalty? *Journal of Marketing*, 63, 33–44.

Parasuraman, A., Berry, L. L. and Zeithaml, V. A. (1991). Refinement and reassessment of the SERVQUAL scale, *Journal of Retailing*, 67(4), 420–450.

Sharp, B. and Ehrenberg-Bass Institute for Marketing Science (Melbourne, Australia) (2010). *How brands grow: What marketers don't know* (Vol. 189). South Melbourne: Oxford University Press.

Sharp, B., Wright, M. and Goodhardt, G. (2002). Purchase loyalty is polarised into either repertoire or subscription patterns. *Australasian Marketing Journal*, 10(3), 7–20.

Wakefield, K. L., Blodgett, J. G. and Sloan, H. J. (1996). Measurement and management of the sportscape. *Journal of Sport Management*, 10(1), 15–31.

Zeithaml, V. A. (1981). How consumer evaluation processes differ between goods and services. *Marketing of Services*, 9(1), 25–32.

18

SPORTS MARKETING PROFESSIONALS' EXPERTISE AND KNOWLEDGE ON CONSUMER BEHAVIOUR[1]

Fabien Ohl and Gary Tribou

There is a variety of models available to comprehend consumer behaviour and a great deal of literature on economic, sociological and psychological determinism, reflecting the existence of multiple processes of influence. Income (Engel, 1857), symbolic dimensions of products purchased (Veblen, 1899) and culture (Halbwachs, 1913) have become pertinent indicators very early on. This pioneering work on consumer behaviour was further extended by including analyses on the influence of tastes, preferences and lifestyles (Bourdieu, 1979; Valette-Florence, 1989). Although most of the research allows us to understand the main trends of consumption, it labours to explain the buyer's decision-making process due to the cultural pluralism of consumers (Lahire, 2004; Peterson and Kern, 1996).

Understanding purchasing decisions has instead drawn from integrative models, attempting to take into account individual choices within the shopping environment. These models are largely based on cognitive and social psychology to understand the influence of individual and situational factors affecting perception, attention, memory and learning (Engel, Kollat and Blackwell, 1968), or to understand, in a broader sense, the attitudes towards brands and products (Howard and Sheth, 1969). Numerous studies have enriched this initial work (including Volle, 2000; Guichard and Vanheems, 2004) and it seems established that the point of sale has a significant influence on consumer behaviour. Most studies show that more than half of the purchasing decisions to buy sporting goods are made in stores.[2] Although the market share of online shopping is growing (18.4% in Europe, however, the weighted average share in Europe in 2014 was 7.2%,[3] in France the growth was +13.5 in 2013 and the market share was 5.5% of the whole retail, but 17% for sporting goods), the experiences of objects and shopping in traditional retailing are at the background of consumers' experiences, pleasure and satisfaction that are in mind and not "exclusively based on the physical experience of using (and owning) an object" (Denegri-Knott and Molesworth, 2010). The internet mass audience also depends on sharing processes of online reviewers and bloggers' comments. More broadly, online word of mouth has increased but it is based on consumers' own experiences (Sandes and Urdan, 2013) in which traditional shopping cannot be neglected. Internet consumers are also using traditional shops to test, touch or try objects they can buy on the internet. Therefore, it is vital to consider the impact of product marketing and product staging (Falk and Campbell, 1997; Barre et al., 2000; Cochois, 2002; Underhill, 2000).

We are not suggesting prolonging these analyses, but rather to understand, in a very pragmatic way, what sports brand marketing managers do in order to incorporate the point of sale effect on consumer purchasing behaviour. We interviewed 11 senior marketing or sales managers in the sports industry to observe how certain sociologists analyse consumer purchasing behaviour with respect to the products they purchase. But prior to considering the elements gathered in the study conducted by the marketing professionals, it is essential to specify the constituents of point of sale.

Dramaturgy in sporting goods stores

For the past ten years in France there have been profound changes in point of sale design. By implementing specific dramaturgy, particularly with the use of suggestive decors, new stores highlight the social importance of the purchasing act, and sometimes go beyond to change the meaning of the goods purchased. Store characteristics (location, window displays, fixtures, decorations, the nobility of materials, lighting, behaviour of personnel, and so on) alter the perception of the articles' intrinsic qualities, which also contribute to a scenic dimension of the store. This promotion of products and location also induces the effect of increasing the value of the consumer themself by symbolically drawing a benefit from their visits and purchases.

The store has gradually become an enchanted space for the consumer (Badot and Dupuis, 2001), a sort of jewellery case providing additional value to the goods sold. Conscious of their image, sports companies seek distribution channels that allow them to promote their products. They aim to associate to their products with sports hero stories or an exceptional physical image and social success, thus providing reference points for the consumer, hence the strategy to offer their own enchanted point of retail space which, themselves, become objects of consumption. Companies have created the concept or flagship store, such as those developed by Nike (Niketown) or Adidas (Adidas Megastore), to provide additional value to the brand and its products (similar to works of art displayed in museums), as well as to the visitor who has just relived a social experience and wants to share it with others in the form of stories (Gerval and Kremer, 2009). The dramaturgy of concept stores includes the design of the façade (in an urban environment it can provide additional value), the interior space and layout (colours, materials, height and format of display shelving, and aisle layout), product merchandising, animated storyboards and digital screens, and posters of sports celebrities referencing high-profile events. All of these elements contribute to increasing the value of the products and consumers who buy them. Penaloza (1998) showed how Nike, the manufacturer, had pushed the boundaries of concept stores by bringing the consumer to live his dream (you can still read on the pediment of the Chicago store: "To all the athletes and their dreams – we dedicate Niketown"). The store seems to answer consumers' expectations to escape everyday life, a desire often felt but not expressed by consumers (Gottdiener, 1995). For instance, Giacomelli Sport stores are known to display sports with an aesthetic flair: you will find boxing rings where customers can be initiated or skateboard ramps where teenagers put on a show. The consumer is attracted to the sporty atmosphere, and with this emotional support takes pleasure in wandering around (so called fun shopping or "retailtainment") in a retail space that feels more like a lifestyle centre rather than a point of sale. If the merchandise is attractive, they may give in to the temptation of some impulse purchases. The increase of online shopping is not in contradiction with the idea of a store as an enchanting place that gives value to the goods. Although there are multichannel retail outlets (Rajagopal, 2011), the store is still a key place for consumers because it is the sole place where they experience goods with all five senses. Furthermore, online shopping is not consumption excluding a bodily experience because internet avatars seems to contribute to a kind of "reembodiment" of the consumer (Belk, 2013).

Purchasing sporting goods is a life experience

We cannot understand purchasing behaviour of sporting goods, often characterised by symbolic tones (Ohl, 2003; Ohl and Tribou, 2004), solely based on utility and rational purchasing models. Without excluding the rationalisation processes (with respect to the quality–price ratio), it seems necessary to consider purchasing as an experience while taking into account perceptions, emotions and passions.

Following in the footsteps of Holbrook and Hirschman (1982), Cova (2000), Ladwein (2003) and Carù and Cova (2006) developed an experiential model that reveals more behavioural traits of sensory and physical stimuli, rather than cognitive characteristics. The studies show how consumers' senses are mobilised at the point of sale: looking at the displays that emphasise products, touching items that the consumer enjoys manipulating (to grab sports equipment or a sports garment contributes to the customer feeling more committed toward the item),[4] listening to sound effects (Holbrook and Gardner, 1993), and smelling scents used to create an olfactory ambiance (Hetzel, 2002; Rieunier, 2009).

The impact of stores on purchasing decisions

In their study on shopping, Kaltcheva and Weitz (2006) showed that the influence of supply is largely dependent on customers' buying motive, emotional state and types of commitment to shopping. Consequently, the same reasoning can be perceived very differently depending on whether something is purchased for pure pleasure or somewhat constrained. But for a retailer or a brand, it is difficult to identify a customer's feelings or buying motive, and especially to affect them. Some tricky merchandising cannot transform purchasing an item from a pleasure purpose into a utilitarian one. Nonetheless, suppliers will try to take advantage of customers' attitudes by adapting the material and human environment of the store as best as they can in order to maximise sales (Miller, 1998). Guichard and Vanheems (2004) spoke of several factors influencing the course of consumer shopping. At first, they highlighted the impact of factors within macro-merchandising, those related to point-of-sale design (such as location of departments when travelling through the store, aisle layout and end displays), as well as micro-merchandising factors (facing items on shelf displays that may grab a customer's attention, dimmed lighting, the warmth, attractiveness and reassuring aspect of colours, and more or less tailored, upbeat background music, and so on). The lack of music seems to reduce the time spent in stores, where the tempo of music played gives a certain rhythm to purchasing, and that the musical style is an efficient means for brand targeting and positioning (Rienier and Daucé, 2002). Other authors observed an average gross sales increase of 12% thanks to music but also mention the complexity of the influence of music. The influence of music depends on the tempo, the mode (major or minor) and can also vary in relation to the level of stimulation that shoppers appreciate (Knoferle et al., 2012) and the way this corresponds to the shopping context (type of store, clients targeted, Woermann and Rokka, 2015). Relations between sales assistants and clients are an essential element in retail (Gremler and Gwinner, 2008; Ewing, Pinto and Soutar, 2001). Consequently, in the field of sports retail, Ohl and Tribou (2004) pinpointed that certain elements in a human environment, as well as those related to sales interactions, respond to a need of sociability and social recognition of buyers. These include the way sales assistants behave (more or less technical, empathetic, warm, sincere, and exemplary), and the way other clients behave (those who give a certain social and cultural flair to the retail space, Péretz, 1992). The scope can also break the purchase routine or purchase intent, or lead to future purchases, by sending a strong signal to consumers. For example, a promotional offer or aggressive advertising will provide immediate satisfaction (by putting forward a less expensive product and providing superior symbolic benefits to the advertising) that will get rid of the persuasion effect exerted upstream. However, we must remain prudent. Conflicting influences were identified depending on the motivational and emotional state of consumers, and on the consumer category and time element (Kaltcheva and Weitz, 2006). More broadly, consumers' experiences depend on the physical set-up of a shop, on the bodily routines and skills, interactions and cultural understanding of a shop (Woermann and Rokka, 2015).

This leads professionals to continuously adapt the layout and design of retail space based on the responsiveness of consumers and their dominant motivations at the moment in order to be able to hold onto clients. It is this managerial approach that we propose to analyse.

Understanding the influence of point of sale: resorting to marketing professionals

We used two main data sources. Box 18.1 shows primary data in the form of interviews with senior marketing managers and sporting good brand managers; shopper studies provide documentary data showing sales results in store departments from conducting experiments with shelving displays. We have not presented a model of consumer behaviour needing validation. Classic models inspired by Engel, Kollat and Blackwell (1968), or even those by Howard and Sheth (1969), multiply the variables that should be taken into account to understand the consumer. If these parameters have undeniable heuristic values, their huge diversity requires limiting a scientific approach to the observation of one of the influencing factors (for example, memory, attention or motivation). However, the managerial limitation of these models centres on the fact that the knowledge they bring does not allow us to understand what the customers are actually doing during a purchase. This explains why we have chosen to use an approach inspired by the Grounded Theory (Glaser and Strauss, 1967), which suggests using observations as a starting point. Our inquiry is similar to that of Bessy and Chateauraynaud (1995) who are interested in analysing how experts or ordinary stakeholders evaluate the objects that surround them. They emphasise the role of perception in developing expertise and take snapshots to assess the value of objects. The term "snapshot" is used to describe the relationship between people and objects, and focuses on all the benchmarks used by the consumer in a position of expertise: perceptions, representations, principles, values and cognitive memory are all confronted when assessing the value of objects. Thus, we can argue that the role of the marketing manager is to provide snapshots to the consumer so that he can positively evaluate objects and so that his willingness to pay is as high as possible (Grewal and Baker, 1994). The staging of the articles in the store and, more specifically, the images and stories that accompany them (especially the reference to sports heroes) will arrange the perception of products in a manner that the consumer can perceive the articles in the most positive way. This requires the indices to converge and for the brand, product packaging, department decorum, materials, posters, lighting, colours, and so on, to help identify the same product quality. Dissonance (for example, a fashion product lost in a handball aisle) can confuse customers, while consistent signs (the same product supported by persuasive advertising) facilitate product expertise and favourably influence the decision-making process.

Box 18.1   Survey approach

In addition to a secondary analysis of quantitative data provided by the shopper studies, eleven marketing and sports brand sales managers were interviewed: Marketing Director of Adidas Sport Style France division (S.R.); Director of France Trade Marketing (M.G.); Marketing Studies Manager, Business Development, Adidas France (H.B.); Director of Marketing of Reebok France (G. de M.); CEO of Puma France (R.T.); Director of Sales, Lifestyle, Puma France (J.R.S.); Director of Marketing, Lacoste World (C.M.); Marketing Manager of Raidlight France (J.T.); Director of Retail Marketing of Skins World (M.G.); Director of Rage, former Director of Marketing, Le Coq Sportif (F.R.); Manager of La Mesure Marketing (M.S.). The interviews were administered face to face in May and June, 2011. We would like to thank the managers, especially I. Calvar-Medec, for their extremely helpful contributions.

The sample was chosen based on three factors. First we wanted to have a homogeneous sample, so the investigation was limited to France. Second, the sample selected was relatively narrow because of the limited number of sports brands. It is also narrow due to the difficulties some sales managers have in sharing their knowledge, because of the competitive market but also out of the fear of being judged. Third, and most important, is that we followed a data saturation principle, inspired by Glaser and Strauss (1967), Grounded Theory. Although more interviews could have been of interest, to explore new questions or analyse the discourses and practices in more detail, or to take into account the effect of the size of the company or the experience of the sales manager, for our very limited subject, the last interviews we realised did not really bring new input, thus confirming a principle of "data saturation".

Interview guide: a three-fold approach:

1. What is the overall impact of the store on purchasing behaviour and more precisely, the impact of the design and layout, props, display of articles, and sales assistants' speech and behaviour?
2. What importance does marketing have on the studies conducted on purchasing behaviour (shopper studies) with respect to consumer studies?
3. How should we apply the findings to trade marketing?

The role of point of sale within sports brand strategies

The interviews indicate that, overall, the point of sale is fully integrated into the brand strategy as a key factor in the purchase decision. According to the marketing director of Reebok, "the organisation of the store is the key factor: first, find what I am looking for, then it is the entrance into the department organised by brand, by purpose, and price, and then comes the dramatisation (props) of the offer, the elements of explanation of the product and the seller". Most agree that the sales assistant is very important; he is "the key number one person responsible to either provide technical explanations or tell the story of the product" (CEO of Puma and Marketing Manager of Raidlight both concur). According to the sales manager of Lifestyle Puma, "if we provide incentives for the sales assistants, we can potentially double the sales of a product". But the sales assistant must act in an opportune environment. For the director of the Rage agency, "the three key elements are the following in order of importance: merchandising, professional development of sales assistants and finally, trade, event and entertainment operations". The Director of Trade Marketing for Adidas commented: "in technical categories such as football and running, the sales assistant is the key factor to direct the client; in impulse purchase categories such as textile training, it is necessary to stage the product". Competition from the web does not seem to challenge the main role played by the point of sale. The marketing director of Lacoste insists that, for her "the store is the only place where there is a real possibility of interaction with the customer". This is also maintained by the Branch Manager of Marketing of La Mesure: "Since the advent of e-commerce, the store has now become the goal of providing the shopper with a life experience; this is a challenge for the web to shop." All agree that the choice of a product goes through three key moments that forge expertise. The first step is the "outstore" experience or that of "pre-shopping", a stage during which media brand communication, influences by family or friends (sometimes in the form of instruction or order) and product placement are crucial tools. The second step is the decision to buy in stores (to which we will return) and which is a critical time of purchasing. The consumer decides when facing a tangible product on shelf-display. The third step is to take into account the use of the product: does the product purchased and utilised meet the expectations in terms of comfort, performance, durability or even design? The positive or negative assessment will generate decisions regarding subsequent purchases of the brand or product. These three steps are the key phases in which the consumer may decide to switch from one brand to another or from one model to another.

Until the late 1990s, brand marketing had focused its resources on the pre-shopping and especially on advertising communication with the widely shared belief, at the time, that a favourable attitude towards the brand after some persuasive action translates into a purchase (Ducrey, 2010). For the last ten years or so, there has been a rebalancing of allocation of resources in favour of actions in the stores (merchandising practices, promotions, advertising, and so on), and even a turnaround in priorities. Thus, according to the Marketing Director of Adidas Sport Style, "the clarity of the offer and staging are more important than the upstream communication: leading the eye, articulating the product range and the product benefit, then seducing by zooming in on the product and finally, reassuring the customer through a sales pitch". "The store has just as much influence as advertising or sponsorship" (F.R., Rage branch) and "it is inside the store that a brand can make the customer live through the strongest experience" (C.M., Lacoste). The Director of Retail Marketing of Skins summarises that "ideally, we should relay actions taken outside of the store inside the store, to support branding with the use of sponsorship or advertising".

These new strategies were the result of repeated studies on the consumer in purchasing situations (often called the shopper). The study findings converge to indicate that, for instance, the power of influence of point of sale is more evident when buying sporting goods compared with buying food. Indeed, it was noted that 60–90% of purchases are decided in store.[5] The lowest score (less than 60%) corresponds to the purchase category of items bundling soccer jerseys and shoes. The highest scores were recorded for running shoes (about 90%) and men's clothing (75%). Among these purchases decided in stores, we find purely impulsive purchases (purchases by consumers who had absolutely no intention of purchasing this type of product) with a score of 10% spent for men's clothing and more than 40% for football jerseys.

Contributions from shopper studies

Beyond the information that allows modulating decisions according to product families, shopper studies lead to a more qualitative decoding of the purchase process. According to G. de M. (Reebok), "these studies are very useful to understand shoppers: they provide a snapshot of the way customers shop". They "complete the panels, store checks and exchanges with the sales assistants" (J.R.S., Puma). "Following the sellout is insufficient (and) it is interesting to cross-reference sellout and studies" (H.B., Adidas). "(The studies) are used to understand what works in optimizing actions and budgets" (M.S., Adidas). Hence, according to the person in charge of Retail Marketing for Skins,

> [B]uying is often an unconscious act (and it is necessary) to truly understand what happens in terms of influences. (Thus,) by cross-referencing shopper studies and store sales, one can make the right decisions in terms of actions. For instance, a conclusion was reached that, in Europe, it is necessary to explain the product benefit and to educate the customer (while in) Australia, the market is more mature and the stake is higher with sales promotion.

There are two types of questions being asked. What are the entry keys that make a buyer go into a department (what makes the buyer frequent this area more specifically rather than another one)? What are the criteria in terms of linear choice, notably the relationship with the brands in each product category (what triggers choice of this specific item of this specific brand)? According to the Director of Trade Marketing for Adidas,

> [W]e use shopper studies to determine the entry keys into each department in order to better segment the department. For instance, in the department devoted to running, the customer expects a segmentation based on use (intense vs. recreational) while in the leisure department, the customer expects a segmentation according to brand or style.

Therefore, "the layout of the products must follow customer expectations and customer uses rather than the range of manufacturers." To answer these questions, marketing professionals muster three types of methods. First, they proceed with gathering consumer groups outside of the store to gauge expectations in terms of departments. For instance, what are the expected legitimate items in a running department? Running shoes, of course, technical clothing as well, but should it also be stocked with specialized luggage, energy food and drinks, stop-watches, goggles, fragrances, and so on? The second method focuses on in-store observation of consumers and interviews of consumers involved in buying.[6] According to S.R., Adidas: "this allows us to see the instinctive elements of decision making as the answers to questionnaires are less reliable." The objective is to better understand the buying logics, notably, the entry criteria into a department and decision criteria (especially compared to brands and prices). Third, experts perform classic quantitative inquiry on buyers in order to measure buying volumes in each segment. It has been observed that in a department devoted to men's all-sports clothing, three types of uses map out to three types of items: one use is for sports practice and involves 35% of the department buyers looking for technical and performance products; another use is for relaxation and leisure and involves 36% of buyers seeking technically simple and comfort items, and a non-sport-oriented usage geared towards group outings, comprising rather young consumers seeking highly-symbolic brands and products exhibiting a remarkable design (about 29%).

Store operationalisation

Marketing professionals leverage the studies in two ways. First, they will draw a decision-tree showing the consumer during the purchasing phase in order to understand how the consumer will mobilise different perceptions of the product in order to assess its value. In other words, in what order will they mobilise their different perceptions of the product attributes in order to guide their purchase? Will they first choose a brand, then a price level, then a product following their usual practice or will they proceed in a different order? The stakes are high as this will lead to choices regarding packaging (what should appear on the front of the package?) and merchandising (product information, labelling, advertising elements). For instance, will a runner base his choice on the type of shoe (a specific shoe for men with reassuring attributes and presentation)? Will the attention focus primarily on the intensity of the practice (beginner, experienced, competitor, short and long distances, occasional or regular user) while ignoring price? Or will it be the reverse? It is also interesting to focus on the way the criteria will be combined to expertly assess the object value. Beyond the psychological price (€80 in 2011), running shoes must stand out for the consumer to make a purchase decision or they must be highly valued among practice experts. All these elements are critical and must factor in the decisions around optimal display organisation so as to translate purchasing intent into actual purchase. If the display organisation does not allow the consumer to reference a perception that gives the purchase some sense, they will postpone their purchase.

The studies previously mentioned also show that the keys to entries into departments vary greatly. In an area devoted to replica soccer jerseys (meaning that they are imitations of official club jerseys), the first key will mostly be the sports club, the sports celebrity or the team, then second, the product type and its technical characteristics. However, in an area devoted to soccer shoes, the first key is the brand. This drives manufacturers and distributors to take joint steps in managing categories by pooling information and their competencies so as to offer the consumer a universe which favours their positive expertise of objects (Lopes, 2011).

Beyond the decision tree, the second way of operationalising the studies consists of identifying purchasing criteria within a department: the price displayed, the product design, highlighting the product technicality, brand, and so on. Remarkable differences arise according to the department and the way objects are valued. For instance, the criterion used to choose a running shoe is comfort and technical nature, while price is the criterion when choosing a textile for a man's shoe; for a leisure shoe, the criterion will more likely be its originality and perception with respect to fashion tenets and tendencies (Ohl, 2003). It would nevertheless appear that sales interactions are rarely taken into consideration in shopper studies even though the literature underscores its importance in general (Gremler and Gwinner, 2008) and specifically for sports (Ohl and Tribou, 2004).

How should we influence the buying process for sports items?

Based on the result of shopper studies, the person in charge of marketing will attempt to accompany the client right through the buying process by guiding perceptions and their consonance. To accomplish this, merchandisers of the brand are entrusted with a mission to work with distributors. They must first drive the customer to look at the product, then make them want to hold it, try it on and then choose it before bringing it to the cashier. Indeed, according to S.R. Adidas, "the main buying triggers are instinctive (meaning spontaneous)". "The classic trade marketing (such as incentives and games) is worn down and only the brand which puts forth something unusual is a winner, the one which attracts attention, which is animated and interacts with the customer" (F.R., Rage).

Give visibility to the product

According to Skins Retail Marketing, "in order to emerge from the plethora of brands and products, one must hail the consumer", and notably "produce break-outs" (H.B. Adidas). To attract gaze, the merchandiser will attempt to make products needing to be promoted stand out. The locations of favourable exposure typically are the window displays that grab the consumer right at the store entrance, the front or end displays at the intersection of high-traffic aisles and the eventful zones in which staging is optimised ("to attract the client into the store hot areas" according to Adidas' H.B.). The brand must be clearly identifiable, which demands that codes be put forth (the logo at a minimum) and communication campaigns highlighting the image of athletes under contract, so as to show coherence and redundancy between the information perceived within and outside of the store (media, posters, and so on). Indeed, upstream communication must be activated within the store in spite of the risk of being overlooked in the context of visible competition between brands (on shelf displays). This is why investments in sports brands with strong competition are particularly common in stores in various new formats: corner location, shelf displays or furniture assuring the brand's visibility. Hence, "for Reebok, the shoe offer has been gathered on a wall space entitled 'Fit For Life' in order to create a breakout island" (G. de M., Reebok). All professionals interviewed insist on the importance of creating such a breakout as "it enables a change in the purchase triggers and a disruption of the codes" (S.R., Adidas) and therefore, "creates a difference in favour of the brand" (G. de M., Reebok).

Giving rise to physical commitment

The first method to bring the consumer to grab the product is organising the department according to its decision-tree. If the consumer is guided by price, then promotional offers should be displayed conspicuously; but this might put the image of technical quality at risk (as it is difficult to put forth several arguments at once). A second method focuses on traffic fluidity among departments (a cluttered aisle dissuades venturing into it) and making available areas where the consumer can handle goods and perform sporting trials (such as testing a shoe by dodging a few racing steps or a racquet by simulating a backhand, and so on) as the difficulties around space restrictions sometime explain poor advertising performance.

Visual perceptions must be confirmed through touch and physical engagement. Therefore, the handling and trying of the products occur in an adapted layout using appropriate furniture: benches to try on shoes, clear areas for tests (for instance, Decathlon provides marked hallways to try bicycles), functional fitting rooms, and even all kinds of sports testing equipment (walking and racing simulators, climbing walls, and so on) Currently, "a lot of work is being done to develop furniture best adapted to these recommendations" (C.M., Lacoste).

Acting on the perception of product value

The commercial success of the process also comes through a theatrical form of the space at two different levels: bend the perception of the product value and trigger positive emotions towards the act of purchase. According to the General Director for Puma France, "one must inject seduction into in-store advertising". For instance, "Lacoste has taken measures which raise its mythical polo shirt to star status (and) a selling ceremonial has been developed for sellers: what speech should be used, what story should be told, what product quality to extol" (C.M.).

Beyond the simple visibility of the products, fixtures are geared to promoting a positive perception, which leads to the consumer attributing a higher value than that of competing products. The quality of materials (wood, metal, glass, plaster or plastic), the type of presentation (isolated product or presented in a lot, facing) or also density, height or width of the departments must contribute to optimising a favourable product expertise. Judgments, especially in sports, can also be influenced by emotions. Mirroring journalistic sportive narratives, objects also embody heroic stories, reflect local or national identities, male or female of a generation reflecting their age, who are celebrated by sporting events. One does not buy an ordinary object but an object which brings to light cultural categories (Douglas and Isherwood, 1979) and, in the case of sports, often reflects passions and identity assertions. Hence, sporting objects can be used as "extended-self", a type of identity extension (Belk, Wallendorf and Sherry, 1989; Ohl, 2003), notably in the case of soccer jerseys (whose purchase generally is motivated by passion and identifying with the champion whose name is on the back of the jersey). Marketing specialists are going to exploit this emotional register by invoking the atmosphere of the games (recordings of stadium clamours, videos of famous matches) and to display soccer celebrities who are contracted sponsors of the brand (some iconic player of a large European club whose image is flashed). The objective is to make the consumer dream, to introduce an emotional and sentimental variable in his decision schema, which will comfort or even replace the cold utilitarian expertise based around the quality-price ratio. However, a running department will not be structured in this way because a consumer who practices running values a technical purchase based on actual usage more highly. Even if an advertisement featuring a marathon runner can move them, the consumer will keep in mind their training constraints and their physical and technical running difficulties (pronator or supinator, with a strong kick or a slender foot, for paved surface or trails, and so on). For this more utilitarian buyer, expertise (and therefore the value attributed to the product) will depend more on technical arguments. It is incumbent to optimise the readability of the information by highlighting technicality, innovative concepts and by sometimes using a pedagogical format. The value attributed to a product can also be strengthened by the expertise of a sales assistant who is recognised as a specialist, someone who can play the role of influencer as long as the customer needs are well defined (sporting use or misuse of purpose?).

Conclusion

Although neglected by sports brands for a long time, today the point of sale is fully integrated into marketing logic. Brands and signs collaborate, combine means and build a common expertise so as to understand consumer behaviours. Nevertheless, two limits threaten this desire for synergy. The first such limit shows up in the strategies of brands developed by distributors who have also become manufacturers and who espouse direct commercial confrontation logic with other brands (by highlighting a better quality-price ratio). A second limit can be found with manufacturers who develop their own distribution networks enabling them to control all the levers of promotional advertising. This market tendency, whereby distributing manufacturers clash with manufacturing distributors, runs the risk of undermining the very concept of trade marketing, which depends on a loyal collaboration between them. Indeed, in order to improve the efficiency of their actions, distributors and sports brands must continue producing knowledge of consumers in a purchase situation.

Let us also underline the need to take into consideration elements of analysis of "ordinary" economic actors (i.e. those who are not academic researchers). Specifically, without referencing scientific models, these actors manage to develop a high level of expertise through simple observation and empirical applications. By systematically observing purchasing behaviours, they treat the consumer the way a consumption sociologist would. It might be fitting to reflect on the famous quote from Becker (2002: p. 12) for whom "whoever produces interesting work about society is a sociologist".

Notes

1. This chapter is based on an article published by the authors in collaboration with I. Calvar-Madec (Calvar-Madec, Ohl and Tribou, 2012).
2. For example, the study, POPAI Dupont *Drugstore Shopper Study*, quoted by Vandercammen (2006, p. 148), indicates that 69% of sporting goods purchasing decisions are made in stores.
3. Center for Retail Research, www.retailresearch.org/onlineretailing.php, and Fevad (French Federation of e-retail and distance shopping), www.fevad.com/uploads/files/enjeux2014/Chiffres_Cles_2014.pdf
4. For instance, the brand Citadium hides price stickers inside the shoes to incite the customer to pick up and feel the shoe first.
5. Interview responses to the question regarding the percentage of purchases decided in stores indicate a range of 50–70% impulse purchases (S.R., G. de M., R.T., J.R.S.). For example, "at Courir, only 25% of customers had a specific idea in mind of what they wanted to buy when entering the store" (J.R.S.).
6. For this purpose, there are ad hoc tools such as "the yes tracking to identify the shopper's journey through the store" (H.B., Adidas) or "the counting video camera that measures the time a consumer spends looking at a shelf display, minimum retaining time: 2 seconds" (M.S., La Mesure Marketing).

References

Badot, O. and Dupuis, M. (2001). Le réenchantement de la distribution. *Les Echos: l'art du management*, 7, pp. 2–3.
Barre, S., Cochois, F. and Dubuisson-Quellier, F. (2000). Designer, packager, merchandiser: trois professionnels pour une même scène marchande. *Sociologie du Travail*, 42–43, pp. 457–482.
Becker, H. S. (2002). *Les ficelles du métier*. Paris: La Découverte.
Belk, R. W. (2013). Extended self in a digital world. *Journal of Consumer Research*, 40(3), pp. 477–500. http://doi.org/10.1086/671052
Belk, R. W., Wallendorf, M. and Sherry, J. F. (1989). The sacred and the profane in consumer behavior: Theodicity on the Odyssey. *Journal of Consumer Research*, 16, pp. 1–38.
Bessy, C. and Chateauraynaud, F. (1995). *Experts et faussaires. Pour une sociologie de la perception*. Paris: Métailié.
Bourdieu, P. (1979). *La distinction, critique sociale du jugement*. Paris: Minuit.
Calvar-Madec, I., Ohl, F. and Tribou, G., coll. (2012). Aménagement du lieu de vente: l'apport des professionnels du marketing du sport à la connaissance du comportement du consommateur. *Management & Avenir*, 6–57, pp. 139–156.
Carù, A. and Cova, B. (2006). Expériences de consommations et marketing expérientiel. *Revue Française de Gestion*, 162, pp. 100–113.
Cochois, F. (2002). *Sociologie du packaging*. Paris: PUF.
Cova, B. (2000). *Au-delà du marché. Quand le lien importe plus que le bien*. Paris: L'Harmattan.
Denegri-Knott, J. and Molesworth, M. (2010). Love it. Buy it. Sell it: Consumer desire and the social drama of eBay. *Journal of Consumer Culture*, 10(1), pp. 56–79. http://doi.org/10.1177/1469540509355025
Douglas, M. and Isherwood, B. (1979). *The world of goods. Toward an anthropology of consumption*. London: Allen Lane.
Ducrey, V. (2010). *Le guide de l'influence*. Paris: Eyrolles.
Engel, E. (1857). Die productions- und consumtionsverhältnisse des Königreichs Sachsen. *Zeitschrift des statistischen Bureaus des Königlich Sächsischen Ministerium des Inneren*, 8–9, pp. 28–29.
Engel, J. F., Kollat, D. T. and Blackwell, R. D. (1968). *Consumer behavior*. New York: Holt, Rinehart and Winston.
Ewing, M. T., Pinto, T. M. and Soutar, G. N. (2001). Agency–client chemistry: demographic and psychographic influences. *International Journal of Advertising*, 20(2), pp. 169–188.

Falk, P. and Campbell, C. (1997). *The shopping experience*. London: Sage.

Gerval, O. and Kremer, E. (2009). *Concept store*. Paris: Eyrolles.

Glaser, B. G. and Strauss, A. (1967). *Discovery of grounded theory. Strategies for qualitative research*. Chicago: Aldine Publishing Company.

Gottdiener, M. (1995). *Postmodern semiotics*. Oxford: Blackwell.

Gremler, D. D. and Gwinner, K. P. (2008). Rapport-building behaviors used by retail employees. *Journal of Retailing*, 84(3) pp. 308–324.

Grewal, D. and Baker, J. (1994). Do retail store environmental factors affect consumers' price acceptability? *International Journal of Research in Marketing*, 11, pp. 107–115.

Guichard, N. and Vanheems, R. (2004). *Comportement du consommateur et de l'acheteur*. Paris: Bréal Editions.

Halbwachs, M. (1913). *La classe ouvrière et les niveaux de vie*. Paris: Alcan.

Hetzel, P. (2002). *Planète conso. Marketing expérientiel et nouveaux univers de consommation*. Paris: Éditions d'Organisation.

Holbrook, M. B. and Gardner, M. P. (1993). An approach to investigating the emotional determinants of consumption durations: Why do people consume what they consume for as long as they consume it? *Journal of Consumer Psychology*, 2, pp. 123–42.

Holbrook, M. and Hirschman, E. (1982). The experiential aspects of consumption: consumer fantasies, feelings and fun. *Journal of Consumer Research*, 9, pp. 132–140.

Howard, J. A. and Sheth, J. N. (1969). *The theory of buyer behavior*. New York: John Wiley.

Kaltcheva, V. and Weitz, B. A. (2006). When should a retailer create an exciting store environment? *Journal of Marketing*, 70, pp. 107–118.

Knoferle, K. M., Spangenberg, E. R., Herrmann, A. and Landwehr, J. R. (2012). It is all in the mix: The interactive effect of music tempo and mode on in-store sales. *Marketing Letters*, 23(1), 325–337. http://doi.org/10.1007/s11002-011-9156-z

Ladwein, R. (2003). *Le comportement du consommateur et de l'acheteur*. Paris: Economica.

Lahire, B. (2004). *La culture des individus*. Paris: La Découverte.

Lopes, C. (2011). *Le guide du category management*. Paris: Eyrolles.

Miller, D. (1998). *A theory of shopping*. Cambridge: Polity Press/Cornell University Press.

Ohl, F. (2003). Les apparences sportives: comment des biens banalisés peuvent constituer des références identitaires. *Anthropologie et Société*, 27–22, pp. 167–184.

Ohl, F. and Tribou, G. (2004). *Les marchés du sport. Consommateurs et distributeurs*. Paris: Armand Colin.

Penaloza, L. (1998). Just doing it: A visual ethnographic study of spectacular consumption behavior at Nike Town. *Consumption, Markets & Culture*, 2, 4, p. 337–400.

Péretz, H. (1992). Le vendeur, la vendeuse et leur cliente. Ethnographie du prêt-à-porter de luxe. *Revue Française de Sociologie*, 33–31, pp. 49–72.

Peterson, R. and Kern, R. (1996). Changing highbrow taste: From snob to omnivore. *American Sociological Review*, 61, pp. 900–907.

Rajagopal. (2011). Determinants of shopping behavior of urban consumers. *Journal of International Consumer Marketing*, 23(2), pp. 83–104, doi.org/10.1080/08961530.2011.543051

Rieunier, S., ed. (2009). *Le marketing sensoriel du point de vente*. Paris: Dunod.

Rieunier, S. and Daucé, B. (2002). Marketing sensoriel du point de vente. *Recherches et Applications en Marketing*, 17–24, pp. 46–65.

Sandes, F. S. and Urdan, A. T. (2013). Electronic word-of-mouth impacts on consumer behavior: Exploratory and experimental studies. *Journal of International Consumer Marketing*, 25(3), 181–197. doi:10.1080/08961530.2013.780850

Underhill, P. (2000). *La science du shopping. Comment le merchandising influence l'achat*. Paris: Village Mondial.

Valette-Florence, P. (1989). *Les styles de vie. Fondement, méthodes et applications*. Paris: Economica.

Vandercammen, M. (2006). *Marketing. L'essentiel pour comprendre, décider, agir*. Bruxelles: De Boeck.

Veblen, T. (1970 [1899]). *Théorie de la classe du loisir*. Paris: Gallimard.

Volle, P. ed. (2000). *Etudes et recherches sur la distribution*. Paris: Economica.

Woermann, N. and Rokka, J. (2015). Timeflow: How consumption practices shape consumers' temporal experiences. *Journal of Consumer Research*, 41(6), pp. 1486–1508. doi:10.1086/680668

19

A METHODOLOGY TO CLASSIFY SPECTATORS

The case of AIK in Stockholm

Sten Söderman

Introduction

Supporters are the lifeblood of professional football. Without its supporters, professional football would be no different from an amateur sport or pastime. While most players and coaches change clubs during their career, supporters retain their commitment through thick and thin and remain faithful to their team, forming the bedrock or foundation of their club. These are the words of the UEFA president (UEFA, 2011).

A significant feature of football is that it is about winning and this focus is transferred to the supporters through emotions. After a loss, the supporters become depressed. Fan experiences are strongest and "direct" in the arena, but it is the "indirect" type of experience that grows strongest. On 22 June 2006, the Sweden vs England game was seen by 52,000 direct viewers present at Köln Stadium, and 56 million people in Europe had an indirect experience as viewers – the digitalized fans – of a televised broadcast. In Asia, a large number saw the game indirectly through their mobile phones or computers (Söderman, 2013: 15).

Professional team sports, like other forms of popular culture, are attractive and highly marketable. Furthermore, technological advances and globalization have expanded the potential marketplace for professional sports organizations. For instance, Barcelona FC has 144,756 club members, whereas Bayern Munich tops Barcelona with 251,000 members (Jarosz, Kornakov and Söderman, 2015: 126). Barcelona is believed to have 70 million supporters worldwide, whereas Manchester United, which boasts more club members, 151,079, is reported to have 659 million fans and supporters worldwide (United, 2012). The income from a game, often referred to as match-day revenue, is a critical factor in the club's economic equation. How does the club learn about the spectator-club development?

The Swedish national football team fell from second place in 1994 to 35th place in 2009, then to 39th place in 2015 in the FIFA global ranking. Some analysts argue that the uncertainty surrounding football governance in Sweden (Gammelsæter, 2009; 2010), coupled with a lack of money in the Swedish football league, makes it difficult to retain the best players, who leave for better European leagues (Gammelsæter, Storm and Söderman, 2011). Due to rapid technology development, it is a challenge to estimate direct and indirect audiences in football. The spectators are scrutinized more and more due to unsuitable and dangerous behavior before, during and after matches inside and outside the stadium. Therefore, the need for knowledge of spectators is vital. A number of control mechanisms are implemented in different countries. There are also a number of driving forces leading to an increase of integrity rules protecting people's privacy.

Who are the spectators visiting the arena – the direct audience – and why do they not stay at home watching TV? A further aspect is the club's constant struggle for revenues using ticketing, sponsorship, media and merchandising (Andreff and Staudohar, 2000) as the four revenue streams. The development of new stadiums based on the cases of Parken in Copenhagen and Ryavallen in Borås, as well as the study by the Association of Swedish Football, recommends better facilities for the audience (Olsson, 2008). Tele2 and Friends arenas in Stockholm, and Swedbank Stadion in Malmö, are three of the many new arenas that were constructed in recent years as a consequence of the aforementioned study. The audience per match in Sweden in Allsvenskan was 6,518 in 2010, 7,326 in 2011, 7,210 in 2012, 7,627 in 2013 and 8,014 in 2014. In 2014 the AIK club had the highest number of spectators (in the new Friends arena).

The construction of an arena can be linked to services. The increase in competition resulting from the continuous development of innovative production techniques brought a general democratization of most consumer products, as well as heterogeneity of products. The mass availability of such products, being goods or services, was the spark to market fragmentation in which individuals would satisfy a variety of needs and buying habits. This situation introduced the necessity for all, including football marketers, to understand how to properly address such changing customers' needs to better position their products and offerings on such emerging markets.

In the late 1950s, Wendell Smith (1956) introduced the concept of market segmentation. In his article he argues that a heterogeneous market can be divided into smaller distinct and homogeneous markets in which customers' characteristics are similar in terms of behavior or needs. This approach changed businesses' approach to marketing. Market segmentation can occur at a business, industrial level or at a customer level (see Shapiro and Bonoma, 1984). Among the latter we find geographic, demographic, psychographic and behavioral segmentation. Geographic segmentation divides the market into different geographical areas. Demographic segmentation focuses on grouping individuals according to variables such as age, sex, income or occupation among other factors. In psychographic segmentation, the grouping occurs based on lifestyle, personality or values. Behavioral segmentation analyzes the customer in terms of knowledge of a product or their attitude toward it. One characteristic that is shared among all the segmentation bases is its dynamic character. The consumer evolves and so does their interaction with the product. Therefore, the segmentation process has to be continuous for it to be efficient and timely respondent.

The football industry as a whole is moving toward becoming a segmented entertainment industry and football in Sweden is creating tougher competition and losing ranks. However, the number of spectators is stable, even slightly increasing.

The aim of this chapter is to develop a methodology enabling a classification of spectators. The structure is organized so that initially, a few problem perspectives are presented, thereby building a practical framework. The literature review is concentrated on three basic references, which include various typologies of audiences. The data collection consists of our two surveys, which are statistically analyzed by using cluster analysis. The fan cluster data is then compared with the three reference studies enquiring as to whether the Råsunda Stadium fans' consumption behavior changed over the period between the two surveys (five years). The methodology is conceptually and stepwise developed based on a number of AIK (in club rank 396 in the FIFA club order) matches.

Practical framework

Today, companies recognize the necessity of better understanding their customers in order to offer more appealing products by using specific marketing mixes. This view applies to a variety of sectors and more recently it has also been introduced in sports. The strong media coverage of sports events introduced a broader classification of the audience. With the advent of television and other real-time communication media, the individual was not required to physically take part in the event. This meant that individuals could sit down at home to watch the event or be in a bar and meet up with friends. The case of this is even clearer in football. A lot of research exists on conceptual frames and performance data in football, however, fewer empirical studies are available on the behavior of football fans.

Important knowledge is needed on the size and the character of the various viewers, i.e. the spectators, and the indirect audience. This knowledge is possessed by the "symbioticians", who are dealmakers, i.e. intermediaries, between the club and the sponsor who make use of this knowledge to influence current and potential sponsors (Söderman, 2013: 197).

The function of selling tickets to events is a feature that football shares with all areas of the entertainment business, and has been associated with the game almost since its inception. For a long time and until the development of the media market and mass marketing, ticketing was the main source of revenue for clubs. The main role of ticketing in a modern club is to manage the sales of matches and season tickets to spectators. From simply paying a fixed amount at the gate, most clubs have developed various levels of seating arrangements, including the creation of various ticket categories within the stands, based on components such as seating comfort, viewing angles and proximity to the playing field. Clubs encourage their supporters to buy match tickets, including promotional season tickets or building match packages to combine more attractive fixtures in order to ensure higher attendances and ultimately, higher revenues for the club (Jarosz et al., 2015: 259). Match-day revenues, based on the ECA Management Guide, are still substantial and account for 21% of the total revenue of a top Polish club's match-day revenues and 25% (163 million euro) of an English top club's revenues (Jarosz et al., 2015: 22).

Fans are also important for a club in terms of creating sponsorship value propositions. Consequently, a major challenge of the club management is to formulate an offering that will reach a potential sponsor's target audience, which is attractive to the sponsor.

There is little doubt that sports elicit intense pleasure, life-long personal attachments, and highly charged memories. The volume of empirical literature that supports this contention is vast and a range of persuasive literature in multiple cultural contexts has demonstrated sport's power to incite, arouse and connect (Guilianotti, 2002). It has even been found that some sports consumers are passionate to the point of addiction (Rein, Kotler and Shields, 2006).

The mechanisms of attachments are not unique to sports and the psycho-emotional benefits of sports consumption are not particularly distinctive from those conferred through other patterns of consumption. While sports fans' experiences meet a number of important psychological, social and cultural needs, ranging from escapism, stimulation and entertainment, to national pride, cultural celebration, and a sense of community and personal identity (Hinch and Higham, 2005), they are not peculiar to sports. Central to this theory is the concept of identification, where sports consumers employ social categories to define others and locate themselves in the social world (Cornwell and Coote, 2003).

Sports fans have a high emotional solidarity and an abiding interest in their sports team or club and are the starting point for the research, as stated by Torsten Schlesinger (2013). Therefore, some but not all sports fans are characterized by loyal consumer behavior toward products of their club (for example, tickets and merchandising products). Fans consume their sports clubs' products on a regular basis, admitting that price and quality only play a secondary role. It is therefore inconceivable that fans with high emotional solidarity are likely to change to another club only because tickets are cheaper, the stadium is nicer or there is a wider range of merchandising products offered.

Comparisons between conventional consumers and sports consumers are also complicated by the tendency of researchers to study extreme forms of sports fandom. While "die hard" and passionate fans are an appealing cohort to examine, the elucidation or their motivation and behavior provides an imbalanced picture of consumption. Sports consumers are not all passionate and fanatical, nor do they all live through their favorite team or player in order to bolster their personal identities. As Smith and Stewart said, "Equally their loyalty can be variable, their attendance irregular, and their interest erratic" (Smith and Stewart, 2013: 532).

Football spectators in previous decades were often quite homogeneous. Through increased media interest, the introduction of satellite and pay television, as well as comfort oriented stadiums, have transformed the traditional football spectators into a more heterogeneous audience (Tapp and Clowes, 2002). As football brings out subjective feelings in the spectator, the audience in modern football is more diverse and the complexity of the industry makes market segmentation a key concept for modern football clubs.

Market research in the sports industry has put great focus on identifying "clear cut" segments in order to assist the clubs in their pursuit for revenue creation through ticketing and merchandising. However, segmentation is a dynamic process that needs to be constantly monitored as the customers seem to change rapidly in terms of characteristics and life experiences.

The use of demographical and behavioral factors to segment a market have been studied by many researchers as previously indicated, but also by Dobson and Goddard (1995), Hunt, Bristol and Bashaw (1999) and Beech, Chadwick and Tapp (2000), who together researched fans' classification with the purpose of understanding fans' motives and needs. Attendance variables as well as the reasons for attending live games have also been studied (Madrigal, 1996; Gwinner and Swanson, 2003; Lonsdale, 2004).

The three frames of references

There are many spectator classifications, but which classes and which services are critical for the club? Behavior is the most important variable for marketers of football. It implies how many games a fan has watched and how loyal a fan is to the club. Football differs from other business ventures in the sense that there is a much higher loyalty to the club than there is to a company's products. To understand this behavior, it is important to view psychographic indicators like lifestyle, personality, activities, interests and opinions. For example, a fan probably spends more time and money on football if he believes that football is more important in life than the family. Of course, it is also interesting to examine indicators like age, gender, income, employment and geographic affinities (Söderman, 2013: 51).

In this study, the audience segmentation was primarily based on three studies: Tapp and Clowes (2002), Kim, Yoo and Pedersen (2007) and Richelieu and Pons (2005). The first two studies perform an analysis on football fans, while the latter study focuses on ice hockey fans. All studies use the single period survey method and the segmentation process concludes in a set number of clusters. All studies focused on the individuals attending the event. However, while in Tapp and Clowes the focus was mainly on the event's selling power, Richelieu and Pons focus primarily on franchise and merchandising. The third study instead concentrates on the marketing mix as the event's value proposition. In particular, Tapp and Clowes' study occurred in two consecutive stages. First, they conducted 25 in-depth interviews with club supporters selected from different sources, who, as an incentive, received a free ticket to a match. The aim was to understand the psychographics in order to better design the questionnaire. In the second stage, 667 supporters completed the questionnaire just before attending the game. Questions were related to personal profile, loyalty, and football as related to entertainment and income. Analysis of the variables created three segments: fanatics, regular and casuals. Among the last classification the authors further divided the group into carefree casuals and committed casuals. Kim et al. (2007) and Richelieu and Pons (2005) used the cluster analysis to create supporters' segmentation. In the former study, the aim was to understand game attendance, while the latter focused on franchise. Kim et al. (2007) surveyed a total of 968 spectators attending a home game in three South Korean cities, and resulted in 967 of the questionnaires being deemed valid. The measures included the factors affecting attendance of the game as well as demographic variables. Four factors were identified explaining the 19 variables influencing attendance, and from those, four clusters were created. The first cluster grouped individuals with strong promotional concerns. The second focused more on place-related factors. In the third cluster, individuals believed that all factors were important to game attendance, while in the last cluster none seemed to be influenced by it. Richelieu and Pons' study was smaller in size and focused on the supporters' orientation toward franchise. They surveyed 280 supporters attending an NHL home game in a major Canadian city. These supporters were randomly selected and 221 questionnaires were considered valid. Variables included game attendance, the purchase of sports-related products, spending on sporting events as well as cognitive, social and emotional variables. From cluster analysis, they identified four groups: super fan, social fan, experiential fan and situational fan.

The conclusion to be drawn is that all of the above studies show the importance of segmentation of the supporters' base in terms of marketing strategies. There seems to be a heterogeneous situation among spectators in terms of attendance, spending and income, where the individuals who consume the most are often classified as fanatics or super fans.

Building on the previous studies highlighted in the literature, the aim of this study is to assess the following research questions: What are the differences and similarities of AIK football club's audience during a five-year period (Stage I)? Should there be a shift in consumer behavior and can patterns be identified (Stage II)?

Crafting the methodology

This study aims to understand whether AIK fans' consuming behavior changed during the five-year period between the two surveys, 2002–2007 (Lyberg and Ingeholm, 2002; Kozanli and Samiei, 2007). The data collection over the stated time period was completed by masters degree students. The study also tries to create clusters for both questionnaires. This will help us understand whether a change in habits is also reflected and in which way it impacts customer segmentation.

To prepare the questionnaire, we interviewed five AIK officials with roles in the organization as managers and marketing officers. This exercise resulted in a 17-question survey with 28 variables (nominal, ordinal and interval scale), which were then coded in SPSS.

To grasp the changing characteristics of the customer, the study was conducted over two periods. The first survey took place in April 2002 and the second five years later, in April 2007. In both cases, the data gathering was performed outside of AIK's home stadium. The data was collected over four home games by interviewing 214 spectators in Study One and

218 in Study Two. The individuals were randomly selected at the entrance and interviewed just before the match.

Stage I: analysis and results

To examine the customers' attitude change we initially considered a broad sub-classification of AIK's fan base. The three resulting groups were originally derived from AIK's marketing, utilizing this categorization in seating position at the Råsunda stadium (which later was replaced by Friends arena), these were:

- Klacken
- Family
- Others

The rationale for it was the assumption that seating was the variable in AIK audience classification. Both Tapp and Clowes and Richelieu and Pons defined supporters in terms of game attendance, while Kim et al. (2007) mostly focused on factors influencing attendance and team-related variables. Our study showed similar segmentation patterns, with Klacken – those attending more than half of the home games – being associated with the Fanatics, and casuals and regulars being closer to the non-Klacken group. This, however, supposed that the Klacken were seated in one section of the stadium, while the family were seated in another section and the rest were displaced throughout the stadium. However, after analysis, this turned out not to be the case.

The sample was regrouped into two broader classifications: Klacken and non-Klacken. The first one represents 34% of the 214 supporters interviewed. From the analysis of variance (ANOVA), 11 of the 28 variables were statistically significant and 8 were used: the "Age category", the "Club member" and the "Number of visited training games" were not considered to explain the differences between the two groups. These variables included: knowledge of the game, purchase decision regarding the season card, number of visited games, importance of prices and of reasonable prices, importance of opponent, importance of club feeling and importance of togetherness.

The first analysis aimed at identifying the biggest gaps between the two groups. Figures 19.1 and 19.2 represent the outcomes of both studies. The comparison of the two studies seems to show a shift in the supporters' profile. As we see from the figures, of the first three variables with the biggest gaps, only one is in common with the two studies and is related to the number of visited games. The result related to the willingness to buy a season card is striking.

In Study One, most Klacken already had a one-season card. It seems from the latest study that:

- The number of seasonal cardholders has decreased.
- Importance of togetherness has increased for both groups; both groups also show the same percentages in relation to the price of tickets.
- Knowledge of the game still shows strong figures, although it slightly contracted for the non-Klacken in the second study while it expanded sensibly for importance of club feeling. These results can be explained in relation to the age shift of the supporters.

In Study One, the average age of Klacken and non-Klacken supporters was 30.26 years and 36.35 years, respectively. It seems from the second study that the spectator age had decreased

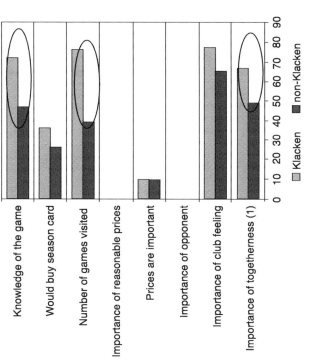

Figure 19.2 Klacken vs non-Klacken, Study Two

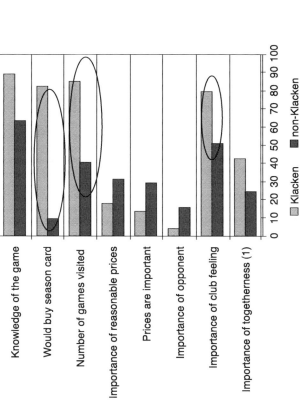

Figure 19.1 Klacken vs non-Klacken, Study One

Table 19.1 The results where Klacken "dominates" the gaps

Study One	Study Two
Would buy season cards.	Number of visited games.
Number of visited games.	Knowledge of the games.
Importance of club feeling.	Importance of togetherness.

to 26.97 for Klacken and 33.54 for non-Klacken. Correlating this result with today's society patterns in terms of the cost of living might help to explain the shift in the cost-related variables. Unfortunately, given that the survey did not address income related variables, this correlation cannot be clearly stated. The finding that two variables from Study One were not anymore statistically significant in Study Two is also interesting. This can be explained by the fact that football is becoming more associated as a cultural event that can be enjoyed with family and friends, rather than a pure sports event to be consumed by specialists. In this regard, we can also explain why the importance of the opponent does not help in explaining the other variables anymore.

Stage II: analysis and results

Building on our previous stage I analysis we conducted a cluster analysis on Study One and Study Two to determine the supporter's classification. The aim was to identify patterns to be used as marketing tools by the marketing managers.

For this purpose, the K-mean cluster analysis was used. To begin we had to perform data normalization of the variables that had been identified as statistically significant in our previous study. Using SPSS we calculated the Z scores so as to have a dimensionless quantity to be used in our cluster analysis.

Analysis of Study One

For Study One, after running the analysis several times we identified a five-cluster solution. These clusters were labelled:

1   Seasonal
2   Casuals
3   Price sensitive
4   Game advocates
5   Occurrence enjoyers

The seasonal cluster included 31 respondents (14.5%). The members of this group showed a strong interest in the seasonal card, while they seem to be not very concerned with pricing. Age-wise, almost 42% of the cluster was under 30.

The second cluster, the casuals, consisted of 58 respondents (27.10%) and showed no strong interest in most variables. Their behavior seemed to lean toward a "per event" consumption and not related to the club colors or acquaintance. For this reason, pricing is not very relevant for this group where again we find that 55.2% are under the age of 30. This group

Table 19.2 Stage II analysis leading to five clusters

- Cluster analysis on Study One and Study Two to determine the audience classification.
- K–mean cluster analysis was used.
- For Study One we identified five clusters.
- For Study Two we identified three clusters.

is a potential challenge in terms of marketing tools, as it appears to have no strong variables to use a pivot.

The third cluster, price sensitive, 57 respondents (26.6%) showed a positive view of pricing as well as the opponent while not so much interest in the club colors. They seem to be selective consumers attending high emotional games, but with a strong price concern. This group shows the highest percentage of under age 30 (64.9%).

The fourth cluster, game advocates, included 46 respondents (26.6%). These individuals showed positive views of game knowledge and negative views of opponent. They appear to love the sport and be very informed about it. They seem to be positive in relation to season card, but not as much as in the first cluster. This segment shows the highest age category value with 43.5% being between 31 and 50.

Finally, in the fifth cluster, occurrence enjoyers, 22 respondents (21.6%) appear to be club supporters who see games as a nice happening and like the social factor such as well as being out with friends or family. Prices also have positive views. This group shows the highest rate for people aged above 50. This group also shows the highest value for women at 27.3%.

From the analysis we determined core patterns in the supporters that can be used to better target marketing products to enhance game attendance, the quality of the event, and last but not the least: profitability. We have seen that in some cases designing marketing tools can be tricky, while in other terms it seems that the determinants are much clearer.

Figure 19.3 Characteristics of the five clusters

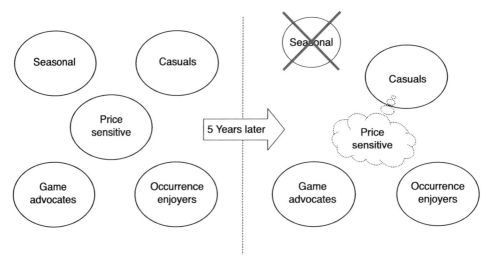

Figure 19.4 From five to three clusters in five years

Analysis of Study Two

For Study Two, the findings were different. This result could be explained by the partially different nature of the answer scheme in the study, where in some cases the variables in Study One were split in Study Two (for example, the variable "friends and family" would become two variables: friends and family). For homogeneity, the authors regrouped these variables to recreate a structural similarity with the Study One questionnaire. A further issue is determined when questions were not completely answered, which resulted in a null value when standardizing the data. Overall, these circumstances created 19 missing cases in the cluster analysis.

In terms of clusters, we found that the respondents would now fit in a three-cluster solution. To retain the cluster naming code of Study One, these clusters are:

1   Casuals
2   Game advocates
3   Occurrence enjoyers

Similar to the findings in our previous study, interest in a season card has dropped in such a significant way that we have not been able to identify a specific cluster. The highest interest for this variable is in the game advocates, but its weight is far from being determinant in the cluster itself. The casual and price sensitive clusters in Study One seem to have merged into a broader casual cluster.

In the casuals cluster, 117 respondents (53.7%) showed a positive view of pricing as well as the opponent, while again, not so much interest in the club colors. Attention to the opponent is important as much as reasonable prices. Once more, this group shows the highest percentage of under age 30 (66.7%).

Game advocates included 59 respondents (27%). These individuals showed positive views of game knowledge and interest in home games, while the opponent in this specific case does not seem to be relevant. This group enjoys football and likes to know its dynamics. It also

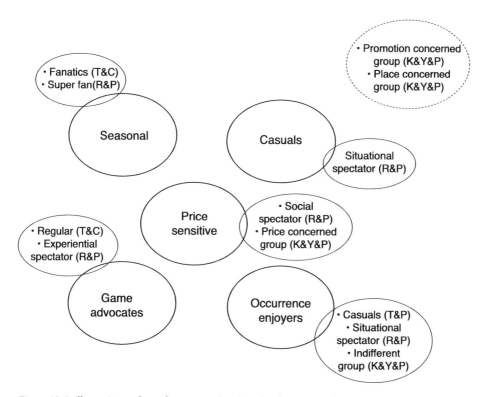

Figure 19.5 Illustrations of our five types related to the three main frames of reference

Note: K&Y&P is Kim et al., 2007; R&P is Richelieu and Pons, 2005; T&C is Tapp and Clowes, 2002.

shows the highest interest in a season card, although this interest does not shape the group itself. This segment is mostly represented by the aged 50+ individuals (36.8%).

Our last cluster is occurrence enjoyers. Here, 42 respondents (19.3%) seem to possess club feelings as well as the will to spend good time with family and relatives. Prices do not seem to be a determinant. This group shows the highest rate for people aged 31–50 (38.1%) as well as highest value for women at 26.2%.

Similar to the findings in our previous study, interest in the season card has dropped in such a significant way that we have not been able to identify a specific cluster.

The highest interest for this variable is in the game advocates, but its weight is far from being determinant in the cluster itself. The casual and price sensitive clusters in Study One seem to have merged into a broader casual cluster.

Further conclusions

In reference to the data collected in the second sample, there seems to be some differences from the first study. At first we immediately noticed that Klacken dominates all variables. The biggest gap in the second study occurs for the variable related to the number of visited games, where 76% of Klacken attends more than half of the home games, compared to only 39% for the non-Klacken.

The comparison of the two studies seems to show a shift in the supporter profile. As we have seen from the first three variables with the biggest gaps, only one appears in the two studies and is related to the number of visited games. The result related to the shrinking willingness to buy a season card and it is striking. Importance of togetherness has increased for both groups and interestingly both groups also show the same percentages in relation to the price of tickets. The heterogeneity at the stands seems to increase at the Råsunda stadium.

Season card drop is serious and contradictory to price sensitivity. Decreasing interest in terms of constant attendance on season card demand seems to indicate increasing interest in sport as an event, as expressed by the casuals and occurrence enjoyers. Does this indicate a need for an occasional service, a package for the marketer to develop?

Implications

There is nothing like a grand theory of classification of fans. The changes during the five year period are observed in our data and they seem to increase. Why? Explanatory factors could be that sports are constantly growing as well as world affluence, and therefore the population of many countries has more time to be involved in sports viewing and sports activities. Most probably the indirect audiences are influenced and affected by various technologies, such as mobile devices. All these factors lead to movements of spectators in and out of the classes and also lead to changes of the border lines between the classes.

Can we use this methodology in other team sports, such as handball, basketball or volleyball? Most likely. One conceptual conclusion of normative character is drawn by comparing the three framework studies and our study. This indicates a need for more creative market segmentations.

Another ambition would be to develop a typology model. Rudimentary sponsors–sponsees theory seems to indicate nothing on managing such relations. Getting relevant data is challenging and very difficult because it needs a lot of interviewers, but it should be possible.

Generalizations need to be drawn. English and Swedish audiences are similar in age and gender distribution. Kim et al. (2007) and Richelieu and Pons (2005) have similar demographics despite different sports as well the "cultural approach" to football in Asia.

Continuation study needs to determine how valuable (i.e. purchasing power) is the individual segment for the club? How stable are the individuals in this class?

This study is about the definitions, such as being classified as being a "visitor", "direct audience" or a "spectator"; all three areas are regarded as equal here. Another concept is a fan, which, as we saw in the Manchester United case, amounted to 659 million worldwide. Finally, the word "consumer", defined as an object that purchases a service or a product. In an aggregate form, this implies the revenue stream for the club.

The reliability in this type of empirical study is limited. We also see the behavior of the audience by studying them when they are in the position of starting to watch the game. Whether their answers are honest, we do not know. However, the repetitive character of the study design is guaranteed because the deviations in the five years were not that big.

Future research

Every club should have a clear idea for describing their customer base in a static as well as in a dynamic perspective, i.e. in order to find fans globally and to predict the future base. This is not an easy task, but an important one, because this analysis shows how the sponsors of big clubs try to reach the audience of the football clubs by signing sponsor contracts and blend classic marketing approaches like getting the sponsor's name on the shirts and capturing the customer base of the club. The existing methodologies to identify these bases and to evaluate the purchasing power of the audience are rare, at least in the official publications.

Future studies should therefore attach more importance to other moderating factors of sponsorship effects (for example, sponsorship levels, prominence of sponsors, and the duration or history of the commitment between sponsor and the club). In this way, the influences of fan identity in relation to the different sponsoring activities can be investigated. Based on this, companies can decide more accurately to what extent sponsorship is an effective communication tool for them (Schlesinger, 2013: 560; Demir and Söderman, 2015).

References

Andreff, W. and Staudohar, P. (2000). The evolving European model of professional sports finance, *Journal of Sports Economics*, 1(3), 257.

Beech, J., Chadwick, S. and Tapp, A. (2000). Emerging trends in the use of the internet: Lessons from the football sector, *Qualitative Market Research*, 3(1), 34–44.

Cornwell, B. and Coote, L. (2003). Corporate sponsorship of a cause: The role of identification in purchase intent, *Journal of Business Research*, 58, 268–276.

Demir, R. and Söderman, S. (2015). Strategic sponsoring professional sport: A review and conceptualization, *European Sport Management Quarterly*, DOI: 10.1080/16184742.2015.1042000.

Dobson, S. and Goddard, J. (1995). The demand for professional league football in England and Wales, 1925–92, *The Statistician*, 44(2), 259–277.

Gammelsæter, H. (2009). The organization of professional football in Scandinavia, *Soccer and Society*, 10(3–4), 305–323.

Gammelsæter, H. (2010). Institutional pluralism and governance in "commercialized" sport clubs, *European Sport Management Quarterly*, 10(5), 569–594.

Gammelsæter, H., Storm, R. K. and Söderman, S. (2011). Diverging Scandinavian approaches to professional football, in *The organization and governance of top football across Europe* (Eds Gammelsæter, H. and Senaux, B.). London: Routledge.

Giulianotti, R. (2002). Supporters, followers, fans, and flaneurs: A taxonomy of spectator identities in football, *Journal of Sport and Social Issues*, 26(1), 25–46.

Gwinner, K. and Swanson, R. S. (2003). A model of fan identification, *Journal of Service Marketing*, 17(3), 275–279.

Hinch, T. and Higham, J. (2005). Sport, tourism and authenticity, *European Sport Management Quarterly*, 5(3), 243–256.

Hunt, A. K., Bristol, R. and Bashaw, E. (1999). A conceptual approach to classifying sports fans, *Journal of Services Marketing*, 13(6), 439–452.

Jarosz, O., Kornakov, K. and Söderman, S. eds (2015). *ECA club management guide*, Nyon, UEFA.

Kim, S., Yoo, E. and Pedersen, P. M. (2007). Market segmentation in the K-League: An analysis of spectators of the Korean professional soccer league, *International Journal of Sports Marketing and Sponsorship*, January, 141–158.

Kozanli, A. and Samiei, M. (Spring 2007). *Segmenting the football audience: A market study based on live attendance*, Master thesis, Stockholm University School of Business.

Lonsdale, C. (2004). Player power: Capturing value in the English football supply network, *Supply Chain Management: An International Journal*, 9(5), 383–391.

Lyberg, L. and Ingeholm, D. (2002). *Styrning i mål: Det balanserade styrkortet för fotbollsvärlden*, Master thesis, 10 credits, Södertörn Högskola.

Madrigal, R. (1995). Cognitive and affective determinants of fan satisfaction with sporting event attendance. *Journal of Leisure Research*, 27, www.questia.com/googleScholar.qst;jsessionid=GL3 MYJFNhyRpDwpZQTc8FH3tblH2cffsqpvLnhvnyn3sQMdg2XJ2!368560910?docId=5000 347796 (accessed 14 May 2007).

Olsson, L. C. (2008). *"Benchmark" slutrapport Allsvenskan*, Nyon 2008-11-10.

Rein, I., Kotler, P. and Shields, B. (2006). *The elusive fan: Reinventing sports in a crowded marketplace*, New York: McGraw-Hill.

Richelieu, A. and Pons, F. (2005). Reconciling managers' strategic vision with fans' expectation, *International Journal of Sports Marketing and Sponsorship*, 6(3), 150–163.

Schlesinger, T. (2013). Brand equity models in the spotlight of sport business. In S. Söderman, H. Dolles (Eds.), *Handbook of Research on Sport and Business*: 435–555. Cheltenham: Edward Elgar.

Shapiro, B. P. and Bonoma, T. V. (1984). How to segment industrial markets, *Harvard Business Review*, 62(3), 104–110.

Smith, W. R. (1956). Product differentiation and market segmentation as alternative marketing strategies, *Journal of Marketing*, 21(1), 3–8.

Smith, A. C. T. and Stewart, B. (2013). The special feature of sport: A critical revisit. In S. Söderman, H. Dolles (Eds.), *Handbook of Research on Sport and Business*: 435–555. Cheltenham: Edward Elgar.

Söderman, S. (2013). *Football and management: Comparisons between sport and enterprise*. Basingstoke: Palgrave Macmillan.

Tapp, A. and Clowes, J. (2002). From "carefree casuals" to "professional wanderers": Segmentation possibilities for football supporters, *European Journal of Marketing*, 36(11), 1248–1269.

UEFA (2011). www.uefa.com/MultimediaFiles/Download/Tech/uefaorg/General/01/84/35/28/1843528_DOWNLOAD.pdf?hc_location=ufi (accessed 29 April 2015).

United (2012). http://unitedsverige.se/united-har-659-miljoner-fans/#.VUCW8fmqqko (accessed 29 April 2015).

PART V

Media

Nicolas Chanavat, Simon Chadwick and Michel Desbordes

Sports and the media have a symbiotic relationship: sports are a source of content for the media, which can be utilised as the basis for drawing in readers and viewers, while the profile and presence of sports is forever built by constant media coverage. Although newspapers and radio were the earliest forms of coverage, over the last fifty years sports have become a major television spectacle. Teams, competitions and events routinely draw millions of viewers, often prompting the global, collective consumption of sports. The power of such occasions is seductive for advertisers and sponsors, but also for the broadcasters themselves. Domestic and global corporations increasingly use sports as the focal points for their schedules and bid large amounts of money for the right to show sports. At the same time, the rise of social media has generated new opportunities and new challenges, which many continue to debate. Although sports are arguably being talked about more frequently and widely than ever before, academics and practitioners remain uncertain about the significance and subsequent impact of social media. The chapters in this part have a twofold focus: sports and their emergence as a form of global entertainment, and sports marketing linked to social media and digital marketing.

20

SPORTS MARKETING AND NEW MEDIA

Value co-creation and intertype competition[1]

Patrizia Zagnoli and Elena Radicchi

Introduction

In recent years, the sports industry has gone through two very significant changes. The first relates to practitioners and spectators (demand). The second to the scope and number of sports activities (supply). Sport, defined broadly, includes all forms of physical and recreational activities expressing physical and mental well-being, and plays a significant role in forming social relationships and obtaining results in competition at all levels.

Sports participation greatly developed in the last third of the twentieth century. It majorly involves:

- An increasing cross-sections of participants (men, women, young, senior, etc.).
- New outdoor and indoor spaces to play (street sports, fitness centers, etc.).
- New organizational format (amateur tournaments, social media recruitment and practice, etc.).
- An increasing phenomenon of spectator sports.

Besides sports participants, the spectator sports segment is an integral part of the contemporary sports industry. Although live sports attendance is still very important, the diffusion of new media has determined an increasing trend towards sports multimedia consumption through digital TV, the internet and smart phones.

According to some global surveys,[2] the mobile will increasingly dominate the digital world, fostering a kind of "ubiquitous connectivity": 1.6 billion active mobile social accounts were registered in January 2015. Facebook is ranked as the top social networking site with about 1.4 billion active users at the beginning of 2015. Other social networks, such as Twitter, Instagram and LinkedIn, saw important growth as well. Besides these rankings, there are other significant trends: instant messenger services continue an impressive expansion, especially WhatsApp, WeChat and Viber; multi-platform use is on the rise, the most popular daily activities on mobile devices are watching videos, playing games and using social media apps. The evolution of new media technologies also affects the way people consume sports, besides offering a sheer number of applications that can be developed by sport organizations.

On the supply side, sports operators have to face typical problems related to high "intensity business industry". Sport enterprises management involves budget drawing up, financial managing, marketing strategies, sponsorship endorsements, communication mix and new media content management. The remarkable economic value of sports requires leagues, federations and clubs to provide managerial processes that should combine the leading variables of the sports industry, typically, strategic and economic management, international events, marketing and sponsorship, brand management, new media, and so on.

Value co-creation in the sport industry: the role of media and new media

To shed light on the dynamics undertaken within a complex social and economic system like the sports sector, it can be helpful to frame sports into a specific approach of the services science, such as the Service-Dominant (S-D) Logic perspective (Vargo and Lusch, 2004; 2008).

The new complexity of the sports industry is combined with the growing level of investment required to be competitive, not only in athletic performance but also in sports business. This leads to the fact that sports organizations, such as professional clubs, third sector sports, leagues and federations, should establish a wide composite "network of collaborative relationships" (Normann and Ramirez, 1993; Lusch and Vargo, 2006) with different stakeholders[3] (Freeman, 1984; Freeman, Harrison and Wicks, 2007) who participate in the implementation of the sports product, such as matches, tournaments, events. Multiple actors with diversified roles and various degrees of involvement are "active participants of value co-creation" (Vargo and Akaka, 2012: p. 208) in the sports industry. Like many other services, sports can be seen as a kind of *ecosystem* (Vargo, Maglio and Akaka, 2008) where individuals (practitioners, fans, spectators, etc.), sporting organizations (professional clubs, non-profit associations, fitness centres, etc.), firms (patron, owners, sponsors, media, suppliers, etc.), governing entities (local municipalities, national governments, international federations, etc.) "work with others in mutually beneficial ways" (p. 149) and co-participate in the creation of sports content through a process of resources exchange and integration (Vargo and Lusch, 2004).

Figure 20.1 illustrates the value co-creation process in the sports industry. The inner part with the indicated bi-directional arrows depicts a non-linear and interactive system, where different actors exchange resources, services and activities to converge into a value creation process. As shown in the outer part of the graphic, value is not only always co-created by a network of stakeholders, it is also contingent to and influenced by a specific context, which is viewed mainly as a "set of unique actors with unique reciprocal links among them" (Chandler and Vargo, 2011: p. 40). The different actors, which play actively in a great variety of spatio-temporal contexts, develop specific transactions and relations. The context is a relational framework where services exchanges take place and where resources (economic, financial, technological, managerial, organizational, skills, capabilities, etc.) are found and integrated by different stakeholders.

The way actors interact is led by shared "social rules" – rules of the game (Vargo and Lusch, 2011) – that both constrain and influence the behaviour of individuals, firms and organizations within a given community. Sports are historically an expression of "social norms" rooted in different contexts and regulated at local, national and international level (for example, athletes' health rules, public order, safety and security, regulations for international events, etc.), thus framing the sports supply's offer, besides influencing the companies' and media's behaviour and the way people act within the sports sector.

Sports clubs compete to gain the best technical performance on the field. Therefore, they need to gain specific resources, such as talented players, venues, facilities, sporting goods and

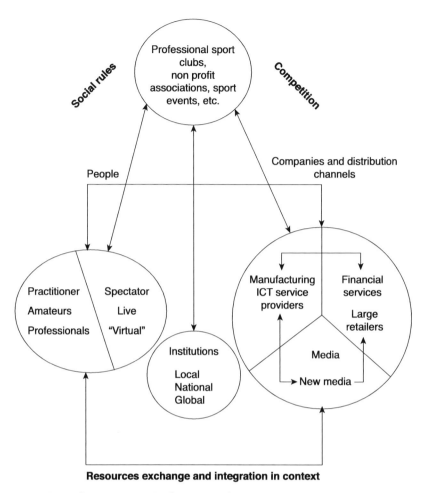

Figure 20.1 Value co-creation in the sports industry

equipment. *Competition* and *cooperation* are in the inner essence of sports. Athletes and teams compete for the best sports record, but they collaborate with each other in order to make harmonic and fruitful results. Competition plays a pivotal role in triggering the value co-creation relations among clubs and other stakeholders (manufacturers, distributors, suppliers, media, etc.). Sports organizations experience business competition as well, because they need to raise funds, gain revenues and cover costs to reach a positive financial performance. This entails the offering of an exciting on-field spectacle, valuable services within stadiums and arena, additional activities (merchandising, restoration, social media services, etc.) to enhance fans' identification with an athlete or a team, to strengthen their brand loyalty and increase the media audience. It is necessary for sports clubs to exchange different kinds of services with multiple actors, such as sponsors, TV networks, sporting equipment suppliers, institutions, marketing agencies, and so on.

In the contemporary sports industry, the whole complex network of relations is driven by a continuous *local-global interplay*, which entails an enrichment and an increase of interactional density, not only among a small number of single actors like club–fans, sponsor–team, etc. ("micro-level"), but also across a variety of sport organizations (federations, leagues, sports governing bodies, etc.) within a specific sport (soccer, volley, fitness, etc.) ("meso level"), to more "macro-level"[4] structures in international and global environments.

In recent years *global corporations* have increasingly secured ownership and control over internationally well-known soccer clubs, Formula 1, motorbikes and cycling teams. Sports are a strategic tool for promoting and selling their products. Buying into a major sports franchise is a business investment that might increase the owners' "trophy status" (Foster, Greyser and Walsh, 2006) and prestige. It can also generate financial gains and might launch investors' products or brands into new markets. Corporations play a strategic role for the development of sports organizations: not only do they integrate their financial resources, providing funds to the team, but they also contribute their strategic and managerial skills in operating them. Sports clubs can overcome organizational and managerial matters with the support of those companies, in terms of financial, human and managerial resources, capabilities and "complementary assets" (Teece, 1986; Teece, Pisano, Shuen, 1997; Pisano, 2006). As an example, consider the Italian soccer teams, AS Roma and FC Internazionale Milano, recently "saved" from a possible financial failure and bought by a North American holding and an Indonesian media tycoon, respectively. In both cases, the new ownership has been beneficial to the continuity of the club. A controversial issue arises if the foreign investors are not concerned to set up a network of ties with local fans, institutions and firms. The unique set of resources (heritage of sports tradition, history, values, and success) embodied in the local context might be impoverished, with the risk of being "destroyed".

Sporting equipment suppliers capitalize on sports teams and events as well. Sporting goods manufactures and distributors supply professional clubs with technologies, materials and components necessary for the sports performance outcome, typically, soccer balls, shoes, fitness equipment, training software, and so on. Sport is a great arena for research and development (R&D) processes and product test. Moreover it is "capable" to add value on marketing actions. This process involves *co-technology* (Zagnoli, 1988a; 1988b) and *co-marketing* (Zagnoli, 1991; Zagnoli and Radicchi, 2011) to improve technical and commercial efficiency (brand awareness). Consider as an example Ferrari: it manufactures an industrial product (the car) based on simulation models and subsystems assembly developed in collaboration with its suppliers. Ferrari's partners provide and integrate the complementary technological resources required for the performance of the focal technology (the car). Gasoline (Shell), tires (Bridgestone), electronic devices (AMD), braking systems (Brembo), power system (Weichai), and so forth, are key supporting technologies whose advancements are crucial to the success of the sports product (car) and its performance on the field. Collaboration is aimed at implementing joint R&D projects and integrating the partners' know-how, with the aim of enhancing the Formula 1 car quality and its performance during the races, improving the complementary technologies' performance and manufacturing a specific car marketable to the final consumer.

Sporting technical partners are increasingly becoming sponsors of teams and events: companies gain many opportunities and synergies, such as the strengthening of their ties with the local context. They can also boost their customers' loyalty, and develop a clear brand identity in order to achieve economic benefits from the investments they have made.

Given the broad appeal of major sporting events it is not surprising that sports have become a crucial and likeable content for *global media companies'* strategies (television networks, mobile companies, internet service providers, online game developers, etc.). Sport is a strategic value added content for new media. This explains why, on a general basis, sport is a core component of new media's market entry strategies. Take as an example the online division of the newspaper corporation "Times of India", which in 2012 acquired the exclusive rights to broadcast the mobile and internet highlights of the English Premier League.[5] Given the growing popularity of soccer in India, this was a strategic partnership to access the increasing number of Indian sports fans using connected devices, thus widening the media company's market share of the Indian mobile telecom industry.

Furthermore, sports events may be appropriate as a means of enhancing the diffusion process of new technologies. For instance, since 2014, Telecom Italia, the leading Italian ICT group has been investing €3.4 billion on the development of new generation technologies and cloud computing. With the goal of reaching, by the end of 2016, 50% of the Italian population with the new optical fibre system and 80% with the mobile network 4G,[6] the ICT company started to offer a range of multimedia content connected to the major sporting events, such as the 2014 FIFA World Cup's games and highlights, which were delivered on mobile devices.

Among the numerous active participants involved within the value co-creation process in the sports sector, *local, national and global institutions*[7] play a meaningful role as well. In recent years, sports activities and events have conquered the role of "proactive" asset with the capability to improve the attractiveness of the host economies. Cities, local governments, regions and countries challenge to bid the host of the Olympics, FIFA World Cups and other major events. Their main goal is to strengthen their local brand image and update infrastructures in terms of telecommunications, transportation, residential areas, and in general a better quality of life. Moreover, city marketers work on the intangible assets of sporting global events, such as social regeneration, strength of local community sense of proudness, change the image of a place, and so on. This creates a "territorial capital" (Bondonio and Guala, 2011) not exclusively linked to tangible assets (infrastructures, roads, redesigning the landscape, etc.), but also to a network of relational and social heritages (Radicchi, 2012). Due to the remarkable power of major sporting events in building economic, social, tourism and infrastructure legacies for the host destination, it is not surprising that emerging countries like Brazil or Qatar strongly invested for the bidding of international games, such as the Olympics and the FIFA World Cup. By hosting a mega event, these growing economies will most likely be able to heighten their role on the global stage.

Fans and *supporters* play a catalytic role in the sport service value co-creation. Their passion, excitement and involvement, are crucial for the event's implementation and value creation. Subscribers and spectators are key supporters to produce the game and to make the sport event happen. They play a meaningful demand function in the value co-creation, involving themselves and dragging friends, family and colleagues as well. Fans are direct consumers of the service provided by the sport club (match). They trigger a virtuous circle where media, suppliers, distributors, institutions, sponsors, club investors, athletes, play complementary roles and create significant value (Zagnoli and Radicchi, 2010).

In this complex relational context, new media are not just mere sports distribution channels. They play a meaningful role in stimulating the development of interactions among a great deal of actors involved within the sports industry. The new communication channels are a kind of "soundboard" of the sports content, and they are strategic promotional tools for sports clubs, sponsors' image and growing brands. With the use of social media, sharing sports content and "voicing" opinions are an important part of the fans' experience (Pine and Gilmore, 2011), that in turn might be engaged both with their favourite teams, athletes and sponsoring brands.

The relationship between new technologies and sports is therefore not merely confined to a distribution role. The new communication channels can be considered as the leading engine of the value co-creation process. They stimulate the people's potential demand, and they also influence directly the strategies of partners involved. Media and new media companies (Sky, Mediaset, Telecom, Vodafone, Google, YouTube, etc.) compete with each other to attract brands from different sectors, thus "multiplying" the spread value of sport contents.

The features of new media

Convergence of computing, telecommunication, and audiovisual technology (Yoffie, 1997; Tapscott, 1996) led to the diffusion of new media, which is any digital media production that is both interactive and digitally distributed, such as websites, social media, and mobile telecommunication (Santomier and Shuart, 2008). New media allows sports organizations and companies to deliver multimedia contents (audio, images, video, graphics, text, animations) through a variety of platforms: users are enabled to enjoy sports everywhere and anytime (see Figure 19.2). People increasingly interact with the world through a "new media network" (Gillis, 2006) composed of digital TV, web, social network and smartphones.

There are two fundamental features that distinguish new media from all other traditional media. In the past, each device usually accomplished some basic tasks: movies were displayed on a television, music came from a tape or a CD, video games were played through a console. Evolution of ICT technologies changed the way content is transmitted and accessed. Multimedia brings together a great variety of devices: television, radio, PC, laptop, tablet, mobile phones and smartphones.

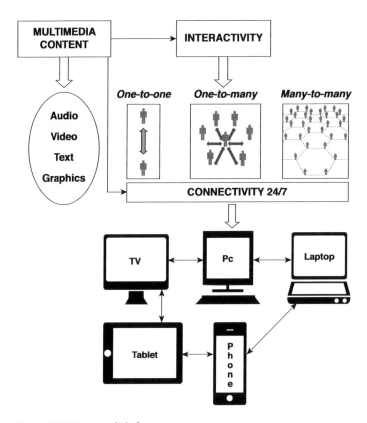

Figure 20.2 New media's features

Technological convergence (Yoffie, 1997) makes it possible for the same sports content (a soccer match, Olympic Games, a Formula 1 race) to be enjoyed using different new media that can provide several functionalities, depending on:

- Equipment devices (TV, PC, tablet, mobile phones).
- Users' location (sitting, mobility, outdoor, indoor).
- Developed infrastructures (wired, wireless, satellite, etc.).

Today a sports game can be watched on television, on a tablet through high speed internet access, or on a smartphone. From the user's perspective, all of those have been interchangeable tools. What makes the difference to the consumer's choice is:

- The context.
- The quality of the image, video, audio, graphics, etc.
- The potential of interactivity.

Spectators do not simply want to sit and watch a sports event on their television. They want to have a "sense of active involvement" in the event. From an experiential perspective (Pine and Gilmore, 2011), the diffusion of new media as a distribution channel of sport gives people the opportunity to live an interactive experience. In the digital society (Tapscott et al., 2000), users can even be a "prosumer"[8] such as active and interactive partners in the production process (Buzzetto Moore, 2013). Furthermore, a major aspect of the changes in new media consumption is the shift in control from broadcaster to viewer.

"Interactivity" refers to the possibility for fans and supporters to be engaged in a wide spectrum of relations, based on the underlying dynamics:

One-to-one: The growing diffusion of "instant" social media, like Twitter, brings out plenty of potentialities to favor a direct interaction between fans and athletes.[9] Every day, sports supporters can take an unprecedented look into the life of their favorite sports "hero". The use of a direct message format that grants immediacy can foster the interactivity with fans, thus increasing their brand loyalty (Price, Farrington and Hall, 2013).

One-to-many: An inner character of new media is the potential of social interaction. Blogs, podcasts and Facebook pages are all ways that users can generate web-based sports content by creating a powerful communication vehicle to convey at the same time messages to passionate fans and spectators.

Many-to-many: Through the new media, fans can share emotions, contents, video, pictures, within a virtual community of people who love the same sports, team or athlete. Take as an example the "Ducati Community" mobile app: through this application, accessible on multiple devices (smartphones, tablets, etc.), fans of the motorbike brand are able to take photographs, film videos, upload contents, follow friends' activities, comment and update their profile. Through this application the Ducati fans' engagement massively increased, doubling its community.[10]

New media technologies allow an increasingly "constant connectivity" (Mazmanian and Erickson, 2014). With smartphones set to overtake the desktop as the primary means by which people browse the internet, it seems that the need to connect with each other is something that is no longer confined to a single space and at a certain time of the day. Compelled to receive constant information updates from their ever expanding peer networks, the average person has been transformed into a "hyper-connected habitué" of social media (Buzzetto Moore, 2013). Sports organizations have to be prepared to respond to this new kind of consumer behavior by creating mobile web experiences and applications to engage fans and increase their brand loyalty (McCarthy et al., 2014).

Multimedia, interactivity and *constant connectivity* are therefore the main dimensions of new media. Sports organizations should try to follow the trend by adopting new media in their content's planning and implementation, since they have the "potential" to positively impact upon fan identification. Furthermore, new media enable sports organizations to interactively test what consumers and fans want and to get the opportunity to influence how their brand is perceived.[11]

The technological convergence process that allows multimedia, interactivity and constant connectivity, requires some features to transmit the sports content enjoyably through different kinds of devices (see Figure 20.2). Despite the evolution of "responsive web design"[12] approaches, each device in the end has different satisfaction levels as regards to images, sound, audio, and so on.

In terms of visualization capability, television is the most appreciated media; home TV screens are getting wider to provide the most detailed viewing experience. Tablet and smartphones have smaller screens but they can be worthwhile in order to enjoy sport games within an outdoor environment or in mobility.[13] Smartphones can also be useful for watching highlights and are used to interact with athletes through Facebook, Twitter, Instagram.

Nevertheless, it is important to specify that major events and popular sports can be broadcasted by big TV networks and mobile service providers. In this case, fans have the choice to select among several devices. However, "minor" sports usually do not have national and international TV contracts. They might pay to appear on local TV. New media are a valuable but less-costly opportunity for niche sports discipline, smaller clubs and federations, which do not provide higher levels of business turnover, to communicate their content to a larger marketplace and to potentially reach their fans on a global scale.

Competition and cooperation in the sports industry

The web (wired and mobile), digital television, digital radio and mobile telecoms are distribution channels of interactive and multimedia content. In each country their presence depends on the existence and development of technological infrastructures (coaxial, twisted pair, optic fiber, wireless, satellite) (see Figure 20.3). Some technologies may or may not be available in different geographical areas. Their expansion might be slower in some contexts than others. For instance, in some large countries where wire and cable are not pervasively diffused (such as India or Brazil), satellite and wireless are very effective transmission technologies. Nevertheless, the diffusion of specific technological infrastructures, with the new media literacy of people, affects users as well, and their attitude towards different kinds of new media devices like mobile phones or digital television.

Indeed, different forms of new media distribution channels require specific technologies to exist and to function. Digital satellite TV necessitates that satellite dishes and mobile telecoms need a wireless wide area network connection. However, over the last few years a "technological convergence" process arisen (see earlier). Existing technologies merged into new forms, bringing together different types of media and applications, enabling people to perform multiple functions through a single device, for example, a song, a game app or a video can all be played using a smartphone.

ICT technological convergence has amplified the competition among communication distribution channels, such as television broadcasters, web service providers, telecom and media companies. Convergence entails the fact that an internet provider may also offer

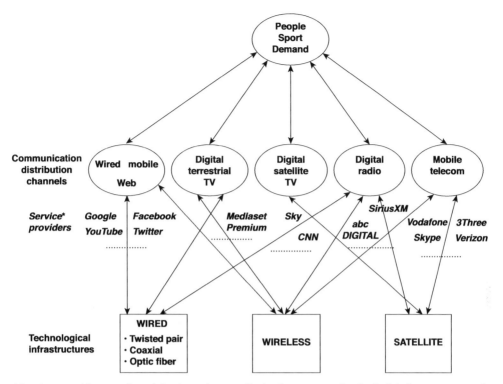

*Service providers are brand business intermediaries between technological infrastructures and communication distribution channels. Intermediation processes in turn enable the sports content's supply to the end-users.

Figure 20.3 The intertype competition in the sports industry

telecommunication services (for example, Skype), an instant messaging operator may offer phone calls (for example, WhatsApp); or even a web search engine, like Google, may provide multimedia and broadcasting services (maps, video, email, blogs, business solutions, etc.).

Developments in digital technologies have opened up the possibility of carrying similar kinds of services over different platforms. Moreover, the process of mergers and acquisitions in the IT industry, induced by both deregulation and digitization (for instance, Google's acquisition of YouTube, Microsoft's acquisition of Nokia and Skype, Facebook's acquisition of Instagram), has contributed to the diffusion of a phenomenon focused on the distribution channels literature, such as *intertype competition*[14] (Varaldo, 1971; Lugli, 2004; 2005; 2007; Levy and Weitz, 2004). Service providers coming from different but technologically convergent industries (telecommunications, IT, TV, media press, etc.) compete in distributing and delivering the same content, for example, soccer games can be watched on terrestrial or satellite TV, internet, smartphones or tablets (see Figure 19.2).

In the sports sector, intertype competition strongly involves 'service providers'. Sports are a key content for media and new media (Barnes, 2005; Santomier and Shuart, 2008; Zagnoli and Radicchi, 2011), they hold the attention of millions of viewers worldwide (through major events like the Olympic Games, Soccer World Championships, Formula 1, international cycling competitions, etc.), they attract advertisers and sponsors who look for opportunities to promote their brands by exploiting the emotions generated from the participation to a sports event, thus gaining meaningful competitive advantages towards their competitors.

Since sports have a global appeal and reach large worldwide audiences, multimedia service providers compete among themselves to acquire broadcasting rights from sports leagues and clubs. Competition among media channels contributes to increase to a large extent the value of media rights, which are becoming a key income source for sports teams, more and more frequently dependent on those revenues.[15] Therefore, new media companies have a tremendous impact on the sports content management, whereas sporting organizations have reduced their power of controlling sports events' diffusion, taken over by multiple and overwhelming media corporations.

As has already emerged in other industries, such as food and large consumer goods retailing or industrial manufacturing (Lugli, 2007), even in the sports sector communication distribution channels have been acquiring progressively more and more power over the content providers (sport clubs, federations, leagues, etc.).

The development of competitive and cooperative relations among new media companies, sports organizations and other sports, and not sport-related enterprises, has a meaningful role in promoting the provision, dissemination and distribution of sports content converging into a value co-creation process.

Hyper (D'Aveni, 1994) and *intertype competition* raise a variety of business models through which sports clubs, leagues and federations attempt to meet the opportunities and challenges offered by the new media diffusion.

A process of *internal growth* has been pursued, for instance by US Major League Baseball. The MLB has been able to properly respond to the contemporary technological complexity by developing strategic new media capabilities through a business unit (MLB Advanced Media) which deals specifically with the League's multimedia contents.

Sports organizations are not always able to stay ahead of the complex and ever-changing new media curve. Instead, they are more likely to be "seized" by the media companies' strategies.

Integration between the distribution channels (media companies) and the content producers (sports clubs) is a very common phenomenon. Over time, several media and entertainment companies have acquired significant equity stakes in strategic sports properties. For example, at the end of the 1990s the New York basketball team, the Knicks, and the ice hockey club, the Rangers, were sold to Cablevision Systems, a North American cable television giant. More recently, since 2010 the British TV company, BSkyB, part-owned by News Corp, with the Italian branch Sky Italia, have become owner and sponsor of the cycling Team Sky.

Through *vertical integration* (Stotlar, 2000), new media companies move towards producing, distributing and selling their own entertainment products (including sports), obtaining access and full control over the team's activity and the programming schedule. The aim for new media channels is to become more powerful and to control content production and delivery in a process that maximizes profits and distribution efficiency. If the benefits of vertical integration include "transaction costs"[16] (Williamson, 1975) saving, realized through the integration of the sports content supplier into the media service provider, this strategy entails the existence of a structured organization and the availability of proper and significant investments, in large extent implemented by corporations and media conglomerates.

Consequently, the sports industry has to face the rise of new business models. Intertype competition opens up market opportunities that bring out more and more potential *scale* and *scope economies* (Porter, 1985). Media services providers and intermediaries are progressively able to capture the value created within the sport sector, whereas sports organizations are incapable of sustaining their bargaining power.

In many countries, sports clubs don't have the capability to strategically manage new media contents and broadcasting rights. Leagues are not able to negotiate directly with TV networks. For example, the Italian soccer "Lega Serie A" is supported by a sports marketing agency, Infront Sports & Media: as "advisor" it handles not only the media rights distribution of the League and its affiliated teams, but also the media content production, besides the clubs' sponsorship and commercialization. Infront plays an intermediary role between service providers and distribution channels (see Figure 20.3), pursuing a strategy of managing and controlling sports contents capable of creating a significant commercial value. From the sports organizations' perspective, there is a "weak appropriability regime" (Teece, 1986): the lack of new media capabilities and managerial knowledge, which should be complementary to the sports technical skills, is one of the main reason that clubs, federations and leagues are often unable to capture the value that flows from sports production. The contractual relationship between sports clubs and "external" services providers can be framed into the "principal-agent"[17] literature (Alchian and Demsetz, 1972; Verheyden, 2004). By transferring to the sports agency the exclusive right of negotiating directly with TV networks and new media service providers, sports clubs actually "empower" their intermediaries, because of the shortage of specific know how and capabilities within the "boundaries" of sports organizations. The new media agencies are increasingly taking advantage of an information asymmetry[18] (Williamson, 1975) that doesn't exclude the risk of opportunistic behavior.[19]

In the contemporary global scenario, the relations of intermediation are increasingly complex. Recently, Infront has been bought by Dalian Wanda Group, China's largest property developer and entertainment conglomerate. The acquisition will give Dalian Wanda the exclusive rights to broadcast Italy's soccer Serie A.[20] Paradoxically, in a country where soccer is very rooted and popular, its system's sustainability depends on the Chinese group that now controls broadcast rights, which in turn account for 60% of the clubs' total revenues;[21] a perverse effect of global competition combined with managerial weaknesses and strategic "dependency" of the sports product controlled by the aggressive sport distribution stakeholders.

Nevertheless, some sports clubs with structured business models are able to interact with media companies without being "overwhelmed" by their strategies, creating an interplay of competitive and collaborative relations. This process generates a variety of agreements – from *unilateral transactions*, to *collaboration* and *cooperation*[22] (Zagnoli and Radicchi, 2011) – which involve sports organizations, media companies, sporting equipment manufacturers, technology firms, and so on.

Unilateral transactions are the most common. Normally sports organizations and media companies sign agreements in which the main focus of the relationship is selling contents (games, highlights, international events, etc.) to a digital network (TV, web, mobile phone, satellite radio, etc.). For example, from 2016/2017, for three seasons the English Premier League's matches will be covered by Sky and BT Sport for an overall value of about £5 billion.[23]

Partnerships between sports organizations and technology providers are also frequently developed (*co-technology*). With all of their features and interactive broadband services, sports clubs websites and other digital platforms require technology partners that permit them to extend their consumer base and optimize their value proposition, providing sports fans worldwide with a consistent, high-quality online experience. Consider the brand new alliance between the NFL franchise, Atlanta Falcons, and IBM: the computing giant will design and deploy a wide range of technologies, including the wi-fi network within the new American football "smart" stadium. The main motivation of this agreement is technology related. Through this partnership, the American football team should be able to acquire IBM's technology expertise, needed to offer a more personalized and immersive in-venue game experience with the aim of enhancing the fans' brand loyalty. Nevertheless, the collaboration between the NFL team and IBM allows the IT company to test in the field of sport its new wi-fi network based on fiber-optical systems, besides getting an extensive advertising and co-branding opportunities.

Different companies from the manufacturing industry, sporting goods suppliers, multimedia service providers and sports clubs develop co-marketing partnerships (Zagnoli, 1991) to access complementary commercial, productive and technological assets, in order to brand entertainment sports contents. In 2015, NBA and Tencent, a leading Chinese internet services provider, announced a five-year expansion of their "digital partnership". Tencent will give Chinese fans access to a record number of live basketball games and highlights[24] using PC and mobile devices. Through this partnership Tencent has been exploiting the growing number of Chinese NBA fans, whereas the US Basketball League might expand its consumer base in China. Furthermore the NBA aims to reduce risk investment by sharing its new product development with the Chinese partner: the league is launching the first NBA League Pass in China,[25] through which fans watch live and on-demand games online and with mobile devices.

The diffusion of new media: from mediate to "social" and virtual sports

The evolution from analogue to digital and then to multimedia systems, greatly impacted the way people have access to sports content. The ever-increasing proliferation of multimedia devices like digital TVs, smartphones, tablets, etc., which provide people with a constant connectivity, has determined an intense intertype competition among multiple distribution channels (telecom, media conglomerates, web service providers, etc.). Sports content is not exclusive for TV broadcasters anymore. TV networks need to re-schedule their sports content programming, thus "modifying" spectators' habits to enjoy sporting events. In the meantime, live sports have seen a great increase in ticket prices and safety and security issues in and out the sports arena.

A decline in the sports games live participation[26] emerges at international level, while the number of people attending a sports event through the lenses of new media channels is increasing. The consumption of sports through mobile devices continues to rise. For example, mobile access of sports in Italy is now 50%, while in the United Arab Emirates 74% of the fans access sport using smartphones. Social media consumption of sports has grown as well: 35% of US fans access sports content through social networks like Twitter and Facebook. Sports games and highlights enjoyed by fans on "second screens" soared recently: 74% of fans in Turkey and 70% in China use a second screen connected device whilst watching sport on TV.

Besides traditional broadcasting channels (free-to-air and cable), a strong growth of content provided through multiple channels has definitely emerged. Moreover, sports new media applications induce an increasing level of "user generated content" besides a progressive growth of collaboration and social interactive relations among fans (see Figure 20.4).

On the sports spectator side, television still dominates worldwide mass market sports media consumption.[27] Despite the fact that TV is the less "social" device, digital satellite and terrestrial television provides many new opportunities for fans and spectators. Compared to live participation, watching a sports event through a digital TV screen is much more entertaining and exciting for the spectator. Fans can benefit from the commentary, instant replays, camera angles, and athlete statistics. Furthermore, through the use of devices like TiVo or MySky,[28] digital television watchers are also able to access programs whenever they want, rather than being bound by a fixed TV schedule.

On the professional clubs side, the development of digital television created increasing opportunities to boost their brand's value through their own TV channels. Most of the top European soccer teams, like Manchester United, Barcelona FC, Juventus FC, have one.

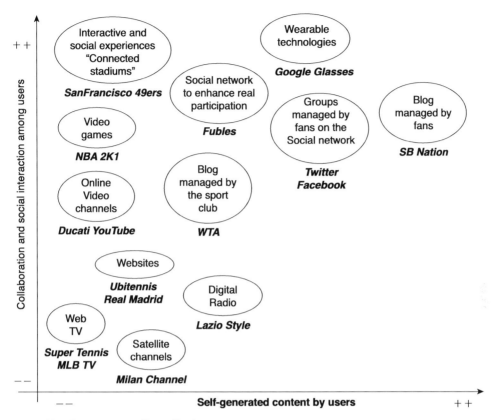

Figure 20.4 Sports new media applications

Communicating on a more regular basis allows them to build a closer relationship with sports fans and grow brand loyalty: a key dimension of the perceived brand equity (Aaker, 1991). New media and social media offer additional services and opportunities either to current sponsors or to attract new ones. Nevertheless, having their own channel remains an important cost issue which can constrain minor and non-professional clubs and organizations from creating TV branded channels.

Digital and multimedia technologies offer new opportunities for building and managing less costly and alternative online media channels such as Web TV. Highlights and full matches can be delivered live or on demand, directly on PC, laptop and mobile devices. For example, the International Federation of Volleyball (FIVB) recently launched a rich and high-quality online TV channel, named "FIVB Web TV". Through this tool, fans can enjoy a lot of exclusive highlights and video live streams from international volleyball competitions, in addition to special programmes, commentaries and full reports on star players. The use of a web TV platform would accelerate the growing popularity of volleyball by uploading video and digital images of players during games. The aim of FIVB is to create a more immersive experience in the world of volleyball, "to raise fans' interest towards this active and exciting sport".[29]

After TV, the second most popular medium to enjoy sports with are websites and social networks. As an example, 50% of Australian sports fans follow a team or a league on social networks, and 52% of Spanish sports fans passionately support their teams over social media.[30] *Web 1.0* was characterized by a mostly one-way communication experience (Weinburg,

2009), providing limited avenues for individuals to communicate and share ideas with others. The most common package of new media services offered through traditional websites are online content to entertain and update fans, keeping them connected to the sports organization. Site content includes players and teams statistics, pictures, and downloads such as screensavers and wallpapers. Interaction occurs through email or message boards, with no potential for instant updates.

In spite of the multimedia technological diffusion, several sport organizations still have websites that are "simple static windows". The latest internet paradigm, the so called *Web 2.0* (O'Reilly, 2005), can be defined as "a collection of open-source, interactive and user-controlled online applications expanding the experiences, knowledge, and market power of users as participants in businesses and social processes" (William and Chinn, 2010).

Social media emerged under the innovative concept of Web 2.0: multimedia and interactive tools that allow the user to partially or totally control content in regards to the creation and distribution processes. Social media, also defined as "Consumer Generated Media" (CGM), such as blogs, forums, news groups, social networks, wiki, podcasts and virtual worlds, allow many-to-many communication and feedback flows. They provide a variety of interactive platforms for sports fans to share, create, discuss, and modify content ("User Generated Content" (UGC)) (see Figure 20.5).

Many sports organizations and franchises have created their own official pages on Facebook, Twitter, Instagram and YouTube. The main purpose is to engage fans, offer exclusives to their followers, start conversations, contribute to the overall supporters' experience. Using social media, sports organizations, leagues and federations may offer innovative and interactive services through the web, such as online sales of tickets, merchandise, memorabilia and collectibles, fantasy, gambling and simulation games, live and archived digital radio broadcasts, live and archived video webcasts of games. Moreover, teams, leagues, and athletes are embracing

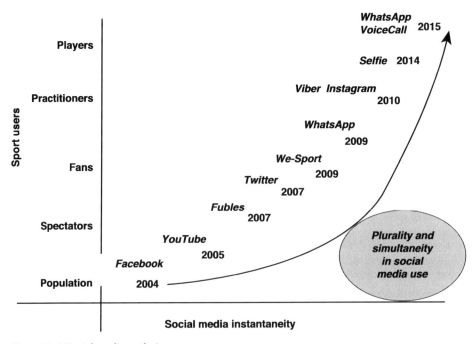

Figure 20.5 Social media evolution

social media and using it to bring fans closer to the game and to the team's brand. By asking fans to submit photos, comments, videos and suggestions, and then highlighting this content on official channels, the sports clubs seem to stimulate fans' loyalty, giving them a role in the team. Social media has led the sports industry to a new concept, providing an instantaneous and low cost way to create connections between the sport club and its fans.

Social networks are able to boost "social" relations among sports fans and spectators as well. These digital tools enable users not only to create virtual many-to-many connections (see Figure 20.2): social platforms can be used to exchange online information, even to organize people meeting in real life. WeSport[31] or Fubles[32] can be mentioned as an example. These are defined as "social sports sharing platforms", location-based, which gives people the possibility of starting a conversation in a virtual environment and then to meet in reality to practice their preferred sports discipline together. In this case, the digital social channel might favor active physical participation by people and enhance the "critical mass practice".

Technology changes, together with decreased costs, allows individuals to have their own websites, host blogs, and connect through social sites using a variety of devices including net books, smartphones, and game consoles (Weinburg, 2009). Social media have therefore strengthened the co-creation of content by the users, who have become their own websites', blogs' and social network's "contributors and developers". For instance SB Nation,[33] the North American-based social blog, is the largest network of the "fan-centric" sports community. This blog is created and managed directly by fans: the editorial team comprises passionate and influential voices of sports fandom and all contents are delivered from a supporter's perspective. The blog has grown so large that it requires a professional structure with locally-based external collaborators.

With the rise of smartphones, mobile devices and social media have become more and more entwined. As such, sports fans like to be connected to their favourite social media outlets 24 hours a day and are increasingly participating at live sports events using their phones, constantly ready to tweet, share, like and take photos. More and more sports fans attend live sports games and use a mobile device either before, during or after the event. Among the most common activities for fans using smartphones during live matches, is calling, texting, and social networking, while the game is actually taking place. In order to increase fans' virtual participation during the events, some professional clubs, such as Liverpool FC, Barcelona FC, Miami Dolphins, San Francisco 49ers,[34] have developed the so called "Connected Stadium". This is a concept where sporting arenas are improved technically and digitally to ensure that the audience is encouraged to interact online from within the stadium. Nevertheless, we are just at the beginning of the process. Indeed, social media applications within sport venues radically change the live event experience. It is a sort of meta-event, a "flagship" innovation, which is still in an experimental phase and requires a sheer amount of investment. This perhaps explains why only a few clubs have been bringing their arenas into the digital and constant connection.

The technological upgrading of multimedia devices have strengthened virtual sports experiences as well. Sports video games, such as Madden Football NFL and NBALive, released by games developer companies (for example, Electronic Arts, 2K Sports, etc.) in connection with teams, are sports simulation products. Most of the time they are enriched with specific features, which give players the control[35] of sports teams or athletes in a virtual environment. Digital gaming is becoming an increasingly popular mode of engagement for sports fans, and many practices of sports fandom might be reinvigorated and reconfigured through the enjoyment with sports videogames (Consalvo, Mitgutsch and Stein, 2013).

The cutting edge frontier of virtual interactive experiences in sports is wearable technologies. These applications enable users to enjoy the sports activity in a real environment with virtual players. As an example, smart watches can be considered "virtual coaches" that help people to play, to improve performance, and to keep their physical activity under control through data like blood pressure, heart rate, burnt calories, and so on. Another example are "smart glasses". These are used during physical practice. They reflect projected digital images like lap time, speed display, route tracking, or "virtual individuals" against whom you can compete and race.[36]

Wearable connected technologies can be defined as "hybrid" realities, since they combine real and virtual objects in the real environment: you play true sports and perform physical activity, but your sporting experience is powered by physical monitoring or virtual and "augmented" contents. Moreover, they encourage "social interaction" among users, since exercise is recorded and each performance can be transmitted to the members of the social media community in specific sports like running, cycling, skiing.

These new wearable devices enrich the "social" value of new media. They actually offer opportunity to diffuse news and appointments to meet people in real life and to practise together.[37] Indeed, by adding a "gamification" (Zichermann, 2013) dimension to specific exercises, these applications might entice more people to become involved in sports practice, spreading the diffusion of physical activity. With no doubt, it is setting bases for monitoring the evolution of people's sports behaviour and promoting a healthy lifestyle.

Concluding remarks

The integration of new media technologies has changed the manner in which sport is produced, marketed, delivered and consumed. On the demand side, fans, spectators and sports enthusiasts increasingly interact through a new media network composed of digital TV, internet, social network, smartphones. The emerging new technologies allow sports consumers to live an interactive and social experience that entails direct "conversations" not only with other fans and supporters, but also with athletes and teams.

On the supply side, new media has created a myriad of innovative possibilities for sports organizations to convey their products and services, and to reach millions of people. New media, especially social networks, by ensuring interactivity and constant connectivity, allow sporting clubs, federations and leagues to communicate more effectively and more often with their "customers", to develop brand awareness and to provide new content. Sports organizations progressively operate as "multi-platform companies". Besides television, which will probably remain the driving force behind the global growth of sports, teams and leagues communicate with their fans through multiple communication distribution channels, such as interactive websites, social media, mobile phones, web TV and digital radio.

New media are not just means of distribution and communication of sports content. The emerging new media channels prompt a dynamic and synergistic network of relations among multiple actors involved in the sports industry and play a pivotal role in value co-creation. Sports organizations use new media platforms to broadcast highlights, video, games, to convey images and messages, to sell tickets and merchandising. By hosting major sporting events, local, national and international contexts gain a significant media exposure that might be decisive to raise the attractiveness of a destination. Telecoms and other media companies, being either sponsor or technology and distribution providers, benefit from the fact that sports are a universal content and implement co-marketing and co-technology strategies to elevate their global presence on the market. Multiple stakeholders like sports clubs, media, technical partners, Institutions, interacting and collaborating with each other, co-create value in providing the sport service. In spite of the fact that this multiplicity of actors compete strenuously, nevertheless the cooperative dimension is embedded in the process of making sport happen. The sports product is a process of exchange and integration of resources, complementary assets and capabilities provided by each "independent" partner. Sports are in the midst of profound social, cultural and media changes that mould the relational context where sports organizations and other actors are involved.

Media and new media attendance induces an important "re-shaping" of the context, mainly with regard to the social norms able to impact the behaviour of practitioners, supporters, companies and sport clubs. The schedules of sport matches are split into different shifts to maximize TV revenues and to grant sponsors and advertisers' visibility. Sports technical rules are changed to make the TV streaming high powered and tense. Finally, the competition of the extreme race to achieve new sports records consists of an attractive and sensational excitement that can induce technological and pharmacological doping, if not corruption.

Nowadays sports organizations face competition embedded in sports activities. Among the sports stakeholders, this process is amplified by the emerging intertype competition over multiple communication distribution channels. These channels, enabling users to enjoy the same kind of sports contents throughout a variety of multimedia devices (TV, laptops, tablet, smartphones, etc.), actually enlarge spectators' fruition and open up new business opportunities that services providers, media corporations and other intermediaries strive to undertake. New media companies are "rivals" in exploiting the economic value linked around international events, tournaments, major sports contests, and so on. With the increase in business and revenue opportunities related to sports as a strategic content, able to catch the attention of millions of people, generating more viewers and followers at global levels, new actors (telecom, TV broadcasters, media conglomerates, and so on) are continuously entering the market and aggressively competing to increase the overall profit generation derived by the sports distribution. In the distribution process of the sports content (events, games, matches, etc.) intense competition prevails in a context of pervasive cooperation on technological infrastructures convergence, in order to make compatible and workable the multimedia platforms.

In the contemporary scenario of relentless sports competition, a remarkable number of minor sporting teams, leagues and federations, frequently facing heavy budget restrictions, do not have proactive skills and attitudes to address the relations with media companies and communication distribution channels. This also entails a strong dependency of sports clubs on media rights fees, as well as a progressive integration throughout acquisition or equity participation of sports teams and leagues by large media corporations. The media's increasing involvement in, and control over, sports has put them in a powerful position to dictate the characteristics of events and matches, to change fundamental game rules and to influence the ways sports content is enjoyed by fans, spectators and sport passionate.

Only a small number of structured sports organizations, mostly among European soccer clubs, US Major Leagues and international governing bodies for the more popular sports (Formula 1, cycling, motor racing, etc.), have been developing an appropriate mix of dynamic capabilities to leverage the potentialities provided by new technological platforms (for example, club channels, web TV, social media, etc.). As a consequence they are fully capable of enhancing their brand image and to boost their fans' loyalty, behaving as "active players" in managing the opportunities offered by new media service providers. Even in the composition of their revenue streams, major sports clubs are able to assure a more sustainable balance in their income, by complementing live stadium attendance with televised and new media sports consumption. Live ticket sales, with sponsorship and merchandising deals, are important revenue sources as well. These prevent sports teams and leagues from relying deeply on the support of TV rights.

However, many professional teams although successful on the field and extremely attractive to a global audience, show a sizeable lack of managerial capabilities. They definitely empower other actors, like sports marketing agencies, to grasp the value created by the sport product. In the countries and the contexts where sports organizations are deeply "product-oriented" and a marketing culture is not rooted and diffused, a strong "asymmetry" emerges between sporting teams and new media companies. Quite often even top sports clubs and leagues are incapable of consciously handling any organizational, marketing and financial structure. Problem solving is almost never coordinated and strategic planning hardly exists.

The way sports organizations manage the intertype competition process brings out different capacities of value appropriability. In many cases, sports content producers are not able to accomplish a powerful role in relation to the other stakeholders (media, sponsor, technological partners, etc.). Consequently, sports might be managed by the communication distribution channels (media and new media) striving to capture the co-created value.

Sports clubs need to develop a more complex and structured organization, which entails a set of strategic new media capabilities, not only to retain the value generated, but also to uphold a higher level of control over their own "identity" content. The wish is that sports might be able to "catch" and manage a significant part of the value created facing global distribution imperatives, without forgetting to maintain the sports essence and nurture the inner dimensions of passion, recreation, participation, integration and entertainment hungered for by spectators, fans and practitioners.

Notes

1. Although the authors have shared their research work, the attribution of authorship is as follows: Patrizia Zagnoli wrote "Competition and cooperation in the sports industry" and Elena Radicchi wrote "Value co-creation in the sport industry: the role of media and new media", "The features of new media", and "The diffusion of new media: from mediate to 'social' and virtual sports". Introduction and Concluding remarks have been jointly developed.
2. See, for example, *We are social*, "Digital, Social and Mobile in 2015", Report March 2015.
3. According to the definition proposed by Freeman, stakeholders are "groups and individuals who can affect, or are affected by the strategic outcomes of a firm". Actors who are vital to the continued growth and survival of the organization can be grouped as primary stakeholders (for example, customers, employees, manager, owners, suppliers, sponsors, local communities), while other groups that can affect or be affected by the focal organization, are called secondary stakeholders (for example, competitors, media, government, consumer advocate groups, special interest groups). See Freeman (1984); Freeman, Harrison and Wicks (2007).
4. For a deeper understanding of "micro-meso-macro contexts" see Chandler and Vargo (2011).
5. Gigaom, "Times of India grabs English soccer highlights for Indians", October 13, 2011, www. gigaom.com (accessed April 19, 2015).
6. Telecom Italia, 2014.
7. The authors of this piece look at institutions, such as local municipalities, sport governing bodies, etc., not only as carriers of "socially created norms" (Vargo and Lusch, 2011), but focusing their role as main active players in sport value co-creation.
8. Alvin Toffler (1980) introduced the concept of proactive consumer, known as the prosumer, to describe common consumers who were predicted to become active so as to influence the design and delivery of goods and services. Social media has brought Toffler's vision to reality by engendering the birth of the social customer, the embodiment of the prosumer. Social networking sites are vital resources of information for the sharing and consumption of products and brands. See also Buzzetto Moore (2013).

9. For example, hundreds of athletes from several professional sport leagues and teams have Twitter accounts. See www.tweeting-athletes.com

10. www.ducati.it

11. Sports clubs can "track" data when fans and supporters are using their laptops, tablets and smartphones. Building big data enables sports organizations to define their fans' patterns of behavior and to combine data and information with their insights, perceptions and preferences. This enables teams, clubs and sponsors to craft services, products and experiences tailored to specific and profiled target segments.

12. Responsive Web Design (RWD) is a web design approach aimed at implementing sites to provide an optimal viewing experience – easy reading and navigation with a minimum of resizing, panning and scrolling – across a range of devices, from mobile phones to desktop computer monitors. This approach proposes addressing the ever-changing landscape of devices, browsers, screen sizes and orientations by creating flexible, fluid and adaptive websites. Instead of responding to today's needs for a desktop web version adapted to the most common screen resolution, along with a particular mobile version (often specific to a single mobile device), the idea is to approach the issue the other way around: use flexible and fluid layouts that adapt to almost any screen. See Marcotte (2010).

13. According to the "Adobe Digital Index", in 2013 TV Everywhere content was viewed mainly on mobile devices, with tablets producing the most at 42%. Video stream growth was driven by sporting events: sports related media content went up 640% from Q1 to Q4 of 2013, compared to non-sports–related content, which increased by 190% during the same period. See Adobe Digital Index (2013, 2014).

14. Levy and Weitz (2004) defined intertype competition as "a kind of competition between different types of retailers selling the same products".

15. See notes 20 and 21.

16. A transaction cost occurs when a good or a service is transferred across a technologically inseparable interface. Transaction costs arise every time a product or service is being conveyed from one production stage to another, where new sets of technological capabilities are needed to make the product or service. Williamson (1975).

17. An agency relationship is a contract under which one or more persons (the principal(s)) engage another person (the agent) to perform some services on their behalf, which involve delegating some decision making authorities to the agent. See Verheyden (2004).

18. An information asymmetry is a situation that favors the more knowledgeable party in a transaction. Potentially, this might lead to an opportunistic behavior, that is "pursuing with astuteness an egoistic goal" by the most powerful party. Williamson (1975).

19. See note 18.

20. Of the €2.3 billion generated by the Italian Serie A soccer clubs, about 60% comes from Infront: €987 million is related to TV rights, €150 million to marketing and sponsorship (FIGC, PwC, Arel, 2015).

21. The Italian Serie A registers the highest impact of broadcasting rights on the total revenues (60%) compared to the other top European soccer leagues: the German Bundesliga (30%), the English Premier League (47%), the French Ligue 1 (48%) and the Spanish La Liga (48%) (Deloitte, 2014).

22. Zagnoli (1988a); Zagnoli (1988b); Zagnoli (1991).

23. www.premierleague.com

24. Such as the NBA preseason and regular-season games, All-Star, Playoffs, the NBA Draft, and so on.

25. The *NBA League Pass* is a service which allows fan to watch every NBA game (regular season, All Star Game, Play Off and NBA Finals), live and on-demand, on all devices (television, tablet, smartphones, video games consoles), www.nba.com

26. Even global sports, such as soccer and baseball, show a drop-off in live games attendance. For example, in Italy the number of live spectators at Serie A, Serie B and Lega Pro's soccer matches has gone down from 14.5 million during the 2008/2009 season, to less than 12 million in 2013/2014 (FIGC, 2014). In the US, popular sports like baseball are experiencing a decreasing trend of live participation as well. Between 2007 and 2013 the number of fans at MLB games went down from more than 79 million to 73 million (*Forbes*, 2014).

27. According to the latest "Global Sports Media Report", in most countries, television is the first medium to access sports events. For example, in Indonesia, in Italy and in Australia respectively, 96%, 95% and 94% of fans consume sports on TV. This report includes data on Australia, Brazil, China,

France, Germany, India, Indonesia, Italy, Japan, Russia, South Africa, Spain, Turkey, UAE, UK, USA. See Perform (2014).

28. BSkyB, through the service *Sky on Demand*, offers hours of sports programming from national soccer championships, Champions League highlights, golf, motor racing, Formula 1, etc. enabling the users to enjoy sports contents from Sky with everything ready to be watched when they want it, as many times as they like. The service *Sky Go* is also available on the move using iPhone, iPad, or laptop.
29. See www.fivb.org/en/media
30. Perform (2014).
31. www.we-sport.com
32. www.fubles.com
33. www.sbnation.com
34. In 2014, the San Francisco 49ers football franchise released the mobile app "Levi's Stadium" to enhance fans' game day experience inside the new sports venue in Santa Clara, in the heart of Silicon Valley. This application provides features such as mobile tickets and parking passes, mobile ordering of food and beverages, a virtual navigation around the building, and a "game center" for high-definition video replays. See www.levisstadium.com/stadium-info/stadium-app/
35. Consider for instance the freestyle control, which enables users to create and execute realistic moves on the screen based on the sequence of motions made with the right analogue stick; the features of the real basketball and football arenas; the reproduction of views, perspectives, or other techniques from television and cinema game play, and so on.
36. See, for example, the application "Race Yourself", www.raceyourself.com
37. In big cities, such as Paris, Madrid, and New York, people, after having met up on a social platform, join groups of other sports enthusiasts in a square, garden or a park to run, cycle or exercise together.

References

Aaker, D. A. (1991). *Managing brand equity*, New York: Free Press.
Adobe Digital Index, The US digital video benchmark, Q4 2013, 2014.
Alchian, A. A. and Demsetz, H. (1972). Production, information costs and economic organization, *American Economic Review*, 62(5), pp. 777–795.
Barnes, C. (2005). Mobile technologies: The opportunities for sports, SportBusiness Report, SportBusiness Group.
Bondonio, P. and Guala, C. (2011). Gran Torino? The 2006 Olympic Winter Games and the tourism revival of an ancient city, *Journal of Sport & Tourism*, 16(4), 303–321.
Buzzetto Moore, N. A. (2013). Social media and prosumerism, *Issues in Informing Sciences and Information Technology*, 10, pp. 67–80.
Chandler, J. D. and Vargo, S. (2011). Contextualization and value-in-context: How context frames exchange, *Marketing Theory*, 11(1), pp. 35–49.
Consalvo, M., Mitgutsch, K. and Stein, A. (2013). *Sports videogames*, London: Routledge.
D'Aveni, R. A. (1994) *Hypercompetition: Managing the dynamics of strategic maneuvering*, New York: Free Press.
Deloitte (2014). Annual Review of Football Finance, June.
FIGC-Arel, PwC (2014). Report Calcio, Stagione 2012–2013.
FIGC, PwC, Arel (2015). Report Calcio 2015, April.
Forbes (2014). Winners and losers: MLB attendance in 2014. Nearly 74 million through the gate, *Forbes*, September 29, www.forbes.com/sites/maurybrown/2014/09/29/winners-and-losers-mlb-attendance-in-2014-nearly-74-million-through-the-gate (accessed 12 November 2014).
Foster, G., Greyser, S. A. and Walsh, B. (2006). *The business of sport: Text and cases on strategy and management*, Mason: Thomson South Western.
Freeman, E. R. (1984). *Strategic management: A stakeholder approach*, Boston: Pitman.
Freeman, R. E., Harrison, J. S. and Wicks, A. C. (2007). *Managing for stakeholders: Survival, reputation, and success*, New Haven: Yale University Press.
Gigaom (2011). Times of India grabs English soccer highlights for Indians, October 13, www.gigaom.com (accessed April 19, 2015).
Gillis, R. (2006). The future of sports marketing, Sport Business Report, SportBusiness Group.
Levy, M. and Weitz, B. A. (2004). *Retailing management*, 5th Edition, Boston: McGraw Hill/Irwin.

Lugli, G. (2004). Food and beverage intertype competition, *Mercati e Competitività*, 1, pp. 17–44.

Lugli, G. (2005). Ampliamento del mercato e intertype competition, in Lugli, G., Pellegrini, L., *Marketing distributivo*, Torino: Utet.

Lugli, G. (2007). *Marketing channel. La creazione di valore nella distribuzione specializzata*, Milano: Utet.

Lusch, R. and Vargo, S. (2006). Service dominant logic: Reactions, reflections and refinements, *Marketing Theory*, 6(3), pp. 281–288.

Marcotte, E. (2010). Responsive web design, *List Apart*, May 25, http://alistapart.com/article/responsive-web-design (accessed 15 September 2014).

Mazmanian, M. and Erikson, I. (2014). The product of availability: Understanding the economic underpinnings of constant connectivity, Paper Proceedings CHI, One of a CHInd, Toronto, Canada, April 26–May 1.

McCarty, J., Rowley, J., Ashworth, C. J. and Pioch, E. (2014). Managing brand presence through social media: The case of UK football clubs, *Internet Research*, 24, pp. 181–204.

Normann, R. and Ramirez, R. (1993). From value chain to value constellation: designing interactive strategy, *Harvard Business Review*, 71(4), pp. 65–77.

O'Reilly, T. (2005). What is Web 2.0. Design patterns and business models for the next generation of software, September 30, www.oreilly.com (accessed on 20 June 2011).

Perform, Kantar Media Sports, TV Sports Markets (2014). Know the fan: Global sports media consumption. Report 2014, June.

Pine, J. and Gilmore, J. H. (2011). *The experience economy*, Boston: Harvard Business Press.

Pisano, G. (2006). Profiting from innovation and the intellectual property revolution, *Research Policy*, 10(35), pp. 1122–1130.

Porter, M. E. (1985). *The competitive advantage: Creating and sustaining superior performance*, New York: Free Press.

Price, J., Farrington, N. and Hall, L. (2013). Changing the game? The impact of Twitter on relationships between football clubs, supporters and the sports media, *Soccer & Society*, 14(4), pp. 446–461.

Radicchi, E. (2012). Megaeventos deportivos y creación de valor para las economías anfitrionas, in Llopis Goig R. (ed.), *Megaeventos deportivos. Perspectivas científicas y estudios de caso*, pp. 25–51, Barcelona: Editorial UOC.

Santomier, J. and Shuart, J. (2008). Sport new media, *International Journal of Sport Management and Marketing*, 4(1), pp. 85–101.

Stotlar, D. (2000). Vertical integration in sport, *Journal of Sport Management*, 14, pp. 1–7.

Tapscott, D. (1996). *The digital economy: Promise and peril in the age of networked intelligence*, New York: McGraw-Hill.

Tapscott, D., Ticoll, D. and Lowy, A. (2000). *Digital capital: Harnessing the power of business webs*, Boston: Harvard Business School Press.

Teece, D. J. (1986). Profiting from technological innovation: implications for integration, collaboration, licensing and public policy, *Research Policy*, 15(6), pp. 285–305.

Teece, D. J., Pisano, G. and Shuen, A. (1997). Dynamic capabilities and strategic management, *Strategic Management Journal*, 18(7), pp. 509–533.

Toffler, A. (1980). *The third wave*, New York: Bantam Books.

Varaldo, R. (1971). *Potere e conflitti nei canali di distribuzione*, Pisa: ETS.

Vargo, S. and Akaka, M. (2012). Value cocreation and service systems (re)formation: A service ecosystem view, *Service Science*, 4(3), pp. 207–217.

Vargo, S. and Lusch, R. (2004). Evolving to a new dominant logic for marketing, *Journal of Marketing*, 68(1), pp. 1–17.

Vargo, S. and Lusch, R. (2008). Service-dominant logic: Continuing the evolution, *Journal of Academy Marketing Science*, 36(1), pp. 1–10.

Vargo, S. and Lusch, R. (2011). It's all B2B . . . and beyond: Toward a systems perspective of the market, *Industrial Marketing Management*, 40(2), pp. 181–187.

Vargo, S., Maglio, P. P. and Akaka, M. (2008). On value and value co-creation: A service systems and service logic perspective, *European Management Journal*, 26(3), pp. 145–152.

Verheyden, D. (2004). *Agent de sportifs. Pleins feux sur une profession en développement*, Paris: Editions du Puits Fleuri.

We are social (2015). Digital, social and mobile in 2015, Report, March.

Weinburg, T. (2009). *The new community rules: Marketing on the social web*, New York: O'Reilly.

Williams, J. and Chinn, S. (2010). Meeting relationship-marketing goals through social media: A conceptual model for sport marketers, *International Journal of Sport Communication*, 3(4), pp. 422–437.

Williamson, O. (1975). *Markets and hierarchies: Analysis antitrust implications*, New York: Free Press.

Yoffie, B. (1997). *Competing in the age of digital convergence*, Boston: Harvard Business School Press.

Zagnoli, P. (1988a). Interfirm high technology agreements: A transaction costs explanation, Working Paper, Center for Research in Management, University of California, Berkeley.

Zagnoli, P. (1988b). Gli accordi di collaborazione tra imprese secondo l'analisi transazionale, *Finanza, Marketing e Produzione*, 4, pp. 81–107.

Zagnoli, P. (1991). *I rapporti tra imprese nei settori ad alta tecnologia*, Torino: Giappichelli.

Zagnoli, P. and Radicchi, E. (2010). The football fan community as a determinant stakeholder in value co-creation, *Sport in Society*, Special Issue "Sport in the city", 13(10), pp. 1532–1551, Abingdon: Routledge.

Zagnoli, P. and Radicchi, E. (2011). *Sport marketing e nuovi media*, Milan: Franco Angeli.

Zichermann, G. (2013). Gamification: the hard truths, *Huffington Post*, January 23, www.huffingtonpost.com (accessed on 12 October 2014).

21

DIGITAL CONTENT AND REAL TIME MARKETING

Strategic challenges for the globalised football brands

Grégory Bolle

Introduction

The aim of this chapter is to explore new developments in sports marketing offered by digital media, with a particular focus on the football industry. Digital media has and continues to transform all aspects of marketing, and this transformation is affecting sports marketing. In today's digital world, sports marketers have to rethink the way they approach sports beyond an experience, an entertainment product, a media platform, or even a unique customer activation. In this new world, sports brands have a tremendous opportunity to use insights and understanding of consumer behaviour through digital media to build their business.

After a decade, the digital industry is delivering upon its initial promise and has developed into a tangible and sustainable global industry. Digital media is now a key component of any media advertising investment decision. In a time where marketing budgets are being squeezed, digital media provides a viable option to marketers who want well-targeted campaigns, using real time bidding techniques (RTB), delivering solutions that are far more cost effective, and focusing on e-transaction purchases to optimise all media advertising return on investment (ROI). Major advertising networks have embraced the technological changes by offering their clients the ability to buy online advertising in a programmatic way. Being able to buy programmatically is revolutionising and changing the face of online advertising. The reason programmatic buying is such a powerful tool for advertisers, is that it automates all of the media buying process to deliver precision in understanding the moments that matter to consumers. This means brand managers can define the budget, goals, and attribution model while the algorithms rapidly adjust dozens of variables in real time based on performance to find the exact campaign settings to achieve the desired ROI. All marketing professionals focus mainly on the complex ratio between the performance and the cost of their advertising campaigns. However, by being more aware of the efficiency offered by real time bidding solutions, they are becoming more demanding towards traditional media performances. Increasingly, brands are becoming even more business results driven and are shifting towards more transactional marketing operations.

Tomorrow's football clubs will learn how to innovate within this new digital paradigm to reach and engage further with their fans. For decades, the hyper-televised football industry promised to be one of the most cost efficient mediums to enable brands to improve reach, and to acquire new customers through their international fan base. Sponsorship was very cost effective when compared to the traditional mass media approach. Today, football, as a lively emotional platform, remains the most followed sport in the world. The football industry undoubtedly provides scale (reach), coverage (frequency) and strong emotional capital (affinity) for any global brand. Mass marketing (brand awareness) and relational marketing (brand preference) are the key axes of the standard football sponsorship model. Global football clubs are still capitalising on these two assets to sign either regional or international sponsorship deals. However, no football club seems to be moving towards the new direction of transactional marketing as they have not yet understood the drastic shift in advertising that has occurred as a result of new digital technologies such as real time bidding or real time marketing. Nevertheless, these new advertising solutions oblige us to rethink our fundamental knowledge of sports marketing and how to further monetise the relationship between the football clubs and their fans. They are encouraging football clubs to become more creative and more audacious in the way they interact with their fans.

Since the democratisation of online networks, the use of digital devices has transformed the "old" sports sponsorship model. Until recently, television – due to its mass visibility – offered the greatest return on investment for brands in terms of reach and frequency (leveraging top-of-mind awareness). Nowadays, the consumption of online video on mobile devices is forever changing the way brands leverage brand-awareness. Most sports marketers understood this "broadcasting" shift and are working towards it. For example, Cas Knight, the managing director of Chelsea FC digital media explained this move: "The huge advances in broadcast quality and capability all add up to a complete viewer experience which enhances the value of sports content significantly" (Merrett, 2011). As technology dictates how we consume content, it has transformed the way football clubs will communicate with their fans. Due to the fast advancements of digital communication, fans have become more complex and more demanding. Fans' expectations have been raised for almost every aspect of products and services. They expect the latest technological product to be of high quality and the digital content to be relevant. Today's sports consumers are sophisticated consumers that expect an exclusive brand experience that includes innovative content and personalised online interactions. New media is encouraging all football clubs to recognise the increasingly important role that digital content and social media play in their business model.

Digital is transforming the sports media industry

Before the digital age, the traditional ways for a football fan to indulge in their passion were the standard ways: watch it on TV, listen it on radio, read about it in the press, attend the game itself, chat about it with friends. The practicality of this for football clubs and leagues was the classic approach of sports marketing 1.0. The digitalisation of sports marketing can be explained by three macro structural transformations.

Broadband internet access

Broadband worldwide penetration is treated as a key economic indicator. Access to broadband services has become essential for the social and economic development of any nation. To promote affordable broadband connectivity many nations – developed and emerging countries

– have created dedicated national broadband plans. Today, the number of internet users in the world has been estimated at 3 billion people, almost 40% of the world population (Klopfer and Ordon, 2009). Broadband has revolutionised the way sports consumers spend their leisure time and has greatly benefited the brands (sponsors) that have harnessed this paradigm shift. In short, broadband brings local and global audiences to sports marketers.

The smartphone age

Nowadays, it seems that everyone wants to stay connected wherever they are. In the US, Far East and European markets just over half of all phones sold were smartphones. According to Nielsen research (Mobile youth around the world, 2010), Italy, Spain, England, America, Germany and China have the highest smartphone usage amongst the 15–34-year-old age bracket in the world. All sports consumers who own a smartphone are looking for more personalised interactions with their favourite sports brands (Smith, 2014). For sports marketers, the world expansion of smartphone offers a wider opportunity to monetise their current fan base and work on new fan acquisition.

Social media phenomena

Since social networks like Facebook, YouTube and Twitter have become mainstream, sports marketing is a whole new ball game. Social media has dramatically and undeniably revolutionised all standards of communication and broadcast approaches. Hence, the way that football clubs, football federations, players, media broadcasters and sponsors discover, experience, access, participate, like and share their love of the game has evolved. In 2014, FIFA digital's global stadium registered a cumulative attendance of one billion and one-third of this audience consumed the FIFA World Cup content on a digital social media platform. It is evident that social media networks are becoming the new virtual stadium for international football fans.

These new sports marketing phenomena perpetuate the successful relationship between mass media and sports. From the late eighteenth century onwards, this relationship has passed through a series of phases. The first of which was parallel growth with the mass media reaching a larger audience through new communication technologies, while sports were attracting an increasing base of paying spectators. Today, thanks to the rapidly evolving digital economy, their routes have converged. Laurent-Eric Le Lay, previous CEO of Eurosport commented:

> The Eurosport Player app demonstrates how we are putting mobile at the core of our online development. We have received positive feedback from sports fans who have downloaded the app and are delighted to be able to now make our unrivalled content available to Android users. Eurosport continues to attract strong audiences across all its available screens, TV, PC, mobile and tablet, and with such an exciting summer of sport ahead we are able to help fans follow the action wherever they are (June 2012).

Football leaders are aware that digital convergence of new media is driving a new marketing paradigm. International fans are more empowered than ever. This new "consumer empowerment" is due to the proliferation of innovative distribution channels, the fusion of offline and online media and, finally, the convergence of content and devices. If we think about it, new technology is helping individuals to better stock, analyse, send and receive more data, information and knowledge. In this sense, new technology influences directly any individual's intellectual faculties, such as memorisation, imagination and reasoning. The practicality of this is that the connected fan will gain more as they will make better use of the content that football clubs, players and sponsors share over the time. Thus, football clubs are learning how to influence sports consumers for the benefit of their daily business operations and respective business models.

With the exponential growth of digital media, international football fans have more access to and more opportunity to engage with their passion. Consequently, football content has become omnipresent. Perhaps the most important aspect of this new sports marketing paradigm is the way fans – with their new social media behaviour – are driving fundamental shifts in how sports businesses operate. After a decade, some online business practices, such as buying tickets and selling merchandise, are becoming common knowledge for sports marketers. However, this know-how is not helping them define how to enrich their conversations through digital fans and thus monetise it. Hence, more interesting is the way in which football clubs need to gain online sports broadcasts, content monetisation and online socialisation.

As fans become broadcasters themselves, football clubs face increasing pressure to control their brand image. Thanks to blogs and social media networks, fans' new mantras have become: "create, communicate, share and connect". These new social behaviours have changed drastically the broadcast media value chain of the sports industry (Figure 21.1). With YouTube being the second largest search engine in the world, football clubs must simply face a new business reality: content sharing is unstoppable. In this new ecosystem where fans are creating and distributing sports content online, clubs simply cannot stop this new societal habit. Instead, they must learn how to surf on this new need and ask for even more participation. To better connect and influence this new type of fan, football clubs need to improve the information that they deliver to their fans by creating new content not directly related to their sporting performances. By being more creative, more educative, more entertaining and more useful, football clubs will be in a better shape to influence the online sports broadcaster communities. Simple content ideas could be fitness programmes, nutrition and health tips, exclusive e-dialogue on FaceTime or Skype, CSR actions, charity auctions, etc. Therefore, the marketing key is to accept more participation from these fan broadcasters to deliver an overall added-value and positive image of your club brand and tacitly its monetisation.

New revenue streams for football clubs

Andrew Keen, the author of *The cult of the amateur* (Keen, 2008), described how digital 2.0 (O'Reilly, 2009) mainly with user-generated content, created an artificial concept where everything was perceived to be for free, which almost eradicated the music industry.

At present, football clubs are facing the challenge of how to monetise content in the digital landscape. The two current digital content monetisation models are that fans are paying for the content (Netflix: subscription model or video on demand) or have free access to sponsored content (YouTube: mass media model). Until now, consumers have been resistant to pay for online content; 85% prefer that content remain free (Covey, 2010).

Football clubs currently follow the free content business model. They compete with each other on content and e-social interactions to generate significant traffic on their online platforms. However, for them to continue to grow their digital following, football clubs need

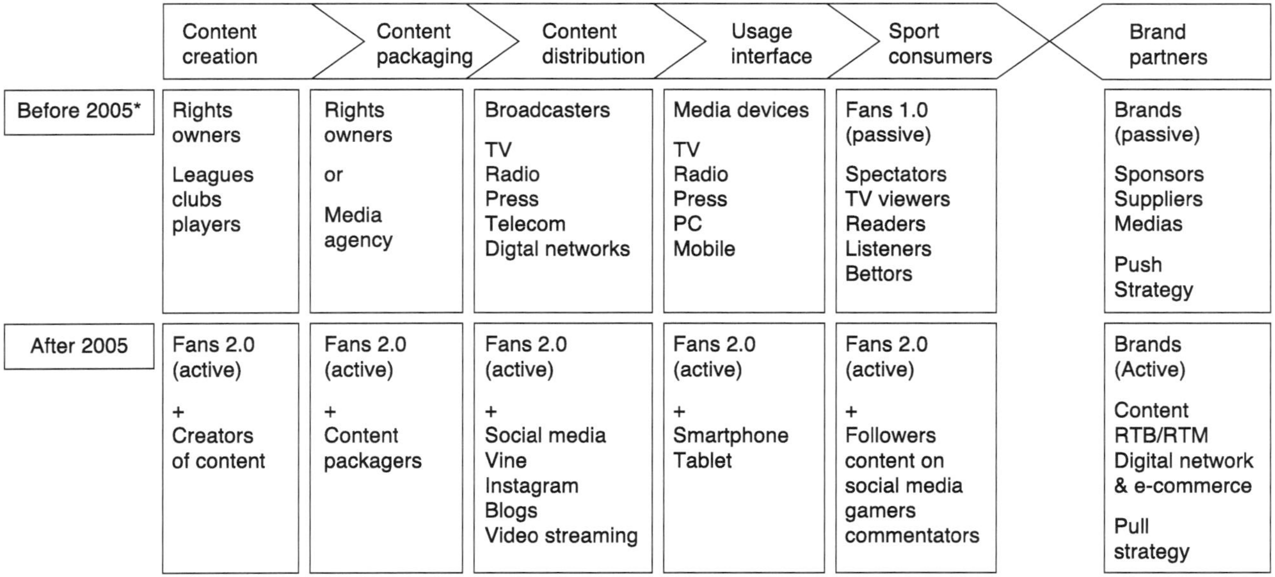

	Content creation	Content packaging	Content distribution	Usage interface	Sport consumers	Brand partners
Before 2005*	Rights owners Leagues clubs players	Rights owners or Media agency	Broadcasters TV Radio Press Telecom Digtal networks	Media devices TV Radio Press PC Mobile	Fans 1.0 (passive) Spectators TV viewers Readers Listeners Bettors	Brands (passive) Sponsors Suppliers Medias Push Strategy
After 2005	Fans 2.0 (active) + Creators of content	Fans 2.0 (active) + Content packagers	Fans 2.0 (active) + Social media Vine Instagram Blogs Video streaming	Fans 2.0 (active) + Smartphone Tablet	Fans 2.0 (active) + Followers content on social media gamers commentators	Brands (Active) Content RTB/RTM Digital network & e-commerce Pull strategy

Figure 21.1 Standard broadcast media value chain in the sports industry

⋆ Web 2.0 is the expression formulated in 2005 by Tim O'Reilly. Web 2.0 describes World Wide Web sites that emphasize user-generated content, usability, and interoperability.

to develop from their existing football centric content assets to innovative, attractive and exclusive content that is not necessarily related to the game.

Nielsen reported that 71% of global consumers said online content of any kind will have to be considerably better than what is currently free before they will pay for it. Nearly 80% would no longer use a website that charges them, presuming they can find the same information at no cost. Thus, for now, earning income with a subscription business model does not seem to be the optimal approach for football clubs. Football clubs will add value to the emotional connection between their sponsors and their fans, by persuading their sponsors to invest in their digital content and gain a more meaningful relationship (return on engagement) with the fan base.

Football clubs will continue to have a mass marketing approach to digital. However, with the fast expansion of the real time bidding model they will progressively move forward towards relationship marketing and ultimately will have to become accountable for their transactional marketing performances.

Due to sponsor demands, football clubs are progressing further on brand engagement and branded content (relationship marketing). It is social media platforms that are behind this phenomenon as they carry and deepen the emotional link between the brand and the fans.

From a sports marketing perspective, social media platforms have fundamentally changed the way sports fans consume sports. The fans no longer need to attend live games to interact with their peers. To enhance the overall experience, football clubs are constantly looking at how their content will enhance the fan's experience, but also how it can supplement sponsorship value.

Football clubs must:

- Listen to the sports consumers before proposing any content.
- Make fans feel like insiders, focus on them not just the products.
- Not just join the conversation, create the conversation.
- Engage in ongoing conversation, sports fans need to feel involved regularly.
- Know what sports consumers want, when they want it.
- Not overwhelm followers with branded content.
- Measure follower engagement, not only membership.
- Plan ahead: not every day has a big game.
- Humanise the message, make it personal.

Football clubs must advocate a model focused on uniting business goals with the sports brand strategy through the eyes of the consumers in the social media space. Simply put, it is marketing that helps build the "shared ideal" between sports brands and the target audience communities (see Figure 21.2). When your content is meaningful, it is likely that fans will engage more often on what they perceive as valuable. In this sense, a straightforward idea such as exclusive player e-chats (Skype, FaceTime) with fans or followers will help in creating a successful social media marketing campaign that clubs could monetise in due course.

The global emergence of new media, combined with new media consumption from fans, will create exciting new sports marketing principles and practices. Football leaders will recognise further opportunities brought about by e-sports marketing solutions (big data, real time marketing, real time bidding, e-commerce, etc.) Traditionally, the essence of sports marketing was activities designed to promote and commercialise the sporting content (TV rights, ticketing) and their directly related products (sponsorship, merchandising, stadium) to meet the needs and wants of sports consumers. With time, football clubs learnt to commercialise

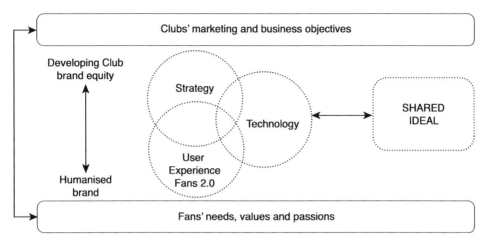

Figure 21.2 Shared ideal to grow meaningful dialogues between clubs and their fans

Source: "The Shared Ideal" Blast Radius, Wunderman Group, WPP

some adjunct sporting content (grassroots, international tournaments, tours, hospitality packages). However, the majority of marketing efforts have been primarily concentrated on enriching their content and unique property: the sporting events or the games. For the coming years, my prognosis is that football clubs need to recognise that they will have to learn how to create new content and new revenue streams from outside of the unique sports fields (Figure 21.3). Today, much of what we see is still traditional sports marketing disguised

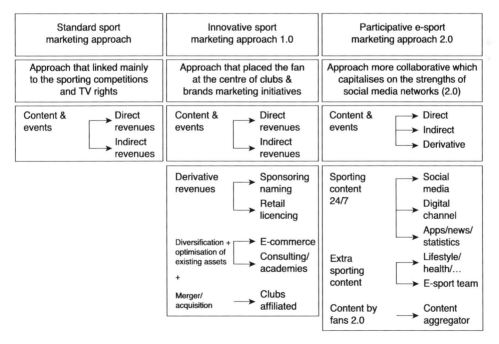

Figure 21.3 A new business model for e-sports marketing

as advertising activations often driven by powerful and innovative brands. All these tactical advertising campaigns are simply surfing on the untapped popularity of sports stars or making sports content further accessible to the fans. The innovation will come only when some clubs start to capitalise on a new business model approach; creating sellable online content not directly linked to their sporting content. These new marketing initiatives will be developed through external partners such as TV house production (Endemol, Talpa Media), video game publishers and developers (Ubisoft, EA Sports, Viacom Multimedia), film studios (Disney, DreamWorks Pictures, Universal), and social media networks (Google, YouTube, Dailymotion, QZone, Youku).

The emergence of a new sports consumer: e-fan

The business to consumer model on social media platforms invites us to reveal some new characteristics of the digital sports consumers: e-fans. However, before defining the distinctive traits of the e-fans, we will need to define the concept of a netizen (internet citizen).

The broad description of a netizen could be any active participant in the online community of the internet. Another definition offered by the French academic, Michel Serres (2008), is what he calls a new and irreversible "digital citizenship". Serres' argument runs as follows. New digital technology has transformed five fundamental aspects of any human life, these are: the notion of time, the spatial dimension, any legal framework, sociability, and, finally, the way we think, operate and work. For Serres, the digitalisation of the world is an enormous cultural and cognitive revolution that justifies the new label of "netizen".

A netizen is well informed, capable of participating and independent-minded, e-fans have developed higher capacities for critical thinking towards a sports brand, its marketing, content, merchandise, etc. This shift makes the sports consumers smarter than ever. The double-edged sword of the digitalisation of sports marketing practices is that football clubs will have greater opportunities to influence their fan behaviours. Not all fans are equally passionate and fanatical, nor use their favourite sporting institution to back their personal identity.

Not all fans are loyal, as some attend sporting events on a regular basis, and others attend only on exceptional occasions. This complexity underpins the need to build business to consumer models of sports consumption that make sense of this disparate fan behaviour. Social media practices can help develop effective fan segmentation and categorise the disparity.

In the past, a true fan was often described as someone who will purchase anything and everything their football club produces. Today, the "digital citizenship" paradigm is placing e-fans at the centre of everything. They are more and more in control and sporting brands need to learn to listen to them. Now, it is all about personalised one-to-one dialogue. The e-fan typology that follows will help football clubs identify the digital experience to fit the particular needs and expected relationships for different categories of fans.

The undecided

This e-fan knows the brand but does not invest emotion into it. Most of the time, this category represents the versatile age of 8 to 14 years old who are also very active users of social media and online gaming platforms.

The opinionist

This category never experienced the club directly but likes to talk about it and express their feelings and suggestions in order to be part of their community conversations. Their streams of information are non-specific media, rumours, moods, clichés, etc. This category can be associated with fans who are geographically distant from the sporting brand, or who spend most of their time engaging in sports chatter and trawling the internet.

The aficionados

The football club is associated directly with their daily lives. These fans use their favourite sporting brand to tell a story about themselves. They buy the tickets, the merchandising, the mug, the scarf, etc. They cannot wait until you issue your next piece of content online. They will consume any content related directly or indirectly to their cherished brand.

The influencers

This category is so emotionally involved with their beloved club that they feel that they have developed a unique expertise that they need to share with others. They want to contribute to the development of the club and more importantly, they want to be rewarded for it.

The creative broadcasters

This is the ultimate category of e-fan: the superfan. They are using your club appeal to create and share their own produced content. In short, they are volunteers who spend time and talent to curate content that other e-fans will consume. They are creating new added-value to your original and emotional brand content. For now, because of their working culture, very few football clubs are willing to work in partnership with the most talented of them.

In the future, football clubs will need to have a more democratic approach towards the generation of their online content and will embrace the web 2.0 participative culture. Football clubs will become more curators and aggregators of digital sporting content produced by the e-fans themselves. To increase their traffic, clubs will capitalise on user-generated content by gathering all this new flow of content towards their "owned media" that they will then monetise into sponsorship packages (ROI). The cumulative audiences of their website, their owned social media pages (see Table 21.1) and the social media audience of their sporting champions (see Table 21.2) will be an always-on digital platform sellable to sponsors.

Table 21.1 Social media audiences of global football clubs in 2015

Ranking	Club	League	Facebook	Twitter	Instagram	YouTube
1	FC Barcelona	Liga	79.1m	13.5m	4.9m	1.6m
2	Real Madrid	Liga	77.2m	13.8m	4.9m	1.6m
3	Manchester United	Premier League	61.6m	3.91m	2.1m	★
4	Chelsea FC	Premier League	38.3m	4.3m	1.4m	380k
5	Arsenal FC	Premier League	30.7m	4.9m	1.3m	166k
6	Bayern Munich	Bundesliga	24.1m	2.32m	1.3m	255k
7	Liverpool FC	Premier League	24m	3.5m	1m	310k
8	AC Milan	Calcio	23.4m	2.31m	660k	254k
9	PSG	Ligue 1	17.9m	2m	1.4m	204k
10	Manchester City	Premier League	16.7m	3.3m	760k	328k

★Manchester United does not have an official YouTube channel.

Source: Forbes.com

Table 21.2 Social media audiences of football players in 2015

Ranking	Name	League	Facebook	Twitter
1	Cristiano Ronaldo	Football Liga	102m	35m
2	Messi	Football Liga	75m	★
3	Neymar	Football Liga	51m	18m
4	Beckham	Retired	50m	★
5	Kaka	US MLS	31m	22m
6	Ronaldinho	Liga Mx	30m	12m
7	Ozil	Premier League	23m	9.89m
8	Iniesta	Football Liga	23m	10m
9	Bale	Football Liga	22m	6m
10	Pique	Football Liga	16m	10m
11	David Villa	US MLS	15m	7.25m
12	Suarez	Football Liga	11m	4m
13	Juan Mata	Premier League	8m	4m
14	Fabregas	Premier League	6m	7m
15	Henry	Retired	8m	1.88m

★Neither Messi nor Beckham have official Twitter accounts.

Source: Facebook and Twitter

Social media audiences are transforming the paradigm of our sports marketing practices. In the past, it was up to the fan to demonstrate their loyalty towards their favourite club. Nowadays, it is the football clubs that are competing on social media, through innovative content and engagement tactics, to increase the numbers of their loyal followers. This new industry reality is articulated by Pete Blackshaw (2011), the global head of digital marketing and social media for Nestlé, S.A. [2011–present], who states: "Sport sponsorship has ceased to be a conversational guarantee for any brands" and "the stadium is flattening. We are all part of a new genre in content creation and consumption called 'fanned media'. The fan voice is louder, infinitely more networked and viral, more inclusive, and questionably – and wonderfully – global."

The new perspectives of e-sports marketing

Fans and the football industry are both changing. Football clubs have done things one way for a long time but with the combined emergence of social media networks and new e-fan behaviours there is simply no going back. Between clubs and fans, it will be increasingly about the one-to-one customised dialogues. Sponsors will focus on investing in those "owned media" channels that deliver high return on engagement. Thus, the role of clubs will be to administer and to broadcast organic sports related content (owned media) and fan-generated content (fanned media) through their various digital platforms (Figure 20.4).

All sports marketers must face this new reality as there is no point ignoring technology and new media, when the creativity of the sports consumers follows it. The backbone of the YouTube business model rests with e-fan contributions; hence, these e-fans will be earned partners to the club's marketing efforts. However, they also create a trust issue within a historically conservative industry, henceforth, football clubs should begin to acclimatise to this new participative reality and embrace its positive attributes.

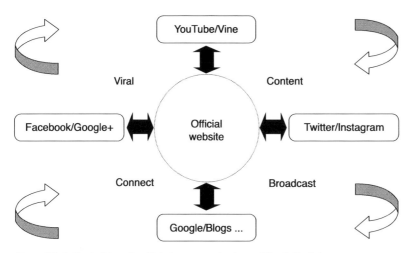

Figure 21.4 Optimising the digital communication of football clubs

Source: Forbes.com

Here are six major e-sports marketing digital opportunities that clubs could investigate in the coming years, they are an amalgamation of the previously discussed realities of digital marketing.

Content marketing

The American author Zig Ziglar taught us that "People do not buy for logical reasons; they buy for emotional reasons" (2014). Football clubs must adopt the power of effective storytelling outside of exclusive sporting content. Sporting institutions are by definition highly charged emotional brands that will continue to support the media industry but could also connect with consumers in different manners. In December 2011, the video game, *Gears of War 3*, sold more than 3 million units globally. A few weeks later, EA Sports' *FIFA 12* sold 3.2 million units in its first week. In 2014, the video gaming industry generated more than $100 billion and became the second-largest segment of the entertainment industry in the world, outstripping films and far surpassing books. In the 1990s, sports marketers had learned from the merchandising expertise of Nike, Adidas, and Umbro. The following decade, they supplemented these learnings with a host of stadium infrastructure enhancements with expertise from Vinci, European Stadium and Safety Management Association, and Populous. The digital and online gaming age is inviting sports marketers to work with a new kind of expertise from the likes of Ubisoft, DreamWorks, Endemol and Playmakers to create, and deliver greater, more immersive content for their fans.

Video content

Football clubs have developed their own online channels on YouTube, Dailymotion and Youku. To get maximum awareness from YouTube, the clubs will either have an internal digital content production team or have to partner with TV production companies, such as Canal Studio, Mediapro, HBS and Bein, to produce exclusive high quality sporting and non-related sporting content. Peripheral content opportunities are numerous, from wellness, fitness, nutrition, portraits of fans, etc. Clubs could also create new content with internet celebrities (Remi Gaillard) or non-sports celebrities (Jason Sudeikis) to reach a fresh new audience such as the 9 million viewers of the Tottenham Hotspur video, *An American Coach in London: NBC Sports Premier League Film featuring Jason Sudeikis* (2013).

Capitalising on a football star's online audiences

In the future, football clubs will have to take the individual rights of their football players into account when negotiating agreements, in order to tap into and capitalise on their individual fanbase to some extent. Since the David Beckham phenomenon, some football players have become international advertising icons for global brands in their own rights. These millions of followers should be aggregated to calculate the cumulative digital audiences of the football clubs and their stars to allow sponsors to develop amplified co-branded campaigns. For instance, the clubs will have the opportunity to develop dedicated online gaming applications, such as *Heads Up with Cristiano Ronaldo*, which was played for more than 225 million minutes by international e-fans.

The first e-sports team

In 2014, an electronic sports (e-sports) competition brought in 27 million viewers for a multiplayer online strategy game (EUM, 2015). More people play and watch e-sports – people playing competitive computer video games such as EA FIFA 2014 – than watched the 2013 NBA Finals (26.3 million), and the 2014 FA Cup (10.1 million). Right now, football clubs are investing more into the niche captive audience of women's football rather than signing new global e-sports super-talents, such as Samad "Samsam" Baïsm, Mike Moreton, Anas "Astank" Sofi, Navid "AdamanT" Borhani, or Sean Allen.

Big data, search and real time marketing

In line with many other industries, football will soon adopt the same techniques of search marketing, real time marketing (Rooney, 2013), online auctions and real time bidding (RTB) to optimise the monetisation of their online assets, such as ticketing, hospitality, and merchandising to their millions of international e-fans and social media followers. Subsequently, the team will share its Big Data with its sponsors and allow them to target their fans with relevant and personalised offers that suit each fan's timely needs and ultimately increase sponsor return on investment (transactional marketing).

Football online betting

"The current estimations, which include both the legal and black markets, suggest the sports match-betting industry is worth anywhere between $700bn and $1tn a year" (Small, 2013). About 70% of that trade has been estimated to come from trading on football.

Football leagues, with clubs' agreement, may soon want to reconsider their position and look at the opportunity to not only collect sponsorship revenues (Bwin, Titanbet, Marathonbet, Unibet, etc.) from this large industry, but also to develop their own online regulated betting platforms in conjunction with their digital strategy.

Interview with Dídac Lee: FC Barcelona board member and director of the new technologies

Grégory Bolle: Could you provide us with some background information – the last five years – on the digital strategy of FC Barcelona?

Dídac Lee: For a little over a year, FC Barcelona has opted for an online team dedicated to making the Club's digital assets profitable. This is why we developed a new web platform that allows us to integrate seamlessly with social media. The tip of the spear, as it were, is our firmly committed dedication to mobile technology as our income generation model on a global scale.

GB: How has the hyper-globalisation of your brand combined with the fast growth of social media networks phenomena reshaped your current digital approach?

DL: FC Barcelona's challenge is to globalise its brand without sacrificing its roots. As a brand, Barça is atypical, in that there isn't another multi-sports club in the world that promotes its unwavering principles to the degree we do. FC Barcelona represents a model of play, a work ethic – like what's taught at La Masía, which is the envy of any sports club – all of this implies an implicit focus on social media. We will not globalise at any cost, perhaps that's one of the unknown factors that helps us promote the Sentiment Blaugrana (Barça feeling) globally.

GB: What are the objectives of the club in terms of digital content generation?

DL: Our objectives can be summed up in three words: audience, engagement, monetisation. Our audience is growing at an incredible pace and our work centers around, more than capture, encouraging loyalty in the fans from around the globe. We have strategic markets that we want to break into, without a doubt, the best way to do that is digitally. With the first team's schedule, it's complicated to plan for a friendly or a worldwide tour. However, downloading a mobile application, for example, is within everybody's reach and it's also dramatically cheaper, at the same time, it allows Barça fans to feel close to the Club.

GB: What is the overall marketing approach in terms of social media networks usage? (Optimisation of social media platforms: Facebook, Twitter, YouTube and Flickr?)

DL: Barça must be present on the main social networks, because that's where the public is. Our approach isn't creating our own platforms seeing that in the market there are magnificent solutions that facilitate access. Our goal is to integrate our efforts with these platforms.

GB: How digital is transforming the marketing and communication approach of a sports institution such as the FC Barcelona? Define the main challenges.

DL: Introducing the Barça brand in China, for example, is a challenge. That's why we have partnered with a solid Chinese organisation. Recently we signed an agreement with Tencent, the deal will open the doors to an enormous market, something that is potentially very important to our interests.

GB: Do you segment your digital strategy in function of your fan base geo-segmentation? If yes, what are the key differentiators between the local fans and the international in terms of user experience?

DL: Segmentation is the basis on which any strategy succeeds. The local public (Catalonia) have interests that don't always coincide with those held by foreign markets. Numerically, the latter constitute about 70% of the traffic to our website. We try to address global concepts, but we don't forsake local interests.

GB: How do FC Barcelona's sponsors benefit from your digital platforms? Are digital rights more critical in terms of sponsorship negotiations? Why?

DL: FC Barcelona's sponsors benefit from aligning with our brand because, as of today, it's one of the most valued brands in the world. Their presence on our website and their integration with various Club associative brand campaigns renders a benefit to them that is difficult to reach any other way.

GB: What was the most successful digital campaign (sponsorship activation) that you operated with one of your sponsors?

DL: More than highlighting a specific campaign or a specific sponsor, we're extremely pleased with the good relationship we have with all of them. It would be unfair to highlight just one sponsor.

GB: From a digital angle, how can we further increase the brand affinity of your sponsors with your local/global fan base?

DL: The campaigns that we plan, in which both parties are comfortable (sponsor and Club), are the ones that directly or indirectly link a product with Barça. With that focus, the possibilities are infinite.

GB: Can you share with us, what are the new digital milestones that FC Barcelona wishes to accomplish in the coming years?

DL: One of our major goals is to create 20 official mobile applications for FC Barcelona for this coming season and to turn the Camp Nou into a "mobile friendly" zone.

GB: Do you see potential scope of work (from a marketing view) between your global brand and one of the major digital channels such as Google, Facebook, YouTube, Microsoft, and Yahoo? If yes, can you elaborate on the same?

DL: We are open to collaborating with large companies that influence the digital world, of course. The challenge is to find common ground on the digital channels and that we gain from the relationship.

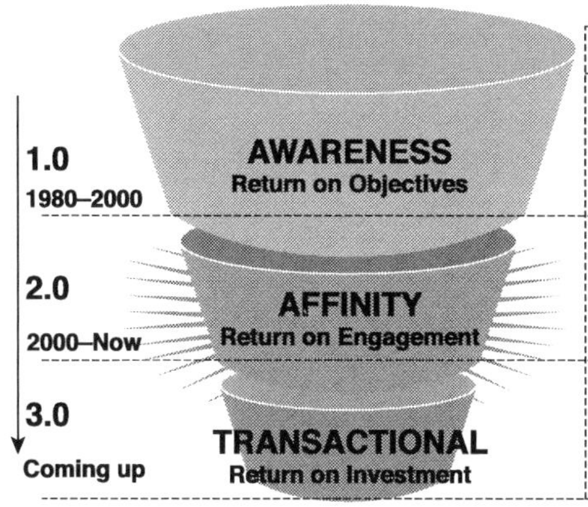

Type	Action	Assets	Expertise
Mass Marketing	Indirect ROI Traffic Reach Frequency	LED Perimeter Shirt Backdrop	IMG Sportfive Infront Mediapro
Relationship Marketing	Engagement Conversation *Content* *RTM*	Social media Schools CRM Technique	Carat Sport Havas S&E Mediacom
Transaction Marketing	E-commerce Big data *RTB* Direct ROI	Exclusive Relevant Personalised Offers	Criteo Xaxis I-prospect

Figure 21.5 The evolution of sponsorship and marketing approaches for football clubs

Source: Facebook & Twitter

Conclusion

The digital economy is a global fast moving and growing sector. New technologies and new digital platforms will not only transform sports marketing, but provide new opportunities for football clubs and their partners. Hence, e-sports marketing will have a fundamental role within any new strategic development of football clubs to network and dialogue with international e-fans. For now, sponsors are satisfied with content marketing, however, with the fast emergence of new disruptive online advertising techniques such as real time bidding and real time marketing, sponsors will soon request more access to the global online fanbase (Big Data) to empower their e-commerce platforms. The football industry will have to shift from a mass marketing approach to a relationship based marketing approach onwards to transactional marketing (Figure 21.5). Then a football club's digital sales performance would attract e-commerce giants, such as Amazon, eBay, Alibaba Group, Souq.com, Booking.com as sponsors, which have to date been disenchanted with the football industry's media supremacy.

Bibliography

Bolle, G. and Desbordes, M. (2005). *Marketing et football: Une perspective internationale*, Presses Universitaires du Sport.
Bolle, G. (2012). Interview of Dídac Lee on the digital strategy of FC Barcelona.
Chanavat, N. and Desbordes, M. (2014). Towards the regulation and restriction of ambush marketing? The case of the first truly social and digital mega sport event: Olympic Games London 2012, *International Journal of Sport Marketing*, 15(3), 151–60.
Covey, N. (2010). Changing models a global perspective on paying for content online, The Nielsen Company.
Desbordes, M. (2001). *Stratégie des entreprises dans le sport: Acteurs et management*, Editions Economica.
Gilbreath, B. (2010). *The next evolution of marketing*, McGraw Hill.
Keen, A. (2008). *The cult of the amateur*, DoubleDay.
Kenneth, C. and Mayer-Schonberger, V. (2013). *Big Data: A revolution that will transform how we live, work, and think*, Eamon Dolan/Houghton Mifflin Harcourt.
Kotler, P. (2007). FAQs marketing, Marshall Cavendish Business.
McCarthy, J., Rowley, J., Ashworth, C. J. and Pioch, E. (2014). Managing brand presence through social media: The case of UK football. *Internet Research*, 24(2), 181–204.

O'Reilly, T. (2009). What is Web 2.0, O'Reilly Media, Inc.

Price, J., Farrington, N. and Hall L. (2012). Changing the game? The impact of Twitter on relationship between football clubs, supporters and the sports media, *Soccer & Society*.

Taleb, N. N. (2014). *Antifragile: Things that gain from disorder*, Random House.

Ziglar, Z. (2014). *Secrets of closing the sale*, Revell.

Webography

Bailleul, A. (2012). L'application Eurosport player débarque sur androïd, Sport Buzz Business, 2012.

Blackshaw, P. (2011). Womma Summit Miami.

Bolle, G. (2013). Using message of sports as the great unifier, Gulf News.

Bolle, G. and Durou, E. (2013). Middle East lags global mobile advertising trend: report Deloitte/WPP, ITP.

Casanovas, J. M. (2011). El club espera doblar los ingresos con la nueva estrategia digital, Sport.es.

Eum, J. (2015). The next multibillion dollar tech trend from Asia: E-sports, VentureBeat.com

Lee, D. (2014). El Barça presenta el nuevo FCB Trivia Fans, Sport.es.

Merrett, G. (2011). The bench launches social games for Barcelona and Chelsea, Social Games Observer.

Serres, M. (2008). Les nouvelles technologies: Révolution culturelle et cognitive, INRIA, YouTube video.

Small, D. (2013). Football betting: The global gambling industry worth billions, BBC.com.

Zeldin, T. (2003). Combien de gens vous comprennent et vous apprécient, YouTube video.

Studies and reports

No Author (2010). Mobile youth around the world, December 2010, The Nielsen Company.

Durou, E. and Saguto, S. (2012). Arab Media Outlook 2011–2015, Dubai Press Club, Deloitte.

Fenez, M. (2011). Changing the game: Outlook for the global sports market to 2015, PWC.

Klopfer, A. and Ordon, K. (2009). Information and communications for development 2009: Extending reach and increasing impact, The World Bank.

Masters, S. (2010). The changing face of sport media, January 2010, The Nielsen Company.

Masters, S. (2011). State of the media: Year in sports 2010, The Nielsen Company.

Rivera, J. (2013). Forecast: Video Game Ecosystem, Worldwide.

Rooney, J. (2013). Behind the scenes of Oreo's real-time Super Bowl slam dunk, Forbes.

Smith, P. (2014). World football, Repucom.

PART VI

Marketing, ethics and development

Nicolas Chanavat, Simon Chadwick and Michel Desbordes

There is no doubt that sports play a number of roles; while the focus in this text is upon the commercial nature of sports marketing, sports have always fulfilled an important social role. It continues to do so: many sports teams, clubs and events are embedded in the communities where they are located; sports are often presented as a force for good, prompting social cohesion, equality of opportunity and healthy living; and sports are a reference point, a source of role models and heroes who influence people of all ages. This means that sports marketing is not simply a commercial activity or one principally associated with revenue generation or customer acquisition. It can entail pursuing CSR goals, promoting sports participation among target groups, or affecting social change. There are other socio-legal issues for sports marketers to consider, linked to the rights of citizens, the legal context of sports and the impact sports can have on people. This final part of the handbook addresses a wide-range of issues from CSR and sponsorship through to consumer perspectives on athlete transgressions, the marketing impact of governance decisions, and beyond.

22

GRASSROOTS SPORTS

Achieving corporate social responsibility through sponsorship

Marc Mazodier, Carolin Plewa, Karen Palmer and Pascale G. Quester

Introduction

The importance of grassroots sporting organizations for the social development of a region has become increasingly apparent, as benefits of community involvement in local sporting clubs are recognized (Houlihan and Green, 2006; Stewart et al., 2004). Grassroots sporting organizations are defined in this chapter as those organizations promoting participation in amateur sports, including local sporting clubs, domestic leagues and local sporting venues. These organizations have strong roots in the community or geographic area in which they operate and often rely on the support of local council funding, sponsorship from local businesses and volunteers from the community in order to operate. Hence, they are by their very nature deemed central to their local social fabric and the "backbone of the voluntary sporting system" (Wicker, Breuer and Hennigs, 2012: p. 318).

Yet research investigating the sponsorship of grassroots or community clubs and events is scarce in comparison to the wealth of information available on the effects of professional sporting sponsorship (Miloch and Lambrecht, 2006). Despite recognition from the sports management literature that grassroots sports sponsorship offers a unique potential to contribute to social development through corporate social responsibility opportunities, only a handful of exploratory studies have addressed this area to date (Pegoraro, O'Reilly and Levallet, 2009). This chapter aims to explore how grassroots sports sponsorship may create consumer perceptions of a sponsor's CSR image and, in turn, lead to desirable sponsorship outcomes, such as brand attitudes, brand trust and purchase intentions. In particular, it examines the importance of members' familiarity with the club's community initiatives, not only for the club but for its sponsors.

Grassroots sports sponsorship

Sponsorship is part of every modern sporting environment, with 69% of all sponsorship investments in North America dedicated to sporting clubs (IEG, 2013). Initially characterized by simple corporate donations, sponsorship has evolved significantly over the years, now reflecting long-term strategic partnerships focused on establishing a competitive advantage (Fahy et al., 2004). Indeed, prolific research has been undertaken to understand those sponsorship environments that offer access to large audiences, coupled with strong media presence and implied high visibility, and thus commercial sporting bodies (d'Astous and Bitz, 1995; Dowling, Robinson and Washington, 2013). Yet many sponsors seek community-based properties, such as grassroots sports organizations to achieve their objectives (Heckmann, 2000) and demonstrate their commitment to the community in which they operate (Lacey, Close and Finney, 2010; Plewa and Quester, 2011).

The advantages grassroots sports organizations hold for sponsors are threefold. First, they are focused typically on a particular geographic region, allowing for a concentrated effort of sponsors leveraging and activation activities (Miloch and Lambrecht, 2006). Second, the audience of grassroots sports organizations are characteristically more homogeneous than larger sports organizations, allowing for a uniform message to be highly effective (Pegoraro et al., 2009). Third, despite a smaller target market, sponsors of these organizations receive a greater return on investment due to the ability to reach consumers with a highly effective and targeted message (Miloch and Lambrecht, 2006). For example, since 2009, the National Australia Bank has sponsored the Australian Football League's (AFL) Auskick program to support more than 2,800 Auskick community centres utilized by more than 168,000 Australian children every week (National Australia Bank, 2013). Thus, the bank uses grassroots sports sponsorship to contribute to social development at the community level, communicate its CSR and benefit from being "a good sponsor".

Research in cause marketing suggests that consumers prefer local causes to national ones (Drumwright, 1996). Although grassroots sports properties offer greater returns on investments (Miloch and Lambrecht, 2006), they also have a strong potential to demonstrate CSR (Pegoraro et al., 2009), because consumers do not view their sponsorships as a form of promotion. Rather, firms appear to provide a service to society by sponsoring properties in need of support (Gwinner, 1997). However, to date, few studies have investigated grassroots sports sponsorship (Misener and Doherty, 2014), despite a wealth of research ascertaining the effects of larger sponsorships. The resultant inadequate understanding of sponsorship at this level limits not only our understanding of grassroots sports sponsorship in the literature but also development of specific guidelines for sponsors seeking to maximize their benefits from such engagement.

Corporate social responsibility in sport

Corporate social responsibility

Organizations are interwoven with the society in which they operate (Wood, 1991) and thus shoulder some responsibility to help ensure society's survival by maximizing benefits and minimizing harmful behaviour. Many authors have argued the case for businesses achieving profit maximization and social performance (Husted and De Jesus Salazar, 2006; Porter and Kramer, 2002). CSR, defined here as "a commitment to improve community well-being through discretionary business practices and contributions of corporate resources" (Kotler and Lee, 2004: p 3), is considered strategic when it provides substantial economic benefits and assists firms in achieving their basic function (Burke and Logsdon, 1996). This occurs when CSR initiatives put in place are central to the context of the firm and provide some benefit for primary stakeholders. Therefore, firms can choose strategically *where* they focus CSR and *how* they go about executing CSR for the purpose of achieving economic and social objectives (Porter and Kramer, 2002).

CSR activities have a unique effect on consumer information processing (Drumwright, 1996), consistent with attribution theory. Originally developed in social psychology literature, attribution theory refers to an area of research rather than one singular theory (Folkes, 1988; Weiner, 2000). It encompasses a number of theories developed to explain how people determine the causes of events they observe (Mizerski, Golden and Kernan, 1979). Human beings naturally search for order and consistency in the world around them and attempt to explain what they observe. In marketing, attribution research has been applied to many levels including consumer attributions of a firm's CSR behaviour (Klein and Dawar, 2004). In brief, attribution theory suggests a cognitive process by which individuals infer motives for an individual's or organization's behaviour; either as self-serving or altruistic (Dean, 2003; Kelley and Michela, 1980). Such inference of motives influences CSR perceptions, or the "associations that reflect a brand's character with respect to its social obligations" (Menon and Kahn, 2003: p. 317). Preliminary evidence shows clear benefits arising from such CSR perceptions, including attitudes, attractiveness, trust, identification, and, ultimately, purchase behaviour (Barone, Miyazaki and Taylor, 2000; Lacey and Kennett-Hensel, 2010; Marin, Ruiz and Rubio, 2009; Sen and Bhattacharya, 2001), showing particularly valuable for organizations in highly competitive markets (Kemper et al., 2013).

Corporate social responsibility in sports sponsorship

A recent amalgamation of CSR and sports management streams has led to a wealth of publications on sports CSR (Godfrey, 2009; Sheth and Babiak, 2010; Walker and Kent, 2009). Sports CSR takes the perspective that sports properties are members of society who are expected to support the communities in which they operate (Anagnostopoulos, Byers and Shilbury, 2014; Berrett and Slack, 2001). Sports teams, as businesses, are thus expected to operate as economic entities, within the existing legal framework and act ethically as society's standards dictate (Sheth and Babiak, 2010). An increase in community foundations developed in the professional sports industry supports this trend (Babiak and Wolfe, 2006; Babiak and Wolfe, 2009). Many sports teams invest in the development of their own socially responsible image and support their local communities in order to attract spectators and sponsors for revenue generation (Godfrey, 2009; Walters, 2009).

In addition, sports teams, leagues, players and venues have the unique ability to be socially responsible, as they sit between business and the community and are considered valuable by most stakeholders in a community. Currently, it is difficult to find a professional sports organization or team without a community program. In addition, professional sports leagues are more commonly implementing social development programs involving professional clubs to address social issues and act in a responsible manner (Walters, 2009), with community-based sports organizations also demonstrating their CSR by not only operating with a local focus but also proactively engaging in their resident community.

Such engagement may take the form of athlete volunteerism, educational initiatives, charitable donations and community initiatives and developments, all of which aim to provide assistance to the local communities in which the sporting clubs operate (Walker and Kent, 2009). Due to limited research dealing specifically with CSR initiatives of sporting clubs, we draw on findings from the broader business literature, which states that such initiatives enable organizations to express their CSR intentions (Gebler, 2006; Geroy, Wright and Jacoby, 2000; Peterson, 2004) and proactively support the well-being of local communities (Zappala and McLaren, 2004).

Despite evidence in the literature of the positive effects of demonstrating community support, research has also shown that consumer awareness of such initiatives in Australia is lacking (Pomering and Dolnicar, 2009), which is likely to explain why such initiatives may not have had the desired effect in practice (Mohr, Webb and Harris, 2001). Hence, we propose the need for consumers to be familiar with the sporting property's involvement in community initiatives, rather than involvement as such, as a predictor of the consumer perceptions of the property's CSR image. Hence:

H1: Familiarity with the property's involvement in community initiatives is positively associated with the property's CSR image.

Despite sports CSR being an emerging area of interest in industry and academia, few studies have explored the influence a sports property's image and the demonstration of its social responsibility in the community may have on the sponsor. Recently, however, Quester et al. (2013) examined the link between club member perceptions of the property's and sponsor's CSR image. Explained by meaning transfer predicted in balance theory (Heider, 1958; McCracken, 1989), positive perceptions related to the property's social responsibility were linked with stronger positive CSR image and goodwill towards the sponsor. Following this argument, we propose that sponsors benefit from the individuals' familiarity with the club's community involvement activities by means of a heightened property CSR image. Hence:

H2: Property CSR image mediates the association between familiarity with the property's involvement in community initiatives and sponsor CSR image.

Corporate image and, more specifically, the image of being a socially responsible corporate citizen, have been a central topic of interest given the deemed positive outcomes for organizations. Although the association between CSR and profit has appeared ambiguous or "equivocal" (Sen and Bhattacharya, 2001: p. 226), researchers have continued to conceptualize and empirically test the impact of CSR activities and image on consumer behaviour, in addition to the responses of other stakeholder groups. CSR activities and image have not only been associated with brand differentiation and a competitive edge (Brønn and Vrioni, 2001), organizations seen as proactively engaging in socially responsible activities can achieve enhanced consumer attitudes and purchase intention (Becker-Olsen, Cudmore and Hill, 2006; McDaniel, 1999). Indeed, research in multiple countries has confirmed its benefits related to patronage and loyalty (Bloom et al., 2006; Maignan, 2001), with Sen and Bhattacharya (2001) confirming a direct impact of CSR on purchase intent for some consumers. In line with extant research, we hypothesize sponsor CSR image to mediate the relationship between property CSR image and outcomes for the sponsor:

H3: Sponsor CSR image mediates the association between property CSR image and sponsor (a) brand attitude, (b) brand trust, and (c) purchase intent.

The model provided in Figure 22.1 summarizes the conceptual framework tested in this study.

Method

The empirical test of this conceptual model relies on an online survey instrument, developed for, and distributed to, the members of a local Australian Rules Football sporting club. This popular sport enjoys a strong following in local communities, and though each club can draw on an existing membership and sponsor base, they also need continuing sponsorship funding to maintain and enhance operations on and off the field. The primary reasons led to the choice of sporting club for this study. First, the club has a long tradition and a loyal fan base

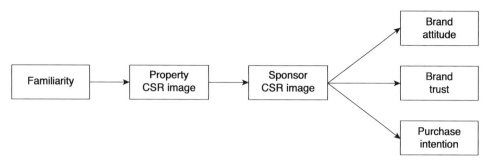

Figure 22.1 Conceptual framework

within the local community. Second, its players are primarily amateur players, many of which started their football career in local junior competitions. Third, the club has a very strong focus on social responsibility by initiating or supporting various programs benefiting the local and regional communities. For this study, we chose one of the focal club's sponsors, a large electrical appliance retailer. Given the activation strategy enacted throughout the season, members' awareness of the association was expected to be high.

The survey items came from existing scales in sponsorship, sports management, and CSR literature (see Table 22.1). An invitation for participation in this research was sent by email to 1,900 members of the club, leading to 319 valid responses. Although 8.5% of the respondents noted that they did not commonly attend games, nearly 30% declared that they attended all games of the season. The demographics of our sample are deemed similar to the club membership, with a majority of male respondents (84.3%) and a mean age of 48 years of age. Although these characteristics are relevant to note, they are not deemed influential in this research, with previous studies illustrating no significant impact of age or gender on sponsorship effectiveness (Coppetti et al., 2009; Stotlar, 1993).

Discussion of results

Path analysis was undertaken to examine the cause and effect relationships between sponsor and property CSR variables, with model fit indices suggesting a suitable model fit ($\chi^2_{(145)}$ = 264.997, p = .000, CFI = .980, SRMR = .047, RMSEA = .051). The results support all three hypotheses of the study. In line with hypothesis 1, familiarity with property CSR initiatives is a significant predictor of sports property CSR, with a standardized path coefficient of .21 (p<.001). Grassroots sporting clubs already possess a close link to the community by means of their regular activities. However, engagement in community initiatives can help to strengthen the consumer's perceived association between the club and community welfare (Walker and Kent, 2009). For such engagement to be acknowledged by consumers and reflects in the club's CSR image, consumers need to be made aware of such engagement. Although research is yet to examine CSR communications in a sporting context, existing literature in other contexts suggests the need for a strategic and balanced approach, as an image can be damaged should an organization be perceived as not delivering on its CSR communications (Polonsky and Jevons, 2009; Reisch, 2006).

To investigate whether property CSR image mediates the relation between familiarity with the CSR initiatives and sponsor CSR image, a path model was tested using Mplus Version 7.1. The indirect effect tested using bootstrapped standard errors was significant

Table 22.1 Measurement items, sources, and item loadings

	Type	Item loadings
Perceived sponsor CSR image (Dean, 2003; Menon and Kahn, 2003)	Likert	
[Brand] fulfils its social responsibilities.		.90
[Brand] gives back to society.		.88
I think that [Brand] acts with society's interests in mind.		.85
[Brand] acts in a socially responsible way.		.85
Perceived sports property CSR image (Dean, 2003; Menon and Kahn, 2003)	Likert	
[Property] fulfils its social responsibilities.		.80
[Property] gives back to society.		.82
I think that [Property] acts with society's interests in mind.		.87
[Property] acts in a socially responsible way.		.87
Congruence (Rifon et al., 2004)	SD	
Not compatible/Compatible		.97
Not a good fit/A good fit		.99
Congruent/Not congruent		.95
Purchase Intent (Mohr and Webb, 2005)	SD	
Unlikely/Very likely		.93
Impossible/Possible		.97
No chance/Certain		.92
Brand trust (Becker-Olsen et al., 2006)	Likert	
[Company] is a business I can trust.		.87
[Company] has strong value system.		.88
[Company] is a business that cares about its customers.		.84
[Company] is a business I believe in.		.85
Brand attitude (Becker-Olsen et al., 2006)	SD	
Good/Bad		.95
Favourable/Unfavourable		.98
Positive/Negative		.96

(β = .093, p<.01), as was the direct effect (β = .179, p<.001). These findings support a partial mediation. Individuals who are familiar with the property's involvement in community initiatives evaluate the sponsor more favourably. Yet this effect is only partly due to the enhanced club's CSR image; with the significant direct effect suggesting an understanding of

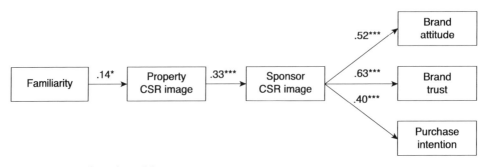

Figure 22.2 Results path model

the wide-reaching effect of sponsors' contributions to the club into various community initiatives. This insight is of particular importance to sponsors seeking to utilize their engagement in grassroots sports to enhance consumer perceptions of the organization's social responsibility. It allows organizations to identify and sponsor those properties that are respected for their social engagement within the organization's target audience.

Tested with the same method, indirect paths from property CSR image to sponsor brand attitude, brand trust and purchase are significant (respectively β = .206, p<.001; β = .254, p<.001; β = .156, p<.001) and the direct paths exhibit non-significance (p>.05). Hence, as expected, the impact of property CSR image on brand attitude, brand trust and purchase intent was fully mediated by sponsor CSR image. In line with extant literature in other contexts, being seen as a socially responsible corporation improves consumer attitudes and behavioural intentions, tested here by means of brand attitude (p=.46, p<.001), brand trust (β =.60, p<.001), and purchase intention (β =.34, p<0.001).

Summary and implications

As sponsors face increasingly uncertain financial environments (O'Reilly, 2009), they must develop a better understanding of how to utilize benefits offered by grassroots sports organizations to support the most effective use of sponsorship budgets. Despite the unique potential of grassroots sports properties for sponsors, few exploratory studies examine sponsorships at community levels (Miloch and Lambrecht, 2006; Pegoraro et al., 2009). In particular, a gap of knowledge remains as to whether the sponsorship of grassroots sports can achieve perceptions of CSR for the sponsor, as well as how the CSR image of a pro-perty may be relevant in this context. This research contributes to the sponsorship, sports marketing and CSR literatures, as we develop our understanding of how grassroots sponsorships may help sponsors establish and foster their CSR image, leading to desirable outcomes for their brand.

Sponsors aiming to achieve CSR image effects from their sponsorship should not only take into account consumer perceptions of the property's CSR image but also the engagement a property shows in enhancing society's perceptions of its social contributions, as well as its communication of such engagement. Familiarity with such engagement appears to be a precondition for it to impact on the property's CSR image and, in turn, benefit the sponsor. Hence, to attract and keep sponsors interested in utilizing sponsorship of grassroots sporting organisation as a CSR initiative, the property needs to devise communication strategies developing a wide-ranging awareness of its community initiatives among the sponsors' target audience. Many grassroots sporting clubs are actively engaged within their community anyway, an asset that can be harnessed not only for the benefit of the community and through their membership base but also when seeking financial support through sponsors.

However, it is important to note that it takes time for consumers to learn about a firm's CSR initiatives, increasing the importance of a strategic approach to CSR communications to enable the club and sponsor to derive value from their respective investments (Mohr and Webb, 2005; Polonsky and Jevons, 2009). Engaging in communication with stakeholders, such as consumers, also allows properties to listen to the market, monitor and respond appropriately to the key issues that are important to these stakeholders (Beckmann, Morsing and Reisch, 2006). Many firms make substantial investments in CSR programs in order to demonstrate affinity with stakeholders, but often with no measurement in place resulting in the inefficient use of corporate resources (Bloom et al., 2006). CSR-focused communications can provide properties with channels through which they can measure response to CSR-initiatives, increasing the efficiency of their initiatives, and contribution to the community in which they operate.

As with all research, some limitations need to be acknowledged. For example, this research investigates only one grassroots sports club and, therefore, our results should be tested in other contexts, for example, with various types of sports, sponsors, and sponsorship scenarios. Rigorous empirical work should determine whether consumers perceive the sponsorship of various grassroots organizations as CSR and what other outcomes sponsors might expect. Further research should also examine how external stakeholders (for example, community members) respond to a sponsorship in terms of attitudes and behaviours towards the sponsor. The cross-sectional nature of the present research limits our ability to draw strong inferences about the variables' sequence. A longitudinal study would offer a robust method to test these causal relationships further and to consider changes in congruence. Future studies may also further investigate fit, for example, considering longitudinal effects through learning (Woisetschläger and Michaelis, 2012) or testing the relevance of separating image and functional fit (Bigné, Currás-Pérez and Aldás-Manzano, 2012).

Acknowledgments

The authors express their sincere gratitude for the support of this research by the Commonwealth Government as part of the ARC Linkage Grant Scheme as well as our industry partner.

References

Anagnostopoulos, C., Byers, T. and Shilbury, D. (2014). Corporate social responsibility in professional team sport organizations: Towards a theory of decision-making. *European Sport Management Quarterly,* DOI: 10.1080/16184742.2014.897736.

Babiak, K. and Wolfe, R. (2006). More than just a game? Corporate social responsibility and Super Bowl XL, *Sport Marketing Quarterly* 15, pp. 214–222.

Babiak, K., and Wolfe, R. (2009). Determinants of corporate social responsibility in professional sport: Internal and external factors. *Journal of Sport Management,* 23, pp. 717–742.

Barone, M. J., Miyazaki, A. D. and Taylor, K. A. (2000). The influence of cause-related marketing on consumer choice: Does one good turn deserve another? *Journal of the Academy of Marketing Science,* 28(2), pp. 248–262.

Becker-Olsen, K. L., Cudmore, B. A. and Hill, R. P. (2006). The impact of perceived corporate social responsibility on consumer behaviour, *Journal of Business Research* 59(1), pp. 46–53.

Beckmann, S. C., Morsing, M. and Reisch, L. (2006). Strategic CSR communications: An emerging field. In M. Morsing and S. C. Beckmann (Eds.), *Strategic CSR Communications* (First ed.). Copenhagen: DJOF Publishing.

Berrett, T. and Slack, T. (2001). A framework for the analysis of strategic approaches employed by non-profit sport organizations in seeking corporate sponsorship, *Sport Management Review*, 4, pp. 21–45.

Bigné, E., Currás-Pérez, R. and Aldás-Manzano, J. (2012). Dual nature of cause-brand fit: Influence on corporate social responsibility consumer perception, *European Journal of Marketing*, 46(3), pp. 575–594.

Bloom, P. N., Hoeffler, S., Lane Keller, K. and Meza, C. E. B. (2006). How social-cause marketing affects consumer perceptions, *MIT Sloan Management Review,* 47(2), pp. 49–55.

Brønn, P. S. and Vrioni, A. B. (2001). Corporate social responsibility and cause-related marketing: An overview, *International Journal of Advertising*, 20, pp. 207–222.

Burke, L. and Logsdon, J. M. (1996). How corporate social responsibility pays off. *Long Range Planning,* 29(4), pp. 495–502.

Coppetti, C., Wentzel, D., Tomczac, T. and Henkel, S. (2009). Improvement of incongruent sponsorships through articulation of the sponsorship and audience participation, *Journal of Marketing Communications,* 15(1), pp. 17–34.

D'Astous, A. and Bitz, P. (1995). Consumer evaluations of sponsorship programs, *European Journal of Marketing*, 29(12), pp. 6–17.

Dean, D. H. (2003). Consumer perceptions of corporate donations, *Journal of Advertising*, 32(4), pp. 91–102.

Dowling, M., Robinson, L. and Washington, M. (2013). Taking advantage of the London 2012 Olympic Games: Corporate social responsibility through sport partnerships. *European Sport Management Quarterly*, 13(3), 269–292.

Drumwright, M. E. (1996). Company advertising with a social dimension: The role of noneconomic criteria, *Journal of Marketing*, 60(4), pp. 71–87.

Fahy, J., Farrelly, F. and Quester, P. G. (2004). Competitive advantage through sponsorship: A conceptual model and research propositions, *European Journal of Marketing*, 38(8), pp. 1013–1030.

Folkes, V. S. (1988). Recent attribution research in consumer behavior: A review and new directions. *Journal of Consumer Research*, 14(4), pp. 548–565.

Gebler, D. (2006). Creating an ethical culture, *Strategic Finance,* 87(11), pp. 28–34.

Geroy, G. D., Wright, P. C. and Jacoby, L. (2000). Toward a conceptual framework of employee volunteerism: An aid for the human resource manager, *Management Decision,* 38(4), pp. 280–286.

Godfrey, P. (2009). Corporate social responsibility in sport: An overview and key issues, *Journal of Sport Management*, 24, pp. 698–716.

Gwinner, K. P. (1997). A model of image creation and image transfer in event sponsorship, *International Marketing Review*, 14(3), pp. 145–158.

Heckman, J. (2000). Sponsorships, *Marketing News*, 34(2), p. 16.

Heider, F. (1958). *The psychology of interpersonal relations*, New York: John Wiley.

Houlihan, B., and Green, M. (2006). The changing status of school sport and physical education: explaining policy change, *Sport, Education and Society,* 11(1), pp. 73–92.

Husted, B. W. and De Jesus Salazar, J. (2006). Taking Friedman seriously: Maximizing profits and social performance. *Journal of Management Studies,* 43(1), pp. 75–91.

IEG. (2013). International Events Group. 2013 Sponsorship outlook: Spending increase is double-edged sword, www.sponsorship.com/iegsr/2013/01/07/2013-Sponsorship-Outlook--Spending-Increase-Is-Dou.aspx (accessed 29 October 2013).

Kelley, H. H. and Michela, J. L. (1980). Attribution theory and research, *Annual Review of Psychology*, 31, pp. 457–501.

Kemper, J., Schilke, O., Reimann, M., Wang, Xuyi and Brettel, M. (2013). Competition-motivated corporate social responsibility, *Journal of Business Research*, 66(10), pp. 1954–1963.

Klein, J. and Dawar, N. (2004). Corporate social responsibility and consumers' attributions and brand evaluations in a product–harm crisis. *International Journal of Research in Marketing,* 21(3), pp. 203–217.

Kotler, P. and Lee, N. (2004). *Corporate social responsibility: Doing the most good for your company and your cause*, Hoboken: John Wiley.

Lacey, R. and Kennett-Hensel, P. A. (2010). Longitudinal effects of corporate social responsibility on customer relationships, *Journal of Business Ethics*, 97(4), pp. 581–597.

Lacey, R., Close, A. G. and Finney, R. Z. (2010). The pivotal roles of product knowledge and corporate social responsibility in event sponsorship effectiveness, *Journal of Business Research*, 63(11), pp. 1222–1228.

Maignan, I. (2001). Consumer perceptions of corporate social responsibilities: A cross-cultural comparison, *Journal of Business Ethics,* 30, pp. 57–72.

Marin, L., Ruiz, S. and Rubio, A. (2009). The role of identity salience in the effects of corporate social responsibility on consumer behaviour, *Journal of Business Ethics*, 84(1), pp. 65–78.

McCracken, G. (1989). Who is the celebrity endorser? Cultural foundations of the endorsement process, *Journal of Consumer Research*, 16(3), pp. 310–321.

McDaniel, S. R. (1999). An investigation of match-up effects in sport sponsorship advertising: The implications of consumer advertising schemas, *Psychology & Marketing*, 16, pp. 163–184.

Menon, S. and Kahn, B. E. (2003). Corporate sponsorships of philanthropic activities: When do they impact perception of sponsor brand?, *Journal of Consumer Psychology*, 13(3), pp. 316–327.

Miloch, K. S. and Lambrecht, K. W. (2006). Consumer awareness of sponsorship at grassroots sport events, *Sport Marketing Quarterly*, 15(3), pp. 147–154.

Misener, K. and Doherty, A. (2014). In support of sport: Examining the relationship between community sport organizations and sponsors. *Sport Management Review*, http://dx.doi.org/10.1016/j.smr.2013.12.002

Mizerski, R. W., Golden, L. L. and Kernan, J. B. (1979). The attribution process in consumer decision making. *Journal of Consumer Research*, 6(2), pp. 123–140.

Mohr, L. A. and Webb, D. J. (2005). The effects of corporate social responsibility and price on consumer responses. *Journal of Consumer Affairs*, 39(1), pp. 121–147.

Mohr, L. A., Webb, D. J. and Harris, K. E. (2001). Do consumers expect companies to be socially responsible? The impact of corporate social responsibility on buying behavior, *Journal of Consumer Affairs*, 35(1), pp. 45–72.

National Australia Bank (2013). NAB AFL Auskick, www.aflauskick.com/nab-competitions/nab-and-the-afl/ (accessed 13 June 2013).

O'Reilly, N. (2009). Sponsorship and the global economic crisis, *Journal of Sponsorship*, 2(2), pp. 111–112.

Pegoraro, A., O'Reilly, N. and Levallet, N. (2009). Gender-based sponsorship of grassroots events as an agent of corporate social responsibility: The case of a national women's triathlon series, *Journal of Sponsorship*, 2(2), pp. 140–151.

Peterson, D. K. (2004). Benefits of participation in corporate volunteer programs: Employees' perceptions, *Personnel Review*, 33(6), pp. 615–627.

Plewa, C. and Quester, P. Q. (2011). Sponsorship and CSR: Is there a link? A conceptual framework, *International Journal of Sport Marketing and Sponsorship*, 12(4), pp. 301–317.

Polonsky, M. J. and Jevons, C. (2009). Global branding and strategic CSR: An overview of three types of complexity, *International Marketing Review*, 26(3), pp. 327–347.

Pomering, A. and Dolnicar, S. (2009). Addressing the prerequisite of successful CSR implementation: Are consumers aware of CSR initiatives? *Journal of Business Ethics*, 85(2), pp. 285–301.

Porter, M. E. and Kramer, M. R. (2002). The competitive advantage of corporate philanthropy, *Harvard Business Review*, 80(12), pp. 56–69.

Quester, P., Plewa, C., Palmer, K. and Mazodier, M. (2013). Determinants of community-based sponsorship impact on self-congruity, *Psychology & Marketing*, 30(11), pp. 996–1007.

Reisch, L. (2006). Communicating CSR to consumers: An empirical study. In M. Morsing and S. C. Beckmann (Eds.), *Strategic CSR Communications*. Copenhagen: DJOF Publishing.

Rifon, N. J., Choi, S. M., Trimble, C. S. and Li, H. (2004). Congruence effects in sponsorship, *Journal of Advertising*, 33(1), pp. 29–42.

Sen, S. and Bhattacharya, C. B. (2001). Does doing good always lead to doing better? Consumer reactions to corporate social responsibility, *Journal of Marketing Research*, 38(2), pp. 225–243.

Sheth, E. and Babiak, K. M. (2010). Beyond the game: Perceptions and practices of corporate social responsibility in the professional sport industry, *Journal of Business Ethics*, 92(3), pp. 433–450.

Stewart, B., Nicholson, M., Smith, A. and Westerbeek, H. (2004). *Australian sport: Better by design?* London: Routledge.

Stotlar, D. K. (1993). Sponsorship and the Olympic Winter Games, *Sport Marketing Quarterly*, 2(1), pp. 35–43.

Walker, M. and Kent, A. (2009). Do fans care? Assessing the influence of corporate social responsibility on consumer attitudes in the sport industry, *Journal of Sport Management*, 23, pp. 743–769.

Walters, G. (2009). Corporate social responsibility through sport: The community sports trust model as a CSR delivery agency. *Journal of Corporate Citizenship*, 35, pp. 81–94.

Weiner, B. (2000). Attributional thoughts about consumer behavior. *Journal of Consumer Research*, 27(3), pp. 382–387.

Wicker, P., Breuer, C. and Hennigs, B. (2012). Understanding the interactions among revenue categories using elasticity measures: Evidence from a longitudinal sample of non-profit sport clubs in Germany, *Sport Management Review*, 15, pp. 318–329.

Woisetschläger, D. M. and Michaelis, M. (2012). Sponsorship congruence and brand image: A pre-post event analysis, *European Journal of Marketing*, 46(3), pp. 509–523.

Wood, D. J. (1991). Corporate social performance revisited, *Academy of Management Review*, 16(4), pp. 691–718.

Zappala, G. and McLaren, J. (2004). A functional approach to employee volunteering: An exploratory study, *Australian Journal on Volunteering*, 9(1), pp. 41–54.

23

MARKETING SPORTS AND RECREATION PARTICIPATION

Kostas Alexandris and Dan Funk

Introduction

Acknowledging the role of sports participation on citizens' quality of life, the European Union adopted a Communication Paper, entitled "Developing the European Dimension in Sport", in which specific actions regarding the societal role of sports were provided. Part of this strategy was the inclusion of a chapter within the Eurobarometer (2014), aiming to collect data on sports participation and provide a comparative report for the EU members. To the best of our knowledge, this is the most detailed report published to date, on cross-cultural aspects of sports participation (EU members). Some of the key findings are the followings:

- 59% of EU citizens never or seldom exercise, while only 41% exercises at least once a week. The proportion of non-participants increased from 39% (2009) to 41% (2013).
- 48% of EU citizens do some form of other physical activity (such as cycling, dancing or gardening) at least once a week, while 30% never do any kind of physical activity.
- 13% of EU citizens do not walk for at least 10 minutes at a time within a week. In addition, on a usual day, about two-thirds (69%) of individuals spend between 2.5 and 8.5 hours sitting, while at other extremes, 11% sit for more than 8.5 hours and 17% sit for 2.5 hours or less.
- Sports or physical activity takes place in a wide range of locations, most commonly in parks and outdoors (40%), at home (36%) or on the journey between home and school, work or shops (25%).

Similar statistics have been reported worldwide. On analyzing global data Hallal et al. (2012) reported that 31% of the adult population worldwide is physically inactive. North America has the highest percentage of inactive residents (43.3%), followed by the Eastern Mediterranean (35%). These figures represent participation in any kind of physical activity (organized and unorganized), which suggests that the participation rates for sports and recreation activities and recreation is likely much lower.

Within the sports participatory market, outdoor managed sports events (for example, rural marathons, mountain biking, obstacle events, triathlon, etc.) has emerged as a poplar activity for individuals over the last decade (Alexandris and Kaplanidou, 2014). Although global trends on participation in such sports events do not exist, country and local statistics show their development, in contrast to the general sports and recreation participation data, which are not the same positive. In the USA, for example, the sports event sector is a prominent one and among the fastest developing markets within sports tourism, as there was a 10.5% event growth from 2010 to 2012 (Schumacher, 2012).

The recent trend in the popularity of organized outdoor sports events highlights the potential benefit of investing in such events for public health officials. Considering that low sports participation rates are related to increased obesity, health problems and medical expenses, and lower low work productivity and quality of life (Min Lee et al., 2012), promoting sports participation within local communities should be a priority among governments worldwide today. In their conceptual paper, Rowe et al. (2013) argued that sports management and marketing literature in the area of active sports participation is limited and represents a promising area for applied and theoretical research in this important sector. Given outdoor events are discretionary activities and highly susceptible to economic and social forces, understanding what influences consumer demand for such events is required. A beneficial means to understand this demand is through the role of decision-making.

A decision-making model of sports participation

In order to develop effective strategies to market sports and recreation participation, we need to understand the key factors that influence an individual's decision-making for taking part. We will discuss some of these factors, taking as a base a general consumer behavior model (Shiffman and Kanuk, 2010), which organizes them into a sequence (see Figure 23.1). According to this model, these factors can be categorized as input factors, process factors and outcome factors. Each of these categories is discussed in the following sections.

The input factors

The Input factors represent a wide range of influential forces that can influence the initial decision to engage in a sports activity (participate or not) as well as subsequent participation (continuation). Inputs are represented by two categories. The marketing mix: product, price, place/channel of distribution, promotion, personnel, physical evidence, and process; and the socio-cultural factors. The discussion of the elements of the marketing mix is beyond the scope of this chapter, and the reader is encouraged to consult a sports marketing textbook (for example, Shilbury et al., 2014). It should be emphasized that the unique characteristics of participatory sports services (for example, intangibility, heterogeneity, perishability, as well as they are consumed in social situations, involve actual participation and personal investment in time and physical effort) should be considered when developing marketing strategies. The factors that influence sports participation and are related to the socio-cultural environment

Figure 23.1 A consumer decision-making process

Source: Adapted from Shiffman and Kanuk (2010)

are diverse. In this chapter we will focus on the following five factors: gender, age, family status, social class, and culture.

Gender

The role of gender on influencing sports participation has been observed in previous research. In most countries, women have traditionally been reported to have lower sports and recreation participation rates than men. In the 2014 Eurobarometer it was reported that in the countries of Belgium, France, Greece, Latvia, Lithuania, Slovakia, Spain, and the UK, men were more likely to report being regularly active in sports than women. In Denmark, Finland, Sweden, and the Netherlands the patterns were reversed (higher sports participation rates for women than men) (Van Tuyckom, Scheerder and Bracke, 2010). Studies have also shown that women's sports participation rates have been increasing over the last ten years, and the gap between men's and women's sports participation rates is closing down (at least in some countries) (Chalabaev et al., 2013; Scheerder and Vos, 2011). Furthermore, there are certain activities (for example, fitness), in which women have higher participation rates than men.

There are key environmental factors that have contributed to the increase in women's sports participation, including changes in women's lifestyle, in their role in the family and society, and in their working status, as well as increased promotion of women's sports in mass and social media, provision of sporting opportunities for women, and increased information about the benefits of sports participation.

TOPICS WITH MARKETING INTEREST

Sports marketers should therefore understand women's unique characteristics and needs before designing marketing strategies for them. Some of the main issues that should be considered include:

- Understanding the cultural aspects influencing women's sports participation (for example, religion, societal roles, family roles, etc.).
- Promoting new sports (for example, outdoors) and not only traditional sports (for example, fitness).
- Promoting family sports for married women.
- Providing sports education by explaining the benefits of sports participation.
- Considering the social aspect of sports program delivery.
- Further segmenting the women's group, according to age and family status.
- Developing targeted promotion and communication strategies.

Age and sports participation

The negative influence of age on recreational sports participation has been well documented. According to Eurobarometer (2014), the amount of regular activity that people do tends to decrease with age: 71% of women and 70% of men in the 55+ age groups never or seldom exercise or play sports. Similar statistics were reported in other countries. In Scotland, it was reported that participation in sports drops from around 80% for adults aged 16–24 to around 45% for people over 55 years old (www.scotland.gov.uk). Similar results were reported in Australia (www.abs.gov.au/ausstats) and Canada (www.pch.gc.ca). In the United States, 29% of individuals who belong within the age group 50–64 years do not participate in any form of physical activity. These figures are further decreasing among individuals more than 65 years old.

Considering the aging of the population in most of the developed countries worldwide (for a detailed discussion see Lee and Masson, 2011) it is clear that marketing efforts should be developed to promote sports and recreation participation among older individuals. It is predicted, for example, that until 2025 more than 25% of the US population will be individuals more than 65 years old.

The argument that older individuals (65+) are not a good target group for sports promotion is a myth today. From a marketing perspective, older individuals (65+) satisfy the main segmentation criteria. First of all, it is a large and increasing market; second, it is a market that can be identified and communicated. There are aging organizations all over the world that are willing to co-operate with sports organizations in order to promote sports participation among them. Third, specific actions can be developed; there are certain sports and recreation programs today that are certified by sports scientists to be appropriate for older individuals (for example, walking, fitness for old people, aqua aerobics, etc.).

OLDER INDIVIDUALS AND MARKETING STRATEGIES

Based on the above discussion, some strategies for promoting sports and recreation participation among old individuals could include:

- Marketing research, used to identify their preferences, needs and constraints for participation.
- Co-operation among local authorities, sports and aging associations in national and international levels.
- Communication campaigns, informing about the benefits of sports and recreation participation for old individuals.
- Sports programs, "packaged" and promoted in an attractive way for old individuals.
- Sports practitioners and providers, trained to design and deliver sports programs for old individuals in an attractive manner.

Family status and sports participation

Marital status is one of the demographic variables, in which mixed results have been reported. Gratton and Taylor (2000) found no significant differences between single and married individuals in terms of sports participation and the same was reported by Van Tuyckom et al. (2010) in a European study. However, in other studies (for example, Alexandris et al., 2009), it was reported that married individuals participate in sports less than single individuals. It could be suggested that a more detailed approach should be adopted in order to study sports and recreation participation, with the application of the family lifecycle concept (Shiffman and Kanuk, 2010). The family lifecycle includes a series of stages, which show the development of an individual from young to aging, in relation to demographic factors and the family. This will help researchers to understand the changes in recreational sports behavior from stage to stage and marketers to develop targeted communication strategies, based on the needs of families in each stage.

Social class

Social class is defined as a homogeneous group of people who have common values, lifestyle and behavior (Shiffman and Kanuk, 2010). Wealth, power, and social status are three elements that relate very much to the definition of social class. Power relates to the ability of an individual to influence aspects of social and professional life, while status relates to social recognition. The three most common variables that define social class are: income, education, occupation. It is expected that these three variables are usually correlated. Lifestyle is a fourth variable that might also relate to social class. The social class variables are used for market segmentation.

In the area of sports and recreation there are studies that tried to investigate the influence of social class on sports and recreation participation, as well as the influence of social class on the selection of specific sports and recreation activities. Most of the studies ended with the conclusion that social class is one of the factors that can be used to predict sports and recreation behavior (for detailed reviews see Beenackers et al., 2012; Scheerder and Vos, 2011). Some conclusions are common to most of the studies. First, sports and recreation participation relates to the level of education. More educated individuals usually have higher participation rates. This shows that with an increase in the level of education we could expect higher sports participation rates. Second, sports and recreation participation relates to income. Individuals with higher income are more likely to participate in sports and recreation activities. Third, sports and recreation participation relates, probably indirectly, to occupation. Classifying the different types of jobs is a difficult task, especially in applying a global model.

Although research on the role of social class on sports and recreation participation is not recent, it could be argued that due to certain changes in the macro environment and the financial situation in many countries (for example, economic crisis), it is an area in which ongoing research should be conducted.

The changing image of some sports in relation to the profile of sports participants is also an issue that deserves to be studied. Sports that used to be elite, such as tennis and skiing, and fast developing sports, such as snowboard and street sports, are good cases that should be studied in relation to social class. Finally, it has to be emphasized that sports and recreation have important social objectives related to social welfare and quality of life. As such, governments and local authorities should identify the disadvantaged social groups in terms of sports and recreation participation and promote sports to them.

Culture and ethnicity

Culture is defined by the set of values, beliefs, and traditions developed from childhood and transferred from generation to generation (Shiffman and Kanuk, 2010). Studying culture is important in the case of international sports marketing. The role of culture should be considered in developing new sports services for entering into new international markets. A very simple example for understanding the role of culture in sports and recreation behavior is the popularity of different sports in different countries. Soccer, for example, is the most popular sport in the United Kingdom, while baseball and (American) football are the most popular in the United States. Cross-cultural studies have shown that sports participation patterns differ among different countries. According to Eurobarometer (2014), citizens in the northern part of the EU are the most physically active. The proportion who exercise or play sports at least once a week is 70% in Sweden, 68% in Denmark, 66% in Finland, 58% in the Netherlands and 54% in Luxembourg. The lowest levels of participation are reported in the southern EU Member States. Most respondents who never exercise or play sports can be found in Bulgaria (78%), Malta (75%), Portugal (64%), Romania (60%) and Italy (60%). These differentiations can be related to cultural issues, but they can also reflect each country's investment in promoting recreational sports participation among their citizens.

Understanding culture is also important in countries where there are different ethnic and racial groups (Pires, Stanton and Stanton, 2011). Studies conducted in North America (for example, Stodoloska and Alexandris, 2004; Stodoloska et al., 2011), have shown how the culture of some groups (for example, Latin American, Asians, etc.) influence their everyday life, leisure behavior and of course sports participation.

TOPICS WITH MARKETING INTEREST

Some issues that sports marketers should consider when targeting different cultural and ethnic groups include:

*   Studying and recognizing the values of the different cultural and ethnic groups.
*   Respecting these values and developing sports in a way to accommodate the needs of these groups.
*   Positioning sports and recreation as a social activity which helps their social integration and inclusion.
*   Promoting sports programs that fit with the culture of the targeted groups (for example, popular sports activities).
*   Use of communication media in the language of the target groups (for example, Latin American, Asians, etc.).
*   Use of communication media that fits with the culture of the targeted groups (for example, formal media and social groups).

The process factors

This includes factors related to internal and psychological constructs, which influence the decision-making process for sports and recreation participation. Three of the most applicable factors in the context of sports and recreation participation are: Needs and motivation, constraints and attitudes.

Needs and motivation

The concept of motivation refers to the forces that initiate, direct and sustain human behavior (Iso-Ahola, 1999). There are several motivation theories that have been applied in the context of participatory sports. One of the most applicable is the self-determination theory (Deci and Ryan, 1985). It was proposed that there are several types of motivation that fall at different points along a self-determination continuum. This continuum runs from high to low levels of self-determination, as one moves from intrinsic motivation to extrinsic motivation, and finally to amotivation. Intrinsic motivation refers to doing an activity for its own sake, for the pleasure and satisfaction derived simply from performing it. When a person is intrinsically motivated, behavior will be performed voluntarily, in the absence of external rewards (Deci and Ryan, 1985). Extrinsic motivation refers to behavior that is engaged in as a means to an end and not for its own sake. It is mainly related to social approval (for example, affiliation to a group and social concern) and external rewards (for example, financial and recognition for accomplishment). Amotivation refers to the stage when an individual has no real incentives to participate in a recreational activity.

The measurement of needs and motivation is a topic with particular interest for marketers. In the context of sports and recreation, the Recreation Experience Preference scale (Manfredo, Driver and Tarrant, 1996) has been applied extensively. Recreation experience was viewed as "the package or bundle of psychological outcomes desired from a recreation engagement"

(p. 189). Individuals are engaged in recreation activities (for example, trekking) in order to achieve certain psychological outcomes (for example, stress relief). It was proposed that since the psychological outcome dimensions covered by the scale are extensive, researchers can determine which are applicable in the context of their studies and use shortened versions of the scale. The most common motivation factors, which have been revealed in participatory sports and recreation studies, are:

- Fun/enjoyment.
- Health/fitness.
- Escape/relaxation.
- Competition/achievement.
- Socialization.
- Learning/skill development.

Research on sports and recreation motivation is useful for marketing purposes. Sports marketers should identify what drives individuals to take part in recreational sports and try to satisfy these needs by packaging and delivering appropriate sports programs and services. There have been studies successfully showing how motivation can be used as a variable to cluster groups of participants. In the study by Alexandris et al. (2007), for example, recreational skiers were categorized into "novice", "multi-interest", "naturalist" and "enthusiast", while in the study by Prayag and Grivel (2014), youth participants in a handball event were segmented into "Indifferent", "Enthusiast", "Socializer", "Competitive". Such segmentations into groups with common motivational patterns are useful in order to guide the development of appropriate marketing and communication strategies. Those, who, for example, are motivated by social needs, should be guided to participate in sports programs that promote socialization (for example, team activities), while those who are motivated by achievement or competition needs should participate in sports programs that include some form of competition (for example, amateur tennis tournaments). An example of how the different needs can be targeted with specific strategies is presented in Table 23.1.

Table 23.1 Motives and strategies

Motives	Strategies
Fun/enjoyment	Emphasis on intrinsic motivation.
	Focus on the entertainment aspect of sports.
	Focus on participants' satisfaction.
Health/fitness	Programs designed to satisfy individual needs (achievement of physiological outcomes).
Escape/relaxation	Outdoor sports programs.
	Recreation in the natural environment (parks/mountains) or relaxation classes (for example, yoga).
Competition/achievement	Individual and team sports with a competition element.
	Participation in tournaments and events.
Socialization	Group activities.
	Social activities as part of sports programs.
Learning/skill development	Teaching of skills.
	Teaching new sports activities.

Constraints

Constraints are "factors that are assumed by researchers and perceived or experienced by individuals to limit the formation of leisure preferences and to inhibit or prohibit participation in leisure activities" (Jackson, 1991: p. 279). Back in 1987, Crawford and Godbey classified constraints into intrapersonal, interpersonal and structural.

Intrapersonal constraints are internal factors that influence an individual's preference for participation. They relate to psychological states and perceptions, such as cultural issues, religious issues, perceived abilities, interest for an activity, self-esteem, and confidence for taking part in an activity. They include the facets of: psychological constraints, cultural issues, limited interest and negative past experiences, and lack of time.

Structural constraints are external factors that influence an individual's decision making for participation, after the preference (for participation) has been developed. They include the facets of: sports facility problems, financial problems, and accessibility issues.

Interpersonal constraints are factors that relate to an individual's interaction with the social environment. They relate to difficulties in finding friends and partners to participate with. They include the facets of: lack of partners and social isolation, and lack of information (for example, available opportunities for participation).

Jackson, Crawford and Godbey (1993) proposed that individuals experience constraints hierarchically. Internal constraints are the most powerful predictors of behavior, while structural constraints are the least powerful. As the most powerful ones, intrapersonal constraints block sports participation, while structural ones might not block it, but they might modify it (for example, participation less frequently or in different activities). Examples of individual constraints that belong to each of the above constraint categories are presented in Table 23.2.

Research on leisure constraints has been extensive over the last twenty years. This is due to the theoretical (Alexandris, Funk and Pritchard, 2011; Godbey, Crawford and Sharon Shen, 2010) but also practical interest (Alexandris et al., 2013; Kennelly et al., 2013, Kim and Trail, 2010; Reis and Correia, 2014) in this topic. The identification of the constraints that individuals face and block or limit their participation can help marketers and practitioners develop strategies in order to remove or at least alleviate the influence of these constraints. Marketing, communication and service delivery should be adjusted in this respect.

Attitudes

Consumer attitudes are an important construct in marketing, since it is a variable used to predict buying behavior. Those who express positive attitudes towards a product or service are likely to buy it. It is important for marketers to design strategies in order to positively influence consumer attitudes towards a sports service. Attitudes are developed based on personal experience (participation in an activity), but they are also influenced by media (traditional and social) and the social environment (significant others). The three-component attitude model is one of the most basic that has been used in the marketing literature (Shiffman and Kanuk, 2010). It proposes three facets of attitudes: cognitive, affective and conative.

Consumers who use the cognitive component evaluate the attributes of a product or service (for example, benefits) in order to make rational decisions. Consumers who use the affective component are more influenced by feelings in their buying behaviour. It is important for marketers to decide which of these elements they want to influence with their

Table 23.2 Constraint factors and examples of individual constraint items

Intrapersonal constraints	
Individual/psychological constraints	Low self-esteem.
	Low perceived skills.
	Fear of getting hurt.
	Does not like exercising in social situations.
Cultural issues	Family roles.
	Religion.
Limited interest and	Participated in the past and did not like.
negative past experiences	Does not like sports participation.
Lack of time	Does not have time because of family commitments.
	Does not have time because of work commitments.
Structural constraints	
Sports facilities problems	Limited recreation places.
	Bad quality of sports facilities.
Financial problems	Cannot afford the expenses required.
Accessibility problems	Does not have transportation.
	Takes time to access the recreation places.
Interpersonal constraints	
Lack of partners/social isolation	No friends to participate with.
	My friends do not like sports participation.
Lack of knowledge	Lack of information on what activity to participate in.
	Lack of information about places to exercise.

communication strategies. If the objective is to influence the cognitive component, it is necessary to develop a communication channel that will be detailed in giving information about the expected benefits of buying a product. In this line, consumers should be informed in detail about the benefits (physical, psychological, social) of participating in a sports or recreation activity. If the objective is to influence the affective component it is important to promote sports in a way to target the individual's feelings. In this line, sports services should be promoted as pleasant and fun experiences with positive psychological outcomes.

More advanced attitude models that have been proposed in literature includes the *Theory of Reasoned Action* (Ajzen and Fishbein, 1980) and its extension, *The Theory of Planned Behavior* (Ajzen, 1985; 1988). According to the TPB, individuals form intentions based on their attitude towards the behavior influenced by opinions of important others as to the appropriateness of the action (subjective norm) and evaluating their own ability to successfully complete it (perceived behavioral control). Perceived behavioral control captures an individual's perception of their capability of successfully performing the behavior (Ajzen, 1985). The attitude is determined by an individual's beliefs concerning the consequences of performing an action and a personal evaluation of the desirability of such consequences. The subjective norm component includes opinions of significant others as to the behavior in question (for example, participation in a specific activity) and the extent to which an individual is motivated to comply with expectations of others (motivation to comply). The inclusion of PBC as a determinant of intention into the model differentiates the theory of planned behavior from the original theory of reasoned action. This extension was introduced in response to criticisms that the theory of reasoned action was based on an assumption of perfect volitional control over behavior and thus, failed to take into account real and perceived constraints that limited individuals' ability to perform the desired actions (Dawson et al., 2001). Perceived behavioral control is positively related to the number of resources and opportunities an individual believes they possess (for example, time, money, skills, cooperation of other people), and negatively associated with the number and intensity of constraints they perceive they experience. The issue of volitional control is particularly important in the context of sports, leisure and recreation settings in which many barriers exist and limit an individual's control over behavior. The TPB has dominated attitude research in health-related behaviors for many years. However, there have been recent critical essays about the value of this theory. In a recent editorial, Sniehotta, Presseaua and Araújo-Soaresa (2014), questioned the predictive validity of the theory on actual behavior and its subsequent utility for practitioners.

ATTITUDE THEORY AND SPORTS MARKETING

On summarizing, attitude research can help sports marketers to:

- Develop communication strategies to influence the cognitive or affective components of sports consumer attitudes.
- Predict actual behavior (participation or not), based on consumer attitudes (positive or negative).
- Determine the factors (subjective norms and perceived behavioral control) that influence the development of positive attitudes towards sports participation.
- Segment current and prospective sports participants, according to the strength of the PBC variable, which has shown to be a predictor of sports participation.
- Understand the role of significant others (subjective norms) on an individual's decision to start taking part in sports (for example, when targeting groups that are influenced by subjective norms, such as women, youths, etc.).

The output factors

One of the most recent and complete theoretical approaches to understand the output factors of an individual's decision-making process for sports participation is the Psychological Continuum Model (Funk and James, 2001; 2006). This model explains the development of commitment to sports participation as a developmental process defined by the stages of awareness, attraction, attachment and allegiance. The model was originally developed to explain fans' commitment to a sports team but it was recently successfully applied to the context of sports participation (Beaton, Funk and Alexandris, 2009; Filo, Funk and Alexandris, 2008). These stages are now briefly defined.

Awareness stage: Before developing any attitudes towards a sports activity, an individual must have some knowledge of the sports activity and opportunities to participate in it. This information comes mainly through socializing agents and formal commercial sources, such as advertising commercials and advertising. Individuals in this stage have not yet developed a preference to participate in the activity (Funk and James, 2001; 2006), but they search for information and explore choices and alternatives (for example, other activities).

Attraction stage: In this stage an individual, based on the experience of having participated the activity, develops a preference for it, associated with positive attitudes towards it (Beaton et al., 2009). These attitudes are still not strong. The experience of participation has been proposed to be an important factor that influences the development of attraction (Beaton et al., 2009). As the positive attitudes towards the activity become stronger, an individual moves to third stage (attachment).

Attachment stage: In this stage, an individual develops strong attitudes and a psychological connection with the activity; these attitudes are now more stable, since individuals are more intrinsically motivated (Funk and James, 2001; 2006). In this stage, the individual attaches affective, symbolic and functional meanings to the activity, which takes more personal meaning (Filo et al., 2008).

Allegiance stage: In this final stage of the model, an individual has developed a strong psychological connection with the activity, which is now stable and enduring. The outcomes of allegiance are behavioral, attitudinal loyalty, persistence and resistance to change (Funk and James, 2001; 2006). Behavioral loyalty is expressed through frequent and lengthy participation in an activity, while attitudinal loyalty is expressed through strong emotions and feelings about the activity (affective behavior).

STAGES OF THE PCM AND SPORTS MARKETING

This PCM model is a useful approach in understanding the outcomes of an individual's decision making for sports participation in a stage to stage approach. From a marketing perspective it can be used for segmenting individuals and categorizing them into the four stages, if used in combination with the levels of recreation involvement. Such an approach can guide marketing actions targeted to segments belonging to each of the four stages. For example:

- Targeting the awareness stage: Formal (for example, media) and informal (for example, socialization agencies) promotional strategies are required for building sports activity (brand) awareness.
- Targeting the attraction stage: This is a key stage, since some of the individuals will move up the next stage, while others will drop out from participation. The main objective should be to maximize the positive participation experience. Research on participants' satisfaction and perceived service quality can help towards this direction.
- Targeting the attachment stage: Individuals at this stage could be considered as "loyal customers". Subsequently, relationship marketing programs should be developed.
- Allegiance stage: Individuals at this stage have developed strong psychological connection with the activity. Individualized and specialized sports services are required. The role of social groups and sports "communities" (for example, runners) should be explored as well as the role of social communication channels (for example, specialized blogs).

Conclusion

Participatory sports (in the forms of free or organized participation or events) are not examples of typical products, since they require an individual's personal investment in effort and time in order to consume them. This is the reason that drop-out rates are usually high and the issue of customer or participant loyalty is a difficult one in this market. While attracting participants is an important task, practitioners have to work on retaining their customers. The study of the factors that influence an individual's decision making for sports participation is important. By using a typical decision-making model as a basis, this chapter aimed to offer a brief discussion of some of the possible factors that should be studied. It is clear that we did not cover all the external, internal and environment factors that could be incorporated in the model. There are also other theoretical models and approaches (for example, the transtheoretical model, Prochaska and Velicer, 1997; socio-ecological models, Rowe et al., 2013), which could be used to explain sports and recreation behavior. It is also clear that the discussion of marketing and promoting sports participation is extensive. In this line, we agree with Rowe et al. (2013), who proposed that this is an area that has great prospects for future sports marketing academic and applied research.

References

Ajzen, I. (1985). From intentions to actions: A theory of planned behavior. In J. Kuhl and J. Beckmann (Eds.). *Action control: From cognition to behavior* (pp. 11–39). Heidelberg: Springer.

Ajzen, I. (1988). *Attitudes, personality and behavior*. Chicago: Dorsey Press.

Ajzen, I. and Fishbein, M. (1980). *Understanding attitudes and predicting social behavior*. Englewood Cliffs: Prentice-Hall.

Alexandris, K. and Kaplanidou, K. (2014). Marketing sport event tourism: sport tourist behaviors and destination provisions. *Sport Marketing Quarterly*, 23(3), 125–126.

Alexandris, K., Funk, D., and Pritchard, M. (2011). The impact of constraints on motivation, activity attachment and skier intentions to continue. *Journal of Leisure Research*, 43, 56–79.

Alexandris, K,, Kouthouris, C., Funk, D. and Giovani, K. (2009). Segmenting winter sport tourists by motivation: The case of recreational skiers. *Journal of Hospitality Marketing and Management*, 10, 480–500.

Alexandris, K., Kouthouris, C., Funk, D. and Tziouma, O. (2013). The use of negotiation strategies among recreational participants with different involvement levels: The case of recreational swimmers. *Leisure Studies*, 1–19.

Beaton, A., Funk, D. and Alexandris, K. (2009). Operationalizing a theory of participation in physically active leisure. *Journal of Leisure Research*, 41(2), 177–203.

Beenackers, M., Kamphuis, C., Giskes, K., Brug, J., Kunst, A., Burdorf, A. and van Lenthe, F. (2012). Socioeconomic inequalities in occupational, leisure-time, and transport related physical activity among European adults: A systematic review. *International Journal of Behavioral Nutrition and Physical Activity*, 9, 116.

Chalabaev, A., Sarrazin, P., Fontayne, P., Boiché, J. and Clément-Guillotin, C. (2013). The influence of sex stereotypes and gender roles on participation and performance in sport and exercise: Review and future directions, *Psychology of Sport and Exercise*, 14, 136–144.

Crawford, D. and Godbey, G. (1987). Reconceptualizing barriers to family leisure. *Leisure Sciences*, 9, 119–127.

Dawson, K. Gyurcsik, N., Culow-Reed, N. and Brawley, L. (2001). Perceived control: A construct that bridges theories of motivated behavior. In G. Roberts (Ed.). *Advances in motivation in sport and exercise* (pp. 321–357). Champaign: Human Kinetics.

Deci, L. and Ryan, M. (1985). *Intrinsic motivation and self-determination in human behavior*. New York: Plenum.

Filo, K., Funk, D. and Alexandris, K. (2008). Exploring the role of brand trust in the relationship between brand associations and brand loyalty in sport and fitness. *International Journal of Sport Management and Marketing*, 3, 39–57.

Funk, D., Beaton, A. and Alexandris, K. (2012). Sport consumer motivation: Autonomy and control orientations that regulate fan behaviors. *Sport Management Review*, 15, 355–367.

Funk, D. C. and James, J. (2001). The psychological continuum model: A conceptual framework for understanding an individual's psychological connection to sport. *Sport Management Review*, 4(2), 119–150.

Funk, D. and James, J. (2006). Consumer loyalty: The meaning of attachment in the development of sport team allegiance. *Journal of Sport Management*, 20(2), 189–217.

Godbey, G., Crawford, D. and Sharon Shen, X. (2010). Assessing hierarchical leisure constraints theory after two decades. *Journal of Leisure Research*, 42(l), 111–134.

Gratton, C. and Taylor, P. (2000). *The economics of sport and recreation*. London: E & FN Spon.

Hallal, P., Andersen, L., Bull, F., Guthold, R., Haskell, W. and Ekelund, U. (2012). Global physical activity levels: surveillance progress, pitfalls, and prospects. *Lancet*, 380, 247–257.

Iso-Ahola, S. (1999). Motivational foundations of leisure. In E. L. Jackson and T. L. Burton (Eds.), *Leisure studies: Prospects for the twenty-first century* (pp. 35–51). State College, PA: Venture Publishing.

Jackson, E. L. (1991). Leisure constraints/constrained leisure: special issue introduction. *Journal of Leisure Research*, 23, 279–285.

Jackson, E., Crawford, D. and Godbey, G. (1993). Negotiation of leisure constraints. *Leisure Sciences*, 15, 1–12.

Kim, Y. and Trail, G. (2010). Constraints and motivators: A new model to explain sport consumer behavior. *Journal of Sport Management*, 24, 190–210.

Lee, R. and Mason, R. (2011). Population aging and the generational economy: A global perspective. Cheltenham: Edward Elgar Publishing Limited.

Manfredo, M., Driver, B. and Tarrant, M. (1996). Measuring leisure motivation: A meta-analysis of the recreation experience preference scales. *Journal of Leisure Research*, 28(3), 188–213.

Min Lee, Shiroma, E., Lobelo, F., Puska, P., Blair, S. and Katzmarzyk, P. (2012). Effect of physical inactivity on major non-communicable diseases worldwide: an analysis of burden of disease and life expectancy. *Lancet*, 380, 219–229.

Pires, G., Stanton, J. and Stanton, P. (2011). Revisiting the substantiality criterion: From ethnic marketing to market segmentation. *Journal of Business Research*, 64, 988–996.

Prayag, G. and Grivel, E. (2014). Motivation, satisfaction and behavioral intentions: Segmenting youth participants at the Interamnia World Cup 2012. *Sport Marketing Quarterly*, 23(3), 148–160.

Prochaska, J. O. and Velicer, W. F. (1997). The transtheoretical model of health behavior change. *American Journal of Health Promotion*, 12, 38–48.

Reis, H. and Correia, A. (2014). Facilitators and constraints in the participation of women golf tourists' perceptions and assessments. *Advances in Culture, Tourism and Hospitality Research*, 8, 137–146.

Rowe, K., Shilbury, D., Ferkins, L. and Hinckson, E. (2013). Sport development and physical activity promotion: An integrated model to enhance collaboration and understanding. *Sport Management Review*, 16, 364–377.

Scheerder, J. and Vos, S. (2011). Social stratification in adults' sports participation from a time-trend perspective: Results from a 40-year household study. *European Journal for Sport and Society*, 8(1/2), 31–44.

Schumacher, D. G. (2012). Report on the sports travel industry. National Associations of Sport Commissions (NASC), www.sportscommissions.org/Portals/sportscommissions/Documents/About/NASC%20Sports%20Travel%20Industry%20Whitepaper.pdf (accessed June 25, 2014).

Shiffman, L. and Kanuk, L. (2010). *Consumer behavior*. Englewood Cliffs: Prentice-Hall.

Shilbury, D., Weesterbeek, H., Quick, S., Funk, D. and Karg, A. (2014). *Strategic sport marketing*. London: Allen & Unwin.

Sniehotta, F., Presseaua, J. and Araújo-Soaresa, V. (2014). Time to retire the theory of planned behaviour. *Health Psychology Review*, 8(1), 1–7.

Special Eurobarometer 412 (2014). Sport and physical activity, European Commission.

Stodolska, M. and Alexandris, K. (2004). The role of recreational sport in the adaptation of first generation immigrants in the United States. *Journal of Leisure Research*, 36, 379–413.

Stodolska, M., Shinew, K. A., Acevedo, J. and Izenstark, D. (2011). Perceptions of urban parks as havens and contested terrains by Mexican-Americans in Chicago neighbourhoods. *Leisure Sciences*, 33, 103–126.

Van Tuyckom, C., Scheerder, J. and Bracke, P. (2010). Gender and age inequalities in regular sports participation: A cross-national study of 25 European countries. *Journal of Sports Sciences*, 28(10), 1077–1084.

Websites

www.scotland.gov.uk
www.abs.gov.au/ausstats
www.pch.gc.ca

24

MANAGING BEHAVIOR

Organizational and consumer perspectives on athlete transgressions

Constantino Stavros, Kate Westberg, Bradley Wilson
and Aaron C. T. Smith

Setting the scene

The San Diego Union-Tribune, a newspaper in California, maintains a page on its website (www.sandiegouniontribune.com) titled NFL Arrests Database. It is a catalogue of National Football League (NFL) players who have been arrested or received citations since 2000 that, according to the site, "were more serious than speeding tickets". As of early May 2015, the database included 792 records ranging from public urination through to murder. As the newspaper highlights, the database cannot be considered comprehensive as some incidents are not reported or records of other events are not easily obtained.

Given the NFL is often perceived as the gold standard of sports marketing excellence, it is evident that not even the best management intentions and strategies can prevent athlete misbehavior. The challenge, therefore, for all sports organizations, is to manage such behavior; with the ideal of prevention often elusive due to issues surrounding wealthy, widely-recognized athletes and their usage of the time and access that their celebrity status affords them.

Many members of society, not just athletes, transgress. One can argue that such behavior is merely representative of our communities. However, the expectations in relation to athlete behavior may be higher given their responsibility to their sports, their team, their sponsors, their fans and even more broadly, as a role-model in society. These complex perspectives are explored in this chapter.

Before beginning our discussion, we suggest the reader consider what they would classify as a transgression. Readers can ponder the scenarios described in the following sections or more specific incidents with which they are familiar. Examples of sports related transgressions, thanks to increased media and public scrutiny, are not difficult to find.

These transgressions can be broadly categorized according to the nature of the transgressor (individual or organization), the type of transgression (moral or legal) and the context (on- or off-field) of the incident. These three areas are explored separately in the following sections, however, they are strongly interrelated.

Who commits the transgression?

This chapter focuses on transgressions committed by athletes and the implications of these incidents. These include instances of doping, assault, inappropriate gambling and drunken behavior, to name a few. Athlete transgressions need to be prevented where possible and if they occur, as is often inevitable, they must be managed. How well this can be done is usually dependent upon the type of transgression and where it occurred. However, transgressive behavior can also happen at organizational levels. This includes match-fixing, salary cap cheating and inappropriate governance. Organizational transgressions can be particularly damaging as they typically involve systematic processes of deception, leading to significant repercussions.

What type of transgression?

Athlete transgressions infringe upon morality or legality. Each of these areas can be further categorized either by rules that pertain to sports, such as certain aspects of what is considered "fair play", or societal expectations. A renowned athlete who cheats on their spouse may be crossing moral boundaries, but is not breaking the law (in most countries). Such behavior might be perceived differently from an athlete who drives in a drunken state, breaking the law and endangering their own life and that of others. Keep in mind that within moral and legal spheres the concept of sports rules and norms might need to be considered and these are often hard to delineate. Some people may feel that an athlete taunting an opposition player in a World Cup final in order to have that player react violently and be sent off is a legitimate part of sport and acceptable, others may feel it is unconscionable behavior.

Where did the transgression occur?

The location of a transgression is particularly important in how a transgression is perceived as it provides a context to which interested parties ascribe particular value judgements. An athlete striking out at an abusive fan while walking off the pitch, or an athlete biting another player, cannot be condoned, but they may be deemed less severe than the same incidents occurring in a city street. The heat of competition in the cauldron of a stadium is part of the modern vernacular where going to a sports event is promoted as akin to witnessing a metaphorical battle. The concept of "white line fever" is often used to explain uncharacteristic acts on sporting fields.

Athletes who blatantly cheat on-field are afforded little understanding, however, as this transgression goes to the very soul and integrity of sports. A golfer who breaks a rule, even inadvertently, is often immediately disqualified from an event to preserve the intentionally high standards of that sport, and many leagues around the world set up their own judicial tribunals to deal with athletes who break their sporting rules. Doping, which can be considered an on-field transgression even though the actual regimen might take place behind the scenes, is particularly reviled around the world. An athlete who is successful as a result of doping is likely to receive little sympathy from fans, even if an excuse along the lines of "everyone else was doing it" is proffered.

Athletes misbehaving off-field are often afforded latitude if the transgression is minor. In some instances this may also be mitigated by timing. Drunken behavior by athletes the night before a big game is less likely to be acceptable to fans than such behavior the night after winning the big game.

These three questions are merely a starting point for considering transgressions and their management. Additional questions regarding when an incident occurred, who was involved, the history of such incidents, zones of tolerance, locus of control and societal expectations all need to be considered. The perspective from which associated stakeholders view such incidents and their various antecedents and layers is also critical. As such the remainder of this chapter will explore three key perspectives, sporting organizations, sponsors and consumers, to shed some light on athlete transgressions and their management.

Introduction

The vast reach and global appeal of sports has established it as a significant aspect of society and culture. Major sporting events help define national identities (Tomlinson and Young, 2006) and teams, such as Manchester United and the New York Yankees, stand side by side with some of the largest commercial brands in the world.

Sports also help shape community expectations and cultural values, providing a lens for the appropriate portrayal of roles in society (Roche, 2000). The term "role model" can have different meanings, but is applied to an individual who is "perceived as exemplary, or worthy of imitation" (Yancey, 1998: p. 254). Role models shape individual and collective attitudes and behavior through personal contact and relationship cues (Ingall, 1997). Brand custodians, such as sponsors, understandably want to associate their brands with positive role models and sport is a fertile space for such endorsers. Sporting administrators and other key stakeholders, however, need to remain cognizant of their responsibility for facilitating and promoting these positive connections and minimizing the potential for negative athlete behavior, including creating and perpetuating inappropriate stereotypes (Wilson, Stavros and Westberg, 2008).

Professional athletes are brands in their own right and significant modern-day celebrities; valued by sponsors to endorse their products; proudly held up by sporting entities as the epitome of success and perceived by many in the community as aspirational leaders. These athletes serve a multitude of stakeholders and, under increasing scrutiny, are expected to perform to high standards on and off the playing field. An insatiable media appetite for insights into their lives, coupled with the pervasiveness of social media and consumer voyeurism, has altered the management of the athlete brand and the sporting organization. This brand management is particularly challenging when transgressions occur.

The marketing literature describes a transgression as the breaking of the implicit or explicit rules outlining relationship performance and evaluation (Aaker, Fournier and Brasel, 2004). Wilson, Stavros and Westberg (2010) note that the violation of such rules or overstepping the standards of normative behavior by athletes can significantly impact sport and its various stakeholders. While they also posit a more detailed typology of crises based on accidents, transgressions, faux pas and terrorism, the term transgression in this chapter is considered more generally, relating to the negative behavior of athletes, which may lead to a crisis if not handled appropriately or act as a degenerative episode in which key relationships are affected (Westberg, Stavros and Wilson, 2011). This position is consistent with the work of Gardial, Flint and Woodruff (1996: p. 36), who highlight the potential relational impact of incidents that are "perceived by the consumer to be out of the ordinary". Aside from the nature and consequences of transgressive events themselves, the attribution of such incidents can also significantly impact the response of stakeholders (Wilson et al., 2010).

This chapter will consider the impact and management of athlete transgressions from three important and interrelated perspectives. We begin with a broad overview of the current context and challenges for sporting entities to which the relationship and branding of many athletes is symbiotically connected. Perspectives on athlete transgressions from sponsors, a key financial and marketing partner to sporting entities, are then presented before the final section considers the under-explored view of the consumer. This chapter consolidates ground-breaking research with sport organizations and sponsors conducted by the authors over a number of years, with the consumer insights gained from their most recent academic inquiries. Suggestions and opportunities for future research are also posited.

Athlete transgressions: sporting entity perspectives

Sporting entities have an elevated status in developed societies. Their codes, regulators, teams and various levels of administration are often closely interwoven with important public, media and government members. Roche (2000) insists that sports are a valuable conduit for spreading a global culture and that many governments harness events as a form of soft power to positively influence public sentiment.

Naturally, when a transgression occurs that disrupts or threatens athlete or sporting code legitimacy, then it becomes newsworthy and concerning. Athlete transgressions (alleged or actual) can harm stakeholder reputations and brands. This is amplified if the event is global and reaches a large audience. An athlete transgression can be a form of crisis for a sporting entity. Coombs (2002) indicated that a crisis can not only disrupt organizational operations, but also damage reputation. Athlete transgressions have the ability to affect associated sporting entities in this manner. This damage can be exacerbated by the sheer variety of transgressions that can occur, their varying consequences and their tendency not to proceed with any routine order (Kersten, 2005).

The limited focus on managing transgressions in sports does not reflect the broader and more established practices in the public relations literature and consumer goods and services (Wilson et al., 2008). While O'Beirne and Ries (1999) posited a sports crisis model that adapted the general prevention, response and recovery processes, the ensuing decade has seen increased emphasis on the need to explore the perspective of sporting entities in more detail.

Wilson et al. (2008), in examining major Australian sporting teams, identified that an *ad hoc* approach was usually taken in the management of transgressive incidents. Some sporting entities had experienced a large number of negative events involving athlete behavior and had garnered valuable experience in dealing with such issues, despite being developed through trial and error.

Research remains in the nascent stages of development from the sporting entity perspective, however, several key issues have been identified. These issues relate to managing the cause and effects of transgressions, managing the depth and complexity of multiple stakeholder relationships, and the importance of transparency (Wilson et al., 2008).

Managing transgressions

Structural changes in media, reflecting its continuity, interactive nature and immediacy, have coincided with sport managers' decreased ability to maintain control of transgression events. Technological advancements, such as the widespread availability of recording devices on phones, feed prying consumer and global media demand for increased reporting of scandals. This freedom and rapid spread of information and subsequent level of transparency requires sports administrators to have sophisticated issues management handling processes in place.

Sports managers need to be prepared for information flows to be asymmetrical and to dynamically evolve for all incidents. Spokespeople must be across a vast array of contexts and interest groups, given the pervasiveness of sports in society. If managers are seeking greater control over the way an issue is played out over time, they may want to deal with relevant stakeholders through a centralized process to mitigate the likelihood of misinformation. The organization's website may be a useful communication vehicle for some stakeholders, such as fans, and some form of internal network is necessary for key groups such as sponsors who will require particularly careful management. This approach also helps to control the timeliness in which administrators respond to the issue at hand. There is a chance that the news of athlete misbehavior will become embellished by fans and the sports media who rush to discuss and report with limited information, while sporting entities must patiently gather all the facts before responding. This gap between news of a transgression and the subsequent response (if any) from a sporting entity can be problematic in the modern 24/7 news cycle.

Sporting entities, therefore, must develop constructive relationships with the media in order to mitigate the potential damage. These organizations should also seek to create awareness of the processes they have in place to minimize athlete transgressions, such as counselling sessions, mentoring programs, responsibility awareness and leadership development. Such knowledge allows sporting entities to potentially affect perceptions of the locus of control and the attributions of blame by key stakeholders, including consumers and sponsors, during these incidents. Notwithstanding this, organizations that continue to experience transgressions caused by their athletes will be judged increasingly negatively, irrespective of preventative strategies put into place.

Nurturing complex interactions for multiple stakeholders

The genesis for managing complex relationships lies within the early literature in services marketing and with relationship marketing. That is, marketing that aims to improve the interactions between stakeholder members (Berry, 1995). Nurturing strong relationships with stakeholders, such as consumers and sponsors, should be a central goal of sporting entity administrators and becomes particularly relevant in the management of a transgression. The importance of consumer-brand relational bonding is considered to be a business imperative (Fournier, 1998) and it is an inherently appealing and compelling goal for sporting entities to build value-laden and strong intimate interactions to continually enhance such bonds. Sports are somewhat unique in that they naturally build close relational bonds between consumer groups, given the levels of identification and motivation ascribed to the context. This is especially true for active supporter groups whose passion is well documented. Ultimately, however, it is still the focus on maintaining a satisfactory service encounter (Shostack, 1985) that ensures that the relational bond remains strong.

Analogies can also be drawn from social network analysis, which maps the complexity of all relations (de Nooy, Mrvar and Batagelj, 2005). Such work has not yet been fully explored in sports, but may offer utility to extend insights into likely future transgression events and information management practices. Given the complexity and array of dynamic interactions occurring with stakeholders as a result of a transgressive event, it is important to consider the recommendations of Wilson et al. (2008: p.104) in facilitating open communication and instigating what are termed "communication posts" that allow true two-way exchanges of dialogue between partners.

Additionally, Wilson et al. (2008) highlight the role of trust in stakeholder communications. Trust is a valuable commodity in times of crisis, facilitating efficiency in communication channels, effectiveness in common messages that may be presented by stakeholders and ensuring that transparency is prioritized. This is particularly important for sporting entities that have formed a significant number of commercial relationships, and who needed to manage these complex relationships at the micro level given the differing needs that may exist, but also holistically to present a solidified and credible persona at the macro level. Relationship partners need to work together when transgressive events occur to ensure they communicate in the same manner and have shared relationship expectations. Benefits from this arrangement are well established in the crisis management literature (Birch, 1994; Couretas, 1985; Fearn-Banks, 1996).

Accommodating and providing necessary transparency

Wilson et al. (2008) found that the typical state of play with athlete misbehavior is that when an event breaks, managers are operating with only partial information. Speculation and misinformation are often rife within the media and the general public. It is within this context that the media feeds the crisis event story to often prematurely impel management action on the actual (or alleged) transgressor. Managers communicate that this is a situation that has led to sub-optimal decision making with only partial facts at their disposal.

Notwithstanding this encumbrance, it is suggested that supporters, and especially sponsors who invest significant financial and relational capital, need to be provided with the facts by sporting entities regarding incidents, and this should happen in a timely fashion given that brand and corporate reputational harm to sports entity and sponsors may be the result of delayed action. Without an established procedure in place, presenting the critical information in a timely fashion may be difficult. Sporting managers will experience some degree of helplessness operating in these difficult circumstances and will need to carefully balance competing pressures. It is not unusual, for example, to have a team be at odds with the governing body of their sport over the impact or severity of an alleged athlete transgression. General public relations practices of proactively developing goodwill with key stakeholders so as to establish credibility, project authority and be allowed time to respond are recommended, and these approaches have been contextualized in the sport literature (for example, Stoldt, Dittmore and Branvold, 2012). Such an investment in goodwill is typically well rewarded for sporting managers, particularly in team sports where athlete transgressions are often not a case of "if" but "when".

Incidents involving athlete misbehavior require management action in terms of determining consequences for the athlete, typically in the form of some "punishment". While we note that this action should be timely and transparent, the dissemination or the organizational response must also be carefully managed. As such, sporting entities need to prioritize the flow of such notification, ensuring that key stakeholders (or the transgressor themselves) do not learn of the action through the general media or various social platforms that exist.

Transparency requires not just clarity around the circumstances of the transgression, but also how the event is then handled by the sporting entity. Sporting entities will need to keep this process-orientated approach in mind as dealing with an event is rarely quick, particularly if subsequent facts emerge that throw the issue back into the spotlight.

Concluding thoughts

Sporting entities are facing growing challenges in dealing with athlete transgressions. Many athletes are increasingly becoming celebrities and often have worldwide media currency. Sport administrators need to carefully manage reputations in line with rising community expectations, but at the same time respond to the imperative to be successful on-field in a world where "win at all costs" is a sporting mantra.

With transgressive actions analysed from multiple perspectives, sporting entities must become skilled at assessing differing viewpoints and responding accordingly to ensure that they meet the expectations of key stakeholders. This process of needs matching or assessing goal congruence helps gain a valuable shared understanding. In taking this approach, sporting entities will need to be conscious of the views of their governing bodies, whose purview of maintaining the overarching integrity of the sport often wields a stricter interpretation of a transgression and its subsequent punishment than a team might anticipate. As has been noted, it is important that athletes are not only trained to recognize and avoid situations that may lead to negative behavior, but also that athletes are mindful of the potential impact such actions may have on the integrity of their sport and their personal reputation and marketability.

The opportunity to guide and mentor athletes in a more rigorous fashion can only be seen as a positive advancement, however, sporting managers also need to increase their awareness and knowledge base to deal with the array of negative behavior they may encounter. Areas of training, such as strategic workshops, crisis plans, preparedness audits, stakeholder training and crisis simulations should all be considered.

Sporting entities also need to assess their own tolerance to their athletes' transgressions and consider how they will reflect on the image of their organization. Some sporting entities, for example, might welcome or cultivate a risk-taking identity, therefore, tolerating more readily some transgressions as part of this personality. A valuable basis for initial discussion in such a scenario may be centred on the sporting entity identifying partners who can (relatively speaking) tolerate transgressions in a similar fashion. Conversely, sporting entities that are particularly risk averse may wish to facilitate and prioritize athlete recruitment programs that minimize potential harm. Given aspiring athletes now come through established and well-monitored pathways, the identification of the potential for problematic behavior is somewhat easier, albeit never certain.

Athlete transgressions: sponsor perspectives

Companies enter into sports sponsorship relationships to achieve brand-related benefits through associating with a sports entity brand. However, as highlighted in the preceding section, athlete transgressions have the potential to threaten the brand of the sporting entity associated with the athlete. This damage can further extend to the brands of associated sponsors and can weaken or even dissolve the sponsorship. The effective management of these transgressions is thus critical, not only in protecting the equity of sporting entity and sponsor brands, but also ultimately the relationships between these organizations.

Sponsorship has been recognized as a powerful platform for building brands (Cliffe and Motion, 2005). Benefits to the sponsor's brand include increasing brand awareness, creating or strengthening image and achieving brand differentiation. These benefits accrue to sponsors through positive associations with the image or excitement of a sporting event (Cornwell, Weeks and Roy, 2005). Sports entities are increasingly acknowledging the role of their brand in influencing relationships with sponsors as well as other key stakeholders, such as their fans and the media. This realization has resulted in more active brand management within many professional sports teams (Kahuni, Rowley and Binsardi, 2009).

Sponsors, too, are seeking to actively enhance their brands and are justifiably concerned about the impact on their brand as a result of transgressions associated with a sponsorship arrangement. These incidents can trigger a change in the sponsorship relationship. The terms "critical event" or "critical incident" have been used to describe an event that causes a radical change in a business environment (Halinen, Salmi and Havila, 1999: p. 786). Negative critical incidents have the ability to cause stakeholders to review long-term relationships and can cause destabilization (van Doorn & Verhoef, 2008).

Athlete transgressions can damage the sponsorship relationship resulting in relational change, including the premature termination of a sponsorship, the nonrenewal of a sponsorship or some form of relationship modification such as the addition of behavioral clauses to the sponsorship contract. Whether these incidents have a negative impact on the sponsorship relationship is determined by a number of aspects related to the incident such as the sponsor's attribution of blame, the sponsor's perceived severity of the incident and the extent of media attention (Westberg et. al., 2011). In addition, the existing quality of the relationship between sports entity and sponsor may have a role to play as well as the sports entity's management of the transgression. These factors will be discussed in the following sections.

Attribution of blame

Attribution theory explains how people interpret behavior (Kelley and Michela, 1980). In the context of athlete transgressions, attribution of blame relates to whether the sponsor believes that the sport entity is accountable for preventing or better managing negative player behavior. For example, numerous incidents may suggest poor management or a fundamental problem with the culture of the sports organization. Further, sponsors may also be concerned as to whether key stakeholders, such as their customers or the community, could perceive their firm to be condoning or supporting this type of behavior due to their continued association.

Perceived severity of the behavior

The sponsor's perceived severity of the behavior can influence whether the incident prompts a change to the sponsorship relationship. For example, whether the negative behavior occurred on- or off-field, the extent to which the behavior infringed upon social norms and whether the behavior related to a sponsor's sensitivities or zones of tolerance (Westberg et al., 2011). While on-field violence or the flagrant disregard for the rules of a sport is not likely to be condoned by sponsors, it may be more understandable as an unfortunate outcome during a passionate game. However, off-field behavior that is either illegal or conflicts with social norms, may be less palatable. For example, incidents such as driving while intoxicated or committing assault are likely to be more harshly regarded by sponsors wanting to associate their brand with positive images and values.

The nature of the sponsor's business may also influence their perceptions of athlete transgressions and the subsequent pressure for them to respond. Negative behavior directly related to a sponsor's business is an obvious concern, for example, an insurance company may be more alarmed by the implications of reckless driving or driving while under the influence of drugs and alcohol, compared to a sportswear company. In addition, certain companies, such as banks, may be more conservative and, therefore, have increased sensitivity to any form of transgression or impropriety. As a result, these sensitivities are likely to impact on a sponsor's tolerance in relation to an incident. When incidents occur outside the zone of tolerance of a sponsor, changes to the relationship may be made (Schurr, Hedaa and Geersbro, 2008).

Media impact

Incidents that attract greater levels of media interest are likely to have more potential for damaging associated brands. The media create awareness of these incidents and have a significant role in shaping the way in which the transgression is presented. The media may also report the story prior to the sports organization being able to ascertain all the facts; the media may also go directly to a major sponsor seeking comment. As a result, media scrutiny of a sports scandal can result in a sponsor's brand receiving significant negative exposure (Kahuni et al., 2009).

Mitigating factors outside of the transgression

In addition to the circumstances surrounding the athlete transgression, there are a number of factors that may influence the sponsor's response to the incident. For example, the quality of the relationship between sponsor and sports organization may influence whether the incident has a negative effect on the relationship and the extent of that effect (Westberg et al., 2011). Fundamental relationship tenets, such as communication, commitment and trust, provide the foundation upon which the sponsor evaluates an incident and determines their response. Communication has been identified as a critical element in maintaining a successful business relationship (Ford and Associates, 2002). Sports organizations need to be proactive in fostering strong relationships with sponsors and to manage these on an ongoing basis.

Further, specific relational investments can also form part of the commitment to the sponsorship relationship (Urriolagoitia and Planellas, 2007). Commitment to a sponsorship relationship can be reflected by length of sponsorship, size of the sponsorship investment as well as the degree to which the sponsorship relationship has been leveraged. The latter refers to specific relationship investments, which are unique to the partnership and, therefore, non-transferable, and have been linked to successful alliances (Dyer and Singh, 1998).

In a business relationship, trust can negate the need for all contingencies to be outlined in a formal contract (Dwyer, Schurr and Oh, 1987). As such, reputation can be an important contributor to trust and to the success of a sponsorship alliance. A critical issue, likely to erode trust in the sponsorship relationship, is the sports entity's inability to prevent athlete transgressions. Depending on the circumstances, sponsors may be unaffected by a single occurrence, however, repeated offences would be of much greater concern.

The management of athlete transgressions is likely to influence the impact that these incidents have on the sponsorship relationship. As previously noted, critical aspects of this process include transparency when dealing with sponsors, timeliness of communication, proactivity and effective media management (Westberg et al., 2011). These four interrelated elements provide open communication allowing for joint problem-solving that is likely to preserve the relationship. Sponsors expect to be informed as a matter of priority, especially as they may be questioned by key constituents such as customers, senior management and the media. Sports entities need to institute processes and procedures to pre-empt and manage potential player crises, thereby providing sponsors with confidence in their abilities. On the other hand, sponsors need to consider not just the benefits of sponsorship but also prepare for the potential unintended consequences of "undesired outcomes of such partnerships" (Kahuni et al., 2009: p. 61).

Concluding thoughts

Sports sponsorship is becoming increasingly complex and strategic. Athlete transgressions present a real threat to managing successful relationships with sponsors. Sports organizations need to be aware that sponsors are prepared to terminate a sponsorship in the event of a severe transgression, especially if the sponsorship relationship has been weakened by factors such as repeated offences or poor communication. An abrupt or premature termination of the contract, whereby the sponsor is explicit in their reasons for termination and leaves no possibility of negotiation, is the most obvious evidence that the relationship has been damaged. However, non-renewal of a contract may be a form of an "indirect or disguised exit strategy" (Alajoutsijarvi, Moller and Tahtinen, 2000: p. 1275), whereby the sponsor may attribute non-renewal to a change in the company's strategy as opposed to the actions of the sports entity. Other less radical changes to the relationship may also occur if the transgression is perceived as less severe and has occurred within a strong alliance, including relational adaptation, such as amending the sponsorship agreement to include exit clauses, fines or other specifications regarding player or sports entity behavior. Sports entities need to be aware that these requests can signal a change in the relationship that may represent the initiation of an "exit strategy". They should also be aware of other signs, such as reduced communication and investment, which may precede relationship dissolution (Alajoutsijarvi et al., 2000).

Sponsors and sports entity managers both need to protect their brands by being prepared for the potential challenges of athlete transgressions. A proactive approach can reduce the impact and duration of the incident, as well as preserving the relationship between the two parties (Wilson et. al., 2008). The presence of a prevention program within sports organizations can also help to manage the expectations of sponsor and sports entity and thus reduce the threat to the sponsorship, as well as the damage to corporate reputations and brand equity. Sponsors can also introduce their own programs aimed at assisting sport entities to formalize preventative measures. This can include fully briefing sports organizations of their expectations, clearly stating their sensitivities (zone of tolerance) and the reactionary measures to be taken if they are breached. This mutual understanding will assist sport entities to adopt a more effective and proactive brand management approach.

Athlete transgressions: consumer perspectives

As consumers increasingly turn to sports for their heroes and role models (Parry, 2009; Rojek, 2006), athletes have become a desirable property on many levels and have been transformed from individuals to brands with considerable value. The previous two sections have considered the impact that athlete transgressions can have on sporting organizations and their sponsors, however, the nexus between these entities and the consumer is arguably the most important to consider. Ultimately most sporting organizations are reliant on attracting fans, spectators and viewers to their games. Similarly, sponsors frequently enter into arrangements with these sports organizations to further consumer-orientated goals. Negative athlete behavior can have significant consequences for achieving these objectives.

From a consumer perspective, athletes can be seen as fulfilling two broad roles: first, as a productive participant, striving for excellence either in an individual or team sports environment and second, as celebrity endorsers or as ambassadors for their sport and its sponsors. Both roles can be affected by negative events that occur on or off a sports playing field. The celebrity status of an athlete has been well researched to determine the positive impact of such endorsement (for example, Erdogan, 1999; Ohanian, 1991; Lafferty, 2002) and how consumer evaluation of a celebrity's credibility can also be affected by transgressions (Zhou and Whitla, 2013). Sports stars can be effective as endorsers, particularly among younger generations (Bush, Martin and Bush, 2004; Dix, Phau and Pougnet, 2010).

Previous research has broadly examined the relational impact of transgressions committed by service employees with whom the consumer has a relationship (for example, Jones, Dacin and Taylor, 2011). However, the consideration of the relationship between an athlete and consumer provides a unique and unexplored scenario. An athlete is an individual, and often a contracted employee of a sporting organization, with whom the consumer has a less direct (and arguably a fantasized or perceived) relationship, even though the levels of personal identification that exist in sports are very high. Attribution theory provides a useful lens for exploring how consumers make sense of negative athlete behavior and how consumers respond, cognitively and emotionally. According to this theory, "people interpret behavior in terms of its causes and that these interpretations play an important role in determining reactions to the behavior" (Kelley and Michela, 1980: p. 458).

Given the dearth of existing research into consumer response to athlete transgressions, the authors of this chapter, as part of a larger study, conducted a series of semi-structured depth interviews with consumers and undertook a content analysis of a variety of discussions on online media platforms pertaining to athlete transgressions. This data was collected to examine consumers' response to athlete transgressions, primarily in relation to team sports, and their perspectives on the role of athletes. Key findings on consumer attributions are presented in the following sections.

General consumer attitudes toward athlete transgressions

In considering the general topic of athlete transgressions, consumers expressed a wide range of responses, often evaluating the transgressive act itself as well as the subsequent management of the incident by the team and governing sporting body. Responses can be noted across a spectrum of emotion from anger and frustration through to empathy and tolerance. However, there also exists a significant degree of circumspection and, in many instances, a desire to seek out further information to help in determining their feelings.

Negative reactions to a transgression typically emanated from females who perceived athletes as role models and by males who viewed athletes who transgressed (and in particular those who repeatedly transgressed) as individuals who were "wasting" a privileged opportunity afforded to few. Such informants viewed their actions with a sense of frustration that an athlete's individual excellence, or contribution to a team, was potentially being impacted by inappropriate behavior.

The perception of the increasing frequency of athlete transgressions has instilled in some informants a notion that a "here we go again" mentality had become normalized and athlete misbehavior was now somewhat routine. Others similarly noted that they were becoming immune to such incidents given their repeated occurrence.

Consumer expectations of athletes' behavior

The concept of athletes as role models was specifically explored. Many people felt that this mantle now "goes with the territory" of a professional athlete. This view, however, was somewhat mediated by the age of the athlete concerned, with younger, inexperienced athletes having their transgressive actions more readily understood, provided they learnt from their behavior and demonstrated contrition. Females specifically noted that many sports followers were children and that their idolization and emulation of athletes instilled perceptions of desirable role model behavior, whether athletes explicitly accepted it as part of their duties or not. Melnick and Jackson (2002) have highlighted that athletes can shape the values and beliefs of adolescents, and as such, contribute to their identity.

The broader perceived role of an athlete was also a significant factor in determining how transgressive behavior was evaluated. Expectations of a standard of conduct were frequently raised and this expectation can be further distilled into on-field and off-field, as well as during the season and during the off-season in the case of off-field actions. Not surprisingly, the actions of athletes in their private time, outside the playing season, is a period where informants felt that the in-season high standards expected on and off-field could potentially be relaxed. However, there was considerable disparity as to how much these expectations could be relaxed, if at all. Many informants believe that the privileges afforded to sport stars mean that implicit behavioral standards exist at all times and that the athlete is always on show. This high level of scrutiny is seen to be compensated by the large salaries many sports stars are now perceived to earn.

Some informants were more empathetic to an athlete's requirement to constantly meet expectations and noted that this pressure was often too much, particularly on younger, less-experienced athletes. Males in particular note that youthful athletes are often ascribed expectations that non-athletes of the same age would never be expected to adhere to.

Making sense of athlete transgressions

In considering athlete transgressions the concept of attribution reflects a comparison between the role of an athlete and expectations of the informant's own behavior in a situation. While it is perfectly normal to accept that one's own standards set a level of expectation in relation to the behavior of others, little compensation is seemingly made for the rarefied situation that star athletes are placed in. The assumption that athletes receive guidance, advice, training, high levels of compensation and various levels of protection mitigates the sense of disparity that might exist when having to perform one's profession, and in many cases private life, under almost constant media scrutiny.

Consumer attributions are influenced by a complex array of factors aside from general norms of behavior. These include whether multiple transgressions had occurred in relation to a player, or a team that they were involved in. Informants, not surprisingly, believe that athletes should not repeat misbehavior, either that of their own or of a teammate.

Internal attributions relate most prominently to demographic characteristics of the athlete, such as age and education, as well as broader psychological aspects such as character and upbringing. External attributions relate to societal expectations of a role-model, the culture of the sport or the presence of an external instigator that could lead to transgressive behavior. Where athlete transgressors were part of a team sport, informants are more likely to blame individual athletes and place less responsibility on the team given the perception that team sports now provide education programs and mentoring to positively modify inappropriate athlete behaviors. Informants were however particularly severe on sporting organizations that permitted repeated negative behavior among members of their team. Allowing such behavior to be highlighted by numerous incidents switched the emphasis to the team lacking the appropriate structure, culture and resolve to properly educate athletes on expected behavior.

Not surprisingly, as has been highlighted throughout this chapter, the severity of the incident was a significant factor. Athletes who break the law were held to account more stringently than those who transgress moral or social boundaries. Actions that contravene the values of sport itself, such as drug taking or cheating, are not easily forgiven by consumers, who view such actions as harming the integrity of competitive sports and that the athlete had a duty to protect this as part of their broader role. As a result, on-field transgressions that ultimately impact upon the enjoyment of a sporting contest are particularly critically evaluated.

Attributions of blame also extended beyond the individual athlete and team. The rarefied and often stereotypical macho culture of sports was seen to promote the normalization of certain behavior, such as heavy alcohol consumption. In considering sports culture, particularly among members of a sporting team, informants describe perceptions of protective behaviors that had the potential to form a cocoon that misaligned athlete behavior with societal norms.

Concluding thoughts

While consumers have an indirect relationship with individual athletes, they also have beliefs and expectations of what constitutes appropriate behavior within that relationship, on and off the playing field. Transgressions by athletes present a real threat to the relationship between consumers and sports entities (or the sport itself) as attributions of blame frequently extend beyond the athlete. This type of conflict has been identified as a form of degenerative episode between sport organizations and their sponsors (Westberg et al., 2011) and may similarly impact on the relationship between consumers and sporting entities.

As the negative impact of conflict can outweigh the positive influence of a firm's relationship marketing strategy (Palmatier et al., 2006) it is critical that sports organizations understand consumer expectations and effectively manage transgressions to minimize relational damage. This harm may not always be visible in the form of customer behavior typically seen with services (complaint or exit), but impacts on commitment to the relationship (Jones et al., 2011). In sports, such damaged relationships can lead to a discontentment that manifests itself in reduced spectating (Kim and Trail, 2011) and reductions in levels of identification and motivation, which are critical to ensuring the levels of engagement needed in sports.

Sports administrators also need to be aware that consumers readily distinguish between a transgressive act by an athlete and how this act is then handled by the athlete or their team. This extended consideration implies that consumers must be carefully monitored and managed throughout the period of a transgression to ensure that not only can they appropriately make sense of the incident, but that the follow-up actions are deemed to be congruent.

Suggested further research

The conceptual domain of athlete transgressions could be further developed to posit frameworks that highlight that it is the collection of many varied episodes (both negative and positive with interventions) that make up the various relationships explored in this chapter. To reveal how these relationships evolve over time is the key as brand harm and relationship dissolution is often not a function of one major crisis or incident (Westberg et al., 2011). The work of Mazodier and Quester (2014) provides some guidance on the rigor necessary to investigate sponsorship topics longitudinally. Tracking relationship and dissolution trajectories for stakeholder partners needs to be implemented and individual trajectories could be estimated with advanced multivariate modelling techniques. An exploration of possible interventions through media or management responses by crisis types may further reveal key factors impacting positive maintenance and longer term key stakeholder relationship continuance.

Drawing further inspiration from the episodic and zone of tolerance perspective of Schurr et al. (2008) in business-to-business research, relationship dissolution for stakeholders occurs at different thresholds. To understand how to measure the threshold level given the stage in the relationship cycle would give sporting administrators a pre-emptive sign when dissolution is near. Management workshops could discuss and highlight between stakeholders how their own respective tolerances and thresholds may be unique.

Future studies should also have sufficient sample sizes and cross-cultural composition to provide a clearer distinction of viewpoints between managers and administrators of teams and also sporting entities. New methods could provide valuable micro-insights such as utilizing automated textual data coding tools and algorithms to reveal nuances missed with human coding.

Sports agents are an important part of the sports management mix and represent an area that has been relatively ignored in the literature regarding this topic. It would be remiss to believe that athletes are not advised carefully in the event of transgressions by their own agents and associated advisors (marketing/celebrity agents, legal teams, social media experts, etc.). Research studies need to include these valuable members.

Finally, it is natural that a relationship might cease because the contract has concluded or an athlete retires (Havila and Wilkinson, 2002) but the sporting celebrity has the potential to do just as much, or more, brand and reputational damage after their career has officially ended. Avenues for future research are many and varied in this respect. Herein is what makes this domain completely fascinating for researchers, in that potentially it never ends over the entire lifetime of the athlete as a brand.

References

Aaker, J., Fournier, S. and Brasel, A. (2004). When good brands do bad, *Journal of Consumer Research*, 31(1), 1–16.

Alajoutsijarvi, K., Moller, K. and Tahtinen, J. (2000). Beautiful exit: how to leave your business partner. *European Journal of Marketing*, 34(11/12), 1270–1290.

Berry, L. L. (1995). Relationship marketing of services: Growing interest, emerging perspectives. *Journal of the Academy of Marketing Science*, 23(4), 236–245.

Birch, J. (1994). New factors in crisis planning and response. *Public Relations Quarterly*, 39(1), 31–34.

Bush, A. J., Martin, C. A. and Bush, V. D. (2004). Sports celebrity influence on the behavioral intentions of generation Y. *Journal of Advertising Research*, 44(1), 108–118.

Cliffe, S. and Motion, J. (2005). Building contemporary brands: A sponsorship based strategy. *Journal of Business Research*, 58(8), 1068–1077.

Coombs, W. T. (2002). Deep and surface threats: Conceptual and practical implications for "crisis" vs "problem". *Public Relations Review*, 28(4), 339–345.

Cornwell, T. B., Weeks, C. and Roy, D. P. (2005). Sponsorship-linked marketing: Opening the black box. *Journal of Advertising*, 31(2), 21–42.

Couretas, J. (1985). Preparing for the worst. *Business Marketing*, 70, 96–100.

de Nooy, W., Mrvar, A. and Batagelj, V. (2005). *Exploratory social network analysis with Pajek*. New York: Cambridge University Press.

Dix, S., Phau, I. and Pougnet, S. (2010). Bend it like Beckham: The influence of sports celebrities on young adult consumers. *Young Consumers*, 11(1), 36–46.

Dwyer, R., Schurr, P. and Oh, S. (1987). Developing buyer-seller relationships. *Journal of Marketing*, 51(2), 11–27.

Dyer, J. H. and Singh, H. (1998). The relational view: cooperative strategy and sources of interorganizational competitive advantage. *The Academy of Management Review*, 23(4), 660–679.

Erdogan, B. F. (1999). Celebrity endorsement: a literature review. *Journal of Marketing Management*, 15(4), 291–314.

Fearn-Banks, K. (1996). *Crisis communications: A casebook approach*. Mahwah: Lawrence Erlbaum and Associates.

Fournier, S. (1998). Consumers and their brands: Developing relationship theory in consumer research. *Journal of Consumer Research*, 24(4), 343–373.

Ford, D. & Associates. (2002). *The business marketing course: Managing in complex networks*. Chichester: John Wiley & Sons.

Gardial, S., Flint, D. and Woodruff, R. (1996). Trigger events: Exploring the relationships between critical events and consumers' evaluations, standards, emotions, values and behavior, *Journal of Consumer Satisfaction, Dissatisfaction and Complaining Behavior*, 9, 35–51.

Halinen, A., Salmi, A. and Havila, V. (1999). From dyadic change to changing networks: An analytical framework. *Journal of Management Studies*, 36(6), 779–794.

Havila, V. and Wilkinson, I. (2002). The principle of the conservation of business relationship energy: Or many kinds of new beginnings, *Industrial Marketing Management*, 31(2), 191–203.

Ingall, C. K. (1997). *Metaphors, maps and mirrors: Moral education in middle schools.* Greenwich: C. T. Ablex Publishing Corporation.

Jones, T., Dacin, P. and Taylor, S. F. (2011). Relational damage and relationship repair: A new look at transgressions in service relationships, *Journal of Service Research*, 14(3), 318–339.

Kahuni, A. T., Rowley, J. and Binsardi, A. (2009). Guilty by association: image 'spill-over' in corporate co-branding. *Corporate Reputation Review*, 12(1), 52–63.

Kelley, H. H. and Michela, J. L. (1980). Attribution theory and research. *Annual Review of Psychology*, 31, 457–501.

Kersten, A. (2005). Crisis as usual: Organizational dysfunction and public relations. *Public Relations Review*, 31(4), 544–549.

Kim, Y. K. and Trail, G. (2011). A conceptual framework for understanding relationships between sport consumers and sport organizations: A relationship quality approach. *Journal of Sport Management*, 25(1), 57–69.

Lafferty, B. A. (2002). The dual credibility model: the influence of corporate and endorser credibility on attitudes and purchase intentions. *Journal of Marketing Theory and Practice*, 10(3), 1–12.

Mazodier, M. and Quester, P. (2014). The role of sponsorship for changing brand affect: A latent growth modeling approach. *International Journal of Research in Marketing,* 31(1), 16–29.

Melnick, M. J. and Jackson, S. J. (2002). Globalization American-style and reference idol selection. *International Review for the Sociology of Sport*, 37, 3–4, 429–448.

O'Beirne, P. and Ries, S. (1999). Extinguishing the fires: Crisis management in sport marketing. *Cyber-Journal of Sport Marketing*, 3(2), http://fulltext.ausport.gov.au/fulltext/1999/cjsm/v3n2/obeirne32.htm (accessed October 20, 2014).

Ohanian, R. (1991). The impact of celebrity spokespersons' perceived image on intention to purchase. *Journal of Advertising Research*, 31(1), 46–54.

Palmatier, R., Dant, R., Grewal, D. and Evans, K. (2006). Factors influencing the effectiveness of relationship marketing: A meta-analysis. *Journal of Marketing*, 70(4), 136–153.

Parry, K. D. (2009). Search for the hero: An investigation into the sports heroes of British sports fans. *Sport in Society: Cultures, Commerce, Media, Politics.* 12(2), 212–226.

Roche, M. (2000). *Mega-events and modernity: Olympics and expos in the growth of global culture.* London: Routledge.

Rojek, C. (2006). Sports celebrity and the civilizing process. *Sport in Society: Cultures, Commerce, Media, Politics*, 9(4), 674–690.

Schurr, P. H., Hedaa, L. and Geersbro, J. (2008). Interaction episodes as engines of relationship change. *Journal of Business Research*, 61(8), 877–884.

Shostack, L. G. (1985). Planning the service encounter. In *The service encounter*, Czepiel, J., Solomon, M. and Surprenant, C. (Eds.), Lexington: D. C. Heath and Co.

Stoldt, G. C., Dittmore, S. and Branvold, S. (2012). *Sport public relations: Managing stakeholder communication.* Champaign: Human Kinetics.

Tomlinson, A. and Young, C. (2006). *National identity and sports events.* Albany: SUNY Press.

Urriolagoitia, L. and Planellas, M. (2007). Sponsorship relationships as strategic alliances: A lifecycle model approach. *Business Horizons*, 50(2), 157–166.

van Doorn, J. and Verhoef, P. C. (2008). Critical incidents and the impact of satisfaction on customer share. *Journal of Marketing,* 72 (July), 123–142.

Westberg, K., Stavros, C. and Wilson, B. (2011). The impact of degenerative episodes on the sponsorship B2B relationship: implications for brand management, *Industrial Marketing Management.* 40(4), 603–611.

Wilson, B., Stavros, C. and Westberg, K. (2008). Player transgressions and the management of the sport sponsor relationship. *Public Relations Review*, 34(2), 99–107.

Wilson, B., Stavros, C. and Westberg, K. (2010). A sport crisis typology: Establishing a pathway for future research. *International Journal of Sport Management and Marketing*, 7, 21–32.

Yancey, A. K. (1998). Building positive self image in adolescents in foster care: The use of role models in an interactive group approach. *Adolescence,* 33(130), 253–268.

Zhou, L. and Whitla, P. (2013). How negative celebrity publicity influences consumer attitudes: The mediating role of moral reputation. *Journal of Business Research,* 66(8), 1013–1020.

25

MARKETING WOMEN'S SPORTS

A European versus North American perspective

Nancy Lough and Ceyda Mumcu

Marketing women's sports: a global perspective

Marketing women's sports has received little attention among scholars. As Toffoletti and Mewett reported, "female voices and perspectives have been largely ignored in sports fan research and in the wider cultural imagination" (2012: p. 1). To date, scholarly work on female fans and spectators has focused on gender differences positioning women as "others" within the masculine domain of sports. Examples include studies examining women's attendance at live sporting events (Fink et al., 2002; Gauthier and Hansen, 1993), female consumption of live television broadcasts of sport events (Clark et al., 2009; Gantz and Wenner, 1995), gender differences relating to motivations for sports spectatorship (Farrell et al., 2011; James and Ridinger, 2002; Lough and Kim, 2004), and fan affinity and fan avidity of female consumers of sports (Armstrong, 2001; Dixon, 2002; Wann et al., 2004). Women as "others" within the domain of sports represents one of the many challenges those marketing women's sports face. The commodification of female sports fans has been noted, suggesting there is an increasing awareness of the potential value aligned with women as sports consumers and women's sports as a product. Within the United States women are responsible for 65% of all apparel purchases, 52% of all new vehicle purchases, 70% of all travel decisions and 80% of family healthcare decisions (Brennan, 2011), suggesting the female economy is ripe for targeting.

Similar to most, the sports industry ignores the women's market. Sports scholars have studied the lack of "women's voices" in the sports context and have attributed women's emergence as sports fans and spectators as being grounded in female marginalization from and in sports (Gosling, 2007). As Hall (1985) explained, the marginalization of woman's voices is attributable to the "gender structuring of sport organizations, the organizational processes and dynamics that structure gender, and the relations of power between women and men within an organizational context" (p. 273). Interestingly, Hall suggested that participation by women in sports could function as an effective source of liberation and sense of inclusion in sports that could combat the historical "silencing" of women in this area. More recently, this silencing has started to shift with increasing numbers of women's teams, events, and sports properties creating a new level of awareness regarding women sports. For example, the 2012 Olympic Games in London were referred to as the Women's Olympics, with a record 4,847 women entering, representing every country for the first time in history (Brown, 2012). The addition of women's boxing for the first time meant women were also represented in all sports, with a record 132 possible medals totaling five more than in Bejing in 2008 (Elliot, 2012).

In today's technology-driven sport landscape, a different type of silencing often occurs. For example, the Women's Sports and Fitness Foundation found only 7% of media coverage was allocated to women's sport in the UK, which points to how the media effectively works to silence women in sports by either ignoring or trivializing it (WSFF, 2014). In contrast, there is a well-established symbiotic relationship between the sports media and mainstream sports organizations. Marketing efforts dedicated to mainstream sports, such as football, can rely on the media for "audience building", which effectively promotes them above and beyond all others (Duncan and Messner, 1998). This strategy has proven effective, with additional value being attributed to men's sports, due to the extended audience reach offered directly by media coverage. Yet this strategy is ineffective for women's sports because of the lack of media coverage, which creates a unique challenge for those marketing women's sports.

When the marketing efforts dedicated to women's sports mimic the typical model for more established men's sports, the result is very limited success. For example, only .4% of the total value for commercial sponsorship in the UK was found to be attributed to women's sport (WSFF, 2014). When no symbiotic relationship between mainstream media and women's sport exists, the potential for additional avenues for promotion and revenue generation also diminish. Arguably, the lack of media coverage diminishes the potential for sponsorship objectives such as extended audience reach and brand exposure, thereby decreasing the value potential attributed to sponsorship of women's sports. Therefore, in today's highly competitive sports landscape, more unique and effective strategies are warranted to effectively promote women's sports, including targeted tactics to reach the women's sport market. To illustrate the current lack of understanding, Lough and Kim (2004) discovered a South Korean women's professional basketball league made continuous efforts to improve the fan experience by enhancing in-game promotions and improving the league website. Yet not all new marketing initiatives were "based on known needs and wants because no research had been done to determine or understand the needs and wants of the fans" (p. 41).

To date, little effort has gone into understanding consumers of women's sports and less effort has emerged in the development of a fan base for most women's sports properties. As we will see from the contrasting models from Europe and the United States, much work remains to fully understand how to best approach the marketing of women's sports. To understand why a strategic marketing focus is needed, we look first at the societal notions of gender and how they have impacted perceptions of women athletes, and thereby diminished the value associated with women's sports as a product. We then consider the media's impact, which typically works against women's sports as it creates a disparity between women's and mainstream men's sports, which then impacts needed investments, such as sponsorships. Little attention has been paid to how the limited media attention impacts women's sports product by creating barriers to communication channels, which limits key marketing objectives of sponsors. Finally, we look to the potential of alternative sources such as dedicated websites and social media to provide innovative strategies needed to provide access for fans and consumers of women's sports.

History of oppression, social acceptance: perception of value of women's sports product

1972 was a milestone for women's sports in the United States. With the passage of Title IX, opportunities to participate in sports expanded for girls and women. According to Women's

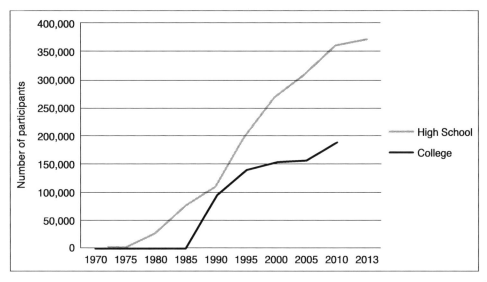

Figure 25.1 Girls' and women's sports participation

Sport Foundation, girls' and women's sport participation increased by 560% at college level and 990% in high schools. Yet society's perception of female athletes and women's sports changed little, even with federal legislation enacted.

Most societies view gender as a dualistic notion, meaning masculinity and femininity are at opposite ends. Female athletes are viewed as violating gender roles due to the fact that sports have long been considered to be male-oriented, masculine activities (Coakley, 2008). Traditionally, the predominant perspective in American society has considered the roles of "female" and "athlete" as being incompatible. Society identifies femininity based on appearance, behaviors and body type with the ideal female image being small, thin and model-like (Krane et al., 2004). Female athletes are typically perceived as not conforming to this feminine ideal due to the amount of strength, muscle and masculine features that they possess.

For example, female athletes have self-confidence, a positive sense of self and solid self-concept, and they recognize themselves as being strong and powerful individuals who are proud of their bodies and identities. Former professional athlete and author, Mariah Burton Nelson, stated her opinion on female athletes and femininity as follows: "It is not feminine to know exactly what you know, then go for it. Femininity is about appearing beautiful and vulnerable and small. It is about winning male approval" (Ross and Shinew, 2008). In general, female athletes are perceived as violating stereotypical female gender roles and because of this, they are typically denied the status, respect or approval provided to their male counterparts based on athletic performance. Explanations for this phenomenon point to the blurred areas between bipolar dimensions of masculinity and femininity that violate societal perceptions of power differentials. As a result, women athletes are often seen as threats to the social order, which is dictated by masculine hegemony in most societies (Bryson, 1987).

Societal perceptions of female athletes reflect on how women's sports are evaluated. Disapproval of female athletes often works to diminish the value attributed to women's sports as a product. Media representations of women athletes contribute significantly to creating impressions of the women's sports as an inferior product. For example, the mainstream sports media very typically emphasizes a female athlete's femininity and presents a sexualized image instead of stressing her sports competence or athleticism. During the 2014 Australian Open, 19-year-old Canadian tennis player, Eugenie Bouchard, was interviewed courtside after qualifying for her first career grand slam semi-finals and instead of getting questions about her performance on the court, she was asked about her dream date (Chase, 2014). In this case, the media's approach belittled Bouchard's success at a major tennis tournament and thereby diminished the potential to build appreciation of the quality of the women's sports product. Similarly, in 2014, after the WNBA All-Star game, Bleacherreport.com published a video composed of bad passes and mistakes from the game while ignoring the highlights of the game, which included Brittney Griner's dunk and Shoni Schimmel's spectacular athletic moves. Too often the sports media chooses to present female athletes as weak and incapable, thereby devaluing women's sports as a product. In comparison, the sports media actively builds audiences for mainstream men's sports, thereby driving ticket sales, improving sponsorship value and increasing salary potential for male athletes (Duncan and Messner, 1998). The devaluation of women's sports by the media results in lower attendance numbers and ticket prices for women's sporting events, which lead to lower salaries for professional women athletes.

Professional women's sports in the US

A review of the history of women's professional team sports reveals that women's sports as a product has had a difficult time thriving in the United States. Throughout the 1990s and early 2000s, many professional leagues were established, only to be disbanded a few years later. The first two women's professional softball and basketball leagues filed for bankruptcy and folded within a few years after their establishment (Elyachar and Moag, 2002; Spencer and McClung, 2001; Wesley, 1999). Women's professional soccer shared the same destiny as women's professional softball and basketball. The Women's United Soccer Association (WUSA) suspended operations with losses of more than $100 million in three years, due to a substantial decline in attendance and television viewership and lack of major sponsorship revenue (Rovell, 2003). Similarly, the second women's professional soccer league, Women's Professional Soccer (WPS) was terminated due to a lack of fan support and media coverage in 2012 (Pethchesky, 2012). In 2014, the National Pro Fastpitch (NPF), Women's National Basketball Association (WNBA) and Women's Soccer League (NWSL) were continuing their businesses with support of their male counterparts, MLB, NBA and MLS. The National Women's Soccer League (NWSL) also received support from the United States Soccer Federation, Canadian Soccer Association and Federation of Mexican Football in an effort to reduce overall expenses and develop a balanced revenue-expense model with potential for sustainability (Foudy, 2013).

Women's sports in Europe

While professional women's team sports struggle to survive in the United States, the state of women's sports varies across Europe. Volleyball and basketball have been the most popular women's sports in Europe. Perhaps this is due to the fact that many countries have a multi-tier league system in women's volleyball and basketball. While teams play in their respective leagues in their country, the top team or two from each league also compete in regional championships organized by Fédération Internationale de Basketball (FIBA) and Confédération Européenne de Volleyball (CEV). Sixteen teams from ten countries compete in FIBA Europe's top tier women's basketball competition-Euroleague, and 31 teams representing 12 countries compete in the second tier competition called EuroCup (The FIBA Europe Championships). Similarly, CEV organizes the Champions League and Challenge Cup among clubs from

Table 25.1 History of women's professional sports in the United States

Baseball Leagues	Founded	Ceased
All-American Girls Professional Baseball League	1943	1954
Ladies League Baseball/Ladies Professional Baseball	1997	1998
Basketball Leagues		
Women's Professional Basketball League	1978	1981
Women's Basketball Association	1993	1995
American Basketball League	1996	1998
Women's National Basketball Association	1997	Current
Football Leagues		
Women's Football Association	2000	2004
Women's Professional Football League	1999	2007
Women's Football Alliance	2009	Current
Hockey League		
National Women's Hockey League	1999	2007
National Women's Hockey League	2015	Current
Softball Leagues		
International Women's Professional Softball Association	1976	1980
Women's Professional Softball League	1997	2001
National Pro Fast-pitch	2002	Current
Soccer Leagues		
Women's United Soccer Association	2001	2004
Women's Professional Soccer league	2007	2011
National Women's Soccer League	2013	Current
Volleyball League		
Major League Volleyball	1987	1989
Women's Professional Volleyball Association	1987	1999
Individual Sports		
Ladies Professional Golf Association	1950	Current
Women's Tennis Association	1973	Current

women's volleyball leagues in Europe (The European Volleyball Confederation Championships). These regional championships are beneficial in many ways. They create rivalries among countries, develop community and country support for women's sports, and also increase awareness and exposure. However, extensions of the champion's leagues and cups in women's sports should not be understood at the same level as the Champions League of men's football in Europe. Clubs receive small funds for participating in these events, unlike men's football, mostly due to the lack of large broadcasting rights.

In more recent years, women's football has also become more popular in Europe. According to UEFA, in 2014 there were professional women's football leagues in 46 countries competing at different levels (division 1, 2 and 3). One of the strongest women's professional football leagues is Sweden's Damallsvenskan, which is the highest division of women's football in the country. Experts believe that the league would never fold and Malmö's coach, Jonas Eidevall, supports this belief by saying "Damallsvenskan can never fold as a league. If one club would fold, another one would be promoted. Maybe not all clubs would be professional, but the league would always live on" ("Women's soccer", 2014).

Table 25.2 UEFA Member associations in women's football by year, number of players and clubs

Member association information	Member association information
Football Association of Albania – 2009 225 & 9	Lithuanian Football Federation – 2001 595 & 23
Austrian Football Association – 2005 17,000 & 265	Luxembourg Football Federation – 1972 1,793 & 38
Football Federation of Belarus – 1992 970 & 5	Malta Football Association – 1995 1,318 & 18
Royal Belgium Football Association – 1971 16,562 & 228	Football Association of Moldova – 1996 360 & 7
Bosnia & Herzegovina Football Federation – 1998 460 players	Royal Netherlands Football Association – 1972 124,100 & 47, 594
Bulgarian Football Union – 1981 350 & 12	Irish Football Association – 1998 1,149 & 49
Croatian Football Federation – 1971 1,732 & 26	Football Association of Norway – 1976 108,400 players
Cyprus Football Association – 1972 879 & 9	Polish Football Federation – 1991 5,000 & 70
Football Association of the Czech Republic – 1992 18,776 & 120	Portuguese Football Federation – 1985 1,683 & 40
Danish Football Association – 1974 71,273 & 339	Football Association of Ireland – 1991 21,590 & 300
English Football Association – 1993 6,600 teams	Romanian Football Federation – 1990 450 & 21
Estonian Football Association – 1994 698 & 22	Russian Football Union – 1987 32,000 & 320
Faroe Islands Football Association – 1984 1,202 players	Scottish Football Association – 1998 2,600 & 60
Football Association of Finland – 1972 26,423 & 250	Football Association of Serbia – 1970 1,230 & 32
French Football Federation – 1970 Not available	Slovak Football Association – 1993 880 & 24
Football Association of the FYR of Macedonia –1948 Not available	Football Association of Slovenia – Not Available Not Available
German Football Association – 1970 250,000 & 5,486	Royal Spanish Football Federation – 1988 61,394 & 104
Hellenic Football Federation – 1989 3,242 & 41	Swedish Football Association – 1988 299,855 players
Hungarian Football Federation – 1982 2,600 & 50	Swiss Football Association – 1993 22,978 & 20
Football Association of Iceland – 1981 6,571 & 26	Turkish Football Federation – 1971 48,691 & 72
Israel Football Association – 1996 948 & 13	Football Federation of Ukraine – 1992 222 & 8
Italian Football Federation – 1974 12,975 & 365	Football Association of Wales – 1993 2,509 & 82
Football Federation of Kazakhstan – 1987 280 & 7	
Latvian Football Federation – 1998 647 & 5	

Source: Information retrieved from www.uefa.com/memberassociations/women/index.html

An important point should be made here to explain why Damallsvenskan would never fold since women's professional leagues in volleyball and basketball would also never fold in Europe; the way sports are structured in Europe is why these leagues will always live on. In Europe, most leagues are organized in a multi-tier system (Li, MacIntosh and Bravo, 2012). In other words, there is a pyramidal hierarchical system in place with promotion and relegation. If a team folds for any reason, a team from the lower tier will be promoted to replace the folded team at the end of the current season. For example, Tyreso of Damallsvenskan, which is one of the best teams in Europe and in the world with a wealth of talent, announced in June 2014 that the team would not finish the season due to financial problems and players were released immediately (Kassauf, 2014). At the end of the 2014 season, in addition to regular promotion and relegation moves of clubs, one more team from division two was then promoted to the Damallsvenskan. Although teams may and do fold, the league will continue to survive due to this system and the fact that there will always be enough teams to continue the league each year.

The multi-tier system is not the only reason women's professional sports leagues have remained in Europe for decades. Existence of multi-sport clubs is another reason for sustainability of women's sports. For example, in Turkey, female athletes compete in professional volleyball and basketball leagues. Some of the teams in these leagues are part of multisport clubs where several sports are supported within the club. Men's football is the mainstream sport at these clubs, which drives the business, whereas women's professional sports and other non-revenue sports are subsidized by total revenues of the club, mostly generated by men's football, sponsorship agreements, broadcasting rights and shares collected from national sports betting.

Although this system keeps women's sports alive, it has weaknesses. There are large discrepancies in the budgets of the teams within leagues, especially women's teams from the three most successful and biggest clubs in Turkey (Galatasaray, Fenerbahçe and Beşiktaş), which are known as the "Big Three" and typically dominate their appropriate leagues. Smaller teams' budgets are not comparable to the teams of the Big Three clubs, which leads to incomparable talent on team rosters and lack of competitive balance in the leagues. In addition to big differences in budgets, not having a draft system allows these teams to create team rosters full of high caliber American and European players with the best domestic players by offering high salaries. For example, in 2010, Diana Taurasi was offered a salary more than four times her WNBA salary by Fenerbahçe (C. Ates, personal communication, November 27, 2013). In 2014, Madelaynne Montano and Caroline Costagrande were paid high salaries of approximately \$1 million each, in the Turkish Professional Women's Volleyball League ("Highest paid European", 2014).

There is an important point to be made here. Although being paid large sums of money makes female athletes professional, it must be understood that women's sports leagues and clubs are not always managed professionally. Even the Big Three clubs in Turkey do not have a full time staff solely responsible to handle the business aspects of women's professional basketball and volleyball. Most often, the business operations of women's sports are handled by the club management (E. Memnun, personal communication, September 6, 2014). This approach results in limited marketing activities and a lack of exposure and awareness, resulting in limited revenue generation. So although the multisport club system has the potential to create profitable women's professional sports teams in Turkey, the clubs' management often does not take a business based approach, and therefore, they fail to capitalize on the marketing opportunities available considering the large fan bases aligned with each of these clubs.

The clubs support women's sports for the love of sports and also due to rivalries among the Big Three. WNBA players, Angel McCoughtry and Seimone Augustus, explain the extent of rivalry among these clubs:

McCoughtry says "You don't know till you come here. It's worse than Yankees–Red Sox. It's deep. It's instilled in you growing up. It's really unique. You're like 'What in the world is this?'" While these types of rivalries are common across Europe in football or in men's basketball, it rarely is heard of on the women's side. Augustus adds "You see Gala fans on one side and Fener on the other. The police are in the middle and somehow fights usually break out in the stands" ("American women know", 2012).

These WNBA players' descriptions of Turkish fans are best explained by what are known of as "fan associations" in Turkey. The Big Three have large followings in Turkey with 35%, 33% and 20% of sports fans identifying as followers of Galatasaray, Fenerbahçe and Beşiktaş, respectively (Fan Percentages of Soccer Clubs in Turkey, 2009). Some of these fans are members of "fan associations", which means they act as an organized fan group, attend games together, cheer together and also fight together.

Although women's professional basketball, volleyball and football leagues have been in existence for decades in Europe, this is not the case for other women's sports. On February 13, 2014, cricket became a professional sport for women in the UK. The England and Wales Cricket Board announced they were creating the first group of full-time women's professional cricketers and would fund the league and players' salaries with revenues from International Cricket Council events held in England ("England to have first", 2014). Similarly, according to BBC Sports, women's rugby players are becoming professional in England as they will be paid for the first time in 2014. The Rugby Football Union (RFU) announced that they will be giving full-time contracts to 20 top players. Women's rugby will be included for the first time in the 2016 Olympic Games and RFU decided on a professional setup in order to allow England to compete effectively against other full-time opponents at the Olympic Games ("Women's Rugby", 2014).

Women's sport disparity

The current status of women's sports in the US and Europe indicates that women's sports are still far from being on par with men's sports. Unfortunately, the media's representation of

Table 25.3 Comparison of WNBA and Turkish Women's Basketball League (TWBL)

	WNBA	TWBL
Founded	1996	1980
Format	Closed league system	Promotion–Relegation System
# of teams in 2014–15	12	14
# of regular season games	34	26
Most titles	Houston Comets (4)	Galatasaray (12)
Highest attendance	22,076	15,000
Average attendance 2014	7,578	Not available
Broadcasters	ESPN/ABC	Turkish Basketball Federation TV
	NBA TV	TV channels of multi-sport clubs
Major revenue sources	Sponsorship fees	Sponsorship fees
	Broadcasting fees	Share from national betting site, Iddia
		No broadcasting revenue
Min–max player salary 2014–2015	$34,500–$107,000	$15,000–$500,000

female athletes and women's sports has contributed to the disparity, by activating negative stereotypes and providing prejudicial treatment of women's sports. Gender marking, language use, familial references made about female athletes, and the sexualization that works to trivialize the accomplishments of female athletes, have all served to diminish the value sports marketers work to create and associate with the women's sports product.

Gender marking is one way the media contributes to the marginalization of women's sports, resulting in this disparity. Women's sports competitions are often labeled as women's events in the media while men's competitions are not specified with any gender. For instance, the NCAA Final Four is used to describe the men's college basketball tournament in the US, while the women's tournament is labeled as the Women's Final Four, even though the events take place in different locations at different times. Similarly, the World Cup is the term used to refer to the men's World Championship in soccer. Although the Women's World Championship is held a year after the men's World Cup, and therefore, there would be no confusion if the women's event was also labeled as the World Cup. Instead, the women's World Championship in soccer is referred as the Women's World Cup. The gender marking of women's competitions implies that men's sports are the mainstream sports and women's sports are the second tier, or substandard to the mainstream men's sport product, which also positions women as the "other".

In addition to gender marking, the language used by commentators contributes to the marginalization of female athletes and women's sports generally. Female athletes are often infantilized by media with comments such as girls. According to Sabo and Jansen (1992), female athletes are most often referred to as girls, while male athletes are referred to as men or young men. For example, in 2014 commentators continued to infantilize female athletes during the Winter Olympic Games in Sochi, as NBC Sport's commentators consistently referred to female athletes competing in the skiing half pipe competition as girls (Feeney, 2014). The media's language use results in infantilization of female athletes, and thereby supports the status quo within the sports industry, giving men's sports privilege and power while actively diminishing the image of female athletes by presenting them as childlike, weak, dependent and passive.

The media also degrades female athletes and women's sports with familial references. According to Kinnick (1998), female athletes' relationships are more often described than those of their male counterparts. *Gender in Televised Sports* by Messner, Cooky, and Hextrum (2010) provides examples of familial references. For example, *SportCenter* reported on two-time Olympic gold medalist track-and-field star, Sanya Richards, but she was introduced as the fiancée of Aaron Ross of the New York Giants. By introducing Richards as Ross' fiancée, *SportsCenter* emphasized her relationship status over her athletic accomplishments. Familial references of female athletes degrade their success as athletes and puts their relationship status at the front as their main identity. Presenting female athletes as childlike and emphasizing their roles as wives and mothers actively downplays the image of female athletes as competent competitors, while supporting traditional gender roles and maintaining male hegemony in the sport industry.

Kane and Maxwell (2011) found women's sports and female athletes have been marketed and represented in the media predominantly using attractiveness. During the 2014 Winter Olympics in Sochi, in a segment about how extreme the course was for skiers, the NBC skiing analyst, Steve Porino, said that the female athletes do "all of that while in a Lycra suit, maybe a little bit of makeup—now that is grace under pressure" (Feeney, 2014). In addition to highlighting female athletes' femininity and attractiveness with comments similar to Porino's, female athletes are often photographed in sexual rather than athletic poses, and female athletes are marketed using their sex appeal (Kim, Sagas and Walker, 2011). According to Kinnick (1998), sexualization of female athletes "frames them as something to be gazed upon for others' pleasure and diminishes their identity as athletes" (p. 212). Presenting female athletes by utilizing their sex appeal does little to increase the popularity of the athlete and women's sports but rather diminishes the value of the female athlete and her sports. Kane and Maxwell's (2011) results challenged the notion that "sportswomen are best served when presented as pretty, 'sexy babes' rather than as highly competent and dedicated athletes" (p. 1). In a clear and important summary, the author's findings provided evidence that "sex does not sell" women's sports.

The media has a strong influence on viewers' perceptions of female athletes and women's sports. Although they cannot directly tell the viewer what to think, they contribute to the creation of societal views using framing of stories. In essence, the media defines the situation and issues for viewers and they actively implant their biased views. Highlighting female athletes' familial roles and describing them as weak, passive and childlike, sexualizing them with trivializing comments and photographs, works to create an inferior image of female athletes and thereby lessens the value and quality of women's sports in the eyes of consumers. Through these approaches, the media contributes to creating disparity between men's and women's sports, and reinforces existing gender roles and power structures while naturalizing masculine hegemony within the sport marketplace.

Improving media coverage

In addition to the content of media coverage, the quantity of media coverage of female athletes and women's sports also results in an important disparity. According to the Media Coverage and Female Athletes report published by Tucker Center for Research on Girls and Women's Sports (2014), 40% of the sports participants are female in the US although women's sports only receive 2–4% of sports media coverage. Furthermore, over the past decade, the visibility of women's sports on TV has declined (Messner, Cooky and Hextrum, 2010). In Europe, media coverage of women's sports is at similar levels. The Women's Sport and Fitness Foundation (WSFF) of England reported women's sports were sidelined, receiving only 5% of the sports media coverage after the historic summer of women's sports attributed to the 2012 Olympics in London (Topping, 2012). Men's and women's sports get more balanced media coverage during the Olympic Games, although during the 2010 Winter Olympics in Vancouver, men's sports received more than 60% of airtime in Canada after researchers excluded mixed gender competitions. Their conclusion was that male athletes were mentioned significantly more often in the media than female athletes (Angelini, MacArthur and Billings, 2012).

This limited media coverage of women's sports is related to a lack of interest among the male dominant media executives. Higher ratings are required to increase coverage of women's sports, to justify their existence in programming and to be profitable for media. However, in order to increase interest, the public needs to be exposed to women's sports and perceive women's sports as quality athletic competitions. Thus, the lack of media coverage conveys the impression that "women's sports are inexistent or have no achievements" that are newsworthy (Kinnick, 1998). In addition, the content of the coverage marginalizes women's sports by presenting female athletes as eye candy for the viewing pleasure of a male audience. Therefore, improved media coverage with higher quality content, based upon athletic competence and achievement is required to develop the positive perceptions of women's sports necessary to increase interest in women's sports and build a sustainable fanbase.

New media

To combat the lack of media exposure, new media has increasingly substantiated the interest in women athletes and women's sports. For example, Serena Williams has more than 4 million Twitter followers and Maria Sharapova has more than 15 million likes on her Facebook page. ESPNW was created in 2010 as an online destination for women's sports content. By 2014, ESPNW was reporting 19.8 million unique page views per month, up 71% from 2013 (ESPNW Summit, 2014). Clearly, women's sports consumers face the challenge of needing to seek out content or coverage for their sport of choice. During the 2014 Winter Olympic Games in Sochi, 1.16 million fans streamed the women's gold medal hockey game when the United States faced Canada. These types of ratings are providing the evidence needed to demonstrate a viable audience exists for women's sports. Social media, such as Twitter, Facebook and Instagram have become the choice for fan engagement among millennials. Fortunately for women's sports fans, new media provides a shift away from the reliance on information pushed by the media, toward consumer's creating content and supporting women sports more directly, and thereby effectively transforming the effect of the traditional "gatekeepers".

Marketing remedy

When women's sports is marketed well, success often follows. For example, the global status of the WTA has been enhanced by the success of celebrity athletes and 54 events played in 33 countries. In 2008, there were only two events in China, by 2016 there will be 11. In contrast, when Billie Jean King founded the WTA, there were 14 events, primarily in the United States. The fortieth anniversary of the WTA in 2013 was marked by a shifting focus toward engaging fans through entertainment as a strategy to grow the product. With a record 5.4 million people attending women's tennis events in 2013, WTA Commissioner Stacy Allaster set a goal to eventually award $180–200 million in prize money, which is a significant increase from the $120 million awarded in 2014. To drive that growth the WTA intends to create compelling events for fans. With increasing levels of sponsorship adding to record tournament earnings, this global women's sports property has contributed to the status of Serena Williams and Maria Sharapova as two of only three women in Forbes' top 100 wealthiest athletes. So while the

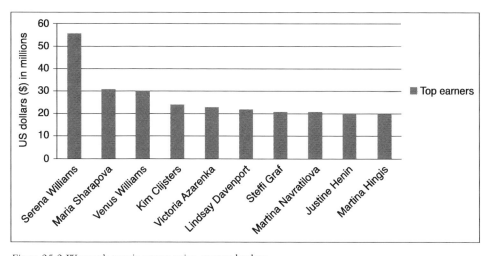

Figure 25.2 Women's tennis career prize money leaders

WTA is well-positioned for growth, more work remains to place this premier women's sports property on equal footing with other mainstream sport leagues.

Women are gaining recognition as a viable target market to grow, with data showing they comprise nearly 50 million avid followers of professional sport (Bush et al., 2005). With sports participation and interest increasing among women globally, the expectation seems reasonable that women's sports properties would be well-positioned for growth globally. Increasing sponsorship support will be tied directly to growth, which points to the need for more innovative strategies such as the use of social media. Additionally, as women increasingly gain recognition as a consumer base to target and grow, women's sports properties will be well-positioned to take advantage of this powerful consumer segment.

Conclusion

To continue to build the fan base for women's sports properties, more accurate data is needed on consumption patterns of women's sports fans. Too little is known and understood about consumers and fans of women's sports. By identifying why fans follow women's sports, the needs of consumers can be addressed more intentionally by marketers. Going forward, sport marketers need to shift their focus away from the typical sport fan demographic and begin to value the purchasing power of more distinct target markets. Both women and men follow the mainstream sports properties, such as the NFL and Euro League, therefore, there is no justification for expecting the fan base of women's sports to be restricted to one gender, only women.

To enhance the marketing of women's sports in the future, enhanced relationships with sponsors will be necessary. Women's sports properties are poised to seek sponsors from new categories, in an effort to recognize the economic power of women. Increasingly, women are recognized for making major purchasing decisions in categories such as insurance, financial, travel, etc., which can then be used to leverage messages of empowerment that resonate more authentically with a women's sports product. This strategy presents less risk to sponsors, and potentially cuts through the clutter apparent in mainstream sport marketing.

Finally, improving the image of sportswomen as being highly competent and dedicated athletes will assist sports marketers in achieving their desired goals. Simply recognizing that "sex does not sell" women's sports, will serve as one significant step toward creating new strategies to promote women's sports. This is an uphill battle, given the media has yet to make this important shift. However, unique approaches and innovative strategies are the hallmark of quality sports marketing. In the twenty-first century, women's sports are well-positioned to use these novel tactics to create a new era of growth.

References

American women know all about Turkish hoop rivalry (2012, July 24). *The Zaman*, www.todayszaman. com/news-287533-american-women-know-all-about-turkish-hoops-rivals.html (accessed 18 August 2015).

Armstrong, K. L. (2001). Self and product image congruency among male and female minor league ice hockey spectators: implications for women's consumption of professional men's sports, *Women in Sport and Physical Activity Journal*, 10(2), 27–39.

Angelini, J. R., MacArthur, P. J. and Billings, A. C. (2012). What's the gendered story? Vancouver's prime time Olympic glory on NBC. *Journal of Broadcasting & Electronic Media*, 56(2), 261–279.

Ates, C. (2013). An unpublished interview with Ceren Ates: Sport Agent/Interviewer: Ceyda Mumcu. New Haven, CT.

Brennan, B. (2011). *Why she buys: The new strategy for reaching the world's most powerful consumers.* New York: Random House.

Bryson, L. (1987). Sport and the maintenance of masculine hegemony. *Women's Studies Forum International*, 10(4), 349–360.

Bush, V. D., Bush, A. F., Clark, P. and Bush, R. P. (2005). Girl power and word-of-mouth behavior in the flourishing sports market. *Journal of Consumer Marketing*, 22(4/5), 257–264.

Chase, C. (2014, January 20). Canadian teen embarrassed after revealing dream date during Australian Open interview. *USA Today*, http://ftw.usatoday.com/2014/01/eugenie-bouchard-genie-justin-bieber-australian-open (accessed 18 August 2015).

Clark, J. S., Apostolopoulou, A. and Gladden, J. M. (2009). Real women watch football: Gender differences in the consumption of the NFL Super Bowl broadcast. *Journal of Promotion Management*, 15(1/2), 165–183.

Coakley, J. (2008). *Sports in society: Issues and controversies*. 8th ed. New York, NY: McGraw Hill.

Dixon, M. A. (2002). Gender differences in perceptions and attitudes toward the LPGA and its tour professionals: An empirical investigation. *Sport Marketing Quarterly*, 11, 44–54.

Duncan, M. C. and Messner, M. A. (1998). The media image of sport and gender. *MediaSport*, 170–185.

Elliot, R. (2012). London 2012 Olympics: The women's Games, www.independent.co.uk/sport/olympics/news/london-2012-olympics-the-womens-games-7976835.html (accessed 6 February 2014).

Elyachar, R. and Moag, L. (2002). The growth of women's sports, www.moagandcompany.com/i_a/Dec_02_womens_sports.pdf (accessed 25 February 2012).

England to have first full-time professional women's team. (2014). www.bbc.com/sport/0/cricket/26171943 (accessed 2 September 2014).

ESPNW (2014). Women + Sports Summit, October 13–15, http://espn.go.com/espnw/w-in-action/2014-summit/ (accessed 9 October 2015).

Fan Percentages of Soccer Clubs in Turkey. (2009). http://spor.haber7.com/spor/haber/415027-4-buyuklerin-taraftar-orani-yuzde-kac (accessed 6 September 2014).

Farrell, A. O., Fink, J. S. and Fields, S. K. (2011). Women's sport spectatorship: An exploration of men's influence. *Journal of Sport Management*, 25, 190–201.

Feeney, N. (2014). A brief history of sexism in TV coverage of the Olympics, www.theatlantic.com/entertainment/archive/2014/02/a-brief-history-of-sexism-in-tv-coverage-of-the-olympics/284003/ (accessed 2 September 2014).

Fink, J. S., Trail, G. T. and Anderson, D. F. (2002). Environmental factors associated with spectator attendance and sport consumption behavior: gender and team differences. *Sport Marketing Quarterly*, 11(1), 8–19.

Foudy, J. (2013). Will NWSL be a success? Well... http://espn.go.com/espnw/news-commentary/article/9161421/espnw-latest-women-professional-soccer-league-success (accessed 24 April 2013).

Gantz, W. and Wenner, L. (1995). Fanship and the television sports viewing experience. *Sociology of Sports Journal*, 12, 56–74.

Gauthier, R. and Hansen, H. (1993). Female spectators: Marketing implications for professional golf events. *Sport Marketing Quarterly*, 2(4), 21–26.

Gosling, V. K. (2007). Girls allowed? The marginalization of female sport fans in J. Gray, C. Sandvoss and C.L. Harrington (eds) *Fandom: Identities and communities in a mediated world*. New York: New York University Press.

Hall, M. A. (1985). Knowledge and gender: Epistemological questions in the social analysis of sport. *Sociology of Sport Journal*, 2, 25–42.

Highest paid European female volleyball players. (2014). www.volleywood.net/volleyball-features/music-style/highest-paid-european-female-volleyball-players/ (accessed 2 September 2014).

James, J. D. and Ridinger, L. L. (2002). Female and male sport fans: A comparison of sport consumption motives. *Journal of Sport Behavior*, 25(3), 260–278.

Kane, M. and Maxwell, H. D. (2011). Expanding the boundaries of sport media research: Using critical theory to explore consumer responses to representations of women's sports. *Journal of Sport Management*, 25(3), 202–216.

Kassauf, J. (2014). Tyreso won't finish season; players released immediately, http://womens.soccerly.com/2014/06/05/tyreso-folds-players-free-agents-wont-play-2014-damallsvenskan/ (accessed 2 September 2014).

Kim, K., Sagas, M. and Walker, N. A. (2011). Replacing athleticism with sexuality: Athlete models in Sports Illustrated Swimsuit Issues. *International Journal of Sport Communication*, 4(2), 148–162.

Kinnick, K. N. (1998). Gender bias in newspaper profiles of 1996 Olympic athletes: A content analysis of five major dailies. *Women's Studies in Communication,* 21(2), 212–237.

Krane, V., Choi, P. Y. L., Baird, S. M., Aimar, C. M. and Kauer, K. J. (2004). Living the paradox: Female athletes negotiate femininity and muscularity. *Sex Roles,* 50, 315–329.

Li, M., MacIntosh, E. W. and Bravo, G. A. (2012). *International sport management.* Champaign: Human Kinetics.

Lough, N. and Kim, A. (2004). Analysis of socio-motivations affecting spectator attendance at women's professional basketball games in South Korea. *Sport Marketing Quarterly,* 13(1), 35–42.

Memnun, E. (2014). An unpublished interview with Ekrem Memnun – Head Coach at Galatasaray Women's Basketball Team/Interviewer: Ceyda Mumcu: New Haven.

Messner, M., Cooky, C. and Hextrum, R. (2010). *Gender in televised sports news and highlights shows, 1989–2009.* University of Southern California: Center for Feminist Research.

Pethchesky, B. (2012). Women's professional soccer is officially dead, http://deadspin.com/5911436/womens-professional-soccer-is-officially-dead (accessed 16 January 2013).

Ross, S. R. and Shinew, K. J. (2008). Perspectives of women college athletes on sport and gender. *Sex Roles,* 58, 40–57.

Rovell, D. (2003). Still a business, not a cause, http://espn.go.com/sportsbusiness/s/2003/0915/1616775.html (accessed 16 January 2013).

Sabo, D. and Jansen, S. C. (1992). Images of men in sport media: The social reproduction of gender order. In Craig., S. (Ed.), *Men, masculinity, and the media* (169–184). Newbury Park: Sage.

Spencer, N. E. and McClung, L. R. (2001). Women and sport in the 1990s: Reflections on embracing starts, ignoring players. *Journal of Sport Management,* 15, 318–349.

The FIBA Europe Championships. www.fibaeurope.com/default.asp (accessed 2 September 2014).

The European Volleyball Confederation Championships. www.cev.lu/default.aspx (accessed 2 September 2014).

Toffoletti, K. and Mewett, P. (2012). *Sport and its female fans.* New York: Routledge.

Topping, A. (2012, October 24). Women's sport is underfunded and ignored, charity claims. *The Guardian,* www.theguardian.com/lifeandstyle/2012/oct/24/womens-sport-underfunded-ignored-charity-claims (accessed 18 August 2015).

Tucker Center for Research on Girls and Women in Sport and tptMN (Producer). (2014). Media coverage and female athletes report, http://video.tpt.org/video/2365132906/

Wann, D. L., Waddill, P. J. and Dunham, M. D. (2004). Using sex and gender role orientation to predict level of sport fandom. *Journal of Sport Behavior,* 27(4), 367–377.

Wesley, A. (1999). Was the 1999 pro softball season a hit with fans? *Amy Love's Real Sports,* 2(3), 46–47.

Women's Rugby: The players to be paid as England Seven turn pro. (2014). www.bbc.com/sport/0/rugby-union/28924321 (accessed 2 September 2014).

Women's soccer show me the money. (2014). www.sportsmyriad.com/2014/03/womens-soccer-show-me-the-money/ (accessed 2 September 2014)

Women's Sports and Fitness Foundation (2014). Say yes to success, www.wsff.org.uk/say-yes-to-success (accessed 6 February 2014).

Women's Sport Foundation (2013, March 18). Title IX Myths and Facts, www.womenssportsfoundation.org/en/home/advocate/title-ix-and-issues/what-is-title-ix/title-ix-myths-and-facts (accessed 2 September 2014).

26

THE ROLE OF SPORTS AS AN AGENT OF SOCIAL CHANGE AND MARKETING PERFORMANCE

Examining the charitable face of Real Madrid

Verónica Baena[1]

The current idea of corporate social responsibility (CSR) dates back to the early twentieth century, when business tycoons, such as Carnegie and Ford, began donating funds to improve social conditions (Sheth and Babiak, 2010). However, although most researchers and professionals agree that CSR has become a necessary business function, there is a great deal of variation in understanding how the term is characterized. More specifically, CSR deviates from the neoclassical economic view that the singular objective of the firm is to maximize shareholder value. In particular, "the challenge facing those who advocate corporate social initiatives then is to find a way to promote what they see as social justice in a world in which this shareholder wealth maximization paradigm reigns" (Margolis and Walsh, 2003: p. 273). Organizations have recently answered this challenge, resulting in a shift from the perception of CSR as a charitable activity to that of an integrated part of strategic management, whereby an organization incorporates CSR activities with business operations that add value to the business (Porter and Kramer, 2006).

Accordingly, the early part of the twenty-first century has ushered in an era of corporate scrutiny, and the heightened accountability that goes with it. Nevertheless, consumer distrust of many corporate entities is high, with the misdeeds of a few tainting the marketplace for the rest. For instance, headline-making companies, such as Enron, Arthur Andersen or Merrill Lynch, have triggered a rapid shift in how companies are viewed legally and by the public at large (Walker and Kent, 2009). Therefore, having a clear understanding of CSR is critical in the evaluation of every organization.

In terms of a definition, CSR is a tortured concept. Definitions among practitioners have proliferated, with groups such as the World Business Council (1999: p. 3) offering their own definition: "corporate social responsibility is the continuing commitment by business to contribute to economic development while improving the quality of life of the workforce and their families as well as of the community and society at large". More recently, while numerous definitions and interpretations of the concept of CSR have been offered, it can be broadly understood as the responsibility of organizations to be ethical and accountable to the needs of their society as well to their stakeholders (Bradish and Cronin, 2009). In short, the general consensus would be that CSR represents a set of actions that appears to further some social good, extend beyond the explicit pecuniary interests of the firm, and are not required by law (McWilliams and Siegel, 2000; Godfrey, 2009).

Based on this, CSR for scholars and practitioners needs to move from traditional business contexts, and expand its reach into economic sectors such as sports (Godfrey, 2009). For instance, Nelson Mandela's statement that sports can change the world holds much ideological sway. In addition, former United Nations Secretary-General, Kofi Annan, once commented that he was interested in the power of football to teach lifelong lessons about playing others' rivals, not enemies (Smith and Westerbeek, 2007). Therefore, sports might be a useful vehicle in the employment of CSR for development in certain situations. This is because sports allow for development initiatives to extend to groups where traditional development schemes tend not to reach, especially youth communities. But where does the use of sports in CSR for development make a difference compared with other CSR or development schemes? There are two distinct benefits that advocates highlight: the ability of sports to reach out to communities that are particularly marginalized by traditional development initiatives, and the capacity to create partnership among institutions that would not normally work together (Levermore, 2010).

In addition, sports can spread understanding and tolerance through the introduction of new cultural values in fan and interactive ways. The obvious example can be found in the opening and closing ceremonies of major sports events, such as the Olympic Games (Smith and Westerbeek, 2007). For these reasons, CSR has become increasingly prevalent in the sports industry. For example, the Fédération Internationale de Football Association (FIFA) has made significant investment regarding social responsibility and "more than 40% of FIFA's income goes directly towards supporting the grassroots of the game, development work, and partnerships with relief organizations" (FIFA, 2004: p. 66). Nevertheless, little academic attention has been paid to the role of CSR in sports organizations (Walters, 2009; Mattera and Baena, 2014). In an attempt to shed light on this topic, this chapter focuses on Real Madrid, one of the most successful sports clubs in the world in terms of worldwide supporters (more than 200 million people), and the most valuable soccer team in the world (Baena, 2015). More specifically, this work attempts to give insights on the role of CSR as a driver of social change and fan engagement.

History and trophies

Founded in 1902 as the Madrid Football Club, the team has traditionally worn a white home uniform ever since. The word Real (royal in Spanish) was conferred on the club by King Alfonso XIII of Spain in 1920 with the royal crown in the emblem. The team has played its home matches in the Santiago Bernabéu Stadium, Madrid, since 1947. In December 2014, Real Madrid had won 32 Ligas (national league trophy), 19 Copas del Rey (the national cup in Spain), 10 European Championship titles, 3 Intercontinental Cup trophies, 2 UEFA SuperCup trophies, 1 Club World Cup, among others. Because of this exceptional number of titles, Real Madrid was named "FIFA Club of the Century" in 2002. Real Madrid is also allowed to wear a multiple-winner badge on their jersey during UEFA Champions League matches as the club has won more than five European Cups. Added to this, on 23 December 2000, Real Madrid was awarded with the recognition of FIFA as Club of the Twentieth Century. More recently, in 2004 it received the FIFA Order of Merit.

As regards brand value, Manchester United, Real Madrid, and Bayern Munich have traditionally been the most successful sports teams in Europe. In 2010, Forbes estimated Real Madrid's worth to be approximately $1,323 million, ranking them second after Manchester United. Nevertheless, Real Madrid has recently usurped Manchester United's long-held title as the most valuable soccer team in the world. More specifically, the 2012/13 season marks the first time since Forbes began tracking the value of soccer teams in 2004 that Manchester United has not ranked first. Therefore, Real Madrid is worth more than any team in the world, a fact that is especially notable in a period of crisis in Europe.

Furthermore, Real Madrid has realized the importance of the brand and grasped the ability to market in a way not seen anywhere else in the world of soccer. In particular, they are one of the most recognizable brands in sports, and are among the top 3 teams in the world in terms of followers and engagement in social media. With some of the world's greatest players on the field, Real Madrid exemplifies that team value is also based on brand management. For example, the fusion of the potent Real Madrid brand with equally powerful global football superstars, such as David Beckham and Cristiano Ronaldo, was a profitable decision. When the two footballers started to wear the Real Madrid jersey, the club was able to dramatically increase the price paid by their major corporate sponsors.

Source: Qualitative interview with Julio González, Managing Director of the Real Madrid Foundation, and official website of the club: www.realmadrid.es

---

Presentation of Real Madrid

Name of the Chairman: Florentino Pérez

Number of subscribers: 67,000

Number of Facebook fans: +80 million

Average number of spectators per match: 72,834 people (capacity of Bernabéu stadium: 81,044 people)

Budget of the club: €540 million

Total income: €603 million

Distribution of revenue: marketing (32%); broadcasting (29%); membership dues, ticketing and stadium revenue (25%); revenues from friendly matches (14%).

Name of sponsors: Adidas, Emirates Airlines, IPIC, Bwin, Mahou, Audi, Microsoft, Turismo de Madrid, BBVA, Nivea Men, STC, Empresas Polar, Yamaha, Solán de Cabras, NBAD, Coca Cola, Samsung, Sanitas et Ooredoo.

Source: Real Madrid Group Management Report 2013/2014, and the official website of the club: www.realmadrid.es

---

Presentation of Julio González

Julio González: Managing Director of the Foundation Real Madrid since 2009.

What is the Real Madrid Foundation?

Concerning socially responsible actions, it is worth mentioning the immense effort that Real Madrid FC has implemented through the "Real Madrid Foundation". This entity is 18 years old and one of the largest sports education institutions in the world, and one of the very few with its own AENOR certificate. In addition, the Foundation serves as an instrument by which Real Madrid is present in society and develops its social and cultural awareness program to achieve the following goal:

> To promote, both in Spain as well as abroad, the values inherent in sports, and the latter's role as an educational tool capable of contributing to the comprehensive development of the personality of those who practice it. In addition, as a means of social integration of those who find themselves suffering from any form of marginalization, as well as to promote and disseminate all the cultural aspects linked to sport.
>
> *www.realmadrid.com*

Caring for infants and youths, the main goal of the Foundation, is achieved through the care of minors in a conflictive family or social situation. By means of nearly 50 socio-sporting football schools, thousands of boys and girls are educated in weekly training sessions with the "They play, we educate" program, through the Foundation's general educational philosophy: "For a REAL Education: Values and Sport". In addition, Real Madrid uses sports to reach out to demographic groups in risk of social exclusion through its Foundation. The team also promotes the development of positive values and competences, such as team work, the acceptance and respect for established rules, and respect for one's fellow man.

In short, the Foundation's main goal is to encourage values inherent in sports, and use this as an educational tool. Because of that, in 2007 the Real Madrid Foundation received the Plaque from the COE (Spanish Olympic Committee) in recognition of "its extraordinary social work". Real Madrid has also been awarded the International Award for Solidarity in Sport, for the "School united by the peace of football (Israel and Palestinian Territories)", as well as the Corporate Social Responsibility Award from the Football is More Foundation, which was created by S.D. Prince Constantin von und zu Liechtenstein, to promote development and peace through football. More recently, the European Club Association (ECA) awarded the prize for the Best Community and Social Responsibility Program 2014 to Real Madrid.

The combination of the aforementioned factors made Real Madrid the appropriate brand to choose for this chapter, representing a leading organization in sports, business, and CSR.

Socially responsible actions for a better world

As stated, Real Madrid is more and more present in the world through its Foundation, helping with its sporting message and its solidarity values; values that Real Madrid transmits. Teamwork, improvement, motivation and respect are the base of its multiple activities. Its work is principally centered on infancy and youngsters, but also in the collectives that can suffer any kind of social difficulty. As Julio González, Managing Director of the Foundation Real Madrid, said: "The power of sport and energy of Real Madrid are definitively capable of attempting to change the terrible reality faced by millions of people every day".[2] For that reason, the Foundation is present in hospitals, help centers, penitentiary centers and nursing homes, among others. In particular, the Foundation's main activities can be grouped into the following areas: educational and sports activities; social insertion and welfare activities; cooperation for social causes; and socially responsible practices as a driver of fan engagement. All of them are now discussed further.

Educational and sports activities

Sports have youth appeal (Smith and Westerbeek, 2007). Children are more likely to engage in social initiatives run by community sports than activities run solely by a local council. It is worth mentioning that in Spain, more than 10,000 people have benefited from 124 projects developed by the Real Madrid Foundation through its Social Sport Schools. The Foundation has opened 229 Social Sport Schools in 70 countries with more than 37,500 direct beneficiaries. These academies are not scouting outposts aiming to find the next Cristiano Ronaldo or Gareth Bale, but educational centers funded by the Foundation and its partners.

As noted by Emilio Butragueño, Director of Institutional Relations of Real Madrid, "The Real Madrid Foundation seeks to promote our values through sports and education, teaching children human values such as commitment, responsibility and teamwork, which will be central to their success in their future work life". That is, at the Foundation's social sports schools "the children participate in training, games and events, while at the same time going to school or taking part in a professional training program... They also benefit from social services adjusted to their specific needs, such as classes and workshops on different themes, medical check-ups, psychological follow-up [and the provision of] snacks and school supplies".[3]

An illustration of how educational activities are important for Real Madrid could be provided by the new schools opened in 2014 in Nasugbu and La Carlota (the Philippines), for more than 200 homeless boys and girls aged between 5 and 12. Beneficiaries were chosen by a social educator from the Roxas Foundation in accordance with their poverty index, by gathering information at the primary schools in which they are enrolled and examining each case. In addition to the football program, breakfast, lunch and an afternoon snack, tournaments and friendly matches were held between all the students at the school. In short, "They play, we teach" is based on socio-educational activities, such as talks on values, classes reinforcing students' studies at school or football talks of a more theoretical nature, including refereeing, the rules of the game and more specific talks on a healthy lifestyle, hygiene and nutrition, among others.

Real Madrid's Campus Experience provides another example of the commitment of Real Madrid with education. Hundreds of boys and girls of many nationalities may spend their time every year at those campuses. With a unique environment for learning, having fun and playing sports, the Campus Experience of Real Madrid provides to be the preferred option for parents, who see it as an extraordinary opportunity for the personal development of their children. Consolidation has also been seen internationally, establishing itself for the first time on all five continents, with campuses in United Kingdom, Brazil, Mexico, Singapore and Poland going from strength to strength, and opening new centers in Australia, Canada, Argentina, Italy, Lebanon and China, among other countries. Nationally, as well as Madrid, the main center, there are also campuses in Alicante, Mallorca and Menorca, and a campus with English classes at King's College in Madrid.

Social insertion and welfare activities

Sports provide the best tool for conflict resolution, the dissolution of guns and the fight against racial discrimination. Sports are also seen as a way to promote understanding of

Figure 26.1 Beneficiaries of the Real Madrid Foundation in the Philippines

Source: www.realmadrid.com (accessed 21 November 2014)

different cultures and strengthen community cohesion. Sports CSR "offers a platform for encouraging social interaction in a functional way" (Smith and Westerbeek, 2007: p. 51). Related to this, Emilio Butragueño remarked that Real Madrid feels "the need to give back to society and to our fan base, by assisting the most vulnerable people, at-risk children and youngsters living in precarious conditions or exposed to violence, poverty, drugs and crime".[4]

By encouraging children to participate in sports activities, they work together and interact. Another way in which sports encourage social interaction is through the delivery of social inclusion programs aimed at disengaged people. Real Madrid knows that, and uses its brand to reach out to demographic groups at risk of social exclusion, through its Foundation. Particularly in Spanish penitentiary centers, the Foundation aims to facilitate the integration of inmates into society through the practice of football or basketball, and promotes the development of positive values and competences, such as team work, the acceptance and respect for established rules, and respect for one's fellow man, among others.

The Foundation also facilitates the social integration of immigrant children and their families through the joint practice of football and complementary education programs. In this sense, "one of the most important goals of the Real Madrid Foundation is to promote values inherent in sports, and to use the latter as an educational tool, both in Spain and the rest of the world".[5] To achieve this goal, the club uses the universal nature of the name, Real Madrid,

Figure 26.2 Socio-sporting schools of Real Madrid in the USA

Source: www.realmadrid.com (accessed 21 November 2014)

to make the rest of the world aware of the importance of teaching values and promoting charitable causes. For instance, in conjunction with the International Studies Foundation, the Real Madrid Foundation recently developed a training course in Worcester (Massachusetts), Arlington (Virginia) and Houston (Texas). The problems mainly faced by the American social schools beneficiaries consist of the difficulty in integrating, as they are boys and girls aged between 6 and 11 of Latin African American and Asian origin, who are at risk of social exclusion, have academic problems, and are at risk of abandoning their education. Through quality time playing sports, Real Madrid offers them training on the positive values that facilitates their integration.

In addition, almost 13 tons of food was collected for the Madrid Food Bank. The food collection campaign, named "tickets for food" was at the Santiago Bernabéu stadium. The campaign was held in 2014 in conjunction with SEUR Foundation on the days before the games against Galatasaray and Olímpic de Xàtiva. It was a success on both occasions.

Another example that may illustrate the role played by Real Madrid to help community is the campaign "at Christmas, no child without a gift". This campaign took toys to more than 2,000 children at shelter homes and community of Madrid participation centers in 2013. Children's sports programs at hospitals should also be noted. The aim of these projects is to provide a normal environment of well-being for children hospitalized for long periods of time, who are receiving treatment for different reasons, as well as providing their parents and families with a place to spend the long days of waiting at hospitals.

Cooperation for social causes

The Sport for Development and Peace International Working Group (SDPIWG)[6] notes that sports contribute to international development in the following categories: individual development for the able bodied and disabled (emphasis on empowerment especially through education); health awareness and disease prevention; promotion of gender equity; social integration (particularly through communication and social mobilization), peace building and conflict prevention or resolution; post-disaster trauma relief; and economic development (including building infrastructure), among others. Moreover, participation in sports improves diet and discourages the use of tobacco, alcohol and drugs. It also helps to reduce violence, enhances functional capacity and promotes social interaction and integration (World Health Organization, 2003).

Based on this, we may argue that sports programs and events provide a natural and non-political arena where partners can meet up and strengthen the interaction of business, NGOs, civil society, and political institutions.

In late 2014, Real Madrid's social initiatives had been carried out in more than 220 socio-sporting schools located in 70 countries across Europe, America, Africa, the Middle East and Asia, helping more than 60,000 people either directly or indirectly. "Thanks to the contributions of institutions and people, each day it works for a more just world, using a common language: sport", remarked Julio González.[7] To achieve this goal, volunteers and collaborating members play a crucial role. For instance, the Real Madrid Foundation is mostly aimed at people between 18 and 55 years old who want to voluntarily support social activities, such as providing assistance in the stadium to people in wheelchairs, helping the coaches at the socio-sporting schools, or working on charity matches and participating in campaigns with charities.

Funding for all these projects comes from the club – the richest in the world – and includes the benefit matches, the Foundation's annual Gala, or benefit concerts, in which it instills values to be emulated by society. Corporate partnerships are also a major source of the Foundation's resources. For example, in 2013 Microsoft provided computer software, worth a reported $1.38 million, to an initiative to reach 20,000 children in Argentina, Brazil, Colombia, Ecuador and Mexico.

Any individual, entity or supporters club may join the Foundation as a collaborating member, paying a yearly fee of €75, with the resulting tax reductions of 25% of the contribution. Collaborators also receive an exclusive gift, as a Collaborating Member as well as Collaborating Member Card. This allows them to enjoy all the benefits of the Foundation and the symbolic recognition of the continuous collaboration of its members over time, with bronze, silver and gold cards issued to those who maintain their collaboration for 5, 10 and 15 years, respectively. Special discounts on activities organized by the Foundation, such as those at the Campuses and Sports Schools, are also offered in conjunction with free attendance of events organized by the Foundation Real Madrid and free subscription to the Foundation Real Madrid's magazine and Report.

The Real Madrid Foundation exists thanks to cooperation with different public authorities, and the generous support it receives from important national and international companies through patronage and sponsorship agreements. Furthermore, this Foundation helps people thanks to the individual donations and support made by thousands of Madrid's fans, who wish to strengthen their bond with Real Madrid. González said, "[T]he Foundation Real Madrid thanks all Madrid fans for their social engagement. With their help we contribute to a better world for all".[8]

Figure 26.3 Real Madrid's legends annual match to raise money for a charitable purpose

Source: www.realmadrid.com (accessed 20 May 2015)

Figure 26.4 Real Madrid campaign (official website and banners) to explain to their followers how to help people through the team's Foundation

Source: www.realmadrid.com (accessed 12 November 2014)

Socially responsible practices as a driver of fan engagement

We operate in a global society, which implies that people are more aware of a firm's actions in terms of social problems (Mattera and Baena, 2014). This fact is especially important in the sports sector, where institutions are facing a public that is increasingly aware of the social aspects of corporate policy, due to the notoriety given to recent corporate misdeeds (Walker and Kent, 2009). Above all, when a consumer identifies closely with a team, a sense of connectedness ensues, and they begin to define themself with the club (Mael and Ashforth, 1992). In other words, sports fans will seek out positive information about elements they endorse. For example, highly identified game attendees may look for the socially responsible activities of teams to reinforce their fanship (Walker and Kent, 2009).

CSR could also be viewed as a form of reputation building (McWilliams, Siegel and Wright, 2006), as well as brand awareness enhancement (Mattera, Baena and Cerviño, 2014). Moreover, there is a link between social initiatives and affective responses by the team followers. Specifically, consumers have an overall positive attitude towards companies associating themselves with causes that benefit society (Walker and Kent, 2009). Therefore, investing in socially responsible activity may be crucial for fan attraction and community commitment.

Based on these arguments, sports teams are often viewed in high regard within their local community. Having a prosocial agenda could mean having a powerful marketing tool that may help to build and shape the team's status, differentiate it in the market, and lead to the organization's competitive edge (Walker and Kent, 2009). In other words, through CSR programs, sports institutions can further enhance their stature in society.

The Real Madrid Foundation exemplifies this discussion as it exists thanks to the collaboration of many different agents (both public and private institutions), but also, thanks the support from thousands of Madridistas (Real Madrid supporters), who wish to reinforce their commitment to the club. This is because when a fan identifies closely with their team, they begin to define themself with the organization (Mael and Ashforth, 1992). Nevertheless, sports marketers have to manage this issue with caution. Although many companies communicate the "good" things they are doing, consumer skepticism of corporate communication is high, making these communications of suspect value. Therefore, the goal is to develop the appropriate marketing communication strategy that provides details about how the team has addressed specific social issues.

Florentino Pérez, Chairman of Real Madrid, argued:

> [A]ll Real Madrid supporters should feel proud of Realmadrid Foundation battle against poverty and injustice. The work of its Foundation increases every day because it has proved to be a guarantee of quality and its huge commitment to its social project. . . The Foundation constantly received the support of many organizations and people that wish to contribute their solidarity. A message that must be conveyed to the entire society.[9]

The club is well aware of the importance of its message reaching all the entities and people that lend or may lend their support, as well as society as a whole. In order to achieve this goal, it is essential that detailed information of all the initiatives that are undertaken by the Real Madrid is made known. More specifically, the team has attempted to develop involvement activities as part of a broader CSR initiative, which can also be used to increase and maintain the bonds between the team and the community. In this sense, the following methods are used to help spread the word about its activities:

1   *Magazine.* A quarterly publication, the magazine has a circulation of 8,000 copies and a distribution of 6,000. Recipients of the magazines are the patrons, associate members, and sponsors.

2   *Annual Report.* The report provides a detailed record of the activities and projects developed by the Foundation Real Madrid. It is published in English and Spanish and includes an evaluation of the economic management and audit.

3   *Publishing.* Through the publication of books, Real Madrid describes the club's history as the values that characterized the institution.

4   *Realmadrid.com.* This website hosts the Foundation's own website. It publishes information on the most important events and activities organized by the entity.

5   *E-Newsletter.* The monthly newsletter provides information to members and associate members of the Real Madrid Foundation on its most relevant activities.

6   *Social Networks.* As a part of its effort to increase its level of support as much as possible, the Real Madrid Foundation has a strong presence on Facebook and Twitter. It has more than 2 million followers on Facebook and 250,000 on Twitter, which makes it the most followed charitable sports institution.

Real Madrid also collaborates with many individual athletes who have set up charitable foundations (for example, the Rafael Nadal Foundation). By doing so, the team increases the number of potential (direct and indirect) beneficiaries as well as the engagement with the team. Besides, Real Madrid's figures all support and promote the team's CSR activities whenever they can. All these actions help to increase the emotional attachment the team followers have for Real Madrid, as well as their identification with the club, creating a shared social identity.

Figure 26.5 Beneficiaries of the Real Madrid Foundation in Guatemala receive a visit from the Chairman of Real Madrid, Florentino Pérez

Source: www.realmadrid.com (accessed 1 June 2015)

Conclusion

A variety of factors have led to the growing importance of CSR for sports organizations. The omnipresence of sports has occasioned the elevation of sports teams as influential members of the global community, especially as they have become big businesses themselves. Sports occupy a unique role in society, consequently having a great impact on the community (issues such as education, social values, etc.). For instance, the link between participating in sports and positive health benefits is well established (Walters, 2009). Therefore, sports offer substantial potential for community return (Smith and Westerbeek, 2004).

Concerning Real Madrid, the team "is fully aware that its strength, power and prestige must focus on fighting inequality and above all, the injustice affecting the most vulnerable, the boys and girls that need us, wherever they are, because for Real Madrid, in the area of solidarity, there are no border".[10] To achieve this goal, the club runs regular sports camps for children around the world, while also working in prisons and hospitals, and with immigrants and individuals with physical or learning difficulties. By doing so, the Real Madrid Foundation is one of the largest sports education institutions in the world. Moreover, it focuses on social welfare and integration by cooperating with public and private agents, having helped more than 60,000 people in 70 countries around the world in 2014.

In addition, socially responsible actions implemented by the Foundation contribute to enhance the emotional attachment that Madridistas (Real Madrid supporters) feel towards their team. More specifically, "thousands of boys and girls see Real Madrid as a reference model that accomplishes the expectations generated by the team tradition and colors... The Real Madrid Foundation is an outstanding symbol of the club and unites all Real Madrid supporters. Therefore, they can proudly say that Real Madrid has achieved success far beyond the football field or basketball court" as González said.[11] In other words, "the Real Madrid Foundation is the proof of fact that using our will, we (the team) can achieve anything. The Foundation shows there is no (caring) challenge unattainable to Real Madrid".[12]

This has resulted in the integration of CSR into the strategic management of the team to deliver a number of benefits that can ultimately create and enhance a sustainable competitive advantage. This chapter confirms that socially responsible actions could be of help to get the followers' commitment. For example, highly identified game attendees may look for the socially responsible activities of teams to reinforce their engagement towards the club. Besides, CSR associations have a strong and direct impact on supporters' attributions, which in turn influence brand evaluations, and purchase intentions.

This work may have implications for sports marketers as well as serve as the starting point for future research. Having a clear understanding of CSR in sports would aid in the evaluation of such efforts in organization. Besides, CSR should be regarded as one of the most important components of contemporary sports management theory and practice. Therefore, this work will contribute to expanding knowledge and understanding the role of sports as an important agent of social change.

Notes

1. The author wishes to thank Emilio Butragueño, Director of Institutional Relations of Real Madrid, and Julio González, Managing Director of the Real Madrid Foundation, for their support and availability.
2. Julio González, interviewed by Professor Verónica Baena, 21 November 2014.
3. Interview published in 2013, www.aljazeera.com/sport/football/2013/10/charitable-face-real-madrid-20131022163236149593.html (accessed 1 April 2015).

4. Extract of interview published in 2013, www.aljazeera.com/sport/football/2013/10/charitable-face-real-madrid-20131022163236149593.html (accessed 1 April 2015).
5. Julio González, interviewed by Professor Verónica Baena, 21 November 2014.
6. This group comprised national governments, the UN and civil society and made recommendations for the integration of sports into international development initiatives.
7. Julio González, interviewed by Professor Verónica Baena, 21 November 2014.
8. Julio González, interviewed by Professor Verónica Baena, 21 November 2014.
9. Letter from the Chairman of Real Madrid published in the Real Madrid Foundation's Annual Report 2013/2014.
10. Florentino Pérez, President of Real Madrid. Real Madrid Foundation Annual Report 2013/2014.
11. Julio González, interviewed by Professor Verónica Baena, 21 November 2014.
12. Letter from the Chairman of Real Madrid published in the Real Madrid Foundation's Annual Report 2013/2014.

References

Baena, V. (2015). Analyzing online and mobile marketing strategies as brand love drivers in sports teams. Findings from Real Madrid, *International Journal of Sport Marketing & Sponsorship* (forthcoming).

Bradish, C. and Cronin, J. (2009). Corporate social responsibility in sport, *Journal of Sport Management*, 28, 691–697.

Godfrey, P. C. (2009). Corporate social responsibility in sport: An overview and key issues, *Journal of Sport Management*, 23, 698–716.

Levermore, R. (2010). CSR for development through sport: examining its potential and limitations, *Third World Quarterly*, 31(2), 223–241.

Mael, F. and Ashforth, B. (1992). Alumni and their alma mater: A partial test of the reformulated model of organizational identification, *Journal of Organizational Behavior*, 13, 103–123.

Margolis, J. and Walsh, J. P. (2003). Misery loves companies: Rethinking social initiatives by business, *Administrative Science Quarterly*, 48(2), 268–305.

Mattera, M. and Baena, V. (2014). Getting brand commitment through internet and mobile sports marketing. An insight on Real Madrid football team in *Strategies in Sports Marketing: Technologies and Emerging Trends*, Chapter 13, 203–218. IGI Global, Pennsylvania, EE.UU.

Mattera, M., Baena, V. and Cerviño, J. (2014). Investing time wisely: Enhancing firms' brand awareness through stakeholder engagement in the service sector, *International Journal of Management Practice*, 7(2), 126–143.

McWilliams, A. and Siegel, D. (2000). Corporate social responsibility and financial performance: Correlation or misspecification? *Strategic Management Journal*, 21(5), 603–609.

McWilliams, A., Siegel, D. and Wright, P. (2006). Corporate social responsibility: Strategic implications, *Journal of Management Studies*, 43, 1–18.

Porter, M. E. and Kramer, M. R. (2006). Strategy and society: The link between competitive advantage and corporate social responsibility, *Harvard Business Review*, December, 78–92.

Sheth, H. and Babiak, K. (2010). Beyond the game: Perceptions and practices of corporate social responsibility in the professional sport industry, *Journal of Business Ethics*, 91, 433–450.

Smith, A. and Westerbeek, H. (2004). *The sport business future*. London: Palgrave Macmillan.

Smith, A. and Westerbeek, H. (2007). Sport as a vehicle for deploying corporate social responsibility, *Journal of Corporate Citizenship*, 25, 43–54.

Walker, M. and Kent, A. (2009). Do fans care? Assessing the influence of corporate social responsibility on consumer attitudes in the sport industry, *Journal of Sport Management*, 23, 743–769.

Walters, G. (2009). Corporate social responsibility through sport. The community sports trust model as a CSR delivery Agency, *Journal of Corporate Citizenship*, 35, 81–94.

Webography

www.aljazeera.com/sport/football/2013/10/charitable-face-real-madrid-20131022163236149593.html Extract of the article, The charitable face of Real Madrid, by Dermot Corriganet, www.aljazeera.com on 22 November 2012 (accessed 1 April 2015).

Reports and practitioner documents

FIFA (2004). *Activity Report: April 2002–March 2004*. 54th FIFA Congress, Paris.

Forbes (2010). *The Business of Soccer*. April, 2010.

Forbes (2013). *Top Forbes' Social Media Rankings*. December, 2013.

Real Madrid Foundation (2014). *Real Madrid Foundation's Annual Report 2013/2014*.

Real Madrid (2014). *Real Madrid Group Management Report 2013/2014, June, 2014.*

World Business Council (1999). *Corporate social responsibility: Meeting changing expectations.* Geneva, DH: World Business Council.

World Health Organization (2003). *Health and development through physical activity and sport*, Geneva.

27

THE MARKETING AND LEGAL IMPLICATIONS OF THE ATP EVENT REORGANIZATION

Mark Dodds, George Vazenios and Justin Lovich

Introduction

Because of the increasing competition for attendance, television revenue and sponsorship dollars over the last two decades, many sports organizations are focusing on generating new revenue streams and markets (Larson, Jensen and Bowman, 2011). Among these new markets is international growth, specifically in emerging markets, and one of these emerging markets is China. China offers a great opportunity for sports organizations looking to take advantage of the world's second biggest economy, its 1.3 billion population, its increasing sports media consumption (sports television channels have the second highest ratings after the news channel) and aggressive city governments wanting to use sporting events to promote their city image in the Chinese and overseas markets (Ho, 2011).

However, laws governing business operations are vastly different in China. Many activities, such as price fixing, are legal in China but violate US antitrust laws (Peng, Wang and Jiang, 2008).

One of the primary goals of the US antitrust law is to enhance consumer welfare by promoting consumer interest, increasing economic efficiency, increasing market competition, and lowering costs (Roberts, 1988). Typically, business practices that increase output while lowering price enhance consumer welfare (Jacobs, 1991). Antitrust law has been applied in a sports context to player-free agency issues, salary spending, restrictions on ownership (Masteralexis, 2013), organizational structure (Jacobs, 1991), player eligibility, discipline and movement (Lazaroff, 1984). These challenges have been brought by players, owners, prospective owners, cities, media entities and prospective owners (Masteralexis, 2013).

In 2009, the Association of Tennis Professionals (ATP) reorganized its worldwide tennis circuit in an effort to increase its popularity and compete against other sports in a global marketplace. This reorganization included a new Tier I event in Shanghai, China and downgrading the ATP tournament in Hamburg, Germany from a Tier I event to a Tier II event. In an effort to retain the event's premier status, the German Tennis Federation brought a lawsuit against the ATP, claiming antitrust violations and alleging the directors of the ATP breached their fiduciary duties (*DTB v. ATP*, 2009). Ultimately, the United States Court of Appeals for the Third Circuit held that the ATP did not violate any antitrust laws and dismissed the breach of fiduciary duty claim (*DTB v. ATP*, 2010a).

Facts

The ATP Tour is a worldwide professional tennis circuit comprising more than 400 professional players, with 61 tournament events organized into three levels: Tier I, Tier II and Tier III (*DTB v. ATP*, 2010a) and a championship event (World Tour Finals) located in 31 countries (About the ATP, n.d.). In an effort to increase its popularity to compete against other sports and entertainment events, the ATP in 2009 instituted the "Brave New World" schedule reorganization, channeling more top-tier players to the top-tier ATP tournaments and reclassifying the tier categories of some tournaments.

In the ATP, players earn prize money and ATP ranking points by playing in ATP tournaments (*DTB v. ATP*, 2010a). These points determine the player's world rankings and seed players in the Grand Slam tennis events (i.e. Australian Open, French Open, Wimbledon, and US Open). Players can earn more prize money and ranking points by playing in higher tiered ATP tournaments. Under the Brave New World plan, the ATP increased the potential ranking points in the tournaments: the Tier I events increased the winner's points from 500 to 1000; Tier II would award 500 points instead of 250–300; and Tier III increased from 175 to 250. These increases were designed to create an incentive for the top tennis players to play in the ATP top-tier events. The top seven players in the ATP rankings qualify for the ATP World Tour finals. The final eighth position is determined by the highest ranked player who won a Grand Slam tennis event between eighth and twentieth position, or, if no player fits this criteria, then the eighth ranked player (Frequently, n.d.).

Although the ATP kept the overall number of Tier I events at nine, it demoted the Hamburg event to Tier II and added a Tier I tournament in Shanghai, China (*DTB v. ATP*, 2010a). The demotion of Hamburg and the creation of the Rio Open increased the number of Tier II events from nine to eleven. Importantly, the ATP requires that qualifying players for the Grand Slam tournaments play all Tier I events, at least four Tier II events and at least two Tier III events. The ATP implemented sanctions such as suspensions and loss of ranking points to enforce this rule change.

- Tier 1 Events (9)
  Cincinnati, USA; Indian Wells, USA; Madrid, Spain; Miami, USA; Monte-Carlo; Montreal, Canada; Quebec, Canada; Paris, France; Rome, Italy; Shanghai, China
- Tier II Events (13)
  Acapulco, Mexico; Barcelona, Spain; Basel, Switzerland; Beijing, China; Dubai, UAE; Haile, Germany; Hamburg, Germany; London-Queen's, UK; Rio de Janeiro, Brazil; Rotterdam, Belgium; Tokyo, Japan; Valencia, Spain; Washington, USA
- Tier III Events (61)
  Atlanta, USA; Auckland, New Zealand; Båstad, Sweden; Bogota, Colombia; Brisbane, Australia; Bucharest, Romania; Buenos Aires, Argentina; Casablanca, Morocco; Chennai, India; Delray Beach, USA; Doha, Qatar; Estoril, Portugal; Geneva, Switzerland; Gstaad, Switzerland; Houston, USA; Istanbul, Turkey; Kitzbühel, Austria; Kuala Lumpur, Malaysia; Marseille, France; Memphis, USA; Metz, France; Montpellier, USA; Moscow, Russia; Munich, Germany; Newport, USA; Nice, France; Nottingham, UK; Quito, Ecuador; Sao Paulo, Brazil; 's-Hertogenbosch, The Netherlands; Shenzhen, China; St. Petersburg, Russia; Stockholm, Sweden; Stuttgart, Germany; Sydney, Australia; Umag, Croatia; Vienna, Austria; Winston-Salem, USA; Zagreb, Croatia
  (Tournaments, n.d.)

The Brave New World plan also created geographic swings that allow top players to play in ATP events in preparation for an upcoming Grand Slam event (*DTB v. ATP*, 2010a). This change can acclimate a player to the general geographic area and the playing surface of the next Grand Slam event. For instance, the New Zealand event is held one week before the Australian Open.

Legal case history and analysis

In response to their reclassification to a Tier II event, the German Tennis Federation ("Federation") brought a lawsuit against the ATP and its directors. Because the ATP is registered as a Delaware (USA) not-for-profit corporation, this case was brought before a US federal court. The lawsuit alleged the ATP's Brave New World plan violated §§ 1 and 2 of the Sherman Act and the ATP's directors breached fiduciary duties owed to the Federation (*DTB v. ATP*, 2009). At trial, the District Court found in favor of the defendant, the ATP. The court dismissed the breach of fiduciary claim as a matter of law. The antitrust claims were submitted to a jury who returned a verdict for the ATP. The jury found the Federation failed to prove their allegations against the ATP. The Federation appealed this decision to the United States Court of Appeals for the Third Circuit.

In order to prevail in an antitrust lawsuit, the plaintiff must prove the defendant entered into a contract, combination or conspiracy with any separate entity under § 1 of the Sherman Act and must establish a relevant product market under § 2 (*DTB v. ATP*, 2010a). Because of its unique situation, legal doctrines created for a more traditional business context are often difficult to apply to the sports industry (Roberts, 1988). Often in sports, there has to be some level of cooperation and agreement between competitors on economic issues (Lazaroff, 1984).

The Federation contended the ATP conspired and combined to control the supply of top men's professional tennis players' services, established a favored class of tournaments in which top-player participation was mandatory, while precluding other tournaments from competing for such player services, in violation of § 1 of the Sherman Act (*DTB v. ATP*, 2010a). Section 1 requires two or more separate entities to agree not to compete in the marketplace. Under a "rule of reason" analysis, the trial jury found the Federation failed to prove the ATP entered into any agreement with a separate entity (*DTB v. ATP*, 2009), thus the § 1 claim failed. Instead of a coalition between the multiple tennis events, the ATP was considered a single entity because each of the tennis events is dependent on the others to produce a single, common product: the marketable professional tennis tour. Thus, tour events function collectively to compete with other forms of sport and entertainment for spectators, television viewers, and sponsors.

The Federation argued the Brave New World plan created a horizontal restraint of competition and should have met the § 1 requirement. Although the individual tennis events agreed to the Brave New World plan, often sport requires separate entities to work together in order to be more competitive in the large sport marketplace (*NCAA v. Board of Regents*, 1984). Overall, the appellate court accepted the pro-competitive effects of the agreement outweighed the negative effects. The § 1 requirements were not met because the modifications to the tour calendar, higher payments to the players, and expanded geographic reach, improved the ATP product in comparison to other worldwide sports options.

The § 2 claim alleged a monopolization, the attempt to monopolize, or conspiracy to monopolize the market for men's professional tennis players' services (*DTB v. ATP*, 2010a). An unlawful monopoly exists when one entity obtains control of the market for a product or service through anticompetitive conduct (U.S. Department of Justice, 2012). Under a § 2 claim, a plaintiff must show that the defendant willfully acquired and maintained monopoly power and these actions injured the plaintiff (Shropshire, 1990). Although the Federation sought to define the relevant product market as, among other things, the market for the production of top-tier men's professional tennis, the trial court found that the market was more expansive, likely including alternative entertainment options available to consumers. Without sufficiently establishing the existence of a relevant product market, the Federation could not show that the ATP illegally acted to create a monopoly (*DTB v. ATP*, 2009).

The dismissal of the breach of fiduciary claims was affirmed by the appellate court by applying the business judgment rule. The business judgment rule "is a presumption that in making a business decision the directors of a corporation acted on an informed basis, in good faith, and in honest belief that the action taken was in the best interests of the company" (*Aronson v. Lewis*, 1984: p. 812). The court held that the directors, individually or as a whole, were "materially self-interested when they voted for the Brave New World plan" (*DTB v. ATP*, 2010a: p. 824). Here, although one voting director also owned a 24% stake in a Tier I event (Indian Wells), the Federation could not show the director received any personal financial benefit from the Brave New World plan.

The Federation appealed this decision from the Court of Appeals. However, the United States Supreme Court decided not to hear the appeal, effectively concluding the Federation's antitrust claims (*DTB v. ATP*, 2010b).

Reorganization impact

From a sponsor's point of view, the decision to give preferable treatment to the Shanghai event makes good business sense for the short-term marketing benefits of the game and sponsor attraction. More importantly, the Shanghai tournament facilitates the long-term benefits of growing the game and business of tennis in China, intended to inspire fan support and develop potential players, and, ultimately, increase sponsorship opportunities.

Indeed, Shanghai is the commercial and business center of China, with a population of over 23 million (World Population Review, 2014). By selecting Shanghai, China as the new event site, the ATP is able to tap into one of the biggest emerging economies for foreign sport entities. For example, the English Premier League (EPL) has marketed itself in China since 2003 and the financial return to the league is so powerful that many game times have been changed to accommodate the Chinese television audience at the expense of the European fan (Sayarer, 2013).

Tennis is a growing sport in China. It is the third most popular sport on television behind soccer and basketball; there are more than 50 million playing tennis in China now (Schlabach, 2012). Perhaps due to the Shanghai ATP event, the Chinese government invested in tennis at the grassroots amateur levels and created world class tennis facilities. This investment has paid off because China has a star of their own in Li Na, who won the Australian Open in 2014 and is more popular than basketball star Yao Ming in the eyes of the Chinese public (Williams, 2014). More than 116 million television viewers watched Li Na play in the 2011 French Open finals (Associated Press, 2011). The market for tennis in China is, indeed, growing.

This new event has proven to be very popular with the players and the fans. The players awarded this tournament the "ATP World Tour Masters 1000 Tournament of the Year" (ANZ Media Release, 2012) and the tournament attracted a worldwide audience of 45 million viewers (ANZ Media Release, 2012).

It is important to note that the ATP did not drop the tournament in Hamburg; it was merely downgraded to a Tier II event. There is still the opportunity for Hamburg to attract players as well as maintain its event sponsors. There might be an opportunity for Hamburg to re-enter the Tier I event classification in the future. Just as the ATP increased the number of Tier II events from nine to eleven, there is a possibility that the ATP may increase the number of Tier I events going forward. The potential for reclassification as a Tier I event exists especially if Hamburg focuses its efforts in surpassing other Tier II events in terms of sponsorship attraction and local marketing presence.

Nevertheless, the negative implications for promoters, marketers, and sponsors of the Hamburg ATP event are clear. The value of a Hamburg ATP sponsorship has been deflated by the event's demotion. As the future classification of the event seems, at best, uncertain, sponsors may recognize ATP events as short-term assets and avoid long-term commitments. In addition, participation in the Hamburg event and other Tier II tournaments is now optional for players; the Federation and similar event organizers must promote the tournament to players as well as fans and sponsors. Thus, the Federation might seek to work creatively with sponsors to make the event enticing to players, thereby drawing the attention of fans so as to synergistically maximize sponsorship value.

Conclusion

Ultimately, the outcome of this case certainly establishes the ability for an international sports tour to reclassify its events in a changing world economy. Under American antitrust law, the tour is allowed to evaluate its events based on the existing business market as well as the potential for growth to determine the best event locations. The existing events do not possess any guarantee that the event cannot be reclassified, or even potentially dropped completely, solely because of previous event history. Sponsors and event promoters have been put on notice that governing bodies are willing to make difficult decisions with individual events in attempting to maximize the economic potential of the overall business enterprise.

Under the rule of reason test, a court will analyze both the pro-competitive and anti-competitive effects of a policy (Lazaroff, 1984). When fans in one city are saddened by a negative action by a sports organization, it is often offset by the fans celebrating in another city (Lazaroff, 1984). Thus, courts analyze the market impact and economic effect of the business decision (Jacobs, 1991).

Most sports leagues would like to create increased foreign interest in their sports. This may be accomplished by having international home teams to generate interest, and increase television viewership and revenues (Shropshire, 1990). Any expansion of other US professional sports leagues into Europe may create new liability, primarily under Articles 81 and 39 of the EC Treaty (Edelman and Doyle, 2009). Sports leagues, such as the NBA and NFL, have age and education requirements, player selection drafts and reserve systems, which most likely violate these laws (Edelman and Doyle, 2009).

References

ANZ Media Release (2012, November 22). ANZ signs five-year Shanghai Rolex masters sponsorship.
Aronson v. Lewis, 473 A.2d 805 (Del. 1984).
Associated Press (2011). 116 million Chinese watch Li Na win, http://sports.espn.go.com/sports/tennis/french11/news/story?id=6641140.
About The ATP. (n.d.). www.atpworldtour.com/Corporate/About.aspx
Deutscher Tennis Bund v. ATP Tour, Inc., 2009 U.S. Dist. LEXIS 97851 (D. Del., Oct. 19, 2009).
Deutscher Tennis Bund v. ATP Tour, Inc. 610 F.3d 820 (3d Cir. 2010a).

Deutscher Tennis Bund v. ATP Tour, Inc., 131 S.Ct. 658, 178 L. Ed. 2d 482, 2010 U.S. LEXIS 9253 (U.S., 2010b).

Edelman, M. and Doyle, B. (2009). Antitrust and "free movement" risks of expanding U.S. professional sports leagues into Europe. *Northwestern Journal of International Law & Business*, 29, 403–438.

Frequently asked questions. (n.d.), www.atpworldtour.com/Rankings/Rankings-FAQ.aspx

Ho, P. (2011). Making your Chinese sponsorship work. *Journal of Sponsorship*, 4(3), 214–219.

Jacobs, M. (1991). Professional sports leagues, antitrust and the single-entity theory: A defense of the status quo. *Indiana Law Journal*, 67, 25–58.

Larson, B., Jensen, R. and Bowman, N. (2011). Developing international sports markets: Professional sports selling to new segments with new promotions. *Journal of International Business Disciplines*, 6(2), 9–24.

Lazaroff, D. (1984). The antitrust implications of franchise relocation restrictions in professional sports. *Fordham Law Review*, 53, 157–220.

Masteralexis, L. (2013). Antitrust and labor law. In D. Cotten and J. Wolohan (Eds.), *Law for recreation and sport managers 6th Ed.* (pp. 626–637). Dubuque, IA: Kendall Hunt.

NCAA v. Board of Regents, 468 U.S. 85 (1984).

Peng, M., Wang, D. and Jiang, T. (2008). An institutional-based view of international business strategy: A focus on emerging economies. *Journal of International Business Studies*, 39(5), 920–936.

Roberts, G. (1988). The evolving confusion of professional sports antitrust, the rule of reason and the doctrine of ancillary restraints. *Southern California Law Review*, 61, 943–1016.

Sayarer, J. (2013, Apr. 7). Socialism in one country and English football's Premier League, www.opendemocracy.net/openeconomy/julian-sayarer/socialism-in-one-country-and-english-footballs-premier-league

Schlabach, N. (2012, Oct. 9). Tennis gaining popularity in China, http://english.cri.cn/7146/2012/10/09/53s726155.htm

Shropshire, K. (1990). Thoughts on international professional sports leagues and the application of United States antitrust laws. *Denver University Law Review*, 67(2), 193–212.

Tournaments. (n.d.), www.atpworldtour.com/tournaments/tournament-landing.aspx

U.S. Department of Justice (2012). Antitrust enforcement and the consumer, www.justice.gov/atr/public/div_stats/antitrust-enfor-consumer.pdf

Williams, S. (2014, Jan. 31). Tennis star's "bonus" sparks Chinese public outrage, www.voanews.com/content/tennis-star-li-nas-bonus-sparks-chinese-public-outrage/1841989.html

World Population Review (2014). Shanghai Population 2013, http://worldpopulationreview.com/world-cities/shanghai-population

CONCLUSION

This book was designed to showcase the latest thinking in sports marketing, written by established researchers in the field and emerging academic talent. In bringing together such an array of authors, the editorial team feels it has achieved its goal and we hope readers will agree with us.

There remains a debate about the precise nature of sports marketing, with the first paper of this volume we hope that researchers and academics in this field can proceed with greater clarity and certainty in the work they undertake. Given the uniqueness of its core product, sports marketing is distinct from other forms of marketing and therefore merits being differentiated from other forms of marketing.

There are nevertheless likely to be ongoing definitional issues for sports marketing, not least in those sports where entertainment and sports appear to be converging. At the same time, issues pertaining to engagement (whether of fans or commercial partners), developments in the organisation and structure of sports, and the role of social media, potentially pose challenges to established notions and definitions of sports marketing. For researchers in the field, we need to ensure in the future that our conceptualisation and definition of sports marketing remains robust and relevant.

The breadth and sophistication of the chapters presented here symbolises how far sports marketing has come over the last decade, though many people from outside the field continue to see the limits of sports marketing as sponsorship and sales. This collection of readings disproves such a notion in the way that it demonstrates the depth and diversity of the discipline.

Sponsors and their relationships with sports properties continue to be an important and fruitful focus for academic research. So, too, is the phenomenon of ambushing; this growing and increasingly innovative activity is being examined by numerous academics across the world and has become a popular subject for analysis.

The next steps for ambush marketing research remain somewhat unclear. Thus far, research has focused on definitional issues as well as on legal and moral considerations related to it. The readings presented here take such issues one-step further, creating the opportunity for this subsequent development to take place. As we now have a clear notion of what ambush marketing is, we are right to anticipate developing insights into how it functions and what its effects are.

How ambushing functions is important in a number of respects as it embraces organisational and managerial issues relating to the development of official sponsor programmes and those devised by ambushers, and which are intended to undermine their official rivals. At the same time, matters of creativity and innovation are important on the part of ambushers seeking to pose a competitive threat and to official sponsors and event owners seeking to ward-off the threat of ambushing.

Furthermore, the sports marketing community must look towards understanding how ambushing impacts upon consumers and upon the perpetrators and targets of it. Although a small amount of research has been undertaken in the field, the consumer effects of ambushing have thus far been weakly explored. There are likely to be cognitive and behavioural issues associated with consumers, but these need to be dealt with by researchers in a much more focused, coherent and formal way.

Consumers, as fans, play a pivotal role in sports; many people refer to them as the heart and soul of sports. In sports marketing terms, on this basis they perform several important roles, not least that they are co-producers of the sports product, generating atmosphere and emotion at events and elsewhere. Consumers are not simply a source of revenue, they have an important, albeit somewhat intangible, role to play too.

The sports marketing literature is replete with studies examining the consumption motives of fans. This is an area that is important and will continue to impact upon academic literature and management practice. Understanding fan engagement, which is distinct from fan motivation, seems to be a pressing need, as does a better understanding of consumers and fans and their use of social media. The globalisation of sports and the internationalisation of fan bases present some opportunities too, and one hopes for some emerging sports marketing literatures in countries such as China.

Often, fan engagement, motivation and consumption are prompted by a brand name. Sports are populated by some of the most appealing, compelling and seductive brands in any industry anywhere in the world. Sadly, the academic literature has thus far failed to capture this dynamism, however, the readings here help to capture some of the key issues in the field and provide a strong basis for further research.

As the chapters identify, the nature and scope of brands in sports are key foci for researchers and practitioners, and how such brands can be brought to life through activation programmes is an interesting new area for sports marketers to consider. Beyond the content covered in this text though, there are several aspects of branding in sports that need urgent attention. For example, sports brands are now being extended into a variety of new and existing product categories, yet the academic literature has failed to keep up with the speed of such developments.

For many of us, our principal means of consuming sports is through the media: newspapers, television, and more recently, through social media and the internet. The latter has inevitably already posed some interesting recent challenges for us all in terms of the phenomenon and the methodologies for analysing it. But television retains a very important role in sports marketing, whether as a means through which consumption takes place, or as a platform for the strategies of broadcasting corporations, or as a marketing communications tool for commercial partners.

Given the symbiotic relationship between sports and the media, one could argue that more research in sports marketing should already have taken place at the intersection between the two. That it has not thus far implies one future research opportunity. Research could also focus on issues such as purchasing behaviour on the internet, the way in which the media contributes to the construction of meaning and experience in sports, the role television plays in promoting a sponsor's products and the way social media can assist in the development of international fan groups.

It is important to remember that sports marketing is neither the preserve nor the sole domain of elite professional sports or events. This book is a clear acknowledgement that sports marketing has a crucial role to play at all levels of sports. In the same way, we implicitly assert that there is also an important socio-legal component to sports marketing. Given the prominence of corruption, doping and transgression in sports, the impact of these practices on the likes of sponsors and consumers will demand analysis if we are to get to grips with them.

The importance of sports marketing at grassroots level is equally as acute. Whether as part of the process of talent management and development or as a means of promoting active, healthy lifestyles, the need for a clear and coherent research agenda is clear. As has already been mentioned, sports marketing is not just about the likes of Beckham, Ferrari and the Olympic Games, it also entails promoting health initiatives, fostering social cohesion and sustainably engaging young people in sports. We hope our section here serves as a prompt to the research that is required in these areas.

There is no doubt that sports marketing has really come into its own since the start of the new millennium. As a result, the discipline is healthy, growing and maturing. The work undertaken over the last fifteen years is testament to the importance of it and to the intellect and commitment of researchers in the field. With the publication of this book, we feel as though we have captured much of what is good right now. Equally, we believe that the range of chapters presented here provide a strong platform for the development of this discipline over the next fifteen years. We look forward to it.

INDEX